FAVORITES OF FORTUNE

· · ·

*Technology, Growth,
and Economic Development
since the Industrial Revolution*

EDITED BY
PATRICE HIGONNET
DAVID S. LANDES
HENRY ROSOVSKY

HARVARD UNIVERSITY PRESS
Cambridge, Massachusetts
London, England
1991

This book is printed on acid-free paper, and its binding materials have been chosen for strength and durability.

Library of Congress Cataloging-in-Publication Data

Favorites of fortune : technology, growth, and economic development
  since the Industrial Revolution / edited by Patrice Higonnet, David S.
  Landes, Henry Rosovsky.
      p.   cm.
  Includes bibliographical references and index.
  ISBN 0-674-29520-X
    1. Technological innovations—Economic aspects—History.
  2. Economic history.   3. Industry—History.   I. Higonnet, Patrice L. R.
  II. Landes, David S.   III. Rosovsky, Henry.
  HC79.T4F38   1991
338'.064'09—dc20   91-12249
                                                       CIP

Acknowledgments

It is always a pleasant task for the editors of a book to thank all those who have collaborated in its publication. To acknowledge debts of friendship is also to be reminded of the importance in our life and work of friends and colleagues. Nor, perhaps, is it irrelevant to our sense of satisfaction that to write a page of acknowledgments is one of the last of the very many assignments that the writing of a book entails!

We are grateful to the Rockefeller Foundation and to the Bellagio Center for Advanced Studies for financial help in hosting the conference on economic change that led to the writing of this volume. We are grateful also for the presence at Bellagio of Judith Vichniac, Director of Studies in the Social Studies Committee at Harvard University, and to Riva Kastoryano of the Centre National de la Recherche Scientifique in Paris. Their organizational and intellectual contributions to that meeting were numerous and are warmly acknowledged. The advice and help of Aida Donald at Harvard University Press were invariably generous and efficient. The editors are particularly mindful of Rebecca Menes' contribution in dealing with the countless queries, proofs, and questions that a complex volume invariably occasions, and we thank Kathy Craig and Amanda Heller for their scrupulous editing of the manuscript.

Our initial purpose in bringing together economic historians from three continents was to exchange ideas on a central issue that challenges not just the discipline of economics, but mankind. Economic growth is primordial, and the various and sundry questions, of method especially, that growth brings to the fore are central to the field of economic history. The relation of the state to growth; the cultural antecedents of change; the industrial, technical logic that change implies for the shape and size of firms or governmental agencies are critical matters that find a common ground in their relevance to a single problem, namely the nature, origins, and future of industrialization and, it would seem, of "postindustrialization" as well.

Our purpose in organizing a conference was to consider one question from many points of view, and the chapters that make up this book deal with a variety of subjects. They range from industrial change to body language, from Victorian housing to early modern diets; economic growth in different places and different times has to be considered on its own terms.

Diversity is inherent in the theory of economic growth, as it is of course in the practice of the theory also, a practice that is often the end result of complex and even contradictory forces. It would be hard to think of any aspects of social and cultural life—some of them complementary, others not—that are not cause or effect of economic change.

There are, then, many mansions in the house of economic history. It was our pleasant surprise that what might have been a babel of confusion proved to be instead a concert of mutually stimulating views. This book, we hope, reflects the sense of happy discovery that marked our Italian stay.

Contents

• • •

Favorites of Fortune

. . .

Introduction: On Technology and Growth

David S. Landes

In the beginning was Smith, and Smith told us not to worry about economic growth: it would take care of itself. Left alone, people would sort things out, do what they did best, make appropriate choices to maximize return. The market would take care of the rest, rewarding reason and quickness and knowledge and punishing the opposite. All of this, moreover, would work to the general advantage, augmenting the wealth of nations and leading them through a natural progression of stages from agriculture to industry to commerce. Long live the invisible hand![1]

To be sure, this sense of immense possibilities for improvement did not last. Malthus and Ricardo in particular developed theses of limits to growth that did much to earn for economics the name of "dismal science." Malthus stressed the tendency in the long run for population to increase to and beyond the limits of subsistence and linked this unhappy outcome to the inexorable operation of arithmetic. For Malthus, natural and man-made disasters—famine, disease, war—were the necessary winnows of a biosphere in disequilibrium. He was not a complete pessimist and recognized the small possibility that self-imposed restraint in reproduction might solve the problem, but given the force of human nature and the prevailing contraceptive technology (to say nothing of the absence of television and other compensating diversions), he was not very hopeful.

Ricardo took the stick from the other end: the limits to the extension of cultivation. As demand for food increased, he argued, ever poorer land would be brought under cultivation, thereby raising the cost of food and wages and crowding out other uses for capital. The motor of growth would simply seize up. The result would be the stationary state.

It would be rash to argue that Malthus and Ricardo were not an integral part of the classical paradigm. Yet their pessimistic lessons were in fact dismissed or, more precisely, put away to be revived another day. In the heady years of nineteenth-century expansion, they seemed at best misguided. It is true that

1

population was growing faster than ever (although there were any number of misconceptions about what had passed before), but food was apparently no problem. On the contrary, the famines of yesteryear disappeared, for many reasons: new staple crops (the potato, maize), the application to the soil of outside nutrients, better rotations, cultivation of virgin lands in and outside of Europe, improved transport.[2] And those regions where population pressed on subsistence were able to export their surplus eaters: the opening of frontier areas overseas seemed to provide an indefinite solution to the Malthusian dilemma.

As a result, the theme of limits to growth simply receded from the intellectual consciousness. Occasionally a lonely voice such as that of Jevons was heard, warning of the exhaustion of the coal supply, but his anxieties were dismissed as parochial, especially after the technological innovations of the Second Industrial Revolution (liquid and gaseous fuels, electricity) transformed the economics of energy.

This "growth is natural" model (though no one would have called it that) remained for well over one hundred years the dominant paradigm; so much so that it became an invisible given of economic thought in general and more or less disappeared as a subject of inquiry. Insofar as some nations had trouble following this path—doing what comes naturally—the explanation was as Smith himself understood it: man and politics had gotten in the way.[3] In particular, the intervention of the state, however well meant, worked to hobble initiatives, distort the market, and cripple the invisible hand.

The same sense of complacency prevailed in regard to distribution. Some nations were clearly richer than others. But that was all right because it was in the nature of things. Of the three factors of production—land, labor, and capital—it was the first that made the difference. Land (which included resources under the land and climate above) was unequally distributed. That was God's work. Those nations more richly endowed with resources were, other things being equal (the saving proviso of economic thinking), bound to be richer. As for the other two factors, labor and capital, the assumption was that in the long run these were homogeneous and equal. People were rational maximizers or could be trained to the role (the jargon term today is *putty*); and money was money, subject to appropriate rates of exchange. Both factors were assumed to be mobile and/or elastic, ready to move to opportunity—labor by migration or population change, capital by transfer or saving. In the meantime, given this natural inequality, it was in the interest of each nation to make the best of what it had. Here Ricardian analysis of comparative advantage reinforced the Smithian model and the contentment that went with it.

It should be said that the Marxian mode of analysis, which presented itself as a dissent, did not reject or seek to alter this paradigm. Marx accepted the naturalness of growth and the positive link between technical advance and wealth. His primary concern was with distribution and the class relations implicit in or derived from the ownership and use of the means of production. In this regard, he never asked questions about the reasons for or determinants of technology or the mode of production—and this for the very simple reason that he did not think there was anything to explain. The pursuit of productivity was a perfectly natural effort to enhance relative surplus, thereby increasing the rate of exploitation, and to promote the accumulation of capital. Besides, for Marx, technological innovation was typically the work of science, and as such, the gratuitous fruit of what he called social labor. The capitalist was a taker. The first to take (to innovate) generally went broke, and the legacy was culled by the jackals of enterprise. "It is, therefore, generally the most worthless and miserable sort of money-capitalists who draw the greatest profit out of all new developments of the universal labour of the human spirit and their social application through combined labour."[4] So much for innovation.

What Marxists (as opposed to Marx and to mainstream economics) did come to concern themselves with was the distribution of wealth among nations. (One can see the analogy to his preoccupation with the question of distribution within the economy.) Specifically, they raised the issue of the economic consequences of imperialism and likened the workers of colonial countries (what we would now call Third World countries) to an external proletariat exploited by the capitalists of imperial states. This analogy, which offered polemical advantages in the attack on the old order, had the additional merit for some Marxists of explaining in politically congenial terms such evidence of improvement as they were willing to concede in the working-class standard of living under capitalism. The argument ran that the capitalists were buying off their own workers and thus buying peace at home by squeezing these outsiders—in effect, by holding them down and back.

Note that this thesis was sharply at variance with Marx's own favorable view of the economic consequences of empire: he castigated its abuses but considered it "objectively" progressive. Nothing else, he thought, could shake the torpor of centuries, otherwise known as the Asiatic mode of production.

Intellectually, however, the Marxist anti-imperialist thesis remained in the master's tradition by accepting the classical paradigm; that is, it saw growth as natural and interpreted colonial poverty and backwardness as products of political exploitation and the wrong kind of interference. It assumed, therefore, that once the burden of captivity was removed, the liberated colonies would be free to pursue their own destiny and develop economically as had their rich oppressors.[5]

For pessimism in my sense of the word, one has to turn not to Marxism, for all its prophecies of capitalist doom, which it saw, of course, as the precondition of socialist happiness (such has always been the nature of apocalyptic expectations), but to the so-called stagnationists of the 1930s. Those were hard times, when most industrial economies proved unexpectedly resistant both to the presumably corrective and restorative processes of classical economics and to the intervention of well-intentioned governments. It was a time for new explanations of persistent unemployment and of inadequate investment (thus, capital-saving innovation or the progressive exhaustion of technological possibilities). To be sure, these pessimists gave themselves an out by suggesting that "appropriate price and other policies" could compensate; but, as Alvin Hansen (who felt he knew what to do) warned, there was no assurance that these would be introduced.

No matter. The war came and unemployment disappeared; and after the war, contrary to expectations based on the post–World War I years, reconstruction, renewed trade, the satisfaction of pent-up consumer demand, and the invention of new techniques and industries fueled the most rapid growth the world had ever seen. So the stagnationists of the 1930s went the way of the Malthusians of the early nineteenth century—into dimly recollected oblivion.[6]

This was the state of the art of growthmanship when the end of World War II ushered in a new era of development promotion, of making up for lost time in the advanced industrial nations and, thanks to imminent decolonization, in the newly baptized Third World.[7] The effect of this new agenda was to shift the attention of economists from those problems of cyclical conjuncture that had preoccupied them before (understandable in the depression of the 1930s) and to restore the problems of growth and development to center stage, for the first time in over a century. In a matter of years, we had a rash of work on the subject, much of it taking the form of growth models of a Keynesian character.[8]

These constructs and lucubrations, though new in theme, were in the old tradition of classical analysis, as modified by the techniques of macroeconomics. They remained within the paradigm. (The Keynesians, who prided themselves on being iconoclasts and custodians of a new orthodoxy, were actually less revolutionary than they thought.) Thus they sought by means of production functions to link output to conventional inputs and took for granted the naturalness of a process that gathered and combined factors and turned them optimally into marketable goods and services.

All of this modeling was schematic and dealt primarily with "stylized," highly simplified versions of modern industrial economies whose connection to reality was at best coincidental. The underlying assumption, as before, was that growth and development were universally available and achievable, hence inevitable. Modern Industry (Marx's term) and Modern Economic Growth (Simon Kuznets') were destiny.[9] Because of this, there was no real effort to probe the sources of the wealth of nations (Hahn and Matthews 1964, p. 890). Rather, the process of growth was taken for cause and explanation; the *how* stood in for the *why*.

This sometimes unspoken faith (unspoken because obvious) was true of the entire political spectrum, right, left, and indifferent. Colin Clark had already set the pattern in his *Conditions of Economic Progress* (1940), with its analysis of shifting proportions from the primary to the secondary to the tertiary sector (the resemblance to Smith is apparent). And Walt Rostow, in his optimistic *Stages of Economic Growth* (1960), described an almost biological progress from one stage to another in the life of a national economy. Soviet spokesmen boasted about their imminent surpassing of capitalist economies such as those of France or the United States (''We shall bury you''). They even found Western sympathizers to echo their brags. Third World economists rejoiced at the prospect of wealth and power: one can read calculations (in effect quantified predictions) by economists and politicians of democratic republic X or ex-colony Y, newly launched on its populist path, showing it duly catching up with capitalist countries A, B, and C by the year 19—— (Patel 1962). Pride goeth . . .

The economic historians—then, unlike now, as often historians as economists—worked essentially in the same paradigm, with one major reservation. The historians necessarily incorporated external, noneconomic influences—politics, power, war, culture—into their explanatory framework. In particular, their analysis of changes in the mode of production—they were prepared to study what the economists took for granted—laid emphasis on the role of exogenous shocks in the form of new knowledge and innovation.

Two figures stand out here. The first was Paul Mantoux, a French historian who chose to do his *thèse d'état,* always a mammoth undertaking, on the subject of the British Industrial Revolution. The French, it should be noted, are singularly parochial in their historical interest, as their library collections and university course offerings show, but they have always made something of an exception for their friendly neighbor and historical enemy Britain; so students of British history include in the canon of classics such magna opera as Halévy's multivolume study of the cultural and political ramifications of industrialization. It was this tradition that legitimated Mantoux's project and prepared the way for its extraordinary intellectual influence in both countries.

This was at the turn of the century, long before we had the statistical data and constructs that make possible national income analysis, and Mantoux, following in the steps of earlier scholars (Arnold Toynbee, Thorold Rogers, W. Cunningham) and still earlier students of specific branches of manufacture (Richard Guest and Edward Baines on cotton, J. Bischoff and J. James on woolen and worsted)—there are always predecessors, as any student of intellectual history knows—set the tone for generations of historians (the book was still being

reprinted and assigned to students 75 years later) by treating the Industrial
Revolution as primarily a technological event, a new way of doing things.

This approach was subsequently reinforced by the historical work of A. P.
Usher, who pushed the emphasis on technology and invention farther than
anyone before, first in a modestly tentative but extraordinarily insightful *Industrial History of England* (1920), and then in *A History of Mechanical Inventions*
(1929), which resonated further in Lewis Mumford's influential *Technics and
Civilization* (1934).

The propagators of these views thought of themselves as adding an extra-
economic dimension and must have cherished the hope that economics itself
would change to take these ideas and findings into account. Yet the character of
economic analysis is that it is less a body of thought (although it is that, as any
graduate student will testify) than a mode of reasoning; and as such, it is
extraordinarily skillful at reducing apparently irregular or nonrational events to
regular, rational patterns, at bringing outside in. So with technology. Economists had no trouble "endogenizing" this phenomenon and incorporating it into
the classical paradigm. Invention and innovation may be exogenous and on
occasion adventitious—kinks in an otherwise smooth curve—but taken as a
large class (the law of large numbers), they could be linked as dependent
variables to conventional factors such as demand and investment. It was possible to show, for example, that the higher the rate of investment, the greater the
incentive to invent and the opportunity to innovate. Sometimes the transformation was little more than terminological. Usher, for example, had had recourse
to Gestalt psychology to account for invention: the inventor, he said, becomes
aware of something missing, something needed to make whole an incomplete
complex or process, and is led to create and act to fill the gap. But that could
be seen as a metaphor for a challenge-and-response (demand-and-supply) sequence of changing marginal rates of return. Subsequent authors had no trouble
defining these responses in economic terms.

Emerging, however, from this economic-historical tradition were two amend-
ments to the Smithian-Ricardian canon. The first was entrepreneurial history, an
offspring of business history and Schumpeterian economics. Headquarters was
the Center for Research in Entrepreneurial History at Harvard, under the direction of Arthur H. Cole. The work of this center, active in the late 1940s and
1950s, was diverse in character and argument; but the thread common to most
of it was the importance and particularity of the human factor, whether for
individual achievement or group patterns of economic behavior. Whereas the
classical paradigm assumed the universal homogeneity of the labor factor,
whether in fact *(Homo economicus)* or in potential (people as putty),[10] the
entrepreneurial school argued that people are different, and that, however ed-

ucable in the long run, they behave in culturally specific ways that shape the course of development.[11]

It should be said that this entrepreneurial approach was seen by most economists as romantic-impressionistic if not heretical and made little impact on mainstream economic thought. It was hard enough to model economic behavior using quantifiable factors without trying to incorporate unmeasurable idiosyncratic and cultural elements. Besides, nothing could shake the economists' fundamental belief in the rationality of human action, or at the least in the ineluctable triumph of rationality over its converse.

The second deviation was largely the contribution of Alexander Gerschenkron of Harvard University, who, be it noted, had little use for the entrepreneurial approach. (It was not until he encountered the Italians that he was prepared to say that maybe economic actors from different countries might themselves be different.) In a seminal article of 1951 (I use that much overused word advisedly) entitled "Economic Backwardness in Historical Perspective," he attacked the question of lateness.[12] Was the process of growth and development, which he assumed was congruent with industrialization, an easy progression, a matter of doing what comes naturally, or rather a difficult task requiring special preparation and effort? Gerschenkron's answer: industrialization is not easy, and latecomers do need to build special institutions to enable them to leap the gap between what they are and what they can be.

By implication, then, the market alone is not enough, even after the removal of political and institutional obstacles. Only Britain could do it the Smithian way. To be sure, there are advantages to coming after, in particular, the chance to learn from the successes and failures of one's predecessors and to exploit an accumulated pool of knowledge and technique. Hence, follower countries grow faster than their predecessors, in a spurt or series of spurts.

But there are also disadvantages. For one thing, the gap grows with time, so that threshold requirements of energy and resources increase. It takes more to do more. For another, the more it takes, the more painful the effort; hence the need for periods of respite. What is more, a backward economy unable to mobilize resources by private enterprise must rely on the state to accomplish this task; and the state can be (and has been, more often than not) a ruthless taskmaster. Gerschenkron's analysis here rested primarily on the Russian, then the Soviet Russian experience, and this was not a pretty story.

Within mainstream economic optimism (in the end, we shall all get there), Gerschenkron's discussion of backwardness was ambiguous. On the one hand, it set out a strategy for overcoming backwardness; on the other, his introduction of somewhat unspecified conditions and his emphasis on the social and political costs of revolution-from-above implied the possibility of failure. He confined his attention to Europe, and above all to those countries that had joined the

industrial parade, and this necessarily gave his analysis a how-to cast. But he
was not unaware of hard cases elsewhere, and his way of looking at the problem
carried its own pessimistic logic.

So it was from the side of economic history that the first breaks came with the
classical paradigm. But even without economic historians, the underlying optimism of classicists, neoclassicists, Keynesians, Marxists, and Third Worlders
must eventually have foundered on the rocks of reality.[13] Three shocks here:

1. *The pain of growth.* The passing years were to show how difficult development can be. Thus, after a generation of peace and effort and sundry political
incantations and promises, the Soviets had not come close to matching the
French, much less the American, standard of living and income per head—and
this, in spite of the promulgation of artificially inflated, blatantly fabricated, and
arrantly deceptive data of performance and the imposition of an absurdly flat-
tering official exchange rate for the ruble. Nor have the Indians matched the
proud predictions of their economists. Not that these pursuers were not growing;
some of them were growing faster than their predecessors of the nineteenth
century ever had. The advanced industrial economies were simply growing
more—that is, the gulf had widened. Meanwhile, a large number of poor
nations actually lost ground and became poorer, while some, apparently well
launched on the path of growth and progress, found their advance impeded or
even reversed by natural and man-made disaster.

2. *The discovery of the so-called residual.* The story of that discovery is
worth recalling. The ground was laid by the developing technique of national
accounting and the growing body of aggregate data on product and income. By
the 1950s it was possible to take the figures of factor inputs (number of workers,
quantity of investment) and relate them to the aggregates by means of production functions—the idea being to assign shares to the various components.
When the returns were in, however, the researchers were astonished to learn
that the conventional factors (land, labor, and capital) could account for less
than half the growth in product; and indeed, that the more advanced the economy, the greater the share of growth not so accounted for. The rest—obviously
the heart of the matter—was labeled the "residual," which was perceived and
understood as "technology"—a not unreasonable stand-in for productivity
gains that increased product beyond what the conventional factors could do.

But science abhors residuals, even when they are defined as something so
familiar as technology.[14] There were two reactions. The first was to get rid of
the residual. This took the form of so redefining the factors as to weight them
for quality as well as quantity—that is, to give up the assumption of
homogeneity—and thereby reduce the residual as much as possible. These
efforts did succeed in swelling the proportions assigned to the conventional

factors, but it is not clear to me that this is more than a clever bookkeeping device. The reality of knowledge, skill, education, work habits, values—the whole set of more or less (mostly less) quantifiable characteristics of the human actors—remained, though now homogenized like cream in milk.[15]

The second consisted in learning more about technology and its consequences. On the theoretical level, economists investigated the nature of technical change—for example, whether labor-saving, capital-saving, or neutral. But, more important, they also studied data on the invention and diffusion of techniques by way of understanding the determinants of change (Schmookler 1966; Mansfield 1968). Most of this work has assimilated technical know-how and hardware to a class of commodities freely available, in substitutable forms, to those who want and can pay for them, because that assumption allows the economist to deal with technology as an endogenous economic phenomenon, that is, as an object of rational calculation and market transactions. Case studies of particular changes or sequences of change continued to be left largely to economic historians and historians of technology, although important exceptions can be cited (for example, Griliches 1958).

Almost all this work, it should be noted, has dealt with technological change in advanced industrial economies. Work has barely begun on the nonrational obstacles to innovation, on the negative influence of institutional, social, and psychological attitudes.[16] And yet experience shows that technology does not always travel well, even on the cognitive level; that there are, for comparable technologies, substantial differences in productivity and in return to investment from one place to another; and that these differences are an important factor in differential rates of growth.

3. *The so-called Japanese miracle of the 1950s and 1960s.* The metaphor is not farfetched in the context of the classical paradigm. By all good economic lights, postwar Japan had little chance of regaining its status as a major economic power. The pounding of Allied bombers had reduced major industrial installations and much of the infrastructure to rubble; and the loss of overseas colonies and protectorates had deprived the country of privileged access to industrial raw material. The likelihood of Japan's returning to successful industrialization was small enough; the probability of attaining a major place in world steel and other branches of heavy industry had to be negligible.

And yet Japan did all this and more, achieving rates of growth never before seen and attaining in the space of less than two generations the second, if not the first, position in the competition for economic leadership. Furthermore, a number of other Asian economies—some, such as Hong Kong and Singapore, very small and special, others, such as Taiwan and lately South Korea, considerably larger—have clearly accomplished an industrial revolution and built similar rates of growth on the development of export manufactures. Note that all of these are former or, in the case of Hong Kong, present colonies, and hence presumably liable to the handicaps widely associated with such status.

All of this has given economists food for thought. It was clear that the classical paradigm could not easily explain these selective gains, any more than it could account for the economic failures that were now marring the landscape of conventional can-do optimism. To be sure, success and failure have different resonances. Many have been comfortable explaining *success* in human terms: the Japanese, for example, are said to be a society with a strong sense of teamwork and collective responsibility. Private enterprises, even though organized for profit, are able to build on these values to promote and enforce high standards of work performance, with direct consequences for efficiency and product reputation.

To explain *failure* in human terms, however, is more difficult, if only because no one likes to disparage the values and attitudes of others. It has been easier to blame external forces (neocolonialism, unequal trade, peripherality) or internal political and social institutions (bad government, the siphoning of surplus to support the life-style of an inherited or self-appointed elite, the follies of overweening military ambitions, the vainglorious and costly pursuit of prestige, the high cost of class conflict and ethnic and tribal divisions, poverty and ill health, and more); and there is truth in all of these. Few economists, however, are ready to look upon them as effects rather than causes, as the consequence of otherwise directed or inefficacious individual and social action.

Not that economists do not recognize and pay obeisance to the influence on growth of human factors. Any reading of the literature will turn up a wide variety of salutes to "attitudes to work, to wealth, to thrift, to having children, to invention, to strangers, to adventure, and so on" (Lewis 1955, pp. 14–16), to "attitudes of the mind and the ability to change them" (Paul Rosenstein-Rodan, in Meier and Seers 1984, pp. 219–220), to Rostow's "propensities" (a rose by any other name), and so on.[17]

Such passing references in the economic literature, however, are typically salutes *pour la forme*—a way of paying tribute to reality. The trouble with attitudes is that they do not measure well (although quantifiable proxies are occasionally available), and hence do not lend themselves to model building and abstract theorizing in the economic mode. Neither do they lend themselves to manipulation, correction, or improvement—at least, not in the short run. Indeed, there are some who look upon allusions to such considerations as vaguely racist, partly because they are attached to large groups of people (although economists have never had trouble with other kinds of group characterizations), partly because some prefer to see them (the easier to criticize them) as somehow genetic or psychologically embedded, hence quasi-unchangeable.

Ironically, they are also dismissed, sometimes by the same scholars, as epiphenomena that yield quickly to rational incentives and material interest. As a result, noneconomic, qualitative human variables, when mentioned, have been honored more in principle than in practice.

Nowhere is this clearer than among the practitioners of applied development. These doers and intenders of good are among the last adherents of the classical paradigm. They have no choice: either one knows what to do or there is no point in doing. Rostow (1990, p. 374) cites Albert Hirschman's recollections of his role as financial adviser to the planning board in Colombia in the 1950s (Hirschman, in Meier and Seers 1984, p. 90):

> I was principally expected to take, as soon as possible, the initiative in formulating some ambitious economic development plan that would spell out investment, domestic savings, growth, and foreign aid targets for the Colombian economy over the next few years. All of this was alleged to be quite simple for experts mastering the new programming technique: apparently there now existed adequate knowledge, even without close study of local surroundings, of the likely ranges of savings and capital-output ratios, and these estimates, joined to the country's latest national income and balance of payments accounts, would yield all the key figures needed.

They are like doctors who, for want of better, are compelled to treat the symptoms rather than the disease.

This confusion of the what and the how for the why, of process and effect for cause—what we may call the economists' sympathetic fallacy, of taking what you know and like for what you need—has had its counterpart among the economic historians, who came somewhat belatedly to the marvelous theories of neoclassical economics and the new quantification and have embraced them with all the enthusiasm of converts more papist than the pope.

This intellectual epiphany shows itself in any number of areas, but nowhere so clearly as in discussions of the Industrial Revolution. As noted earlier, this topic was traditionally studied as a revolution in technology, with all manner of consequences for product and income, internal and external terms of trade, distribution of product and employment by branch and sector, and similar conventional economic variables. Moreover, insofar as historians sought to understand this process, which, as we saw, was more than most economists were ready to do, the causality went from technique to economic consequences. And insofar as some sought to go deeper and understand why the changes in technique, the explanations took the form of naturally rational proclivities (as in Usher's Gestalt model) or of special social and cultural circumstances that led some people or definable groups into intellectual exploration, material invention, innovation, and enterprise.

There were, however, attempts to specify economic determinants of technical change. These focused originally on the supply of factors: capital (Earl J. Hamilton and the windfall profits of inflation [1929, 1941–42, 1952]; sundry Indian historians and the pillage of Indian wealth; T. S. Ashton and a falling rate of interest over the course of the eighteenth century [1949]; Eric Williams and the profits of the slave trade and sugar plantations [1966]); then land and its products (J. U. Nef and a "first industrial revolution" based on coal [1933, 1958]; and Kerridge, Bairoch [1973], Wrigley, and divers other scholars emphasizing the necessity and sufficiency of a prior agricultural revolution). Still others found the prime mover in the stimulus of demand, whether as a support for increased output (Eric Williams 1966; Solow and Engerman 1987; O'Brien and Engerman 1988) or as a source of pressure on the mode of production (Landes 1965, 1969, 1986).[18]

Things changed radically, it seems to me, when the economists first and the historians second got caught up in the question of the numerical criteria of an industrial transition or revolution. Once the development of the techniques of national accounting gave them numbers to work with, it was as though they had tasted of the fruit of the tree of knowledge and knew they were naked. In particular, a number of scholars followed the economists in arguing that industrialization would be marked by an increase in the rate of capital formation from, say, under 5 to over 10 percent of income. From there it was easy to confuse symptoms with etiology; the increased capital was seen as making, or making possible, the Industrial Revolution.[19]

Macroeconomic argument requires macroeconomic data, and "stylized" facts are subject to factual verification. The outcome was foreseeable, indeed inevitable. Beginning with Phyllis Deane, economic historians began to estimate, revise, and refine the national accounts of Britain in the eighteenth and early nineteenth centuries and found that the rise in the rate of capital formation was surprisingly gradual. No quick jump: the transition to a higher, postindustrial level took three-quarters of a century; moreover, the rates moved up to the higher level only after the introduction of the railway, with its much larger capital requirements (Deane and Cole 1962; Rostow 1963; Floud and McCloskey 1981; Crafts 1985). Factory industry alone was not enough.

The lessons of this reevaluation seemed to be confirmed by the national income data (Crafts 1989, pp. 64–65). Overall growth was slower than had been thought on the basis of the production series of those branches directly touched by the new technology. The economy obviously was a lot bigger than industry, a fortiori than the modern industrial sector, and changes in one part took time to ramify. In effect, the emphasis of J. H. Clapham, half a century earlier, on the tenacity of the older modes and branches and the gradualness of change was confirmed by the aggregate numbers (Clapham 1932, chap. 2).

But what conclusion to draw? One extreme reaction was to revive the debate about nomenclature: Did the Industrial Revolution deserve to be called a revolution? How could anything so gradual claim such a name? My own sense is that such quarrels are otiose, unless one is ready to give them substance by saying that there is no kink in the curves, no break in the previous pattern that signals a change in rhythm and mode. Some may be ready to say this, but such an assertion would fly in the face of the same statistical "facts" that have been used to argue the reverse. As slow as growth was in Britain from the late eighteenth century on (rising from 1.3 percent per annum in 1780–1801 to 2.5 percent in 1831–1860, according to Crafts 1989, p. 66), it was substantially faster than what had gone before (0.7 percent in 1700–1780); so that if one were to extrapolate backward, one would quickly arrive at near-zero levels of product and income.

There was a break, then, and this kink in the curve, however modest to start with, was indeed revolutionary in its import. It consisted in new ways of doing things, supported by new ways of thinking about the problems and tasks of production. These remain for me the heart of the matter, and the efforts of some historians to dismiss or decry the "technicist interpretation" strike me as misguided. They tell more about their authors than about industrial history.[20]

Shielded as they were from the tranquilizing reassurances of today's cliometricians (don't worry, be happy; you're doing better than you know), foreign contemporaries of the Industrial Revolution were anxiously aware that something momentous was going on in Britain that threatened to upset not only commercial relationships but the international order. More even than so perspicacious an observer as Smith, who was not conscious of the fact that he was living in an age of technological revolution, the mercantilist and cameralist functionaries of continental Europe understood that Britain's innovations were a challenge to the balance of power and the autonomy of other nations.[21] And what this means is that any attempt to understand why—why the change and why the sequence of change, within the economy and among nations—must begin with the character and sources of technological innovation. Not with the symptoms, not with the aggregate consequences, but with the causes.

A parallel reconstruction of the rates of growth of the so-called early follower countries (France, Belgium, Germany, the United States) has produced a comparable revisionism. There was a time when France in particular was seen as the very symbol of slow industrialization, to the point where some asked whether that country had gone through a revolution or an evolution. The contrast was especially marked with Germany, the model of rapid late development, and the exploration of these differences gave rise to a shelfful of interpretation and debate (Clapham 1921; Clough 1946; Landes 1949, 1950, 1953–54, 1954–55; Gerschenkron 1953–54, 1954–55; Cameron 1985).

It is clear to me now that this literature was in part a function of the condition of France in the interwar and immediate postwar periods, say 1920 to 1950. (In spite of all determination to resist temptation and work from the past forward, history is never free of anachronistic impulse.) France had suffered grievous industrial losses in World War I and, by the usual measures of economic power—income per head, consumption of energy, stock of consumer durables—had continued to lag behind; so that visitors there in the immediate post–World War II years had the sense of a country that had changed little since 1914.

France made up this lag in the next two decades (1950–1970), and her image changed accordingly. Meanwhile, research by French scholars into the aggregate statistics of growth gave a more favorable picture of French performance in the nineteenth century (Marczewski 1965; Markovitch 1965–66; Lévy-Leboyer 1968; Crouzet 1970); and this in turn provided ammunition for an incipient interest in alternative paths of growth: if France could do so well with smaller-scale enterprises, a larger agrarian sector, more light industry than heavy, and high-quality, even customized products, well, then, maybe our conventional assumption that a proper industrial revolution had to be built on heavy industry, bigness, and mass production was unjustified and contrary to fact. Note that this conventional assumption held even more for Marxists and, until recently, for most development economists than for neoclassical economists. Gerschenkron's work was symptomatic here, though he would not have been happy to be put in the same bed with socialist planners.

For a time. The disappointments of development programs, which even when reasonably successful could not satisfy the impatience of the poor and hungry, and in particular the repeated failure of attempts to follow the "big is better" formula, promoted an interest in less ambitious strategies of "appropriate technology." And this in turn was reinforced by a growing sensitivity to the dangers and penalties of big industry at any cost.

Some of the newer work in European history responded and gave support to these concerns. First there was the O'Brien and Keyder reinterpretation, *Economic Growth in Britain and France, 1780–1914: Two Paths to the Twentieth Century* (1978), which tried to argue from numbers that France did at least as well as Britain over the course of the Industrial Revolution. This is no easy affirmation to quantify, because as everyone knows, international comparisons across currencies depend on imputed equivalences. The index of exchange rates is crucial to the procedure, and the O'Brien-Keyder index leaves much to be desired (this must be the only price series anywhere that finds British coal to be more costly than French). Yet, even while putting the best possible face on French performance (by, among other things, excluding services from national product), the authors find British wages and consumption to be substantially greater than the French over the course of the century. To be sure, one man's "substantial" is another man's "trivial." They do not think the difference mattered much ("a gap of 15 per cent or so [in average consumption] is not very wide," p. 197); and besides, quantitative differences do not take into account quality considerations: they feel that *bifteck pommes frites* is better than fish and chips. De gustibus . . .

In the same intellectual tendency, though largely number-free, is the work of the "small is beautiful" school (my label) represented by Michael Piore, Charles Sabel, and Jonathan Zeitlin. This argues, along lines adumbrated by Stephen Marglin (1974, 1984), though with different motivation, that the bigness–mass production strategy is not only *not* the sole path to wealth but also not necessarily the most efficient; and that an emphasis on smaller-scale, more flexible enterprise would have produced a happier society and a more stable economy. The argument (as made in Sabel and Zeitlin 1985) is supported by evidence of the success of such enterprise in times and places past, and it has achieved special popularity in a country such as Italy, where recent industrial growth and prosperity have rested to a large degree on the success of such "small and flexible" firms in finding and exploiting niches in the market.

It does not seem to me that these strategies are mutually exclusive.[22] The technology of the Industrial Revolution gave important advantages to large-scale mass production, and these persist in branches making homogeneous or easily standardizable products. But there has always been a place for the smaller, more versatile enterprise, and what is more, such enterprise has often worked in productive symbiosis with the big producers, which are more comfortable with longer runs and fewer lines. Even so, the smaller enterprises have a special problem with continuity. If they are successful, they may grow to where they are no longer small and flexible; or they may look appetizing to bigger fish that have the ability to swallow them. And if they are not successful, they often do not have the resources to resist; hence a frequent pattern of brutal wage cuts and intensification of labor to a degree unacceptable, even unthinkable, in larger enterprises.

So, it is important to see the "small and medium-sized enterprises" for what they are, taking the bad with the good; to admire their creativity and artfulness while recognizing their weaknesses. They are seen by some today as a panacea for the ills of bigness and boredom, and an attempt to view them dispassionately is somehow felt to be counterprogressive. But these enterprises will not be the worse for realistic appraisal—or the better—unless one is talking more about politics than business. That kind of ideological loading is not economic history or economics; it is a yearning after utopia.[23]

I would give one more example of the difficulties of historical interpretation, the more instructive because it combines the two sources of temptation and error I have noted. On the one hand, it illustrates the dangers of taking the consequence for the cause, of the *how* and *what* for the *why;* on the other, of allowing programmatic ideology to call the tune.

I am referring here to the effort to understand the economic and technological superiority of Europe over the rest of the world and its translation into political power. Here too, as with the Industrial Revolution, we have the statistical paradox: the apparent contradiction of the achievement and the numbers. On the level of technology, one has by about 1500 a Europe so much stronger than other civilizations that it can plant itself just about anywhere on the surface of the globe within reach of naval guns. (Note that this represented a monumental change in relations: the Europe of the millennium had been weak and insecure, liable to aggression from all sides, too poor in its production techniques to sell more than some occasional minerals and above all people—a sure sign that there was not much else to sell.) This new hegemony, moreover, was related not only to knowledge and know-how, where Europe had already pulled ahead of other cultures, but to such related values as curiosity, adventurousness, and greed. The Europeans of the sixteenth century were ferocious in their appetites. Not a commendable quality, but powerful and devilishly effective.

The history of the confrontation between an expansionist West and the rest of the world is marked by repeated affirmations of this inequality, already well established before the Industrial Revolution. One could select examples at will, but perhaps the most revealing is the encounter of Britain and China, the most advanced of the new rich and the greatest of the old. At the end of the eighteenth century, when Britain was barely launched on its course of growth, China had thirty times the population and was far richer in the aggregate. This disparity, rather than intimidating, was irresistibly tempting to a Britain in full technological revolution and bursting with stocks of manufactures for export, the more so as Britain had a growing appetite for things Chinese, while the Chinese did not seem to want or need anything British, with the exception of such "toys" as clocks for the imperial court.

So Britain sent Lord Macartney at the head of a flotilla of men-of-war, laden with cannon and with gifts for the emperor, to treat as equal with equal, but really as advanced with backward. The gifts were chosen to convince the Chinese of Britain's scientific and technological superiority, to make them understand why Britain ruled the seas and hence the globe, to persuade them to make a permanent place in the capital for British representatives, to make them want to buy British. The Chinese, however, who knew that they were the celestial empire, navel of the universe, were in no mood for any subtle intimations of weakness or inferiority; for them, the British, like all barbarians, were come to bring tribute. So they took the gifts and sent the embassy back with a few of their own—but yielded no trade concessions. The British tried again, in vain, some twenty years later. After that, in 1839, they tried gunboats—that is, superior armament—and made their point.[24]

Now, one might well expect that this kind of technological and political superiority would be an expression of, and translate into, differences in productivity and product per head. Europe should have been rich by comparison with its more backward rivals (although these would not necessarily have thought of themselves as such) and getting richer.[25]

But this, we are told by Paul Bairoch (1979), is not what the figures say. They seem to say that there was little difference in income per head between Europe and the other major civilizations in the eighteenth century, and that the great gap between what we now see as First and Third World came as a result of the Industrial Revolution—indirect evidence, by the way, for the revolutionary character of that transformation. To be sure, the meaning of such figures depends on definition (What is the Europe we are comparing with the outside?) and perhaps on distribution (Is the average of an aggregate misleading? Is income distributed more widely in one than the other?). And of course, the figures are not comparable in their accuracy to those developed by modern statistical bureaus. They are the product of ingenious guesswork and the heroic use of proxies. One does not have to believe them at all.

Yet, let us believe them, because then we have to confront the same kind of problem we considered in regard to European industrialization: namely, where is the cause and what is the timing?

Cause first: the *primum mobile* is the acquisition and application of knowledge. Wealth alone is not enough, nor even growth of wealth.[26] The disparity of power comes not from wealth but from its uses. Differences in power in turn translate easily into aggression and domination, for politics, like nature, abhors a vacuum, and the stronger, or at least some of the stronger (conquistadores, for example) will use the disparity for their advantage.

In this process, trajectory is more important than levels. A passing vehicle starts behind, comes abreast, and pulls away. Its superior acceleration anticipates, announces the change in relative position. And so for West and East: European technological superiority built up over time, appearing in one or two branches to start with (like the leading sectors in the Industrial Revolution)— and not just any branches, but rather critical branches such as navigation and armament, and not by chance, not by windfall gifts, but on the basis of new forms of knowledge and know-how. For many years—centuries—the legacy of accumulated wealth and pride comforted the laggards and losers, though only for a time.

These changes in capability and productivity, moreover, were related to profound differences in structures and values between Europe and the rest of the world. They did not rest on chance or luck. This is no small matter, for it has political and ideological implications. It has been comforting and useful to what we may call development historians (by analogy with development economists) of a radical or anti-Western persuasion to argue that Western dominance was the product of a small, better yet accidental, moment of superiority, which was then successfully nourished and fortified. A small gap became a gulf, especially after an industrial revolution that was itself the reward of imperial dominance and exploitation. Such an interpretation may be helpful in delegitimizing Western wealth ("They never really earned it") and in justifying claims for compensatory damages. It may also serve the useful purpose of moderating the complacency and pride of the haves over against the humiliation and deprivation of the have-nots. But it is not history. Marx, following Hegel, said that history abhors leaps, and so it does. It also abhors stunted chains of causality, big consequences derived from small accidents.

In all these matters of analysis and controversy, we are talking in effect of two ways of viewing economic change. These two ways divide in essence economics proper and economic history. They do not necessarily have to divide them, because they do not represent incompatible perspectives on reality. On the contrary, each is needed to complete the other. Yet they stand apart, regarding each other across a divide of method, temperament, congeniality, philosophy. These are not small reasons for divergence, in spite of a common allegiance to "scientific method" and truth.

The diversity of the essays in this collection reflects this methodological divide, as well as more conventional differences in topic as grouped under the three main headings of Technology, Entrepreneurialism, and Paths of Economic Growth. In this they testify to the richness of the larger problem of economic development, whether from the point of view of sources, process, or consequences—a richness that invites and requires a variegated response. There is a history of technology by James Burke (1978) that has the potent one-word title *Connections* and emphasizes the way in which one thing leads to another: the whole process of inquiry and discovery is one of linkage and ramification. So with problem-oriented research.

So, then, with the topic of technology—which, in spite of its frequently exogenous character, remains at the heart of the larger process of economic development. We have Paul Bairoch, Paul David, and Joel Mokyr on the sources and choices of technological change, Robert Fogel and Wolfram Fischer on the working-out of such change in two very different areas of application, and Rudolf Braun (as always, an intellectual pioneer and outlier, but then, he comes to history from the side of ethnography) on the biological constraints and implications of the new industrial technologies.

The same with entrepreneurship (which I prefer to *entrepreneurialism;* the word has enough syllables already). This is, on the level of choices and decisions, the point of intersection of conventional factors and human responses. This is the theme of the Robert Allen and Peter Temin essays, and also of

Jonathan Hughes's pioneering exploration of bureaucratic enterprise— pioneering because the salient characteristic of that piece in my opinion is the mapping of a problem in economics and economic history onto a topic that is normally left to students of political science. This is another instance of the "connections" syndrome: method transcends disciplinary boundaries, and economists, the most self-assured of "social scientists," are natural imperialists.

François Jequier, on the other hand, is pure historian: he tells the story of the successes and tribulations of the Swiss watch industry in terms of owners and managers, pride and complacency, standards and competition, old techniques and new. It reads as narrative, but a story well told is an implicit analysis. François Crouzet does the same, although he treats not of industry but of trade and finance. (He also provides an uncommonly rich prosopography, in the best Namierian tradition, of his dramatis personae: those Protestant merchants and bankers who had come to Britain usually poor, as refugees from religious persecution, and profited from bonds of language and memory, kinship and marriage, while working to dissolve these same bonds in the melt of an easy assimilation.) Both deal with a community of entrepreneurs, defined in each instance by common activities and concerns—for the Swiss watch industry by industrial history and tradition, and for the Huguenots by religious history (persecution and dispersion) and a set of values that Weber called an ethic. Implicit in both, then, is the notion that these common characteristics have an influence on economic performance: rationality and optimization are not the whole story.

William Lazonick poses a more general problem, one that concerns all of us (including me in this essay) because of its seeming intractability: how to marry economic history and economics. The two parties esteem and need each other, but is there love? And can a marriage without love succeed? Lazonick is more hopeful than I. For one thing, he believes in radical economics as an appropriate and effective incorporation of history and politics with theory. For another, he feels he has found an answer in his own work and teaching, that is, that he has found a way to marry these discrepant but complementary partners. And he quotes the nearest thing to Scripture in the good cause: Schumpeter, who said that if he could do it over, he would do economic history.

Schumpeter, incidentally, has not been alone. One can think of other instances of economists turning to economic history in their later years, not so much perhaps in penance as in an effort to compensate for their failure to stay abreast of new developments in economics. Shifting comparative advantage rewards these field shifts. In an increasingly mathematized discipline, time is a fearsome enemy. As everyone knows, mathematicians are at their most original and best when they are very young. More and more, the same is true of economists. This is the reverse of a field such as history, where intellectual buildup should be cumulative and one is supposed to grow wiser with age. As economic history becomes more quantitative, it becomes more open and welcoming to retread economists.

Both Lazonick and Temin use the same material to pursue very different paths. Lazonick states his personal debt to Stephen Marglin's essay "What Do Bosses Do?" (1974) and deplores my own want of appreciation of a bold challenge to conventional wisdom that made use (wanted to make use?) of historical data (Landes 1986). I should, he says, have welcomed this recourse to history and rejoiced. Instead I laid great stress on the evidential weaknesses of the essay, inter alia, a focus that no doubt reflects my own methodological biases as historian: if one is to do history, evidence matters. Mea culpa. Be that as it may, it is one more proof of the difficulty of this marriage.

Temin, on the other hand, looks at the debate and suggests that there is need for refinement—specifically, for the distinction between Schumpeterian innovative entrepreneurship and ordinary, routinized enterprise (my term, with a bow to Max Weber), which he calls management. This distinction goes back a long way; it was one of the recurrent themes of Arthur Cole's Center for Research in Entrepreneurial History in the 1950s, where most of us were reluctant to limit the entrepreneurial factor to great and small leaps forward. It is a distinction still worth making on the analytic level, but one frequently and necessarily transcended in real life by entrepreneur-managers who do both. Besides, as Harvey Leibenstein has shown, even apparent routine lends itself to creative change and important gains in productivity.

The interweaving and ramification of themes shows in the ambiguous character of the ordering of the essays: it is hard to know, for example, why Walt Rostow's survey of theory should not be paired with Robert Allen's excursion, or why Alfred Chandler's piece in Part III should not be included with the others on entrepreneurship. Rostow's essay, along with Lazonick's, is a particularly helpful example of one of history's major functions: the rescue of thought and wisdom from neglect and oblivion. This is no small matter in a field that has a desperate yearning for quick obsolescence. It's all in the role model. Insofar as economics strives to be scientific, it imitates the natural sciences in its rush to obliterate the past by improving on it. Physicists do not feel the need to do the history of physics. Why should economists have to reckon with their predecessors, except perhaps to stand on their shoulders (or backs)? Well, for one thing, the best of these predecessors were as smart and wise as the best of their successors; for another, much of what they said is relevant to our problems today.

The other essays are studies of the working-out of technical change. Jeff Williamson examines in this regard an aspect of what may well be the most tenacious and passionate (as much as these things can become passionate) debate in European economic history: Was the Industrial Revolution good or bad? Using the methods of cliometric history to examine the urban landscape, he argues that, whatever gains were made in industry, social overhead (housing and related amenities) was sorely neglected; indeed, that it was this neglect that released capital for industrialization. By implication, British growth—already seen by the so-called new economic history as slower than had been thought—was slower yet. This widening of the historian's perspective to include related social costs is an important argument, not unrelated to the current debate on the incorporation of negative environmental effects into national income accounts.

Irma Adelman, Anne Krueger, and Claudia Goldin are more positive in tone. All are concerned with the bottom line, which has a way of revealing what the year-in, year-out tribulations tend to conceal or obscure behind a curtain of static.

Adelman's analysis draws on a large body of empirical data of growth and their statistical analysis (see, inter alia, Morris and Adelman 1988). The results show what is already widely known, namely, that rates of growth in the twentieth century are higher than in the nineteenth. But there are surprises, in particular the relative importance of institutional innovation in comparison with technological change. One could, of course, do some bookkeeping sleight of hand (as with the "emptying" of the residual) and define technology to include institutional arrangements as well as equipment and processes; there is certainly warrant for such a definition. But that would be evading the issue, and a more fruitful approach would be to explore the reasons, which are probably related among other things to the potential returns of the two types of innovation in labor-abundant economies.

Krueger builds similarly on the numbers and notes the especially favorable conjuncture of the decades following World War II, when the international economy grew at an unprecedented rate and conditions were never more favorable to poor countries trying to catch the rich. Some took advantage, and some did not, and Krueger would find the principal distinction in the adoption by the former of policies that facilitated integration into the international market and exploitation of its opportunities. Her explanation for bad choices (with apologies to materialist colleagues) is largely ideological: a postcolonial legacy of aggravated nationalism, the belief in government as an all-powerful provider, and the memories of market failure during the period of the Great Depression. I would add in this connection only the influence of radical, anticapitalist doctrines., which have argued that integration into the world market is an invitation to dependency and exploitation, and hence to be avoided. My own sense is that economists in Third World countries have been more influenced by Prebisch and company than by Ragnar Nurkse. With all this, Krueger remains hopeful, because there is always room for self-amendment and self-improvement. (It is easier to be discouraged about the past than the future.)

This underlying optimism (can we afford anything else?) of the "quantitativists" reminds me that the introduction of numbers into the debate on the consequences of the Industrial Revolution similarly tilted the verdict toward the positive; to the point where the "pessimist" critics chose to shift the emphasis away from real wages and consumption data toward the qualitative aspects of life. Even if material conditions improved, the argument ran, the quality of life deteriorated. And that may well be, since quality is surely much a matter of perception, so that even in times of amelioration, expectations may outstrip reality. Today one could make a similarly pessimistic argument about growth in Third World countries, where morbidity and ecological data remain discouraging, to say nothing of the unhappy politics of social discontent and bad government. But one can hope that the long run will prove favorable on all counts, as it has in industrializing Europe, that knowledge and technology will do their work.

These are examples of the limitations of data, even numerical data: they are a necessary but not sufficient condition of persuasion and conviction.

These differences underline the fact that economic history, for all its increasing quantification, remains an art rather than a science. And where there is art, there is the artistry and the diversity of understanding, interpretation, and persuasion. That comes across very well in the essays presented here, which approach a common concern with considerable assurance and a variety of technique; which talk to one another but in somewhat different tongues; which come up with answers small and large, but leave room for amendment and contradiction. Would it be better if there were one valid answer to the problem of growth and we knew it? No doubt; but we are talking here about an intensely human phenomenon, hence immensely complex and in its totality ungraspable. On the material level, that can be very painful as well as gratifying. On the intellectual level also.

It is good to think that we have come a long way since our predecessors, even people as clever as Smith and Marshall. Our successors will presumably be able to say the same.

Notes

1. E. A. Wrigley (1987, pp. 21–45) presents Smith differently. In a suggestive and original essay, "The Classical Economists and the Industrial Revolution," he pairs him with Malthus and Ricardo as someone who "discounted the possibility of a sustained, progressive rise in real incomes" (p. 23).

I do not agree. It is true that Smith, anticipating Malthus, speaks of the "natural" propensity of "every species of animals" to multiply "in proportion to the means of their subsistence" (although he associates this behavior in "civilized society" with the "inferior ranks of people"); also that he finds the condition of the "labouring poor" at its best when society is in the "progressive state": "It is hard in the stationary, and miserable in the declining state." And he goes on to say, "The progressive state is in reality the cheerful and the hearty state to all the different orders of the society. The stationary is dull; the declining melancholy" ([1776] 1937, p. 81).

Smith never defines these "states," and there is nothing in his exposition to indicate that they are some kind of unhappy progression. (My own sense is that they represent conditions or conjunctures, characteristic of one or another nation at one or another time.) On the contrary, he is, as Wrigley notes, conscious of the substantial improvement in the condition of labor over the course of his lifetime; he was also well aware of the fact that labor often receives a better-than-subsistence wage. And while he did not realize that the England of his day had entered upon an industrial revolution, he thought of technology and the mode of production as responsive and malleable. The same chapter, "Of the Wages of Labour" (chap. 8), ends on this note: "The same cause, however, which raises the wages of labour, the increase of stock, tends to increase its productive powers, and to make a smaller quantity of labour produce a greater quantity of work. The owner of the stock which employs a great number of labourers, necessarily endeavours, for his own advantage, to make such a proper division and distribution of employment, that they may be enabled to produce the greatest quantity of work possible. For the same reason, he endeavours to supply them with the best machinery which either he or they can think of."

Smith goes on to say that what takes place in the workplace also takes place in the society as a whole: the greater the number, the greater the division of labor. Moreover, "more heads are occupied in inventing the most proper machinery for executing the work of each, and it is, therefore, more likely to be invented."

Smith was an optimist.

2. The one major exception to this happy picture was the great Irish famine of the mid-1840s. It should not pass uncommemorated as a monument to human mismanagement, incompetence, and indifference. There were also less severe local famines, as in Flanders in the early 1840s. Famines on the other side of the world, as in India or Japan, made little or no impression on Europeans.

3. See, on this point, Smith's analysis of China's "stationary" state: the country "had probably long ago acquired that full complement of riches which is consistent with the nature of its laws and institutions. But this complement may be much inferior to what, with other laws and institutions, the nature of its soil, climate, and situation might admit of" ([1776] 1937, p. 95).

4. Marx [1894] 1962, chap. 5, sec. 5, p. 103. See Bober 1968, pp. 282–283.

5. This is a condensed, homogenized version of a diverse literature. Marxist critiques of imperialism range from simple land-drain arguments—that it is a system for growing the cash crops and emptying the mines with cheap forced or semiforced labor of a kind one could not employ at home—to conspiracy theories about capitalist unwillingness to help colonies develop industrially in competition with the mother country. For a guide to some of this diversity, much of which takes the form of rediscovering old news, see Griffin and Gurley 1985.

Note, of course, that this criticism of capitalist rule was system specific; that is, it applied to capitalist or bourgeois government, not to socialist regimes. In this regard, the Marxists, as collectivists, were far closer to the Tories than to classical economic liberals. Cf. Lipset 1988, p. 30.

6. On 1930s pessimism and the bullish rebuttal of business journalists who may have been motivated by self-interest but proved to have had better judgment than the panjandrums of economics, see Landes 1969, pp. 480–485.

7. The origin of the term is French, *tiers monde,* first used by Georges Balandier and Alfred Sauvy in 1956. Ironically, they did not intend it at first in the sense that it has since taken on, of a third world alongside and in between the first world of the advanced capitalist countries and a competitive second world of socialist nations. Rather, they were thinking of the Tiers Etat of revolutionary France, also a majority and also powerless: "What is the Tiers Etat? Nothing. What does it want to be? Everything" (Gilbert 1985, p. 678).

8. By way of a quick statistical probe, I have compared the volume of publication of articles on

growth and development theory (which, in spite of the designation, includes empirical studies) in the *Index of Economic Journals* of the American Economic Association: for the period 1925–1939, a little over one page of citations; for 1940–1949, a little over two pages; for 1950–1954, over seven pages; and for the next quinquennium, sixteen pages. Even if one allows for the overall growth in publication, the increase of 1955–1959 over 1950–1954 is over 60 percent. A new subdiscipline had been born.

9. Kuznets himself was more careful. He noted that the expectation that "underdeveloped" countries would develop was based on three considerations: (1) there are other countries where production and growth per capita are at much higher levels; (2) over the last two centuries "strikingly high rates of growth" have been achieved; and (3) the stock of useful knowledge is large, has been growing fast, and is there for the using. But, he stressed, this expectation was a presumption, and we should be wary about inferring from the successes of perhaps a fifth of mankind the prospects of the underdeveloped rest (Kuznets 1965, p. 177).

10. A codicil to the classical paradigm argues that even if there are differences in the quality of the human factors of production, these can be compensated by hire: "High-grade managerial and technological skill is always on sale at a competitive price, and provided it can adapt itself to local conditions . . . is cheap almost regardless of its price . . . Managerial and engineering 'know-how' are the most mobile internationally of economic goods" (Viner 1953, p. 104).

11. This approach was subsequently reinforced, at least implicitly, by a revival (recollection) of Joseph Schumpeter's theory of the entrepreneur—an outlier, well out of the mainstream of the discipline of economics. Economic historians had not really noticed it before, but then again, not many economic historians kept abreast of the economics literature.

12. He was, of course, not the first to raise the issue. Thorstein Veblen had anticipated him in his *Imperial Germany and the Industrial Revolution* (1915), which is, once one gets past the introductory material, the locus classicus for the effects of "lateness" on economic development. Indeed, practical concern with problems of backwardness goes back to the eighteenth century, when the countries of continental Europe became aware of British technological advance and realized that they could not afford not to follow. The assumption then was that the state, in the best mercantilist tradition, would take the necessary steps to catch up—by sending missions of inspection, overt and covert, by financing and otherwise facilitating new forms of enterprise, and so on. And then, after the end of a generation of revolutionary and imperial wars, when the European governments found themselves short of resources, private enterprise came forward with suggestions of institutional innovations to accomplish what the state could or would no longer do. In particular, we have numerous proposals for the creation of investment banks and joint-stock ventures with the specific aim of mobilizing capital to meet the larger industrial requirements of the new technologies. These proposals, coming from experienced businessmen such as Gustav Mevissen and political economists such as Friedrich List (himself influenced by Alexander Hamilton's "Report on Manufactures" of 1791), are every bit as conscious of the specificities of backwardness as the work over a century later of Gerschenkron. But when Gerschenkron wrote, this older stream of thought had faded into the oblivion of seeming irrelevance, a program rendered obsolete (as List thought it should be) by the passage of the earlier follower countries from backwardness to industrial maturity.

13. One of the best discussions of the tension between theory and reality is to be found in Jacob Viner's little book *International Trade and Economic Development* (1953), originally delivered as lectures at the National University of Brazil in July and August 1950. A number of his points are worth repeating. He warns, for example, of "the general tendency, inherent in the nature of theory, to be unsuitable for practical application unless . . . adequate consideration is given to the need for its adaptation to the realities and the complexities of the specific situation" (p. 1). He notes the "great temptation for the theorist" to reduce and simplify, and suggests that this practice is encouraged by "the doctrine of ancient origin, but nevertheless of highly questionable validity for the social sciences, that the progress of scientific analysis is marked by the substitution of simple for complex solutions to problems and of precise and definite for qualified and contingent answers to questions" (p. 2). He deplores the tendency to select problems for their interest as intellectual exercises: "We are, like all professions, a

kept profession, and we must supply to the public who hire us the merchandise which they need, although not necessarily the merchandise they ask for. *We must be relevant*" (p. 4). And without mentioning mathematics, he tells his fellows to be suspicious of "a trend toward greater simplicity and rigor of models in economics at a time when it is apparent to even the man in the street that the real economic world has been getting more complicated and its problems less susceptible of exact and clean-cut solutions" (p. 3).

14. Cf. E. A. G. Robinson at the conclusion of a conference on the role of technology in economic growth: "We can't have an amorphous residual factor for which there is no explanation" (B. R. Williams 1973, p. xi, cited in Rostow 1990, p. 333).

15. Among the economists most active in this still controversial reevaluation of the factors of production has been Dale Jorgenson, who sees things differently. He agrees that the discovery of the residual was a major shock to the assumptions and conventions of economics, as great as or greater in its significance than the so-called Keynesian revolution. Yet he argues that the effort to reorder the analysis of growth along new lines, emphasizing technological innovation (that is, shifts in the production function) as against substitution effects (movements along the isoquants) was mistaken; in other words, that after the dust has settled, the classical paradigm has been confirmed. By his calculations, gains in productivity—that is, advances in technology—accounted for only 27 percent of United States growth during the period 1870–1914 and only 24 percent for the period 1948–1979. See Jorgenson and Griliches 1967, 1972a, 1972b; and Jorgenson 1988 and unpublished ms. and the literature cited there. I have problems with this approach. For me, it is not simply a move along the isoquant; the very character of the isoquant has been transformed by the introduction of new techniques.

16. There is, however, a substantial literature on the politics and culture of technological change in Third World countries, much of it in the kind of regional or local scholarly journal not often read by "mainstream" economists. See, for example, Bhattacharya 1966 for the influence of caste arrangements on the adoption and diffusion of modest but highly remunerative innovations in Indian craft industry; or Attwood 1984 and 1985 on the use of irrigation in the Indian sugar industry.

17. I have been led to these quotes by Walt Rostow's survey of thought on development (1990), which is a mine of information on the intellectual evolution and fashions of the subject.

18. For a rebuttal to demand-driven models, see Mokyr 1977 and McCloskey, in Floud and McCloskey 1981, pp. 120–123. McCloskey's argument is based on a static analysis of a closed system illustrated by parables drawn, inter alia, from Robinson Crusoe and pretends to a rare and superior common sense. "In the aggregate," he writes (p. 120), "demand is not an independent factor causing income to grow . . . Judging from the frequency with which it has eluded writers on the industrial revolution the point is an elusive one." Indeed. The exposition is laced with spoken and unspoken assumptions of equal returns at the margin, of full and optimum employment of inputs, and of technological autonomy, plus a few metaphors, and any connection with what really happened in eighteenth-century England is largely coincidental.

19. Much to the distress of Rostow, who laments the misunderstanding (1990, p. 434): "My colleagues insisted on regarding the rise in the investment rate in the takeoff as a primal cause in the manner, say, of a Harrod-Domar growth model . . . a part of the fault was certainly mine. If I had it to do over again, I would state emphatically, right at the beginning, . . . [that the] emergence of a rate of net investment sufficient to outstrip the rate of increase of population and to yield a positive net rate of growth is at least as much the result of prior sectoral growth as a cause of growth."

20. For a dismayingly accepting appreciation of recent revisionist writing on this subject, see Jones 1988, chap. 1, "A Know-All's Guide to the Industrial Revolution." The quoted phrase is from p. 19.

21. In another strange excursion, Donald McCloskey tries to decouple Britain's economic lead from the strategic interests of other countries by arguing that industrial power was not a vital ingredient of political and military power: "In economics there are substitutes, even if there are not in chemistry" (1988, p. 647). That inference from theory strikes me as dead wrong, but even if it were right, it would not be relevant to the decisions of contemporaries of the Industrial Revolution, who thought otherwise. But then they had not had the benefit of courses in neoclassical economics.

22. The argument, insofar as it is historical and not programmatic, relies among other things on grandiose counterfactuals, what one might call the Big If: if, two hundred years ago, we had done this instead of that . . . Such exercises in conjecture have a strong optative component and are not amenable to testing: historical fun and games. See on this Landes, "Piccolo è bello. Ma è bello davvero?" in Landes 1987, pp. 162–178.

23. For an earlier, similar presentation of ideology with historical argument, see Marglin, "What Do Bosses Do?" (1974) and "Knowledge and Power" (1984), and a response in Landes, "What Do Bosses Really Do?" (1986). Marglin also engages in counterfactual hypothesizing: his alternative path is one in which enterprises are owned collectively and run unhierarchically, without division of labor and stultifying specialization. And, like Sabel and Zeitlin, he feels that the victory of mass-production, factory-based technology rests not on superior technology and efficiency but on a succession of political acts.

24. See especially Peyrefitte 1989, which is based not only on the traditional sources, the published memoirs of British participants, but on hitherto unexploited and in part unknown Chinese, British, and French archives: a tour de force.

25. It is interesting in this regard to read Adam Smith on the subject of China. China, he tells us, "has long been one of the richest, that is, one of the most fertile, best cultivated, most industrious, and most populous nations in the world." But China has been "stationary" for centuries and seems to be no better (or worse off) than it was in the time of Marco Polo. This lack of growth explains the low wages of labor, so that, although peasants, workers, and artisans labor and run hard all day, "the poverty of the lower ranks of people in China far surpasses that of the most beggarly nations in Europe" ([1776] 1937, pp. 71–72). Smith relies here on what we would call anecdotal evidence—the reports of travelers on the Canton area, in particular concerning the behavior of the poor. One sentence is well worth remembering: "Marriage is encouraged in China, not by the profitableness of children, but by the liberty of destroying them."

26. In *Growth Recurring* (1988), Eric Jones argues that what matters is not so much technical innovation as "intensive growth," that is, growth in product or income per head; and that while technology no doubt contributes mightily to such growth, it is not necessary to it. I disagree. What I would call windfall growth—that is, growth that is not based on gains in productivity derived from advances in technique and organization—is intrinsically precarious and ephemeral. For the experience of today's Third World countries in this regard, see Fagerberg 1988, p. 451.

References

Ashton, T. S. 1949. *The Industrial Revolution, 1760–1830*. London: Home University Library.

Attwood, Donald W. 1984. "Capital and the Transformation of Agrarian Class Systems: Sugar Production in India." In M. Desai, S. Rudolph, and A. Rudra, eds., *Agrarian Power and Agricultural Productivity in South Asia*, pp. 20–50. Delhi: Oxford University Press.

———— 1985. "Peasants vs. Capitalists in the Indian Sugar Industry: Impact of the Irrigation Frontier." *Journal of Asian Studies* 45, no. 1:59–80.

Bairoch, Paul. 1973. "Agriculture and the Industrial Revolution, 1700–1914." In Carlo M. Cipolla, ed., *The Fontana Economic History of Europe: The Industrial Revolution*. London: Collins/Fontana Books.

———— 1979. "Ecarts internationaux des niveaux de vie avant la Révolution industrielle." *Annales: économies, sociétés, civilisations* 34 (January–February):145–171.

Bhattacharya, S. 1966. "Cultural and Social Constraints on Technological Innovation and Economic Development: Some Case Studies." *Indian Economic and Social History Review* 3, no. 3 (September):240–267.

Blusse, L., H. L. Wesseling, and G. D. Winius, eds. 1980. *History and Underdevelopment: Essays on*

Underdevelopment and European Expansion in Asia and Africa. Leiden: University of Leiden, Center for the Study of European Expansion.

Bober, M. M. [1927] 1968. *Karl Marx's Interpretation of History*. 2nd ed., rev. Cambridge, Mass.: Harvard University Press.

Burke, James. 1978. *Connections*. Boston: Little, Brown.

Cameron, Rondo. 1985. "A New View of European Industrialization." *Economic History Review*, 2nd ser., 38:1–23.

Clapham, John H. 1921. *The Economic Development of France and Germany*. Cambridge: Cambridge University Press.

———— 1932. *An Economic History of Modern Britain*. Vol. 2. *Free Trade and Steel, 1850–1886*. Cambridge: Cambridge University Press.

Clark, Colin. [1940] 1951. *The Conditions of Economic Progress*. London: Macmillan.

Clough, Shepherd B. 1946. "Retardative Factors in French Economic Development in the Nineteenth and Twentieth Centuries." *Journal of Economic History* 3 (supp.):91–102.

Crafts, N. F. R. 1985. *British Economic Growth during the Industrial Revolution*. Oxford: Clarendon.

———— 1989. "The Industrial Revolution: Economic Growth in Britain, 1700–1860." In Anne Digby and Charles Feinstein, eds., *New Directions in Economic and Social History*. Chicago: Lyceum.

Crouzet, François. 1970. "Essai de construction d'un indice annuel de la production industrielle française au XIXe siècle." *Annales: économies, sociétés, civilisations* 25, no. 1 (January–February):56–99.

Deane, Phyllis, and W. A. Cole. 1962. *British Economic Growth, 1688–1959*. Cambridge: Cambridge University Press.

Fagerberg, Jan. 1988. "Why Growth Rates Differ." In Giovanni Dosi et al., *Technical Change and Economic Theory*. London: Pinter.

Felix, David. 1956. "Profit Inflation and Industrial Growth: The Historic Record and Contemporary Analogies." *Quarterly Journal of Economics* 70:441–463.

Floud, Roderick, and Donald McCloskey, eds. 1981. *The Economic History of Britain since 1700*. 2 vols. Cambridge: Cambridge University Press.

Gerschenkron, Alexander. 1953–54. "Social Attitudes, Entrepreneurship, and Economic Development." *Explorations in Entrepreneurial History* 6, no. 1 (November):1–15. Reprinted in A. Gerschenkron, *Economic Backwardness in Historical Perspective*, pp. 52–71. Cambridge, Mass.: Harvard University Press, 1962.

———— 1954–55. "Some Further Notes on 'Social Attitudes, Entrepreneurship, and Economic Development.' " *Explorations in Entrepreneurial History* 7, no. 2 (December):111–119.

Gilbert, Pierre, ed. 1985. *Dictionnaire des mots contemporains*. New ed. Paris: Les usuels du Robert.

Griffin, Keith, and John Gurley. 1985. "Radical Analyses of Imperialism, the Third World, and the Transition to Socialism: A Survey Article." *Journal of Economic Literature* 23 (September):1089–1143.

Griliches, Zvi. 1958. "Research Costs and Social Returns: Hybrid Corn and Related Innovations." *Journal of Political Economy* 66, no. 5 (October):419–431.

Hahn, F. H., and R. C. O. Matthews. 1964. "The Theory of Economic Growth: A Survey." *Economic Journal* 74, no. 296 (December):779–902.

Hamilton, Earl J. 1929. "American Treasure and the Rise of Capitalism, 1500–1700." *Economica* 9:338–357.

———— 1941–42. "Profit Inflation and the Industrial Revolution." *Quarterly Journal of Economics* 56:257–270.

———— 1952. "Prices and Progress." *Journal of Economic History* 12:325–349.

Jones, Eric. 1988. *Growth Recurring: Economic Change in World History*. Oxford: Clarendon.

Jorgenson, Dale. 1988. "Productivity and Postwar U.S. Economic Growth." *Journal of Economic Perspectives* 2, no. 4 (Fall):23–41.

———— Unpublished ms. "Productivity and Economic Growth." Harvard Institute of Economic Research.

Jorgenson, Dale, and Zvi Griliches. 1967. "The Explanation of Productivity Change." *Review of Economic Studies* 34 (3), no. 99 (July):249–283.

———— 1972a. "Issues of Growth Accounting: A Reply to Edward F. Denison." *Survey of Current Business* 52, no. 5 (May):65–94.

———— 1972b. "Issues in Growth Accounting: Final Reply." *Survey of Current Business* 52, no. 5 (May):111.

Kuznets, Simon. 1965. *Economic Growth and Structure: Selected Essays*. London: Heinemann.

Landes, David S. 1949. "French Entrepreneurship and Industrial Growth in the Nineteenth Century." *Journal of Economic History* 9 (May):45–61.

———— 1950. "French Business and the Businessmen in Social and Cultural Analysis." In E. M. Earle, ed., *Modern France*, pp. 334–353. Princeton: Princeton University Press.

———— 1953–54. "Social Attitudes, Entrepreneurship, and Economic Development: A Comment." *Explorations in Entrepreneurial History* 6, no. 4:245–272.

———— 1954–55. "Further Comment." *Explorations in Entrepreneurial History* 7, no. 2 (December): 119–120.

———— 1965. "Technological Change and Development in Western Europe, 1750–1914." In *The Cambridge Economic History of Europe*. Vol. 6. *The Industrial Revolutions and After*. Pt. I, pp. 274–601. Cambridge: Cambridge University Press.

———— 1969. *The Unbound Prometheus: Technological Change and Industrial Development in Western Europe from 1750 to the Present*. Cambridge: Cambridge University Press.

———— 1986. "What Do Bosses Really Do?" *Journal of Economic History* 46, no. 3 (September): 585–623.

Landes, David S., ed. 1987. *A che servono i padroni? Le alternative storiche dell'industrializzazione*. Turin: Bollati Boringhieri.

Lévy-Leboyer, Maurice. 1968. "La croissance économique en France au XIXe siècle: resultats preliminaires." *Annales: économies, sociétés, civilisations* 23 (July–August):788–807.

Lewis, Arthur. 1955. *The Theory of Economic Growth*. London: Allen & Unwin.

Lipset, S. Martin. 1988. "Neoconservatism: Myth and Reality." *Society* (July–August):29–37.

Mansfield, Edwin. 1968. *The Economics of Technological Change*. New York: W. W. Norton.

Mantoux, Paul. [1906] 1959. *La révolution industrielle au XVIIIe siècle*. Paris: Cornély. English edition, rev., 1961. *The Industrial Revolution in the Eighteenth Century*. London: Jonathan Cape.

Marczewski, J. 1965. "Le produit physique de l'économie française de 1789 à 1913 (comparaison avec la Grande-Bretagne). *Cahiers de l'ISEA* (Institut de Statistique économique appliquée) 4 (July).

Marglin, Stephen. 1974. "What Do Bosses Do?" *Review of Radical Political Economy* 6 (Summer):60–112. Reprinted in Andre Gorz, ed., *The Division of Labour: The Labour Process and Class Struggle in Modern Capitalism*, pp. 13–54. Hassocks: Harvester, 1978.

———— 1984. "Knowledge and Power." In Frank H. Stephen, ed., *Firms, Organization, and Labour: Approaches to the Economics of Work Organization*. New York: St. Martin's Press.

Markovitch, T. J. 1965–66. "L'industrie française de 1789 à 1964." *Cahiers de l'ISEA* (Institut de Statistique économique appliquée) 4 (July 1965); "Analyse des faits," 5 (May 1966); "Analyse des faits (suite)," 6 (June 1966); "Conclusions generales," 7 (November 1966).

Marx, Karl. [1894] 1962. *Capital*. Vol. 1. New York: Modern Library.

McCloskey, Donald. 1988. "The Storied Character of Economics." *Tijdschrift voor Geschiedenis* 101:643–654. Reprinted in *If You're So Smart: The Narrative of Economic Expertise*, pp 41–43. Chicago: University of Chicago Press, 1990.

Meier, Gerald M., and Dudley Seers, eds. 1984. *Pioneers in Development*. N.p.: Oxford University Press for the World Bank.

Mokyr, Joel. 1977. "Demand vs. Supply in the Industrial Revolution." *Journal of Economic History* 37:981–1008.

Morris, Cynthia Taft, and Irma Adelman. 1988. *Comparative Patterns of Economic Development, 1850–1914*. Baltimore: Johns Hopkins University Press.

Mumford, Lewis. 1934. *Technics and Civilization*. New York: Harcourt Brace.

Nef, John U. 1933. *The Rise of the British Coal Industry*. 2 vols. London: Routledge.

———— 1958. *Cultural Foundations of Industrial Civilization*. Cambridge, Mass.: Harvard University Press.

O'Brien, Patrick K., and Stanley L. Engerman. 1988. "Exports and the Growth of the British Economy, 1688–1802." Paper prepared for a conference, "Slavery and the Rise of the Atlantic System," Harvard University.

O'Brien, Patrick K., and Caglar Keyder. 1978. *Economic Growth in Britain and France, 1780–1914: Two Paths to the Twentieth Century*. London: Allen & Unwin.

Patel, Surendra J. 1962. "Rates of Industrial Growth in the Last Century, 1860–1958." *Economic Development and Cultural Change* 9:316–330.

Peyrefitte, Alain. 1989. *L'empire immobile: le choc des mondes*. Paris: Fayard.

Piore, Michael J., and Charles Sabel. 1984. *The Second Industrial Divide: Possibilities of Prosperity*. New York: Basic Books.

Rostow, Walt W. [1960] 1971. *The Stages of Economic Growth*. Cambridge: Cambridge University Press.

———— 1990. *Theorists of Economic Growth from David Hume to the Present, with a Perspective on the Next Century*. New York: Oxford University Press.

————, ed. 1963. *The Economics of Take-Off into Sustained Growth*. London: Macmillan.

Sabel, Charles, and Jonathan Zeitlin. 1985. "Historical Alternatives to Mass Production: Politics, Markets, and Technology in Nineteenth-Century Industrialization." *Past & Present* 108:133–176.

Schmookler, Jacob. 1966. *Invention and Economic Growth*. Cambridge, Mass.: Harvard University Press.

Smith, Adam. [1776] 1937. *An Inquiry into the Nature and Causes of the Wealth of Nations*. New York: Modern Library.

Solow, Barbara. 1988. "Slavery and Colonization." Paper prepared for a conference, "Slavery and the Rise of the Atlantic System," Harvard University.

Solow, Barbara, and Stanley L. Engerman, eds. 1987. *British Capitalism and Caribbean Slavery: The Legacy of Eric Williams*. Cambridge: Cambridge University Press.

Usher, Abbott Payson. 1920. *An Introduction to the Industrial History of England*. Boston: Houghton Mifflin.

———— [1929] 1954. *A History of Mechanical Inventions*. Cambridge, Mass.: Harvard University Press.

Van Dam, Ferdinand. 1980. "North-South Relations Reconsidered." In L. Blusse, H. L. Wesseling, and G. D. Winius, eds., *History and Underdevelopment*. Leiden: University of Leiden, Center for the History of European Expansion.

Viner, Jacob. 1953. *International Trade and Economic Development*. Oxford: Clarendon Press.

Williams, B. R., ed. 1973. *Science and Technology in Economic Growth*. London: Macmillan.

Williams, Eric. 1966. *Capitalism and Slavery*. New York: Capricorn Books.

Wrigley, E. A. 1987. *People, Cities, and Wealth: The Transformation of Traditional Society*. Oxford: Basil Blackwell.

I
‥
TECHNOLOGY

1

...

The Conquest of High Mortality and Hunger in Europe and America: Timing and Mechanisms

Robert W. Fogel

Recent findings in economic and demographic history as well as in the biomedical sciences have shed new light on the struggle to escape from high mortality and hunger in western Europe and the United States. Although some of the investigations are still at an early stage, the outline of a new interpretation has begun to emerge. Attempts to predict now what the final picture will look like are necessarily risky. Nevertheless, I believe that it is useful to draw together various aspects of these findings in a way that indicates where we stand and what issues require further investigation, and to conjecture about how the pieces might ultimately fit together. Provided that due caution is exercised, such a provisional interpretation not only suggests the wider significance of what otherwise appear to be disjointed investigations, but also helps contribute to the social agenda for the next round of research.

I will first present this provisional interpretation as a set of theses and then in the balance of this chapter discuss several of them. The evidence suggesting these theses is drawn primarily, but not exclusively, from Great Britain, France, and the United States.

Eleven Theses

Thesis 1: The modern secular decline in mortality in western Europe did not begin until the 1780s, and the first wave of improvement was over by 1830 in England and by 1840 in France.

Thesis 2: The elimination of crisis mortality played only a secondary role in the first wave of the secular decline in mortality, and virtually none thereafter. Over 90 percent of the initial decline was due to the reduction in ''normal'' mortality.

Thesis 3: The famines that plagued England and France between 1500 and

1800 were man-made, resulting from a failure of government policy rather than natural calamities or inadequate technology, and could have been eliminated nearly two centuries earlier than they were.

Thesis 4: The elimination of famines played only a minor role in the initial escape from high mortality, accounting at most for 6 percent of the initial decline.

Thesis 5: While the elimination of famines played only a minor role in the first wave of the mortality decline, reductions in chronic malnutrition were much more important and may have accounted for most of the initial improvement.

Thesis 6: Chronic malnutrition, which was a major factor in the high mortality rates prevailing before 1780, could not have been eliminated merely by more humane national policies, but required major advances in productive technology.

Thesis 7: Although there were some improvements in the health, nutritional status, and longevity of the lower classes in England and France between 1830 and the end of the nineteenth century, these advances were modest and unstable, and included some reversals. An even larger reversal occurred among the lower classes in the United States.

Thesis 8: Although the technological progress, industrialization, and urbanization of the nineteenth century laid the basis for a remarkable advance in health and nutritional status during the first half of the twentieth century, their effects on the conditions of life of the lower classes were mixed, at least until the 1870s or 1880s. In the United States the negative effects probably exceeded the positive ones through the 1870s, while in western Europe the outcome of the conflicting factors was more even and may have been slightly positive.

Thesis 9: The great gains of the lower classes in nutritional status, health, and longevity began later and moved more swiftly in both western Europe and the United States than is often presumed. Most of the gains were concentrated in the 65 years between 1890 and 1955.

Thesis 10: The principal mechanisms for the escape from high mortality and poor health were the elimination of chronic malnutrition, the advances in public health, the improvement of housing, the reduced consumption of toxic substances, and advances in medical technology. The relative importance of each of these factors in the escape is still a matter of controversy, however.

Thesis 11: Improvement in nutrition and health may account for as much as 30 percent of the growth in conventionally measured per capita income between 1790 and 1980 in western Europe, but for a much smaller proportion in the United States.

Demographic Crises, Famines, and the Secular Decline in Mortality: Theses 1–4

The evidence on the timing of the secular decline in mortality (Thesis 1) comes mainly from Wrigley and Schofield (1981) and from Weir (1984), who in turn relied on data developed by the Institut National d'Etudes Démographiques (1977) for the period 1740–1829. Both the English and French time series show that the crude death rates were high until the 1780s, when the English series begins to decline (see Figure 1.1).[1] It bottoms at about 22 per thousand and remains stable until the beginning of the 1870s. The French series begins to decline about half a decade later than the English, but proceeds at a much more rapid rate, reducing the original gap of about 9 per thousand to about 2 per thousand by the late 1830s, after which the French death rate stabilizes at about 24 per thousand.

The evidence to support Thesis 2 also comes from Wrigley and Schofield (1981), who, for the first time, had a sample of parishes large enough in number and wide enough in geographic scope to permit an estimate of the national impact of mortality crises on the annual crude death rate in early modern England. Over the 331 years covered in their study, they found 45 crisis years, defined as years in which the annual crude death rate (cdr) was more than 10 percent above a 25-year moving average of crude death rates. By combining the information from two of their tables, we can assess the impact of crisis mortality on the average crude death rate. The result of the computation is summarized in

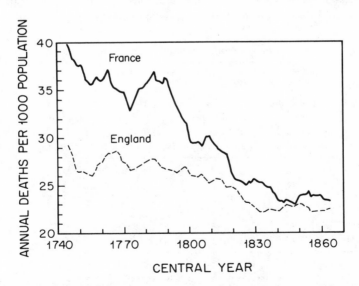

Figure 1.1   Crude death rates in France and England, 1740–1869. See note 1 for sources.

Table 1.1. Perhaps the most significant aspect of their data is that they drastically diminish the role of crisis mortality as an explanation for the high average mortality rates that prevailed before 1750. During the 210 years ending with that date, crisis mortality accounted for less than 6 percent of total mortality. When crisis mortality is expressed as a percentage not of total contemporary mortality but of "premature" mortality (the excess of the average cdr for the period less the English death rate in 1980), the figure rises to 13.2 percent.[2] An implication of Table 1.1 more directly relevant for Thesis 2 is that just 6 percent of the decline in the annual crude death rate between the third quarter of the eighteenth century (18-III) and the second quarter of the nineteenth century (19-II) was a result of the elimination of crisis mortality (0.27 + 4.70 = 0.057).

Table 1.1 also has a bearing on Thesis 4, since it follows that even if every mortality crisis identified by Wrigley and Schofield were owing to famines, then the elimination of famines would account for at most 6 percent of the first wave of the secular decline in mortality. As Wrigley, Schofield, and Lee have demonstrated, however, most crisis mortality was unrelated to subsistence crises (Wrigley and Schofield 1981, pp. 332–373; Lee 1981; Schofield 1983). Using procedures different from those that they followed, I have estimated that less than 10 percent of all crisis mortality during the 331 years that they covered was due to famines (Fogel 1986b, pp. 494–495; Fogel 1988a, appendix). These findings should not be taken to imply that there were not times when local famines produced large increases in local mortality rates. Too much evidence of local disasters induced by food shortages has accumulated to rule out such phenomena. In light of the evidence developed by Wrigley and Schofield,

Table 1.1   The impact of crisis mortality on the average crude death rate, 1541–1871.

Period	Crude death rate per thousand person-years	Crisis mortality per thousand person-years	Crude death rate after factoring out crisis mortality (per thousand)	Crisis mortality as % of average mortality	Crisis mortality as % of premature[a] mortality
1541–1750	27.66	1.57	26.09	5.68	13.16
1751–1775	27.28	0.40	26.88	1.47	1.97
1776–1800	26.85	0.55	26.30	2.05	2.77
1801–1825	25.40	0.15	25.25	0.59	0.82
1826–1850	22.58	0.13	22.45	0.58	0.83
1851–1871	22.42	0.13	22.29	0.58	0.85

Source: See Fogel (1988a, pp. 6–7).

[a] Premature mortality is defined as the crude death rate for a given period minus the English death rate of 1980 standardized on the English age structure of 1701–1705.

however, it now seems likely that, dramatic as famines were, their elimination could not have accounted for as much as 6 percent of the decline in annual mortality between the third quarter of the eighteenth century and the second quarter of the nineteenth.

The evidence for Thesis 3 has been developed in the course of efforts to assess the types of valid inferences that can be made about the supply of food from data on grain prices. Attempts to make such inferences date back beyond Gregory King, although he was the first to propose explicitly something approaching a demand curve—the famous King's law. After King, a host of political mathematicians and economists proposed variants of King's law to predict the shortfalls in annual grain yields from the annual deviations of grain prices around their trend. In recent years this procedure was invoked by economic historians in France (Labrousse 1944) and Britain (Hoskins 1964, 1968) to identify subsistence crises. Hoskins, using annual deviations from a 30-year moving average of wheat prices to identify subsistence crises, concluded that there was a major wheat shortage once every six years between 1480 and 1759. He attributed the sequences of high prices that he found not primarily to weather cycles but to the low (between 4 and 5) yield-to-seed ratio. Hoskins suggested that one bad harvest tended to generate another because starving farmers were forced to consume their reserve for seeds. Wrigley and Schofield, using annual deviations from a 25-year moving average of an index of real wages (basically the inverse of an index of food prices), found a pattern of subsistence crises quite similar to that of Hoskins, but little connection between subsistence and mortality crises.

The problem with this approach to the measurement of subsistence crises lies not in its logic but in the difficulty of estimating the price elasticity. If the elasticity of the demand for grain were known, the shortfall in the supply would follow directly from the deviation in price. Efforts to estimate that parameter from King's law or variants of it (such as the formulas of Davenant, Jevons, and Bouniatian) imply values of ϵ in the neighborhood of 0.4 (Wrigley 1987; Fogel 1988a). The difficulty with these estimates is that they are based on the implicit assumption that the annual supply of grains varied directly with the annual per acre yield. That assumption would be correct only if carryover inventories at the beginning of the harvest were zero. Yet carryover inventories ran between four and five months of annual consumption. When King's law is reestimated allowing for the effect of these stocks, the value of ϵ declines from 0.40 to 0.25. Additional evidence bearing on the exceedingly inelastic demand for inventories by those who held them indicates that the best estimate of ϵ is in the neighborhood of 0.18 (Fogel 1988a).

A price elasticity of 0.18 implies that even relatively small declines in supply would lead to sharp rises in prices. Moreover, because of large differences in the

elasticity of demand for grain between the upper and lower classes, a reduction
in the supply of grain by as little as 5 percent would set off a spiral rise in prices
that would cut the consumption of the laboring classes by a third (Fogel 1988a).
Thus the typical subsistence crises took place not because there was not enough
grain to go around, but because the demand for inventories pushed prices so
high that laborers lacked the cash to purchase the grain. Even in the largest
deviation of wheat prices above trend during Hoskins' entire 280-year period or
Wrigley and Schofield's 331-year period involved a manageable shortfall in the
supply of food. Although carryover stocks were diminished, more than two-
thirds the normal amount—in excess of a three-months' supply—remained over
and above all claims for seed, feed, and human consumption.

During the Tudor era authorities recognized that famines were man-made
rather than natural disasters because the available surpluses were more than
adequate to feed the lower classes. The basic strategy of the Crown was to leave
the grain market to its own devices during times of plenty. But in years of
famine for the lower classes, the state became increasingly bold in overriding
the complaints of traders, merchants, brewers, bakers, and other processors
about its meddling in the market. Since mere denunciations of engrossers did
not work, in 1587 the Privy Council issued a "Book of Orders," which in-
structed local magistrates to determine the extent of private inventories of grain
and to force their owners to supply grain to artificers and laborers at low prices.
Although it took more than a decade to overcome local resistance to these
orders, by the year 1600 local authorities were vigorously responding to the
directives of the Crown. Historians are generally agreed about the diligence of
the authorities during the reigns of James I and Charles I, but not over whether
their paternalistic policies actually worked. In any case, the paternalistic system
began to unravel with the Civil War. Since the heavy-handed intervention of the
Crown in grain markets was one of the grievances of the opposition to Charles,
Parliament developed a legislative program aimed at unshackling farmers, producers, and merchants from the restraints that had been imposed on them. Some
scholars view the new grain policies as acts of self-aggrandizement by the
landlords, traders, and merchants who controlled Parliament, while others argue
that the new policies were aimed at stimulating a depressed agriculture, improving marketing and transportation, and promoting industry (Leonard 1965;
Lipson 1971; Jordan 1959; Supple 1964; Barnes 1930; R. B. Rose 1961; Everitt
1967; Thirsk 1985a, 1985b; Chartres 1985).

Whatever the motivation for the switch in policy, it was the abandonment of
the Tudor-Stuart program of food relief, not natural disasters or the technological backwardness of agriculture, that subjected England to periodic famines for
two additional centuries. Analysis of variance indicates that during the period
from 1600 to 1640, when government relief efforts were at their apogee, the

variance of wheat prices around trend declined to less than a third of the level of the preceding era. That large a drop cannot be explained plausibly by chance variations in weather, since the F-value is statistically significant at the 0.0001 level. Nor is it likely that the sharp rise in the variance of wheat prices during the last six decades of the seventeenth century was the result of chance variations in weather (Fogel 1988a).[3]

In the absence of government action to reduce prices during grain shortages, workers took to the streets, and price-fixing riots became a standard feature of the eighteenth century. During the early decades of the century the government sought to cope with such outbreaks by enforcing vagrancy and settlement laws and by force (Lipson 1971, III, 457–467; R. B. Rose 1961). During the late 1750s, however, after food riots of unprecedented scope and intensity, proposals reemerged for the government to intervene vigorously in the grain market (that is, to return to the Tudor-Stuart policies), including proposals to reestablish public granaries. As the battle over these questions ebbed and flowed during the next half-century, the government, at the local and national levels, gradually shifted toward more active intervention. It was not until the nineteenth century, however, that government control over stocks became adequate to reduce the variance in wheat prices to the level that had prevailed at the apogee of Tudor-Stuart paternalism. By the middle of the nineteenth century, famines had been conquered, not because the weather had changed, or because of improvements in technology, but because government policy (at least with respect to its own people)[4] had unalterably shifted back to the ideas and practices of commonweal that had prevailed during the years 1600–1640 (Barnes 1930, pp. 31–45; Post 1977).

The Extent and Significance of Chronic Malnutrition: Theses 5 and 6

Although the possibility that famines might have had only a small impact on aggregate mortality had been anticipated (Lebrun 1971; Flinn 1974, 1981), Wrigley and Schofield (1981) provided the data needed to measure the national impact. By demonstrating that famines and famine mortality are a secondary issue in the escape from the high aggregate mortality of the early modern era, they have indirectly pushed to the top of research agendas the issue of chronic malnutrition and its relationship to the secular decline in mortality. It is clear that the new questions cannot be addressed by relating annual deviations of mortality (around trend) to annual deviations of supplies of food (from their trend). What is now at issue is how the trend in malnutrition might be related to the trend in mortality and how to identify the factors that determined each of these secular trends.

The new problems require new data and new analytical procedures. In this connection one must come to grips with the thorny issue of the distinction between diet (which represents gross nutrition) and nutritional status (which represents net nutrition: the nutrients available to sustain physical development). I will not dwell on this distinction here (see Fogel 1986b) but will only emphasize that when I mean gross nutrition I will use the term *diet,* and that other terms such as *malnutrition, undernutrition, net nutrition,* and *nutritional status* are meant to designate the balance between the nutrient intake (diet) and the claims on that intake.

Malnutrition can be caused either by an inadequate diet or by claims on that diet (including work and disease) so great as to produce widespread undernutrition despite a nutrient intake that in other circumstances might be deemed adequate. There can be little doubt that the high disease rates prevalent during the early modern era would have caused malnutrition even with extraordinary diets, that is, with diets high in calories, proteins, and most other critical nutrients. I believe that the United States during the period 1820–1880 is a case in point, and I will return to that example later. Recent research indicates, however, that for many European nations prior to the middle of the nineteenth century, the national production of food was at such low levels that the lower classes were bound to have been malnourished under any conceivable circumstance, and that the high disease rates of the period were not merely a cause of malnutrition but undoubtedly, to a considerable degree, a consequence of exceedingly poor diets.

Recently developed biomedical techniques, when integrated with several standard economic techniques, make it possible to probe deeply into the extent and the demographic consequences of chronic malnutrition during the eighteenth and nineteenth centuries. The biomedical techniques include improved approaches to the estimation of survival levels of caloric consumption and of the caloric requirements of various types of labor; epidemiological studies of the connection between stature and the risk of both mortality and chronic diseases; and epidemiological studies of the connection between body mass indexes (BMI) and the risk of mortality. The economic techniques include various methods of characterizing size distributions of income and of calories, as well as methods of relating measures of nutrition to measures of income and productivity.

Energy Cost Accounting: Britain and France during the Last Quarter of the Eighteenth Century

In developed countries today, and even more so in the less developed nations of both the past and the present, the basal metabolic rate (BMR) is the principal component of the total energy requirement. The BMR, which varies with age, sex, and body weight, is the amount of energy required to maintain the body while at rest: that is, it is the amount of energy required to maintain body temperature and to sustain the functioning of the heart, liver, brain, and other organs. For adult males aged 20–39 living in moderate climates, BMR normally ranges between 1,350 and 2,000 kilocalories, depending on height and weight (FAO/WHO/UNU 1985, pp. 71–72; Davidson et al. 1979, pp. 19–25; Quenouille et al. 1951), and for reasonably well-fed persons normally represents somewhere in the range of 45 to 65 percent of total calorie requirements (FAO/WHO/UNU 1985, pp. 71–77). Since the BMR does not allow for the energy required to eat and digest food, nor for essential hygiene, an individual cannot survive on the calories needed for basal metabolism. The energy required for these additional essential activities over a period of 24 hours is estimated at 0.27 of BMR or 0.40 of BMR during waking hours. In other words, a survival diet is 1.27 BMR. Such a diet, it should be emphasized, contains no allowance for the energy required to earn a living, to prepare food, or for any movements beyond those connected with eating and essential hygiene. It is not sufficient to maintain long-term health but represents the short-term maintenance level "of totally inactive dependent people" (FAO/WHO/UNU 1985, p. 73).

Energy requirements beyond maintenance depend primarily on how individuals spend their time beyond sleeping, eating, and essential hygiene. This residual time will normally be divided between work and discretionary activity such as walking, community activities, games, optional household tasks, and athletics or other forms of exercise. For a typical well-fed adult male engaged in heavy work, BMR and maintenance require about 60 percent of energy consumption, work 39 percent, and discretionary activity just 1 percent. For a well-fed adult male engaged in sedentary work (such as an office clerk), a typical distribution would be: BMR and maintenance 83 percent, work 5 percent, discretionary activity 13 percent. For a 25-year-old adult male engaged in subsistence farming in contemporary Asia, a typical distribution would be: BMR and maintenance 71 percent, work 21 percent, and discretionary activity 8 percent. Similar distributions of energy requirements have been developed for women as well as for children and adolescents of both sexes. In addition, the energy requirements of a large number of specific activities (expressed as a multiple of the BMR requirement per minute of an activity) have been worked out (see Table 1.2 for some examples). In order to standardize for the age and sex distribution of a population, it is convenient to convert the per capita consumption of calories into consumption per equivalent adult male aged 20–39 (referred to as a consuming unit).

Historical estimates of mean caloric consumption per capita have been derived from several principal sources: national food balance sheets; household

Table 1.2   Examples of the energy requirements for common activities, expressed as a multiple of the basal metabolic rate (BMR), for males and females.

Activity	Males	Females
Sleeping	1.0[a]	1.0[a]
Standing quietly	1.4	1.5
Strolling	2.5	2.4
Walking at normal pace	3.2	3.4
Walking with 10-kg load	3.5	4.0
Walking uphill at normal pace	5.7	4.6
Sitting and sewing	1.5	1.4
Sitting and sharpening machete	2.2	—
Cooking	1.8	1.8
Tailoring	2.5	—
Carpentry	3.5	—
Common labor in building trade	5.2	—
Milking cows by hand	2.9	—
Hoeing	—	5.3–7.5
Collecting and spreading manure	6.4	—
Binding sheaves	5.4–7.5	3.3–5.4
Uprooting sweet potatoes	3.5	3.1
Weeding	2.5–5.0	2.9
Ploughing	4.6–6.8	—
Cleaning house	—	2.2
Child care	—	2.2
Threshing	—	4.2
Cutting grass with machete	—	5.0
Laundry work	—	3.4
Felling trees	7.5	—

Sources: FAO/WHO/UNU (1985, pp. 76–78, 186–191); Durnin and Passmore (1967, pp. 31, 66, 67, 72). Rates in Durnin and Passmore given in kilocalories per minute were converted into multiples of BMR, using kilocalories per minute of a 65-kg man and a 55-kg woman of average build (p. 31).
[a] That is, BMR × 1.0.

consumption surveys; food allotments in hospitals, poorhouses, prisons, the armed forces, and other lower-class institutions; food entitlements to widows in wills; and food allotments in noble households, abbeys, and similar wealthy institutions. National food balance sheets estimate the national supply of food by subtracting from the national annual production of each crop, allowances for seed and feed, losses in processing, changes in inventories, and net exports (positive or negative) to obtain a residual of grains and vegetables available for consumption. In the case of meats, the estimates begin with the stock of livestock, which is turned into an annual flow of meat by using estimates of the annual slaughter ratio and live weight of each type of livestock. To estimate the meat available for consumption, it is necessary to estimate the ratio of dressed to live or carcass weight, as well as the distribution of dressed weight among lean meat, fat, and bones (Fogel and Engerman 1990; 1974, II, 91–99).

Household surveys are based on interviews with families who are asked to recall their diets for a period as short as one day (the previous day) or their average diet over a period of a week, a month, a year, or an undefined period designated as their "normal diet." In recent times, such surveys may be based on a daily record of the food consumed, which is kept either by a member of the family or by a professional investigator. Institutional food allowances are based on allotments for each class of individuals laid down as a guide for provisions purchased by the institution (as in the case of victualing allowances for military organizations and daily diet schedules adopted in abbeys, noble households, schools, workhouses, hospitals, and prisons) as well as descriptions of meals actually served and actual purchases of food for given numbers of individuals over particular time periods (Oddy 1970; Appleby 1979; Morell 1983; Dyer 1983). Food entitlements for widows and aged parents were specified in wills and contracts for maintenance between parents and children or other heirs (in anticipation of the surrender of a customary holding to an heir). Such food entitlements have been analyzed for England, France, the United States, and other countries at intermittent dates between the thirteenth century and the present (Bernard 1975; Dyer 1983; McMahon 1981; for studies of other countries, see Hémardinquer 1970).

Although these sources contain valuable information on the average consumption of nutrients, they are also fraught with difficulties. In the case of the national food balance sheets, for example, the accuracy of the estimates depends in the first instance on the accuracy of the production figures and on the various coefficients used to transform outputs of grains and stocks of animals into food available for human consumption. Even if the outputs and factors used to produce the national food supply are accurate, however, the average amount of nutrients produced is not necessarily equal to the average amount consumed. There are storage and food processing losses not only before the supply reaches the household but within the household as well. There is also the question of the amount of food put on an individual's plate that is not consumed (plate waste and feeding to pets).

Household food surveys, especially those of past times, have their own set of problems. They are focused largely on lower-class diets and are generally judgment samples. Hence it is difficult to know precisely where they are located in the national distributions of calories and other nutrients. Since these surveys

sometimes include information on the income of households, it is possible to
relate the average consumption of diets to the average income (or expenditures)
of households. Such studies for English budgets generally indicate an income
elasticity of the demand for food between the 1780s and the mid-1850s that is
at the high end of those found for less developed nations today, which is not
inconsistent with estimates of English per capita income for that period. Scholars are in disagreement, however, over whether these households were below or
above the middle of the English income distribution for their period, and whether
the reported income understates or overstates the true household income. Although information on the size distribution of income before World War I is
sparse, that which is available can be used to locate households in nutrient
distributions (Crafts 1981; Woodward 1981; Shammas 1983, 1984).

Sources of information about food allotments in institutions and of food
entitlements in wills often suffer from a common problem: lack of information
on the age and sex of the recipients. Caloric requirements vary so significantly
by age and sex that failure to standardize for these characteristics can cause
misleading interpretations of the adequacy of diets, and shifts in the age-sex
structure over time may bias the estimated trends in nutrition. Food wasting
varied greatly by institutions, so the proportion of the food supply actually
consumed was much lower in noble households than in poor households. No
one, for example, could have consumed regularly the daily allowance at the
royal households in Sweden of foods containing 6,400 kilocalories (Heckscher
1954, pp. 21–22, 68–70). Even allowing for heavy work and cold climate, a
third to a half of the allowance must have been wasted in storage, in preparation, and on the plate.

Toutain (1971), on the basis of a national food balance sheet, has estimated
that the per capita consumption of kilocalories in France was 1,753 during
1781–1790 and 1,846 during 1803–1812. Converted into kilocalories per consuming unit (equivalent adult male), the figures become about 2,290 and 2,410
kilocalories. Data in the household budget studies recently reexamined by economic historians indicate that English daily consumption during 1785–1795
averaged about 2,700 kilocalories per consuming unit (Fogel 1988b; cf. Shammas 1984).

One way of assessing these two estimates is by considering their distributional implications. As has been noted elsewhere, all of the known distributions
of the average daily consumption of calories of populations are not only reasonably well described by the lognormal distribution but have coefficients of
variation that lie between 0.2 and 0.4—a narrow range determined at the top
end by the human capacity to use energy and the distribution of body builds, and
at the bottom end by the requirement for basal metabolism and the prevailing
death rate (Fogel 1988b). Consideration of available evidence on mortality rates

(Bourgeois-Pichat 1965; Weir 1984) and the findings of Goubert (1960, 1973), Bernard (1975), Hufton (1974), Kaplan (1976), and others on the condition of the lower classes in France during the late ancien régime rule out either 0.2 or 0.4 as plausible estimates of the coefficient of variation and suggest that 0.3 is the best approximation in the light of current knowledge.[5]

Table 1.3 displays the caloric distribution for England and France implied by the available evidence. Several points about these distributions that lend support to Toutain's estimate for the French and the estimates derived for the English from the budget studies are worth noting. First, the average levels are not out of keeping with recent experiences in the less developed nations. Low as it is, Toutain's estimate of the French supply of calories is above the average supply of kilocalories in 1965 estimated for nations such as Pakistan, Rwanda, and Algeria, and only slightly less than that of Indonesia (39 kcal). The English estimate is above that for 30 less developed nations in 1965, including China, Bolivia, the Philippines, and Honduras, and only slightly below India (37 kcal) (World Bank 1987).

Second, the distributional implications of the two estimates are consistent with both qualitative and quantitative descriptions of the diets of various social classes (Hufton 1974, 1983; Goubert 1973; L. A. Tilly 1971; C. Tilly 1975;

Table 1.3 A comparison of the probable French and English distributions of the daily consumption of kilocalories per consuming unit toward the end of the eighteenth century.

	Distribution A France c. 1785 $\bar{X} = 2,290$ $(s/\bar{X}) = 0.3$		Distribution B England c. 1790 $\bar{X} = 2,700$ $(s/\bar{X}) = 0.3$	
Decile	Daily kcal consumption	Cumulative %	Daily kcal consumption	Cumulative %
Highest	3,672	100	4,329	100
Ninth	2,981	84	3,514	84
Eighth	2,676	71	3,155	71
Seventh	2,457	59	2,897	59
Sixth	2,276	48	2,684	48
Fifth	2,114	38	2,492	38
Fourth	1,958	29	2,309	29
Third	1,798	21	2,120	21
Second	1,614	13	1,903	13
First	1,310	6	1,545	6

Source: See Fogel (1988b, esp. tables 4 and 5 and n. 6).

Frijhoff and Julia 1979; Blum 1978; Cole and Postgate 1938; M. E. Rose 1971; Drummond and Wilbraham 1958; Pullar 1970; Wilson 1973; Burnett 1979; Mennell 1985). For example, Bernard's study (1975) of marriage contracts made in the Gévaudan during the third quarter of the eighteenth century revealed that the average ration provided in complete pensions was about 1,674 kilocalories. Since the average age of a male parent at the marriage of his first surviving child was about 59, the preceding figure implies a diet of about 2,146 kilocalories per consuming unit (Fogel 1988b). That figure falls at the 47th centile of the estimated French distribution (Table 1.3, distribution A), which is quite consistent with the class of peasants described by Bernard.

The two estimates are also consistent with the death rates of each nation. The crude death rate in France around 1785 was about 38.0 per thousand, while the figure for England circa 1790 was about 26.8 (Weir 1984; Wrigley and Schofield 1981). It is plausible that much of the difference was due to the larger proportion of French than English who were literally starving (Scrimshaw 1987). The French distribution of calories implies that 2.48 percent of the population had caloric consumption below basal metabolism, most of them presumably concentrated at very young and old ages. Table 1.3 implies that the proportion of the English below basal metabolism was 0.66 percent. If a quarter of these starving individuals died each year (cf. Chen, Chowdhury, and Huffman 1981), they would account for about a sixth (6.6 per thousand) of the French crude death rate, but only about a sixteenth of the English rate (1.7 per thousand) and for about 40 percent of the gap between the crude death rates of the two nations.[6]

What, then, are the principal provisional findings about caloric consumption at the end of the eighteenth century in France and England? One is the exceedingly low level of food production, especially in France, at the start of the Industrial Revolution. Another is the extremely low level of work capacity permitted by the food supply, even after we allow for the reduced requirements for maintenance owing to small stature and reduced body mass (cf. Freudenberger and Cummins 1976): In France the bottom 10 percent of the labor force lacked the energy for regular work, and the next 10 percent had enough energy for less than three hours of light work daily (0.52 hour of heavy work). Although the English situation was somewhat better, the bottom 3 percent of its labor force lacked the energy for any work, but the balance of the bottom 20 percent had enough energy for about six hours of light work (or 1.09 hours of heavy work) each day.[7]

That the English ultrapoor were better off than the French ultrapoor was partly a result of the greater productivity of English agriculture (as measured by the per capita production of calories). The distribution of income was so unequal in England, however, that had it not been for the English system of poor relief, the proportion of the English who starved would have been nearly as great as that of the French. In response to the bread riots of the eighteenth century, English authorities substantially expanded the system of poor relief. Between 1750 and 1801, poor relief increased at a real rate of 2.3 percent per annum, which was nearly three times as fast as the growth of either GNP or the pauper class (Crafts 1985, p. 45; M. E. Rose 1971, pp. 40–41; Marshall 1968, p. 26; Mitchell and Deane 1962, p. 469). Consequently, by around 1790 relief payments to the ultrapoor had become substantial, more than doubling the income of households in the lowest decile of the English income distribution. In prerevolutionary France, on the other hand, the average annual relief provided to the ultrapoor could purchase daily only about one ounce of bread per person (Fogel 1988b, nn. 17, 18). The responsiveness of the British government to the bread riots of the poor (Barnes 1930; R. B. Rose 1961; Marshall 1968) not only kept the English death rate from soaring but may have spared Britain a revolution of the French type.

Implications of Stature and Body Mass Indexes for Explaining Secular Trends in Morbidity and Mortality

The available data on stature and on body mass tend to confirm the basic results of the analysis based on energy cost accounting: chronic malnutrition was widespread in Europe during the eighteenth and nineteenth centuries. Recent advances in biomedical knowledge make it possible to use anthropometric data for the eighteenth and nineteenth centuries to study secular trends in European nutrition, health, and risks of mortality. Extensive clinical and epidemiological studies over the past two decades have shown that height at given ages, weight at given ages, and weight-for-height (a body mass index) are effective predictors of the risk of morbidity and mortality. Until recently most of the studies have focused on children under 5, using one or more of the anthropometric indicators at these ages to assess risks of morbidity and mortality in early childhood, and it was at these ages that the relevance of anthropometric measures was established most firmly (Sommer and Lowenstein 1975; Chen, Chowdhury, and Huffman 1980; Billewicz and McGregor 1982; Kielmann et al. 1983; Martorell 1985). During the last few years, however, a considerable body of evidence has accumulated suggesting that height at maturity is also an important predictor of the probability of dying and of developing chronic diseases at middle and late ages (Marmot, Shipley, and Rose 1984; Waaler 1984; Fogel et al. 1986). Body mass indexes have similar predictive properties (Heywood 1983; Waaler 1984; Martorell 1985).

Height and body mass indexes measure different aspects of malnutrition and health. Height is a net rather than a gross measure of nutrition. Moreover, although changes in height during the growing years are sensitive to current levels of nutrition, mean final height reflects the accumulated past nutritional experience of individuals over all of their growing years, including the fetal period. Thus it follows that when final heights are used to explain differences in adult mortality rates, they reveal the effect not of adult levels of nutrition on adult mortality rates, but of nutritional levels during infancy, childhood, and adolescence on adult mortality rates. A weight-for-height index, by contrast, reflects primarily the current nutritional status. It is also a net measure in the sense that a body mass index (BMI) reflects the balance between intakes and the claims on those intakes. Although height is determined by the cumulative nutritional status during an entire developmental age span, the BMI fluctuates with the current balance between nutrient intakes and energy demands. A person who is short relative to the modern U.S. or West European standard is referred to as "stunted." Those with low BMIs are referred to as "wasted."

The predictive power of height and body mass indexes with respect to morbidity and mortality is indicated by Figures 1.2 and 1.3. The left-hand side of Figure 1.2 reproduces a diagram by Waaler (1984). It shows that short Norwegian men aged 40–59 at risk between 1963 and 1979 were much more likely to die than tall men. Indeed, the risk of mortality for men with heights of 165 centimeters (65.0 inches) was on average 71 percent greater than that of men who measured 182.5 centimeters (71.9 inches). The right-hand side of the figure shows that height is also a significant predictor of the relative likelihood that men aged 23–49 would be rejected from the Union Army during 1861–1865 because of chronic diseases. Despite significant differences in mean height, ethnicity, environmental circumstances, the array and severity of dis-

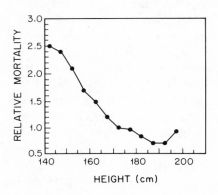
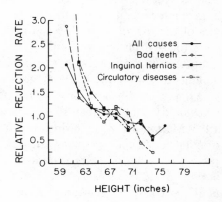

Figure 1.2   The relationship between body height and relative risk in two populations. *Left:* Relative mortality rates of Norwegian men aged 40–59, between 1963 and 1979 (source: Waaler 1984). *Right:* Relative rejection rates for chronic conditions in a sample of 4,245 men aged 23–49 examined for the Union Army (source: Fogel et al. 1986).

eases, and time, the functional relationship between height and relative risk are strikingly similar. Both the Norwegian curve and the U.S. all-causes curve have relative risks that reach a minimum of between 0.6 and 0.7 at a height of about 187.5 centimeters. Both reach a relative risk of about 2 at about 152.5 centimeters. The similarity of the two risk curves in Figure 1.2, despite the differences in conditions and attendant circumstances, suggests that the relative risk of morbidity and mortality depends on the deviation of height not from the current mean but from an ideal mean: the mean associated with full genetic potential.[8]

Waaler (1984) has also studied the relationship in Norway between a BMI and the risk of death in a sample of 1.8 million individuals. Curves summarizing his findings are shown in Figure 1.3 for both males and females. Although the observed values of the BMI (kg/m^2) ranged between 17 and 39, over 90 percent of the males had BMIs within the range 20–29. Within this range the curve is fairly flat, with the relative risk of mortality hovering close to 1.0. At BMIs of less than 20 and over 29, however, the risk of death rises quite sharply as the BMI moves away from its mean value.[9] The BMI curves are much more symmetrical than the height curves in Figure 1.2, which indicates that high BMIs are as risky as low ones.

Not only do adult height and the BMI measure different aspects of nutritional status, but their correlation in cross-sections is relatively low, both within

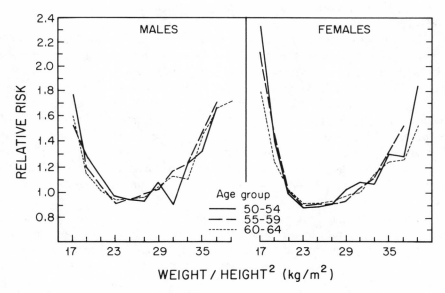

Figure 1.3 The relationship between BMI and prospective risk among Norwegian adults aged 50–64 at risk between 1963 and 1979 (source: Waaler 1984).

populations and over them (Benn 1971; Billewicz, Kemsley, and Thomson 1962; Waaler 1984; Fogel et al. 1986). The low correlation is explained by two important aspects of the biology of nutrition. Not only is stunting due to mal-nutrition during developmental ages, but it appears that most stunting occurs under age 3, after which even badly stunted children generally move along a given height centile; that is, they develop without incurring further height def-icits (Tanner 1982; Billewicz and MacGregor 1982; Martorell 1985). Second, no matter how badly stunted an adult might be, it is still possible to have an optimum (or good) weight for that height. Thus, for example, a Norwegian male stunted by 2 inches during his developmental ages could still have a normal risk if his BMI were about 26.

The fact that even badly stunted populations may have quite normal BMIs reflects the capacity of human beings to adapt their behavior to the limitations of their food supply. Adaptation takes place in three dimensions. Small people have lower basal metabolism, because less energy is needed to maintain body temperature and sustain the function of vital organs. Since small people need less food, they require less energy for consuming their food and for vital hygiene. The third aspect of adaptation comes in the curtailment of work and discretionary activity. If a small (56 kg) man confined himself to a few hours of light work each day, he could remain in energy balance and maintain his BMI at a satisfactory level with as little as 2,000 or 2,100 kilocalories, whereas a larger man (79 kg) engaged in heavy work for 8 hours per day would require about 4,030 kilocalories to maintain his energy balance at a BMI of 24 (FAO/WHO/UNU 1985).

The fact that stunted individuals are in energy balance at a good BMI does not imply that they are not at greater risk than persons not stunted, but only that the demands on their energy intake leave them in balance at a satisfactory level—without causing them to consume tissue in order to sustain their energy output. As Figure 1.4 shows, there is an optimum weight for a 160-centimeter male, a weight that puts his relative mortality risk at a minimum. At a weight of 66 kilograms (BMI = 25.8), the risk of a 160-centimeter male is about 30 percent less than that of a similarly stunted male of just 51 kilograms (BMI = 19.9). Yet, even at his optimum weight, a 160-centimeter male is at about a 60 percent greater risk than a 180-centimeter male of optimum mass (79.4 kg and BMI = 24.5).

What implications do these new analytical tools have for the interpretation of secular trends in nutritional status and mortality? Table 1.4 compares the final heights of six populations for which such figures have been estimated for the period 1750–1875. They are all severely stunted by modern standards (see bottom line of table). The French cohort of 18-IV is the most stunted, measur-ing only 160.5 centimeters (63.2 inches). The next two shortest cohorts are

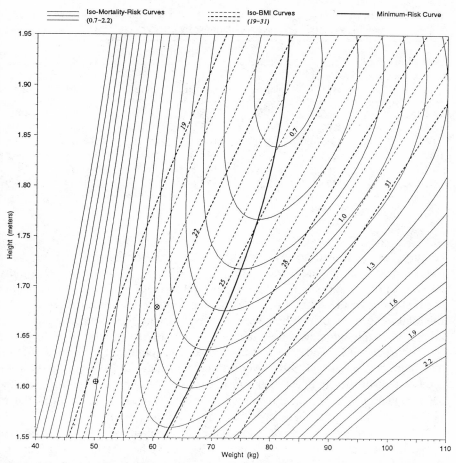

Figure 1.4   Isomortality curves of relative risk for height and weight of Norwegian males aged 50–64. Note: ⊕ = the possible location of adult French males aged 25–34 circa 1785 on the isomortality map; ⊗ = the possible location of comparable English males circa 1790. All risks are measured relative to the average risk of mortality (calculated over all heights and weights) among Norwegian males aged 50–64.

those of Norway for 18-III and Hungary for 19-I, which both measured 163.9 centimeters (64.5 inches). Britain and Sweden had the tallest populations between 1775 and 1875, although by the end of the period, Norway nearly matched the leaders.

France may have experienced the most rapid early growth rate of any nation shown in Table 1.4, with stature increasing by 1.24 centimeters per decade between 18-IV and 19-II. French heights declined slightly over the next quarter-

Table 1.4   Estimated average final heights of men who reached maturity between 1750
and 1875 in six European populations, by quarter-centuries.

Date of maturity by century and quarter	Height (cm)					
	Great Britain	Norway	Sweden	France	Denmark	Hungary
18-III	165.9	163.9	168.1	—	—	168.7
18-IV	167.9	—	166.7	160.5	165.7	165.8
19-I	168.0	—	166.7	165.1	165.4	163.9
19-II	171.6	—	168.0	166.7	166.8	164.2
19-III	169.3	168.6	169.5	166.4	165.3	—
20-III	175.0	178.3	177.6	172.0	176.0	170.9

Source: Fogel (1988b, table 7).

century, however, and hovered between 165.3 and 166.7 until the turn of the
twentieth century (Floud 1983a). British heights also increased quite rapidly
(0.76 cm per decade) and for a longer period than the French. The increase over
the first 75 years (18-III to 19-II) was 5.7 centimeters, more than three-fifths of
the total increase in British heights between 18-III and the current generation of
adults. British heights, however, like those of the French, declined slightly with
the cohort of 19-III and also remained level for about half a century (Floud,
Wachter, and Gregory 1990). Swedish heights appear to have declined during
the last half of the eighteenth century but then rose sharply beginning with the
second quarter of the nineteenth century, initiating the marked secular increases
in Swedish heights that have continued down to the present day.

Indeed, over the last century the three Scandinavian countries (shown in
Table 1.4) and the Netherlands (Chamla 1983) have had the most vigorous and
sustained increases in stature in the Western world, outpacing Britain and the
United States (Fogel 1986b). Hungary's growth pattern differs from that of all
the other European nations. Its cohort of 18-III was taller than that of Sweden,
but then Hungarian heights declined sharply for half a century and, despite a
turnabout in the nineteenth century, remained among the shortest in Europe
(Komlos 1990). The mean height in Hungary today is below the level achieved
by the British cohort of 19-II.

Data on body mass indexes for France and Great Britain during the late
eighteenth and most of the nineteenth centuries are much more patchy than
those on stature. Consequently, attempts to compare British and French BMIs
during this period are necessarily conjectural. It appears that around 1790 the
average English BMI for males of about age 30 was between 21 and 22, which
is roughly 10 percent below current levels. The corresponding figure for French

males circa 1790 may have been only between 19 and 20, which is around 20 percent below current levels (Fogel 1988b). The conjectural nature of these figures makes the attempt to go from the anthropometric data to differential mortality rates more illustrative than substantive. Figure 1.4 indicates the apparent location of French and English males of 18-IV on the iso-mortality map generated from Waaler's data. These points imply that the French mortality rate should have been about 38 percent higher than the English, which is quite close to the relative mortality rates indicated by Figure 1.1.[10] In other words, the available data suggest that in 18-IV both France and Great Britain were characterized by the same mortality risk surface (that is, the same mortality regimen) and that differences in their average mortality rates are explained largely by differences in their distributions of height and weight-for-height.

This result raises a question about how much of the decline in European mortality rates since 18-IV can be explained merely by increases in stature and BMIs, that is, merely by movements along an unchanging mortality risk surface. For the three countries for which even patchy data are available—England, France, and Sweden—it appears that nearly all of the decline in mortality between 18-IV and 19-III was the result of movements along the Waaler mortality surface, since the estimated changes in height and BMI appear to explain virtually the entire decline in mortality during this three-quarters of a century. Movements along the Waaler surface would appear to explain only about 50 to 75 percent of the decline in mortality rates after 1875, however. After 1875 increases in longevity involved factors other than those that exercise their influence through stature and body mass (Fogel 1988b).

The Instability of Improvements in Health and Nutritional Status for the Lower Classes before the Twentieth Century and Achievements during the Twentieth Century: Theses 7, 8, and 9

Although the period from the middle of the eighteenth century to the end of the nineteenth has been hailed justly as an industrial revolution, a great transformation in social organization, and a revolution in science, these advances brought only modest and uneven improvements in the health, nutritional status, and longevity of the lower classes before 1890. It was not until well into the twentieth century that ordinary people in Europe and America began to enjoy regularly the levels of nutrition and longevity that characterize our age. Whatever contribution the technological and scientific advances of the eighteenth and nineteenth centuries may have made ultimately to this breakthrough, escape from hunger and high mortality did not become a reality for most ordinary people until the twentieth century.

Figure 1.5 summarizes the available data on U.S. secular trends in both stature and mortality since 1720. The time series of final heights shown in the upper portion of the figure are for native-born white males and are given as averages for five-year birth cohorts. The time series in stature is controlled for shifts in the distribution of the region of birth, of occupation, and of several other characteristics, while the life expectancy series is not, but merely gives the mean life expectancy at age 10 of all of the individuals at risk during each period in the sample from which it was constructed. Since southerners were deficient in the sample of life spans, an attempt to correct for this deficiency is shown by the line with short dashes. A line indicating the trend in life expectancy in Maryland during the eighteenth century is also displayed.

Both the series on stature and on life expectancy contain striking cycles. Both series rise during most of the eighteenth century, attaining substantially greater heights and life expectations than prevailed in England during the same period (Floud 1985). Life expectancy began to decline during the 1790s and continued to do so for about half a century. There may have been a slight decline in the

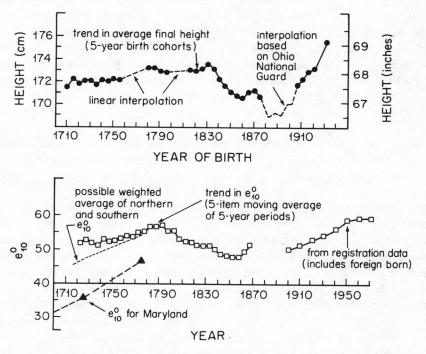

Figure 1.5   The trend in the mean final weight of native-born white American males and the trend in their life expectancy at age 10 (e_{10}^0) (height by birth cohort; e_{10}^0 by period).

heights of cohorts born between 1785 and 1820, but the sharp decline, which probably lasted about half a century, began with cohorts born around 1830. A new rise in heights, the one with which we have long been familiar, probably began with cohorts born during the last decade of the nineteenth century and continued for about 60 years.

Data on final heights in America are not available for cohorts born before 1710, but the relatively flat profile from around 1710 to around 1750 and the tall stature compared with that of the English in 1750 suggests that heights were probably rising rapidly for several decades before our series begins. This inference is supported by data on food consumption in Massachusetts discovered by McMahon (1981). Wills deposited in Middlesex County between 1654 and 1830 indicate a sharp rise in the average amount of meat annually allotted to widows for their consumption. Between 1675 and 1750 the average allotment increased from approximately 80 to approximately 168 pounds per annum, with about half the increase taking place by 1710. The evidence both on stature and on food allotments suggests that Americans achieved an average level of meat consumption by the middle of the eighteenth century that was not achieved in Europe until well into the twentieth (McMahon 1981; Holmes 1907; Fogel 1986).

Figure 1.5 reveals not only that Americans achieved modern heights by the middle of the eighteenth century, but also that they reached levels of life expectancy that were not attained by the general population of England or even by the British peerage until the first quarter of the twentieth century (Fogel 1986b, p. 467). The early attainment of modern stature and relatively long life expectancy is surprising. Yet in light of the evidence that has accumulated in recent years, it is by no means unreasonable. By the second quarter of the eighteenth century, Americans had achieved diets that were remarkably nutritious by European standards, and particularly rich in protein. The American population was low in density, probably below the threshold needed to sustain major epidemics of diseases such as smallpox. The low density probably also reduced exposure to the crowd diseases of the nineteenth century that took a heavy toll of life in both England and America. This is not to say that there were no epidemics in America between 1725 and 1800, but with the exception of a few port cities, outbreaks of epidemic diseases appear to have been much milder than in England.

Similar cycles in height appear to have occurred in Europe. Table 1.4 indicates that average Swedish heights declined by 1.4 centimeters between 18-III and 18-IV. Hungarian heights declined sharply (4.8 cm) between 18-III and 19-I. There may also have been a slight decline in the mean final height of the French between the second and third quarters of the nineteenth century. Although Table 1.4 does not reveal it because heights are averaged over quarter-centuries, there also appears to have been regular cycling in English final heights throughout the nineteenth century. Although the amplitude of these cycles was moderate, they are statistically significant (Floud, Wachter, and Gregory 1990). The use of quarter-century averages in Table 1.4 also disguises some height cycles in Sweden. During the second half of the 1840s and in the 1850s, heights declined sharply in Stockholm and in southern Sweden generally. This decline in heights was accompanied by a rise in infant mortality rates (Sandberg and Steckel 1988).

This evidence of cycling in stature and mortality rates between 18-III and 19-III in both Europe and America is puzzling. The overall improvement in health and longevity during this period is less than might be expected from the rapid increases in per capita income indicated by national income accounts for most of the countries in question (Maddison 1982; Crafts 1985). More puzzling are the decades of sharp decline in height and life expectation, some of which occurred during eras of undeniably vigorous economic growth. This conflict between vigorous economic growth and very limited improvements, or reversals, in the nutritional status and health of the majority of the population suggests that the modernization of the nineteenth century was a mixed blessing for those who lived through it. The problem at hand, then, is to identify and measure the negative aspects of modernization that temporarily offset such benefits as the leap forward in scientific knowledge, the remarkable technological innovations in agriculture, transportation, industry, and commerce, and the marked gains in labor productivity.

Research into this problem has focused so far on four principal possibilities. These are rapid urbanization, increased geographic mobility, more rapid increases in population than in the food supply, and increases in the inequality in the distribution of income. At the present stage of knowledge, discussion of the relative roles of these factors in temporarily offsetting the benefits of increased productivity must of necessity be speculative, but may suggest fruitful lines of further research.

Although the mix of factors tending to retard improvements in nutritional status and health varied from one country to another, one factor stands out more than any other: rapid urbanization. In both Europe and America the population of cities during the nineteenth century grew far more rapidly than at any other time in history (Wrigley 1969; Bairoch 1988). The mortality rate appears to have been influenced both by the size of the city and by the rapidity of its rate of growth. In the case of the United States around 1830, cities with 50,000 or more persons had more than twice the death rates of rural areas (Vinovskis 1972; Fogel et al. 1978), and similar patterns have been observed for Europe (Weber 1899; Woods 1984; Bairoch 1988). The exact threshold at which city size began to affect mortality rates varied with time, place, and circumstance, but in the United States during the mid-nineteenth century, cities of about 25,000 persons appear to have been the threshold of significant elevation in mortality rates.[11]

Increased geographic mobility had an independent effect on mortality rates. A classic example is the spread of the cholera epidemic of 1849–50 in the United States. This epidemic was brought to American shores in December 1848 by two ships carrying German immigrants, one bound for New York, the other for New Orleans. Although New York–bound passengers who were sick with cholera when the ship arrived were kept in quarantine, others were allowed to enter the city. Within a few days cholera broke out in the immigrant districts of New York; later it spread to the predominantly native-born, lower-class districts nearby, and eventually to upper-class districts. In the case of the ship bound for New Orleans, public health officials were able not only to tie the spread of the disease to New Orleans with the disembarkation of the immigrants there, but to follow the movement of cholera up the Mississippi and its tributaries. As immigrants from the infected ship boarded river steamers, cholera broke out aboard these ships and then in the cities at which the steamers called, including Memphis, Nashville, Louisville, Cincinnati, Wheeling (now West Virginia), Pittsburgh, and St. Louis. Soon after it reached these cities, cholera broke out in the surrounding countryside (U.S. Surgeon General's Office 1875).

Despite the drama of the cholera epidemic, internal migration was probably more instrumental than foreign immigration in spreading disease in the United States during the nineteenth century. The migration of many easterners to the Midwest via New Orleans appears to have been a major factor in making malaria endemic in the Midwest as far north as Madison, Wisconsin, during the 1820s, 1830s, and 1840s (Boyd 1941; Ackernecht 1945, 1952; Drake 1850, 1854; Coolidge 1856). The upsurge of malaria in the North following the Civil War appears to have been the consequence of the return of large numbers of Union Army men who became infected with the plasmodium while serving in the South (Ackernecht 1945; Boyd 1941).

In addition to their independent effects, urbanization and migration had an important interactive effect. The overcrowded housing, the crisis in public sanitation brought on by decades of exceptionally rapid population growth, and the poor personal hygiene of tenement dwellers made the large cities of Europe and America reservoirs of disease that not only undermined the health of urban residents but also served to infect the surrounding rural areas. The mechanisms through which urban diseases were transmitted to the countryside were trade (Landes 1969) and the rotation of labor between the cities and the surrounding countryside. Studies have revealed that in addition to providing a supply of permanent migrants to the city, the countryside produced a large stream of temporary laborers. Perhaps two or three times as many rural residents rotated work between the city and the countryside as left the countryside permanently (Goubert 1973; Vries 1984). Thus trade and labor rotation carried such diseases as typhoid, typhus, dysentery, cholera, and other major killers of the nineteenth century from the city to the countryside.

The pressure of population on the food supply may have played some role in the cycling of heights. Komlos (1985, 1988) argues that this was the case in Hungary between 18-III and 19-I, and Sandberg and Steckel (1988) provide a similar explanation for the decline in heights and the rise of infant mortality rates in southern Sweden from about 1840 to 1860. Such general pressure on the food supply, however, does not seem to be a likely explanation for the United States' decline in heights and in life expectation, shown in Figure 1.5. Calories available for human consumption appear to have increased between 1840 and 1860.[12] In any case, both average calorie and protein consumption were high throughout the period of decreasing stature and life expectation, exceeding 3,600 kilocalories and 120 grams of protein per consuming unit daily.[13] These levels are in excess of current recommended daily allowances for males engaged in heavy work for 3,300 hours annually (FAO/WHO/UNU 1985, pp. 71, 77, 79).

The fact that the average food consumption of Americans (gross nutrition) remained high during the period 1830–1860 does not imply that the average amount of nutrients available to sustain physical development (net nutrition) remained high. Indeed, the fact that average stature declined by several centimeters implies either that an increasing amount of the food ingested failed to be metabolized or that claims on the intake of food were increased. The growing prevalence of malaria in the North, associated with the migration of persons bound for the Midwest through New Orleans; the apparent rise in diarrheal diseases (including cholera and typhoid) in both the cities and the countryside; and the increased incidence of typhus, tuberculosis, and respiratory infections, measles, and other crowding diseases associated with rapid urbanization after 1820 provide the mechanism necessary to reconcile a high level of food consumption with the observed decline in stature (Ackernecht 1945; Boyd 1941; Smillie 1955). Increases in the incidence of such diseases could have reduced the nutrients available for growth because of the diversion of nutrients to fighting the diseases, decreased absorption of nutrients, reduced appetite, and the poorer quality diets that are often fed to the sick (*Journal of Interdisciplinary History* 1983; Taylor 1983; Scrimshaw, Taylor, and Gordon 1968).

Since permanent stunting occurs largely at ages under 3 (Tanner 1982; Billewicz and MacGregor 1982; Horton 1984; Martorell 1985; Martorell and Habicht 1986), declines in final heights during the nineteenth century raise questions about the synergism between nutritional status and disease in utero and in early childhood. Physical development before age 3 could have been retarded because of increased infections of pregnant mothers, increased contamination of foods fed to young children, or increased use of elixirs containing opiates to pacify infants, or because weaning and early childhood diets were low in protein. Early childhood diets that were marginally inadequate in protein when exposure to disease was low could have become severely inadequate as the incidence of disease increased. Since disease interrupts growth, the amount of protein required to bring about full catch-up growth following an episode of infection may be many times the normal requirement (Scrimshaw, private communication; Whitehead 1977). In the United States, an increase in the proportion of time in which children under age 3 were sick or in the process of recovery could explain the sharp decline in final heights despite the large and relatively constant quantities of meat consumed by older persons during the period 1830–1860.

Increases in the inequality of the distribution of income (and hence of the consumption of nutrients) could also explain the periodic declines in stature during the nineteenth century. This factor could have been at work, particularly during depressions that sharply increased unemployment among manual workers and reduced their real wages. The fact that the heights of the British upper classes did not exhibit the same cycling as found among the laboring classes, and the correlation between the real wages of urban workers and stature, suggests that there may have been cyclical surges in inequality, even if there was no marked secular increase in inequality in Britain between 18-III and 19-III (Floud, Wachter, and Gregory 1990; Lindert and Williamson 1982, 1983; Williamson 1985; Feinstein 1988). Sharp declines in the real wages of nonagricultural manual workers appear to have been a factor in the United States as well (Williamson 1976; Margo and Villaflor 1987; Fogel and Engerman 1990; Fogel, Galantine, and Manning 1991). But even those who prospered between 1840 and 1860, such as the farmers, experienced sharp decreases in stature. In the American case about four-fifths of the decline in average stature between 1830 and 1860 took place among rural populations that prospered (Fogel 1986b).

Principal Mechanisms for Escaping High Mortality: Thesis 10

The decline in mortality rates over the past hundred years is one of the greatest events in human history. The paper published by McKeown and Brown in 1955 marked a turning point in the effort to provide a warranted explanation for this decline. Bridging the worlds of social scientists and medical specialists, they brought into the discussion most of the range of issues that have been under debate since that time. That debate not only defined the issues more clearly than

previously, but it also revealed that the critical differences were quantitative
rather than qualitative. Nearly all the specialists agree that improved nutrition,
better public and personal sanitation, decontamination of food and water, improved housing, and advances in medical technology were responsible for the
decline in mortality, but they have had quite different views about the relative
importance of each of the factors. The unresolved issue, therefore, is not really
whether a particular factor was involved in the decline, but how much each of
the various factors contributed to it. Resolution of the issue is essentially an
accounting exercise of a particularly complicated nature, which involves measuring not only the direct effect of certain factors but also their indirect effects
and their interactions with other factors.

The complexity of the measurement problem is indicated by my earlier statement that 50 to 75 percent of the decline in mortality rates in England, France,
and Sweden between 18-IV and 19-III was due to improvements in stature and
body mass. These results indicate that the elimination of chronic malnutrition
was a major factor in the decline in mortality, but they do not indicate how
much of this portion of the decline was the result of improvements in diet and
how much was the result of other factors that affected stature and body mass,
such as the decline in the incidence of infectious diseases. Although work on
this question is still at an early stage, and the eventual outcomes of many issues
are hard to predict, several points already established are worth noting.

It appears that the average level of caloric intake and of protein consumption
was so low during the last quarter of the eighteenth century in both England and
France that large proportions of the population were bound to have been vulnerable to high morbidity and mortality rates. Moreover, while there were
improvements in both the per capita supply of food and its distribution between
18-III and 19-III, the improvements were modest by comparison with the advances of the twentieth century. In France, for example, it was not until 19-II
that average daily caloric consumption reached levels currently prevailing in
India. Although French caloric intake increased by nearly 50 percent from
around 1830 to 1880, meat consumption remained relatively low, averaging just
69 pounds per capita during 19-III, or less than two-fifths of the U.S. level of
consumption in 1880 (Toutain 1971; Holmes 1907; Bennett and Pierce 1961).

To see the figure on average meat consumption in its proper perspective, we
must keep in mind that the distribution of meat was much more unequal than
that of calories. We do not yet have reliable estimates of the inequality of the
meat distribution for European nations in the mid-nineteenth century. Even a
highly egalitarian distribution (Gini = 0.22), however, implies that the average annual meat consumption of the bottom half of the French population during
19-III was about 47 pounds, and a distribution of meat as unequal as that for
income in England during the nineteenth century (Gini = 0.5) implies that the

lower half of the population consumed an average of just 23 pounds annually (Feinstein 1988). So even when France approached adequate average levels of meat consumption, perhaps as much as a quarter of the population were still consuming less than an ounce of meat per day.

Such low levels of meat consumption, when compared with current standards, were not confined to France. Available evidence suggests that annual meat consumption at the turn of the twentieth century was below 75 pounds per capita in Sweden, Norway, and Austria-Hungary. British consumption, the highest in Europe, probably averaged about 100 pounds per capita annually (Holmes 1907; Fogel 1989).[14] It was not until after World War II that these nations reached levels of meat consumption achieved in the United States more than a century earlier (U.S. Bureau of the Census 1960, p. 774; U.S. Central Intelligence Agency 1980; Peach and Constantin 1972).

The fact that the U.S. diet of the mid-nineteenth century provided enough high-grade protein to permit considerable catch-up from the interruption in growth caused by disease goes a long way toward explaining why the final heights of native northern white farmers born circa 1830 averaged 68.7 inches. Yet without any apparent deterioration in diet, the final heights of farmers born circa 1860 averaged only 67.2 inches, 1.5 inch below the earlier level and almost 3 inches below levels of white American males born circa 1955 (Fogel 1986b; U.S. Department of Health and Human Services, 1987).[15] These differentials suggest the magnitude of stunting of even well-fed males in a severe disease environment. The apparent final height of the London poor circa 1800, which was about 62 inches (Tanner 1982), may be taken as representing the combined effect of exceedingly poor diet and exposure to extremely severe disease environments, while 70 inches (the average final height of white males in the United States today) may be taken to approximate the combined effects of a relatively good diet and a mild disease environment. These figures suggest that even with good diets, continuous exposure to a severe disease environment will lead to stunting of about 3 inches, which is about 40 percent ($\frac{3}{8} = 0.4$) of the stunting associated with the combined impact of severe exposure and diets barely above maintenance. Moreover, with the BMI held at its optimal level, 3 inches of stunting increases the risk of death by about 21 percent.

Contribution of Improved Nutrition and Health to the Growth of Labor Productivity: Thesis 11

The first law of thermodynamics applies as strictly to the human engine as to mechanical engines. Since, moreover, the overwhelming share of calories consumed among malnourished populations is required for BMR and essential maintenance, it is quite clear that in energy-poor populations, such as those of Europe during the second half of the eighteenth century, the typical individual in the labor force had relatively small amounts of energy available for work. This observation does not preclude the possibility that malnourished French peasants worked hard for relatively long hours at certain times of the year, as at harvest time. Such work could have been sustained either by consuming more calories than normal during such periods, or by drawing on body mass to provide the needed energy. That level of work, however, could not have been sustained over the entire year. On average, the median individual in the French caloric distribution of 18-IV had only enough energy, over and above maintenance, to sustain regularly about 2.1 hours of heavy work or about 3.7 hours of moderate work per day.[16]

It is quite clear, then, that the increase in the amount of calories available for work over the past 200 years must have made a nontrivial contribution to the growth rate of the per capita income of countries such as France and Great Britain. That contribution had two effects. First, it increased the labor force participation rate by bringing into the labor force the bottom 20 percent of the consuming units, who, even assuming highly stunted individuals and low BMIs, had had only enough energy above maintenance for a few hours of strolling each day—about the amount needed for a career in begging—but less on average than that needed for just one hour of heavy manual labor.[17] Consequently, merely the elimination of the large class of paupers and beggars, which was accomplished in England mainly during the last half of the nineteenth century (Lindert and Williamson 1982, 1983; Himmelfarb 1983; Williamson 1985), contributed significantly to the growth of national product. The increase in the labor force participation rate by itself contributed 0.11 percent to the annual British growth rate between 1780 and 1980 ($1.25^{0.005} - 1 = 0.0011$).

In addition to raising the labor force participation rate, however, the increased supply of calories also raised the average consumption of calories by those in the labor force from 2,944 kilocalories per consuming unit circa 1790 to 3,701 kilocalories per consuming unit in 1980.[18] Of these amounts, 1,009 kilocalories were available for work in 1790 and 1,569 in 1980, so that calories available for work increased by about 56 percent during the past two centuries.[19] We do not know exactly how this supply of energy was divided between discretionary activities and work in 1790, but we do know that the preindustrial and early industrial routine included numerous holidays, absentee days, and short days (Thompson 1967; Landes 1969). If it is assumed that the proportion of the available energy devoted to work has been unchanged between the end points of the period,[20] then the increase in the amount of energy available for work contributed about 0.23 percent per annum to the annual growth rate of per capita income ($1.56^{0.0053} - 1 = 0.0023$).

Between 1780 and 1979, British per capita income grew at an annual rate of about 1.15 percent (Maddison 1982; Crafts 1985). Thus, in combination, bringing the ultrapoor into the labor force and raising the energy available for work by those in the labor force explains about 30 percent of the British growth in per capita income over the past two centuries.

At the present stage of research, the last figure should be considered more illustrative than substantive since it rests on two implicit assumptions that have yet to be explored adequately. The first is that the share of energy above maintenance allocated to work was the same in 1980 as in circa 1790. It is difficult to measure the extent or even the net direction of the bias caused by this assumption. On the one hand, absenteeism appears to have been much more frequent in the past than at present, owing either to poor health or to a lack of labor discipline (Landes 1969).[21] On the other hand, work weeks are shorter today than in the past, and a large share of energy may be devoted to recreation or other activities whose values are excluded from the national income accounts. Although it is my guess that these two influences tend to cancel each other out, it may be that the share of energy above maintenance allocated to work (measured GNP) is lower now than in the past. In that event the estimate of the share of British economic growth accounted for by improved nutrition and health would be overstated. The other implicit assumption is that the efficiency with which tall people convert energy into work output is the same as that of short people. An enormous literature has developed on this question, but the evidence amassed so far is inconclusive.[22] Even if both of these assumptions tend to bias upward the share of British economic growth attributed to improved nutrition, however, it is quite unlikely that the bias could be as much as 50 percent. Hence, it appears that improved nutrition and health accounted for at least 20 percent of British economic growth, and the best estimate could be as high as 30 percent.

Notes

1. I am indebted to David Weir for supplying Figure 1.1, which corrects a typographical error in the version of that diagram published in Weir 1984. Both the French and the English series are 11-year moving averages, centered on the years shown. Weir's sources were Wrigley and Schofield (1981, pp. 531–535); INED (1977, pp. 332–333); and Mitchell (1980, pp. 116–119).

2. The English cdr in 1980, both sexes combined, and standardized on the age structure of 1701–1705, is 7 per thousand (Fogel 1986b, p. 440).

3. The F-values for S_3^2/S_2^2 and S_4^2/S_2^2 are significant at the 0.004 level (the periods referred to by the three subscripts are 1600–1640 for 2, 1641–1699 for 3, and 1700–1745 for 4).

4. For a more extended discussion of this point, see Fogel 1988b, sec. 2.1.

5. The main conclusions summarized in this section are robust to any value of the coefficient of variation in the range 0.3 ± 0.1.

6. This discussion takes account only of the incidence of mortality among those in each country whose consumption of calories was below basal metabolism. There were many other individuals, however, who were at increased risk of death because they were malnourished, even though the degree of malnourishment was less extreme. See note 10.

7. Even small amounts of common agricultural or urban manual labor would have put such malnourished individuals on a path toward consuming their own tissue, and if continued long enough would sooner or later have resulted in death. These are the people who constituted Marx's "Lumpenproletariat," Mayhew's "street fold," Huxley's "substrata," King's "unproductive classes," consuming more than they produced, and the French *gens de néant* (Himmelfarb 1983; Laslett 1984).

8. For a further discussion of this possibility, see Fogel 1988b. It is important to keep in mind that the denominator of the relative risk curve is the average mortality rate computed over all heights. Consequently, the curve will shift as the overall mortality shifts. What appears to be stable over a wide range of mortality regimens are the height-specific relative rates.

9. As with height, these curves have the average mortality rate, calculated over all BMIs, in the denominator. Compare the discussion in note 8. The body mass index used here, weight—measured in kilograms—divided by height—measured in meters squared—or kg/m^2, is referred to as the Quetolet index. Epidemiologists use height squared rather than height in the denominator because that transformation reduces the correlation between weight and the BMI to close to zero in cross-section.

10. The English cdr circa 1790 is 26.7, and 1.38 times that number is 36.8, which is close to a French cdr of 36.1 derived from Weir's (1984) data.

11. This statement relies on the use of height data as a proxy for mortality rates. In regressions relating final heights of native-born white males to socioeconomic factors, dummy variables for city size did not become significantly negative until the dummy for 25,000–49,999. For similar results based on direct measurement of mortality, see Vinovskis 1972.

12. Komlos (1987) has argued for a slight decline in caloric intake between 1839 and 1859, but this result is based on the assumption that human corn consumption was just 4 bushels per capita throughout the period, despite the rise in output per capita and in output per consuming unit (including livestock) of about 56 percent (Fogel 1965, p. 206). An increase of human corn consumption by about half a bushel per capita annually between 1840 and 1860 wipes out the small decline in calories postulated by Komlos. The large increase in corn feed per consuming unit also casts doubt on his assumption that the slaughter weight of livestock remained constant.

13. See Fogel and Engerman 1974, II, 92–99, and 1989b for the procedures followed in obtaining these estimates. It should be kept in mind that corn, peas, and other widely consumed vegetables are major sources of protein. Consequently, contrary to Komlos' (1987) assumption that average protein consumption per capita declined between 1839 and 1859, it may have increased slightly not only because average meat consumption may have increased but also because of an increase in the availability of vegetable sources of protein. In any case, Komlos' estimates (1987, table 8) imply that during the 1840s and 1850s consumption per equivalent adult male was about 3,700 kilocalories and 125 grams of protein.

14. It should be noted that the figures in Holmes' (1907) table 59 need to be converted from dressed weight to edible weight. In the British case, I followed him in assuming that imports were close to edible weight but that domestic production represented dressed weight. To convert dressed to edible weight (excluding lard) I used 0.64 (0.47/0.73 = 0.64). This is the factor for swine and is somewhat higher than for cattle and sheep (Holmes 1907, pp. 60–63).

15. The content of the diet of northern farm children under age 3 circa 1850 is still an open issue.

16. I have assumed a height of 160.5 centimeters and a weight of about 49 kilograms. These assumptions imply a BMR of 1,372 kilocalories and 1,742 kilocalories for maintenance, leaving about 451 kilocalories for work. Heavy work (including rest breaks) requires 219 kilocalories per hour, moderate work (including breaks) 122. Hours of work per day are calculated on a basis of 365 days. If one assumes a work year of 250 days, allowing for holidays and sickness, then the figures become 3.1 hours of heavy work and 5.4 hours of moderate work *per working day*. The last pair of figures still does not standardize for slack days and inclement days, when only indoor work of a sedentary nature was

performed. Adjusting for such days would further increase the number of hours of heavy work and moderate work normally performed during such key seasons as planting and harvesting.

17. It was assumed that the bottom 20 percent of the English consuming units were 157 centimeters tall, with a weight of about 47 kilograms, which implies a BMR of about 1,342 kilocalories and about 1,704 kilocalories for maintenance. The estimated average caloric intake of the second decile of the English caloric distribution in 18-IV was 1,903 kilocalories. Strolling requires about 76.56 kilocalories above maintenance, so that such an individual could stroll for about 2.6 hours. One hour of heavy manual labor, including rest breaks, requires 219 kilocalories above maintenance, and 335 kilocalories above maintenance while engaged. Computed from the requirements in FAO/WHO/UNU 1985, p. 76.

18. Calories per capita in 1980 were converted to calories per consuming unit, using the age/sex structure of the British population in 1980 *(Annual Abstract* 1987).

19. It was assumed that in 18-IV mature males aged 23–29 were 167.9 centimeters tall, with a BMI of 21.7 (see Fogel 1988b; Table 1.4 above), so that their mean weight was 61.2 kilograms. Such men would require 1,524 kilocalories for BMR and 1,935 for maintenance. The corresponding figures for 19-III were 175 centimeters, BMI of 24.0, and 73.5 kilograms. The BMI figure is the average of those for the British Petroleum staff and business executives in Eveleth and Tanner (1976, p. 285). These imply 1,679 kilocalories for BMR and 2,132 for maintenance (Quenouille et al. 1951).

20. There was probably an increase in hours worked per week between 18-IV and 19-II and a decrease thereafter. Intensity of work per hour may have increased steadily in Britain throughout the past two centuries, however.

21. Not a great deal is known about how disability days have varied over time. It has been estimated that U.S. slaves circa 1850 had an average of 12.7 disability days. U.S. blacks averaged 14.8 days in the late 1890s, 16.2 days in 1970, and 21.7 in 1981. For the entire civilian U.S. population the annual number of disability days rose from 16.4 per capita in 1965 to 19.1 in 1981. Interestingly, over this period the number of disability days per capita rose for persons under age 65 but not for those over 65, which suggests that this measure may be strongly influenced by cultural or social norms including the days of sickness pay in labor contracts (Fogel and Engerman 1974, II, 101; U.S. Bureau of the Census 1983, p. 121). Riley and Alter (1987) have found an upward shift in the age-specific schedule for the duration of illness between the periods 1866–1870 and 1893–1897 in a sample of English Odd Fellows, which they attribute to a decline in the case mortality rate.

22. See Osmani 1991 for an extended summary of the literature.

References

Ackernecht, E. H. 1945. *Malaria in the Upper Mississippi Valley, 1760–1900.* Baltimore: Johns Hopkins University Press.

——— 1952. "Diseases in the Middle West." In *Essays in the History of Medicine in Honor of David J. Davis.* Urbana: University of Illinois Press.

Annual Abstract. 1987. *Annual Abstract of Statistics,* no. 123. Great Britain Central Statistical Office. London: Her Majesty's Stationery Office.

Appleby, A. B. 1979. "Diet in Sixteenth-Century England: Sources, Problems, Possibilities." In *Health, Medicine, and Mortality in the Sixteenth Century,* ed. C. Webster. Cambridge: Cambridge University Press.

Bairoch, P. 1988. *Cities and Economic Development: From the Dawn of History to the Present,* trans. C. Braider. Chicago: University of Chicago Press.

Barnes, D. G. 1930. *A History of the English Corn Laws from 1669 to 1846.* London: George Routledge and Sons.

Benn, R. T. 1971. "Some Mathematical Properties of Weight-for-Height Indices and as Measures of Adiposity." *British Journal of Preventive Medicine* 25:42–50.

Bennett, M. K., and R. H. Pierce. 1961. "Changes in the American National Diet, 1879–1959." *Food Research Institute Studies* 2:95–119.

Bernard, R.-J. [1969] 1975. "Peasant Diet in Eighteenth-Century Gévaudan." In *European Diet from Pre-Industrial to Modern Times*, ed. E. Forster and R. Forster. New York: Harper & Row.

Billewicz, W. Z., and I. A. MacGregor. 1982. "A Birth-to-Maturity Longitudinal Study of Heights and Weights in Two West African (Gambian) Villages, 1951–1975." *Annals of Human Biology* 9, no. 4:309–320.

Billewicz, W. Z., W. F. F. Kemsley, and A. M. Thomson. 1962. "Indices of Adiposity." *British Journal of Preventive Social Medicine* 16:183–188.

Blum, J. 1978. *The End of the Old Order in Rural Europe*. Princeton: Princeton University Press.

Bourgeois-Pichat, J. 1965. "The General Development of the Population of France since the Eighteenth Century." In *Population in History: Essays in Historical Demography*, ed. D. V. Glass and D. E. C. Eversley. Chicago: Aldine.

Boyd, M. F. 1941. "An Historical Sketch of the Prevalence of Malaria in North America." *American Journal of Tropical Medicine* 21:223–244.

Burnett, John. 1979. *Plenty and Want*. 2nd ed. London: Scholar Press.

Chamla, M. C. L. 1983. "L'évolution récente de la stature en Europe occidentale (période 1960–1980)." *Bulletin et mémoire de la Société d'anthropologie de Paris* 10, no. 13:195–224.

Chartres, J. A. 1985. "The Marketing of Agricultural Produce." In *The Agrarian History of England and Wales*. Vol. 2. *Agrarian Change*, ed. J. Thirsk. Cambridge: Cambridge University Press.

Chen, L., A. K. M. Chowdhury, and S. L. Huffman. 1980. "Anthropometric Assessment of Energy-Protein Malnutrition and Subsequent Risk of Mortality among Pre-School–Aged Children." *American Journal of Clinical Nutrition* 33:1836–45.

——— 1981. "The Use of Anthropometry for Nutritional Surveillance in Mortality Control Programs." Letter to the editor. *American Journal of Clinical Nutrition* 34:2596–99.

Cippola, C. M. 1980. *Before the Industrial Revolution: European Society and Economy, 1000–1700*. New York: Norton.

Cole, G. D. H., and R. Postgate. 1939. *The British Common People, 1746–1930*. New York: Knopf.

Coolidge, R. H. 1856. *Statistical Report on Sickness and Mortality in the Army of the United States*. Washington, D.C.: A. O. P. Nicholson.

Crafts, N. F. R. 1980. "Income Elasticities of Demand and the Release of Labor by Agriculture during the British Industrial Revolution." *Journal of European Economic History* 9:153–168.

——— 1981. "The Eighteenth Century: A Survey." In *The Economic History of Britain since 1700*, ed. R. C. Floud and D. N. McCloskey. Vol. 1. Cambridge: Cambridge University Press.

——— 1985. *British Economic Growth during the Industrial Revolution*. Oxford: Clarendon Press.

Davidson, S., et al. 1979. *Human Nutrition and Dietetics*. Edinburgh: Churchill Livingstone.

Drake, D. 1850, 1854. *A Systematic Treatise, etc. on the Principal Diseases of the Interior Valley of North America*. 2 vols. Cincinnati.

Drummond, J. C., and A. Wilbraham. 1958. *The Englishman's Food: A History of Five Centuries of English Diet*. 2nd ed. London: Jonathan Cape.

Durnin, J., and R. Passmore. 1967. *Energy, Work, and Leisure*. London: Heinemann.

Dyer, C. 1983. "English Diet in the Later Middle Ages." In *Social Relations and Ideas: Essays in Honour of R. H. Hilton*, ed. T. H. Aston et al. Cambridge: Cambridge University Press.

Essemer, M. 1983. "Food Consumption and Standard of Living: Studies on Food Consumption among Different Strata of the Swedish Population, 1686–1933." *Uppsala Papers in Economic History*. Research Report no. 2.

Essemer, M., and M. Morell. 1986. "Changes in Swedish Nutrition." In *Long-Term Change in Nutrition and the Standard of Living*, ed. R. W. Fogel. Bern: Ninth International Economic History Congress.

Eveleth, P. B., and J. M. Tanner. 1976. *Worldwide Variation in Human Growth*. Cambridge: Cambridge University Press.

Everitt, A. 1967. "The Marketing of Agricultural Produce." In *The Agrarian History of England and Wales*. Vol. 4. *1500–1640*, ed. J. Thirsk. Cambridge: Cambridge University Press.

FAO/WHO/UNU. 1985. *Energy and Protein Requirements*. Report of a Joint FAO/WHO/UNU Expert Consultation. Technical Report Series no. 724. Geneva: World Health Organization.

Feinstein, C. 1988. "The Rise and Fall of the Williamson Curve." Typescript. Nuffield College, Oxford.

Flinn, M. W. 1974. "The Stabilization of Mortality in Pre-Industrial Western Europe." *Journal of European Economic History* 3:285–318.

——— 1981. *The European Demographic System, 1500–1820*. Baltimore: Johns Hopkins University Press.

Floud, R. 1983a. "The Heights of Europeans since 1750: A New Source for European Economic History." Mimeograph. National Bureau of Economic Research.

——— 1983b. "Inference from the Heights of Volunteer Soldiers and Sailors." Mimeograph. Birkbeck College, London.

——— 1985. "Two Cultures? British and American Heights in the Nineteenth Century." Mimeograph. Birkbeck College, London.

Floud, R., K. Wachter, and A. Gregory. 1990. *Height, Health and History: Nutritional Status in the United Kingdom, 1750–1980*. Cambridge: Cambridge University Press.

Fogel, R. W. 1965. "A Provisional View of the 'New Economic History.' " In *New Views on American Economic Development*, ed. R. L. Andreano. Cambridge, Mass.: Schenkman.

——— 1986a. "Physical Growth as a Measure of the Economic Well-Being of Populations: The Eighteenth and Nineteenth Centuries." In *Human Growth*, ed. F. Falkner and J. M. Tanner. Vol. 3. 2nd ed. New York: Plenum.

——— 1986b. "Nutrition and the Decline in Mortality since 1700: Some Additional Preliminary Findings." In *Long-Term Factors in American Economic Growth*, ed. S. L. Engerman and R. E. Gallman. Conference in Research in Income and Wealth. Vol. 41. Chicago: University of Chicago Press.

——— 1988a. "Second Thoughts on the European Escape from Hunger: Famines, Chronic Malnutrition, and Mortality." Presented at the Conference on Poverty, Undernutrition, and Living Standards. UNU/WIDER, Helsinki, Finland, July 17–31.

——— 1988b. "Biomedical Approaches to the Estimation and Interpretation of Secular Trends in Labor Productivity, Equity, Morbidity, and Mortality in Western Europe and America, 1780–1980." Typescript. University of Chicago.

——— 1989. *Without Consent or Contract: The Rise and Fall of American Slavery*. Vol. 1. New York: Norton.

Fogel, R. W., and S. L. Engerman. 1974. *Time on the Cross: The Economics of American Negro Slavery*. 2 vols. Boston: Little, Brown.

——— 1990. "The Slave Diet on Large Plantations in 1860." In *Without Consent or Contract*. Vol. 2. *Evidence and Methods*. New York: Norton.

Fogel, R. W., S. L. Engerman, J. Trussell, R. Floud, C. Pope, and L. T. Wimmer. 1978. "The Economics of Mortality in North America, 1650–1910: A Description of a Research Project." *Historical Methods* 11 (Spring):75–108.

Fogel, R. W., R. A. Galantine, and R. L. Manning, eds. 1991. *Without Consent or Contract: Evidence and Methods*. New York: Norton.

Fogel, R. W., C. L. Pope, S. H. Preston, N. Scrimshaw, P. Temin, and L. T. Wimmer. 1986. "The Aging of Union Army Men: A Longitudinal Study." Photocopy. Cambridge, Mass.

Freudenberger, H., and G. Cummins. 1976. "Health, Work, and Leisure before the Industrial Revolution." *Explorations in Economic History* 13:1–12.

Frijhoff, W., and D. Julia. 1979. "The Diet in Boarding Schools at the End of the Ancien Régime." In *Food and Drink in History: Selections from the Annals*. Vol. 5. *Economies, Societies, Civilizations*, ed. R. Forster and O. Ranum, trans. E. Forster and P. M. Ranum. Baltimore: Johns Hopkins University Press.

Goubert, P. 1960. *Beauvais et le Beauvaisis de 1600 à 1730*. Paris.

———— 1973. *The Ancien Régime*. New York: Harper & Row.

Heckscher, E. F. 1954. *An Economic History of Sweden*, trans. G. Ohlin. Cambridge, Mass.: Harvard University Press.

Hémardinquer, J.-J. 1970. *Pour une histoire de l'alimentation*. Cahiers des Annales no. 28. Paris: Colin.

Heywood, P. F. 1983. "Growth and Nutrition in Papua New Guinea." *Journal of Human Evolution* 12.

Himmelfarb, Gertrude. 1983. *The Idea of Poverty: England in the Early Industrial Age*. New York: Random House.

Holmes, G. K. 1907. "Meat Supply and Surplus." *U.S. Bureau of Statistics*. Bulletin 55.

Horton, S. 1984. "Human Resources and Living Standards Measurement." Mimeograph. World Bank Living Standards Measurement Study.

———— 1986. "Child Nutrition and Family Size: Results from the Philippines." *Journal of Development Economics* 23:161–176.

Hoskins, W. G. 1964. "Harvest Fluctuations and English Economic History, 1480–1619." *Agricultural History Review* 12:28–46.

———— 1968. "Harvest Fluctuations and English Economic History, 1620–1759." *Agricultural History Review* 16:15–31.

Hufton, O. H. 1974. *The Poor of Eighteenth-Century France*. Oxford: Clarendon Press.

———— 1983. "Social Conflict and the Grain Supply in Eighteenth-Century France." *Journal of Interdisciplinary History* 14:303–331.

Institut National d'Etudes Démographiques. 1977. "Sixième rapport sur la situation démographique de la France." *Population* 32:253–338.

Jordan, W. K. 1959. *Philanthropy in England, 1480–1660*. London: George Allen and Unwin.

Journal of Interdisciplinary History. 1983. "The Relationship of Nutrition, Disease, and Social Conditions: A Graphical Presentation." *Journal of Interdisciplinary History* 14:503–506.

Kaplan, S. L. 1976. *Bread, Politics, and Political Economy in the Reign of Louis XV*. The Hague: Martinus Nijhoff.

Kielmann, A. A., et al. 1983. *Child and Maternal Health Services in Rural India: The Narangwal Experiment*. Vol. 1. *Integrated Nutrition and Health*. Baltimore: Johns Hopkins University Press.

Koenker, R. 1977. "Was Bread Giffen? The Demand for Food in England circa 1790." *Review of Economics and Statistics* 59:225–229.

Komlos, John. 1985. "Stature and Nutrition in the Habsburg Monarchy: The Standard of Living and Economic Development in the Eighteenth Century." *American Historical Review* 90:1149–61.

———— 1987. "The Height and Weight of West Point Cadets: Dietary Change in Antebellum America." *Journal of Economic History* 47 (December):897–927.

———— 1990. "Stature, Nutrition, and Economic Development in the Eighteenth-Century Habsburg Monarchy: The 'Austrian' Model of the Industrial Revolution." Ph.D. diss., University of Chicago.

Labrousse, C. E. 1944. *La crise de l'économie française à la fin de l'ancien régime et au début de la Révolution*. Paris: Presses Universitaires de France.

Landes, D. S. 1969. *The Unbound Prometheus: Technological Change and Industrial Development in Western Europe from 1750 to the Present*. Cambridge: Cambridge University Press.

Laslett, P. [1965] 1984. *The World We Have Lost: England before the Industrial Age*. New York: Scribner's.

Lebrun, F. 1971. *Les hommes et la mort en Anjou au 17e et 18e siècles*. Paris.

Lee, R. 1981. "Short-Term Variation: Vital Rates, Prices, and Weather." In *The Population History of England, 1541–1871: A Reconstruction*, ed. E. A. Wrigley and R. S. Schofield. Cambridge, Mass.: Harvard University Press.

Leonard, E. M. 1965. *The Early History of English Poor Relief*. New York: Barnes and Noble.

Lindert, P. H., and J. G. Williamson. 1982. "Revising England's Social Tables, 1688–1812." *Explorations in Economic History* 19:385–408.

————— 1983. "Reinterpreting Britain's Social Tables, 1683–1913." *Explorations in Economic History* 20:94–109.

Lipson, E. 1971. *The Economic History of England.* Vols. 2 and 3. *The Age of Mercantilism.* London: Adam and Charles Black.

Lipton, M. 1983. "Poverty, Undernutrition, and Hunger." World Bank Staff Working Papers no. 597. Washington, D.C.: World Bank.

Maddison, A. 1982. *Phases of Capitalist Development.* Oxford: Oxford University Press.

Margo, R. A., and G. Villaflor. 1987. "The Growth of Wages in Antebellum America: New Evidence." Working paper, National Bureau of Economic Research.

Marmot, M. G., Shipley, and Rose. 1984. "Inequalities of Death-Specific Explanations of a General Pattern." *Lancet* 1:1003–6.

Marshall, J. D. 1968. *The Old Poor Law, 1795–1834.* London: Macmillan.

Martorell, R. 1985. "Child Growth Retardation: A Discussion of Its Causes and Its Relationship to Health." In *Nutritional Adaptation in Man,* ed. K. Blaxter and J. C. Waterlow. London: John Libby.

Martorell, R., and J.-P. Habicht. 1986. "Growth in Early Childhood in Developing Countries." In *Human Growth.* Vol. 3. *Methodology,* ed. F. Falkner and J. M. Tanner. 2nd ed. New York: Plenum.

McKeown, T., and R. G. Brown. 1955. "Medical Evidence Related to English Population Changes in the Eighteenth Century." *Population Studies* 9:119–141.

McMahon, S. F. 1981. "Provisions Laid Up for the Family." *Historical Methods* 14:4–21.

Mennell, S. 1985. *All Manners of Food.* London: Basil Blackwell.

Mitchell, B. R. 1980. *European Historical Statistics, 1750–1975,* 2nd ed. London: Macmillan.

Mitchell, B. R., and P. Deane. 1962. *Abstract of British Historical Statistics.* Cambridge: Cambridge University Press.

Mokyr, J. 1985. *Why Ireland Starved: A Quantitative and Analytical History of the Irish Economy, 1800–1850.* London: George Allen and Unwin.

Morell, M. 1983. "Food Consumption among Inmates of Swedish Hospitals during the Eighteenth and Early Nineteenth Centuries." Paper presented at "Colloquium on the Standard of Living in Europe since 1850," Uppsala University, Sweden.

Oddy, D. J. 1970. "Working-Class Diets in Late-Nineteenth-Century Britain." *Economic History Review* 23:314–323.

Osmani, S. R. 1991. "Nutrition and the Economics of Food: Implications of Some Recent Controversies." In *Nutrition and Poverty,* ed. S. R. Osmani. Oxford: Clarendon Press.

Payne, P. 1991. "Undernutrition: Measurement and Implications." In *Nutrition and Poverty,* ed. S. R. Osmani. Oxford: Clarendon Press.

Peach, W. N., and J. A. Constantin. 1972. *Zimmermann's World Resources and Industries.* 3rd ed. New York: Harper & Row.

Post, J. D. 1977. *The Last Great Subsistence Crisis in the Western World.* Baltimore: Johns Hopkins University Press.

Pullar, P. 1970. *Consuming Passions: Being an Historic Inquiry into Certain English Appetites.* Boston: Little, Brown.

Quenouille, M. H., A. W. Boyne, W. B. Fisher, and I. Leitch. 1951. *Statistical Studies of Recorded Energy Expenditure in Man.* Technical Communication no. 17. Aberdeenshire, Scotland: Commonwealth Bureau of Animal Nutrition.

Richardson, T. L. 1976. "The Agricultural Labourer's Standard of Living in Kent, 1790–1860." In *The Making of the Modern British Diet,* ed. D. Oddy and D. Miller. London: Croom Helm.

Riley, J. C., and G. Alter. 1987. "The Epidemiologic Transition and the Morbidity Trend: Sickness Risk by Age and Form." Presented at Social Science History Association Conference, New Orleans, October 29–November 1.

Rose, M. E. 1971. *The Relief of Poverty, 1834–1914.* Studies in Economic History. London: Macmillan.

Rose, R. B. 1961. "Eighteenth-Century Price Riots and Public Policy in England." *International Review of Social History* 6:277–292.

Sandberg, L. G., and R. H. Steckel. 1988. "Overpopulation and Malnutrition Rediscovered: Hard Times in Nineteenth-Century Sweden." *Explorations in Economic History* 25:1–19.

Schofield, R. 1983. "The Impact of Scarcity and Plenty on Population Change in England, 1541–1871." *Journal of Interdisciplinary History* 14:265–291.

Scrimshaw, N. S. 1987. "The Phenomenon of Famine." *Annual Review of Nutrition* 7:1–21.

Scrimshaw, N. S., C. E. Taylor, and J. E. Gordon. 1968. *Interactions of Nutrition and Infection.* Geneva: World Health Organization.

Shammas, C. 1983. "Food Expenditures and Economic Well-Being in Early Modern England." *Journal of Economic History* 43:89–100.

———— 1984. "The Eighteenth-Century English Diet and Economic Change." *Explorations in Economic History* 21:254–269.

Smillie, W. G. 1955. *Public Health: Its Promise for the Future.* New York: Macmillan.

Sommer, A., and M. S. Lowenstein. 1975. "Nutritional Status and Mortality: A Prospective Validation of the QUAC Stick." *American Journal of Clinical Nutrition* 28:287–292.

Srinivasen, T. N. 1983. "Malnutrition in Developing Countries: The State of Knowledge of the Extent of Its Prevalence, Its Causes, and Its Consequences." Background paper prepared for FAO's Fifth World Food Survey, Economic Growth Center, Yale University.

Stigler, C. J. 1974. "The Early History of Empirical Studies of Consumer Behavior." *Journal of Political Economy* 62:95–113.

Supple, B. E. 1964. *Commercial Crisis and Change in England, 1600–1642.* Cambridge: Cambridge University Press.

Tanner, J. M. 1982. "The Potential of Auxological Data for Monitoring Economic and Social Well-Being." *Social Scientific History* 6:571–581.

Taylor, C. E. 1983. "Synergy among Mass Infections, Famines, and Poverty." *Journal of Interdisciplinary History* 14:483–501.

Thirsk, J. 1985a. "Agricultural Policy: Public Debate and Legislation." In *The Agrarian History of England and Wales.* Vol. 2. *Agrarian Change,* ed. J. Thirsk. Cambridge: Cambridge University Press.

———— 1985b. "Agricultural Innovations and Their Diffusions." In *The Agrarian History of England and Wales.* Vol. 2. *Agrarian Change,* ed. J. Thirsk. Cambridge: Cambridge University Press.

Thompson, E. P. 1967. "Time, Work-Discipline, and Industrial Capitalism." *Past and Present* 38: 57–97.

Tilly, C. 1975. "Food Supply and Public Order in Modern Europe." In *The Formation of National States in Western Europe,* ed. C. Tilly. Princeton: Princeton University Press.

Tilly, L. A. 1971. "The Food Riot as a Form of Political Conflict in France." *Journal of Interdisciplinary History* 2:23–57.

Toutain, J. 1971. "La consommation alimentaire en France de 1789 à 1964." *Economies et sociétés, Cahiers de l'ISEA* (Institut de Statistique économique appliquée) 5, no. 11:1909–2049.

U.S. Bureau of the Census. 1960. *Historical Statistics of the United States, Colonial Times to 1957.* Washington, D.C.: Government Printing Office.

———— 1983. *Statistical Abstract of the United States, 1984.* Washington, D.C.: Government Printing Office.

U.S. Central Intelligence Agency. 1980. *National Intelligence Fact Book.* Washington, D.C.: Government Printing Office.

U.S. Department of Health and Human Services. 1987. "Anthropometric Reference Data and Prevalence of Overweight." *Vital and Health Statistics,* ser. 11, no. 238.

U.S. Surgeon General's Office. 1875. *The Cholera Epidemic of 1873 in the United States.* Washington, D.C.: Government Printing Office.

Vinovskis, M. A. 1972. "Mortality Rates and Trends in Massachusetts before 1860." *Journal of Economic History* 32:184–213.

Vries, J. de. 1984. *European Urbanization, 1500–1800*. Cambridge, Mass.: Harvard University Press.

Waaler, H. T. 1984. "Height, Weight, and Mortality: The Norwegian Experience." *Acta Medica Scandinavica,* supplement no. 679. Stockholm.

Weber, A. F. [1899] 1963. *The Growth of Cities in the Nineteenth Century: A Study in Statistics.* Ithaca: Cornell University Press.

Weir, D. R. 1984. "Life under Pressure: France and England, 1670–1870." *Journal of Economic History* 44:27–47.

Whitehead, R. G. 1977. "Protein and Energy Requirements of Young Children Living in the Developing Countries to Allow for Catch-Up Growth after Infections." *American Journal of Clinical Nutrition* 30:1545–47.

Williamson, J. G. 1976. "American Prices and Urban Inequality since 1820." *Journal of Economic History* 2:303–333.

———— 1985. *Did British Capitalism Breed Inequality?* Boston: Allen and Unwin.

Wilson, C. A. 1973. *Food and Drink in Britain: From the Stone Age to Recent Times.* London: Constable.

Woods, R. 1984. "Mortality Patterns in the Nineteenth Century." In *Urban Diseases and Mortality in Nineteenth-Century England,* ed. R. Woods and J. Woodward. New York: St. Martin's Press.

Woodward, D. 1981. "Wage Rates and Living Standards in Pre-Industrial England." *Past and Present* 91:28–45.

World Bank. 1987. *World Development Report, 1987.* Oxford: Oxford University Press.

Wrigley, E. A. 1969. *Population and History.* London: Weidenfeld and Nicolson.

———— 1987. "Some Reflections on Corn Yields and Prices in Pre-Industrial Economies." In E. A. Wrigley, *People, Cities, and Wealth: The Transformation of Traditional Society.* Oxford: Basil Blackwell.

Wrigley, E. A., and R. S. Schofield. 1981. *The Population History of England, 1541–1871: A Reconstruction.* Cambridge, Mass.: Harvard University Press.

2

...

The Hero and the Herd in Technological History: Reflections on Thomas Edison and the Battle of the Systems

Paul A. David

The story to be told here is about the early period in the development of electric lighting and power supply networks.[1] Since this tale is one whose broad outlines probably are familiar to many readers from previous recountings,[2] I must have a special reason to return to it on the present occasion. My motivation lies in the bearing which some less well known details of the rivalry between direct current and alternating current systems of electricity supply will be seen to have upon a difficult, far broader issue. That subject concerns the precise place to be accorded individual economic actions in the evolution of modern technological systems.

What causal role properly can be assigned to particular decision makers in the build-up of those complex production systems that form the material infrastructure of modern societies? When do specific actions, taken purposively and implemented by identifiable agents (say, entrepreneurs) have the power to alter significantly the course of technological history? Or should we hold that the economic analyst of technical change, being occupied for the most part with the progress of armies that have few generals and need none, will find only misleading metaphors in the heroic deeds chronicled by traditional political and military historians?[3] Rather than being "made" by any*one* at any particular time, does not technology simply accumulate from the incremental, almost imperceptible changes wrought by the jostling interactions among the herd of small decision makers—the dreamers and scientists, tinkerers and engineers, inventors and innovators, tycoons and managers, artisans and operatives—all of whose separate motions have somehow been coordinated and channeled by markets under the system of capitalism? Should we not then insist that the nature of technical progress is best conveyed by conceptualizing it as a continuous flow, and forswear narratives that dwell on a succession of unique actions and discrete historical "events"? These questions are daunting, and I have no

72

definitive answers to them. But surely they cannot be inappropriate, especially now that innovation, entrepreneurship, and, indeed, "intrapreneurship," are on the lips of those in business and politics who concern themselves with preserving competitiveness by fostering technological dynamism.

Views of Technological Change: Herds or Heroes?
Continuities or Events?

From the way that I have phrased my agenda, one might surmise that I am preparing to plunge into the thick of the recurring debate over Schumpeter's representation of entrepreneurs as individuals who form a distinct sociological category—those heroic few to whom in each era is assigned the function of innovation, and without whom the capitalist economic system soon would settle down to a dismal stationary state.[4] I do not mean, however, to focus squarely on this question of what it is that entrepreneurs and "bosses" do, really do, or may have done in the past.[5] Instead, I want to take up a different problem, which, being more general, is logically antecedent to that subject of ongoing controversy among economic historians: When, if at all, in the development of society's technological knowledge and apparatus, could the actions of some individual participants in a market process be expected to exert a perceptible influence over the eventual outcome—in effect, to determine the characteristics of the particular trajectory of diffusion and development along which some branch of technology becomes channeled?[6] For this, one must admit, there is no need that the vital actors be cast as visionary heroes, or essential contributors to enhancing economic efficiency. Scoundrels and fools, or merely men with weak stomachs for the perils of entrepreneurial voyages, may serve just as well in teaching us when it is that big consequences are most likely to flow from historical events petty enough to be the work of ordinary mortals.

Oddly enough, many who now are studying technological and economic history would not care to be asked to concentrate on the actions of specific individuals, and so to emphasize the role those persons had in producing changes consequent upon "events."[7] At least two causes can be found for this state of affairs. For the first, there is the dominant historiographic tradition regarding the progress of technology. As elsewhere in the writing of social science history, this tradition perpetuates Darwin's approach to the study of evolution. Changes, in this ahistorical view, are produced by slow, continuous adaptations in an "eventless" world.[8] It is, of course, a strong tradition that can draw upon Karl Marx, A. P. Usher, and C. S. Gilfillan for elaborations of the view of technical progress as a social process, consisting of the steady accretion of innumerable minor improvements and modifications.[9] It therefore supports the conceptualization of "technology" as a powerful flux, a broad and mighty river reshaping the economic and social landscape and, in the process, sweeping puny individual actors—inventors, businessmen, workers, customers, politicians—along in its currents. Thus, although the dominant tradition in the historiography of modern technological change has firmly embraced the Schumpeterian vision of a distinctly capitalist process of development situated in historical time, its adherents paradoxically still resist Schumpeter's emphasis on the discontinuous nature of technological progress.

For a second cause we can turn closer to home. In the era of cliometrics, especially, economic theory has not been without an influence on the way that technological history has come to be studied.[10] Mainstream economics since the "Marginalist Revolution," and certainly since Alfred Marshall, has subscribed to the characterization of change as being so incremental as to constitute an "eventless" continuum. Moreover, although modern microeconomists show no hesitancy in producing formal theories of human action, they appear to be most comfortable with the assumption that actual individuals (in the past and present) somehow or other manage to cancel one another out, so that changes emerge from the ensemble of their behaviors—that is, from the action of the anonymous masses. As a consequence of the neoclassical economists' efforts to expose the workings of mechanisms that would cause invention and innovation to respond like other resource-using activities to signals and incentives emanating from markets, Adam Smith's metaphoric "invisible hand" has now reached deep into the technological historians' bailiwick. The actions of many individual human minds and muscles are thus depicted naturally as being subject to coordination by nonhierarchical social organizations, including markets, thereby permitting very substantial decentralization of control in the creation of technological achievements of tremendous complexity.[11] On this view it would appear that no technoeconomic entrepreneurs of extraordinary stature are required for the creation of such things as railroads, electrical supply systems, or telephone networks.

While I am prepared to demur from this opinion, I seek no quarrel with those who say that technological progress is a collective, social process, many important aspects of which are characterized by continuity. Nor would I dispute the case for treating invention and innovation as endogenous to the resource allocation process conducted by means of markets. But I do want to counteract or at least to qualify the suggestion—one that is strongly conveyed by some recent contributions to the history of technology—that individuals essentially have no real points of leverage from which to control the outcomes of such a macrocosmic societal process; that decision-making agents either are rationally moving with the tide of technical change, or, by failing to heed the proper signals, are running the risk of being swept aside by it.

Rather than formulating an alternative vision of the way the world works in fairly general and abstract terms, as I have attempted to do elsewhere, I shall try here to advance my argument by means of a concrete historical illustration.[12] I will use the story of a technological rivalry—the Battle of the Systems, so-called, between the late-nineteenth-century commercial proponents of direct current and alternating current systems of electricity supply—to suggest that sometimes we should expect to find critical moments, or points of *bifurcation*, in the dynamic process of technical change. Such points, really more like narrow windows in the domain of time, are especially prone to appear at early stages of the incremental development of integrated production and distribution systems that are characterized by strong elements of localized positive feedback, or increasing returns to the more extensive utilization of one or another among the available technical formulations. In this context, specific technical formulations represent variants of a particular *technological system paradigm* and tend to undergo further development and elaboration along rather narrowly defined *trajectories* which lead away from these historical bifurcation points.[13] It is at such junctures, I suggest, that individual economic agents do briefly hold substantial power to direct the flow of subsequent events along one path rather than another. Unfortunately, in the very nature of those circumstances it is difficult to gauge just how quickly seemingly similar paths may begin to diverge, or to foresee exactly the eventual alternative outcomes toward which they lead.

Looked at in retrospect, however, things often take on an appearance of having been rather more preordained. In the case at hand, modern commentators have been inclined to downplay as historically insignificant the rivalry that arose in the late 1880s between Thomas Alva Edison and George Westinghouse, then the publicly prominent champions, respectively, of direct current and alternating current in the United States. The actors in these events hardly rank as pygmies on the stage of American technical innovation and entrepreneurship, and their supporting cast in this particular drama includes Elihu Thomson, Nikola Tesla, Henry Villard, J. Pierpont Morgan, and Samuel Insull. Yet such is the strength of the currently dominant historiographic tradition that some satisfaction has been taken in showing even an Edison to have been utterly without power to prevent the technical "progress of civilization" from pushing aside his own previous achievements in the field of direct current, and moving forward in the new form of polyphase alternating current. Edison has been portrayed as foolishly deluded, stubbornly egotistical, and worse for launching a campaign against the Westinghouse electricity supply system on the grounds that it constituted a menace to public safety.[14] Most historians of the episode have supposed that the Wizard of Menlo Park and his colleagues meant to "do in" their rivals by blocking the future commercial application of alternating current in the United States, and so they present Edison's failure to achieve that result as testimony to the proposition that there is not much scope for either individual heroism or knavery where technical change is concerned. This would tell us that the momentum of technological progress is overwhelming, that it raises up its heroes and casts down those who try to thwart or redirect it for their own irrational ends. Although the thought may be comforting to some, I reject it as a myth that has encouraged flawed interpretations of the facts and the extraction of quite the wrong moral from the historical episode in question.

The reinterpretation of the Battle of the Systems that I offer here argues for a different way of thinking about the process of technological change. We should become more consciously reconciled and, perhaps, even comfortable with its contingent nature, acknowledging that some and possibly many episodes in the progress of technology will be marked by a high degree of *ex ante* indeterminacy. I would prefer to see careful qualifications placed around such bald propositions as: "There is nothing in the character of a previous event or decision—the choice of one path or another—that implies reversibility. Even an accident changes the future irremediably."[15] But where localized positive feedback mechanisms *are* operative, there the element of chance or historical accident—in the form of idiosyncratic personal perceptions and predilections of the actors, as well as extraneous and transient circumstances surrounding their decision making at such junctures—is most likely to acquire sufficient power to shape the eventual outcomes. Such adventitious influences must render the task of prediction an unproductive one for all but the closest and most acute observers.

The point I wish to underscore by example is therefore a modest one, concerning the special scope which the development of network technologies creates for individuals to influence the course of history, as innovating entrepreneurs, or in other roles. As a result, *some* important and obtrusive features of the rich technological environment that surrounds us may be the uncalculated consequences of actions taken long ago by heroes and scoundrels. The accretion of technological innovations inherited from the past therefore cannot legitimately be presumed to constitute socially optimal solutions provided for us, either by heroic entrepreneurs or by herds of rational managers operating in efficient markets.

Network Technologies and Accidents of History

The recent wave of improvements in information, computing, and communications technologies has heightened popular awareness of some of the special opportunities and difficulties created by competitions waged by commercial sponsors of alternative technical formulations for new, complex products and production methods. Brief reference to our contemporary experience therefore can assist in forming an intuitive appreciation for the highly contingent way in which the technology of the electrical manufacturing and supply industries came to be elaborated at the end of the nineteenth century, and the significance of the rapid emergence in the United States of de facto technical standards for a universal electrical supply system based on alternating rather than direct current. Recall that during the early 1980s the burning issue in the market for videotape recorders (VCRs more specifically) was whether to commit to the Betamax format developed and sponsored by Sony, or cast one's lot with the VHS format group that had formed around the Japan Victor Corporation.[16] Who among us has not wrestled with the question of whether our desktop computer is to be an IBM PC-compatible system or an Apple system like the Macintosh? Or paused to consider the call of the International Dvorak Society to reconfigure our computer keyboards, learn to touch-type on the DSK keyboard patented in 1932 by August Dvorak and W. L. Dealey, and thereby escape a perpetual bondage to the inefficient QWERTY layout (see David 1985, 1986a)? Such quandaries seem all too commonplace nowadays.

Two features are significant concerning the prosaically modern choice-of-technique dilemmas just described. First, they involve technologies characterized by *increasing returns to scale* of use or production, and second, they entail choices in which considerations of *technical interrelatedness* among the components forming alternative systems cannot be ignored. These are attributes of "network technologies," which, because they may give rise to pecuniary and technical *externalities,* create special problems as well as economic opportunities for private and public decision makers. It is now quite widely recognized that users of a network technology are at the mercy of the social mechanisms available for maintaining efficient system performance by providing compatibility among all its constituent elements. Network technologies may, of course, be developed in a coordinated way through private commercial sponsorship of an integrated system: all the necessarily interrelated components of a product or production facility can, in many instances, be packaged together by a single provider who develops and maintains the required interface specifications. A difficulty can arise, however, when the entailed fixed capital costs are so large that they pose effective barriers to the entry of competitive formulations of the basic technology; the gains in operating efficiency ensured by integrated supply then may be obtained at the expense of the inefficiencies that come with "natural monopoly" and too little diversity to suit the varied needs of end users. Yet, when coordination of a network or technological system is left to the decentralized resource allocation processes of competitive markets, these have generally led to an insufficiently high degree of standardization, or compatibility, to avoid efficiency losses in systems operations.[17]

A different point, which has only lately come to be more fully appreciated among economic analysts, is that when private agents in pursuit of profits set about solving what seem to be reasonably straightforward problems of operating more efficiently with the technologies already at hand, the ensemble of suppliers and users can easily become committed to an unfavorable implicit trade-off against dynamic gains from further basic innovations in fundamental systems design. When the relative attractiveness of adopting a technical solution tends to increase as that particular practice or device gains adherents, and durable commitments are being made sequentially by different agents under conditions of imperfect information, the ultimate outcome of the process can turn on the detailed timing of small events—even happenings of a nature so extraneous as to appear random.[18]

Such commitment, moreover, is most likely to occur within a narrow frame of time, positioned near the beginning of the technology's trajectory of diffusion and development. What defines these critical phases, or windows in time, and causes them to close down quickly, is essentially the growing weight that attaches to considerations of "network externalities"—the shaping of individual technological choices by the context formed through the prior decisions of other agents. For it is the distribution of the already "installed base" that will come to count more and more heavily in determining choices about interrelated capital investments, which must be made in respect to both supplying and using the network technology.

Government intervention, therefore, is not the only potential source of standardization errors; markets also can make early and costly technological mistakes that subsequently prove difficult to undo. Under competitive conditions, and in the absence of public policy interventions, the existence of significant increasing returns to scale, or analogous positive feedback mechanisms such as learning by doing and by using, can give the result that one particular formulation of a network technology—VHS-formatted VCRs, for example, or QWERTY-formatted keyboards—will be able to drive out other variants and so emerge as the de facto standard for the industry. By no means need the commercial victor in this kind of systems rivalry be more efficient than the available alternatives. Nor need it be the one that adopters would have chosen if a different sequence of actions on the part of others had preceded their own.[19]

Yet by the same token it is entirely conceivable that for reasons having little to do with the ability of economic agents to foresee the future, or with anything more than an accidental and possibly quite transitory alignment of their private interests with the economic welfare of future generations, technological development may take a particular path that does prove eventually to have been superior to any available alternative. This is a disquieting message for those who assume that the invisible hand of market competition, assisted sometimes by the visible hand of farsighted management, somehow has worked to shape ours into the most economically efficient of all possible worlds. But recognition of the importance of network externalities naturally predisposes one to be extremely skeptical about the claims of that proposition to any general validity. We must acknowledge that where network technologies are involved, one cannot justifiably suppose that the system that has evolved most fully is really superior to others whose development might have been carried further but was not. Nor should we rely on the presumption that the "right" economic reasons were responsible for the emergence of a technological system that has in fact turned out to be superior to any of the alternatives available.

Some History of "Current" Affairs

The years 1887–1892 witnessed an episode of intense rivalry involving the proponents of two technologies vying for the electricity supply market. The contestants were, on the one side, the incumbent direct or "continuous" current system sponsored by the complex of manufacturing and financial interests that had been built up around Edison's 1878 patent for a carbon filament incandescent lamp and its sequelae;[20] and, on the other side, the challenging alternating current technology which at the time was represented on the American scene primarily by the Westinghouse and Thomson-Houston companies. This was not a competition of long standing, for the first commercial AC system was built during the autumn of 1886 in Buffalo, New York, by the Westinghouse Electric Company, an enterprise that had received its corporate charter from the state of Pennsylvania only as recently as January of the same year (see Prout 1921, pp. 94–95, 113; Sharlin 1963, pp. 195–196). George Westinghouse, whose fame and fortune already had been established by more than a score of patents which he had secured for railroad air-brake apparatus in the years 1869–1873, was thus a comparative latecomer to the young electrical lighting industry.[21] In 1886 the Edison Electric Light Company had already been installing isolated plant electric supply systems for five years, and, having commercially implemented its system of incandescent lighting in 1882 by opening the Pearl Street Station in New York City and the Holborn Viaduct Station in London, was well launched in the business of building central generating plants (Fleming 1921, p. 225).

Although Thomas Edison's inspiration had propelled direct current into an early position of leadership as the basis for a commercially implemented technology for electricity supply and application, the fundamental principles of generating alternating current with dynamos were not new. Indeed, the invention of the first direct current dynamo, by H. Pixii, in 1832, had involved the addition of a commutator to the alternating current dynamo he had built immediately following Michael Faraday's formulation of the dynamo principle in the preceding year. Furthermore, knowledge of the fundamental "inductance" or self-induction property of electric conductors (which formed the basis for the technique of distributing alternating current at reduced voltage by means of step-down transformers) dated from the same era. It had been discovered by Faraday in 1834, and even before him by an American professor, Joseph Henry.[22]

Commercial exploitation of AC had awaited the demonstration—by the Frenchman Lucian Gaulard and his English business partner, J. D. Gibbs—that by using higher-voltage alternating current and step-down transformers, it was possible to achieve substantial reductions in the costs of moving energy, while making electrical power available at the low voltages then suitable for application to incandescent lamps (Sharlin 1963, pp. 192–193; T. P. Hughes 1983, pp. 86–91). The beauty of the thing was that transformers could be used essentially without loss of power to substitute voltage for amperage in order to reduce the need for the high-conductivity, heavy-gauge copper wire transmission lines that were associated with DC lighting systems (thereby saving greatly on fixed capital costs), and then employed again in reversing the process to make low voltages available for local distribution at points of consumption.[23] The critical portion of the detailed chronology with which we shall be concerned (see Table 2.1) is therefore the part that commences in 1882, when a patent was awarded to Gaulard and Gibbs in Britain.

There were, however, practical problems with the Gaulard-Gibbs transformer system, and it was not until 1885 that these were remedied by William Stanley, an American inventor in the private employ of George Westinghouse. The latter had become actively interested in the potentialities of alternating current during the previous year, and had moved quickly in securing the American rights to the Gaulard-Gibbs transformer patent. Within the same year, 1885, S. Z. de Ferranti was installing an AC lighting system with transformers wired in parallel in London's Grosvenor Gallery.[24] In the United States, commercial use of alternating current for lighting followed close on the heels of these developments. An experimental lighting system had been set up by Stanley in Great Barrington, Massachusetts, and successfully demonstrated for Westinghouse in March 1886; within six months Stanley's work was being put to use in Buffalo by the Westinghouse Electric Company (T. P. Hughes 1983, pp. 101–105; Passer 1972, pp. 131–138). Thus, on both sides of the Atlantic, Thomas Edison in 1886 was quite suddenly confronted by potential commercial rivals who had begun to explore an alternative technological trajectory.

Initially the two systems did not compete directly. Instead, they staked out distinct portions of the market which were determined primarily by the differences in their inherent technical constraints. Two distance-related problems

Table 2.1 Chronology of key events in the Battle of the Systems episode in the United States.

Direct current system development	Alternating current system development
1878 December: Swan carbon lamp exhibited in Newcastle, England	1878– Different "alternators" (AC generators) designed by Gramme, Ferranti, and others
1879 Edison patents filament lamp in U.S. and Britain; builds bipolar dynamo	
1880 Edison electric lighting system at Menlo Park First commercial carbon filament lamps produced	
1882 Edison central stations at Pearl St., N.Y., Holborn Viaduct, London	1882 Gaulard and Gibbs file British patent for distribution by transformers
1883 Edison-Hopkinson 3-wire distribution system patented and installed	1883 Parallel wiring of generators demonstrated, following Hopkinson
1885 Van Depoele streetcar system in New Orleans, South Bend, etc.	1885 Stanley patents improvement of GG transformer; Zipernowsky, Deri, and Blathy also patent improvement Ferranti installs AC system with transformers in parallel in Grosvenor Gallery
1886 November: Edison sanguine about Westinghouse competition, raises "safety issue" in memo to Johnson Villard returns with "proposal"	1886 November: Westinghouse Co. completes first AC central station in Buffalo, N.Y. March: Stanley demonstrates experimental AC system for Westinghouse at Great Barrington, Mass.
1887 Sprague electric traction system successful in Richmond, Va. Edison and associates engaged in animal experiments at West Orange, N.J.	1887 Induction motor research by Tesla, Ferraris Thompson-Houston enter production and sale of AC lighting system March: Bradley patents polyphase induction motor October: Tesla files first AC motor patent
1888 July: Brown demonstration at Columbia; campaign to persuade N.Y. legislature to set voltage limit	1888 May: Bradley files for patent on rotary converter April–June: Shallenberger develops AC meter based on induction motor

Table 2.1   (continued)

Direct current system development	Alternating current system development
1889 January: Edison General Electric Co. organized	July: Westinghouse acquires Tesla patents
1890 Edison liquidates personal holdings in EGE Co.	1890 Westinghouse Electric and Manufacturing Co. reorganized and refinanced by Belmont syndicate
1892 General Electric formed by Thompson-Houston & Morgan— backing for acquisition of EGE Co.	1891 Westinghouse power system at Telluride Demonstration of transmission with 3-phase alternators driving synchronous motors, at Lauffen-Frankfurt Niagara project commits to electricity
	1893 Westinghouse demonstrates "universal" 3-phase system at Chicago World's Fair Westinghouse and GE submit AC generator designs for Niagara project

hampered immediate widespread application of the DC technology. First, despite implementation (beginning in 1883) of Edison's three-wire distribution design, which reduced the cost of wiring by two-thirds relative to the previous two-wire scheme,[25] the cost of copper wire in the transmission lines continued to define what constituted an economically viable distance in competition with illuminating gas. Moreover, even if lower-cost conductors were to be found, or new wiring systems devised, the low-voltage DC system was distance-constrained on technical grounds having to do with "voltage drop." In other words, the farther a current traveled, the larger the voltage loss on the lines between the point of generation and the point of consumption. The earliest Edison systems, which typically were confined to a fairly small service area (approximately one mile in diameter), made allowance for this problem by generating at 105–110 volts in order to ensure the delivery of at least 100 volts at the point of consumption, this being the voltage for which household lamps and other appliances were then being designed.[26] Beyond a certain transmission distance, however, this type of adjustment would no longer prove adequate; the system would deliver too broad a spectrum of voltages along the transmission lines.

Like others, George Westinghouse had seen these limitations of the direct current system as leaving an opening through which the alternative Gaulard-Gibbs formulation could be used to make a significant inroad into the promising electricity supply business dominated by Edison. Transmission of alternating current at higher voltages meant that with a given amount of generating capacity and a given weight of copper wire, the distance over which it remained economically feasible to deliver electric power would increase substantially. Indeed, for a given amount of power input, and a wire conductor of specified material and cross-sectional area, transmission distance increases as the square of voltage.[27] The economic implication of this was that expansion of supply from existing AC generating capacity—which allowed the further spreading of fixed capital charges—would be *comparatively* unconstrained by the costs of reaching customers over a wider area. Situating generating facilities at locations where ground rents were not as high as those found in urban central business districts, where electric energy demand for lighting, generally, was most concentrated, was another potential source of economic advantage. Transmitting alternating current at high voltage and then employing step-down transformers at substations, or "bumping down" at the point of consumption, also greatly ameliorated the voltage-drop problem encountered in operating DC systems.

Nevertheless, at this stage Edison's system remained the better positioned of the two to dominate the more densely populated urban markets. Part of the reason was that there, peak-load lighting demands could be matched with Edison's larger, more efficient generators, leaving the AC supply systems to work the surrounding territory. Reinforcing this territorial division were numerous absolute disadvantages that blunted the ability of the early, single-phase AC technology to penetrate the urban market in competition with DC.

At least four generic difficulties with AC remained to be resolved at the end of 1886. First was the fact—alluded to already—that the early Westinghouse and Thomson-Houston "alternators" (the AC equivalent to dynamo generators) were only 70 percent efficient, whereas 90 percent efficiency was being achieved with DC dynamos, especially the large "jumbo" design introduced by Edison. Second, the DC system was able to provide metered electric supply, whereas no AC meter had yet been developed, a deficiency that greatly reduced the system's attractiveness to central station operators. A third drawback for the AC technology at this stage of its development was that although the principle of operating alternators in parallel had been demonstrated in 1883 (following the theoretical work of John Hopkinson), it remained to be translated into practical central station operations. The ability to connect dynamos in parallel rather than in series gave the DC system a distinct advantage: its generators could be disconnected and reconnected to the mains in response to varying load, thereby saving power inputs and wear and tear. Furthermore, DC generators could be shut down for repair and maintenance—or might even break down—without disruption of the entire system.[28] Fourth, at a time when central stations employing the Edison system were beginning to spread fixed generating costs by supplying electricity for power as well as lighting, the AC system's ability to compete in urban markets was restricted by the lack of any satisfactory secondary motor available to be used with alternating current.

In addition to depriving electricity supply companies who chose to install alternators of the ability to serve industrial and commercial power customers, the lack of a motor became an increasingly pronounced comparative disadvantage with the success of the experimental electric streetcar systems installed during 1885 by Charles J. Van Depoele in New Orleans, South Bend, and Minneapolis. Its ability to deliver high torque at low rpm made the direct current motor particularly well suited in such applications as traction, where continuous speed control was important. The "traction boom" based on DC was well and truly launched in 1887, with the completion of the superior streetcar system developed for the city of Richmond, Virginia, by Frank J. Sprague, a talented but erratic inventor formerly employed by Edison, in partnership with another Edison associate, Edward Johnson. There would be 154 electric street railway systems in operation in the United States by the close of 1889.[29]

It should be emphasized that up until 1888 the underlying technological and economic considerations were not such as to allow much scope for the commercial realization of conventional scale economies and positive network externalities in the electricity supply business, as distinguished from the business of manufacturing electrical supply equipment and appliances such as lamps. Within *local* territories served by utility companies, of course, there were significant fixed-cost requirements for generation and transmission, and these were sufficient to produce some "exclusion effects," or "first-mover advantages," which created incentive for racing between the sponsors of rival systems.[30] As has already been noted, however, rather than being symmetrically positioned with regard to every market, DC and AC systems both could find some markets in which they would enjoy certain advantages in preempting entry by the other. Furthermore, such economies of scale as each could exploit in the generation of current remained definitely bounded by rising marginal distribution costs, with the geographical bounds owing to transmission costs being more tightly constricted around the central generating stations in the case of DC systems. On the other side of the ledger, the possibilities of enjoying economies of scale in generation by achieving greater load diversity, and consequently higher load factors for plants of given capacity, were far more limited for AC systems at this stage, for these were still restricted to serving only the segment of the market (for incandescent lighting) that was characterized by very high peak load in power usage. In the case of residential lighting demands, the load factor—

defined as the ratio of the average load to the maximum load of a customer, group of customers, or an entire system during a specified period—typically might be as low as 10 to 20 percent.[31]

All things considered, in 1886 Edison was perhaps quite justified in his rather sanguine view of the challenge represented by AC and the recent entry by Westinghouse into the central station business. November of that year found him writing to Edward Johnson: "Just as certain as death Westinghouse will kill a customer within 6 months after he puts in a system of any size. He has got a new thing and *it will require a great deal of experimenting to get it working practically* . . . None of his plans worry me in the least; only thing that disturbs me is that Westinghouse is a great man for flooding the country with agents and travelers. He is ubiquitous and will form numerous companies before we know anything about it."[32] One cannot be sure of the bases for Edison's assessment of the situation at this point. Had he been thinking primarily of the commercial advantages that his DC-based enterprises derived from their head start in acquiring experience and expertise in engineering design, component manufacturing, and operation of central stations supplying incandescent lighting, he could have viewed the safety problem as indicative of some of the many practical improvements that remained to be made in the AC system. Quite possibly he also had in mind the disadvantage at which the AC lighting technology would be placed in competing against a more comprehensive ("universal") electrical system which could supply lighting, power, and traction customers—such as the one that was beginning to be implemented on the basis of DC under Edison's sponsorship.[33]

Data on the number of central stations and lamps associated with each of the rival formulations suggest that by the years 1888 and 1889 the diffusion of AC technology was rapidly catching up with that of the DC technology in the United States. As of October 1888, the Westinghouse Electric Company already could count 116 central stations (some of which, however, actually were DC plants) with a total capacity to run 196,850 lamps, in comparison with the 185 Edison central stations operating 385,840 lamps. By 1891 AC had pulled ahead in the area of lighting, but the available estimates of generating capacity for that date indicate that when electricity supply for power and traction is included, DC remained preponderant.[34] The catch-up that occurred during the latter 1880s mainly reflected the AC companies' move into the electrification of smaller cities and towns not well served by DC, rather than penetration into the Edison system's "natural" territory in the spatially more dense urban lighting market.

There surely were some geographic markets in which the two variants were approximately balanced in their advantages, at least from the viewpoint of the cost of supplying electricity for lighting—larger territory for AC being offset by the impossibility of load balancing through connections to industrial power users and traction companies. In such circumstances one might well expect that competition would feature the use of marketing tactics of all kinds, designed to tip the balance in one direction or another between competing system sponsors. And in fact it is precisely against this background of an apparent technological standoff in the late 1880s that historians of technology and economic historians who have studied the electric supply industry have set the ensuing episode known as the Battle of the Systems. Nevertheless, the events which marked this period of intense and open rivalry between the proponents of direct and alternating current become fully comprehensible, in my view, only when they are seen to have been precipitated by a fundamental transformation of the underlying technoeconomic situation. That disruption of the status quo ante occurred in 1887–88.

The Electricity Supply Battlefield Revisited

As it has been recounted by more than one historian of technology and business enterprise, the battle that burst into public view during 1887–1892 was remarkable—even bizarre in some aspects—and regrettable in transgressing the normal boundaries for both market competition between different formulations of a new and highly promising technological paradigm and professional disputation among scientists and engineers with regard to their comparative technical merits.[35] Spilling over from the marketplace and the academy into the legal and political arenas, the "contest of the currents" between DC and AC took the form of courtroom struggles over patent rights, attempts to pass anticompetitive legislation, and public relations schemes aimed at discrediting the opposition and frightening its customers. The conjuncture of these events in time has contributed to the impression that they all were facets of a concerted and unbridled counterattack launched by the Edison camp, parts of an irrational effort to turn back the tide of technological progress that had brought an unwelcome influx of competition into the electrical supply business. But some of the temporal coincidences are rather misleading. So it is necessary to begin by disentangling two of the major strands that appear intertwined.

Throughout the late 1880s claims and counterclaims regarding infringement of electrical patent rights flew back and forth, both between members of the DC and AC camps and among parties belonging to the same camp.[36] Virtually from their inception the companies associated with Edison, and their financial backers, had approached the development and commercial exploitation of electricity for lighting and other uses within the paradigm of an integrated system, originally conceived of by the inventor through a conscious analogy drawn with existing systems of lighting, based on the generation and distribution of illuminating gas.[37] The owners of these companies had an obvious collective motivation to block competition from a major variant system. In claiming patent rights to some components that were utilized by the AC alternative, the Edison interests might well have hoped to delay the marketing of a rival integrated electrical supply system, if only by inducing would-be competitors to take the time and trouble to "invent around" Edison's patents. Indeed, there were several occasions on which Westinghouse's company was induced to go to great lengths to circumvent Edison patents, particularly those linked to the incandescent lamp (Passer 1972, pp. 149–164). Legal contests of this form are not costless, however; time, energy, and money were expended by all parties involved, and the costs often were deemed particularly steep by the more talented inventors, who were drawn away from their laboratories in order to defend proprietary rights to previous inventions—even though they had sometimes ceased to hold a major ownership stake in those putative rights.[38]

Edison's personal financial stake in patents he had received relating to lighting diminished greatly from the outset of his incandescent lamp project in 1878, when he had slightly over a 50 percent share; by 1886, after several rounds of raising more capital—first for the lighting enterprise, and then to expand his companies engaged in manufacturing components—he had sold nearly all his shares of the Edison Electric Light Company, the paper entity that legally held the patents and licensed use of the devices they covered to local light and power utilities (see Josephson 1959, p. 351). Throughout 1880–1885, neither Edison nor the holding company's directors showed much interest in litigating over patent infringements, even though Edison maintained that his incandescent lamp invention preempted the claims of both Sawyer-Man and Maxim. Edison had been involved in enough patent litigation to know that such battles could stretch out over many years and entail very considerable expenses; it was also true that the Edison lamp at this time was far superior to the others being offered, and that during the pioneering phase of their development of the DC electric supply system, the Edison people were more concerned with competing against gas than against the sponsors of rival electric lighting systems.

Moreover, the subsidiary enterprises engaged in manufacturing dynamos, motors, conducting mains and components, lamps, and other appliances required for lighting plants using the Edison system were proving quite profitable even in these early years. The manufacturing part of the business constituted the primary source of income not only for the inventor but also for his original colleagues at Menlo Park; Johnson, Batchelor, Upton, and Bergman had become responsible for the running of these subsidiary enterprises in which they had co-ownership interests with Edison.[39]

Beginning in 1885, however, the Edison Electric Light Company's passive stance vis-à-vis patent infringers was altered. At that time a reorganization of the board of the holding company occurred, which resulted in a weakening of the power of Edison and his original co-workers, particularly Batchelor and Upton. The new board was almost entirely representative of the financiers behind the company, and so was primarily interested in protecting the revenues derived from the proprietary rights of the Edison patents. A policy decision was therefore made to go after the infringers; lawsuits were initiated and customers were notified that the other sellers of lamps would be prosecuted.[40] The patent fights that reached the courts in the late 1880s and dragged on into the early 1890s thus had been set in motion well beforehand and bore little direct connection with Edison's own responses to the intrusion of competition from the AC suppliers.

Of course, the patent litigation was only one aspect of the conflict and not the one that has caused the Battle of the Systems to be characterized as bizarre. The most striking events of this episode revealed the lengths to which Edison and his immediate associates were prepared to go in order to convince the public that alternating current was an unsafe basis for an electricity supply system. Their campaign was waged through a barrage of scare propaganda, supported by the grisly "evidence" the Edison group produced by experimenting with AC at their laboratory in West Orange, New Jersey. As Edison's biographer, Matthew Josephson, relates: "There, on any day in 1887, one might have found Edison and his assistants occupied in certain cruel and lugubrious experiments: the electrocution of stray cats and dogs by means of high-tension currents. In the presence of newspaper reporters and other invited guests, Edison and Batchelor would edge a little dog onto a sheet of tin to which were attached wires from an a-c generator supplying current at 1,000 volts" (Josephson 1959, p. 347). In July 1888 Harold Brown, a former Edison laboratory assistant, electric pen salesman, and self-styled "Professor," put on a demonstration of the harmful effects of AC at Columbia College's School of Mines: the electrocution of a large dog was featured.[41] Meanwhile, a scarlet-covered book had been issued under the title "A Warning from the Edison Electric Light Company," in which competitor companies were accused of patent theft, fraud, and dishonest financing (including personal attacks on George Westinghouse); it gave descriptive details of the death and in some instances the cremation by electrocution of unfortunates who came into contact with wires carrying alternating current (Woodbury 1960, pp. 170–171).

During 1888 the "West Orange gang," consisting of Edison, Johnson, and young Samuel Insull, aided by Brown and other assistants, succeeded in bringing off a related, stunning achievement in the art of negative promotion: they persuaded the state of New York to substitute electrocution by administration of an *alternating current* for hanging, as the means of executing convicted criminals. Edison himself had lobbied for this action before the New York legislature, and Brown—engaged as a consultant to the state on capital punishment by means of electrocution—surreptitiously purchased three Westinghouse alternators which he then announced had been selected as the type most suitable for such work.[42] The Edison group proceeded to milk the legislature's decision for all the publicity it was worth, circulating leaflets that, in warning the public about the dangers of high-voltage AC, used the term "to Westinghouse" in referring to electrocution by alternating current.[43]

Now, some warnings concerning the dangers involved with the new technology would not have been unwarranted when alternating current was first suggested as the basis of an incandescent lighting system. The source of the problem, however, lay not in the nature of the current but in the fact that the proposed AC system would transmit energy on its mains at a higher voltage; direct current is always more deadly than alternating current at an equivalent voltage.[44] Back in the fall of 1886, when the Westinghouse Electric Company commercially introduced its alternating current lighting system, Edison was being overly optimistic only in predicting that there soon would be some accidental electrocutions of Westinghouse's customers. His view of the danger at the time was supported as reasonable by some experts within the AC camp.[45] Professor Elihu Thomson, co-founder of the Thomson-Houston Company of Pittsburgh, advised his company to refrain from marketing an AC lighting system for home use until better safeguards were developed, despite the fact that he had already employed alternating current in the company's commercial arc-lighting systems, and had developed an AC incandescent lighting system concurrently with the one that Westinghouse was marketing. As one of Thomson's biographers has put it: "There was enough truth in the contention [that high-voltage AC is deadly] to hold the Pittsburgh firm back and use up much of its time and money in making counterclaims [to those of the Edison forces]" (Woodbury 1960, pp. 169–172). Thus it was that while the Westinghouse Electric Company and Edison interests were engaged in head-to-head battle in the incandescent lighting field, the Thomas-Houston firm held off for a year and developed a simple method of preventing accidental electrocution in the unlikely event a transformer short-circuited.

Following this safety improvement, however, the Edison group did not relent in their propaganda campaign. Right through to 1889 Edison continued to participate in publicizing the undesirability of high-voltage AC (HVAC) on grounds of safety, by criticizing the technical means given for rendering AC less hazardous. In an article "The Dangers of Electric Lighting," published originally in the *North American Review,* Edison stated that the undergrounding of high-voltage lines (an often-suggested means of increasing their safety) would serve only to make them more dangerous; furthermore, he claimed that there was no means of effectively insulating overhead high-voltage wires, and concluded that "the only way in which safety can be secured is to restrict electrical pressure (voltage)" (*Electrical World,* November 2, 1889, pp. 292–293).

With the benefit of hindsight, and a seeming predisposition toward the "Whig" interpretation of technological history, previous chroniclers of this episode have been almost unanimous in portraying Edison as economically irrational in stubbornly championing the direct current system, and uncharacteristically but deplorably unscientific in his dogmatic public opposition to the rival alternating current technology sponsored by Thomson-Houston and the Westinghouse Electric Company.[46] Harold Passer described Edison's transformation bluntly in the following terms: "In 1879, Edison was a bold and courageous innovator. In 1889, he was a cautious and conservative defender of the *status quo.*"[47]

The reputation of Thomas Edison in American history books is in all other respects so little in need of rehabilitation that there is no call to repair it in this one regard, even if such a defense were plainly warranted by the facts. The concern here, accordingly, lies less with the way the conduct of the Battle of the Systems has colored modern appraisals of Edison the man, and more with the proper appreciation of the strategic goals and constraints which shaped the decisions that he and his close associates made and implemented in this episode.

Initial safety concerns about the hazards of a house-to-house incandescent lighting system based on AC notwithstanding, practical experience in the industry soon revealed that grounding and insulation methods worked quite reliably (Woodbury 1960, pp. 172–173; Josephson 1959, p. 345). It is therefore difficult to credit the view that Edison continued to pronounce AC "unsafe" because he remained ill informed or foolishly obstinate. Presumably he had a purpose in going on with the campaign until 1889, but not continuing it beyond that year. Indeed, the existence of some deeper, goal-directed strategy has been supposed even by some historians who had expressed disapproval of the tactics used.[48] An immediate purpose is not too hard to find. The objective of the animal execution demonstrations, the initiation of the electric chair, and the volumes of published material detailing the actual and potential hazards of AC was not, however, that of gaining sales in contested markets by influencing the choices made by purchasers of lighting systems, or their ultimate customers. Rather, the proximate goal was the creation of a climate of popular opinion in which further inroads by AC systems in the Edison companies' share of the incandescent lighting market might be prevented by legislative restraint, ostensibly justified on grounds of public safety. The gruesome promotional campaign was designed to persuade lawmakers to limit electric circuits to 800 volts, thereby stripping the rival system of the source of its transmission cost advantage. In at least two states, Ohio and Virginia, these efforts came closer to succeeding than in New York, where, having adopted the electric chair, the legislature balked at the intended sequel (T. P. Hughes 1983, p. 108).

Edison's actions can be construed as an economically rational, albeit cynical response on the part of an inventor-entrepreneur whose long-term plan to be the sole sponsor of a "universal" electrical supply system suddenly had gone awry. On this view, far from being foolishly obtuse, Edison was more likely than any of the other interested parties to have perceived during 1887 that the world in which he was operating had been abruptly altered; specifically, that a number of unexpected and serious blows had been dealt to his previous hopes of profiting greatly from control of the key technological components of a system that could supply energy for public arc lamps, residential and commercial lighting, industrial power, and traction. This sudden reversal of his fortunes in the direct current electricity business came from the concatenation of two fundamentally unrelated sets of developments. One was a clustering of technological innovations that opened the way for alternating current to become the basis of an alternative, fully competitive universal electricity supply system; the other was the deterioration of Edison's personal financial position, along with that of the companies in which he was most directly involved. We have now to consider the nature of these critical technological and financial developments, taking them in turn. Coming together, they precipitated a course of action well designed to salvage for Edison and his immediate associates as much as was possible before he left the industry to embark on other ventures.

The Advent of Polyphase AC and Its Significance

The original standoff situation, which had left DC and AC in 1885–86 with respective markets within which each held a clear, technically derived advantage, was in reality a condition of transient equilibrium, a temporary balance soon disturbed by the realization of a differentially faster rate of technological advance along the AC system trajectory.[49] In the alternating current field, three new and interrelated innovations abruptly removed the disadvantages that had formerly restrained AC supply companies from penetrating the DC lighting and power markets: (1) the induction motor; (2) the AC meter; and (3) the rotary converter.

Between 1885 and 1888 Nikola Tesla in the United States, Galileo Ferraris in Italy, and Michael Osipowitch von Dolivo Dobrowolsky in Germany had each discovered that two alternating currents differing in phase by 90 degrees, or three alternating currents differing in phase by 120 degrees, could be used to rotate a magnetic field; that by placing in such a field a pivoted bar of iron, or a drum of laminated iron on which were wound self-closed coils of copper wire, one could construct a two- or three-phase induction motor.[50] Invention of the motor led directly to the development of a special polyphase generator and system of distribution.

Tesla's first two patents on the alternating current motor were filed in October 1887, and three more patents pertaining to the system were filed in November. The Westinghouse Electric Company acquired these patents in July 1888, by which time Westinghouse already had persuaded Ferraris to permit it to file an American patent on the rotating magnetic-field motor that he claimed he had built three years before.[51] Coincidentally, in April 1888 Oliver B. Shallenberger, an engineer working for Westinghouse, came upon the polyphase induction phenomenon and applied it to solve the problem of designing an effective meter for alternating current; by June he had shown that such meters could be built in quantity. Hence, by 1889 Westinghouse Electric Company was able to put into commercial production a meter that enhanced the scope for AC in central station lighting operations, and the technological basis for penetrating portions of the electric power market.[52]

While the AC induction motor and meter posed an obvious threat, they did not immediately give rise to commercial challenges to Edison's manufacturing companies in urban markets where DC power supply was already established. Despite the greater than 50 percent market share that AC had achieved in the field of lighting by 1891, there was a considerable amount of momentum built into the growth of DC supply systems. Two forces were behind this momentum. First, where a local electric supply system did constitute a natural monopoly and there already existed an installed DC generating and distribution system, the unamortized investment in DC plant was so large that it discouraged replacement with polyphase AC; by adopting a mixed system, the local utility would lose the scale advantages associated with a single system.[53] Second, as long as a sizable portion of the urban market was held firmly by DC—namely, the market for traction power, and to a lesser degree industrial electrolysis, as distinguished from that for secondary-motor power for elevators, factories, and other such applications—the local DC central stations meeting this (traction) demand would necessarily also supply the other electricity needs in the area; rivals could not penetrate the market because the DC system, with its load-balancing advantage, could underprice them. Hence, unless some "gateway" or interface technology emerged, a partial commitment to perpetuation of the DC technology would remain for some time to come.

Viewed from this perspective it was another technical innovation, part of a new "gateway" technology coincident to and dependent on the development of polyphase AC, that was critical in delivering the coup de grace to a comprehensive electric supply system based entirely on a DC technology.[54] The rotary converter was a device that combined an AC induction motor with a DC dynamo to make possible the connection of high-voltage AC transmission lines to DC distribution networks. A former Edison employee, Charles S. Bradley, who had already applied for a patent on a polyphase generator and a synchronous motor in March 1887 (actually before Tesla), successfully patented the rotary converter in the United States during the following year.[55]

The major significance of the rotary converter lay in the fact that it enabled the old DC central station and traction distribution networks to be coupled with new long-distance high-voltage AC transmission mains. These "gateway devices" thereby made possible the formation of a more flexible "hybrid" system, the advantages of which were recognized in the electrical engineering press as early as 1887.[56] By the early 1890s Bradley had set up his own factory to produce the converter in Yonkers, New York, a plant that would soon be acquired along with the patent by the General Electric Company. The potential profitability of the business of supplying rotary converters likewise drew the Westinghouse Electric Company into further development work on such devices.[57] Converters were also developed to couple existing single-phase AC with the newer and more efficient polyphase technology. In fact, by the middle of the 1890s there would exist devices to convert in any direction. Conversion of DC to polyphase AC proved an immediately attractive application in some locales, such as Chicago, where Samuel Insull saw it would permit raising the load factors on existing DC plant by transmitting current over a much more extensive area in which the load was more diverse.[58]

What had happened during 1887–88, in essence, was the dramatic appearance of a new technological variant—the polyphase AC system—induced by the opportunities inherent in the limitations of DC and single-phase AC as bases for a "universal" electricity supply system. It was the polyphase AC technology that would diffuse rapidly, becoming the de facto network standard for electricity generation and transmission in the United States, penetrating the core urban markets for electric light and power, and thereby realizing the greater economies of scale which fostered the emergence of extensive natural monopolies in the electric supply industry.

Although Edison may not have foreseen the whole evolution of the network technology that would be created to exploit the transmission cost advantages of alternating current, his course of action from 1887 onwards reflected, in my view, an astute grasp of the precarious, unstable nature of a competitive situation that was unfolding with unexpected speed from the successful experiments with polyphase AC motors. That perception would have reinforced whatever other considerations might have disposed him to leave the electricity industry, instead of girding himself to participate in an inventive race against the emerging AC-based universal system.[59]

As Thomas Hughes has emphasized, Edison's talents inclined him toward the invention of devices that were interrelated within a *system* context, and he naturally preferred to work on components whose improvement would lead to enhanced performance and value throughout a system whose parameters he could control—and thereby draw the greater profit from (T. P. Hughes 1983, pp. 22–23). Yet in the circumstances of the electricity supply industry during 1887–88, reasonable expectations of extracting significant rents on any incremental, strictly DC-compatible inventions had largely been vitiated by the developments leading to Bradley's rotary converter. Furthermore, the DC system elaborated under Edison's sponsorship was now at a disadvantage; additional research and development resources would have to be devoted to reducing distribution costs just for it to be able to hold its own in competition with polyphase AC systems. What profit to an inventor undertaking that uncertain mission, when the limiting value of the improvement would be that set by the cost of the rotary converters installed to transform DC to AC, and/or AC back to DC for local distribution and traction uses? Edison had more tempting projects in which to engage his laboratory staff and his own inventive genius.[60]

The unorthodox and rather desperate tactics adopted by the "West Orange Gang" in their safety campaign against Westinghouse takes on a different appearance when set in this context, especially their focus on invoking some regulatory intervention to deprive alternating current–based systems of the transmission advantages deriving from use of high voltages. The campaign looks more like a temporary holding operation meant to delay the competition so as to permit Edison to stage a more orderly and profitable exit from the industry, and less like a serious counteroffensive. Had it been Edison's hope and intention permanently to cripple the competitive system of electricity supply, it would hardly have made sense for him to accelerate his withdrawal from the business of manufacturing and selling the key components of the DC system that would be left in command of the field. Yet that is precisely what he was doing.[61] It was a decision, however, that owed something also to the financial straits in which Edison unexpectedly found himself just when he was moving into research and development projects in other areas, pursuing costly undertakings that were still quite far from the commercialization stage.

The End of the Sponsored-Systems Rivalry

Edison's decision to get out of the electricity business was significant, because it would lead shortly to the disappearance from the United States' electrical manufacturing industry of a commercial sponsor whose proprietary interests lay exclusively in the DC technology.[62] It had its roots not only in the burst of polyphase AC developments just reviewed, but also in the evolution of Edison's relationship with the holding company (Edison Electric Light) in charge of his lighting patents and the various entities, such as Edison Lamp and (Edison) Machine Works, that actually manufactured the components of the system and serviced them. Recall that by the mid-1880s Edison and his associates had little stake in and less control over the holding company that drew royalties on the use of the lighting patents by central station companies and other companies set up to license the construction of isolated lighting plants; whereas Edison remained the principal owner of the factories from which he and his associates had been drawing their main income. During 1886–1888, however, the precarious financial situation of these enterprises came to be perceived as tremendously burdensome to their owners. Much of the equipment supplied previously by the manufacturers to central stations had been paid for with hard-to-negotiate shares in those fledgling enterprises, resulting in severe cash-flow problems for the Edison concerns. With the recovery from the business recession of 1885, electrical equipment orders were coming in faster than the factories had resources to produce and deliver. But it was proving difficult to finance the expansion on short-term credit, and to solve this problem by permitting the Morgan banking group (who already dominated Edison Electric Light) to extend their control over the manufacturing enterprises in exchange for long-term loans was hardly an appealing prospect. Thus, at the same time that Edison was fretting over the possibility that his overexpanded manufacturing businesses might be forced into bankruptcy, he was also sending his financially skillful young colleague, Samuel Insull, off to borrow the extra sums needed for the West Orange, New Jersey, laboratory's expanding program of nonelectrical research (Josephson 1959, p. 340; McDonald 1962, p. 38).

Consequently, the return of Henry Villard from Germany in 1886, bearing a commission from the Deutsche Bank to negotiate with Drexel, Morgan and Company about the acquisition of holdings in American businesses, came at a most fortuitous moment. Edison was much relieved to be presented soon thereafter with Villard's proposed plan for the consolidation of all the Edison-related enterprises (including the patent-holding company, and Sprague Electric Railway and Motor Company) into one new corporation with backing from the Deutsche Bank, the Allgemeine Elektrizitäts Gesellschaft, and the firm of Siemens and Halske of Berlin. The inventor saw in this a welcome opportunity both to extricate himself from the worries and distractions of managerial and financial responsibility for the manufacturing business, and to raise sufficient capital to place his laboratory on firmer financial foundations.[63] Ultimately, the terms to which J. P. Morgan was willing to agree turned out to be somewhat less favorable to Edison and the manufacturing company owners than those initially proposed, and, not surprisingly, more generous to the holders of the lighting patent with whom Morgan was directly involved. Nevertheless, they gave the inventor $1,750,000 in cash, 10 percent of the shares, and a place on the board of the new company (McDonald 1962, pp. 40–41).

In this way the Edison General Electric Company came to be organized in January 1889. Within a few months the consolidations were formally effected, and Edison himself no longer had direct influence in the running of the manufacturing side of the business. By 1890 he had largely completed the liquidation of his remaining 10 percent shareholding in the new company and was taking no active role on its board of directors. On February 8 he wrote to ask Villard not to oppose his "retirement from the lighting business, which will enable me to enter into fresh and congenial fields of work" (Josephson 1959, p. 361). The propaganda war against the Westinghouse AC system, which had been brought to its peak in the midst of the consolidation negotiations, was rapidly wound down in 1889. It would seem to have served the real purpose of supporting the perceived value of the Edison enterprises which were at the time wholly committed to manufacturing the components of a DC-based electric light and power system, and thereby improving the terms on which Edison and his close associates were able to "cash out."

Elements within the American financial community, among which the Morgan interests were most prominent, were moving at this time to consolidate and hence "rationalize" another network industry—the railroads.[64] The control and consolidation of the electrical manufacturing and supply business represented a parallel undertaking. A major step was effectively accomplished by joining Thomas-Houston Company and the Edison General Electric Company; in 1892 the former, under the leadership of Charles A. Coffin, received Morgan's support in buying out the latter, thereby forming the General Electric Company.[65] This turn of events meant that by 1892 Edison, who had earlier been adamantly opposed to the idea of forming a combine with Thomson-Houston and doubtless would have remained so, had withdrawn entirely from the business, so that no solely DC-oriented manufacturing entity existed in the American market.

Westinghouse's enterprise, however, was able to elude the Morgan group's aspirations for an all-encompassing rationalization of the industry, paradoxically, because its shaky condition had forced it to put its affairs in order and line up banking support from other quarters at the very beginning of the decade. Finding his business undercapitalized to weather the aftermath of the Baring "crisis" in 1890, and unable to obtain a half-million dollars on satisfactory terms from the Pittsburgh business banking community, George Westinghouse was obliged to turn for backing to a New York–based financial syndicate headed by August Belmont and to reorganize his company.[66] Work on the development of Tesla's induction motor and three-phase system was brought to a halt during these difficulties in 1890–91, but it soon was resumed—once Tesla had been induced not to hold Westinghouse to the terms of the royalty agreements concluded between them in 1888–89.[67]

The electrical manufacturing business in the United States thus came to be dominated by two large firms from 1892 onward, but the industry also had become essentially homogeneous with regard to the basic formulation of its technology. By 1893, the General Electric and the Westinghouse Electric and Manufacturing companies both were marketing some version of a polyphase alternating current system, and both had entered the profitable business of manufacturing rotary converters.[68] The era of rivalry between commercial sponsors of technologically distinct systems in the United States' electrical supply industry was brought to a close within six years of its commencement.

Diffusion of the New Technology—and the Path Not Taken

Yet the question of the superiority of one form of current over the other remained unresolved within the engineering community. Whether direct or alternating current was to be generated by the hydroelectric power project being undertaken at Niagara Falls was still very much an open question during 1892 (Fleming 1921, pp. 238–239). The proponents of DC at Niagara had argued that for conditions of varying load, as was the case in a lighting system, DC was much the more efficient of the two.[69] While this may have held true in 1890, following the 1891 demonstration by Oscar Muller and the Swiss firm of Boveri and Company that polyphase current could be transmitted 110 miles from Lauffen on the Upper Neckar River to Frankfurt am Main,[70] and the equally impressive Westinghouse Electric Company polyphase system exposition (including the rotary converter) at the Chicago World's Fair in 1893, it was evident that lighting was no longer the only factor to consider in discussing the load and efficiency characteristics of the AC and DC system variants.[71] With the extension of AC to power users, and to traction users as a result of the invention of the rotary converter, the decision between AC and DC came down to one of which could distribute power over a distance more efficiently and cheaply. And, as the distance from Niagara to the nearest concentration of customers, in Buffalo, New York, was 20 miles, AC could reduce the loss of power on transmission lines to a far greater extent than was possible with DC. In 1893 both the Westinghouse Electric Company and the newly formed General Electric Company submitted plans to the Cataract Construction Company (which was pioneering the Niagara development), specifying an AC system consisting of generators, transformers, and transmission lines.[72]

Beginning in 1896, central stations began being converted into substations hooked up to AC transmission lines, and by 1898 a constant-current transformer had been developed to make possible the linking up of arc lighting distribution networks with AC transmission lines (National Electrical Manufacturers Association 1946, p. 74). Hence, the flexibility and capabilities of this new coupling technology led to a rapid diffusion of the AC polyphase technology and the integration of smaller urban electricity supply systems into larger networks which eventually formed regional grids.[73] Once the systems competition had tipped in this direction, lighting plants also came to be reequipped with AC technology as the previous DC distribution networks wore out; other things being equal, transformers stepping down high-voltage AC were a much simpler and cheaper technology for lighting purposes than the use of rotary converters to feed local DC distribution networks from high-voltage AC transmission lines (Byatt 1979, p. 76). Converters continued to be employed well into the twentieth century, however, most notably in the traction field, where DC remained the current preferred at the point of consumption (Byatt 1979, chap. 4; Sharlin 1963, pp. 185, 188).

A de facto standard, in the form of alternating current as the basis of a "universal" electrical supply system, had emerged by the 1920s both in the United States and abroad. While diffusion data for the 1890s are not available, the figures assembled in Table 2.2 show that in America the fraction of central station generating capacity accounted for by AC rose from 736.3 kilowatts out of a total capacity of 1,066.4 kilowatts, or 69 percent, in 1902, to 8,557.7

Table 2.2   Distribution of generating and end-use electric capacity between direct current and alternating current, excluding power generation by electric railways, in the United States, 1902–1917.

Technological characteristic	Kilowatt capacity (thousands)			
	1902	1907	1912	1917
Dynamos				
DC: constant voltage	330.1	406.5	432.4	418.6
AC and polyphase	736.3	2,221.8	4,689.2	8,557.7
Rotary converters	232.2	363.4	1,009.1	1,898.6
Transformers	560.4	1,693.5	4,103.9	9,499.0
DC share in total generating capacity[a]	0.31	0.16	0.08	0.05
DC share in end-use capacity[b]	0.53	0.29	0.28	0.26
Ratio of transformer capacity to AC capacity	0.76	0.76	0.88	1.11

Sources: Dynamo data: Bureau of the Census (1920, table 40, p. 63, for 1907, 1912, and 1917); transformer data: Bureau of the Census (1920, table 110, pp. 170–171, for 1917); Bureau of the Census (1915, table 65, p. 104, for 1912); Bureau of the Census (1906, tables 118 and 119, pp. 134–137, for 1902).

[a] DC share in generating capacity is calculated by dividing DC dynamo capacity into the sum of DC and AC dynamo capacity.

[b] DC share in end-use capacity is calculated by subtracting rotary converter capacity from the AC polyphase dynamo capacity, adding rotary converter capacity to DC dynamo capacity, and then recalculating DC's share of total capacity.

kilowatts out of a total of 8,976.3 kilowatts, or 95 percent, in 1917. Moreover, one can discern in this the large role played by the rotary converter. This appears from the absolute rise in rotary converter capacity installed and also from the fact that the DC share of end-use capacity fell far less sharply than its share in generating capacity. Indeed, the former remained essentially unchanged after 1907. At the engineering level, therefore, the Battle of the Systems did not end with the capitulation and withdrawal of one of the contenders, as the Edison-Westinghouse business rivalry had done. The technological denouement has been described by Thomas Parke Hughes (1983)[74] as a peaceful resolution to the conflict: no outright defeat for DC, but rather a graceful and apparently efficient absorption within a transitional "mixed" system, prior to its gradual disappearance from the American electrical scene.

The perspective of hindsight may impart to this story an impression of inevitability, and even a supposition of optimality, both of which should be resisted. Meaningful global evaluations of efficiency are difficult if not impossible to make between alternative technological systems whose influences ramify so widely and are so profound that they are capable of utterly transforming the economic and social environments into which they have been introduced.[75] As a guard against the strong temptation to suppose in matters of technological advance that "what is, ought to have been," it is always useful at least to notice the existence of other paths that were not taken.

From the technical journals and magazines of the period it is apparent that no immediate consensus emerged on the engineering merits of the two currents; there were well-respected inventors and scientists, many of whom were founders of the industry, who would not testify to the technical superiority of alternating current.[76] For the DC technology also showed itself quite capable of being further elaborated in directions that both heightened its special advantages and broadened the range of conditions under which it was economically competitive. As was the case with AC, the possibility of lowering the cost of the DC systems by raising the voltage was being actively explored. As early as 1883 Charles F. Brush had attempted a high-voltage DC system that could more fully utilize fixed generating capacity and increase the radius of profitable transmission by using "accumulators" (storage batteries) to handle some of the peak lighting load and to accomplish the reduction of voltage for local distribution. Because of a combination of problems associated with the battery technology available at the time, the dangers of operating a high-potential system having dynamos wired in series, and the usual run of financial difficulties, this particular project never took off, and the concept was not pursued further in the United States (Stanley 1912, p. 565).

Abroad, however, the English from the mid-1880s onward attempted to implement a variety of high-voltage direct current (HVDC) electricity supply schemes.[77] The earliest of these met much the same fate as that of Brush—too many troubles with expensive primitive batteries and myriad financial woes arising from inadequate demand and insufficient capital. But several innovations introduced late in the 1880s did prove successful. Notable among these was the Oxford system, an approach first employed in 1889, which transmitted high-voltage DC to substations, where it was "bumped down" to usable voltage levels via either a battery arrangement or a direct current transformer.[78] On balance, the major advantages of the HVDC battery technology lay in ensuring continuity of supply when generating plants failed or were shut down for maintenance, and in reducing the amount of fixed capacity required to meet peak loads on the system.[79] In Britain, then, the story unfolded along lines very different from those in the United States; there, the "competition of the currents" was tipped during the 1890s toward DC by the possibility of using accumulators in combination with high voltage.[80]

Concurrently, on the European continent, M. Thury was developing a system of transmitting direct current at very high voltages from constant-current generators worked in series, and commonly coupled mechanically in pairs or larger groups driven by a single prime mover. This offered advantages in easier line insulation than was required at half the voltage with alternating current, and removal of difficulties of line inductance and capacity encountered in high-voltage AC transmission. The high-voltage constant-current plant lent itself to greater ease of operation in emergencies (over a grounded circuit, for example) and permitted the design of comparatively simple and inexpensive switchboard arrangements. Notwithstanding the fact that the direct current generators used in this system were relatively expensive and their individual output was inconveniently small for large transmission work, around 1910 even a contemporary American authority gave it as his view that "the possibilities of improvement in the system have by no means been worked out, and although it has been overshadowed by the enormous growth of polyphase transmission it must still be considered seriously."[81]

Unlike the battery-using HVDC, the AC version of the "universal" electricity system concept inexorably pushed Samuel Insull and others who pioneered it in the United States toward "load balancing" as the way to mitigate the wastage imposed by having to build enough generating capacity to meet peak loads. The search for a diversified load over a wider region, with high fixed costs in place, created problems of natural monopolies which would not have existed to the same degree under the HVDC battery technology. Of course, it must be acknowledged that without strong increasing returns effects via load balancing, a DC-battery–DC technology might simply have allowed more leeway to the forces making for too great a degree of diversity in voltages, current, and AC frequencies. Such could be said to have been the experience of the industry in Britain. Yet if regulatory intervention is accepted as a proper solution to the natural monopoly problem which soon arose in the United States in the case of electric utilities, presumably public intervention could have imposed some standardization of DC voltages to permit realization of scale economies in the production of motors, lamps, and other end uses. Moreover, further down the road, when social efficiency was deemed to be achieved through the development of a larger network or "grid," the U.S. state and local regulatory structure, which by then had actually been imposed in response to the condition of local monopoly, would prove to have discouraged local utilities from integrating and supplying still wider geographical markets.

Such skepticism about the long-run economic optimality and consequent inevitability of the de facto standard that emerged in the United States is, of course, reinforced by the foregoing detailed recounting of its historical roots in the Battle of the Systems. Given the urgency of the utility companies' drive to achieve scale economies in electric supply, their move to the polyphase AC–based universal system was certainly little affected by weighing the potentialities for long-run technical improvement offered by alternative systems. Just as short-run liquidity considerations had figured prominently in Edison's decisions during the formation of Edison General Electric, so short-run maximization of rents on the existing stock of proprietary technology seems to be the best algorithm descriptive of the course of action pursued by the dominant successor firms engaged in manufacturing and marketing electric supply equipment in the United States during the years before World War I.

Reflections on Network Technologies and Schumpeterian Entrepreneurs

The Battle of the Systems has been presented by previous narrators as a colorful and cautionary tale. Many of them, it seems, would have us find in it the moral that even an individual possessing extraordinarily inventive and entrepreneurial talents may sink to foolish knavery by exchanging the role of technological progress's steadfast champion to become, instead, a defender of the status quo. As we have had to be taught that the progress of invention and technical change is a complex social and economic process, which transcends the intentions and efforts of individual men and women, and that technology is best regarded as "socially constructed"—a cumulative result of the work of many minds and hands under the guidance of unseen forces—we naturally suppose ourselves to have a clearer view than that held by the individual participants in the process. In a sense this leaves one predisposed to fault even Thomas Alva Edison for his supposed hubris in hoping singlehandedly to stay this advance.

Although there are contexts in which such a moral is well worth remembering, it does not strike me as the best one to recall in conjunction with this
particular episode in technological and industrial history. Indeed, the perspective offered by recent contributions to economic theory on the early phases of
the evolution of a paradigmatic network industry such as electricity supply
should prepare us to recognize the degree to which discrete events of a largely
adventitious nature, among them the specific courses of action chosen by individual agents occupying key decision-making positions, really do have the
potential to set important technological parameters defining the industry's future
trajectory. This is not to say that great consequences can be expected to follow
from every move made by the drama's principal human actors; only that if we
are concerned to understand a thing such as how and why one particular technical variant rather than some other eventually came to be widely adopted and
further elaborated, recognition of the presence of "localized positive feedback
effects" should make us especially skeptical of modes of explanation that
presuppose the inevitability of one outcome and the impotence of individual
agents to alter it. These individuals, in such circumstances, may well have the
power to take *early* actions which, in effect, will turn out to have strongly
directed the ensuing course of developments.

In the story as retold here, the actions of Edison and his associates during the
years 1887–1892 do not stand out as having run counter to an immanent flow of
events leading the electrical supply industry in America away from direct current and rapidly toward a universal integrated system designed around polyphase alternating current. Rather than vainly seeking to block the further development of the competitive AC electrical supply technology and so preserve
a monopoly of the field for his DC system, Edison, in the present account, sees
the juggernaut of a competitive technical system bearing down upon his own
immediate economic interests with a swiftness that he has not anticipated. He
undertakes expedient actions aimed to slow the pace of its advance enough to
allow him to get his inventive resources and financial assets safely out of the
way. The propaganda campaign thus launched against high-voltage AC in general and Westinghouse in particular, with its threat of crippling restraints by
safety legislation, makes considerable economic sense in the context, however
unscrupulous it may have been.

Did it also make more sense than the other, more direct, and probably more
reliable modes of commercial competition that were available to the Edison
enterprises, but apparently went untried? That remains less clear, for it seems
that Edison had reasons for seeking to exit from the industry promptly. A
supplier of direct current dynamos, lighting and other appliances, and traction
motors who had sought to hold onto a dominant market share might have moved
immediately to explore ways in which the new rotary converter technology

could be supplied cheaply for application in lowering the costs of transmission (via high-voltage AC mains) between DC-based generating plants and end users. As has been shown, this kind of mixed, or "patched," system, which was already being discussed in the engineering periodicals in 1887, was entirely feasible and came to be implemented by electric utility companies in the following decade.

Additionally, or alternatively, "promotional" pricing of DC generators and compatible equipment by the Edison manufacturing companies might well have sufficed in the late 1880s further to entrench that system in urban markets. The principal immediate beneficiaries from this short-run revenue sacrifice, it is true, would have been the financiers around Morgan, because it was they who held the rights to the patent royalties on sales of DC central stations and isolated electrical plants. But had Edison wanted to remain in the business, the occasion of the negotiations opened by Villard during 1887–88 might have been used to arrange a share in some of the royalties that would thereby be secured during the remaining seven to eight years of life on his basic lighting patents. Perhaps it would have proved impossible ultimately to negotiate such an arrangement. What is significant is that there are no indications from the published sources based on the relevant archives that Edison and those around him ever considered it, or were exploring other ways of using their substantial initial position to compete against the commercial sponsors of alternating current. Westinghouse, if not Thomson-Houston as well, might have proved vulnerable to attack at just that point. The former enterprise evidently was undercapitalized to meet a head-on challenge, so much so that George Westinghouse found himself obliged during 1890–91 to turn for financial help to August Belmont, and to persuade Nikola Tesla to relinquish his legal claim to a fortune in patent royalties.

But far from fighting to drive out competition and stem further technological advances based on polyphase AC, Edison responded to the cluster of innovations related to the AC induction motor by refusing to engage the opposition in an economically costly market rivalry, and to conduct a rapid but orderly financial withdrawal under the diversionary cover of a "talking war." I have suggested that it was not unreasonable in the circumstances, much less irrational, for Edison to have seized upon the Villard proposal to consolidate all Edison-related electrical enterprises as a fortuitous opportunity to exit profitably from the electrical manufacturing business. The evidence presented here, however, does not speak to the question of whether or not, in withdrawing and turning his attention to the improvement of his phonograph, the movies, and mining technology, the inventor was following an unexpected private wealth-maximizing strategy. Evidently Edison's decision was influenced by the short-run asset constraints, indeed, by the distracting liquidity constraints, under which both the manufacturing operations and the laboratory at West Orange were perceived to be working. In any event, had he chosen otherwise, or been prevailed upon by others to remain in the industry and sacrifice short-run earnings in an attempt to block the commercial development of universal electricity supply systems based entirely on polyphase AC, the outcome could well have been very different.

The bunching of related induction-motor inventions by Tesla, Shallenberger, and Bradley, which appears as the most probable cause of Edison's precipitate retirement from the electricity business, had a direct bearing on the outcome, which is also worth keeping in mind.[82] The induction motor made polyphase AC a rival standard around which to develop a universal system of electricity generation, transmission, distribution, and application, such as was originally conceived by Edison. This was so in large measure because it permitted comparatively inexpensive conversion from AC to DC for application to high-torque–low-rpm motors most suitable for traction work. Yet by the same principal, the rotary converter could have been used more extensively to expand the market territory served by existing DC central stations, thereby depriving commercial AC-generation technologies of part of the widening basis for incremental improvements that they came to enjoy. Just as DC traction motors became a specialty application of electrical energy through the mediation of rotary converters, so converters could have been employed to transform DC into AC for specialized application in textile mills, mines, and other industrial contexts where "sparkless" AC motors were advantageous. The resulting system by 1914 would quite probably not have been more efficient in an engineering sense than the one that was in existence in the United States at that date; it would, perhaps, have resembled the situation that obtained in Britain. But that is beside the main point, which is that the advent of polyphase AC generators and motors brought into existence a multiplicity of feasible equilibriums in the design and configuration of electricity supply systems.

Might-have-beens are difficult for the historian to articulate, in that they call for very precise specifications of the contingent unfolding structure of counterfactual worlds. There was nothing foreordained, much less evidently optimal, about the determination that Edison's reactions contributed to making among these possibilities. Holding more closely to what did happen in this particular episode, I should simply say that those who seem to view with approval the outcome of the Battle of the Systems in the United States have unjustifiably withheld from Edison due recognition for his inglorious part in the avoidance of what could have been a protracted market competition of uncertain result between the contending currents.

Little can be taken from this conclusion, even by granting that AC really was the economically and technically superior basis for a universal electricity supply system rather than being simply the more cost-effective form of current for long-distance transmission work. "Good guys" are not automatically winners when network technologies compete. One may note that if a new network technology were economically superior to an incumbent system once everyone has switched to it, complete information in the possession of all agents would be sufficient to induce everyone to decide independently to make the necessary switchover. But given the state of uncertainty and conflicting opinion among the scientists and engineers of the day, complete information simply was not in the cards.[83] One may also note that technological "sponsorship" sometimes will be adequate to prevent the installation or retention of an inferior network technology as the unintended consequence of mere "accidents of history." Where patent holdings give commercial sponsors property rights in particular technical standards, as in the case at hand, they may be able to capture the benefits that otherwise would accrue to producers and users from subsequent network expansion. A firm convinced that the system whose benefits it can internalize will be superior in the future to the present incumbent system therefore may find it well worthwhile to subsidize the initial adoption of its technological variant by pricing the equipment or service below cost.[84] Yet an incumbent confronted by challengers sponsoring a potentially superior technology (the benefits of which it cannot expect fully to share) may successfully defend its position if it has enough financial resources to engage and outlast those rivals in a war of attrition.

In view of the latter possibility, I have thought it important in the foregoing account to indicate some reasons why Edison apparently turned away from such a course of action. Although these have been sufficiently idiosyncratic to underscore my emphasis on the working of chance, one should observe that the strategy of counterattack in such circumstances generally would require access to financial backers with deep pockets and widely diversified portfolios.[85] Lacking that, short-run asset constraints may prevent superior technologies from acquiring sponsors with sufficient capital to unseat inefficient incumbents, just as they may precipitate the premature capitulation of an established technology sponsor faced with the entry of an alternative technology.

Thus, while exercises in applied microeconomics can tell us that rather special circumstances are required for an inefficient formulation of a technological system to become accidentally "locked in," we may also see that these were the very conditions that obtained when the electricity supply business—and possibly some other paradigmatic network industries in the fields of transportation and communications—were beginning to take shape. Most of the complex, multicomponent, and multiagent systems of production with which we are familiar did not emerge full-blown in the forms that they have come to assume. Large-scale technological systems such as railroads, electrical utilities, and telephone networks have been built up sequentially, through an evolutionary process in which the design and operation of constituent components undergoes both continuous and discrete adaptation to the specific technical, economic, and politico-legal circumstances in which new opportunities and problems are perceived. And those perceptions, in turn, are often formed on the basis of experience acquired through the operation of preexisting systems having some of the same functions, or ones directly analogous to the technology in question. So it was that Edison in the 1870s had before him the model of then-existing illuminating gas supply systems—with their generators, distribution mains, meters, and lamps—when he conceived of an integrated lighting and power system based on electricity. To recognize this calls for acknowledgment of the importance of chance factors in the precise timing of events, including, naturally enough, the sequential development of technical and organizational innovations that shape the competitive strategies followed by commercial sponsors of different network formulations. But as traditional historians intuitively have understood, the timing and character of "small events" are more likely to be capable of exerting real leverage when these occur close to the beginnings of a sequential development process.

Of course, the temporal location and brevity of those critical phases, in which there is maximum scope for individual decision makers to alter the direction of a decentralized process of technology diffusion and development, must be a relative matter. The comparison indicated here is with the full course of the market competition which may ensue as one system or another progresses toward establishment as the de facto universal standard for the industry. Actual temporal durations depend on the rate at which system suppliers and users become sequentially committed to one technical formulation, with its attendant compatibility requirements, or another; cyclical booms, during which high rates of investment are undertaken to embody specific technologies in long-lived physical facilities, thus can contribute to narrowing the time window within which truly formative decisions can occur. Viewed from this angle, it is the fleeting context created by an emergent network technology that creates the opportunity for one or another innovating agent to take specific initiatives which can be held to have directed the subsequent course of events.

Although I began with the question of what role individual entrepreneurial actions could have in the social construction of technological progress, I should therefore close with the observation that the relationship of interest now appears to be a reflexive one. A special kind of competitive struggle, involving the formation of technological or organizational systems characterized by localized positive feedback, holds a special role in the creation of Schumpeterian innovators. This is so if only because these "battles" evolve as dynamic processes in which chance actions on a human scale can prove determinative. Moreover, as such actions are more likely to be those which have occurred before battle lines became clearly drawn and large forces were engaged, if archetypal entrepreneurs are to be found anywhere by retrospective observers, surely they can be singled out more readily from among the ranks of the early participants in emergent network industries. "Innovation," then, in the sense of an unanticipated impulse imparting a cumulative motion to the economic system, is perhaps less a product of unique individual attitudes and special social incentives, and more a matter of being pivotally situated during those comparatively brief passages of industrial history when the balance of collective choice can be tipped one way or another. Thomas Edison demonstrated this, as much by abandoning the electric manufacture and supply business as by launching it.

Notes

1. The research assistance of Julie Bunn was indispensable to me in preparing this chapter. Much of the historical material presented here has been drawn (without further attribution) from sections of our collaborative paper (David with Bunn 1987). Numerous debts incurred in that connection have been acknowledged in the proper place. It remains a pleasant necessity to record here my thanks to Patrice Higgonet and Henry Rosovsky, and to Peter Temin, for their excellent editorial advice about the best way to structure this essay; to Jonathan Hughes for sharing insights into Edison's nature and generously welcoming disagreement over points of emphasis; and to W. Edward Steinmueller and Gavin Wright for characteristically perceptive and helpful suggestions of ways to sharpen the presentation of my arguments. Financial support for this research was provided under the High Technology Impact Program of the Center for Economic Policy Research at Stanford University. I wish also to thank Kenneth S. Ryan for a personal gift of pertinent reference materials, which proved to be a considerable convenience to me in this research.

2. Landes (1969, pp. 281–290) gives a concise and pithy account of the main electrical developments in Britain, France, and Germany up to 1913, drawing largely on Jarvis (1967a, 1967b) for technical details. Among works appearing subsequently that deal primarily with the British and American sides of the story, in chronological order, see Hennessey (1971), Passer (1972), Byatt (1979), Hannah (1979), Bowers (1982), and T. P. Hughes (1983). The work by Hughes also treats the experience of Germany.

3. On the argument's other side, Jonathan Hughes (1986, p. 3) writes: "In too many accounts the economy lies silently in the background growing miraculously to support and nourish the actions of the gods and heroes the professional historians so love to study in war and politics. But just as men must be mobilized and led in war, voters organized and persuaded in politics, so economic resources must be mobilized and directed intelligently for economic growth to occur."

4. See Clemence and Doody (1950) for a useful account of the Schumpeterian system, and the recent, sympathetic overview by Stolper (1981). Streissler (1981, pp. 65–67) makes the interesting observation that to have emphasized the *creative* role of the entrepreneur was no revolutionary intellectual departure on Schumpeter's part, nor even on the part of his main teacher, Friedrich von Wieser. Rather, what was novel and somewhat shocking to Schumpeter's contemporaries was the stress he placed on the *destruction* and *disorder* that entrepreneurs caused with their innovations. The potential for competing network technologies to displace one another completely in actual use, and the associated properties of randomness and unpredictability that adhere to such competitions, make the novel aspect of Schumpeter's untidy vision of economic development particularly congenial to the major themes of this essay.

5. The long-standing controversy among economic historians over the nature and essentiality of the entrepreneur's role has most recently been renewed and refreshed by Landes' (1986) critique of Marglin (1974) and Temin's (1987) effort to distinguish questions about the genesis and advantages of large-scale, hierarchically structured production activities from other historical questions concerning the control and management of hierarchical organizations, including those addressed by Clark (1984).

6. David and Olsen (1986) provide a formal model of the generation of a "diffusion-cum-development trajectory," along which the adoption and incremental improvement of a capital-embodied technology are intertwined. That analysis, however, leaves aside the mathematically more difficult stochastic aspects of the actual matter, which are the focus of interest here.

7. I concede that I would have numbered myself among them, at least until 1975. Jonathan Hughes complained of this state of affairs among professional economists in his introduction to the 1965 edition of *The Vital Few,* and has reiterated it more recently, while noting the recent rejuvenation of interest in the subject of entrepreneurship among business and political circles. See J. Hughes (1986, pp. ix, 2).

8. This concept of change as timeless and constant of course holds a strong grip on other areas of the natural sciences, and the social sciences that have made them their model—whence, ironically, it has come to conflict with the narrative tradition in the writing of history. See the perceptive and too little noticed work of Teggart (1925, esp. chaps. 7–12), more recent use of which has been made by Eldredge (1985, chap. 1 and pp. 141–146). In this respect it may be seen that the pioneering work of Nelson and Winter (1982) on "evolutionary models" of economic change has been well designed to influence economists at ease with the eventless Darwinian conception of continuous modification through (competitive) natural selection. The incorporation of the Markov property in Nelson and Winter's models has served the same purpose, as has been noted elsewhere (for example, David 1975, p. 76).

9. Gilfillan (1935b) explicitly stressed the Darwinian evolutionary analogy in placing "the continuity of development" first among his 38 "social principles of invention," and documented it *in extenso* by references to the merchant ship (1935a). For Marx's views of technology, see Rosenberg (1976), who calls attention to their fruition in the emphasis Usher (1954) accorded to social processes in "setting the stage" for invention, as well as in the accumulation of small improvements. I will, perhaps, be forgiven for noticing that this particular chain of influence extends at least one important link further, to Landes; in a related context Landes (1986, p. 602) declares himself to be among the descendants of the (intellectual) House of Usher.

10. See Rosenberg (1982, chap. 1) for a subject review.

11. Williamson (1975, 1985), and related work on organizational structure, contracting, and hierarchical control, has, of course, reacted against the more extreme formulations of this position, on the grounds that they left unexplained the boundaries between firms and the market, and the internal institutional features of modern business enterprises. Chandler (1977), much occupied with the rise of large and complex business organizations within which were developed modes of resource allocation alternative to the market, casts the emerging technology of large-scale production in the role of the principal exogenous force inducing these organizational adaptations. Where the new technology was coming from, and whether its development was occurring primarily under the guidance of a visible hand (rather than its invisible, market counterpart), remains inexplicit in Chandler's scheme of things.

12. See, for example, David (1975, pp. 6–16, 50–91; 1987) for formalizations of the underlying view of the nature of the stochastic process that generates path-dependent technological progress. The heuristic value of vivid illustration, such as the tale of the QWERTY typewriter keyboard layout recounted in David (1986), has been masterfully demonstrated by Gould (1987).

13. This is a highly compressed and necessarily abstract statement of complicated matters that have been set out more fully elsewhere. See David (1975, chap. 1) on localized stochastic learning, the channeling of technical innovations along particular "cones" in factor input space defining available production processes (techniques), and the influence of historical events in causing industries or economies to become committed to a particular path or trajectory of development associated with such techniques. The notion of a technological paradigm, which Dosi (1982, 1984) has introduced and elaborated upon, is quite usefully applied to the concept of a "universal" electrical system, that is, an

integrated network for electricity supply and use. This concept, the paradigm, embraces variant technical formulations of such a system, notably the alternative designs based on DC, single-phase AC, and polyphase AC. Each of these, as will be seen, would carry some peculiar implications for the subsequent experience of the regions and economies that became committed to one or another specific trajectory of technological and industrial development.

14. The following passage from Prout (1921), the American Society of Mechanical Engineers' official biographer of Westinghouse, exemplifies this tradition of interpretation: "As soon as it became evident that Westinghouse proposed to exploit extensively the alternating-current system great opposition was developed. Looking back at history, one is surprised at the stupidity and puerility of some of this opposition. Men of great repute gave their names and their help to methods of which they must now be thoroughly ashamed. They know now that if they had succeeded, the progress of civilization would have been delayed—how much and how long we cannot even guess . . . It is needless to enlarge upon this [Battle of the Systems] aspect of the development. Every well-informed human being knows Westinghouse was right, the alternating electric current being now used to generate and convey 95 percent of the electric use in power and lighting in the United States" (p. 115). More recent versions, to be examined later in this chapter, do not even contemplate the possibility that Edison could have succeeded, had it been his intention to block these developments.

15. Landes (1986, p. 622), speaking of the historical evolution of the factory system.

16. A sequel confronted the home video or "camcorder" enthusiast and the manufacturers of videocamera and VCR equipment: whether to preserve the half-inch (12.7 mm) tape width for VCRs as a standard or to switch to systems based on the 8-millimeter format pioneered by Sony. See Rosenbloom (1985) on the background; Cusumano (1985) on details of the VCR rivalry from the producers' side.

17. The normative literature on the economics of standardization recognizes that while the evident failure of markets would call out for remedies in the form of government efforts to promote the exploitation of economies of scale obtainable via network coordination and system integration, such interventions may all too easily result in choices of technology that prove to be "mistakes." See Brock (1975), Kindleberger (1983), Carlton and Klamer (1983), Katz and Shapiro (1985a, 1985b), Farrell and Saloner (1985a, 1985b, 1985c). David (1987) reviews this literature in fuller detail.

18. Under such conditions—where, as I observed some years ago, "marked divergences between ultimate outcomes may flow from seemingly negligible differences in remote beginnings" (David, 1975, p. 16)—market rivalries among variant technological systems do exhibit a strictly *historical* character, in the sense that they are nonergodic; the dynamic process cannot shake itself loose from the grip of past events, and its outcome therefore can properly be described as *path-dependent*.

19. It should be emphasized that this form of (hindsight) recognition that rational decision making had nonetheless resulted in an inferior path's being mistaken for the "right" one could not arise under conditions of constant or decreasing returns; in the latter cases the eventual outcomes would be *path-independent*. See Arthur (1984, 1989) and Arthur, Ermoliev, and Kaniovsky (1985) for more formal (mathematical) treatment, and David (1987) for further exposition.

20. In 1882, according to Jones (1940, p. 41), this complex of enterprises included: (1) the Edison Electric Light Company, which had been formed to finance the invention, patenting, and development of Edison's electric lighting system, and which licensed its use; (2) the Edison Electric Illuminating Company of New York, the first of the Edison municipal lighting utilities; (3) the Edison Machine Works, organized to manufacture the dynamos covered by Edison's patents; (4) the (Edison) Electric Tube Company, set up to manufacture the underground conductors for electric power distribution in the lighting system; and (5) the Edison Lamp Works.

21. On the previous career of Westinghouse, see Leupp (1919), Prout (1921).

22. See, for example, Sharlin (1963, pp. 136–147) and Jarvis (1967a, 1967b) for convenient subject reviews. More details of the history of alternating current technology prior to 1880 can be found in *Electrical World* (March 1887); Sumpner (1890); *Encyclopaedia Britannica* (1910–1911, IX, 179–203); Fleming (1921, p. 44).

23. A *transformer,* in modern electrical parlance, refers to a device by which the electromotive force

(emf) of a source of alternating current may be increased or decreased. (For the reader whose recollection of the introductory physics of electricity has grown as hazy as was mine: the difference in potential, which may be thought of as a kind of driving force behind the electrons forming the current, is sometimes called the emf and is measured by V, the voltage. Electric current is analogous to the flow of water through a pipe, the rate of flow being measured by I, the amperage. Power (P), measured in watts, is W/t, the time rate at which energy (W) is developed or expended.) Unlike a dynamo used in generation, a transformer needs no moving parts. It has a primary winding (whose terminals are attached to an AC source), and a secondary winding, both of which pass in coils around an iron core. The first such device was the closed-core transformer made by Faraday, the core of which had the form of an iron ring. Step-down transformers have a larger number of turns of wire in the primary winding than in the secondary winding, since the ratio of primary (or impressed) voltage to secondary voltage is equal to the ratio of the number of turns in the respective windings. Although it may seem, on first consideration, that the boost in voltage achieved by means of a step-up transformer somehow violates the law of conservation of energy, such obviously cannot be the case; the power supplied at the primary is just equal to that delivered at the secondary. In general, when the voltage is stepped up (or, as English electrical engineers say, "bumped up"), the current is "bumped down" by the same proportion.

24. See Stanley (1912, pp. 564–565) and Passer (1972, pp. 136–138) on Gaulard and Gibbs, Stanley and Westinghouse, and the still more comprehensive account in T. P. Hughes (1983, pp. 95–105). The challenge of solving the practical problems arising from the connection of the primary coils of the transformers in series by Gaulard and Gibbs also drew a response in the same year from the Hungarian team of Zipernowsky, Bláthy, and Déri of Budapest. Like Stanley, they found that transformers can be worked independently if the different primary circuits are arranged in parallel between two high-voltage mains (1,000 V in their patent), like the rungs on a ladder; the secondary circuits of the transformers were kept isolated, with incandescent lamps placed on them in parallel.

25. Josephson (1959, pp. 231–232); Jarvis (1967b, chap. 10, p. 229); T. P. Hughes (1983, pp. 83–84); Byatt (1979, p. 99).

26. Jarvis (1967b, p. 229). The 110-volt standard for electricity consumption that came to be established in the United States was selected by Edison on the basis of electrical circuit theory and the maximum-resistance lamp filament that he was able to obtain circa 1879. How the Europeans, following the Berliners' example, came to establish a 220-volt standard is another story (see T. P. Hughes 1983, p. 193).

27. Using the standard notation introduced in note 23, the power equation for direct current is $P = VI$; but for the case of alternating current, power has to be thought of in an "average" sense, and the equation takes the root mean square form: $P = V_{rms} I_{rms} \cos \phi$. Here $V_{rms} = V_{max}/(2)^{1/2}$ and $I_{rms} = I_{max}/(2)^{1/2}$. The power factor, $\cos \phi$, depends on the phase angle ϕ, which measures the amount by which the electron current in the line leads or lags the impressed voltage. For current of any kind, however, Ohm's law gives the resistance, R, measured in ohms, as $R = I/V$. Note that the resistance of a wire connecting two points is directly proportional to its length, L, and inversely proportional to its cross-sectional area, A, with the factor of proportionality being the "resistivity" β: $R = \beta(L/A)$. This relation, combined with Ohm's law, and the AÇ power equation, yields the voltage-distance relationship cited in the text: $L = (V^2/P)B$, where the constant is implicitly defined as $B = [A(\cos\phi)]/2\beta$.

28. See Passer (1972, pp. 137–144, 165–167); Byatt (1979, pp. 102–107); Evans (1892, p. 52).

29. See Passer (1972, pp. 237–249 on Sprague and Johnson, pp. 216–255 on electric street railways; also McDonald (1962, p. 36).

30. And also between the main competitive suppliers of AC lighting plant—the Thomson-Houston and Westinghouse electric companies. On "first-mover advantages," and incentives for preemption by suppliers of new technologies and goods and services based on them, see the theoretical analysis developed by Fudenberg and Tirole (1985); and Bresnahan and David (1986), for an effort at empirical application.

31. See, for example, T. P. Hughes (1983, pp. 217–219). A 10 to 12 percent load factor is given as the average for a simple lighting load in the article contributed by J. A. Fleming, "Electricity Supply," in *Encyclopaedia Britannica* (1910–11, IX, 194).

32. Quoted in Josephson (1959, p. 346; emphasis added). Josephson's source was an Edison mem-

orandum to E. H. Johnson, commenting on a report that had been obtained from the engineers of Siemens and Halske (Berlin) evaluating the version of the AC lighting system that had been developed by Zipernowsky, Bláthy, and Déri (note 24).

33. According to Prout (1921, p. 95), Westinghouse had begun installing isolated DC lighting plants earlier in 1886, and had practically completed his company's first DC central station in Trenton, New Jersey, in August. Direct current installations in other towns were under way. Quite probably it was this bustle of activity—an incursion into markets that otherwise might "naturally" fall to the Edison Electric Lighting Company—that Edison felt was more disturbing than the first AC central station completed by Westinghouse Electric Company in November.

34. See Passer (1972, table 19, p. 150) for lighting capacity data for the three leading companies in 1891.

35. For a sample of the best modern accounts in each genre, see Stillwell (1934); Passer (1972, chap. 5); T. P. Hughes (1983, chap. 6, esp. pp. 106–111); J. Hughes (1986, pp. 192–198). McDonald (1962, pp. 43–46) recounts the affair from the viewpoint of Samuel Insull.

36. For example, in addition to the patent suits mentioned later in this chapter, Westinghouse filed a claim for patent infringement against Thomson-Houston when that firm began production and sale of an AC incandescent lighting system. The two companies worked out an agreement under which control of the Consolidated and Sawyer-Man patents in possession of Thomson-Houston was relinquished to Westinghouse. See Passer (1972, p. 139).

37. See T. P. Hughes (1983, pp. 22–23), and references therein, on Edison as a "systems inventor," a point of some further significance later on in my discussion.

38. For example, Woodbury (1960, pp. 184–185) gives an account of the inordinate amount of time and worry that Elihu Thomson had to devote to problems connected with patent litigation. Josephson (1959, pp. 354–358) details Edison's vexations with the protracted "war" with Westinghouse over the carbon filament patent of 1878, in which he was called to testify during 1890. The suit cost the victorious Edison General Electric Company, holder of the patent, about $2 million by the time it was concluded in 1891, when the lamp patent had less than three years of life remaining. Sheer vanity aside, *economically* motivated reputational considerations can account for the willingness of inventors to spend time defending claims to proprietary rights which they have already sold; the value to purchasers of patent rights, which a self-employed inventor might wish to sell in the future, will be directly and indirectly affected by this form of commitment.

39. See Josephson (1959, pp. 295–297); also T. P. Hughes (1983, pp. 38–41).

40. See Josephson (1959, p. 299); also *Electrical World* (January 1, 1887) for details on the eleven suits the Edison Electric Company began against the Westinghouse Electric Company on December 23, 1886, for injunctions and damages for the infringement of electric lighting patents; the patents in question covered the entire central station system.

41. See Josephson (1959, pp. 347–348); also T. P. Hughes (1983, pp. 108–109); Woodbury (1960, p. 174).

42. George Westinghouse reportedly was outraged. One of these alternators was in place at the Auburn State Prison in August 1890, where it produced the current lethal to the first victim of the electric chair, William Kemmler, a convicted ax murderer. See Leupp (1919, pp. 132–155) for details of the controversy over this execution, and the unfounded suspicions at the time that Westinghouse was financing the opponents of capital punishment who mobilized on the occasion.

43. See Josephson (1959, pp. 348–349); Cheney (1981, p. 43); T. P. Hughes (1976, p. 108).

44. See *Electrical World* (August 1887, September 1888); Woodbury (1960, p. 174). The lesser hazard of accidental electrocution from AC derives from the tendency of the current to repel a body from the mains, breaking the contact, whereas DC does not have this effect. Although the text follows contemporary popular discussions by speaking of the harm done by high voltage, V, strictly, the damage done by a current is dependent on the volume of the flow, that is, the amperage, I. By Ohm's law, however, the latter is proportional to the emf, V—the proportionality constant being the resistance of the conducting body, R (see note 27).

45. Josephson (1959, p. 345). In addition to the early concern expressed by Elihu Thomson, Franklin Pope in the United States and both Dr. Werner Von Siemens and Lord Kelvin—recognized "scientific authorities" on electricity—warned against the dangers of the AC system of transmission at higher voltages.

46. See the influential account given by Josephson (1959, pp. 313–338, 349–350, 361–362), emphasizing Edison's resistance to the advice of others to follow Westinghouse and Thomson-Houston into the AC electricity supply field.

47. Passer (1972, p. 74). This summation in Passer's 1954 study is quoted approvingly in the biography by Josephson (1959, p. 350). Alterations in the inventor's objective economic and institutional circumstances are cited by Passer in explanation of this transformation, whereas Josephson attributes Edison's unwillingness to pursue developments in AC technology to "the fear that all the effort, equipment, and capital invested in the old system would quickly be made obsolete by the new," seemingly without crediting Edison with an awareness that if his efforts could produce that result, it also could happen at the hands of others.

McDonald (1962, pp. 32–33) takes a different explanatory tack in suggesting that a profound psychological change had occurred with the death of Edison's wife, Mary Stilwell Edison, in 1884: "Edison's creative period as an electric innovator [sic] ended with his wife's death, and in the future he not only contributed little to the success of his electric companies, but sometimes actually impeded their progress [by opposing alternating current applications]. From the greatest single asset a collection of electrical enterprises could possibly have, he suddenly became a burden." An awkward fact, omitted from McDonald's account, is that within a year of Mary's death Edison had courted and successfully proposed marriage to Mina Miller, and appeared to his friends to have drawn a renewed vitality and pleasure in anticipating life with his second wife (see Josephson 1959, pp. 301–308). As for the suggested waning of Edison's inventive powers, McDonald's assertion (p. 33, n. 16) that "after 1884, virtually all Edison's inventions were relatively trivial, and some of them were almost foolish" is refuted within ten pages by his own, more accurate statement (p. 43): "To be sure, some of his greatest achievements were yet to come—among them the perfected phonograph and the motion picture—but none of them was in the electric field."

More severe is the judgment offered by Jonathan Hughes's (1986) spirited account, according to which, by 1886–87 Edison "had lost touch with the rapidly changing technology, or was fast losing touch. He had been a stanch, and then a rabid, opponent of alternating current transmission . . . For some reason Edison could not comprehend the a.c. system. He was convinced that, transformers or not, the high-voltage of the a.c. system made it extraordinarily dangerous . . . Arguments got nowhere with Edison on this issue. The fact that he considered the main proponents of the a.c. system to be common thieves made him even more unwilling to see any virtue in their arguments . . . There was no part of Edison's career that was so unworthy of the man and, in fact, sordid" (pp. 193–194). This account bears indications of the influence of Josephson's (1959, p. 349) view that the "whole dreadful controversy can be attributed only to an extreme bitterness of feeling towards his [Edison's] opponents that completely overbalanced his judgment."

48. See, for example, McDonald (1962, p. 62); T. P. Hughes (1983, pp. 107–109).

49. See T. P. Hughes (1983, pp. 106–111) for a discussion suggesting that this differential rate of progress was somehow elicited because electrical engineers, having used AC to overcome the transmission cost constraints that encumbered the expansion of DC distribution networks, quickly encountered numerous obstacles in getting an AC electricity supply system to emulate the functions that existing DC systems were capable of performing—particularly the provision of power to secondary motors. While such constraints may have served as "focusing devices" (see Rosenberg 1969), directing engineering efforts toward projects which were more likely to have high commercial payoff if the technical problems could be overcome, they could not have signaled the possibility of actually solving those problems.

50. See Fleming (1921, pp. 146–147) for details of motor development and construction.

51. T. P. Hughes (1983, pp. 115–117) gives full details on the filing, issuance, and acquisition dates of the key Tesla patents and others.

52. See Prout (1921, pp. 128–129). Development of an AC meter was regarded as sufficiently

important that Westinghouse himself filed patents on one such device, in June 1887, and on another in October 1887, developed jointly with one of his engineers, Phillip Lange. Patents were issued for these meters in May 1888, but by then they had been superseded by Shallenberger's design.

53. T. P. Hughes (1983, p. 120) also notes that the electrical equipment manufacturing companies "remained partially committed to direct current" by virtue of the specialized facilities and patent positions, as well as the experience and expertise they had built up in that field.

54. The role of "gateway" innovations in network technology evolution is explicitly considered with reference to the rotary converter by David with Bunn (1988), and is discussed more generally in regard to standardization policy issues by David (1987).

55. Passer (1972, pp. 300–301); T. P. Hughes (1983, p. 118). The courts eventually ruled against the patent application by Bradley for the generator and synchronous motor, on the ground that Tesla's patent was fuller and more complete.

56. See Pfannkuche (1887) for discussion of an "all-purpose" system involving DC dynamos and AC transmission.

57. Lamme (1926, chap. 6) recounts his early work for Westinghouse on rotary converters.

58. See McDonald (1962, pp. 69–70) on the work of Chicago Edison's chief engineer Louis Ferguson circa 1894, who installed rotary converters at both the generating and local distribution ends— using polyphase AC for transmission only. On the technology of rotary (or, in some English usage, "rotatory") converters, as well as rotary transformers (used in changing the voltage of direct current), and the Ferranti rectifier (used in transforming an alternating single-phase current into a direct pulsating current for arc lighting), see the article "Transformers" contributed by J. A. Fleming, in *Encyclopaedia Britannica* (1910–11, XXVII, 178–179). More generally, on the significance of converters, see T. P. Hughes (1983, pp. 121–122).

59. Edison, in a 1908 encounter with George Stanley, the son of William Stanley, whose improvement on the Gaulard Gibbs patent had been the basis for Westinghouse's AC system, is said to have remarked, "Oh, by the way, tell your father I was wrong." Josephson (1959, p. 349), in reporting this, interprets Edison to have thereby acknowledged that he had made "his greatest blunder" by not following Westinghouse into AC technology. Apart from the issue of whether Edison had made a blunder or a justifiable decision, it remains quite unclear exactly what Edison felt he had been "wrong" about. Possibly it was his mistaken expectation, in 1886, that a great deal of experimenting and a long period of further practical development would be needed before a system based on AC could be brought to the point of challenging his own.

60. Thus it is not surprising that after the spring of 1887 Edison should have allowed himself to become increasingly preoccupied with renewed experimental work on his phonograph—entering an inventive race against workers in the laboratory of Alexander Bell, who had undertaken to improve on the original Edison device of 1877. Josephson (1959, pp. 317–331) relates the story of this project, which was brought to a successful culmination by Edison's famous 72-hour frenzy of nonstop work in June 1888; and of the disappointing sequel, in which J. Lippincott and Edison's unscrupulous associates swindled the inventor out of a major part of the value of the rights to the new phonograph patent and an exclusive manufacturing license.

61. In response to this interpretation, Jonathan Hughes in private correspondence with me (March 5, 1987) wrote: "I hope you're right about how clever Edison was in getting out of the way of the a. c. 'juggernaut.' So far as actual verbal evidence goes, Edison could have done what he did for no more reasons than ignorance and cunning . . . I am willing to grant that he had a certain peasant cunning *(Bauernschlauheit)* that would make him see that a campaign of dust-in-your-eyes about a.c. would allow him to sell out and get out. It is reasonable. The evidence that he was running from what he did not and could not understand is pretty strong too."

62. See Josephson (1959, pp. 350–366) and McDonald (1962, pp. 30–39) for a fuller account of the formation of the Edison General Electric Company (EGE) and then the General Electric Company.

63. Josephson (1959, pp. 351–353). On Villard's role, see also McDonald (1962, pp. 39–40) and T. P. Hughes (1983, pp. 76–77).

64. See, for example, Daggett (1908), Campbell (1938), Kolko (1965, chap. 4, esp. pp. 64–67).

65. See McDonald (1962, pp. 48–51). Villard, at the head of EGE, previously had sought a consolidation with the Westinghouse Electric Company, but when priority was awarded to Edison's carbon filament patent in 1891, he felt his hand sufficiently strengthened to seek to acquire a supposedly weakened competitor, and opened negotiations with Thomson-Houston. In the end, Morgan agreed with Coffin that Thomson-Houston was in a stronger financial position, and so should purchase EGE. There is a nice but unresolved and probably unresolvable question: whether EGE's comparatively weaker financial condition owed something to the effect of Edison's propaganda campaign against AC, which supported an inflation of the price EGE paid for its constituent DC-system companies.

66. See Leupp (1919, pp. 157–181). Under Belmont's direction, two electric lighting companies that had been controlled by the Westinghouse interests (the United States and the Consolidated) were absorbed into the reorganized firm, and their stockholders were given the new preferred and common stock issued by the Westinghouse Electric and Manufacturing Company. The stockholders of the main company surrendered 40 percent of their old stock, and were asked to take second preference shares in the reorganized firm in lieu of the rest. By these measures the original outstanding liability of more than $10 million (on which the annual interest charges exceeded $180,000) was reduced to less than $9 million, all in equity.

67. See Cheney (1981, pp. 48–49). According to the memos exchanged between Westinghouse and Tesla in 1888 and 1889, the former was to pay the Tesla Electric Company $2.50 per hp of electric power sold. It was said that by 1893 the accrued royalties that would have been owed Tesla under these agreements would have amounted to $12 million—considerably more than the assets of the Westinghouse Electric and Manufacturing Company at that date. Tesla, by then, had already been talked out of his royalties by George Westinghouse, who reportedly had told him, "Your decision determines the fate of the Westinghouse Company." Were Tesla not to give up his contract, Westinghouse suggested, there was nothing to ensure that his inventions would be implemented commercially: "In that event you would have to deal with the bankers, for I would no longer have any power in the situation."

68. Passer (1972, pp. 298–303); Sharlin (1963, pp. 187–188). Bradley's patents and facilities were bought up by General Electric, and the Westinghouse Electric Company developed its own rotary converters over the same period.

69. "One engineer estimated that under such conditions, the d.c. system would be twice as efficient as an a.c. system" (Sharlin 1963, p. 200, quoting from a statement in 1900 by the British electrical engineering authority J. A. Fleming).

70. See Landes (1969, p. 286) and Fleming (1921, pp. 238ff.) for technical details.

71. On the Westinghouse exhibit at the Columbian Exposition in 1893, see, for example, Prout (1921, pp. 134–140); Sharlin (1963, pp. 206–211).

72. See Sharlin (1963, pp. 195–210) for a discussion of the choice of technology at Niagara.

73. See Byatt (1979, p. 114), Bowers (1982, p. 162), Lardner (1903) for discussion of regional grid development.

74. T. P. Hughes's (1983, pp. 120–121) succinct formulation bears quotation: "Because 'the battle of the systems' had become far more complicated than a technical problem awaiting a simple technical solution, it ended without the dramatic vanquishing of one system by the other, or a revolutionary transition from one paradigm to another. The conflict was resolved by synthesis, by a combination of coupling and merging. The coupling took place on the technical level; the merging, on the institutional level."

75. This is a difficulty with which efforts to quantify the effects of major transport innovations, such as the canal and railroad systems, have had to contend (see, for example, David 1975, chap. 6); I am grateful to Edward Constant, who has reminded me of its relevance in the present connection.

76. Throughout the Battle of the Systems, electrical engineers debated the advantages and disadvantages of the variant systems in the pages of *Electrical World* (see, for example, the issues of February 26, 1887; January 21, 1888; March 31, 1888). In addition to Lord Kelvin and Dr. Werner von Siemens, two of the more distinguished industry personalities who argued on behalf of direct current until late in the nineteenth century, there were many other engineers who continued to debate the merits of the two systems at the turn of the century (see, for example, Barstow 1901; Scott 1901).

77. The voltages these involved were much lower than those in modern high-voltage direct current systems, which have reemerged as a technological area of active research and development interest to the electricity industry in the United States. See, for example, Alvarado and Lansetter (1984), Weeks (1981), Zorpette (1985).

78. See Parsons (1940, chap. 4, pp. 52–70) for a discussion of early HVDC systems in England. According to the *Encyclopaedia Britannica* (1910–11, IX, 196) the Oxford system was distinguished by the use of "continuous" (direct) current transformers to accomplish the drop in voltage from the 1,000–2,000-volt range at which the current was transmitted from the generating stations to the 100–150 volts supplied by distributing mains to users. Although 3,000 volts came to be regarded as the practical limiting voltage for individual DC dynamos (owing to the problems of sparking at the commutator brushes when run at faster speeds), two or more such machines could be wired in series in order to secure much greater voltages for purposes of transmission. In France, for example, on the Thury direct current system, energy was transmitted a distance of 115 miles (between Moutiers and Lyons) at voltages upwards of 45,000 volts, using four groups of dynamos in series, each group consisting of four machines in series. See *Encyclopaedia Britannica* (1910–11, VIII, 778).

79. Byatt (1979, p. 100). One additional advantage of the Oxford system was that existing DC arc lamps for street lighting could be worked off the high-voltage mains in sets of 20 to 40 (see *Encyclopaedia Britannica*, 1910–11, IX, 196; also Lineff 1888).

80. Landes (1969, pp. 285–286) summarizes this with the statement that "the two systems competed fiercely in Britain for many years. In the long run, however, victory lay with centralized generators and long-distance transmission." Although the latter is indisputable, there is a point in noticing that the "victory" was not an indigenous evolutionary outcome. In came the 1920s, with the transplantation to Britain of the electric utility system technology which had become the dominant engineering style in the United States. The interruption of World War I had contributed to leaving Britain's electricity supply industry in a rather dilapidated state, considerably behind American practice in terms of generator size and efficiency and load factors. Compared with British "average practice" circa 1920, American methods looked far superior. But the long-run outcome of the British "contest" cannot be offered in support of the optimality of the course of technological evolution which the industry had followed in the United States. It was not an independent experiment; indeed, had the AC-DC rivalry not been resolved in the American market so far before, allowing time for much improvement in the design and actual operation of electricity networks, borrowing technology from the United States might hardly have been so attractive to the British in the 1920s.

81. Louis Bell, "Power Transmission," in *Encyclopaedia Britannica* (1910–11, XXII, 234). Bell was chief engineer of the Electric Power Transmission Department of General Electric Company and former editor of *Electrical World*. See also Weeks (1981, pp. 267–271).

82. The significance of the rotary converter as an example of a neutral "gateway" innovation, which may have had important effects in tipping the balance between a sponsored systems rivalry, is further explored by David with Bunn (1987).

83. See Farrell and Saloner (1985a). The indicated route of escape from being "locked in" to a suboptimal technological system depends on a rigorous backward induction process, which leads the last decision-making unit to switch, given that all others have switched; and the next-to-last correctly to anticipate the decision of the last, and so to switch, given that all before him have already switched; and so on, back to the first decision maker, who will rationally switch in the expectation that all following him will do likewise. It is a pretty piece of logic, but incomplete information readily breaks this chain, and therefore would prevent it from even beginning to form.

84. This point has been developed by Katz and Shapiro (1985b). Westinghouse is said to have acted from just such considerations: submitting a successful but money-losing low bid for the contract to light the Columbian Exposition in Chicago in 1893, conscious that the demonstration value would ultimately pay off, possibly by affecting the outcome of the competition for the contract to build AC generators for the Niagara project (see Leupp 1919, pp. 162–170).

85. Moreover, just those bankers with the financial resources adequate to the task may be the ones

most concerned, as was J. P. Morgan, to avert "destructive" price competition, and to seek the pooling of patent rights as a basis for the cartelization or outright monopolization of the industry in question.

References

Alvarado, F. L., and F. H. Lansetter. 1984. "Methodology for Analysis of Multi-Terminal HVDC Systems." In *Trends in Electric Utility Research*, ed. C. W. Bullard and P. J. Womeldorff. New York: Pergamon.

Arthur, W.B. 1984. "Why a Silicon Valley? The Pure Theory of Locational Choice." Technological Innovation Project Workshop paper. Department of Economics, Stanford University, November.

———— 1989. "Competing Technologies, Increasing Returns, and Lock-in by Historical Events." *Economic Journal*, 99(March):116–131.

Arthur, W. B., Y. M. Ermoliev, and Y. M. Kaniovsky. 1985. "Strong Laws for a Class of Path-Dependent Urn Processes." In *Proceedings of the International Conference on Stochastic Optimization, Kiev, 1984*. Munich: Springer-Verlag.

Barstow, W. S. 1901. "Notes on the Alternating Current System of Distribution." *AIEE Transactions* 18:849–853.

Bowers, B. 1982. *A History of Electric Light and Power*. New York: Peter Peregrinus.

Bresnahan, T. R., and P. A. David. 1986. "Strategic Effects in the Diffusion of Innovations: Testable Implication and Preliminary Findings for the Case of Automatic Teller Machines in U.S. Banking Markets." Paper presented to the Conference on Innovation Diffusion at the University of Venice, March 17–22, 1986. Technical Papers Series of the High Technology Impact Program, Center for Economic Policy Research, Stanford University.

Brittain, J. E. 1977. *Turning Points in American Electrical History*. New York: IEEE Press.

Brock, G. 1975. "Competition, Standards, and Self-Regulation in the Computer Industry." In *Regulating the Product: Quality and Variety*, ed. R. Caves and M. Roberts. Cambridge, Mass.: Ballinger.

Bureau of the Census, U.S. Department of Commerce and Labor. 1906. *Special Reports of the Bureau of Census: Electrical Industries, 1902*. Washington, D.C.: Government Printing Office.

———— 1910. *Special Reports of the Bureau of Census: Electric Light and Power Stations, 1907*. Washington, D.C.: Government Printing Office.

Bureau of the Census, U.S. Department of Commerce. 1915. *Census of Electrical Industries, 1912*. Washington, D.C.: Government Printing Office.

———— 1920. *Census of Electrical Industries, 1917*. Washington, D.C.: Government Printing Office.

Byatt, I. C. R. 1979. *The British Electrical Industry, 1875–1914: The Economic Returns to a New Technology*. Oxford: Clarendon Press.

Campbell, S. G. 1938. *The Reorganization of the American Railroad System, 1893–1900*. New York: Columbia University Press.

Carlton, D. W., and J. M. Klamer. 1983. "The Need for Coordination among Firms, with Special Reference to Network Industries." *University of Chicago Law Review* 50:446–465.

Chandler, A. E., Jr. 1977. *The Visible Hand: The Managerial Revolution in American Business*. Cambridge, Mass.: Belknap.

Cheney, M. 1981. *Tesla: Man Out of Time*. Englewood Cliffs, N.J.: Prentice-Hall.

Clark, G. 1984. "Authority and Efficiency: The Labor Market and the Managerial Revolution of the Late Nineteenth Century." *Journal of Economic History* 44, no. 1 (December):1069–83.

Clemence, R. V., and F. S. Doody. 1950. *The Schumpeterian System*. Cambridge, Mass.: Addison-Wesley.

Cusumano, M. 1985. "Note on VTR Industry and Market Development: Japan, the U.S., and Europe, ca. 1975–1985." Harvard Business School.

Daggett, S. 1908. *Railroad Reorganization*. Boston: Houghton Mifflin.

David, P.A. 1975. *Technical Choice, Innovation, and Economic Growth: Essays on American and British Experience in the Nineteenth Century.* New York: Cambridge University Press.

———— 1985. "Clio and the Economics of QWERTY." *American Economic Review* 75, no. 2 (May):332–337.

———— 1986. "Understanding the Economics of QWERTY: The Necessity of History." In *Economics History and the Modern Economist*, ed. W. N. Parker. Oxford: Basil Blackwell.

———— 1987. "Some New Standards for the Economics of Standardization in the Information Age." In *Economic Policy and Technological Performance*, ed. Partha Dasgupta and Paul Stoneman. Cambridge: Cambridge University Press.

David, P. A., with J. A. Bunn. 1987. "The 'Battle of the Systems' and the Evolutionary Dynamics of Network Technology Rivalries." High Technology Impact Program Working Paper no. 15, Center for Economic Policy Research, Stanford University, January.

David, P. A., and J. A. Bunn. 1988. "The Economics of Gateway Technologies and Network Evolution: Lessons from Electricity Supply History." *Information Economics and Policy* 3:165–202.

David, P. A., and T. E. Olsen. 1986. "The Equilibrium Dynamics of Diffusion when Incremental Technological Innovations Are Foreseen." *Ricerche economiche* (Special Supplement on Innovation and Diffusion) no. 4.

Dosi, G. 1982. "Technological Paradigms and Technological Trajectories: A Suggested Interpretation of the Determinants and Directions of Technical Change." *Research Policy* 13, no. 1 (February):3–20.

———— 1984. *Technical Change and Industrial Transformation.* London: Macmillan.

Eldredge, N. 1985. *Time Frames: The Rethinking of Darwinian Evolution and the Theory of Punctuated Equilibria.* New York: Simon and Schuster.

Electrical World. 1887. "Edison vs. Westinghouse." 9 (January 1):7–8.

———— 1887. "Incandescent Lights on High-Tension Circuits." 9 (February 26):110.

———— 1887. "The Distribution of Electricity by Secondary Generators." 9 (March 26):156–158.

———— 1887. "Report on the Committee on Electrical Distribution by Alternating Currents." 10 (August 20):92–93.

———— 1888. "Alternating Current or Storage Battery." 11 (January 21):25.

———— 1888. "Alternating vs. Continuous Current." 11 (March 31):159.

———— 1888. "The Comparative Danger of Alternating vs. Direct Current." 12 (September 8):126.

———— 1889. "Mr. Edison on the Dangers of Electric Lighting." 14 (November 2):292–293.

Evans, G. T. 1892. "Some Phases of the Alternating Current." *Electrical World* 19 (January 23):52.

Farrell, J., and G. Saloner. 1985a. "Standardization, Compatibility and Innovation." *Rand Journal of Economics* 16 (Spring):70–83.

———— 1985b. "Economic Issues in Standardization." Working Paper no. 393, Department of Economics, Massachusetts Institute of Technology, October.

———— 1985c. "Installed Base and Compatibility, with Implications for Product Preannouncements." Working Paper no. 385, Department of Economics, Massachusetts Institute of Technology, August.

Fleming, J. A. 1921. *Fifty Years of Electricity: The Memories of an Electrical Engineer.* London: Wireless World.

Fudenberg, T., and J. Tirole. 1985. *Dynamic Models of Oligopoly.* Fundamentals of Pure and Applied Economics series. Vol. 3. Theory of the Firm and Industrial Organization Section. London: Harwood Academic Publishers.

Gilfillan, S. C. 1935a. *Inventing the Ship.* Chicago: Follet.

———— 1935b. *The Sociology of Invention.* Chicago: Follet.

Gould, S. J. 1987. "The Panda's Thumb of Technology." *Natural History* 1 (January):14–23.

Hannah, L. 1979. *Electricity before Nationalism: A Study of the Development of the Electricity Supply Industry in Britain to 1948.* Baltimore: Johns Hopkins University Press.

Hennessey, R. A. S. 1971. *The Electric Revolution.* Newcastle upon Tyne: Oriel Press.

Hughes, J. 1986. *The Vital Few.* New York: Oxford University Press.

Hughes, T. P. 1976. "The Science Technology Interaction: The Case of High Voltage Power Transmission Systems." *Technology and Culture* 17 (October):654–659.

——— 1983. *Networks of Power: Electrification in Western Society, 1880–1939*. Baltimore: Johns Hopkins University Press.

Jarvis, C. M. 1967a. "The Generation of Electricity." In *A History of Technology*. Vol. 5. *Late Nineteenth Century, 1850–1900*, ed. C. Singer, E. J. Holmyard, A. R. Hall, and T. I. Williams. Oxford: Clarendon Press.

——— 1967b. "The Distribution and Utilization of Electricity." In *A History of Technology*. Vol. 5. *Late Nineteenth Century, 1850–1900*, ed. C. Singer, E. J. Holmyard, A. R. Hall, and T. I. Williams. Oxford: Clarendon Press.

Jones, P. 1940. *A Power History of the Consolidated Edison System*. New York: New York Consolidated Edison.

Josephson, M. 1959. *Edison: A Biography*. New York: McGraw-Hill.

Katz, M. L., and C. Shapiro. 1985a. "Network Externalities, Competition, and Compatibility." *American Economic Review* 75 (May):424–440.

——— 1985b. "Technology Adoption in the Presence of Network Externalities." Discussion Paper in Economics no. 96, Woodrow Wilson School, Princeton University.

Kindleberger, C. P. 1983. "Standards as Public, Collective and Private Goods." *Kyklos* 36: 377–396.

Kolko, G. 1965. *Railroad and Regulation, 1877–1916*. Princeton: Princeton University Press.

Lamme, B. G. 1926. *Benjamin Garver Lamme, Electrical Engineer: An Autobiography*. New York: Putnam's Sons.

Landes, D. S. 1969. *The Unbound Prometheus: Technological Change and Industrial Development in Western Europe from 1750 to the Present*. Cambridge: Cambridge University Press.

——— 1986. "What Do Bosses Really Do?" *Journal of Economic History* 46, no. 3 (September): 585–624.

Lardner, H. A. 1903. "Economical and Safe Limits in the Size of Capital Stations." *AIEE Transactions* 21:407–416.

Leupp, F. E. 1919. *George Westinghouse: His Life and Achievements*. London: John Murray.

Lineff, W. 1888. "Accumulators versus Direct Currents for Electric Traction." *Electrical World* 11 (April 14).

Marglin, S. 1974. "What Do Bosses Do? Part I." *Review of Radical Political Economy* 6 (Summer): 60–112.

McDonald, F. 1962. *Insull*. Chicago: University of Chicago Press.

National Electrical Manufacturers Association. 1946. *A Chronological History of Electrical Development*. New York: NEMA.

Nelson, R. R., and S. G. Winter. 1982. *An Evolutionary Theory of Economic Change*. Cambridge, Mass: Belknap.

Parsons, R. H. 1940. *The Early Days of the Power Station Industry*. Cambridge: Cambridge University Press.

Passer, H. C. 1972. *The Electrical Manufacturers, 1875–1900: A Study in Competition, Entrepreneurship, Technical Change, and Economic Growth*. New York: Arno.

Pfannkuche, A. 1887. "Long-Distance Distribution of Electric Energy." *Electrical World* 9 (April 12):170–171.

Prout, H. G. 1921. *A Life of George Westinghouse*. New York: American Society of Mechanical Engineers.

Rosenberg, N. 1969. "The Direction of Technological Change: Inducement Mechanisms and Focusing Devices." *Economic Development and Cultural Change* 18, no. 1 (October):1–24.

——— 1976. "Marx as a Student of Technology." *Monthly Review* 28(July–August):56–77. Reprinted in N. Rosenberg, *Inside the Black Box: Technology and Economics*, chap. 2. Cambridge: Cambridge University Press, 1982.

———— 1982. *Inside the Black Box: Technology and Economics.* New York: Cambridge University Press.

Rosenbloom, R. 1985. "Managing Technology for the Longer Term." In *The Uneasy Alliance,* ed. K. Clark et al. New York: Praeger.

Scott, C. F. 1901. "Alternating Current as a Factor in General Distribution for Light and Power." *AIEE Transactions* 18:843–848.

Sharlin, H. I. 1963. *The Making of the Electrical Age.* New York: Abelard-Schuman.

Stanley, W. 1912. "Alternating Current Development in America." *Franklin Institute Journal* 68: 568–573.

Stillwell, L. B. 1934. "Alternating Current versus Direct Current." *Electrical Engineering* 53, no. 5:708–710.

Stolper, W. F. 1981. "Aspects of Schumpeter's Theory of Evolution." In *Schumpeterian Economics,* ed. H. Frisch. New York: Praeger.

Streissler, E. 1981. "Schumpeter's Vienna and the Role of Credit in Innovation." In *Schumpeterian Economics,* ed. H. Frisch. New York: Praeger.

Sumpner, W. E. 1890. "Some Peculiarities of Alternate Currents." *Electrical World* 15 (January 11):33.

Teggart, F. J. 1925. *Theory of History.* New Haven: Yale University Press.

Temin, P. 1987. "Bosses and Technical Change." Paper presented to the conference in honor of David S. Landes in Bellagio, Italy, August 30–September 4. Revised and presented in this volume as Chapter 12, "Entrepreneurs and Managers."

Usher, A. P. [1929] 1954. *A History of Mechanical Inventions,* 2nd ed. Cambridge, Mass.: Harvard University Press.

Weeks, W. 1981. *Transmission and Distribution of Electrical Energy.* New York: Harper & Row.

Williamson, O. E. 1975. *Markets and Hierarchies: Analysis and Anti-Trust Implications.* New York: Free Press.

———— 1985. *The Economic Institutions of Capitalism.* New York: Free Press.

Woodbury, D. O. [1944] 1960. *Elihu Thomson: Beloved Scientist, 1853–1937.* Boston: Museum of Science.

Zorpette, G. 1985. "HVDC: Wheeling Lots of Power." *IEEE Spectrum* (June):30–36.

3

...

The "Docile" Body as an Economic-Industrial Growth Factor*

Rudolf Braun

Je ne me trompe point, le corps humain est une horloge, mais immense, et construite avec tant d'Artifice et d'Habileté, que si la roue qui sert à marquer les secondes vient à s'arrêter; celle des minutes tourne et va toujours son train.

If I am not mistaken, the human body is a clock, but huge and built with such artifice and cunning that if the second wheel stops, the minutes wheel continues to turn all the same.

J. O. de la Mettrie, *L'homme machine*, 1748

One of the classic topics in economic history is the question of capital funds: their mobilization, their allocation, and finally the way they are turned to effective use. This process of capital formation was and is in a state of continual motion, even with the global option and futures markets with their computer-controlled practices. Is it so farfetched to disregard, for once, this process of capital formation and focus instead on the process of "human capital formation"—the substitution of the "docile body" for "docile capital"? This, too, is a process which was and is in continuous motion, even to the extent of gene diagnostics as an instrument for career selection. In this chapter I will try to sketch this process, though the outline can be no more than rough and cursory. The sociocultural change and its scientific-ideological components will constitute the center of my interest. Practice, the working world itself, will be illuminated by several entr'actes. The reader will see, I hope, the processes of capital formation and those of human capital formation as an amalgamation.

At the beginning of the so-called Industrial Revolution, during the second half of the eighteenth century, there existed various forms of physical discipline and a culture of movement, in a coherence of the incoherent. We have, to begin with, the court culture of the late baroque period, epitomized in the art of

* Translated by Brigitte Helbling.

dancing: among the key words of this culture of body and movement were _air, grace,_ and _balance,_ signifying discipline, style, and sublimation. Elements of the dance were part of overall communicative behavior, and elements of behavior a part of dancing. Dancing lessons were the central means for instilling and solidifying behavioral patterns and distinctions of estate; they were, moreover, a basic requirement for making one's way in the highly differentiated hierarchy of court society.

Underlying this was a development of two hundred years' duration: Castiglione's *Book of the Courtier* (1528) experienced a rapid distribution in numerous translations and was widely acknowledged in an abundance of "courtesy literature."[1] The "polite learning" that was required for acquiring, demonstrating, putting to use, and thus amortizing the virtues and skills of an ideal courtier called for long-term investments with high opportunity costs and considerable risks. Idleness and dilettantism were part of the ritual self-portrayal of an "ideal courtier": the celebration of leisure instead of time saving, *l'art pour l'art* instead of the "useful arts," most strikingly manifest in the highly complex art mechanics, the baroque industry of automated figures. And, like these automatons, which were in need of an audience, the "ideal courtier" was continually on stage, subjected to unceasing constraints from within and without. He was expected to demonstrate a dainty, natural, seemingly innate "air," "grace," and "balance," but underlying these were constraints, inflicted by the self and the outside world, which can be compared with the mechanics of the automatons—mechanics that were controlled from outside.[2]

Nature was regarded as something that can be brought to bear only in the human determination to create—in domestication, in "mechanical laws"—a sort of second nature. This understanding of "nature" corresponds with the architecture, the landscape gardening, the literature, music, dance, and overall attitude toward movement of the late baroque period: "Like trees that are pruned and planted in symmetrical patterns, like the dancing master meticulously prescribing one's carriage, from head to feet and to the fingers, like the minuet, which is danced in set geometrical figures, such is the way in which the whole being of man is approached. Out of his 'first' nature, which is bulky and awkward, a 'second,' graceful nature is generated. Only those men that are thus domesticated and civilized can correctly occupy the place assigned to them by the society of estates according to ascribed rules" (Gugerli 1988, p. 23). One can speak of a "habitus," as Pierre Bourdieu did, meaning a system made up out of "organic or mental dispositions and unconscious patterns of thought, observation, and action" (Bourdieu 1974, p. 40).

The reverse side of the coin was a practice of physical discipline in the outgoing ancien régime based on severe constraints, coming from both the self and the outside world, which formed a contrasting picture to the "air," the "grace," the "balance": the new military drill. For hours on end, soldiers were taught how to stand and walk correctly, with or without arms, as if peasant boys from the Campagna or the Altmark were babies meant to be converted into automatons. Thus, for example, the Prussian "Royal Decree of June first 1776, in accordance with which the Exercitium Dero of the whole Infantry is to be established—upon Highest Command, translated from French into German" describes in detail "how the recruits shall be trained step by step." Under "the soldier's bearing," we read that he is to be accustomed "to immobility," and his "bearing" is described minutely, down to the very position of the eyes. This is followed by sections on "the recruit's first instruction in steps" or "points to be kept in mind during the drillmaster's first instruction in steps as well as the bearing for falling in with arms" (pp. 17ff.).

In this context, the Royal Decree maintains that "the ultimate objective attained by this step is above all the following: to approximate through mechanical laws the natural gait as closely as possible." Here, then, as well, "mechanical laws" are required to instill "natural" movement (p. 20). Contemporary literature, based on Descartes, compares the human body in various ways with a machine, especially with clockworks, notably in a book published in 1748 in Leyden under the title *L'homme machine*. The author, J. O. de la Mettrie, arrived, after "numerous physical observations," at the conclusion that human beings respond to the same mechanical principles of movement as a machine he had constructed (see Gendolla 1980, pp. 13ff.). Automated figures and human automatons: in the assembly rooms and the machinery cabinets of the princely courts of Europe, automated figures moved according to complex mechanical laws, while the movements of the court society—from paying reverence to dancing the minuet—were directed by complex social control mechanisms and automated regulations of behavior that had the effect of curbing spontaneous outbursts of emotion by formalizing and stylizing them. Outdoors, on the parade ground, soldiers were learning to become human automatons. Referring to these military drilling methods, Foucault remarks: "Thus, a politics of constraints is established, working at the body, calculating and manipulating its elements, its gestures, its reactions. The human body enters into a machinery of power, which penetrates it, takes it apart, and puts it together again" (Foucault 1979, p. 135).

In this culture of the body, as in so many other spheres of human life and cohabitation, the ancien régime forged the very arms that would ultimately defeat it.[3] This holds true in the first place for its physical education: even a passing look at the philanthropic-bourgeois reformist education, especially its new physical training and bodily education, provides sufficient evidence of the extent to which military drilling methods were incorporated in it. This is true although its underlying motivations, goals, and purposes were completely different, not least because of their hidden, unpolitical—thus exactly political—

opposition to the ancien régime's cultivation of the body, of movement and behavior, and its aristocratic exercise: as part of a performance syndrome— measurements, competitions, merit point collecting, speed and strength—the conduct of drill-like physical exercises by the collective, on command and under rigorous control, was recommended as an important element of reformist education as a whole.[4] In the case of bourgeois reformist education, the preparation of the human body as an obedient and submissive part of a machinery of power was already oriented toward work, competition, and performance, as, for example, when J. H. Pestalozzi (in Fetz 1973, 85) calls for a "sequence of artistic and force exercises" aiming at the improvement of "striking, pushing, turning, swinging, lifting, and kicking"; elementary physical education of this kind was seen as a "means to the method" in "effecting and establishing a trade force and industry."

In the second place, dancing in this period was literally undergoing a revolution in the couple-oriented round dance, especially the waltz. Unlike in the court dances, there was no geometry, symmetry, choreography, and artistry of gesture; an arbitrary number of couples were the unit of order and related only to themselves in close physical contact; "air" and "grace" were replaced by free, whirling, mechanical movements; speed produced an intoxicating—even erotically intoxicating—ecstasy; the nature of dancing was egalitarian and individualized rather than hierarchical.[5]

Certainly the way was paved for the breakthrough of this caesura in dance and movement behavior in part by court society: especially after the middle of the eighteenth century, choreographed self-constraints oriented toward hierarchy of estate led to an escapism, to a desire for rural idyll, for a simple way of life that expressed itself in, among other things, the dancing of country waltzes at fancy dress balls; "country weddings" were very popular.[6] The bourgeois revolution in dance, however, the waltz craze, cannot be seen as escapism in this way. This kind of dancing was, in the first place, a part of the emancipation of the bourgeoisie; precisely in the apolitical must we look for the politically oppositional. Second, the closed-couple, individualized speed dances served the quest of the bourgeoisie for self-discovery and self-representation. They expressed bourgeois and especially pietistical forms of relationship, soul friendship, the exchange of self-awareness, the heightened and intensified experience of the self in the reflection and analysis of the partner, partnerlike units of separate households, of inner lives, and so forth. Third, the dance revolution can be seen as the manifestation of a central phenomenon in this so-called *Sattelzeit* (the transitional generation in the late eighteenth century that marks the threshold of modernity)—a term we owe to the semantic studies of Koselleck—a transformation in the awareness of things, the modernity of which distinguishes itself by the institution of a new and more dynamic temporality *(Verzeitlichung).*[7]

Indeed, the new physical education of reformist education and the new style of dancing were part of the turning-point syndrome and must be interpreted in the light of this larger context. In a brilliant essay, Wolfgang Kemp draws attention to this wider perspective:

> Natural science thus inclined to classification is the basis for the development of the doctrine of physiognomy, mimicry, phrenology and proportions in the late 18th century, a science, therefore, that deducts the inside from the outward appearance—a doctrine of expression. It represents the effort to overcome the disturbed interaction of individuals through knowledge, doctrine and exercise. Pragmatic anthropology (Kant), the result of these efforts, is formed in an animated interrelation with all kinds of disciplines: the cult of the antique, which spills over into many domains, fundamental changes in the theatre and on the dance floor, in painting and sculpture, in fashion, education and above all in the new physical education must be taken into consideration as determining factors. (Kemp 1975, p. 118)

The disciplines referred to by Kemp as standing in animated interrelation have this in common: the human body as a field of research is surveyed with an inquiring, scientifically classifying eye, as if it held the promise of new ground to be broken. Behind these efforts was the desire to provide a counterpart to the aristocratic court repertoire of body language and personality-shaping forms of physical expression and interaction, a counterpart as varied as the pictures in a kaleidoscope and bearing the traits of the bourgeois working world and experience of life, thus serving as self-justification and self-portrayal; last but by no means least, it shows the fundamental difference "between a life that produces the means of subsistence, and one that only consumes them" (Kemp 1975, p. 119).

These efforts are founded, in part, on the awareness of a constitutive deficit in this area. This already finds expression in the writings of the reformist pedagogues, but most effectively in Goethe's *Wilhelm Meister's Apprenticeship and Travels*. Kemp devotes to this set of problems a subtle analysis at which I can merely hint: Wilhelm is eager to approach the ideal of a genteel life-style and thereby discovers the importance of outward appearance, the mimicry of body and face. He realizes that mere imitation can never be a practicable approach for the bourgeois—a dilemma which, apparently, cannot be resolved. Goethe writes:

> The bourgeois can earn himself a reputation and—at the utmost—cultivate his mind; but his personality loses out, whatever he may do . . . If a gentleman offers everything through the representation of his person, then the bourgeois gives nothing through his personality and is not expected to. The one is allowed and expected to put on appearances, the other must only be what he is and if he tries to put on appearances, the result is ridiculous and vulgar . . . It is not the presumptuousness of nobility and the pliability of the bourgeois that is responsible for this distinction, but the state of society.

Kemp sums up his analysis as follows: "The history of bourgeois behavior patterns is a story that has no end, no solution, a story made up out of half-hearted, even self-forgetful compromises."[8]

It is a telling fact that, for a bourgeois, one of the basic requirements for a genteel life-style, the cultivation of leisure, can be achieved only by thriftily calculating and saving time, so as to eke out some of it for leisure—a paradox: leisure is turned into leisure time. Free disposal of time for cultivating mind, body, and soul is one of the prerequisites of an enlightened concept of freedom; it is an "inalienable right" in a concept of freedom that is understood in temporal terms, a concept of freedom as free time. This has far-reaching consequences, above all in an increasingly sharpened contrast between working hours and spare time, between behavior patterns at work and in leisure hours, as well as an increasingly secularized thriftiness with time—consequences that are as self-evident as their long-term effects on economic-industrial development and the conflicts that are bound to arise with the reaction of employees to these demands and behavior (see Nahrstedt 1972, pp. 279ff.). The constitutive deficit of the bourgeois is not eliminated by this time-oriented concept of freedom, however, but in fact is reinforced, and certainly becomes increasingly obvious: for him, time is and remains money. His skills and ambitions are oriented toward efficiency; they are functionalized and used as instruments with respect to socioeconomic ends—a *vita activa*. By contrast, the essence of a genteel life-style embraces leisure and dilletantism—a secular *vita contemplativa*. Time and property are indispensable constitutive prerequisites.[9]

The bourgeois self-discovery, self-justification, and self-portrayal cannot direct itself toward the external, toward appearances; its object is the internal, the being. Therefore, in the light of genteel life-styles, the interior is analyzed, classified, and formed: the military drill methods and their incorporation into the physical education of the bourgeois; the new dance style; new disciplinary methods, not least those that are put into practice in the wake of reformist education in the elementary schools (seating order, physical discipline, punctuality, cleanliness, control of instincts, and so on); the striving for a personal body language; a scientific doctrine of expression; a new physical awareness of the body, hygiene, and health—this syndrome, which is by no means complete, can be taken as a new bourgeois "habitus," as defined by Pierre Bourdieu. It is based on a new understanding of "nature" that looks not to outer forms and structures but to those inside: "What mattered before in the location of the human body within the coordinates of geometry and proportion, as with the court dance, is now drawn into the body of the being dancing in the world. It is now expected to subjugate itself from within to those principles that had until then served it in the acquisition of the object world with the aim of governing it."[10] Because of this, new educational methods and, as a part of them, new physical training gain a special importance, since the economic, social, and political processes of emancipation must be coupled with an inner firmness and discipline, with the incorporation of constraints inflicted by the self and the outside world, with the domination of nature in one's own body.[11]

Max Weber convincingly demonstrated the religious-dogmatic roots of this new bourgeois "habitus," an interior asceticism, a rationalization of one's conduct of life to the glory of God and as an impetus for the methodical control of the degree of the state of grace; a state of grace that must be documented and controlled both through interior asceticism and with rational methods, precisely because of its irrationality of a twofold predestination. It is particularly for this reason that the rational organization of existence oriented toward God's will becomes accessible for secularization—a secularization in quest of the way inside, the domination of nature in one's own body by the means of an ethic-moral humanistic compass. A largely secularized ethos in matters of profession, acquisition, and work is part of the new "habitus," although the work ethos, which is detached from the acquisition ethos, is also instilled—through indoc-trination and constraints—in the worker. The new "habitus" of the bourgeoisie serves as an underlay for the conception and practical introduction of a new way of working with and at the machine in the centralized production sites of the manufacturing system, a way of working that tries to gain control over the body of those afflicted by it, "not only so they will do what they are told, but also that they will work the way one wants them to: with the techniques, with the speed, with the efficiency that is required. Discipline in this way produces subjugated and trained bodies, pliant and docile bodies" (Foucault 1979, p. 138).

Entr'acte: Glimpses of Concrete Early Industrial Work Requirements and Working Conditions

Let us first take a look at an early industrial, albeit hardly mechanized, enter-prise, a cotton printery in the Swiss canton of Glarus. A feature of this mountain region after 1800 is its early printing industry. Omitting all background infor-mation, I shall confine myself to the conditions at one workplace[12]: the hand-block printers in a factory with 500 workers in the 1860s. The work process was based on the division of labor, and yet was already archaic for that day and age: the cylinder printing machine, which had been in existence for some time, had not yet been introduced. The cantonal factory inspector, as well as a committee of experts appointed by the cantonal government, undertook an investigation of these archaic working conditions. The committee at one point provided the following description of the work of the block printers: "The unchanging mo-tion from the printing table to the dyes, and then back again to the printing table, which is repeated hundreds of times a day, as well as the mechanically regular application of the block, are performed with such haste and speed as to dumbfound the unbiased observer at first." The blocks of the head printer—a man's work—weighed up to 14 kilograms; in subsequent printing processes, where women were also employed, the blocks used were lighter (some weighing only 1 kilogram). The task of the head printer required physical strength and assiduity as well as precision, skill, and concentration; each error was visible and could not be corrected. During a ten-hour workday the head printer immersed his heavy block 1,100 to 1,400 times into the so-called chassis (pad for dyeing the blocks) and applied it 1,100 to 1,400 times to the cloth, using a wooden mallet to pound it down four times with each application. A tear-boy replaced the dye in the chassis and spread it. This operation took place twice a minute. Since the Glarus cotton printery specialized in producing cheap mass articles, speedy work was essential, and for months on end the same block and the same color dye were used for the same article in endless monotony. The conditions at the workplace were characterized by a lack of space (despite the large workroom), heat, humidity, and an atmosphere polluted by vapors from the dyes that varied according to color in their degree of toxicity and physical irritation. These conditions were often aggravated by the fact that the printers tended to skip their dinner break and instead refreshed themselves, with dye-stained fingers, at their work station, in the midst of heat, dust, and vapors.

Reports from the factory inspector (a physician, Dr. Schuler) and the experts committee discuss in detail the effects of printing on health and body. The work itself was performed standing, in a slightly stooped position, so that the printing block could be applied precisely to the cloth. This led to physical deformations: "Thus, feeble, thin calves and overdeveloped, strongly protruding chest and arm muscles, a stooping carriage, considerable impressions in the lower region of the thorax are common among our workers," Dr. Schuler writes, and the report of the experts mentions "malformations that explain many an appearance among the Glarus working population." The vapor from the dyes—acetic acid, hydrochloric acid, turpentine, aniline dye, mercurials—caused an "irritation of the mucous membrane, the respiratory organs, and the eyes" and led to a loss of weight and appetite, a sensation of thirst, headaches, and rashes, among other things.

There is no ignoring the objection: we all know about early industrial manufacturing systems and their exploitation of the human work force, but all this was abolished with the development of mechanical engineering and technological progress. The cylinder printing machine did in fact put an end to such working conditions as those outlined herein. As early as 1835, Edward Baines (1835, pp. 265ff.) enthusiastically describes a cotton-printing manufacture equipped with a cylinder printing machine as "a wonderful triumph of science

. . . a splendid and matchless exhibition of science applied to the arts,'' and goes on to calculate how many hands can be spared by the machine.

Certainly, workhands were saved, the increase in productivity was immense, and the purely physical exertion during work was in no way comparable to that of the hand-block printer. But the "pliant and docile" body, with its potential for adaptation, was now compelled to meet new demands: the speed and the working rhythm of the machine. The "British Parliamentary Papers" contain pages and pages of reports on working conditions and the workloads of men, women, and children operating the cylinder machine. Environmental influences were no less damaging than with hand-block printing, and here too we find numerous complaints about meals being taken at the work station so that the machines could be kept running. What it means to be driven by a machine is recorded in the memoirs of Robert Blincoe, who started working at the Lowdham cotton mill in 1799, when he was only seven, and was put to work at a roving winder. "Being too short of stature to reach his work, standing on the floor, he was placed on a block; but this expedient remedied only a part of the evil; for he was not able, by any possible exertion to keep pace with the machinery. In vain, the poor child declared it was not in his power to move quicker. He was beaten by the overseer with great severity and cursed and reviled from morning to night." In these memoirs there is also an example of how the rhythm of the machine was used as an instrument in the education and punishment of the body to make it docile: "On one occasion, an overseer had hung Blincoe above a machine so that he had to lift his leg, to avoid losing it, every time the machine turned."[13]

But let us return to the more general point, the question of man in correlation with, on the one hand, his "docile" body, and, on the other hand, the machine, the organization of work, and the working process.

Adam Smith tries to explain the division of labor on the basis of human nature. Andrew Ure turns it into an apologetic "philosophy": "The adaption of the worker to every specialized operation forms the very essence of the division of labour" (cited in Marx [1887], I, 330, n. 4). Marx refers to Ure in *Kapital*, although naturally his analysis is devoid of any spirit of apology:

> After Manufacture has once separated, made independent, and isolated the various operations, the labourers are divided, classified, and grouped according to their predominating qualities. If their natural endowments are, on the one hand, the foundation on which the division of labour is built up, on the other hand, Manufacture, once introduced, develops in them new powers that are by nature fitted only for limited and special functions . . . The habit of doing only one thing converts him [the worker] into a never failing instrument, while his connexion with the whole mechanism compels him to work with the regularity of the parts of a machine.   (Marx [1887], I, 330)

To elucidate this last statement, Marx quotes the reply of a factory manager to a question from an inspector of the Children's Employment Commission (1865) on how children can be kept at their work: "They cannot well neglect their work; when they once begin, they must go on; they are just the same as parts of a machine" (I, 330, n. 3). They are treated, according to Dugald Stewart, as "living automatons" (I, 340, n. 2); living automatons whose behavioral characteristics, precisely when they are independent and creative, represent an interference factor in the overall mechanism. For Andrew Ure, "by the infirmity of human nature, it happens that the more skilful the work man, the more self-willed and intractable he is apt to become, and of course the less fit a component of a mechanical system in which . . . he may do great damage to the whole" (I, 346–347). Selection, indoctrination, reward, and constraint—either from the machine itself or from factory discipline—are the means for adapting man and his "docile" body to the rhythm of the machine, the organization of work, and the working process. In the manufacturing system, "social organization of the working process can only be attained by chaining the same worker to the same detail." The maximization of profit, not the devil, is in the details (I, 365).

While Andrew Ure and other advocates of economic liberation praise mechanical engineering almost euphorically, it is seen by others as a menace to mankind, above all by the educated middle classes: "The prevalence of mechanical engineering distresses and frightens me: slowly, slowly, like a thunder storm, it is rolling towards us, but it has taken its course and will eventually hit its mark." It is symptomatic that Goethe puts these much-quoted words into the mouth of Wilhelm Meister.[14] It is equally symptomatic that during this time (from about 1790 to 1820), the automaton gains a central importance in the literature of romanticism, a subject which is associated with nightmarish fears (in German literature, above all in the writings of Jean Paul and E. T. H. Hoffmann). Peter Gendolla (1980) has studied this problem: the mechanical man as a fatal threat to mankind in the literature of romanticism is not, according to Gendolla, an immediate danger, as with the golem legend or modern science fiction, but rather one that is indirect, and all the greater for that reason. Artificial man carries traits that bear a frightening resemblance to natural man. An intangible force seems to control the thoughts, emotions, and physical movements of natural man: "Like a puppet, the human body responds to an external will, but this will no longer has metaphysical origins, but instead arises from and takes effect in social behavior." The confrontation with mechanical man exposes the human machine: "Therein, he perceives the construction of the self, the living interior is just as prone to artificial or technical manipulation"; and because of this, the mechanical men are destroyed in self-defense.[15]

It is telling that the mechanical arts during the close of the ancien régime— *l'art pour l'art,* the delight of princes and courtiers—served as an inspiration for the "useful arts" in the bourgeois milieu: a chess player automaton that was exhibited in London (and later turned out to be a fake) inspired the clerical gentleman Edmund Cartwright to construct the mechanical loom in 1785.[16] But it is precisely these "useful arts," inventions oriented toward work and productivity, as well as the working conditions and working organizations established in the wake of their implementation, that are responsible for the alarmed awareness of the educated middle classes concerning the adaptation of human beings to automatons. The automaton metaphor is interpreted in a new light as a thing controlled from inside—a side effect in the new bourgeois "habitus" of the so-called *Sattelzeit*.[17]

Can this romantic literature of the automaton also be interpreted as an early recognition of a change in paradigm? In any case, these threatening, hominoid puppets open up new prospects that look within, prospects that are linked with the displacement of patterns of interpretation and behavior based on theological and philosophical moral concepts by scientific-biologistical patterns of thought, order, and classification. I will mention only biological characterizations of the role of the sexes, the hygienization of living and cohabitation, the setting up of standards for health care, eating habits, and the control of instincts. Underlying these are complex processes related to scientific history and scientific ideology that can themselves be associated with sociocultural changes during the second half of the nineteenth century. They can be touched on here only as key words. In the tradewind of faith in science and progress, the nineteenth century produces a wide range of specialized scientific disciplines striving for independence, professionalization, and incorporation into the curriculum of universities and technical colleges, as well as sociopolitical and socioeconomic recognition and influence. The research into the human body plays a large role in this process.[18]

The adoption of the concept of energy from physics as a model for thought, organization, and experiment by H. von Helmholtz in the middle of the nineteenth century can be seen as an important caesura. "Energy became the highest principle of nature," observes A. Rabinbach (1985), in a study of the utmost importance for our subject. He demonstrates how the metaphor of the mechanical man was rendered obsolete by the adoption of the concept of energy:

> What arrives in its place is the energumen, the creator of movement or energy—the motor. This change is at the heart of the new metaphor, articulated by Hermann von Helmholtz, who in 1854 proclaimed that the human machine more accurately resembles a power machine, which transforms matter into "work-energy" . . . What distinguished the Helmholtzian paradigm from that of the mechanists was the universality of energy in all manifestations of nature . . . The capacity for energy production became the leitmotif of a body seen as a system of economics of force with quantifiable rules.[19]

This transference of the concept of energy to the "docile" body, and the "human motor" as a new metaphor, defines the automatic inner control in terms of biology and physiology. This has far-reaching consequences, for scientific history as well as for social ideology; Rabinbach (1985, p. 18) writes: "Social Helmholtzianism thus offered the promise of a labor force that did not have to be inculcated with eternal truth about the importance of will, the sin of idleness, or the value of work. Moral exhortations, the idealization of the 'sublime' worker, and even the reflections of the political economists on the worker's 'system of need' began to appear obsolete. In their place emerged a scientific and medicalized discourse on labor, corporal physics instead of appeals to conscience."[20]

The way is now cleared for adjusting the "docile" body as a working body, a "human motor" with psychophysical and physiological peculiarities, to the conditions at work and the workplace, selecting, controlling, correcting, stimulating, in such a way as to attain an optimum of efficiency and productivity in the time assigned to work. Not until now does the "docile" body truly enter into "a machinery of power that penetrates it, takes it apart and puts it together again" (Foucault 1977). New prospects in research are opened up; new specialized scientific disciplines are put into service for this task or offer their services in striving toward professionalization: experimental psychology (estranged from philosophy and oriented toward physiology) splits up into subsections such as applied psychology, behavioralism, industrial psychology, psychotechnics—which are all experimentally active in, above all, the area of selection, motivation, stimulation—and personality evaluations with laboratory experiments, testing methods, and a variety of apparatus. All these subsections are geared to the practical side. Experimental hygienics develops into industrial physiology and, more generally, industrial medicine, which deals with constitutional types and reactions as well as with biochemical and biogenetic cybernetics, work-related neurological and somatic problems, and so on: it looks as if the hitherto unfathomable interior may now be deciphered.

A basic issue in these studies is the question of limiting values; from limiting values during work efforts to limiting values in the resorption of noxious emissions at the workplace. This concept of limiting values—which has today, more than ever, a sociopolitical relevance and vital importance in connection with environmental pollution—provides industrial medicine with exclusive control of thresholds and checkpoints. At the same time, studies of constitutional types and selection tests gain an additional importance for the assignment of work (see Milles and Müller 1987, pp. 20ff.).

Contemporary trends in social science served as an ideological underlay and as connecting links: theories of heredity and race, determinism, social Darwinism, natural selection. They could also be used as justificational ideologies in pseudoscientific studies and practices. "Time and motion" studies, for example, provided the Taylor system with a scientific rationale: right after the turn of the century, this system was developed by Frederick W. Taylor and applied in practice; a system that measures the worker's movements, down to the smallest conceivable unit, in order to study them, translate them into mathematical formulas, and bring them into line with optimal efficiency. It goes without saying that limiting values was what Taylorism aspired to as well.

These examples must suffice. All of these efforts in research have gained in practical relevance since the late nineteenth century; after World War I they interlocked into what is summed up in the term *scientific management*. Economic-industrial changes during this time further enhanced this development: the so-called Great Depression; innovations in the area of technology and factory organization; so-called organized capitalism; wartime economy. It is an interesting fact that the "docile" body was subjected to being "taken apart and put together again" by other contemporary interest groups as well. The era of imperialism and militarism produced, especially in Germany, an abundance of "studies and manuals on the physical economy of drill and other aspects of military training."[21] The sports movement, spreading from England throughout the world since the last quarter of the nineteenth century and establishing a forum for international contests with the Olympic games, provided the basis for a new sports medicine, looking toward the ever higher, farther, faster. Its methods and aims in research are comparable to, even interchangeable with, those figuring in industrial medicine or "scientific management."

Entr'acte: An Example from the Origins of "Scientific Management"

The Bally shoe factory was the first industrial enterprise in Switzerland to send—even before World War I—a delegation to the United States to learn about "scientific management" and to visit Hugo Munsterberg, a pioneer of industrial psychology, and Taylor. This study trip was conducted in the autumn of 1913 and is even mentioned in the German translation of Taylor's *Shop Management* under the heading "latest successes": "Vier Herren dieser Firma (Bally & Co.) sind augenblicklich mit dem eingehenden Studium der Verfahren in den Vereinigten Staaten beschäftigt" (Four gentlemen of this company [Bally & Co.] are at this moment occupied with a thorough study of the procedures in the United States).[22]

The delegation was well prepared for its task: "rationalizations" toward an optimum increase in efficiency and performance had already been introduced into various departments of the enterprise during the preceding years. Thus, for example, time studies had led to a modification of day rates in the sewing of trimmings during the year before the study trip: 6.40 francs for 80 sets, as compared with 7.91 francs for 43 sets. Conditions for the performance of such a masterpiece of rationalization were favorable: some years before, the company had made a clean sweep of all trade union activities within its premises, and Bally held almost exclusive control over the local job market, which consisted mainly of worker-peasants. In short, everything was ready for the reception of Munsterberg and Taylor. To see the thing through properly, a young member of the delegation, a qualified engineer from the Federal Institute of Technology, was left behind in the United States for half a year to study Taylorism on the spot, that is, in the factory. On his return, he was appointed head of the Department of Organization and Wages and set about Taylorizing the Bally shoe factory step by step.

Jaun (1986) has reconstructed the different stages; our interest lies in the fact that this was a *Hamlet* without the prince, that is, Taylorism without the high wage policy. Although various measures and devices had resulted in a considerable increase in the already existing piece-rate tasks (which fixed the number of pieces to be attained per shift), the profit was skimmed off by the management, day wages had been set beforehand, and the quota was fixed on such a scale as to render it virtually impossible to exceed the day wage through increased performance. For the employee, the ratio of wage to performance worsened considerably. A new system of supervision carried a "hitherto unknown amount of rationality and transparency into the organization of labor. Output and wages can be controlled daily, apparent extra earnings and a lowered performance are immediately visible and open to correction" (Jaun 1986). In the company's staff newspaper *Schwyzerhusli*, the Taylor system is portrayed to the staff as an energy-saving work method or division of labor, equally applicable to the watering of vegetables during leisure time as to fashionable shoe production. The management does not allow this genre picture to be marred: when a worker wishes to hold a lecture on the Taylor system, this is prevented and the worker is reprimanded.

The absence of the stimulus of high wages and the special conditions in the job market, with a regionally limited recruiting pool that permits rigorous hiring and firing, raises the notion of special methods in training, motivation, and stimulation as well as aptitude tests. Ivan Bally, impressed by the writings of Munsterberg, made the acquaintance of the Zurich experimental psychologist Jules Suter—later head of the Institute for Psychotechnology—in 1914. From 1915 to 1917, Suter conducted work-psychology experiments in various departments at C. F. Bally: aptitude tests, a sewing school for training tests, a regulation of breaks, and so on. The underlying creed was the interesting point: the goal, totally in line with Taylor, was the achievement of an optimal continuous performance. Thus, for example, Suter drew the following conclusion from his investigations: "The present performance graph from room V is still far from reaching the maximum that is attainable and in no way injurious to the worker"—limiting values as a given aim! Qualification tests were used for the achievement of an optimal continuous performance: mechanical devices measured the visual power, speed of movement, freedom of movement, tactile sensitivity, and speed of reaction. Proceeding from the "decisive fact" that human beings have "more or less differentiated and fixed behavioral habits that have little or nothing in common with the rational economic activity that modern work calls for," Suter, influenced by Pestalozzi, conceived a sewing school, where young workwomen were trained step by step to achieve a steady top-level performance. Suter gave all the credit for the astonishing increase in performance to his experiments, whose efficacy can, of course, be doubted. A gratuity, received in advance from the management, was accepted with the assurance of earning "your trust and cooperation." It presumably paid off: the "docile" body as growth factor—"links to larger processes of economic development"!

After World War I and a brief but violent postwar recession (1920–1922), the adoption and propagation of "scientific management" was speeded up, thus acquiring the characteristics of a syndrome: the interdisciplinary scientific instrumentary was constantly enlarged and refined, the human body tested, controlled, and corrected down to its very secretion of adrenaline, its responses to stimuli and exhaustion, its susceptibility to stress, its powers of concentration, and so on. A varied technical arsenal was brought in for the dissection: photo cells and work films documented every work-oriented movement, which was subsequently evaluated by a sequential timekeeper; electrodes registered the stimulus response of the central nervous system, while the Fusion Frequency Test examined the irritability of the eyes; musical accompaniment, short breaks, alternating work stations, all were studied with respect to their effect on an increase in efficiency, performance, and concentration; the running speed of assembly lines was regulated according to prior tests of concentration and exhaustion, in such a way as to achieve the maximum output per shift. One could carry on this enumeration endlessly. Workers were studied, selected, motivated, stimulated, and controlled as if they were white mice or laboratory rats.

In our day the diagnosis of genes in laboratories already includes their evaluation for a selection at the workplace; will we be spared the next step, the manipulation of genes in the service of work selection?[23] Even white-collar workers are no longer spared the testing and control apparatus of "scientific management": their work-specific behavior is studied as well as their general attitude, from personality ratings to the electronic calculation and control of the number of strokes per minute at the typewriter; from stress analysis to an abbreviation of the response times on the computer screen meant to increase the powers of concentration. Naturally, this "scientific management" has no lack of apologists and creators of justifying ideologies, the Andrew Ures of the twentieth century, from Henry Ford to the human relations experts who open up the sphere of family and leisure to research on "scientific management," and wrap up the whole in appealing phrases such as "objectivity in wage-setting and collective bargaining," "the basis for a reduction of work hours," and "humanizing the world of labor." Skepticism, let alone any critical objection, is warded off skillfully: "That is no more than an inability to come to terms with a past ridden with class struggle. The humanization of work is an economic necessity and a social progress" *(Industrielle organisation* 1973, p. 560).

A further feature of the expanding syndrome of "scientific management" is the fact that the numerous disciplines are not only dovetailed and complementary to one another, but also assist one another in opening up new fields of research, experiment, and possible profit. Studies of motion and time concerning an optimum increase in output give access to physio-psychological fields of research in the domain of exhaustion, monotony, stimulus response, stress, causes of accidents, and so forth. Answers are sought that hold the promise of new areas of expertise in industry and economy, as in aptitude tests and new training methods. If, for example, accident research tends to be oriented solely toward the worker, neglecting the technical organization of the overall environment, then aptitude tests and selection expertise may step in with the promise of eliminating an accident-prone employee. The fact that "scientific management" makes use of theories and methods from natural science, such as experiments, laboratory tests, mathematical classification systems, and quantification, also requires that its results be represented as science, free of value judgments, to the economic system and society. This has the further advantage that there is no need to accept responsibility: the goal is set and the overall conditions fixed; man must be adapted to his work and not the work adapted to man. This does not need to be expressed as explicitly as in Munsterberg (1912, p. 188):

> Thus applied industrial psychology is totally dominated by the notion of economic ends. We must immediately complete this observation with another one: One must emphasize that industrial psychotechnology does not concern itself with an investigation of the end it serves. Like every technical science, applied psychology establishes what must be done, but only in such a way as to say: If you want to gain a certain end, you must follow this course, you must employ this and this device. It is no concern of technical science whether the end itself is the right one.[24]

Such a straightforward text can of course be encoded in numerous ways; and there is no shortage of encoded texts that have been incorporated as ideologies during the process of change in which the "scientific management" expert turns professional—from psychotechnicians to timekeepers, and from work physiologists to human relations experts and economic moral philosophers. A further factor is that any efforts or aims in "scientific management" that tend toward an improvement in the employee's situation (concerning wages or conditions at the workplace) are often not put into practice, as is illustrated by the example of the Bally Company.

The development of the syndrome of "scientific management" after World War I coincides with a new perception and culture of the body: an enthusiasm for new, accelerated rhythms, movements, dances, sports, gymnastics, parades, and musical shows, together with the assimilation of jazz and other styles of music with faster motor rhythms, as well as for new fashions and physical care accentuating the body and geared to youth. Acceleration coupled with disciplined precision exerts fascination; the legs of chorus girls seem to reflect the assembly lines in the collective precision of their movements. In 1922 Pierre Winter writes in the magazine *Esprit nouveau:* "It [sport] introduces the law of that equilibrium which governs work and breaks. It imparts to us a precision in our gestures and their coordination. It trains us to react fast. It gives the factor of time its due position in modern life." Some weeks before, in an article with the title "Le corps nouveau" in the same magazine, Winter had predicted: "The exaltation of athletes is conquering the world, and their charisma will be immeasurable. Painters, sculptors, poets, you all will come to feel it."[25] And feel it they did; as, for example, Fernand Léger, who made the new culture of the body into one of the central motifs in his work and was commissioned to create a suitable monumental mural for the "hall for the culture of the body" in the French pavilion at the World's Fair in Brussels in 1935. This spirit of the time seems to echo the *Sattelzeit;* all spheres of life are dovetailed into a kind of syndrome, undergoing a process of change: from the new perception of time in the theory of relativity to dance, from fashion to pictorial arts. This new "habitus" condenses in a cultic, excessive elevation of sports and physical culture. In an essay in the 1925 *Europa-Almanach* with a book jacket designed by Léger, Hermann Kasack (cited in Mauer 1988) sees sport as the "most up-to-date embodiment of the spirit." The new perception and culture of the body develop into a mass phenomenon. Scientific sports literature begins to fill libraries: biomechanics, physiology, and psychology of tests, training doctrines, and so on. The results and aims as well as the way they are put into practice correspond to those of industrial medicine and "scientific management." The main concern in both cases is an increase in efficiency, expanding the limits of capacity, conquering the limits of exhaustion by hook or by crook—right down to the use of illegal drugs; in both cases the goal set is new limiting values.[26]

The planning of recreational activities and dealing with free time become the reproduction of planning and accomplishment at work: competitive sports, jogging, exercising, constant exposure to multimedia stimuli in disco dancing, listening to the Walkman while doing homework, playing computer games, and so forth. The education of children—with computers and telecommunication—already emphasizes a steady, concentrated occupation with video screens, signs, symbols, and formal-logical procedures during work time—a process of socialization which is growing more and more important in the course of mastering one's life and making one's way in the working world, and which has a vital though hardly calculable significance in its consequences for the individual and society.

Computers bear a growing resemblance to human beings: they play chess; they are looked on as friends who are always available; they even trigger a state of dependence similar to that with a lover. Preschool children already discuss the question of whether computers are "alive" and what might be the difference between computers and themselves.[27] The line between man and computer seems to be growing indistinct. On the one hand, computers and programs are constructed after the model of man: the professed aim of artificial intelligence is to develop programs that can think and speak like human beings. As long as this is not possible, computers can at least simulate these abilities; this is called "user-friendliness": programs that "understand" natural language, or blink a friendly "welcome" from the screen.

On the other hand, people bear more and more resemblance to computers: in their capacity for digesting stimuli, in the way they are programmed for work and free time, and, above all, in the fact that the mechanics of the computer are used as a model for self-perception. Expressions originating in the field of computer technology are gradually infiltrating psychology, as well as the psychology of everyday life: "You're programmed all wrong." "There's a bug in your system." These are expressions that point to a shift from the psychoanalytical to the computer model of man, where there is hardly room for the subconscious and the unconscious: Freudianism is being devalued. In our day computers have already become, in J. D. Bolter's words, a "defining technology," a technology that influences our view of society, nature, and man, as did clockworks or the steam engine in former times.

> A defining technology develops links, metaphorical or otherwise, with a culture's science, philosophy, or literature; it is always available to serve as a metaphor, example, model, or symbol . . . Plato compared the created universe to a spindle, Descartes thought of animals as clockwork mechanisms, and scientists in the nineteenth century and early twentieth century have regularly compared the universe to a heat engine that is slowly squandering its fuel. Today the computer is constantly serving as a metaphor for the human mind or brain: psychologists speak of the input and output, sometimes even the hardware and software, of the brain; linguists treat human language as if it were a programming code; and everyone speaks of making computers "think."[28]

What cannot be integrated into this rational model of psychic procedures—intuition and creativity, for example, irrational, subcognitive layers of human knowledge—is gradually pushed aside as unimportant or even looked on as an interference factor in the smooth running of the machinery.

The metaphor of the "human computer" has become a household expression, and "being programmed" is used by schoolchildren for describing human communicative behavior. Therefore, once again, metaphors for the human body are precipitations of a "habitus," in Bourdieu's sense of the term, meaning a system made up of "organic or mental dispositions and unconscious patterns of thought, observation, and action." They determine and set the limits for, among other things, an awareness of problems, their definition, and the ability to solve them. The integration of the metaphor of "human computers" into everyday language has far-reaching consequences; we should take this into account.

The "docile body" as an economic-industrial growth factor: ergonomy is the science of the adaptation of work to human beings. Industry and economy have been and still are hesitant to accept ergonomic propositions: ergonomy does not yet bear the promise of a gold mine. Will the postmodern developments—computerization, microelectronics, telecommunication—give ergonomy a second chance? One of the most important preconditions would be that the "docile body" be given more attention in an analysis and evaluation of "larger processes of economic development."

Notes

1. For England, see Wigham (1984, chap. 1); on court society in general, see Elias (1983).

2. Contemporary dancing compendiums contain not only chapters on the "regulated carriage" or the "well-regulated gait," but also others on taking off and putting on one's hat, making different reverences, and so on. See, for example, Taubert (1717). Note that these externally controlled mechanics correspond with contemporary scientific research, in particular with the formulation of the laws of kinetics.

3. On the same phenomenon in other spheres of life, see Braun (1984, pp. 282ff.).

4. Vieth (in Fetz 1970, VIII, 9ff.), for instance, states that "a kind of military drill" should be enforced in gymnastic exercises.

5. See also J. W. Goethe, *Die Leiden des jungen Werther,* letter of June 16.

6. This is described by many contemporary writers; see, for instance, Casanova (1965, VI, 56ff.). "Air," "grace," and "balance" were replaced by coarsely rural, closed-couple dances accompanied by crudely sensual vulgarities instead of refined, subtly erotic sign language.

7. See also the introduction to Brunner, Conze, and Koselleck (1972, I, xiiiff). Koselleck emphasizes that the *Verzeitlichung* of terms may not be seen as isolated: "All specified criteria— democratization, temporalization, ideologizability, and politicization—are linked to one another" (p. xviii). The propagation of a connection between waltz rhythms and/or velocity dances and the new mechanical engineering seems to suggest itself, and is sometimes attempted. This seems to me a rather questionable, short-circuited association, however.

8. Kemp (1975, p. 120). Quotation from Goethe, p. 124; general analysis of *Wilhelm Meister,* pp. 122–130.

9. As a kind of substitution or deficit compensation, the bourgeois woman in the nineteenth century is entrusted with the demonstration and celebration of leisure, dilettantism, and *l'art pour l'art.*

10. Gugerli (1988, p. 232). The interior is mysterious, unfathomable: precisely because of this comes the attempt to judge the inside by the outside (as in studies in physiognomy, for example).

11. Rudolf zur Lippe's thesis belongs in this context: "The tendency of instrumental action on nature and the institutionalization of relations between members of a society converge in this form of dominating nature in one's own body" (cited in Gugerli 1988, p. 232).

12. See also Heer and Kern (1989, chap. 3, pp. 89–185) for details.

13. Blincoe (1977, pp. 29, 56). On factory discipline in general, see the already classic work by Sidney Pollard (1965); Pollard stresses the fact that discipline was a new, crucial, even vital problem for the early industrial entrepreneur.

14. Goethe-Quelle, see Kemp (1975, p. 128).

15. Gendolla (1980, pp. 4ff.); also: "In this sense—as a reflection of the relation between inner forces and outward appearances—automatons enter the field of literature, at a time when the real automatons had already lost the attention of society and were gathering dust in the collections of a few amateurs" (p. 10).

16. Guest (1823, pp. 44ff.), cited in Smelser (1960, p. 131). During a conversation with some gentlemen of Manchester on the excessive supply of cotton, Cartwright observed that in this case, Arkwright would have to invent the weaving mill. The gentlemen rejected the idea as impracticable. "And in defence of their opinion, they adduced arguments which I certainly was incompetent to answer or even to comprehend, being totally ignorant of the subject, having never at the time seen a person weave. I controverted, however, the impracticability of the thing, by remarking that there had lately been exhibited in London, an automation figure, which played at chess. Now you will not assert, gentlemen, said I, that it is more difficult to construct a machine that shall weave, than one which shall make all the variety of moves which are required in that complicated game."

17. Surely it may be seen as a symptom that the automatons in the nineteenth century, especially in the second half, were used as toys for upper-middle-class children, toys that were controlled from inside instead of outside: dolls that could move, open their eyes, speak (by means of a built-in phonograph), play music, and so on.

18. Bear in mind specialized disciplines such as physiology, psychology, psychiatry, biology, biochemistry, hygienics, neurology, pathology, and all the rest; there exists an extensive literature on the development of these specialized disciplines and their national differentiations.

19. Rabinbach (1985, pp. 5ff.); see also Akert (1986–87, pp. 3ff.).

20. Rabinbach (1985, p. 8). This social Helmholtzianism coupled with the time-related concept of freedom and its practical interpretation (leisure time versus work hours) means that the body is hardly ever made into a topic in negotiations between employers and employees; the regulation of salary and work hours are the first, even exclusive issues. Michel Foucault (1977) speaks of a "bio-force" and writes: "Surely, this bio-force was an indispensable component in the evolution of capitalism, which would not have been possible without the controlled participation of the body in production plants and without the adaptation of phenomena in the population to economic processes" (p. 168). See also Labisch (1987, pp. 7ff.); this study is important for our subject in other respects as well.

Unfortunately, the limits of this chapter do not allow a differentiation and separate study of the set of problems concerning the man-woman topic. I would therefore like to point to the concluding chapter in Gendolla (1980), which contains a digression bearing the title "Exkurs: 'Die Eva der Zukunft,' oder Warum der Automat Eine Frau Ist." On the special interest in terms of woman in the research of industrial medicine in connection with "bio-force" and social Helmholtzianism, see also Milles and Müller (1987, pp. 27ff.), where we read: "Since the end of the century, woman has become a main factor in research and argumentation whenever the object was the consolidation of the male norm biography."

21. Rabinbach (1985, p. 18); here we find biographical data on this research oriented toward sports and the military system.

22. Rudolf Jaun (1986, chap. 3) discusses this Bally example in detail.

23. On this subject, see Daele (1985); also Chargaff (1986).

24. See also Ruegsegger (1986).

25. Cited in Mauer (1988, pp. 31ff.). Milles and Müller (1987, p. 5) write: "One observes a new way of dealing with the body; the cleaning and strengthening of one's body stand in the center of the modern feeling of life . . . The body can be experienced and formed, it renders possible a confirmation and control of the self." In this context they quote from an essay by Mrazek and Rittner (1986, p. 62): "The new forms of attention to the body seem in all probability to stand in connection to the stress of the industrial society, and therefore have a vital importance."

26. For all that, it is remarkable that these phenomena can be observed on both sides of the Iron Curtain. Taylorism and "scientific management" were discussed in the USSR as early as the 1920s; in the area of sports medicine as well as in other areas concerned with the achievement of record performances in sports, Eastern Europe took the lead after World War II. It would be illustrative to enter into the methods of selection, training and conditioning, daily and seasonal planning, and so on, from motivation to nutrition, from the protraction of the limits of exhaustion to autogenous training and psychological care by experts. We must forgo this, however, and also forgo entering into the concrete situation at the workplace in the era of computers and workers at their video display terminals, for instance, or in computer-controlled production facilities.

27. See on this the treatise by Turkle (1984) on the cultural-consequential effects of computerization.

28. Bolter 1986, p. 11. I should like to thank Bettine Heintz, who is working on a dissertation on the cultural significance of computers in connection with the processes of social change, for the references to Turkle and Bolter.

References

Akert, K. 1986–87. *Gedanken über die psychische Energie.* University of Zurich, Annual Report.

Baines, E. 1835. *History of the Cotton Manufacture in Great Britain.* London.

Blincoe, R. [1825] 1977. *A Memoir of Robert Blincoe, an Orphan Boy,* ed. J. Brown. Manchester.

Bolter, J. D. 1986. *Turing's Man: Western Culture in the Computer Age.* Middlesex.

Bourdieu, P. 1974. *Zur Soziologie der symbolischen Formen.* Frankfurt am Main.

Braun, R. 1984. *Das ausgehende Ancien Régime in der Schweiz.* Göttingen.

Brunner, O., W. Conze, and R. Koselleck, eds. 1972–85. *Geschichtliche Grundbegriffe: Historisches Lexikon zur politisch-sozialen Sprache in Deutschland.* 5 vols. Stuttgart.

Casanova, G. 1965. *Geschichte meines Lebens,* ed. E. Loos. Berlin.

Chargaff, E. 1986. "Der kunstgestopfte Schleier der Moderne: Betrachtungen zur Gentechnologie." *Merkur: Deutsche Zeitschrift fur europäisches Denken,* no. 450 (August).

Daele, W. van den. 1985. *Mensch nach Mass? Ethische Probleme der Genmanipulation und Gentherapie.* Munich.

Elias, N. 1983. *Die höfische Gesellschaft.* Frankfurt am Main.

Fetz, F. 1970, 1973. *Studientexte zur Leibeserziehung.* 2 vols. Frankfurt am Main.

Foucault, M. 1977. *Sexualität und Wahrheit: Der Wille zum Wissen.* Frankfurt am Main.

——— 1979. *Discipline and Punish: The Birth of the Prison,* trans. A. Sheridan. New York.

Gendolla, P. 1980. *Die lebenden Maschinen: Zur Geschichte der Maschinenmenschen bei Jean Paul, E. T. H. Hoffmann, und Villiers de l'Isle Adam.* Marburg/Lahn.

Guest, R. 1823. *A Compendious History of the Cotton Manufacture.* Manchester.

Gugerli, D. 1988. *Zwischen Pfrund und Predigt: Die protestantische Pfarrfamilie auf der Zürcher Landschaft im ausgehenden 18. Jahrhundert.* Zurich.

Heer, G., and U. Kern. 1989. "Industrialisierung und Fabrikarbeiterschaft am Beispiel der Glarner Tuckdruckerei im 19. Jahrhundert." Master's thesis, University of Zurich.

Industrielle organisation. 1973. Vol. 42, no. 12.

Jaun, R. 1986. "Bally Schuhfabriken: Taylorisierung nach dem Leitsatz 'Prufe alles, behalte das

Beste.' " In R. Jaun, *Management und Arbeiterschaft: Verwissenschaftlichung, Amerikanisierung, und Rationalisierung der Arbeitsverhaltnisse in der Schweiz, 1873–1959*. Zurich.

Kemp, W. 1975. "Die Beredsamkeit des Körpers: Körpersprache als künstlerisches und gesellschaftliches Problem der bürgerlichen Emanzipation." *Stadel-Jahrbuch, NF,* p. 118.

Labisch, A. 1987. "Industriegesellschaft—Arbeit—Gesundheit/Krankheit—Ein medizinsociologischer/ medizinhistorischer Versuch." Manuscript. University of Zurich.

Marx, K. [1887], n.d. *Capital: A Critical Analysis of Capitalist Production.* Vol. 1. Moscow.

Mauer, K. von. 1988. "Korperkultur und Rhythmus: Léger und das Ideal des 'neuen Menschen.' " In *Fernand Léger: Zeichnungen, Bilder, Zyklen, 1930–1955,* ed. N. Serota. Catalogue of the Léger exhibition in the Stuttgarter Staatsgalerie, March 26–June 19.

Milles, D., and R. Müller. 1987. "Der Korper von Arbeitern in arbeitsmedizinischer Sicht: Ein historischer Ueberblick." Manuscript. University of Zurich.

Mrazek, J., and V. Rittner. 1986. "Wünschobjekt Körper." *Psychologie heute* 12.

Munsterberg, H. 1912. *Psychologie und Wirtschaftsleben.* Leipzig.

Nahrstedt, W. 1972. *Die Entstehung der Freizeit.* Göttingen.

Pollard, S. 1965. *The Genesis of Modern Management: A Study of the Industrial Revolution in Great Britain.* London.

Rabinbach, A. 1985. "The European Science of Work: The Economy of the Body at the End of the Nineteenth Century." Manuscript.

Ruegsegger, R. 1986. *Die Geschichte der Angewandten Psychologie, 1900–1940: Ein internationaler Vergleich am Beispiel der Entwicklung in Zurich, Bern, Stuttgart.* Toronto.

Smelser, N. J. 1959. *Social Change in the Industrial Revolution: An Application of Theory to the British Cotton Industry, 1770–1840.* Chicago.

Taubert, G. 1717. *Rechtschaffener Tanzmeister oder gründliche Erklärung der französischen Tanzkunst.* Leipzig.

Turkle, S. 1984. *Die Wunschmaschine: Vom Entstehen der Computerkultur.* Hamburg.

Wigham, F. 1984. *Ambition and Privilege: The Social Tropes of Elizabethan Courtesy Theory.* Berkeley.

4

• • •

The Choice of Technique: Entrepreneurial Decisions in the Nineteenth-Century European Cotton and Steel Industries

Wolfram Fischer

Technological change is never automatic. It means the displacement of established methods, damage to vested interests, often serious human dislocations. Under the circumstances, there usually must be a combination of considerations to call forth such a departure and make it possible: (1) an opportunity for improvement owing to the inadequacy of prevailing techniques, or a need for improvement created by autonomous increases in factor costs; and (2) a degree of superiority such that the new methods pay sufficiently to cover the costs of the change. Implicit in the latter is the assumption that, however much the users of older, less efficient methods may attempt to survive by compressing the costs of the human factors of production, entrepreneurial or labor, the new techniques are enough of an improvement to enable progressive producers to outprice them and displace them (Landes 1969, p. 42).

In such a circumspect way David Landes introduced more than two decades ago his arguments on why the Industrial Revolution occurred first in Britain. But his statement is more general: it applies to the conditions of technological progress irrespective of time, nation, or industry. Reversed, it should also hold for the lack of technological change, for stagnation. Much has been written in the meantime about both subjects: how economic growth came about via technical improvements and why certain industries and certain countries fell behind others. Insofar as countries are compared, the comparison is mostly restricted to pairs of countries: Britain and America, Britain and France, Britain and Germany. This essay aims not at such a comparison, nor at reviewing the progress (or decline) economic historians have made since Landes' seminal work; it selects only two industries—cotton spinning and steel making—in several western European countries, particularly Britain, Germany, and Switzerland, and to a certain degree also Belgium and France, which have been scrutinized in various studies.[1]

These studies demonstrate several common features. They do not concentrate on a comparison of national behavior, though Fremdling's (1986) and Wengenroth's (1986) titles suggest they do. Industries and their technologies are seen in an international environment, and as far as spatial peculiarities come into focus, they refer more often to regions than to nation-states: the cotton industry of Lancashire as it compares to that in Alsace or the Zurich Oberland: the iron industries of Wales, the Midlands, or Scotland in comparison to the same industries in the Ruhr area, the Sambre-Meuze region between Charleroi and Liège, or the Département of the Haute-Marne. This confirms a trend away from the economic history of nations toward a more regional or industry-type approach.[2]

Another common feature is the emphasis on the macroeconomic level, which has its parallel in America in some of the writings of Paul David and Nathan Rosenberg.[3] David (1975, pp. 4ff.) portrays the diffusion of technology "as a reflection of a changing (equilibrium) distribution of production among different techniques, each one chosen rationally by the members of a *heterogeneous* population of firms, a population for which it could not be said that the latest method that has become available at any moment *ipso facto* constituted the dominant, best-practice technique." And he suggests that "a deeper understanding of the conditions affecting the speed and ultimate extent of an innovation's diffusion is to be obtained only by explicitly analyzing the specific choice of technique problem."

This is exactly what some of these historical studies do in a more concrete way. They try to explain why certain firms, or certain entrepreneurs, chose a particular technique in spinning or steel making despite the fact that others were available to them, or why, although they stayed with seemingly outdated methods of production, they were economically successful, at least for several decades, sometimes even for half a century. In these observations some distinct patterns occur across nations. The Swiss spinning mill owners in the 1840s who refused to use the self-actor and stayed with the mule or transferred to the semi–self-actor, and the British iron companies in the 1880s that adopted the Siemens-Martin process or even clung to the Bessemer process (instead of adopting the Thomas process) in steel making, demonstrated rational business attitudes as much as did the owners of blast furnaces in France and southwest Germany who obstinately used charcoal in iron making up to the middle of the nineteenth century whereas British and Belgian iron companies had adopted coke smelting decades (or, in Coalbrookdale, even a century) earlier.

Dudzik (1987) distinguishes between technologically oriented and commercially oriented entrepreneurs in the Swiss textile industry. While the first category would tend to get an advantage out of adopting new machines or rearranging the flow of materials, the other would use old machinery when it was written off, speculate on the raw cotton market or switch over from coarser to finer yarns (or the other way around) as soon as the market favored one or the other. Which of these entrepreneurial "types" is more successful in business terms depends on a variety of circumstances. Although Dudzik states that in the long run the technologically oriented firm survives better, in the short run the commercially oriented one may reap higher benefits. Therefore, much depends on timing in the choice of a particular technique: if it is adopted too early—for example, earlier than the management can handle it—the firm may be damaged as much as if it is adopted too late. Being among the first pays only for the technically competent; otherwise it is preferable to stay with a proven method of production and let the others try and err. It may be possible to acquire the new technique later at a lower price when it has already been tried and perhaps simplified. But one ought not to miss the train altogether. To make the decision at the right time may be as crucial as making the right decision. Entrepreneurs rarely had a clear-cut choice; nearly always there existed several feasible techniques to choose from, and the cautious businessman may have been well advised if he tried first to improve on what he had and what his foremen and workmen could handle before switching over to a totally new technique for which the labor force was not prepared.

The availability of local resources was another point to be taken into account. Swiss spinning mills used water power for most of the nineteenth century. Coal was expensive in Switzerland; therefore it paid to use a more efficient water turbine rather than a steam engine. By the same token, for many decades it paid, in the traditional iron-working regions, to stick with charcoal, even if its price was somewhat higher than that of coke; charcoal-made wrought iron commanded higher prices because of its greater tenacity and malleability. If ironworks had traditional customers nearby, such as toolmakers, they could compete with the cheaper coke-made iron by saving transport costs; these conditions lasted in many regions of western Europe at least until the 1830s.

All this has been known for a long time. What recent research has added are (1) more exact calculations, some from the firms themselves, some by the researcher, and (2) more sophisticated arguments. Let us now follow some examples in greater detail.

Around 1825 the superiority of British spinning mills was still uncontested, although quite a number of mules existed on the Continent as well. William Smart reported in his economic annals of the nineteenth century: "In Cotton, it could not be denied that we were superior to all other countries: we could undersell all competitors in markets open alike to them and us—even in the East Indies" (Smart 1910–1917, II, 276). At about the same time, William Fairbank reported that the Alsatian spinning mills were still very backward in comparison to British ones. Only eight years later Alsatian and Swiss visitors to England discovered that, except for finer yarns, both regions could indeed keep up with Lancashire. When, after 1834, English machinery could be imported legally, Swiss entrepreneurs found that their own machinery from Escher Wyss or Rieter, or the Alsatian equipment from Risler & Dixon, Nicolas Schlumberger and Company, or André Koechlin and Company, was as good as or better than the English. About the same time (1822) a British mill owner stated before Parliament that British firms had difficulty in keeping up with progress on the Continent: only in operating the mills were they still more experienced and, therefore, more efficient. A few years later (1839) the British factory inspector J. C. Symons explained why Escher Wyss and other Swiss machine-building shops were ahead of the British: "The fact is that foreign engineers borrow our inventions, cull and combine the advantages of our various patents (which we cannot do ourselves), and bribe our workmen to make them . . . Machine making is advancing rapidly in perfection, and the aptitude of the work-people is advancing also; but when these elements in the race are matured, I do not believe that, after the carriage is added, our yarn will find any sale in Switzerland, or immediately adjacent countries" (Dudzik 1987, p. 150).

One reason why technologically oriented entrepreneurs in Switzerland were getting ahead of the British was Johann George Bodmer, a Swiss-born mechanical genius, who exercised what we today call technology transfer. He had been recruited by the government of Baden to bring employment into the Upper Black Forest region after the ancient Benedictine monastery in St. Blasien had been secularized and the monks had gone to Austria. There he opened the first German shop that built spinning machinery of its own design (together with a spinning mill and a gun factory that used exchangeable parts). For his inventions he took out French patents, and he cooperated closely with the French inventor Charles Albert in Paris. In 1820 he left the Continent for Britain, and worked on many improvements and inventions in close cooperation with that country's leading machine builders. He not only gave his Swiss compatriots free access to his inventions, which they sometimes could use before they had won a British patent, but also trained young Swiss mechanics in his shop.[4]

Some of Bodmer's inventions were diffused widely elsewhere before they took hold in Britain. The railway system for the teasel Bodmer had conceived while he was still working in St. Blasien[5] received a British patent in 1824, and improvements were patented there in 1835, 1838, and 1842. But it was first introduced in Alsace in 1827. In the 1830s it was widely used in Germany and Switzerland, where J. C. Symons saw it in 1839. (It was built by Escher Wyss and by Rieter, who both had been licensed by Bodmer.) In the 1840s it was common in France and at the same time it was introduced in the United States and in Scotland. In 1847 a French observer called it "one of the most beautiful innovations, which has had the greatest and most favorable effect on spinning in recent times'' (Alcan 1847, p. 233; Dudzik 1987, p. 156). But in England it was barely known even in the 1850s. Evan Leigh, one of the leading authorities in textile engineering, saw the reason for this delay in the fact that the first English models had been poorly constructed and had therefore received a bad reputation. British spinning mills also seem to have refused the ring throstle between the 1830s and the 1880s because they formed an early bias about the quality of the yarn spun at it, which hindered them from recognizing later improvements made in America (Leigh 1877, p. 176; Dudzik 1987, p. 157).

Reluctance to introduce innovations that had been tried and proven useful elsewhere can also be found outside of Britain. Some Swiss mill owners would not introduce the self-actor because they thought they would need steam power, whereas in fact improvements in their waterwheels, the introduction of a water turbine, or rearrangements in water supply would have been enough to make the existing system adequate.

Often, however, what seemed an irrational bias against a certain machine or method of production to an engineer was not without an economic or social rationale. If entrepreneurs hesitated to introduce a complicated mechanism because they feared that their workers might not yet be able to master it or that it might break down too often, incurring costs, they had a valid reason, though they might have tried harder to overcome the difficulties. In Switzerland, at least during business downswings or during periods of social insecurity, entrepreneurs hesitated to use the most modern technology because they feared public resistance. After the mechanical weaving establishment of Trümpler & Gysi in Oberuster was burned down in 1832—the only example of Luddism in Switzerland—many entrepreneurs postponed their decision to build one or avoided the canton of Zurich, where this had happened. Until 1831, no other establishment was erected in this canton. Even the Zurich textile entrepreneurs themselves built their weaving factories in other regions: "The result of the machine breaking in Uster was a division of founding activities in the mechanical weaving away from the canton of Zurich into the other parts of Switzerland for about ten years'' (Dudzik 1987, p. 188). When hand-loom weaving then really lost ground in the 1840s, weavers in the Zurich Oberland were worse off because only a few could find occupation in mechanical weaving establishments.

Whether animosity toward the new English technology played a role is less clear, since negative opinions about the consequences of the mechanization of spinning were offset by positive ones that asserted that without mechanization, Switzerland would soon be overwhelmed by British imports. But such animosities existed already at the end of the eighteenth century and were loudly expressed during the depression following the end of the Napoleonic Wars.[6]

The most important reasons for the reluctance to adopt new techniques were, however, economic. Early industrial entrepreneurs did calculate. Their calculations may have been rudimentary by twentieth-century standards, but they calculated the costs of their investments (including interest rates), of raw materials and wages, and they calculated probable returns. The commercially oriented entrepreneur would soon find out that he could do without greater investments if he saved on other costs, used written-off machinery until its physical death, employed less or cheaper labor, and bought his raw materials at other places or switched over to more lucrative yarns and fabrics, for example by following fashion more closely. Fairly often he would open up new establishments in regions of cheap labor and water power, or even close down a factory when costs ran too high.

Interestingly enough, entrepreneurs responded differently to different innovations in the same industry. The flyer, the most important part of the prespinning process, was introduced quickly nearly everywhere, while the self-actor, the heart of the spinning process, was chosen on the Continent only by the more technologically oriented entrepreneurs, while it spread fast in Britain, and the ring spindle (throstle), which was invented at about the same time (around 1830) and conquered New England quickly, was rejected not only on the European continent but also in Britain for about 35 years. Let us look at the reasons for these differences in some more detail.

The flyer had already been labeled as indispensable in 1823 by Johann Caspar Escher, a spinning mill owner and one of the foremost spinning machine builders of Switzerland, during one of his journeys to England. He called it "one of the most beautiful inventions in mechanical cotton spinning" (Dudzik 1987, p. 159). A few years later, Christoph Bernoulli characterized it as "the most considerable invention which has been made in machine-spinning in thirty years" (Bernoulli 1829, p. 245). Thirty years later, Andrew Ure judged that "this beautiful machine has arrived at its present state of perfection through more numerous efforts of ingenuity, and by the cooperative agency of a greater variety of individuals, than any other mechanism in the cotton trade" (Ure 1861, II, 49).

Originally invented in 1813 and improved upon between 1815 and 1821 in England, the flyer was equipped with differential gears by the American Asa Arnold. Henry Houldsworth of Manchester improved the gears, built them into the English flyer, and received a patent in 1826. Andrew Ure later called Houldsworth's differential gears "perhaps the most refined specimen of the automatic equating principle to be found in the whole compass of science and art" (Ure 1861, II, 55). In the 1830s Alsatian machine builders joined the phalanx of innovators of the flyer using cogwheels as a drive, while Dyer in Manchester introduced a pressfinger. Thus the flyer became one of the most complicated machines in the whole spinning process (for details, see Dudzik 1987, pp. 171ff). It improved the quality of the prespun yarn so considerably, and raised productivity and lowered costs to such a degree, that even the most commercially oriented entrepreneur did not reject the new technique.

The flyer spread in England during the 1820s. Johann Caspar Escher ordered a model right away after he had first seen the machine in 1823. Since legal export from Britain was still impossible, it took three years until all parts had arrived in Zurich. He would soon begin to produce flyers for his own mills, as did his Swiss competitor Rieter and the machine builders in Alsace. Although its price was originally high, the requirement for power not negligible, and the durability of its product questionable, the most formidable hindrance during the first years was the inexperience of the machine masters in the continental spinning mills. Nevertheless, between 1827 and 1834 the flyer spread quickly through Alsace and only a few years later through Switzerland as well, where in the mid-1830s Escher Wyss and Rieter began to build it for customers. The newly established mills, in particular, ordered it right away. The same was true for the (mainly Swiss-owned) spinning mills in Baden, which had been founded when Baden joined the Zollverein in 1836 in order to bypass its customs. By 1850 the replacement of the older machines by the flyer was completed in the more advanced spinning regions. Finally, the introduction of mechanical weaving helped this breakthrough, since the finer yarn needed for the new machines made the flyer indispensable in the prespinning process.

For about 20 years the flyer had to compete against another device, which had been patented in 1824 by four construction engineers of the Taunton works. It became known as the tube frame or double speeder. It was simpler in construction and delivered more prespun yarn per worker and per hour, but only for the very coarse grades below 30.[7] It was also improved in England, and in 1833 about a thousand such machines were installed there. In Switzerland, Escher Wyss produced it too. But since European spinners replaced the coarser yarns more and more with finer ones, the flyer soon prevailed. In the United States, however, coarse yarn remained much longer the leading product, and the double speeder was able to compete with the flyer for about 20 years.

The same difference in the demand for certain qualities of yarn accounted for the fact that as far as the spinning machine itself was concerned, Europe and America went different ways. While it took about 35 years from the first beginnings to the complete diffusion of the flyer, it took about the same time for the self-actor to *begin* to replace the older mules and semi–self-actors on the Continent and even longer before the Danforth throstle and finally the ring machine, both American inventions, got a real foothold in Europe, though all three were invented about the same time as the immediately successful semi–self-actor, in the late 1820s and early 1830s (for details see Dudzik 1987, pp. 171ff.).

The semi–self-actor was an improvement over the usual mule that saved labor costs, because the number of spindles on a single machine could be raised and two machines could be served by one spinner. One spinner could now work up to 1,200 spindles as against about 300 on a traditional mule. The self-actor as developed by Richard Roberts between 1825 and 1830 was, however, a nearly automatic machine. It needed more power and saved even more labor since one spinner (now called a minder) could, with the help of two or three boys, work 1,600 spindles at a time (Chapman 1972, p. 27). Soon it was used for all grades of yarn. While all these spinning machines grew out of Crompton's original mule of 1779, the Danforth throstle was an improvement of Arkwright's water frame. "There was no flyer, and the spindles were stationary but covered by a conical cap which revolved at a high speed . . . The value of this machine was its simple construction and its speed. It produced yarn softer and more fleecy . . . but it also made more waste" (Mann 1958, p. 291). Another child of the throstle was the ring machine, likewise invented in the United States around 1830.[8] It worked on different principles because it had only one moving part, the spindle.[9] It produced more yarn per worker than any other device, but for a long period only in lower grades usable for weft, not for warp, and it needed even more power than the self-actor.

How would an entrepreneur choose between these different techniques? Leading cotton machinery builders produced all or several types of spinning machines but sold quite different quantities. The books of Escher Wyss in Zurich show that between 1832 and 1847, they produced 750 mules, 159 self-actors, and 127 throstles, but no ring spindles; mules were on the agenda from the beginning; throstles were first introduced in 1836, eight years after John Thorp and Charles Danforth had developed them independently in the United States. It took about the same amount of time to put the Roberts self-actor into the program of this Swiss firm (if we take 1830 as the year of its completion). From 1838 to 1847, while all three machines were available, Escher Wyss built 426 mules, 224 throstles, and 159 self-actors. Besides using them in their own mills, they delivered some of the self-actors to other Swiss firms; but most preferred mules and semi–self-actors, even in the late 1840s, which is reflected by the fact that during the two-year period 1846–47, Escher Wyss built 207 mules but only 43 self-actors and 24 throstles.

Most customers maintained that the self-actor was too complicated, but Dudzik (1987) thinks that this was not the real reason, since the flyer, which they had accepted, was no less sophisticated. He sees the difference in the introduction date: the flyer was already a proven machine when the great business upswing began in the early 1830s, while the self-actor was still in an experimental stage. According to him, entrepreneurs were optimistic about the future of their trade in the early years of the decade, while in the late 1830s and the 1840s insecurity spread and cautious behavior prevailed. In this atmosphere most firms would rely on a trusted technology:

A comparison of the diffusion process of the flyer and the self-actor in the 1840s demonstrates that the spread of a new technology is essentially determined by the economic, social, and political situation of the time of its first application. During a generally unfavorable climate for investments the entrepreneurs were not prepared for a rational estimation of the advantages of an innovation like the self-actor but justified their rejection with a whole series of biases: the self-actor was too complicated a machine, it was not suitable for spinning finer yarns, its use would not be economical, taking the low wages on the Continent into account. (Dudzik 1987, pp. 202ff.)

In 1854 only 8 percent of all spindles in Switzerland were on self-actors, in the middle of the 1860s still only 32 percent, and in the main spinning regions only 18 percent, while in Alsace the figure was 67 percent and in southern Germany 72 percent. Even a decade later, in the three major spinning districts of Switzerland, the cantons of Zurich, Glarus, and Solothorn, no more than 52 percent of the spindles were running on self-actors, while in Alsace the number had now risen to 95 percent and in southern Germany to 87 percent (Dudzik 1987, p. 257). But it was precisely in these regions of Switzerland that some of the finest yarns in the world were spun, matching the standards of Bolton in England. While American scholars (Sandberg 1974b) ask why the British clung to the self-actor and did not introduce the ring machine, Swiss researchers raise the question of why it took the Swiss mills 50 years to accept fully even the self-actors and why they were successful nevertheless.

There is no single answer to these questions but rather a combination: one Swiss entrepreneur in the 1840s thought that lower wages and higher prices for the machines were responsible, while another one mentioned the greater difficulty of changing quickly from one grade of yarn to another if the market favored that particular grade. In addition, entrepreneurs were reluctant to transfer part of their authority to specialists who understood the working of the complicated machinery, and they always feared that water power might not be sufficient. At the shareholders' meeting of one Swiss spinning mill in 1866, a shareholder suggested changing over to self-actors, which were more profitable than the old hand mules; another warned him, however, "not to replace too hastily the old mules which have been earning so much in former times and still are very profitable at other places. One should not forget that self-actors need more water power, more repairs, and more careful attention . . . At any rate the matter had to be considered carefully before changes were initiated" (Dudzik 1987, p. 301).

The ring spinning machine met even more skepticism in Switzerland. A report from the Paris World's Fair of 1867 passes over it with the following remark: "The throstle spinning machine of Platt Brothers & Co. seems to be a machine of the future: therefore we prefer to postpone judgment to the next World's Fair." In the same year another report concludes: "A few years ago people believed that the American ring throstle would be adopted here also. This idea has been fairly well abandoned today. The ring throstle requires very great motive power, renders a lot quantitatively but little qualitatively; therefore its application might be impractical for our conditions.'' At the next World's Fair in 1878, Swiss judgment was not much friendlier: ''The admirers of this fashionable machine seem, however, to diminish. It is today an undisputed fact that the ring throstle is qualitatively far inferior to the flyer throstle. Moreover, the machine is, in spite of a reduction in price which has recently occurred, still much too expensive for medium qualities in purchase as well as in operational costs'' (Dudzik 1987, pp. 322ff.).

In the following years reports emphasize that the ring throstle was still in a stage of experimentation: slowly, however, advantages and disadvantages were calculated more soberly. Between 1878 and 1882 it became possible to spin yarns of grades 50 to 80 on it in sufficient quality, and the ring spindle seemed to Swiss textile technicians to be well enough developed to serve as an alternative to the mule and the self-actor. Among its advantages they counted its compact size, and its higher output for lower wage costs. Both factors had been important in America for several decades; therefore it was introduced there much earlier than in Europe.

But perhaps strict calculations never played the foremost role in investment decisions of the Swiss textile industrialists. As long as moderate profits could be earned by an existing technique, as long as an alternative was not an outright threat to the existence of the firm, all but the most courageous or technologically oriented entrepreneurs kept the proven machinery until it was worn out—and that could be 40 to 50 years in textile mills. This generally cautious attitude, which characterized the majority of Swiss entrepreneurs, was also observed from the outside, as a Frenchman remarked: ''He understands, in effect, that the Swiss industry . . . can only survive on two conditions: modest profits for the boss, poor wages for the worker'' (Reybaud 1863, quoted in Dudzik 1987, p. 301). In other words, Swiss textile entrepreneurs were more risk avoiders than profit maximizers.

Since very similar arguments have been put forward as explanations of why the British spinners stuck to the very same self-actor that the Swiss were so hesitant to accept, a more general explanation may be offered: there was just no clear-cut economic superiority of any of the types of machinery available in nineteenth-century spinning. As today electrical energy can be produced economically by water power in some places (among them Switzerland) or coal in others (for example, lignite coal in the Rhineland, hard coal in America or Australia), these techniques continue to be used while in places where such natural resources are not easily available atomic power clearly has an advantage; and here again three different technical solutions are available. Thus governments and firms have several options as far as the choice of technique is concerned. If they are not profit maximizers but survivors, the degree of freedom is even greater as long as they keep in touch with newer developments. If they do not, they may not survive. There is no evidence that British or continental European textile entrepreneurs did not observe developments in other firms and other countries fairly closely. Some chose a more advanced technique whenever it was available, but most of them waited until their machinery was worn out and decided then on either a big step forward or a more cautious and piecemeal improvement. Both could coexist as long as the market grew as rapidly as it did, at least up to the latter part of the nineteenth century. Some of the more sophisticated entrepreneurs gave up mass production before competition in low-wage regions and countries became too fierce; they looked for the more profitable niches and specialties, or they changed from consumer goods to investment goods in the same industry. Others had to give up after a drawn-out battle for profitability and survival. By the outbreak of World War I, Lancashire, Alsace, and Switzerland still belonged to the most flourishing textile regions in the world, irrespective of the technology preferred by their firms.

Let us now ask how the experience of the iron industry compares with that of the spinning mills. Here the traditional form of iron smelting with charcoal lasted even longer after the superior technique of using coke had been introduced in Coalbrookdale and had spread throughout Britain by the late eighteenth century. Landes (1969, p. 126) posed the problem in the following terms: "In view of the enormous economic superiority of these innovations, one would expect the rest to have followed automatically. To understand why it did not—why even the quickest nations marked time until the third and fourth decade of the nineteenth century—is to understand not only a good part of the history of these countries but also something of the problem of economic development in general."

Rainer Fremdling (1986) gives a somewhat different answer for the iron industry of the Continent. According to him there was for many decades no clear-cut *economic* advantage, but only a *technical* one. "The experience that technical achievements are being overestimated in their economic significance—today as then—requires a theoretical and methodological grasp which does *not separate* technical and economic considerations" (p. 19). Since in Belgium coal and iron ore were located close to each other as in Britain, a quick transfer of British technology as early as the 1820s was an economically successful strategy. In the old iron regions of France and western Germany, however, those firms were more successful that took over only part of the new technology, particularly puddling and rolling, but kept charcoal—because it was close at hand—as fuel for the blast furnace, while firms that adopted the

British production process fully had not only to master the new technique, which was difficult enough for most of them, but also had to face higher transport costs while producing iron and steel of lower quality and value. For decades, at least for one generation, the best entrepreneurial decision was to use coke only for puddling, but to improve the traditional decentralized charcoal furnaces in which the iron ore was smelted down to pig iron. Just as the sailing ships were able to compete with the steamer for several decades thanks to better design, so charcoal furnaces could be and were made more productive by the use of new techniques to feed and run them and by building larger units without radically changing the technology. In many cases it also was economical to keep water as moving power instead of introducing the steam engine, which needed the expensive coal. The rural character of the industry also meant lower wages and the use of traditional skills. Only puddlers and sometimes rollers had to be imported from Britain. Moreover, these entrepreneurial decisions helped to keep regions economically viable that otherwise would have turned earlier into depressed areas.

This situation changed with the improvement of the transport system, which, unlike the case in England, did not come with the canals but came only with the railways—that is, half a century later. Slowly beginning in the 1830s, more quickly with the later 1850s, continental iron works found it cheaper to import pig iron from Britain than to produce it, and then concentrate on puddling and rolling. Only where coal was easily available, as in Belgium and Luxembourg, northern France or Lorraine, and particularly in the Ruhr, could an iron industry that used the most modern technology be economically built up in the second half of the nineteenth century. Fremdling (1986, pp. 372ff.) concludes that the timing of this process differed locally not so much because some entrepreneurs were more innovative than others but because of the very different local conditions. The new technology did not penetrate quickly as basic innovations are supposed to do. Only in retrospect does it look superior also in economic terms. "If, however, the long drawn-out transitional period offers a number of economically viable options to the contemporary observer and actor, the relationship between a certain technology and certain economic stage is much more open than can be assumed from traditional historical experience. The result of this research on the iron industry is that when the new techniques arrived, it was not possible to decide which of all methods finally would be the cheapest" (p. 375).

Ulrich Wengenroth (1986) argues along similar lines regarding the choice of technique among the three methods of steel production developed during the 1860s and 1870s that were available during the "great depression" (1873–1879): Bessemer, Thomas-Gilchrist, or Siemens-Martin. He refutes particularly the assertion that the British steel mills chose the "wrong" technique when they either improved on the Bessemer process or changed over to the Siemens-Martin one rather than to the Thomas-Gilchrist process. But he also disagrees with McCloskey's (1973) conclusions on the grounds that McCloskey made some mistaken assumptions about the conditions under which British entrepreneurs acted. Had he looked at the actually existing choices and the motives for their decisions—that is, the metallurgical peculiarities of raw materials, transport costs, or the requirements of the main purchasers—he would have found that the British railway companies wanted Bessemer steel until the 1890s, and the shipbuilding and bridge construction industries preferred Siemens-Martin and not basic (Thomas) steel (Wengenroth 1986, pp. 272ff.).

Wengenroth states, for example, that the high content of silicon in the iron ore of the Midlands made it unsuitable for the Thomas procedure. There was no lack of experiments, no lack of readiness for innovations; but the problem could be overcome only after decades. It was solved finally with the help of American research in the 1930s. Therefore British firms imported German Thomas steel, which British steelworks could not have produced themselves as cheaply; yet, not only British but also German shipbuilders preferred British steel plates made from Siemens-Martin steel, and the German steelworks had to take great pains to convince the German shipbuilders to change over to the domestic product (Scholl 1983). German competitors acknowledged that the British steelworks were, as far as technology was concerned, equally good. The main difference was workmanship: "As far as the method of production is concerned, the mechanical equipment of the English works is at the height of the time. As far as order and accurate work is concerned, the Rhenish-Westphalian works are superior. If the Englishmen would work with the same accuracy as we do, they would be even more dangerous to us."[10]

As in the textile industry, steel experts exchanged opinions and watched one another's experiments across national borders. The best German iron and steel experts were members of the British Iron and Steel Institute. They discussed their experiences there, and British steelworks sent their experts to their competitors in Essen or Bochum to compare the advantages of different methods of steel production. John Brown in Sheffield and Alfred Krupp in Essen made the same technical decisions when they were confronted with the new Bessemer process in the late 1850s (Wengenroth 1986, pp. 44ff., 257). Krupp engaged the Englishman Longsdon and made him responsible for technical affairs; Longsdon, of course, kept his connections to English steel experts (Wengenroth 1986, p. 91). Krupp modeled his steelworks after Dowlais in South Wales. By following the advice of his British expert and neglecting the contradictory opinion of his commission on the Bessemer process, he copied the "fast process" (Schnellbetrieb), which was developed at Dowlais, and did not change over from the Bessemer to the basic (Thomas) steel process until the 1890s, since he co-owned, with Dowlais, Consett, and the Spanish firm Ybarra, large mines of nonphosphoric iron ore in Spain that gave him an advantage over his immediate competitors in the Ruhr. His works were technically, therefore, very "British." Dowlais as well as Krupp used iron scrap and Bessemer pig iron from their own works to produce Siemens-Martin steel. "The similarities in steel production between both works were . . . sometimes striking" (Wengenroth 1986, pp. 211, 214ff., 225).

Choices of technology and investment decisions were not taken by nations, as some historians seem to believe, but by firms, and they were taken under uncertain conditions. Sometimes good reasons led to wrong decisions and wrong assumptions to decisions that turned out to be right after all. Thus the Consett ironworks, for example, decided in 1879 not to close down their old facilities and move to Cleveland to use phosphoric iron ore but to build two Siemens-Martin furnaces and wait for the Bessemer process to demonstrate its ultimate superiority. Although it turned out that their premise was wrong—Bessemer never came to dominate Siemens-Martin—in building Siemens-Martin furnaces they had made the right decision (Wengenroth 1986, pp. 257ff.).

National differences seem to have prevailed, however, as far as the marketing strategy was concerned. The German iron industry turned to collective action, cartels, and tariffs to protect itself against the older, more efficient British steel industry. British firms remained more independent in their decisions even when they became relatively weaker in comparison to the American or German industries, with their growing domestic markets. As Peter Temin has remarked, the British steel industry was bound to lose relative to those two industries because of their faster-growing home market, even if it retained its leadership in third markets (Temin 1966, pp. 148–151). But it remained more profitable than its German counterpart, at least in the 1870s and 1880s. When the demand weakened worldwide, most British enterprises chose to produce less while German firms tried to keep their production up, get their home market protected, and dump the surplus production on neighboring countries. Right through the decades of the depression, the German steel industry felt endangered by British firms. If the German (and American) steel industries grew much faster than the British, particularly in the great upswing after 1895, they did so not because of wrong technical decisions on the part of the British but because their domestic customers grew stronger—particularly the construction and investment industries, which used steel in great quantities and a wide variety of qualities. Wengenroth concludes from his analysis that, looking back, one could accuse the British steel industrialists of not having used their collective market power in time. "In this respect, not in the realm of production technology, they stood behind their German colleagues" (Wengenroth 1986, p. 292).

What can we learn from these examples? I think the main message is that the choice of technology in most historical situations is not technologically determined. Nearly always several different possibilities exist, particularly in new industries (such as the computer industry since the 1950s). What seems to be the logical choice at a certain date or place may turn out a decade later to have been a less than optimal one. Sometimes one particular technique becomes a worldwide standard, but at its introduction it may compete with several others that seem equal or even superior, as the introduction of three different systems of video recorders has recently demonstrated. All techniques are being improved on constantly, and often only after a long period of small improvements does a particular technique turn out to be superior. Often different techniques have very similar results. In the case of the spinning machines as well as in the case of iron and steel production, the economic viability of a particular technique in a particular environment depended on the specifications of the raw materials used—long or short raw cotton, phosphoric or silicon content in iron ore—but also from a variety of economic and social conditions, such as the available moving power, transport costs, the skill of engineers and workers, and their wage level or attitudes toward work and organizational patterns. Legal and political conditions could be added, though they were not as influential in the nineteenth-century environment as they are today, where government regulations or public opinion may favor one and disfavor another technique (for example, in the use of coal or atomic power to generate electricity). Certainly, entrepreneurial attitudes, biases, and virtues belong to the array of parameters that have to be observed. But before we judge them, giving one group good marks against another group, we should carefully look into all of the conditions under which the groups made their decisions.

Notes

1. This contribution is based mainly on the findings of Peter Dudzik (1987) and Michel Hau (1987) for the textile industries of Switzerland and Alsace, and those of Rainer Fremdling (1986) and Ulrich Wengenroth (1986) for the west European iron and steel industries.

2. Some recent examples are Pollard (1980, 1981), Tipton (1976), Fremdling and Tilly (1979), and Kiesewetter and Fremdling (1985). Of course, monographic studies of regional industrialization abound in each country. A bibliography would fill a small book. But cross-country comparisons of regions are still rare (for the nineteenth century, Wrigley [1962] is still an exception). They are more frequent for the period of "protoindustrialization." See, for example, Kriedte, Medick, and Schlumbohm (1977).

3. For example, David (1975) and his contribution to this volume; Rosenberg (1976).

4. On Bodmer, see Roe (1916); Brownlie (1926); Fischer (1972a; 1972b, particularly p. 430 with further literature pp. 530–532); also Dudzik (1987, pp. 112, 151ff., 164, 173–178).

5. The owner of the factory, Freiherr von Eichthal, a Jewish merchant banker from Karlsruhe, would not allow him to develop his idea because he thought, like many commercially oriented entrepreneurs on the European continent, that such a device would have been introduced in England if it were of any use. He later complained that Bodmer had cost him his fortune because he used the spinning mill as an experimental station to improve his machines instead of running them to produce yarn (Fischer 1972a, pp. 418ff.).

6. In 1817 a pamphlet appeared in St. Gallen under the title "England's Industry and the Mechanical Inventions Are the Ruin of the Continent. Demonstrated as a reminder for the powerful and rich on behalf of the unemployed poor." Its author developed the typical rhetoric of the enemies of technical progress in this time: "Now to call a thing by its name, poverty is spread from East to West, from North to South. These are the names of the human inventions: spinning machinery; fly shuttle in weaving; machine printing; chemical bleaches; and, subsequently, steam engines where fuel is available. These inventions bring honor to the human spirit, but no blessing. They require gushing wealth from some and lay the basis for the unhappiness and ruin of hundreds, nay, of thousands" (Dudzik 1987, pp. 67ff).

7. The standard grade of yarn was number 40, and finer yarns went up to 120 at first, then to 240 and higher.

8. Farnie (1965, p. 577), gives 1828 as the date; Sandberg (1974a, p. 20) gives 1831 and "a certain Mr. Jenks" as the inventor. Sandberg relies on Copeland (1912, pp. 9, 66).

9. Johann Georg Bodmer claimed to have used the same principle previously at his spinning mill in St. Blasien, and he saw himself as a forerunner of Danforth: "I made there the 'goblets' or 'bells' which became known later as 'Danford throstle.' I set the spindle, not the bobbin in motion. Many thousands of them were working. I received a patent in France but did not do anything with it . . . Nothing was understood or desired,—it was too early" (Dudzik 1987, p. 173).

10. Director Thielen of the Phönix in 1879. Quoted in Wengenroth (1986, p. 118).

References

Alcan, M. 1847. *Essai sur l'industrie des matières textiles.* Paris.

Bernoulli, C. 1829. *Rationelle oder theoretisch praktische Darstellung der gesammten mechanischen Bauwollspinnerei.* Basel.

Brownlie, D. 1926. "John Georg Bodmer: His Life and Work, Particularly in Relation to the Evolution of Mechanical Stoking." *Transactions of the Newcomen Society for the Study of the History of Engineering and Technology* 6:86–110.

Chapman, S. D. 1972. *The Cotton Industry in the Industrial Revolution.* London: Macmillan.

Copeland, M. T. 1912. *The Cotton Manufacturing Industry of the United States.* Cambridge, Mass.: Harvard University Press.

David, P. A. 1975. *Technical Choice, Innovation, and Economic Growth: Essays on American and British Experience in the Nineteenth Century.* Cambridge: Cambridge University Press.

Dudzik, P. 1987. *Innovation and Investition: Technische Entwicklung und Unternehmerentscheide in der schweizerischen Baumwollspinnerei, 1800 bis 1916.* Zurich: Chronos.

Farnie, D. A. 1965. "The Textile Industrie: Woven Fabrics." In *A History of Technology*, ed. C. Singer et al. Vol. 5. Oxford: Clarendon.

Fischer, W. 1972a. "Die Anfänge der Fabrik von St. Blasien (1809–1848): Ein Beitrag zur Frühgeschichte der Industrialisierung." In W. Fischer, *Wirtschaft und Gesellschaft im Zeitalter der Industrialisierung: Aufsätze-Studien-Vorträge.* Göttingen: Vandenhoeck & Ruprecht.

——— 1972b. "Drei Schweizer Pioniere der Industrie: Johann Conrad Fischer (1773–1854), Johann Caspar Escher (1775–1859), Johann Georg Bodmer (1786–1864)." In W. Fischer, *Wirtschaft und Gesellschaft im Zeitalter der Industrialisierung: Aufsätze-Studien-Vorträge.* Göttingen: Vandenhoeck & Ruprecht.

Fremdling, R. 1986. *Technologischer Wandel und internationaler Handel im 18. und 19. Jahrhundert: Die Eisenindustrien in Grossbritannien, Belgien, Frankreich, und Deutschland.* Berlin: Duncker & Humboldt.

Fremdling, R., and R. H. Tilly, eds. 1979. *Industrialisierung und Raum: Studien zur regionalen Differenzierung im Deutschland des 19. Jahrhunderts.* Stuttgart: Klett-Cotta.

Hau, M. 1987. *L'industrialisation de l'Alsace (1803–1939).* Strasbourg: Association des Publications près les Universités de Strasbourg.

Kiesewetter, H., and R. Fremdling, eds. 1985. *Staat, Region, und Industrialisierung.* Ostfildern: Scripta Mercaturae.

Kriedte, P., H. Medick, and J. Schlumbohm. 1977. *Industrialisierung vor der Industrialisierung.* Gottingen: Vandenhoeck & Ruprecht.

Landes, D. S. 1969. *The Unbound Prometheus: Technological Change and Industrial Development in Western Europe from 1750 to the Present.* Cambridge: Cambridge University Press.

Leigh, E. 1877. *The Science of Modern Cotton Spinning.* 4th ed. 2 vols. Manchester.

Mann, J. de L. 1958. "The Textile Industry: Machinery for Cotton, Flax, Wool, 1760–1850." In *A History of Technology,* ed. C. Singer et al. Vol. 4. Oxford: Clarendon.

McCloskey, D. N. 1973. *Economic Maturity and Entrepreneurial Decline: British Iron and Steel, 1870–1913.* Cambridge, Mass.: Harvard University Press.

McCloskey, D. N., and L. G. Sandberg. 1971. "From Damnation to Redemption: Judgments on the Late Victorian Entrepreneur." *Explorations in Economic History* 9:89–108.

Pollard, S. 1981. *Peaceful Conquest: The Industrialization of Europe, 1760–1970.* Oxford: Oxford University Press.

————, ed. 1980. *Region und Industrialisierung.* Göttingen: Vandenhoeck & Ruprecht.

Reybaud, L. 1863. *Le coton: Son régime—ses problèmes: Son influence en Europe.* Nouvelle série des études sur le régime des manufactures. Paris.

Roe, J. W. 1916. *English and American Tool Builders.* New Haven: Yale University Press.

Rosenberg, N. 1976. *Perspectives on Technology.* Cambridge: Cambridge University Press.

Rosovsky, H., ed. 1966. *Industrialization in Two Systems: Essays in Honor of Alexander Gerschenkron.* New York: Wiley & Sons.

Sandberg, L. G. 1974a. *Lancashire in Decline: A Study in Entrepreneurship, Technology, and International Trade.* Columbus: Ohio State University Press.

———— 1974b. "American Rings and English Mules." In L. G. Sandberg, *Lancashire in Decline: A Study in Entrepreneurship, Technology, and International Trade.* Columbus: Ohio State University Press.

Scholl, L. U. 1983. "Im Schlepptau Grossbritanniens: Abhängigkeit und Befreiung des deutschen Schiffbaus von britischem Know-How im 19. Jahrhundert." *Technikgeschichte* 50:213–223.

Singer, C., et al., eds. 1965. *A History of Technology.* Vol. 4. Oxford: Clarendon.

Smart, W. 1910–1917. *Economic Annals of the Nineteenth Century, 1801–1830.* 2 vols. London.

Temin, P. 1966. "The Relative Decline of the British Steel Industry, 1880–1913." In *Industrialization in Two Systems: Essays in Honor of Alexander Gerschenkron,* ed. H. Rosovsky. New York: Wiley.

Tipton, F. B. 1976. *Regional Variations in the Economic Development of Germany during the Nineteenth Century.* Middletown, Conn.: Wesleyan University Press.

Ure, A. 1861. *The Cotton Manufacture of Great Britain Investigated and Illustrated.* 2 vols. London.

Wengenroth, U. 1986. *Unternehmensstrategien und technischer Fortschritt: Die deutsche und die britische Stahlindustrie, 1865–1895.* Göttingen: Vandenhoeck & Ruprecht.

Wrigley, E. A. 1962. *Industrial Growth and Population Change.* Cambridge: Cambridge University Press.

5

...

The City and Technological Innovation

Paul Bairoch

The city has benefited greatly from the enormous technological advances of the nineteenth and twentieth centuries. There is no doubt that, without this rich harvest of technological innovation, the process of urbanization would have come to a standstill, owing in particular to a halt in the growth of the larger cities. There is also converging evidence that the building cycles (especially the urban building cycles) are linked to technological changes even if other, especially demographic, factors also play a major role. The research on building cycles is closely related to what is now called the Kuznets cycle, whose thesis dates to the 1930s.[1] The links between technology and building cycles seem to be confirmed by more recent research. As Barras (1987, p. 5) writes: "[The] urban development cycles of 20–30 years' duration . . . have created successive waves of urbanization in the British economy since the Industrial Revolution and . . . can be related to successive long waves of technological development."

If we leave aside the cyclical evolution, it is also obvious that traditional technology, that of the period leading up to the Industrial Revolution, would have been incapable of solving the myriad problems caused by the urban explosion of the postindustrial world. Supposing such an explosion had occurred without the technological developments of the past 200 years, how would one have organized the transport required to ship the food and fuel needed in cities of 2 to 5 million people or more? And how would urban transportation have been provided inside these cities? How, above all, would the serious public sanitation problems arising in cities of this size have been solved without progress in mechanical construction and chemistry? Even the transmission of information would have proven a distinct obstacle without the telephone, which, as the reader will recall, came into practical use as early as the end of 1870, that is, at a time when the largest city in the world, London, had a population of 3 million and the second largest, Paris, a population of 2 million people. By 1885 there were already some 260,000 telephones in service, almost all of them in the cities of developed countries. The number had risen to about 2.5 million in 1900 and 14.5 million on the eve of World War I.

The objection that immediately springs to mind in this connection is that, necessity being the mother of invention, the bottlenecks created by urban growth would have engendered their own solutions. Here, indeed, lies the crux of the problem of the link between technological innovation and the economy in general, and between technical innovation and the city in particular. While it is unquestionably the case that the city has profited from technological advances, has it not also had a considerable hand both in stimulating innovation and in ensuring its diffusion?

These considerations lead me to open my discussion with a brief review of the relations between technology and economic development. This question is very important, for if technology were to turn out to be an independent variable in the life of the economy, this would considerably reinforce our appreciation of the role the city has played in technological innovation. Indeed, if technology is an independent variable, it implies that progress in technology results from the general advance of science in the broadest sense of the term. And it is obvious that the growth of science is intimately bound up with urban life. Be it noted, however, that, if we conclude that technology takes its cue from economic factors, this would not reduce the city's role to zero. But in this case, the contribution would have been made not by the urban factor, properly speaking, but by the economic component of urban life. I will have occasion to return to this aspect of the question later.

Technology, Science, and the Industrial Revolution

The old, classic view is that the Industrial Revolution was the fruit of the progress made in the sciences during the century of the Enlightenment, itself the offspring of the continuous flowering since the end of the Middle Ages of what is conventionally referred to as Western civilization. Although containing significant errors, this view should not be abandoned altogether. There is no doubt that by the start of the eighteenth century, western Europe had reached a level of "civilization" it had never known before. It is even likely that, thanks to its openness to the rest of the world—a spirit, besides, almost unique to western Europe which enabled it to seek out and above all assimilate the offerings of other cultures—European civilization was at that time if not the most advanced, then certainly one of the most advanced in scientific and technical terms. Although the gap between Europe and Asia was not at this point very wide, Arab algebra, Chinese printing, the American potato, the renewed interest in the attainments of the ancient world, all of these things, together with many other borrowings, fertilized by the original researches performed by the Europeans of the sixteenth and seventeenth centuries, had by the start of the eighteenth century probably brought European society to a height no other civilization had reached.

I shall omit here the controversy about the role of religion, and especially, following Weber, that of Protestantism, on European achievement. But more convincing is David Landes' (1969) proposition that "European science and technology derived considerable advantage from the fact that the continent was divided into nation-states, rather than united under the rule of an ecumenical empire" (p. 31).

Doubtless so high a level of scientific and technological development, and such open-mindedness, at once the cause and the consequence of scientific and technological advance, made the West fertile ground first for the agricultural revolution and then for the Industrial Revolution that came after it. But economic history and the history of technology compel us to modify this picture of things. To be sure, it is very seductive to think of a continuous evolution, a direct thread running from the Gutenberg printing press to Stevenson's locomotive by way of the achievements of Leonardo da Vinci, Copernicus, Galileo, Bacon, Descartes, Newton, Papin, Lavoisier, and Watt, to cite only a few names picked at random from the cast of characters in the saga of European progress in science and technology. The fact remains, however, that practically all of the technological advances accompanying the agricultural revolution and especially the Industrial Revolution during its first 70 to 100 years were not the work of scientists: they were rather the work of craftsmen, very often illiterate, who, proceeding along purely empirical lines, perfected or improved the machines on which these revolutions relied. I speak of perfecting and improving rather than inventing them because, in most cases, the machines used during the opening phases of the Industrial Revolution had been invented long before the date of their first real practical application; nor did they necessarily originate in the West.

Science, then, played almost no part in the technological developments associated with the beginnings of industrialization. And the same was true in just about every other sector of development. The first operational steam engine, dating from around 1710, constructed by Savary, and especially those introduced by Newcomen, who was a blacksmith, owed nothing to science. And this continued to be the case with the improvements realized during the next six decades and more.

In the textile industry, which acted as a driving force in industrialization until the middle of the nineteenth century, craftsmen guided by empirical experience were also responsible for creating, perfecting, and improving the first mechanized machines. The figures marking the stages of progress in the mechanization of work in the textile mills, while they may not all have been directly linked to work in this sector, were still like Arkwright, whose career was far removed from scientific life. Arkwright was a barber who "received but a very indifferent education . . . and later amassed a little property from dealing in human hair and dyeing it by a process of his own" *(Encyclopaedia Britannica,* 13th ed., 1910). Besides, during the first decades of the mechanization of the textile industry, the machines were as a rule manufactured by textile concerns themselves. It was only later, probably largely as a result of the substitution of iron for wood in the construction of industrial equipment, that independent workshops took over the fabrication of these machines. This made possible a specialization favoring the introduction of improvements requiring a higher degree of technical qualification. But the fact remains that the original impetus came from inside the industry itself as the fruit of purely practical training and experiment. The same process occurred in the iron and steel industry and in other areas as well. Nor was this lack of ties with science characteristic of industrial technology alone; in the initial phases of their development, agricultural techniques too were influenced only a very little by science.[2]

The farther they advanced, the more complex the new technologies became, drawing more and more frequently on science, which had for its part also progressed very rapidly. The successive transitions from the use of wood (continuing up to around 1820), to the use of iron or cast iron, then to the use of steel (dating from 1860) in the construction of machines represented stages in a process of growing complexity involving, both in manufacturing and in maintenance, more highly developed techniques and more highly evolved equipment.

Thus, the nearer one comes to the end of the nineteenth century, and then the deeper one goes into the twentieth, the more one finds an evolving technology characterized by ceaselessly growing complexity. This complexity gradually led to a break with traditional techniques, a break notably accentuated during the early years of the twentieth century by the generalized introduction of electricity and the internal combustion engine, and becoming total with the numerous applications of electronics and nuclear energy. The chief result of an evolution of this sort lies in the growing independence of technology with respect to the economy.

One may nevertheless wonder whether technology was not already very independent in the second half of the nineteenth century and even more so during the first half of the twentieth century. Since the 1960s this independence has appeared to be extremely great owing notably to the scale of the by-products of arms research and space exploration, and also to the mass of basic research carried out during this period. It suffices in this context to think of the swelling numbers of scientific and technical researchers (the barriers between the two fields being very porous and often nonexistent) to realize the leap that has been made since before World War II. In our particular perspective here, moreover, what matters is the phase of urbanization spanning the nineteenth century and the first years of the twentieth, that is, the period during which the contemporary urban world took shape.

Despite the enormous value and interest attaching to the empirical analysis of the links between technological innovations and the economy, studies in this area are paradoxically rare. Schmookler's (1966) was the most important, because it furnished a starting point for the principal inquiries that have been made into specific aspects of relations between techniques and the city. This study, whose title, *Invention and Economic Growth,* gives a clear indication of its aim, is based on a review of inventions and the course of economic events between 1800 and 1955 in four sectors of the economy of the United States: agriculture and the oil, paper, and railroad equipment industries. Schmookler drew two conclusions from this review. First, despite the widespread belief that the impetus for technological inventions designed for specific applications has come from scientific breakthroughs and major technological innovations, the study of developments in these four sectors of the American economy reveals no case in which a relation of this sort unequivocally came into play. On the other hand, cases abound in which the stimulus for new inventions was provided by the existence of specific technological problems demanding solutions. More precisely, new inventions occurred where there was the promise of large savings (costly procedures being required to get around existing technical difficulties) or where there was the promise of profits accruing to whoever should come up with a new technique or device helping to solve some definite technological problem.

Schmookler's second conclusion was that there was a very close link between the curve tracking the state of the economy and the rate at which patents of invention were filed. That a link of this kind existed has been observed many times. The main point emerging from Schmookler's analysis, however, is that the state of the economy turns out to have been the driving force, upswings in the economy preceding surges in the pace of invention.

He explains these findings by the fact that invention is largely an economic activity carried out, like all other economic activities, for profit. Then again, the profits expected are a function of sales. So even more than his findings, flowing as they do directly from his empirical analysis, the explanations Schmookler offers have the unmistakable ring of the "American way of life." But it should be noted that, as concerns events in the first half of the nineteenth century, a consensus has formed even in the case of Europe regarding the primacy of economics over invention. Furthermore, from the years 1850 to 1860 onward, the United States occupied a central place in technological innovation in the West, its role becoming decisive between 1890 and 1910.[3]

Technological Innovation and the City

Let us now move on to analyze more specifically relations between technological innovation and the city. In undertaking this analysis, I have unfortunately had to rely almost entirely on the work of American researchers. While this would not necessarily have been a bad thing in and of itself, the fact that American students of the question quite naturally direct most of their attention to the United States alone has proved something of a drawback.

The first modern scholar to address this problem was Pred (1966), with his seminal analysis of the dynamics of urban and industrial growth in the United States. He computed the relation between the number of patents pending and the population of the 35 largest American cities from 1860 to 1910. While, to be sure, the course of invention is only imperfectly glimpsed through patents, Pred's calculations point unmistakably to the concentration of invention in the cities. About 1860, the number of patents per inhabitant in the 35 principal cities of the United States was 4.1 times the national average, even though this average reflected the figures furnished for other cities. This ratio nevertheless exhibits a downward trend, falling by 1910 to only 1.6, indicating a diminution of the inventive function of cities. It is true, however, that by around 1910, the 35 largest cities accounted for a higher proportion of the overall urban population than in 1860. And since the urban part of the population of the United States had also increased sharply during this time, the largest cities themselves made up a correspondingly greater share of the national average, thereby mitigating somewhat the force of this downward movement. In any event, though to a somewhat declining extent toward the end of the period, the city played a predominant role in invention in the United States, a fact linked, according to Pred, to the amount of industrial employment located there.

Still with regard to the United States, Higgs (1971) has shown that, throughout the period 1870 to 1920, the relation linking the level of urbanization in the United States as a whole to the number of patents pending was very close and highly significant. The correlation between these two variables proves even tighter than that between the number of patents pending and the proportion of the working population employed in manufacturing.

More specific are the analyses carried out by Feller (1971, 1973). The first of these two studies confirms the findings reached by Pred and Higgs. But Feller tried to isolate more exactly the urban contribution to invention. He argues that while, as Schmookler has shown, invention is unquestionably determined by contact with technological needs, the urban way of life increases the frequency of such contact. Similarly, while invention occurs only when bottlenecks are found to arise in industry, the city makes it possible for a greater number of people to become aware of these bottlenecks.

Since the 1970–1973 period, research has become even more scant on this subject. Among the more recent research I could locate only two papers, both dealing with the contemporary period.[4] The first one (Rees, Briggs, and Oakey 1984), dealing more with the diffusion of innovation, will be discussed later. The second one (Pellenbarg and Kok 1985) deals with a very urbanized country, the Netherlands, where it is difficult to speak of rural areas. And this is probably the reason why the authors' conclusion on small and medium-sized innovative firms is that "there is no clear relationship between the innovation activities and the urban production milieu" (p. 252). This is to some degree a confirmation of the diminished role of cities; we shall come back to this important issue.

Faced with the small number of inquiries into these problems in the framework of European societies and the periods leading up to 1900, I initiated some research in this area within the Department of Economic History at the University of Geneva. This work was chiefly the topic of a dissertation written under my direction by Isabelle Martin (1977), helped in part by a visiting assistant in the department, Gilbert Eggimann. The aim of this study was to explore the relation between the size of cities and technological innovation. It can still very usefully serve our present purpose because the lower limit defining urban centers was fixed at 5,000 inhabitants and because account was taken of developments in rural districts.

A systematic census was taken of all inventors in the field of technology using the histories of techniques available for the three countries included in the study, the United Kingdom, France, and Germany. Martin tried to establish short biographies of the inventors, concentrating on the place of birth, place of education, and place of residence during the period of their major inventions. This proved possible for 535 of the 1,358 inventors on the master list. For each country and for periods set at intervals of 25 or 50 years, Martin compared the size structure of the cities of the country at large to the city size structure of the inventors' birthplaces at the moment at which their most important invention took place.

As may be seen in Table 5.1, technological innovation proves to have been of distinctly urban origin in the European countries studied. In all three, as concerns both the inventors' place of birth and the place in which their inventions occurred, the city largely predominates. The predominance of cities in the case of places of birth can obviously be explained in large part by the close link between place of birth and place of residence. Almost all of the future innovators born in a city still lived in such an environment when their discoveries or inventions took place. Nonetheless, given the fact that the migratory flow of the population ran predominantly from the countryside toward the towns, one would normally expect to find higher indices of urban concentration pointing to a

Table 5.1 Indexes of urban concentration of technical innovation according to inventor's place of birth and place of residence at time of most important innovation.

	Place of birth		Place of invention	
Country	Period	Index of urban concentration of innovation[a]	Period	Index of urban concentration of innovation[a]
United Kingdom	1700–1779	2.6	1760–1819	3.9
	1780–1819	3.3	1820–1879	2.3
	1820–1859	1.8	1880–1899	1.4
France	1800–1829	5.3	1800–1849	6.1
	1830–1879	3.6	1850–1899	3.6
Germany	1800–1839	5.5	1800–1849	7.1
	1840–1859	4.9	1850–1899	3.2

Source: Based on I. Martin, "Inventions techniques et urbanisation en Europe au XIXe siècle: Allemagne, France, et Royaume uni" (degree dissertation, Department of Economic History, University of Geneva, 1977).

[a] Relation between relative size of population of urban places where inventors were born or resided and relative size of urban population.

greater role for cities in the case of places of invention than in the case of places of birth. This does not emerge, however, from a cursory analysis of the figures set forth in Table 5.1, a fact that may be accounted for in part by statistical bias. But it also reflects the gradual decline over time of the specifically urban contribution to innovation, since at least 10 and, as a rule, between 30 and 40 years separate the inventors' birth from the date of their inventions.

Another trend can be seen in Table 5.1: namely, the decline over time of the specifically urban contribution to innovation. The case of these three major European countries confirms the results of the analyses done for the United States, but we shall see later that the same is also true of the diffusion of innovation; I will provide some tentative explanation for such a trend.

Another finding Martin's study enables us to verify, but which takes us a little beyond the framework established here, concerns the positive impact of the size of cities on innovation.

In all three countries there is a clear relation between the size of cities and the intensity of technological innovations. Table 5.2 concerns the place of invention, but the results are very close for the place of birth. It should be noted that in the cases of France and the United Kingdom, the class of cities above the 500,000 limit includes the capitals of those countries, which certainly reinforces the "innovative" function. This effect results largely from migratory move-

Table 5.2   Index of concentration of technical innovation according to inventor's place of residence at time of most important innovation.

Place of invention	United Kingdom		France		Germany	
	1760–1820	1820–1880	1800–1850	1850–1900	1800–1850	1850–1900
Rural areas	0.29	0.14	0.03	0.03	0.10	0.12
Urban areas	3.88	2.28	6.70	3.86	7.18	3.37
City by size (thousands)						
5–19	2.13	0.81	1.62	0.51	4.79	1.60
20–99	4.31	1.28	3.54	N.A.	7.18	3.37
100–199	N.A.	4.50	7.33	N.A.	16.50	7.24
200–499	N.A.	3.63	N.A.	N.A.		2.71
500 and more	5.25	4.11	58.80	19.34	N.A.	7.86

Source: Based on I. Martin, "Inventions techniques et urbanisation en Europe au XIXe siècle: Allemagne, France, et Royaume uni" (degree dissertation, Department of Economic History, University of Geneva, 1977).

N.A. = not applicable because of absence or small number of cities of this size.

ments, since in this case the findings for the place of birth are much lower.

In this area, too, the only two other available studies (albeit not as thorough as the others I have cited) bear solely on the case of the United States. Like their successors, making use in their articles of statistics on patents, Rose (1948) and Ogburn and Duncan (1964) had already reached the conclusion that the larger the city, the greater the number of patents pending per inhabitant. Viewed in a certain light, this relation between the size of cities and innovation is very important, for it reinforces, ipso facto, our apprehension of the urban component of innovation. Indeed, assuming the city made no particular contribution to innovation, there would be little reason for the size of cities to have such an effect.

Empirical analysis, then, fully confirms the predictions suggested by deductive reasoning, which has in just about every case assigned the city a leading role in innovation in the broadest sense of the word, one obviously including technological invention. And this has proven true for preindustrial societies as much as for those issuing from the Industrial Revolution.

In addition to the size element, it is certain that many other urban characteristics have an impact on the innovative potential of a city. Among those the four most significant are probably (1) the quantity and specificity of educational institutions, (2) the industrial structure (including firm sizes), (3) the geographic location (especially in relation to transportation networks), and (4) the mobility of the city's inhabitants. Such an empirical study calls for a large and costly effort, and this explains why it has not been done before.

And now, one other aspect of the question needs to be dealt with: the role of cities in the diffusion of new technology.

The City and the Diffusion of Technological Innovations

Here the problem is at once much simpler and much more delicate. It is simpler because the fact that the urban environment is a more favorable milieu for the diffusion of technological innovations than the rural environment requires no demonstration; it is difficult to see how it could be otherwise. It is more delicate, however, by reason of this very self-evidence which has made empirical studies specifically devoted to this problem exceedingly rare: proving something that is already perfectly obvious is not very exciting. It is also more delicate because it is often much more difficult to follow the subsequent itinerary of an innovation than to locate its place of origin. Still, there is no want of studies bearing on the general problems surrounding the diffusion of innovation. In the bibliography to the second edition of Rogers' (1971) work on this subject, we find 1,640 titles (1,230 of them relating to empirical studies on diffusion), not counting 170 general references dealing with subjects touching on this question. (Rogers modestly says that his work is the distillation of more than 1,500 publications.) The appendix to Rogers' book, which presents, for a hundred or so different propositions, the number of studies treating the given question, the relevant references and the percentage of studies proving or disproving the given thesis, constitutes a wonderful research tool. (It is true, however, that this reader at least was left wondering whether the fact that 95 percent of the studies devoted to the matter reject a given hypothesis necessarily means it is false.)

We must set such considerations aside, however, valuable though they are, because absolute certainties are very rare. In any case, it does distinctly appear that, at least as a general rule, the city favors the diffusion of technological innovation more than the countryside. Symptomatic of the lack of investigation bearing on the specific matter at hand here is the fact that, of the hundred-odd headings under which Rogers classifies the studies on diffusion analyzed in his book, none explicitly relates to the problem of differences in diffusion between cities and the countryside. In a certain way this problem does, however, invoke one of the most fundamental distinctions between urban and rural districts, that concerning the mentality and behavior of their respective populations. In his classic study *The City* (1958), first published in 1921, the sociologist Max Weber distinguishes between the behavior of town and country folk by means of two basic oppositions: the role of the rational as against that of the traditional, and the role of contacts as against that of customs. Although Weber's observations specifically relate to conditions at the time of his writing, the same distinction will be found to have existed much farther back in history, for the uniqueness of urban behavior has always stood out very clearly.

A rational outlook on the world and the frequency of contacts between people: the importance of these two concepts with regard to the general problem of innovation springs readily to mind. To be sure, there is room for nuance. In a now famous article, "Urbanism as a Way of Life," Wirth (1938) notes that the very large number of people one sustains relationships with in the city makes genuine contact impossible. From our point of view here, however, the number is the decisive thing: it is the possibility of encountering or having knowledge of new inventions that counts. For my own part, moreover, I would be inclined to consider the development of a rational outlook as resulting from the enhanced possibilities of contacts with other people; or rather, putting it the other way around, I would regard the maintenance of a traditional outlook as resulting from the absence of such contacts. But this is as much as to say that, as concerns the second of the two distinctions drawn by Weber, the opposition between town and country seems somewhat more doubtful; but one should not disregard the social constraint which leads in rural areas to a more traditional way of life. Data based on the mid-1970s show that even then in the United States the rural-urban "attitudinal and behavioral variation . . . is more than negligible and that there is little reason to believe that its importance is diminishing" (Glenn and Hill 1977, p. 50). Finally, the very fact that urbanism can be associated with tolerance[5] is an additional element leading to the diffusion of innovation.

Modern analyses of the city's role in the diffusion of innovation have chiefly been carried out by Anglo-Saxons and Swedes. Haegerstrand (1967) has made one of the best-known contributions in this area. He insists on the importance of proximity and of interpersonal contacts. It is worth noting the distinction Pedersen (1970) draws with respect to the diffusion of innovation between what he calls business-related innovations and household-related innovations. A good example illustrating this difference is television. In the United States and the other countries in which private broadcasting systems exist, the setting up of a TV station is the business of the entrepreneur; the diffusion of television sets, on the other hand, depends on decisions made in the home. But while this distinction is interesting, one ought to stress the fact that both of these processes of diffusion have a key role in economic development and are, besides, interdependent: the diffusion of new broadcasting stations moves all the faster as more households in other regions buy TV sets.

When all is said and done, there are extremely few attributes specific to urban life that do not favor the diffusion of innovation. Following Haegerstrand, one can speak of increased interpersonal contacts. But let us take other aspects of urban living and see what Rogers' synthesis has to say. In terms of education, 74 percent of the 275 studies Rogers analyzes conclude that the higher the level of education, the more readily innovations are adopted. In terms of social mobility, all five of the relevant studies show that this factor is everywhere correlated with the adoption of innovations. The same holds in the case of the proportion of the general population accounted for by the upper social classes (68 percent), in the case of the cosmopolitan complexion of the population (76 percent), in the case of exposure to the mass media (69 percent), and in the case of the populations of cities belonging to modern urban systems (70 percent). Thus, the studies ''prove'' what already seemed self-evident: the city promotes the diffusion of innovations more than the country.

The Size of Cities and the Diffusion of Technological Innovations

As in the case of innovation itself, the role played by the size of cities brings additional evidence of the urban component in the diffusion of innovations. The studies carried out in this area are hardly more numerous than those relating to the urban contribution generally: an exhaustive bibliography would contain certainly no more than 20 titles or so. The great majority of existing studies bear on and were carried out in the United States. There are two reasons for this dominance in the field: the amount of money made available for this kind of research and the size of the country, which makes the findings of empirical research statistically more significant.

The earliest study is apparently that undertaken by Bowers (1937). It is in any case always cited as such, a circumstance that by no means rules out the possibility of precursors, especially in languages other than English. Bowers' study relates to the growth in the United States of the number of ham radios, broken down by region and by size of city. The analysis concerning the period from 1914 to 1930 shows that this ''innovation'' first gained acceptance in cities of 25,000 to 100,000 people, progressively spreading to smaller towns thereafter. Cities of more than 100,000 people, however, were throughout less affected than the others. The reason for this is not hard to imagine: the diversions offered by larger cities were more abundant.

This type of analysis started again after World War II with Crain (1966) in his investigation of the diffusion of the practice of fluoridating water. This study shows very clearly that a relation exists between the size of cities and their openness to this practice. More evidence of the positive relations between the size of cities and readiness to adopt innovations is found in Haegerstrand's (1967) work. The few other tests relating the diffusion of other innovations to the size of cities all confirm the same thing. Be it nevertheless noted that the relevant studies practically always bear on the contemporary era and the United States.

Robson (1973), however, reached the same conclusion after a detailed study of the diffusion of three innovations through the urban network in nineteenth-century England: the establishment of gas plants from 1820 to 1840, of house-building contractors in 1853 and from 1862 to 1894, and of telephone exchanges from 1881 to 1892. In addition to the size factor, however, Robson quite properly stresses the role of "proximity": the diffusion of innovations from large towns to smaller ones as a function of their proximity to them. For Robson, as for Pred and most other students of these problems, the flow of innovations is a significant factor in the growth of urban populations, and the slowdown in the growth of the larger English cities during the last quarter of the nineteenth century was due to the slowdown in the flow of innovations. Robson's conclusion on telephone exchanges is confirmed by Boyer's (1987) study of France and the Netherlands during the 1879–1892 period.

If we remain in the field of what can be called city equipment, the role of city size remains valid even, or, I should say, even more, for preindustrial periods. This is especially the case of public clocks. In late medieval Europe (1300–1500), in addition to such factors as industrial specialization (notably in textiles), city size was a crucial factor in the spread of public clocks (Dohrn van Rossum, 1987). And this brings us back to Landes (1983).

In the nineteenth century the analysis by Lepetit (1987) shows that in France the strongest factor in the introduction of savings banks during the 1818–1848 period was the size of cities. In Germany, however, the role of the state was a strong element in the diffusion of savings banks (Wysocki 1987).

Thus, the analyses once again prove that the larger the city, the more rapidly innovations take hold. One must nevertheless regret the extreme rarity of analyses of this kind regarding technological innovation in the productive sector of the economy. This is another example of the necessary distinction between business-related innovations and household-related innovations. And it should be remembered that of the two, the former is the more decisive. To what extent, for example, in the nineteenth or twentieth century, did the spinning mills in the large towns tend more readily to convert to modern equipment than their counterparts in smaller towns? The chances are that industry properly speaking follows the rule. The study by Tornqvist (1970), showing the part played by "contacts" (already stressed by Haegerstrand) in industry, lends indirect support to this assertion.

But I must stress the fact that there is very little empirical research on this topic. The only relatively recent publication on this subject, Rees, Briggs, and Oakey (1984), which concerns mainly information processing, shows that if for nearly all types of inventions the adoption rates are lower in rural areas, the difference is not a significant one. Furthermore, the analyses "suggest that the largest urban areas are not necessarily the most conducive environment for companies that use the latest available technologies" (p. 497).

Some Elements of the Declining Urban-Rural Difference

This remark seems to be a confirmation of the trend shown before, for the role of cities in the origins of technology and innovation: the urban component of innovation was more important in the nineteenth century, and the diminishing role of cities is obviously linked to the diffusion of information and contact and also the more even distribution of educational opportunities.

And education is probably the most explanatory factor since, as we have seen, the urban-rural attitudinal and behavioral variation is still present even today. During the nineteenth century the main changes in education took place at the first level (primary schools). Especially in western Europe, school enrollment rose so quickly that illiteracy rates even in rural areas must have declined sharply. According to estimates for the total population, the share of the population over the age of 15 that was illiterate in western Europe[6] declined from 43 to 45 percent around 1800 to 34 to 36 percent around 1850 and to 5 to 6 percent in 1910. There were no dramatic changes in the interwar period, but since the end of World War II, and even more so during the last two decades or so, great progress has been made in secondary and higher education. Table 5.3 shows that the gap in educational level between urban and rural population has narrowed considerably for the 35–44 age group. The fact that I have chosen to follow the changes in educational levels by using age data reduces strongly the bias that would have resulted from comparing data over time. In this case the changes in the notion of rural and urban would have introduced a strong distortion. The fact that the educational level of the rural population is approaching closer and closer that of the city population does not necessarily rule out different attitudes toward everyday life, but it is certainly a factor that in professional life may lead to a more receptive attitude toward technological innovations.

Conclusions

Despite the relatively small amount of research existing in this area of the history of technology, and the almost complete lack of recent research, it seems that fairly valid conclusions can be drawn. Leaving aside the role of cities in technological innovation before the Industrial Revolution, we see that since this revolution the city has played a leading role in the origins of technological

Table 5.3 Urban-rural educational rates[a] of population by age for selected developed countries.

Country	Age		
	35–44 years	45–54 years	55–64 years
Canada (1981)			
Secondary education			
Urban rate	60.5	57.1	53.2
Rural rate	58.5	51.3	44.1
Difference (%)	13.4	11.3	12.0
Higher education			
Urban rate	23.0	14.7	11.8
Rural rate	13.6	8.1	6.5
Difference (%)	69.1	81.5	81.5
Japan (1980)			
Secondary education			
Urban rate	49.2	43.3	30.2
Rural rate	40.3	27.3	16.5
Difference (%)	22.1	58.6	83.0
Higher education			
Urban rate	16.2	12.6	9.3
Rural rate	8.1	4.8	3.6
Difference (%)	100.0	162.5	158.3
Poland (1978)			
Secondary education			
Urban rate	48.5	35.8	28.7
Rural rate	20.3	9.2	4.9
Difference (%)	138.9	289.1	485.7
Higher education			
Urban rate	11.0	8.6	5.2
Rural rate	1.7	0.9	0.4
Difference (%)	547.1	855.6	1,200.0

Source: Derived from United Nations, *Demographic Yearbook, 1983* (New York: United Nations, 1985), pp. 1008–23.

[a] Percentage of population of age having the specific education level.

innovations as well as in the diffusion of those innovations. It is obvious that part of this role, and even an important one, derives from the concentration of economic activities in cities, but other, more specific components of urban life also play a large part.

Two key elements emerge. First, there is a relation between city size and innovations (and diffusion of innovations). That is, the urban concentration of innovation rises with the size of cities, and innovation spreads more rapidly in bigger cities than in smaller ones. The second element is that the urban concentration of innovation (or of diffusion) decreases over time and is actually becoming very marginal. Two of the major reasons for such an evolution are the diminishing difference between urban and rural educational levels and the increased flow of information in rural areas. Among other factors explaining this there is also the fact, as Malecki (1980, p. 232) stresses, that "technological change is taking place unceasingly through the R and D of large multilocational firms. Although this has long been true of the American economy, the role of large corporations has also become important in other Western countries. Thus, the process of technological change relies considerably on the strategies and structures of corporations with respect to R and D . . . with consequences affecting regional development."

The location or relocation of the laboratories of big firms (and in some cases of smaller firms) in the countryside can certainly not be counted as "rural innovation," but it is also difficult to include it in "urban innovation." Yet, the creation of "technological cities" leads to an "urban" concentration of innovation. This and other elements result in what are beginning to be called *technical systems*.[7]

The diminishing role of cities as such in innovation and those new forms of scientific and technological organizations is certainly not a positive element in the Third World urban inflation problem. But in this area the lack of research has even more potent results. And yet the paucity of research in the area of the history of technology has a positive side: there is still room for very interesting work in this field.

Notes

1. Kuznets (1930). The first paper specifically on construction cycles seems to have been Burns (1935). As Burns himself points out (p. 65), he based his analysis mainly on two previous studies: that of Hoyt (1933) and especially that of Riggleman (1933).

2. These conclusions are largely drawn from my study on the Industrial Revolution (Bairoch 1963); the research I have done since has not much changed my point of view, which in fact reflects the predominant if not unanimous opinions of the more "technical" specialists of the history of technology. In his overview of the role of technology in industrialized countries, Caron (1985) emphasized strongly the "divorce" between science and technology in the major sectors of industry in the nineteenth century.

3. To a very large extent, this general conclusion is supported by Utterback (1974), and enriched by questions raised by another pioneer in the history of technology, Nathan Rosenberg (1974, p. 107): "Given the state of the sciences, *at what costs* can a technological end be attained?" For more recent additions, see the study edited by Griliches (1984).

4. To a certain extent the paper of Oakey, Thwaites, and Nash (1980) can be included in this short list.

5. For research on this topic, see Wilson (1985), and for an essay on the role of cities in preindustrial

Europe on a very specific aspect of innovation, "la conscience moderne du corps," see Gélis (1985).

6. For this calculation western Europe includes the following countries: Belgium, Denmark, France, Germany, the Netherlands, Norway, Sweden, Switzerland, and the United Kingdom.

7. Technical systems can be defined as "large-scale, centrally coordinated technological enterprises" (Shrum, Wuthnow, and Beniger 1985, p. 46).

References

Bairoch, P. 1963. *Révolution industrielle et sous-développement*. Paris.

―――― 1985. *De Jéricho à México: villes et économie dans l'histoire*. Paris.

Barras, R. 1987. "Technical Change and the Urban Development Cycle." *Urban Studies* 24, no. 1 (February):5–30.

Bowers, R. V. 1937. "The Direction of Intra-Societal Diffusion." *American Sociological Review* 2, no. 6 (December):826–836.

Boyer, J. C. 1987. "Les débuts du téléphone en France, en Angleterre, et aux Pays-Bas, 1879–1892." In Lepetit and Hoock 1987.

Burns, A. F. 1935. "Long Cycles in Residential Construction." In *Economic Essays in Honor of Wesley Clair Mitchell*. New York.

Caron, F. 1985. *Le résistible déclin des sociétés industrielles*. Paris.

Crain, R. L. 1966. "Fluoridation: The Diffusion of an Innovation among Cities." *Social Forces* 44:467–476.

Dohrn van Rossum, G. 1987. "The Diffusion of the Public Clocks in the Cities of Late Medieval Europe, 1300–1500." In Lepetit and Hoock 1987.

Feller, I. 1971. "The Urban Location of United States Invention, 1860–1913." *Explorations in Economic History* 8 (Spring):285–303.

―――― 1973. "Determinant of the Composition of Urban Invention." *Economic Geography* 49, no. 1 (January):48–58.

Gélis, J. 1985. "La ville et la diffusion de la conscience moderne du corps: le révélateur de l'obstétrique (XVI–XVIIIe siècles)." *Démographic historique, Bulletin d'information* no. 45 (November):2–13.

Glenn, N. D., and L. Hill, Jr. 1977. "Rural-Urban Differences in Attitudes and Behavior in the United States." *Annals of the American Academy of Political and Social Science*, no. 429 (January):36–50.

Griliches, Z., ed. 1984. *R & D, Patents, and Productivity*. Chicago.

Haegerstrand, T. 1967. *Innovation Diffusion as a Spatial Process*. Chicago.

Higgs, R. 1971. "American Inventiveness, 1879–1920." *Journal of Political Economy* 79 (May–June):661–667.

Hoyt, H. 1933. *One Hundred Years of Land Values in Chicago: The Relationship of the Growth of Chicago and the Rise of Land Values, 1830–1933*. Chicago.

Kuznets, S. 1930. *Secular Movements in Production and Prices*. Boston.

Landes, D. S. 1969. *The Unbound Prometheus: Technological Change and Industrial Development in Western Europe from 1750 to the Present*. Cambridge.

―――― 1983. *Revolution in Time: Clocks and the Making of the Modern World*. Cambridge, Mass.

Lepetit, B. 1987. "Réseau urbain et diffusion de l'innovation dans la France préindustrielle: la création des caisses d'épargne, 1818–1848." In Lepetit and Hoock 1987.

Lepetit, B., and J. Hoock, eds. 1987. *La ville et l'innovation en Europe, XIV–XIX siècles*. Paris.

Malecki, E. J. 1980. "Corporate Organization of R and D and the Location of Technological Activities." *Regional Studies* 14, no. 3:219–234.

Martin, I. 1977. "Inventions, techniques, et urbanisation en Europe au XIXe siècle: Allemagne, France, et Royaume-Uni." Dissertation, Department of Economic History, University of Geneva.

Oakey, R. P., A. T. Thwaites, and P. A. Nash. 1980. "The Regional Distribution of Innovative Manufacturing Establishments in Britain." *Regional Studies* 14, no. 3:235–253.

Ogburn, W. F., and O. D. Duncan. 1964. "City Size as a Sociological Variable." In *Contributions to Urban Sociology*, ed. E. W. Burgess and D. J. Bogue. Chicago.

Pedersen, P. O. 1970. "Innovation Diffusion within and between National Urban Systems." *Geographical Analysis* 2:203–254.

Pellenbarg, P. H., and J. A. A. M. Kok. 1985. "Small and Medium-Sized Innovative Firms in the Netherlands' Urban and Rural Regions." *Tijdschrift voor Economische en Sociale Geografie* 76, no. 4:242–252.

Pred, A. R. 1966. *The Spatial Dynamics of U.S. Urban Industrial Growth, 1800–1914*. Cambridge, Mass.

Rees, J., R. Briggs, and R. Oakey. 1984. "The Adoption of New Technology in the American Machinery Industry." *Regional Studies* 18, no. 6:489–504.

Riggleman, J. R. 1933. "Building Cycles in the United States: 1875–1932." *Journal of the American Statistical Association* 28, no. 182 (June):174–183.

Robson, B. T. 1973. *Urban Growth: An Approach*. London.

Rogers, E. M., with F. F. Shoemaker. 1971. *Communication of Innovations: A Cross-Cultural Approach*. 2nd ed. New York.

Rose, E. 1948. "Innovation in American Culture." *Social Forces* 26, no. 3 (March):255–272.

Rosenberg, N. 1974. "Science, Invention, and Economic Growth." *Economic Journal* 84 (March): 90–108.

Schmookler, J. 1966. *Invention and Economic Growth*. Cambridge, Mass.

Shrum, W., R. Wuthnow, and J. Beniger. 1985. "The Organization of Technology in Advanced Industrial Society: A Hypothesis on Technical Systems." *Social Forces* 64, no. 1 (September): 46–63.

Tornqvist, G. 1970. *Contact Systems and Regional Development*. Lund.

Utterback, J. M. 1974. "Innovation in Industry and the Diffusion of Technology." *Science* 183 (February):620–626.

Weber, M. [1921] 1958. *The City*. Glencoe, Ill.

Wilson, T. C. 1985. "Urbanism and Tolerance: A Test of Some Hypotheses Drawn from Wirth and Stouffer." *American Sociological Review* 50, no. 1 (February):117–123.

Wirth, L. 1938. "Urbanism as a Way of Life." *American Journal of Sociology* 44 (July):3–24.

Wysocki, J. 1987. "La fondation de caisses d'épargne communales dans les villes allemandes au 19e siècle." In Lepetit and Hoock 1987.

6

• • •

Dear Labor, Cheap Labor, and the Industrial Revolution

Joel Mokyr

What was the relation between income distribution and the Industrial Revolution?[1] Before we turn to that question, it is worthwhile to ask whether the concept of an *industrial* revolution is not too narrow for its subject. Some recent writing seems to suggest that the term has outlived its useful life and should be dropped, but Landes, in his *Unbound Prometheus* (1969), had few doubts on the matter: "The words [Industrial Revolution], when capitalized, . . . denote the first historical instance of a breakthrough from an agrarian, handicraft economy to one dominated by industry and machine manufacture." Decades after these lines were first written, I still see very little to be added to that definition.[2] In spite of the importance of the political, social, and demographic factors, changes in technology remain at the heart of the matter.

The Industrial Revolution, wrote Landes (1969, p. 1) "spread . . . [from England] in *unequal fashion* to the countries of Continental Europe" (emphasis added). He referred to this process as "Continental Emulation." Sidney Pollard subsequently termed the same process "Peaceful Conquest." The implication is that Britain, by being the first, was in some sense a success story, whereas on the Continent, the later the Industrial Revolution occurred, the more backward an area was. More recent scholarship has qualified these notions of success and failure. Especially France and the Netherlands, it has been maintained, were different but not backward. From a purely technological point of view, however, Britain's lead is as obvious now as it was to contemporaries. Continental observers felt Britain's technical superiority all too keenly. "To take away British steam engines today would amount to . . . ruining her means of prosperity and destroying her great power," wrote the French scientist Sadi Carnot in 1824.[3] Economic historians today might dispute that judgment for the steam engine alone, but surely not for the totality of inventions in power technology, materials, textiles, chemicals, machine tools, and so on. Although it could also be argued that the *really* interesting question about the Industrial Revolution is not why did it happen 70 years earlier in Britain than in Germany but rather why

177

did it happen at all, and why in Europe and not in the Ottoman Empire, tropical
Africa, or China, the variety within Europe poses an important challenge to
economic historians, perhaps because the more limited scope of the problem
makes it possible to resolve it.

Let us consider two aspects of successful industrialization during the Industrial Revolution: the generation and development of new knowledge in the
production of goods and services, and the factors that determine the rate of
diffusion and adoption of techniques that are already known. The two processes
were governed by quite different forces. It is clear that Britain did not monop-
olize invention, but it remained for a long time the stage of the technological
action. Continental inventions, from the Jacquard loom to the Leblanc soda
process, eventually found a more fertile soil in Britain than on their own spawning grounds. Can we explain this? I think we can, and I have made some efforts
to extend attempts in that direction (Mokyr 1990). But when we are discussing
western Europe between 1760 and 1850, the history of the Industrial Revolution
is in large part one of adoption and diffusion, and not only of the causes of
technological change (or its absence). Technical knowledge, despite some attempts to keep it confined to Britain, was quite mobile, and entrepreneurs on the
Continent learned British techniques rapidly and cheaply, often through British
engineers and technicians roaming through Europe. Yet knowledge did not
translate into uniform adoption of new techniques, even when they were unambiguously superior.

What could explain these delays? It struck me some years ago that one way
to think about the problem was to focus on the income distribution *at the outset*
of the process. I arrived at this suggestion working with a model incorporating
a number of what seemed widely accepted, unoriginal, and unobtrusive assumptions reflecting stylized historical fact rather than necessarily analytical
convenience. Precisely because my conclusions appear to be at variance with
the facts in many cases, it seems important to review these assumptions so that
the model may be examined. Because the model is not, strictly speaking, a
growth model (it has few implications for the overall growth rate of the economy) but deals more with the composition and technological practices of some
sectors, I term it a "growing-up" model (Mokyr 1976a, 1976b). The assumptions are as follows:

1. Capital goods "embodied" the new technology. Then, as now, that assumption seemed to me almost too obvious to need justification. The new power
technology, the buildings in which the mills were housed, the implements,
tools, inventories of spare parts and raw materials, all were essential to the new
technology. This is not to deny the significance of disembodied technological
change. It implies, however, that a lack of fixed capital could retard the transformation. The reverse does not hold: an abundant supply of capital did not

guarantee the adoption of technological changes and the emergence of factories, because the owners of the capital could not be relied on to lend it to aspiring factory owners. What mattered was venture capital, not aggregate savings.

2. The rate of accumulation depended crucially on the rate of profit. In the simplest model, in which factory owners could not borrow and had to rely on retained profits to finance new investment, this conclusion is trivial. In models in which financial institutions played a role, however, this relation is not weakened as long as the past performance of the firm is used as an indicator of its future profitability.

3. Wages were the main cost to the firm. If labor productivity is primarily determined by technological parameters, and the prices of output are given, the rate of wages is inversely related to the rate of profit through the factor-price frontier. In other words, because the productivity of labor depended on the technology in use, which was accessible to all economies, the main reason why profit rates differed across economies was different wage levels.

4. The modern sector used a fixed-coefficients technology in which labor and capital were employed in a given "dosage."

5. Goods were internationally mobile, while labor and capital were not. It is assumed that labor was mobile only *within* a region, whereas capital markets were irrelevant as a source of industrial finance. Hence, if there were no important differences in the propensities of capitalists to reinvest profits in their firms, the model predicts that areas that for some reason started off with low wages would undergo an industrial revolution at a faster rate.

The growing-up model is different from the standard growth models in that it is a disequilibrium model. Its dynamics depend on the coexistence of the "old" and the "new" technologies. The traditional technologies, which produce the same good (or a close substitute) as the factories, can continue their existence for a long time after the process has started, because the modern sector is still too small to supplant them altogether. As long as the two sectors coexist, the modern sector earns a "quasi-rent," a disequilibrium payment that will eventually disappear when the manual industries have disappeared. The model differs radically from neoclassical models that predict that high wages will stimulate technological change and capital-intensive techniques (see Landes 1969, p. 116, for a discussion of the pros and cons of cheap labor). Instead, it predicts quite the reverse: high-wage economies would have lower profits, lower rates of accumulation, and thus a slower and later industrial revolution. Second, the model also predicts that wages in the modern sector would grow slowly if at all as long as the traditional sector remained a large employer. In this sense the model is comparable to the labor-surplus models of Lewis and Fei-Ranis popular in the 1970s. In contrast to these models, however, the growing-up model does not have to make any deus ex machina assumptions about the wage rate. The modern sector is small enough relative to the rest of the economy to take the wage parametrically (an assumption I shall modify later in this chapter); hence, the lower the wage set in the traditional economy, the faster the modern sector could grow.[4]

The application of the model to the mysterious "failure" of the Netherlands seemed obvious enough.[5] Of all the continental economies, the absence of an industrial revolution in the Netherlands is the most difficult to explain. A highly urbanized and commercialized economy with unusually good internal transportation, a colonial empire, and a large supply of capital, it seemed an obvious candidate for following the British example in adopting the factory system. Yet no such response occurred. Whether the bleak picture of the Dutch economy that contemporaries painted is somewhat exaggerated remains to be seen (De Meere 1982). Yet there seems to be little question that before 1870 the Industrial Revolution basically passed the Netherlands by. Nor has any serious doubt been raised as to the high level of wages in the Dutch cities. Contemporaries from Adam Smith to the Frenchman Sérionne writing in the 1770s to the Dutch political economist Van Der Boon Mesch writing in 1843 were unanimous about high Dutch wages and their negative effect on profits, and thus on the modernization of Dutch manufacturing (Mokyr 1976a, pp. 168–170). The quantitative evidence of the 1819 census utilized by Griffiths and myself points in the same direction. Although the source is imprecise enough to leave some room for interpretation, the assumption of unusually high wages in the Dutch maritime provinces has not been seriously contested (see De Meere 1982, p. 72; Van Zanden 1985b). To link the high-wage phenomenon with industrial retardation seems natural enough and is theoretically sound.

The story of Belgium, the obverse in my comparative study of the Low Countries, also seemed consistent with the simple income-distribution model. Belgium became the closest follower of Britain in adopting novel techniques in textile, metallurgic, and other industries. It became, in a phrase, the "Second Industrial Nation." How does one explain this phenomenon? In Belgium, I argued, the existence of a large premodern industrial sector in the form of cottage industries in the Flemish and Walloon countryside created a large supply of cheap and willing labor that made it possible for Belgian capitalists to realize high profits and thus grow rapidly. Although other mechanisms that created a link between existing cottage industries and the Industrial Revolution can be thought of, they appear secondary. For instance, the factories seem to have drawn entrepreneurs and some capital from the traditional merchant-industrialists who controlled much of rural industry.[6] One could, of course, produce alternative models of Belgium's speed and effectiveness in overhauling its traditional industries, but the failure of anybody to come up with an alternative story that is coherent and consistent may be taken as an indication of the difficulty of the problem.[7]

In spite of the simplicity of the assumptions, and the story's fit to the Low Countries' experience, the relation between wages and the diffusion of the Industrial Revolution does not hold up for other parts of Europe. The growing-up model in its simple form does not seem to explain the facts very well. In what follows I shall try to explore other ways in which income distribution could have affected the diffusion and implementation of novel technologies. I then turn to the issue of the standard of living and the change in wages resulting from the Industrial Revolution.

One glaring contradiction that the growing-up model runs into is the experience of the British Isles themselves. If low wages were beneficial to rapid accumulation and high wages inhibited it, how does Britain's industrial miracle coupled to Ireland's debacle square with the theory? The confusion on the question of the effect of labor supplies on the Industrial Revolution in Britain is enormous. Some writers have in fact found "abundant cheap labor" in Britain, which was a "crucial factor in maintaining the impetus of the Industrial Revolution" (Deane 1979, p. 148). British wages were, however, higher than elsewhere in Europe, a fact that has prompted speculation that technological progress during the Industrial Revolution was generated to save on these labor costs. In the growing-up model I assumed that generation of the new technology itself was independent of income distribution, and that it was more efficient than the old techniques at any factor-price combination. Only its diffusion, dependent as it was on capital formation, was a function of wages. These assumptions differed from those made by Habakkuk in his celebrated *American and British Technology in the Nineteenth Century*.[8] He argued that technological change depended on factor prices, and that high wages "might" have stimulated technical progress, in a formulation so cautious it led Landes to remark that Habakkuk's is "history in the subjunctive and conditional modes" (Landes 1965, p. 17).

Much ink has been spilled on the Habakkuk thesis. The view that factor prices actually affect the generation of new technological knowledge has been especially controversial. Technological creativity is a deep and mysterious social force. It is simply implausible that high wages were responsible for the bursts of invention that made the Industrial Revolution in Britain. Economic parameters such as income distribution, resource availability, and the structure of demand can be influential in helping decide the direction in which new technology moves, but they will typically not determine the level of technological creativity in a society. The *primum mobile* of technological change has to be sought elsewhere; it is the engine that makes the car run, not the steering wheel. To be sure, the steering wheel determines whether a car is driven onto a highway or into a blind alley: hence the arguments made by David, Rosenberg, and others in which these parameters are viewed as central to the generation of new technologies. Without denying the specific validity of their arguments, I would separate incidentals from fundamentals. These variables are, in Rosenberg's felicitous phrase, "focusing devices." Yet a focusing device is useless without an external source of light. What made Britain more creative and successful than Spain or Russia has to be sought at a more profound level.

An alternative version of the Habakkuk thesis examines a hypothetical *choice* of technique. In this interpretation, the Industrial Revolution created a new isoquant, with many feasible points corresponding to different capital-labor ratios. Could it be that the empirical difficulties of the growing-up model are resolved if we allow for a choice of many modern techniques rather than just one? A moment's reflection suffices to show that if the other assumptions are granted, such a model *strengthens* the conclusion that low wages were a positive factor in the rate of accumulation (though we have to remain in the conditional mode). Habakkuk argued that high-wage economies such as the United States' will use capital-intensive techniques. These techniques may eventually lead to an all-around more efficient world if they tend to permit more "localized" learning, as Paul David pointed out over a decade ago. But if they require *more* capital, and yet wages are *higher,* it may well be that it will take a lot longer to get the economy to accumulate enough capital to make the new technique realistic. Profits may or may not be higher, depending on the ratio between the wage rates and the productivities in the two economies. But more capital has to be accumulated in the high-wage economy; a longer road has to be traveled at a speed that may well be slower.[9]

To be sure, if the modern sector can draw freely on the capital supplies of the economy (or, better still, of the world), the constraint that present profits limit current investment no longer necessarily holds. But the starting point of any model that tries to capture the economics of the Industrial Revolution has to be that defects in the capital market introduced an element of disequilibrium that was, in my judgment, better captured by the Ricardian and Marxian models of accumulation than by neoclassical theories of growth. Habakkuk-type theories operate, I believe, primarily in a microeconomic world of substitution or quasi-substitution occurring along an isoquant, and must assume that there were no serious constraints on capital supplies. The difficulty is that in many senses there was no such thing as "the" supply of capital.[10]

Could it be that the weakness of the growing-up model is in its assumptions concerning capital markets? To what extent was the supply of capital a binding constraint? Cottrell (1980, p. 267) has argued that established firms "did not issue primary financial instruments to attract savings from surplus units and households in order to . . . grow at a rate faster than that supported by the accumulation of internal resources," but adds that he thinks that this phenomenon did not seriously affect the rate of growth of the manufacturing sector of the economy before 1860. In other words, capital markets were largely internal, but the rate of accumulation was not substantially affected by that. His reasoning (purely conjectural, as he admits) is that profits were very high because of a lack of competition and a strong position of employers in the labor market. Moreover, Cottrell argues that investment projects were small and divisible.

Cottrell's analysis of the working of capital markets is unexceptionable, but his counterfactual—that with better capital markets, the rate of accumulation would not have been substantially different—is open to question. Jeffrey Williamson (1987) has tried to estimate the impact of factor market failures. He concludes that these failures *did* matter in an aggregate sense, although the really significant failure was in capital markets. Capital markets starved industry for capital, and thus led to low total profits. Had capital markets functioned better, manufacturing output in 1831 would have been 64 percent higher than it actually was, and employment (unskilled labor only) in manufacturing would have been 40 percent higher. The lack of competition in product markets (giving the modern sector a monopoly rent in addition to the quasi-rents generated by its superior technology) seems hard to believe, given the large number of firms and the integration of the British market.[11] Finally, Cottrell's point about labor markets is, of course, very much in the spirit of the growing-up model, but whether it is right and applicable to Britain is unclear.[12] In short, the assumption that capital markets were imperfect so accumulation depended on retained profits seems to remain a reasonable part of the model.

If this was true for Britain, it was doubly true for other economies that were trying to emulate it. One example strikes me as worth citing. In the 1810s, a flourishing cotton industry grew in the Lagan Valley around Belfast. The failure of this industry, and Ireland's failure to grow a modern sector in Ulster that could have assumed the same role in Irish economic history that the Scottish Lowlands did for Scotland, must remain one of the most fascinating issues in the economic history of England's Celtic fringe. Although other factors played a role, capital scarcity facing modern industry is too powerful an effect to be relegated to the "also-ran" category. When mechanized linen spinning became a technological reality in the mid-1820s, Ulster switched from cotton to linen. Henry Inglis (1834, II, 254) pointed out that "the new spinning mills in Belfast [involved] not the investment of new capital but the transfer of capital from the cotton trade."[13] Why could linen and cotton not have coexisted and developed together in Ulster, as they did in England, Scotland, and even Flanders?

The recognition that by improving capital markets continental countries could catch up faster with Britain was widespread. As early as 1822, when King William I formed the Société Générale in Belgium, statesmen and political economists emphasized the importance of investment banks. In France, Germany, Austria, and Italy, these investment banks eventually played roles in the modernization process, though these roles varied a great deal from country to country. After 1850, therefore, the assumptions regarding capital markets become less realistic, particularly when capital accumulated in Britain and other early industrializers was used to modernize latecomers.

The empirical paradox posed by the growing-up model can be briefly stated. Why did economies which had demonstrably low wages, had access to modern technology, and were integrated into world markets fail to undergo an industrial revolution? Ireland is, needless to say, the most striking example of such an economy. Mutatis mutandis, the argument may well be made for France and southern Europe as well. Still, Ireland was an extreme case, and it may well be worth examining in some detail why a model which apparently predicts Ireland to become a leader in modern industry fails so clearly in this case.

Some explanations of this phenomenon have been put forward in my book *Why Ireland Starved* (1983). A central argument I launched there was that the growing-up model assumes that labor is immobile internationally, though mobile up to a point within a country and very mobile within smaller regions. The British case before 1850 is well described by this assumption. For the case of Ireland, however, it is patently violated in the first half of the nineteenth century. Hundreds of thousands of Irish men and women emigrated both to North America and to Britain. Irish cheap labor thus helped other economies accumulate capital goods, and the Irish Industrial Revolution simply took place in Lancashire and Massachusetts. Ulster was more than proportionally represented in this emigration. Emigration from other regions of Ireland to Ulster was modest: of the roughly 17,000 people residing in Belfast in 1841 who were not born there, almost 14,000 originated in other parts of Ulster (*Census of Ireland* 1843, pp. 446–447). What seems to have happened is that migration was either over a very short distance or overseas. Medium-distance migration within a country was rare before 1850. Under the assumption of a homogeneous labor force, all this may not have mattered much. Emigration, though much larger in Ireland than in other countries before 1850, did not keep the Irish population from growing, and what little evidence there is on Irish wages shows no evidence that emigration deprived the country of its potential factory labor factor, creating labor scarcities and rising wages (see Mokyr and O Grada 1988).

But labor was far from homogeneous, and emigration mattered primarily because emigrants were a self-selected group. If the characteristics of the emigrants were correlated with those of the best factory workers, the effect of emigration on the accumulation and modernization of industry could be much larger than what is implied in the raw numbers of emigrants.[14] Precisely because Ireland was the only European economy to suffer from large-scale out-migration in the first half of the nineteenth century, it seems natural to turn to emigration to explain the paradox of Ireland's failure to industrialize.

Yet there must have been more to it. The one assumption that the growing-up model had to make is that the productivity of labor is the same across different economies. The basis for that assumption was that labor productivity depended on technology and capital intensity alone, and thus output per worker in the modern sector was the same regardless of country. Yet that assumption cannot be realistic. In a paper dealing with a somewhat later period, Gregory Clark (1987) shows the strong correlation of labor productivity with nominal wages, even using the same technology and capital intensity. Clark demonstrates that the high labor cost in the Atlantic economies (always excepting Ireland) was essentially offset by higher productivity of workers in high-wage countries. He concludes that "real labor costs turn out to be as high as those in Britain in most of the other countries except for the very low wage competitors in Asia. The per worker wage rate tells us very little about the true costs of labor" (p. 11). If this finding is sustained and can be generalized, it implies a major modification to the generality of the growing-up model.[15] Labor productivity becomes an independent variable in the model rather than wholly determined by technology and factor proportions.

The problem is that labor productivity estimates independent of wages are very difficult to come by. What we do have, however, are observations by many contemporaries convinced that cheap labor was dear labor because high wages were associated with high productivity and vice versa. Adam Smith and Arthur Young, those warhorses of casual observation about the second half of the eighteenth century, agreed on the issue.[16] The lower productivity of the Irish workers was specifically mentioned by many observers. Arthur Young himself stressed in his *Tour in Ireland* (1892, II, 278, 306) that in Ireland "husbandry labor is very low priced but by no means cheap" because of "skill, goodness of work + c." In 1845 the Irish physician and political economist Robert Kane made the same argument. It was well known, said Kane, that Irish wages were much lower than wages elsewhere in Europe. However, "this nominal cheapness is . . . by no means necessarily economy in final cost . . . British labourers . . . would probably be paid at least twice as much money per day but in the end the work would not cost the employer more; although the wages in the former example [Ireland] were lower, labour was not cheaper, on the contrary, somewhat higher" (Kane 1845, pp. 397–398). The standard complaint about the cotton industry in Ulster in the 1810s and 1820s was that it could not compete with the Scottish and English industries. Apart from differences in labor efficiency, I see little that could have given the Lagan Valley in Ulster a cost disadvantage with respect to British industrial regions, especially after 1830, when declining transport costs reduced the differentials Irish manufacturers had to pay for fuel and raw cotton.

What explains the low productivity of poorly paid workers? Despite the ingenuity with which it poses the question, Clark's essay remains mute on the

possible resolution of the riddle. One type of model that seemingly would lend
itself to the question is an "efficiency wage" model that explicitly links productivity with workers' wages by means of nutrition. Poorly paid workers could
be poorly fed workers. The connection between caloric intake and energy output
of workers is well known. Workers on an insufficient diet do not necessarily get
sick or die; they simply slow down their entire metabolism, to the detriment of
their productivity (see Scrimshaw 1983, pp. 211–213). This argument, it seems,
may not work well for the Irish-British comparison. The cost of nutrition in
Ireland, where food intake was based on potatoes, was substantially lower than
in Britain. As a result, the prefamine Irish, poor as they were, were better fed
than the British.[17] In France, matters may have been quite different, and a
significant segment of the population was apparently underfed. Fogel (n.d.; see
also Chapter 1 of this volume) has concluded that on the eve of the Revolution,
a large proportion of the French labor force could carry out little or no heavy
work because of the insufficiency of food. This startling finding is consistent
with the small stature and the short life expectancy of the French at this time.
During his visit to France, Arthur Young (1929) argued emphatically that
"labour is *in reality* the cheapest where it is *nominally* the dearest . . . If [the
workman] be well nourished and clothed . . . he will perform incomparably
better than a man whose poverty allows but a scanty nourishment" (p. 311;
emphasis in original).

Productivity, however, depended on more than nutrition. Adam Smith
([1776] 1937, p. 81) thought that "the wages of labour are the encouragement
of industry, which like every other quality, improves in proportion to the encouragement it receives. A plentiful subsistence increases the bodily strength of
the laborer . . . where wages are high, accordingly, we shall always find the
workmen more active, diligent, and expeditious, than where they are low."
What Smith seems to be describing, however, is an upward-sloping supply
curve of labor, which makes people work *more* if the wage is higher. The
question is, however, what makes people work *better* or harder per unit of time?

Recent thinking about the efficiency wage hypothesis has shown that labor
productivity can depend on the real wage paid to workers in a variety of ways
(see Yellen 1984; Akerlof 1984). A simple model of this type is the shirking
model, in which it is expensive to monitor the effort the worker puts in. High
wages are a mechanism by which the employer extracts more effort from the
worker because a worker caught shirking risks being fired and losing his high-
paying job. High wages could also increase productivity through reduced turnover. Another model derives a correlation between productivity and wages
through an "adverse selection" mechanism: the worst-quality workers agree to
work for less (Weiss 1980). Sociological studies, too, confirm that, all other
things being equal, workers with lower pay produce less output.[18]

While we cannot measure labor productivity directly, we can measure some properties of the labor force that could be correlated with it. It is often thought that skill differences between nations or regions are crucial in explaining differences in the performance of labor.[19] Unfortunately, skills are difficult to measure, and in societies with primitive systems of formal education in which most workers were self-employed, measuring human capital through such standard proxies as education and experience is all but impossible. The great Irish census of 1841, possibly the most detailed statistical document of the first half of the nineteenth century, provides us with enough county-level data to make some statements about the quality of the labor force. We shall employ four of them: the literacy rate (defined as the percentage of adult males who could both read and write), the age-heaping variable (defined as the proportion of males declaring to be aged 30 divided by the males declaring ages 30–34), the proportion of adult males who listed as their occupation "laborers and servants," and the proportion of adult males in each county whose occupation fell under the heading of "ministering to education." We would expect the first and the last proxies to correlate positively with productivity or ability, while the second and third proxies should correlate negatively.[20]

The regressions cited herein are reduced forms. I do not propose to test whether high wages imply high productivity, as the efficiency wage models imply, or whether the reverse is the case, as human capital theory suggests. All we need do is establish that high wages and "high-quality" labor were correlated. If this correlation is strong enough, then one of the assumptions of the growing-up model has been violated, and we can regard the result as support for the "cheap labor is dear labor" hypothesis.[21]

In Table 6.1 I list the results of regressions in which the county wage levels are the dependent variable and the four proxies of labor quality are the independent variables. Two wage variables are employed: the mean wage, which is total wage earnings per capita (*not* per worker), including the earnings of women and children) and a male wage *rate* (annual, not corrected for unemployment). To avoid spurious correlations, I ran all regressions with a control variable that correlates with wages in each regression. Two controls were used: the percentage of the population living in urban areas (which would vary positively with wages) and the proportion of the labor force in cottage industries.[22]

The table indicates clearly that a positive and strong association between wages and the "labor quality" variables is maintained regardless of specification and the "control" variable chosen. The data also show that cottage industries tend to depress the wage—as predicted by the growing-up model—but the effect becomes very weak when literacy is included. Yet the results also indicate that "labor quality" does not explain Irish wages altogether. If the relations reported in Table 6.1 are approximately linear, we can assess how much Irish

Table 6.1   Wage equations, Ireland (*t*-statistics in parentheses).

Variable or parameter	Equation							
	1	2	3	4	5	6	7	8
Wage variable	Mean	Mean	Mean	Mean	Male	Male	Male	Male
Constant	0.70	4.76	6.26	0.99	4.74	18.17	21.95	4.86
	(2.67)	(5.28)	(12.33)	(3.66)	(4.58)	(5.17)	(10.54)	(4.89)
Literacy	5.69				17.78			
	(7.46)				(5.88)			
Heaping		−5.85				−19.78		
		(−3.06)				(−2.66)		
Proportion laborers			−0.61				−0.19	
			(−7.81)				(−5.86)	
Percent teachers				1.77				6.93
				(3.96)				(4.21)
Proportion urban		3.22		0.70		10.07		0.06
		(6.46)		(0.86)		(5.18)		(0.02)
Cottage industry	0.61		−3.42		2.05		−10.36	
	(.94)		(−4.45)		(0.80)		(−3.29)	
R^2	0.66	0.66	0.68	0.70	0.54	0.56	0.54	0.66

Source: See note 22.

wages could have been raised by changes in "labor quality." For instance, doubling the literacy rate—a tall order—would have raised the "mean" wage by about 45 percent, while raising the "skill" levels by halving the proportion of workers declaring themselves to be "laborers" would have raised the mean wage by 67 percent. Those substantial raises would still have kept Irish wages considerably below British levels.

All in all, then, we have a double-barreled hypothesis explaining why low wages in Ireland were not necessarily an advantage in terms of accumulation. The first is that emigration deprived Ireland of its most efficient workers, thus reducing the average "quality" of laborers at home. The second is that Irish workers were inherently less efficient than British workers. Whether we can ever measure "efficiency" sufficiently precisely to test this hypothesis remains to be seen.

A different possible explanation for the failure of some low-wage economies to switch to modern industry can be found in another modification of the growing-up model. In its simplest version, cottage industries are considered to be competitive with modern industries in both the product and the labor markets. Modern industry is more efficient, and it is only because of the capital formation constraint that the modern sector does not eliminate the traditional sector right away. Yet such a model ignores the complementarities between the two sectors. The technological history of manufacturing during the Industrial Revolution shows that the appearance of new techniques rarely affected handicraft industries across the board. It usually increased supplies in one part and increased demand in another. At later stages, previously positively affected industries would start to suffer, but often new demands were created. In textiles, for instance, there was a stage, lasting about two or three decades, during which spinning and preparing were mechanized and carried out in factories, but weaving was still carried out in the cottage industry because the technical difficulties in power weaving tended to be more complex. The temporary effect of the revolution in spinning technology on hand-loom weaving was thus positive. In cotton this stage lasted from 1780 to about 1815, while in linen it lasted between 1825 and about 1855. Ireland's large supply of cottage-industrial workers, the accumulation constraints discussed earlier, and the long tradition of Ulster and Connacht in linen working saw to it that Ireland found linen more attractive than the more mechanized cotton industry. Linen, however, did not become a growth industry, and its market shrank relative to cotton. The cheap labor in Ireland's cottage industries thus gave the market a signal to specialize in linen. As it turned out, it was the wrong signal from the point of view of long-term development. But without perfect foresight it is not clear how that kind of event could have been avoided.

In the final analysis, then, cheap labor could have been detrimental to industrialization through a variety of mechanisms. It could and probably did mean in some places that workers were underfed and possibly handicapped in other ways. Cheap labor could mean unmotivated, quarrelsome workers, poorly adapted to the discipline and rigor of factory and mining life. It meant poor labor relations, low morale, high turnover, and absenteeism. Cheap labor could mean that workers were illiterate, unskilled, and incapable of making the adjustments required by changing techniques. Cheap labor, however, could also send a wrong signal, not only in terms of choosing a labor-intensive technique but also through specialization in the product market.[23] Yet, all things considered, low wages, when they were not offset by lower productivity, remained an advantage. Since I know of no evidence that Dutch labor productivity was significantly higher than that in Belgium, the growing-up model still holds for that case.

The other side of real wages is the standard of living. Low wages may have meant higher profits, and therefore faster rates of accumulation. They also meant, however, that the distribution of income was unequal and the working classes experienced low living standards compared to workers in high-wage economies. The import of the literature on the standard of living is that rising real wages were the mechanism through which the fruits of technological and economic progress were transmitted to the bulk of the population. At the same time, rising living standards would, all other things being equal, slow down the accumulation process. On both accounts, therefore, the dynamics of the Industrial Revolution and the standard of living of the workers were closely linked.

I will argue that existing evidence does not allow us to reject the hypothesis that the occurrence of an industrial revolution and the emergence of a modern sector did not have a large effect one way or another on what is usually defined as the standard of living before the middle of the nineteenth century. The standard of living is different from the microeconomic concept of utility and the macroeconomic concept of income per capita. It should be regarded as an objective measure of an individual's ability to sustain himself or herself and function, both physically and mentally.[24] The "pessimistic" conclusion has to be modified in a major way if we extend the concept of living standards to include the ability to cope with disastrous supply shocks such as the Irish famine. But apart from that, I submit that before the mid-1840s at the very earliest, the living standards of the masses in western Europe were *on average* practically unaffected by the Industrial Revolution. Some groups gained, but these gains were largely offset by the losses of others. The consumption of some items, such as textiles, increased in per capita terms, but before the middle of the nineteenth century these goods remained in the minority. The slowness of living standards to respond to the Industrial Revolution is consistent with the classical models, whether they are Ricardian, Marxian, or in the Arthur Lewis tradition. This argument can be supported by a look at evidence from four economies: Britain, Ireland, the Netherlands, and Belgium.

The hypothesis is surely to be most controversial in the case of Britain. In their research, Williamson and Lindert have provided substantial evidence for a central argument made by pessimists, namely that inequality during the Industrial Revolution followed a Kuznets curve: an increase in inequality followed by a decrease (see especially Lindert and Williamson 1983a; Williamson 1985). Yet at the same time, they have infused new life into the optimist position. Their 1983 paper could well be said to have out-Hartwelled R. M. Hartwell himself in its rather stunning claim of a 1.8 percent growth rate in real wages between 1819 and 1851 (Williamson and Lindert 1983a). These two positions are not *necessarily* inconsistent with each other, because overall growth *could* have been so fast that a mild increase in inequality would not be sufficient to offset the strong current of overall improvement.

The new optimism has not persuaded everyone.[25] I have argued elsewhere (Mokyr 1988) that the Lindert and Williamson data may well reflect rising wages in that part of the labor force that worked for an employer and received a formal wage, but that for the large number of workers who were self-employed or who worked for putting-out entrepreneurs on a piece-wage basis, matters may have been different. The argument rests on consumption data. If Lindert and Williamson are right and living standards were improving markedly after 1819, we should be able to observe an increase in consumption. Feinstein's aggregate consumption data do indeed reflect that increase (Feinstein 1981, I, 136; Crafts 1985, p. 95). But the aggregate series is a residual—the difference between two highly aggregate and speculative series—and Feinstein was careful not to equate his findings with a rise in living standards for the working classes. It seems preferable to look at microeconomic series of consumption, and to use them in conjunction with some plausible estimates regarding price and income elasticities to "retrocast" a time series of a synthetic living standards variable. Employing this procedure has two marked advantages: first, it reflects the living standards of wage laborers as well as the self-employed (since consumption of such goods as tea and tobacco was universal). Second, because the marginal propensity to consume these goods was probably falling with income, changes in income distribution would be reflected in them. A mean-preserving, variance-increasing change in income distribution would reduce the consumption of these goods and thus be registered as a deterioration in living standards, as well it should. The results indicate that there was an insignificant rise in overall living standards between 1820 and 1845, with a marked improvement occurring only in the 1840s (and not in the early 1820s, as Lindert and Williamson maintain).

Further doubt is cast on the new optimism by two other independent sources. One is the agricultural consumption (cereals and vegetable products only) series pieced together by Gertrud Helling from fragmentary data (1977; see Mokyr 1988, p. 90). The second is the picture slowly emerging from the various projects analyzing average male heights. Although the results are still preliminary, they show little support for the "new optimism." Between 1770 and 1867 there seems to have been no tendency for military recruits to grow taller (Floud 1986). If living standards and real incomes were rising, was none of the increment spent on better nutrition, health care, housing, hygiene, and other goods that would eventually raise average statures?[26] The possibility cannot be excluded, but suspending disbelief becomes increasingly difficult.

How much doubt do these results cast on Lindert and Williamson's careful reworking of the price and wage data? The growing-up model implies that the Industrial Revolution was a process of change in which the old and the new coexisted and interacted in a complex way over long periods. The modern sector included those industries in which technological change was most rapid, and in which workers tended to be formally employed, and so we have records of their wages. In the traditional sector of small handicraft workers, peddlers, shopkeepers, carters, and so on, workers tended to be self-employed or work on a loose basis for a merchant-entrepreneur. Many workers, especially occasional laborers, were involved part-time in both sectors, supplementing the meager earnings of a small business with seasonal wages. The neoclassical intuition is that wages in the modern and in the traditional sector would be strongly correlated, but in practice that does not seem always to have been the case. Wages in the modern sector were increasing on average, while those in the traditional sector were not, by and large. The result was redistribution of income, with living standards in the South of Britain falling behind those of the industrializing North and the commercial towns.

The picture is complicated by the mixed effects that the growth of modern industry had on workers in the traditional sectors.[27] Five separate effects can be distinguished. First, certain consumer goods such as clothing became cheaper simply because the technological changes of the Industrial Revolution reduced prices and improved quality. Second, the increase in the demand for agricultural products and improving terms of trade raised the living standards of most people involved in agricultural production, especially livestock products, but reduced those of people living on purchased agricultural goods. Third, the Industrial Revolution increased the demand for certain complementary industrial activities, such as the weaving of fine grades of yarn, the combing of worsted, millinery, and apparel making, which for many decades remained firmly in the traditional domestic industries. Fourth, technological change in both manufacturing and agriculture affected wages and employment differentially: male labor and female labor were touched in different ways, with mechanization altering the sexual division of labor profoundly (see especially Snell 1985, chap. 1). Thus, inferring living standards from male wages could be misleading. Regionally, too, there were significant divergences, and any attempt to infer national trends from small regional samples might be difficult to interpret.[28] Fifth, those traditional industries that competed directly with the modern sector—the handloom weavers, the nailers, the button and buckle makers, blacksmiths working at small domestic forges, the carters and the craftsmen—were mercilessly ground into the dust by the new techniques, unless they were willing to adopt them and join the modern sector, either as manufacturers or, more frequently, as wage laborers. Until about the middle of the nineteenth century, these powerful but contradictory forces seem to have balanced one another out, and little net improvement for the British working classes as a whole can be discerned. After 1825, the factories and mechanization expanded into more and more products, and the traditional domestic industries experienced increasingly difficult times.[29]

Irish trends in living standards are difficult to discern because of the absence of time series on wages and most other indicators on living standards. Research on heights is currently in progress, and should increase our knowledge of what happened between 1800 and 1860. What we know from fragmentary data, however, indicates that the absence of an industrial revolution did not significantly reduce living standards in Ireland before the famine. True, it may well have deprived Ireland of the *stock* of wealth that could have saved many lives during the rainy days of the Great Famine, as it did in other industrialized regions such as Scotland and Belgium. Yet in the years between 1800 and 1845 we cannot find strong indications of rapid immiseration in the Irish economy in spite of continuing population growth (see Mokyr and O Grada 1988). The Irish were becoming more literate; they seem to have consumed more of desirable consumer goods such as tobacco; and there are few indications of sharply declining nutritional standards. The regions that were the most industrialized seem to have suffered the most, because the rise of modern industry could not compensate for the decline in cottage industries and traditional occupations.

A similar picture emerges for an economy that in other ways was vastly different—that of Belgium. Contemporaries were struck by the failure of Belgian living standards to improve during industrialization. In the late 1830s, before the crisis of 1845, Natalis de Briavoinne, an astute observer of the Belgian economy, pointed out that despite a certain progress, "the fate of the majority is still to suffer . . . the expectations have been disappointed, the efforts have been in vain" (Briavoinne 1839, I, 206). Briavoinne thought that the chief gainers from the Belgian Industrial Revolution (he used the term) were consumers of cheaper goods who mostly lived abroad, and landowners. Others saw the problem squarely in terms of the classical model of political economy. The Dutch political economist Van Hogendorp wrote in 1817 from Verviers that "whenever business booms and machines are being introduced so that goods can be produced at a lower cost than the [current] market price, the workers continue to receive the same wages, while the manufacturers gain thousands" (Van Hogendorp 1825, II, 269).

Recent research on two Belgian towns, Ghent and Antwerp, reaffirms the pessimist view (see Vandenbroeke 1973; Lis and Soly 1977; Lis 1986). Ghent, a center of successful industrialization, and Antwerp, a commercial and port city with some manufacturing, reflected different sides of the modern sector, though both contained large segments that were still traditional. In both, the consumption of cereals, meat, fish, and alcoholic drinks remained more or less stagnant until the 1850s.[30] If meat consumption per capita is any indicator, things were even worse in the industrial centers of Wallonia. The aggregate consumption of sugar and alcoholic beverages in Belgium stagnated before 1850 (Van den Eeckhout and Scholliers 1983). Paradoxically, nutritional standards may not have deteriorated all that much because of the increasing importance of potatoes in working-class diets. Potatoes tended to be an inferior good almost everywhere in Europe, so increases in their consumption are indicative of impoverishment. The net effect of the potato prior to the mid-1840s, however, was to improve the physical well-being of the population. The threat to economies such as that of Belgium was to become more and more like Ireland's. The reason this did not happen in Belgium was, beyond doubt, the Industrial Revolution. Catharina Lis's (1986, p. 163) unequivocal indictment of industrialization as entailing "new and massive impoverishment in the third world as well as in the Western hemisphere" is thus only partly true: things did not much improve in Belgium before the middle of the nineteenth century, but Belgium, unlike Ireland, did not undergo a Great Famine.

In the Netherlands, too, there seems to be little evidence of any improvement. Its prosperous agriculture continued to be the most successful sector of the Dutch economy, although total productivity grew slowly between 1810 and 1850, consumption per capita of meat and dairy products declined, and agricultural real wages fell in this period (Van Zanden 1985a, pp. 117, 136, 139). Outside agriculture, nominal wages grew very slowly if at all. Between 1819 and 1850 the wages of adult unskilled male workers rose no more than 10 percent, most of it toward the end of the period (De Meere 1982, pp. 71–72). The movement of prices, with which this movement in nomimal wages should be compared, is hard to discern. Because 1816 and 1817 were years of unusual dearth, there is an appearance of a (slight) increase in real wages. The high standard errors around the trends of prices make inferences very difficult, and an optimist or pessimist conclusion can be made or unmade by the appropriate choice of starting and end period. Here, too, the study of stature can shed considerable light on living standards in the absence of accurate data on consumption trends. The Dutch data on heights, collected by De Meere, show a somewhat mixed picture. In the four provinces for which there are data on the percentages of recruits rejected for insufficient stature (height less than 157 centimeters), the provinces of North Holland and Groningen show a deterioration, while the southern provinces of Zeeland and North Brabant show an improvement (De Meere 1982, pp. 98–100). Overall, this difference is hard to explain, and De Meere's attempt to connect it to the ratio of cereals to potatoes seems implausible, especially in light of the Irish-British comparison mentioned before. An interesting point in this regard is that, as in Ireland, the Dutch recruits from rural areas tended to be taller than their urban counterparts (see Mokyr and O Grada 1986; De Meere 1982, p. 110). This urban-rural differential seems not to hold for Britain, implying that although the Industrial Revolution may not have raised living standards overall, the geographical distribution of economic welfare may have shifted between city and countryside. A fuller analysis of this issue must await the completion of research projects on stature in the British Isles.

Whether the Industrial Revolution was clearly taking place, as in Britain and in Belgium, or whether it was absent, as in Ireland and the Netherlands, living standards seem to have been unaffected. The interpretation of this finding has to take into account the relatively limited scope of the modern sector even in the more advanced economies. Since living standards are nationwide aggregates, the effects of the modernization process were inevitably diluted by the large traditional sector. Beyond that, however, it is clear that the successful economies relied on a reservoir of cheap, elastically supplied labor, and that it took more than half a century for technological progress, commercialization, and capital accumulation to bid up real wages and raise living standards.

To sum up, are high wages a good thing? In this formulation, the answer is trivial. High wages reflect a higher productivity, a higher quality of labor, a higher level of efficiency, and imply a higher standard of living. A higher standard of living must be the principal objective of the efforts that go into economic growth. The lesson to be learned from the experience of European countries during the Industrial Revolution is that low wages, all other things being equal, facilitated the accumulation of capital necessary for the diffusion of the new technologies, and that eventually these new technologies raised wages, thus eventually eliminating the conditions that made their acceptance possible. There was, however, a long lag between the first appearance of the new technologies and their eventual effect on the standard of living. During this period living standards remained on average little changed.

At the heart of the growing-up model is a dialectical process in which low wages under the right circumstances eliminate themselves by capital accumulation. Rising wages and living standards are the reward that society reaps for the diligence, abstinence, and ingenuity of past generations. To attribute any kind of economic woes or ''declining competitiveness'' to wages that are ''too high,'' as is fashionable today, strikes me as foolhardy. The objective of all economic activity is consumption, not production, and the objective of economic growth is raising living standards, not maintaining a competitive position. There is no contradiction between my contention that, in certain historical situations, low wages (relative to labor productivity) enhanced industrialization and the view that such a situation is inherently undesirable and that it is the objective of growth to eliminate it. It is no more contradictory than to say that high rates of growth tend to be associated with low starting points. Nobody would infer from this association that if growth is desirable, it is advantageous to start as a very poor country.

The trade-off between high and low wages is analogous to the standard problem of saving and intertemporal substitution. A low-wage industrializing economy sacrifices the welfare of one generation for the benefit of its descendants. There is little in economic theory to suggest guidelines on how such choices ought to be made. One might be tempted to draw other lessons for the contemporary world from the European experience during the Industrial Revolution, but such conclusions could be hazardous and even misleading. Thus, for example, the attempts of the Korean government to block wage raises to protect its export industries seem to be unjustified unless it feels that foreign consumers and some future Korean generation are more entitled to the fruits of the toils of the present generation of adult Koreans. It is, on the other hand, perhaps justified in resisting wage demands based on demonstration effects from other sectors or countries when they are not accompanied by increased labor productivity. But such inferences assume some kind of social rate of discount that weighs the consumption of the present generation against that of its children.

All that historians can say to development economists is that income distribution determined to some extent the divergence of the economic experiences of the European economies in the nineteenth century. The way in which economic history can help development economics is not to provide parallels but to train economists to ask certain kinds of questions, to show them how to go about answering them, and to demonstrate how dangerous simple, monocausal theories can be. The growing-up model and its contemporary analogue, the labor-surplus model, provide a good illustration for that view.

Notes

1. I am indebted to Charles Calomiris, Albert Fishlow, Patrice Higonnet, Jonathan Hughes, and Cormac O Grada for their comments on earlier versions of this chapter.

2. For a more detailed discussion of the definitions of the Industrial Revolution, see Mokyr (1985a, pp. 3–6, 44).

3. Cited by Cardwell (1972, p. 130). Other admiring statements of well-informed Frenchmen on Britain's lead in industry can be cited. See, for instance, Say (1841, pp. 82–84); Blanqui (1880, pp. 430–441).

4. The logic of the model has been since adopted by other writers interested in other regions. In his work on the southern cotton industry, summarized in his *Old South, New South* (1987, pp. 76, 124), Gavin Wright explicitly points to the South's emergence as a "low-wage region in a high-wage economy" as the main reason for its success in establishing a thriving textile industry after 1880. Much in Wright's analysis of postbellum southern industry has analogues in the growing-up model, especially his assumptions on labor and capital markets.

5. For a later work corroborating my conclusions, see Griffiths (1979).

6. The magnitude of this effect can be assessed from François Crouzet's (1985) work on Britain, in which he finds that about 42 percent of the 316 industrialists in his sample had manufacturing occupations, though only 29.2 percent had fathers whose occupations were in manufacturing.

7. For some attempts in this direction, see Lebrun (1979) and Mokyr (1981).

8. Habakkuk himself was clearly aware of the paradox and in fact delineated a prototype of the classical low-wage–rapid-accumulation model (1962, pp. 43–45).

9. For that reason, Habakkuk's explanation of the difference between Germany and Britain after 1879 should be considered the weakest part of the argument. The paradox here is that the lower-wage

economy adopted (and developed) new technologies at a rate much faster than the high-wage economy (Britain). Landes (1965, p. 29) had an easy time showing the logical flaws in Habakkuk's resolution of this paradox by means of differences in demand.

10. This point was stated most cogently by Postan (1972, pp. 70–83) in a famous but neglected paper first published in 1935. A similar point is made by Cottrell (1980, p. 267).

11. For a diametrically opposite view, see Church (1980).

12. Cottrell's point that investment projects were small and divisible is of course correct: if projects were sufficiently large and indivisible, an accumulation process based exclusively on self-finance could not occur because there would be no way for it to get started. Once accumulation is started, however, the indivisibility of investment projects still affects the time pattern of accumulation, but will not materially slow it down.

13. For a different view, see Geary (1981). The continuing confusion about this issue is once more illustrated by Philip Ollerenshaw (1985, p. 67), who argues (following Geary) that the Ulster cotton industry did not suffer from a capital scarcity, but then adds that linen spinning provided an alternative into which cotton spinners could move without massive new investment.

14. See Mokyr (1983, chap. 8), and Mokyr and O Grada (1982). We concluded that although brain-drain models of the Irish economy seemed logical and were frequently mentioned by contemporaries, the evidence of Irish emigrants to the United States did not support that view. More recent research suggests, however, that this conclusion may not hold for emigration to Britain, and that the Irish migrating to Britain were more skilled, literate, and possibly more productive than those who stayed behind. See Nicholas and Shergold (1987).

15. For a similar argument, applied to the difference between Ontario and Quebec, see Altman (1988).

16. Some other, less prominent political economists also made this point. See Coats (1958).

17. For references see Mokyr (1983, p. 9). The finding that the Irish recruits to the East India Army in the first decade of the nineteenth century were significantly taller than their British colleagues strengthens this view; see Mokyr and O Grada (1986).

18. Most of this work was carried out in a different context, primarily to test J. S. Adams' "equity theory." Experimental data show that workers who were made to believe that they were underpaid produced both less and lower-quality output, and the reverse was true for subjects who believed they were overpaid. An economist's interpretation would be that effort is correlated with the costs the workers associate with dismissal, which rises with the ratio between pay and opportunity cost. For a summary, see Mowday (1979).

19. See, for instance, De Meere (1982, pp. 38–40), who maintains that Dutch workers were inferior in skills to German immigrant workers. The evidence for such statements tends to be anecdotal (in this case one example regarding peat cutting), and it is never made clear where skills come from and how they are produced.

20. For a rationale for the use of age-heaping variables, see Mokyr (1983, chap. 8).

21. The results *could* be spurious if the "labor quality" proxies were entirely demand-determined (that is, the demand for education were income-elastic so that high-income counties consumed more of it) *and* there were in fact no relation between such variables as literacy or the number of teachers and productivity.

22. The occupational and labor force statistics, as well as the literacy and age-heaping data, were computed from the 1841 *Census of Ireland*. For the wage data, see Mokyr (1983, chap. 2).

23. The view that low wages were inconsistent with the high level of demand necessary for an industrial revolution to occur seems to me not to square with economic logic as well as with historical experience (see my essay "Demand vs. Supply in the Industrial Revolution," in Mokyr 1985a, pp. 97–118).

24. See Sen (1987) for a more detailed analysis of the concept of standard of living and its uses.

25. See, for instance, the biting comments in Walton (1987, chap. 9).

26. The data for housing are, if possible, even less reliable, but if Feinstein's estimates are even close

to the truth, there cannot have been much of an improvement in average housing quality. The stock of housing per capita (1851–1860 replacement prices) grew at an annual rate of less than 0.1 percent between 1800 and 1830, and at about 0.2 percent between 1830 and 1860. Before 1801, Feinstein's residential dwellings were interpolated on the basis of population, and thus per capita figures are meaningless. The absence of technological change in construction may be misleading, because declining transport costs made brick construction cheaper. Yet brick output—a poor indicator of construction for dwellings—grew at a significantly greater rate than population only after 1843, and bricks were also used for industrial purposes and canals (see Feinstein 1978, p. 42).

27. As Maxine Berg (1985, pp. 228–233) has emphasized, there were many forms of factory organization, and many forms of traditional industry, and "there was obviously no through road to the factory system" (p. 232). Yet although the line between the modern and the traditional sectors may be hard to draw in individual industries, she recognizes that the effects of technological change on the handicraft industries of Britain or Belgium, capitalist or not, were inexorable.

28. For a critique of recent work along these lines, see Hunt and Botham (1987).

29. For an analysis of the story of the handloom weavers, see Lyons (1989).

30. Lis (1986, p. 93) is perplexed by the increase in coffee consumption during the first half of the nineteenth century. As I have shown (see Mokyr 1988), coffee consumption in Britain moved perversely and should not be taken as an indication of living standards.

References

Adams, J. S. et al. 1976. *Equity Theory: Toward a General Theory of Social Interaction,* ed. L. Berkowitz and E. Walster. New York.

Akerlof, G. 1984. "Gift Exchange and Efficiency-Wage Theory." *American Economic Review* 74 (May):79–83.

Akerlof, G., and J. L. Yellen, eds. 1986. *Efficiency Wage Models of the Labor Market.* Cambridge.

Altman, M. 1988. "Economic Development with High Wages: An Historical Perspective." *Explorations in Economic History* 25 (April):198–224.

Berg, M. 1985. *The Age of Manufactures, 1700–1820.* London.

Blanqui, J.-A. [1837] 1880. *History of Political Economy.* Trans. from the 4th French ed. New York.

Briavoinne, N. de. 1839. *De l'industrie en Belgique.* Vol. 1. Brussels.

Cardwell, D. S. L. 1972. *Turning Points in Western Technology.* New York.

Census of Ireland. 1843. Great Britain, *Parliamentary Papers.* Vol. 24. "Reports of the Commissioners Appointed to Take the Census of Ireland in the Year 1841."

Church, R. A., ed. 1980. *The Dynamics of Victorian Business.* London.

Clark, G. 1987. "Why Isn't the Whole World Developed? Lessons from the Cotton Mills." *Journal of Economic History* 47 (March):141–173.

Coats, A. W. 1958. "Changing Attitudes to Labour in the Eighteenth Century." *Economic History Review* 10 (March):35–51.

Cottrell, P. L. 1980. *Industrial Finance, 1830–1914.* London.

Crafts, N. 1985. *British Economic Growth during the Industrial Revolution.* Oxford.

Crouzet, F. 1985. *The First Industrialists: The Problem of Origins.* Cambridge.

Deane, P. 1979. *The First Industrial Revolution.* 2nd ed. Cambridge.

De Meere, J. M. M. 1982. *Economische Ontwikkeling en Levensstandaard in Nederland gedurende de Eerste Helft van de Negenteinde Eeuw.* The Hague.

Feinstein, C. 1978. "Capital Formation in Great Britain." In *The Cambridge Economic History of Europe,* ed. P. Mathias and M. M. Postan. Cambridge.

———— 1981. "Capital Accumulation and the Industrial Revolution." In *The Economic History of Britain since 1700,* ed. R. Floud and D. N. McCloskey. Cambridge.

Floud, R. 1986. "New Dimensions of the Industrial Revolution." Paper prepared for the Social Science History Association meeting, St. Louis, October.

Fogel, R. W. N.d. "Biomedical Approaches to the Estimation and Interpretation of Secular Trends in Equity, Morbidity, Mortality, and Labor Productivity in Europe, 1750–1980." University of Chicago.

Geary, F. 1981. "The Rise and Fall of the Belfast Cotton Industry: Some Problems." *Irish Economic and Social History* 8:30–49.

Griffiths, R. 1979. *Industrial Retardation in the Netherlands.* The Hague.

Habakkuk, H. J. 1962. *American and British Technology in the Nineteenth Century.* Cambridge.

Helling, G. 1977. *Nahrungsmittel: Produktion und Weltaussenhandel seit Anfang des 19. Jahrhunderts.* Berlin.

Hunt, E. W., and F. W. Botham. 1987. "Wages in Britain during the Industrial Revolution." *Economic History Review* 2nd ser., 40 (August):380–399.

Inglis, H. D. 1834. *A Journey throughout Ireland during 1834.* London.

Kane, R. 1845. *The Industrial Resources of Ireland.* 2nd ed. Dublin.

Landes, D. S. 1965. "Factor Costs and Demand: Determinants of Economic Growth." *Business History* 7 (January):15–33.

——— 1969. *The Unbound Prometheus: Technological Change and Industrial Development in Western Europe from 1750 to the Present.* Cambridge.

Lebrun, P. 1979. "Conclusions Générales." In P. Lebrun et al., *Essai sur la Révolution industrielle en Belgique, 1770–1847.* Brussels.

Lindert, P., and Williamson, J. G. 1983a. "Reinterpreting Britain's Social Tables, 1688–1913." *Explorations in Economic History* 20 (January):94–109.

——— 1983b. "English Workers' Living Standards during the Industrial Revolution." *Economic History Review* 36 (February):1–25.

Lis, C. 1986. *Social Change and the Labouring Poor: Antwerp, 1770–1860.* New Haven.

Lis, C., and H. Soly. 1977. "Food Consumption in Antwerp between 1807 and 1859: A Contribution to the Standard of Living Debate." *Economic History Review* 2nd ser., 30 (August):460–486.

Lyons, J. S. 1989. "Family Response to Economic Decline: Handloom Weavers in Early Nineteenth-Century Lancashire." *Research in Economic History* 12:45–91.

Mokyr, J. 1976a. *Industrialization in the Low Countries.* New Haven.

——— 1976b. "Growing-Up and the Industrial Revolution in Europe." *Explorations in Economic History* 13 (October):371–396.

——— 1981. "Industrialization in Two Languages." *Economic History Review* 34 (February): 143–149.

——— 1983. *Why Ireland Starved.* London.

———, ed. 1985a. *The Economics of the Industrial Revolution.* London.

——— 1985b. "The Industrial Revolution and the New Economic History." In Mokyr 1985a.

——— 1988. "Is There Still Life in the Pessimist Case?" *Journal of Economic History* 48 (March): 69–92.

——— 1990. *The Lever of Riches: Technological Creativity and Economic Progress.* New York.

Mokyr, J., and C. O Grada. 1982. "Emigration and Poverty in Prefamine Ireland." *Explorations in Economic History* 19 (October):360–384.

——— 1986. "Living Standards in Ireland and Britain, 1800–1850: The East India Company Army Data." Paper presented to the Social Science History Association, St. Louis, October.

——— 1988. "Poor and Getting Poorer? Living Standards in Ireland before the Famine." *Economic History Review* 2nd ser., 41 (May):209–235.

Mowday, R. 1979. "Equity Theory Predictions of Behavior in Organizations." In *Motivation and Work Behavior,* ed. R. Steers and L. Porter. 2nd ed. New York.

Nicholas, S., and P. R. Shergold. 1987. "Human Capital and Pre-Famine Irish Emigration to England." *Explorations in Economic History* 24 (April):158–177.

Ollerenshaw, P. 1985. "Industry." In *An Economic History of Ulster, 1820–1939,* ed. L. Kennedy and P. Ollerenshaw. Manchester.

Postan, M. M. 1972. "Recent Trends in the Accumulation of Capital." In *Capital Formation in the Industrial Revolution*, ed. F. Crouzet. London.

Say, J.-B. 1841. "Traité d'économie politique. 6th ed. Paris.

Scrimshaw, N. S. 1983. "Functional Consequences of Malnutrition for Human Populations." In *Hunger and History*, ed. R. I. Rotberg and T. K. Rabb. Cambridge.

Sen, A. 1987. *The Standard of Living*. Cambridge.

Smith, A. [1776] 1937. *Wealth of Nations*. New York.

Snell, K. D. 1985. *Annals of the Labouring Poor*. Cambridge.

Vandenbroeke, C. 1973. "Voedingstoestanden te Gent Tijdens de Eerste Helft van de Negenteinde Eeuw." *Belgisch Tijdschrift voor de Nieuwste Geschiedenis* 4, no. 2:109–169.

Van den Eeckhout, P., and P. Scholliers. 1983. "De Hoofdelijke Voedselconsumptie in Belgie, 1831–1939." *Tijdschrift voor Sociale Geschiedenis* 9, no. 31 (August):273–301.

Van Hogendorp, K. G. 1825. *Bijdragen tot de Huishouding van Staat in het Koninkrijk der Nederlanden*. Vol. 2. Amsterdam.

Van Zanden, J. L. 1985a. *De Economische Ontwikkeling van de Nederlandse Landbouw in de Negentiende Eeuw, 1800–1914*. Wageningen.

——— 1985b. "Kosten van Levensonderhoud en Loonvorming in Holland en Oost Nederland, 1600–1850." *Tijdschrift voor Sociale Geschiedenis* 11, no. 4 (November):309–323.

Walton, J. 1987. *A Social History of Lancashire*. Manchester.

Weiss, A. 1980. "Job Queues and Layoffs in Labor Markets with Flexible Wages." *Journal of Political Economy* 88 (June):526–538.

Williamson, J. G. 1985. *Did British Capitalism Breed Inequality?* Boston.

——— 1987. "Did English Factor Markets Fail during the Industrial Revolution?" *Oxford Economic Papers* 39:641–678.

Wright, G. 1987. *Old South, New South*. New York.

Yellen, J. L. 1984. "Efficiency Wage Models of Unemployment." *American Economic Review* 74 (May):200–205.

Young, A. 1892. *Arthur Young's Tour in Ireland (1776–79)*, ed. A. W. Hutton. Vol. 2. London.

——— 1929. *Travels in France during the Years 1787, 1788, and 1789*, ed. C. Maxwell. Cambridge.

II

...

Entrepreneurialism

7

...

Entrepreneurship, Total Factor Productivity, and Economic Efficiency: Landes, Solow, and Farrell Thirty Years Later

Robert C. Allen

Nineteen fifty-seven was a turning point for understanding productivity.[1] Robert Solow published his paper "Technical Change and the Aggregate Production Function," which provided a theoretical basis for total factor productivity indices by deriving the Divisia index from a neoclassical production function. In the same year David Landes began the manuscript that became *The Unbound Prometheus* (1969), that survey of European economic history that emphasized technical progress as the source of prosperity and entrepreneurs as the font of that progress (p. viii). Also in 1957 M. J. Farrell published his paper "The Measurement of Productive Efficiency." He distinguished technical inefficiency (the equiproportional use of more of all inputs than is socially necessary) from price inefficiency (the use of inputs in the wrong proportions) and defined economic inefficiency as the impact on costs of both sources of inefficiency.

The three works have had a major influence on subsequent research. Landes' writing has put technical change at the center of much historical research. Solow's paper has become the most often-cited article written in the 1950s by an economist. It gave rise to, among other things, the enterprise of growth accounting. Farrell's contribution has led to several procedures for measuring inefficiency.

The major interaction between these traditions has been between Landes' and Solow's. Growth accounting is a framework that purports to distinguish the separate contributions of technical change, capital accumulation, education, and so forth in raising per capita income. National economic histories written in English by economists are now organized around the metaphor of a shifting production function with output growing faster than the inputs.[2] These exercises are always a confrontation with Landes' hypothesis that technical change caused the growth in per capita income. Some—but not all—of these investigations have vindicated Landes.

203

Britain's relative decline was one historical puzzle in which total factor productivity indices confuted Landes' views, at least at first. Landes had explained Britain's decline by its failing to match the productivity growth achieved in Germany and America after 1870, and he attributed that failure to the poor performance of Britain's entrepreneurs. Iron and steel was one of his most compelling examples, and so it was a shock when McCloskey (1968, 1973) produced Total Factor Productivity (TFP) estimates that showed the British and American steel industries equally efficient on the eve of the Great War. Where was Britain's failure?

I was a graduate student when McCloskey's work appeared, and I remember Professor Landes' telling me that there must be a bias in the method. Since then several studies have shown that McCloskey's procedures underestimated the gap between Britain and its rivals in the treatment of monopoly profits. In fact, the German and American industries were 10 to 15 percent more efficient than the British (Allen 1979, p. 919; Webb 1980, p. 322).

This chapter, however, is about a more fundamental way in which total factor productivity calculations are biased against finding entrepreneurial failure. The bias I will discuss affects most, if not all, tests of entrepreneurial failure that use TFP indices—including my own. All such tests that I know of are justified by Solow's 1957 argument. In terms of a comparison of two firms (or countries), that argument assumes that entrepreneurs in both cases have minimized cost and then asks how technical knowledge (the capacity to convert inputs into output) differs in the two instances. But doesn't that argument preclude exactly what concerned Landes—namely, whether entrepreneurs in the two countries were in fact minimizing cost? It would be more appropriate to reverse the assumptions and posit that entrepreneurs in both places had access to the same knowledge and inquire whether they were equally effective in using it, that is, in producing at low cost. But to ask that question is to move us out of Solow's framework and into Farrell's, which allows firms to choose expensive, not least-cost, bundles of inputs. In this chapter I will extend Solow's theory of index numbers to include the nonoptimal behavior discussed by Farrell. That extension provides a more satisfactory framework for pursuing the questions that Landes (1969) raised.

The Conventional, Optimizing Model of Productivity Measurement

I will call the conventional approach to productivity measurement the *optimizing model* since it assumes that the data being analyzed were generated by firms that minimized cost. As a point of departure, I will summarize that approach. Solow analyzed a single firm (or country) evolving through time, but I will consider the comparison of two firms (or countries) at the same time.

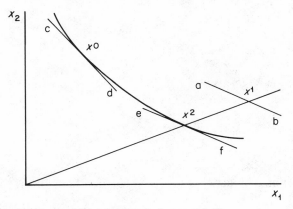

Figure 7.1 The optimizing model (note: *ab* and *ef* are parallel).

For each firm, output and the quantity and price of all inputs are observed. I call these numbers Q^0, Q^1, z^0, z^1, w^0, and w^1, where the superscripts 0 and 1 distinguish the firms and where Q is output, z is the vector of the quantities of the n inputs, and w the corresponding vector of their n prices. I assume that the production functions of the two firms are identical up to a multiplicative efficiency coefficient: $Q^0 = A^0f(z^0)$ and $Q^1 = A^1f(z^1)$. I assume f to be a linearly homogeneous neoclassical production function. I also assume that the supply of inputs is perfectly elastic to each firm at prices w^0 and w^1 and that both firms minimize cost.

There are two questions to answer: (1) how do the firms compare in terms of the ability to convert inputs into output; that is, how can A^1/A^0 be computed? And (2) why do unit costs differ in the two instances? I first derive a theoretical decomposition and then explain how to measure its arguments in practice.

Figure 7.1 illustrates the problem in two dimensions. Since linear homogeneity of f is assumed, I can work with unit isoquants. Let $x^0 = z^0/Q^0$ and $x^1 = z^1/Q^1$. I observe x^0 and x^1 and the slopes of the lines *cd* and *ab*, which equal the observed input price ratios w_1^0/w_2^0 and w_1^1/w_2^1, respectively. I analyze these data by constructing the ray from the origin through x^1 and the isoquant through x^0. Label the intersection of the isoquant and the ray as x^2. This point is *not* observed. Yet, cost minimization by firm 1 and linear homogeneity of f imply that *ef*, which is parallel to *ab*, is tangent to the isoquant at x^2.

The following identity is obviously true:

$$(7.1) \qquad \frac{w^1 \cdot x^1}{w^1 \cdot x^2} \cdot \frac{w^1 \cdot x^2}{w^0 \cdot x^0} = \frac{w^1 \cdot x^1}{w^0 \cdot x^0}.$$

The symbol $\cdot$ indicates products. Since x^1 and x^2 are on the same ray:

(7.2) $x^2 = u \cdot x^1$.

Also $w^0 \cdot x^0 = c(w^0)$ *and* $w^1 \cdot x^2 = c(w^1)$, where $c(w)$ is the unit cost function dual to $f(x)$. Hence equation (7.1) can be rewritten as

(7.3) $\dfrac{1}{u} \cdot \dfrac{c(w^1)}{c(w^0)} = \dfrac{w^1 \cdot x^1}{w^0 \cdot x^0}.$

Equation (7.2) in conjunction with the production functions $Q^0 = A^0 f(z^0)$ and $Q^1 = A^1 f(z^1)$ implies:

(7.4) $u = \dfrac{A^1}{A^0} = \dfrac{Q^1/Q^0}{f(z^1)/f(z^0)}$

where u is a conventional total factor productivity index. The first question has been answered.

To answer the second question, substitute equation (7.4) into equation (7.3):

(7.5) $\dfrac{A^0}{A^1} \cdot \dfrac{c(w^1)}{c(w^0)} = \dfrac{w^1 \cdot x^1}{w^0 \cdot x^0}.$

The right-hand side of equation (7.5) is the ratio of observed unit costs, and the left-hand side of the equation indicates how it can be partitioned into efficiency and input price components. The second question can be answered using equation (7.5).

It should also be noted that equation (7.5) can be rewritten as

(7.6) $\dfrac{A^1}{A^0} = \dfrac{Q^1/Q^0}{f(z^1)/f(z^0)} = \dfrac{c(w^1)/c(w^0)}{w^1 \cdot x^1/w^0 \cdot x^0}.$

Efficiency can be measured either in terms of the relationship between outputs and inputs or in terms of the relationship of input prices and unit costs.

Empirical Implementation of the Optimizing Model

How is this model applied to a historical problem? If there were enough data, one could estimate f and c econometrically and the two left-hand-side terms of equation (7.5) could be calculated directly. The modern index number approach, however, aims to effect the calculations solely using Q^0, Q^1, z^0, z^1, w^0, and w^1. The notion of "exactness" provides the basis. An input quantity index $I(z^0, z^1, w^0, w^1)$ is said to be exact for the production function f if

(7.7) $$\frac{f(z^1)}{f(z^0)} = I(z^0, z^1, w^0, w^1).$$

The input price index $P(z^0, z^1, w^0, w^1)$ is said to be exact for $f(z)$ if $c(w)$ is the unit cost function dual to $f(z)$ and if

(7.8) $$\frac{c(w^1)}{c(w^0)} = P(z^0, z^1, w^0, w^1).$$

Most applications of TFP indices by economic historians have used Paasche, Laspeyres, or geometric indices to compute $f(z^1)/f(z^0)$ and $c(w^1)/c(w^0)$. These indices are exact for the Leontief production function (in the first two cases) and the Cobb-Douglas function (in the third case). Both of these functions are first-order approximations to an arbitrary neoclassical production function.

Modern best-practice productivity measurement has abandoned Paasche, Laspeyres, and geometric indices for what Diewert (1976) calls "superlative" indices. The Fisher ideal and the Törnqvist (often called the Divisia) indices are the most common examples. All superlative indices are exact for functions that can provide a second-order approximation to an arbitrary neoclassical production function. Since superlative indices are exact for a function that can provide a closer approximation to the true function, whatever it is, productivity estimates and cost decompositions using superlative indices are more accurate than those obtained using Paasche, Laspeyres, and geometric indices. That is the original reason for preferring superlative indices.

There is a second reason why superlative index numbers should be used when data are being analyzed within the conventional cost-minimization framework. That reason is clarified by comparing the index numbers displayed in Table 7.1. The Paasche, Laspeyres, and geometric input indices—the nonsuperlative indices—incorporate only *one* of the two sets of input prices. *Both* sets of input prices appear (as factors in the shares) in all of the superlative indices. In the exactness proofs, prices are introduced as observable counterparts to marginal products: that is, the presence of an input price vector corresponds to the assumption that the firm has minimized costs. Superlative index numbers thus presume that both firms (or countries) have minimized costs in view of the prices they face, while the Paasche, Laspeyres, and geometric indices incor-

Table 7.1 Exact and superlative quantity indices.

Input quantity index number		Corresponding production function	
Name	Formula	Name	Formula
Part I Nonsuperlative indices			
Laspeyres	$\dfrac{f(Z^1)}{f(Z^0)} = \dfrac{\sum\limits_{i=1}^{n} w_i^0 Z_i^1}{\sum\limits_{i=1}^{n} w_i^0 Z_i^0}$	Leontief	$f(Z) = \min\left\{ \dfrac{Z_1}{b_1}, \ldots, \dfrac{Z_r}{b_r} \right.$
Paasche	$\dfrac{f(Z^1)}{f(Z^0)} = \dfrac{\sum\limits_{i=1}^{n} w_i^1 Z_i^1}{\sum\limits_{i=1}^{n} w_i^1 Z_i^0}$		
Geometric	$\dfrac{f(Z^1)}{f(Z^0)} = \prod\limits_{i=1}^{n} \left[\dfrac{Z_i^1}{Z_i^0} \right]^{s_i}$	Cobb-Douglas	$\ln f(Z) = \alpha_0 + \sum\limits_{i=1}^{n} \alpha_i \ln Z_i$ where $\sum\limits_{i=1}^{n} \alpha_i = 1$
Part II Superlative indices			
Fisher ideal	$\dfrac{f(Z^1)}{f(Z^0)} = \left[\dfrac{\sum\limits_{i=1}^{n} w_i^0 Z_i^1}{\sum\limits_{i=1}^{n} w_i^0 Z_i^0} \right]^{1/2} \left[\dfrac{\sum\limits_{i=1}^{n} w_i^1 Z_i^1}{\sum\limits_{i=1}^{n} w_i^1 Z_i^0} \right]^{1/2}$	Square-root quadratic	$f(Z) = \left[\sum\limits_{i=1}^{n} \sum\limits_{j=1}^{n} a_{ji} Z_i Z_j \right]^{1/2}$ where $a_{ij} = a_{ji}$ for all ij
Törnqvist	$\dfrac{f(Z^1)}{f(Z^0)} = \prod\limits_{i=1}^{n} \left[\dfrac{Z_i^1}{Z_i^0} \right]^{(s_i^0 + s_i^1)/2}$	Translog	$\ln f(Z) = 0 + \sum\limits_{i=1}^{n} \alpha_1 \ln Z_i$ $+ \sum\limits_{i=1}^{n} \sum\limits_{j=1}^{n} \alpha_{ij} \ln Z_i \ln$ where $\sum\limits_{i=1}^{n} \alpha_i = 1$, $\alpha_{ij} = \alpha_{ji}$ for all i,j and $\sum\limits_{i=1}^{n} \alpha_{ij} = 0$ for $i = 1, \ldots$
—	$\dfrac{f(Z^1)}{f(Z^0)} = \left[\sum\limits_{i=1}^{n} S_i^0 \left(\dfrac{Z_i^1}{Z_i^0} \right)^{r/2} \right]^{1/r} \left[\sum\limits_{j=1}^{n} S_j^1 \left(\dfrac{Z_j^1}{Z_j^0} \right)^{-r/2} \right]^{-1/r}$	Quadratic mean of order r	$f(Z) = \left[\sum\limits_{i=1}^{n} \sum\limits_{j=1}^{n} \alpha_{ij} Z_i^{r/2} z_j^{r/2} \right]1$ Same restrictions as translog

porate the assumption that only one firm (or country) has minimized cost. In the conventional approach to productivity measurement, both firms are assumed to have minimized costs, so consistency requires the use of superlative index numbers.

A Nonoptimizing Model of Productivity Measurement and Cost Decomposition

Now that I have reviewed the conventional approach to productivity measurement—the approach that assumes that both countries being compared have minimized costs—I can allow for entrepreneurial failure. To get anywhere, I must still assume that one country has minimized costs, but I do not have to require that of both. In an assessment of Victorian entrepreneurs, for instance, one might assume that American or German firms were efficient while investigating whether British firms were not. Following Farrell (1957, pp. 254–255), I allow for two kinds of inefficiency—technical and price. A firm is technically inefficient if it could produce the same output with an equiproportional reduction in the use of all inputs. Technical efficiency is thus total factor productivity by a different name. A firm is price-inefficient if it is not producing with the least-cost mix of inputs. Price inefficiency was assumed not to occur in the conventional, optimizing approach. Overall economic inefficiency is the increase in costs from both sources.

There are now three questions to answer: (1) How much technical inefficiency is there? (2) How much price inefficiency? (3) Why do unit costs differ between the two firms (or countries)? As with the optimizing model, I first derive a theoretical decomposition and then consider how to implement it empirically.

Figure 7.2 illustrates technical and price inefficiency and points to a way to measure them. As before, x^0 and x^1 are the observed input bundles, and the slopes of ab and cd are again equal to the ratios of the input prices. As in the cost-minimization framework, these are the only data observed. To analyze them, I assume that firm 0 is technically and price-efficient. I construct the ray from the origin through x^1 and the isoquant through x^0. The isoquant and ray intersect at x^2 and ef and gh are parallel to ab. Firm 1 is technically inefficient since it uses x^1 to produce one unit of output, while an efficient firm could produce one unit with x^2 (an unobserved point). Firm 1 is also price-inefficient since ef is not tangent to the isoquant at x^2; x^3 is the input combination that minimizes unit costs at prices w^1.

In the nonoptimizing model, the following identity holds:

$$(7.9) \qquad \frac{w^1 \cdot x^1}{w^1 \cdot x^2} \cdot \frac{w^1 \cdot x^2}{w^1 \cdot x^3} \cdot \frac{w^1 \cdot x^3}{w^0 \cdot x^0} = \frac{w^1 \cdot x^1}{w^0 \cdot x^0}.$$

For the same reasons as with the optimizing model, $w^1 \cdot x^3 / w^0 \cdot x^0 = c(w^1)/c(w^0)$

$$(7.10) \qquad \frac{w^1 \cdot x^2}{w^1 \cdot x^1} = u = \frac{Q^1/Q^0}{f(z^1)/f(z^0)}.$$

and

As in equation (7.4), u measures technical efficiency or total factor productivity. Its computation answers the first question.

The other questions can be answered by rewriting equation (7.9) as

$$(7.11) \qquad \frac{1}{u} \cdot \frac{w^1 \cdot x^2}{w^1 \cdot x^3} \cdot \frac{c(w^1)}{c(w^0)} = \frac{w^1 \cdot x^1}{w^0 \cdot x^0}.$$

The right-hand side is observed relative unit costs, and the left-hand side shows how to decompose that ratio into the technical efficiency effect ($1/u$), the price effect [$c(w^1)/c(w^0)$], and the middle term, which measures the impact on cost of price inefficiency, that is, the choice of the wrong input mix. This term may be computed as a residual.[3] Equation (7.11) answers the third question, and the computation of $w^1 \cdot x^2/w^1 \cdot x^3$ answers the second question.

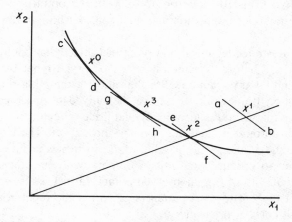

Figure 7.2 The nonoptimizing model (note: *ab, ef,* and *gh* are parallel).

Implementing the Nonoptimizing Model

To apply equation (7.11) to a historical problem, I have to compute the total factor productivity term $(1/u)$ and the input price term $c(w^1)/c(w^1)$. I could use index numbers to approximate them, but which ones? Certainly I should not use superlative indices and impose the condition that ef in Figure 7.2 be parallel to ab, for that would preclude the discovery of price inefficiency. Instead, I should use indices like the Laspeyres or geometric that only impose the tangency of the total cost line to the isoquant for firm (or country) 0. Using the Laspeyres index corresponds to assuming the isoquant through x^0 is Leontief, while using the geometric corresponds to assuming it is Cobb-Douglas. Table 7.2 shows the formulas for computing the technical inefficiency and input price effects in equation (7.11) under these assumptions.

The assumption of a Cobb-Douglas production function is especially interesting since our index number model becomes very similar to the Lau-Yotopoulos model of economic performance.[4] This model was devised to compare the efficiency of large and small farms in developing countries.

The Lau-Yotopoulos model is an econometric specification that allows technical and price efficiency to be measured. Technical efficiency is measured, essentially, as total factor productivity. Price efficiency is measured by introducing a set of n parameters k_i that equal the ratio of the marginal product of each input to its price. If $k_i = 1$, then the input has been optimally chosen; otherwise it has not. Lau and Yotopoulos estimate the k_i econometrically. The price inefficiency term in the index number model presented here depends on the n parameters k_i and equals one if those parameters all equal one. When a

Table 7.2 Technical efficiency and input price effects for Leontief and Cobb-Douglas technologies.

	Leontief	Cobb-Douglas
Technical efficiency (u)	$\dfrac{Q^1/Q^0}{\displaystyle\sum_{i=1}^{n}\dfrac{W_i^0 Z_i^1}{W_i^0 Z_i^0}}$	$\dfrac{Q_i^1/Q^0}{\displaystyle\prod_{i=1}^{n}\left(\dfrac{Z_i^1}{Z_i^0}\right)^{S_i^0}}$
Input price effect $C(W^1)/C(W^0)$	$\displaystyle\sum_{i=1}^{n}\dfrac{W_i^1 Z_i^0}{W_i^0 Z_i^0}$	$\displaystyle\prod_{i=1}^{n}\left(\dfrac{W_i}{W_i^0}\right)^{S_i^0}$

Note: $S_i^0 = W_i^0 Z_i^0 \Big/ \displaystyle\sum_{i=1}^{n} W_i^0 Z_i^0.$

Cobb-Douglas specification is chosen, this result provides further justification for calling $w^1 \cdot x^2 / w^1 \cdot x^3$ a measure of price efficiency.

The Efficiency of the British Iron and Steel Industry in 1907

Let us use the nonoptimizing model to assess the performance of the British steel industry in 1907. The American steel industry in 1909 will be our standard of performance. I will measure output as the tonnage of final iron and steel products, labor as the number of employees, and capital as installed horse-power. These numbers are all taken from my earlier study of this industry (Allen 1979, p. 919). Labor and capital are combined to make value added, and I assume that value added and the various materials are used in fixed proportions that are the same in the two countries. As a result, I need consider only the relationship between capital, labor, and output to assess performance.

To measure price efficiency, I need to compare the prices of labor and capital in the United States and Britain. I take the wage rate to be average annual earnings per worker, as reported by McCloskey (1973, p. 122). The price of capital is the rental price of capital services $r - (i + d) \cdot P_K$, where i is the interest rate, d the depreciation rate, and P_K the purchase or construction price of a unit of capital. Following Berck (1978, pp. 884–885), I assumed that $i = .06$ for the United States and $.05$ for Britain, while $d = .04$ for both countries. Since I measured the quantity of capital as the number of installed horsepower, I measured P_K for the United States as the value of the capital stock for blast furnaces, steelworks, and rolling mills divided by the number of horsepower. I determined the British value for P_K by converting the American P_K to sterling at the rate of $4.86 per pound and then adjusting for the difference in blast furnace construction costs deduced by Berck (p. 883) from reports in the late 1880s. These numbers are displayed in Table 7.3.

From these numbers I can compute the costs of value added per ton of steel in the two countries. For the United States the result is $13.89 and for Britain £2.48. In terms of a common currency, the British cost of value added was 87 percent of the American cost. Britain's cost disadvantage in steel production came from high raw material costs, not the high cost of labor and capital (cf. Allen 1979, p. 932).

Table 7.4 shows how the relative cost of steelmaking can be decomposed into terms of technical efficiency, price efficiency, and price difference under the assumption of Leontief and Cobb-Douglas technologies. The decompositions agree exactly (to two decimal places) as to how much of the cost difference is due to input price differences, but they disagree radically in the measurement of technical efficiency and price efficiency. Both show the British industry to be

Table 7.3 British and American steelmaking data, 1907–1909.

Quantity and price	Great Britain	America
Output[a]	12,418,000	25,643,871
Labor[b]	261,666	303,823
Capital[c]	138,359	327,440
Wage per year	£84.5	$679
Rental price of capital	£63.3	$456

Sources: For output, labor, and capital, see Allen (1979, p. 919). The wage rates are from McCloskey (1973, p. 122). See text for the rental price of capital.

   [a] Output is the net production in tons of blast furnaces, iron and steel works, and rolling mills.

   [b] Labor is the number of employees.

   [c] Capital is the number of installed horsepower, divided by 10.

price-inefficient. The Cobb-Douglas specification also shows it technically inefficient, but the Leontief specification shows Britain technically superior to the American steel industry. What can one make of these inconsistent results?

Figure 7.3 plots the input combinations and factor price lines for the two countries. America is x^0, while Britain is x^1. The Leontief and Cobb-Douglas unit isoquants are also shown. It is clear why the two specifications give such divergent results: x^1 lies between the Leontief isoquant and the origin, so that isoquant shows the British industry as technically more efficient than the American. On the other hand, the Cobb-Douglas isoquant passes between x^1 and the origin, so that production function shows the American industry as technically the more efficient. Since the slope of the Cobb-Douglas isoquant (compared to

Table 7.4 Relative inefficiency, prices, and costs in the United States and Great Britain: Leontief and Cobb-Douglas decompositions.[a]

Production function	Technical inefficiency	Price inefficiency	Input price difference	Relative cost
Leontief	0.72	1.91	0.63	0.87
Cobb-Douglas	1.31	1.04	0.63	0.87

Source: The data are from Table 7.3. Technical inefficiency was computed as $1/u$ by means of the formulas in Table 7.2. The input price difference was calculated as $c(w^1)/c(w^0)$, also from the formulas in Table 7.2. Price inefficiency was computed from equation (7.11). In these calculations Britain was one and America was zero.

   [a] The figures in the table are British values relative to American values.

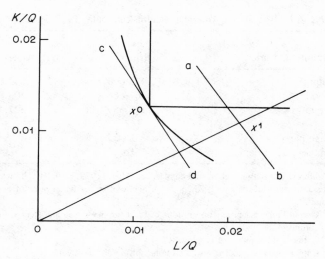

Figure 7.3 British and American steelmaking data.

the slope of the Leontief isoquant) is closer to the slope of the British factor price line when the isoquants cut the ray through x^1, the Cobb-Douglas specification shows less price inefficiency than does the Leontief specification.

Figure 7.3 shows geometrically how the cost decomposition in equation (7.11) works. I pass an isoquant through x^0. Tangency with the input price line gives the isoquant its trajectory. The curvature of the isoquant then determines the intersection with the ray through x^1 and thus the amount of technical inefficiency. The input price index provides a sort of midcourse correction that decomposes what is left into the input price effect and price inefficiency. Evidently, the decomposition depends critically on the curvature of the isoquant.

Unfortunately, the possible decompositions are infinite. The elasticity of substitution is a measure of the curvature of the isoquant. It ranges from zero (the Leontief case) through one (the Cobb-Douglas case) to infinity, which corresponds to a straight line collinear with the total cost line through x^0. The Constant Elasticity of Substitution (CES) production function represents these possibilities parametrically. In the two-input, constant-returns-to-scale case, with which I am concerned, that function is:

$$(7.12) \qquad Q = A[dk^{-P} + (1 - d)L^{-P}]^{1/-P}.$$

Q, K, and L are the quantities of output, capital, and labor, respectively. A indicates technical efficiency or total factor productivity; p is a parameter related to the elasticity of substitution e by the equation $e = 1/(1 + p)$. Equation

(7.12) is undefined for $p = 0$, but in that case the Cobb-Douglas function is its limit.

Table 7.5 shows how the decomposition of costs varies with the elasticity of substitution. With $e = 0$, Britain is technically more efficient than America. With $e = .145$, the isoquant through x^0 passes through x^1, so technical efficiency is equal. Larger and larger values of e show America progressively more efficient since the isoquant is cutting the ray through x^1 closer to the origin. Conversely, British input price inefficiency is very high with $e = 0$, but it declines as e increases. In the vicinity of $e = 2$, no British price inefficiency remains. It disappears since the isoquant then parallels Britain's total cost line while cutting the ray through x^1. At larger values of e, the isoquant is steeper than the total cost line, so input price inefficiency reappears and increases with e.

A striking feature of Table 7.5 is that the input price term is virtually constant

Table 7.5 Constant elasticity of substitution (CES) decompositions.

Elasticity of substitution	Technical inefficiency[a]	Price inefficiency[b]	Input price difference[c]	Relative cost[d]
0.0	0.72	1.91	0.63	0.87
0.1	0.95	1.45	0.64	0.87
0.2	1.06	1.30	0.63	0.87
0.4	1.19	1.14	0.64	0.87
0.6	1.26	1.08	0.64	0.87
0.8	1.29	1.05	0.64	0.87
1.0	1.31	1.04	0.63	0.87
1.5	1.34	1.01	0.64	0.87
2.0	1.35	1.00	0.64	0.87
100.0	1.39	1.02	0.61	0.87

Sources: Entries for elasticity of substitution equal to zero and one were taken from Table 7.4.

[a] Technical inefficiency is the reciprocal of British total factor productivity relative to American and is computed from equation (7.12).

[b] Price inefficiency computed with equation (7.11).

[c] The input price difference is the ratio of the cost function equal to equation (7.12) evaluated at British input prices, relative to the same function evaluated at American input prices:

$$\frac{\{(r''/d)^r + [w''/(1-d)]^r\}^{1/r}}{\{(r'/d)^r + [w'/(1-d)]^r\}^{1/r}}$$

Here $r = -p/(-p-1)$, where r'' and w'' are the British rental price and wage rate and r' and w' are the corresponding American prices. The input prices are from Table 7.3, except that the British prices were multiplied by 4.86 to convert them to dollars.

[d] The cost difference is the ratio of British to American labor and capital costs per ton of iron and steel from Table 7.3. British costs were expressed in American dollars by multiplying British input prices by 4.86.

throughout. That constancy is a feature of the example and not inherent in the model. The input price effect equals the difference in the American unit cost function resulting from the difference in British and American input prices: $c(w^1)/c(w^0)$. That ratio is necessarily bounded by the highest and lowest input price ratios (Samuelson 1947; Pollak 1971). The ratios are .60 (= 84.5 · 4.86/ 679) for labor and .67 (= 63.3 · 4.86/456) for capital. Thus labor was slightly cheaper in Britain than was capital—but not much.[5] As a result, there was little variation in the input price index. If the relative input prices were more divergent, then the input price effect would vary with the elasticity of substitution. The combined effects of technical and price inefficiency on cost would then also vary.

We have reached the limit of what index numbers can do for us. Contingent on an estimate of the elasticity of substitution, one can use index numbers to measure British technical and price inefficiency, but there is not enough information in x^0, w^0, x^1, and w^1 also to identify that parameter. The only solution is to use extraneous information.

The American census, which is the source for most of the American numbers shown in Table 7.3, also provides enough information to estimate the elasticity of substitution. A data set with states as the unit of observation was drawn from the 1899, 1909, and 1919 census of manufactures.[6] The industry was the blast furnace industry plus the steelworks and rolling mills industry. The quantity of labor was the sum of total employment in those industries, while the quantity of capital was the sum of horsepower in them. Output was taken as the tonnage of finished rolled products and forgings plus pig iron produced minus pig iron consumed by steelworks and rolling mills. Total wage payments divided by total employment was taken to be the price of labor. The rental price of capital was computed in a similar fashion to that already described for the Anglo-American comparison.

Since I am presuming that the American industry chose the cost-minimizing combination of inputs in view of the prices it faced, the appropriate way to estimate the elasticity of substitution is with the CES relative share equation:

(7.13) $r \cdot K / w \cdot L = (d/[1 - d])^{1/(1 + P)} (w/r)^{-P/(1 + P)}.$

Here r is the rental price of capital, and w is the wage rate. The ordinary least squares estimate of that equation is:

(7.14) $\ln (r \cdot K / w \cdot L) = .021699 - .19545 \ln(w/r).$

The estimated coefficient of $-.19545$ implies an elasticity of substitution of .8. This value is close to the Cobb-Douglas value of one. Indeed, since the standard error of the coefficient of $\ln(w/r)$ is .246010, the hypothesis that the coefficient equals zero cannot be rejected, and a zero coefficient implies a Cobb-Douglas function. Moreover, R^2 is only .05, so statistically there was little relationship between the shares of capital and labor and their prices. All of these features of the regression imply that iron and steel production function was slightly less elastic than a Cobb-Douglas, but not much.

Our extraneous estimate of e allows us to choose the right decomposition in Table 7.5. That is the decomposition with $e = .8$. It shows that America was technically more efficient than Britain. It also shows some British price inefficiency. Price inefficiency has not been identified before since the optimizing model precludes it by assumption.

This result, however, must be regarded as suggestive rather than definitive. While I have been able to relax the assumption that British firms were price-efficient, the model still retains several standard assumptions that it would be desirable to relax. These include constant returns to scale, the assumption that the American industry made no errors in cost minimization, and (most important) the assumption that the observed choice of inputs was the production of current decisions. If the British were stuck with an older capital stock than the Americans, however, and if that capital stock was chosen from a more limited set of alternatives in the face of different input and output prices, then the measured price inefficiency may simply be a burden of the past. The reason these assumptions are necessary is that a limited amount of information is available in Table 7.3. If one had large samples of plant-level data for both countries, the theoretical assumptions could be replaced with empirical observations. Nevertheless, the results presented here suggest that entrepreneurial failure was even more widespread than measurements based on the optimizing model have indicated.

I have been able to integrate Farrell's distinction between price and technical efficiency into the standard theory of productivity measurement that derives from Solow. This allows me to measure inefficiency more thoroughly than the conventional approach. Indeed, in the case of the pre–World War I British steel industry, I found evidence of price inefficiency. This kind of inefficiency was not detected in earlier investigations since their assumptions precluded it. Landes' intuition that total factor productivity indices were biased against the hypothesis of entrepreneurial failure is, therefore, correct.

This result raises a troubling methodological question: What is the proper role of mathematics in historical research? Since the late 1950s quantitative work in economic history has exploded. Proponents of mathematical methods have claimed that they yield firmer, more certain conclusions than traditional methods. But the debate on Victorian entrepreneurship has shown that such certainty is not automatic. Mathematical models can establish conclusions that might otherwise be beyond reach, but these methods can also mislead the historian by obscuring patterns in the data.

To see why mathematics can have such divergent results, it is useful to review one of the most forceful defenses of mathematical methods—Robert Fogel's survey "The New Economic History" in *Economic History Review* (Fogel 1966). In discussing the relationship of mathematical theory and statistical methods, he wrote:

> Some historians have held that there is no point in applying powerful statistical methods to economic history because the available data are too poor. In actual practice, the correlation often runs the other way. When the data are very good, simple statistical procedures will usually suffice. The poorer the data, the more powerful are the methods which have to be employed. Nevertheless, it is often true that the volume of data available is frequently below the minimum required for standard statistical procedures. In such instances the crucial determinant of success is the ability of the investigator to devise methods that are exceedingly efficient in the utilization of data—that is, to find a method that will permit one to achieve a solution with the limited data that are available. (pp. 652–653)

This analysis does embody an important truth. Fitting lines to the available data allows the investigator to fill in gaps by interpolation and extrapolation. Theory may be a guide in this, but it can also mislead. Victorian entrepreneurship is a case in point. One can make sense of limited data such as in Table 7.3 by analyzing them with index numbers, which amounts to fitting arbitrary isoquants to the data. But if our theory precludes price inefficiency, we will never discover it!

With the benefit of over 20 years' hindsight, I would modify Fogel's discussion in two respects. The first is the guidance it gives to historians. If we are working on a problem and "the volume of data available is . . . below the minimum required for standard statistical procedures," the one thing we should *not* do is develop ever more sophisticated models to fill in the gaps. Instead we should find more data. Indeed, this has been Fogel's own procedure. When a historian is substituting theory for measurement, there is a great danger that the mathematics will mislead rather than enlighten.

The second difficulty with Fogel's discussion is that it fails to give credit to mathematical theory when credit is due. Thus, even where data are abundant, theory is still useful, and, indeed, only then can it come into its own. In the case of the Victorian steel industry, suppose that we had large samples of plant-level data for Britain, America, and Germany. (Indeed, one of the remarkable features about that debate is that such samples have not yet been assembled.) The extrapolation implicit in index numbers could then be avoided, and the best practice isoquant for all three countries could be directly measured. Price and technical efficiency of the average firm in each country could be computed. The impact of old plant and equipment could be measured. If data on capital formation were also available, then investment behavior across countries could also be compared. These exercises would allow a variety of tests of entrepreneurial performance. Theory and mathematical methods would be involved in all of these calculations—not to aid extrapolation with limited information but to test hypotheses about business decision making.

Historians who use mathematical models will always have to be sensitive lest their methods preclude the phenomenon they are searching for. The best chance for mathematical methods to enlighten rather than distort comes when they are applied to large bodies of relevant data. Collecting and assessing that information, as well as posing the questions and framing the tests, requires all the skills of the nonmathematical historian.

Notes

1. I should like to thank C. Blackorby, W. E. Diewert, A. Redish, and W. Schworm for comments on an earlier version of this chapter. Any remaining errors are my own.

2. For instance, Davis, Easterlin, and Parker (1972) for the United States, Floud and McCloskey (1981) for Britain, and Marr and Paterson (1980) for Canada.

3. In the optimizing model it was possible to compute efficiency differences in two ways, as shown by equation (6). Equation (11) shows that the presence of price inefficiency breaks the equality of the putative productivity measures in equation (6).

4. Lau and Yotopoulos (1971) and Yotopoulos and Lau (1973). The Lau-Yotopoulos model differs from the model developed in this essay by treating some inputs as fixed, by developing the analysis with a variable profit function rather than a cost function, and by estimating the price inefficiency parameters for both sets of firms.

5. This result may seem odd since it usually assumed that the relative wage was exceptionally high in America. As Berck's (1978, p. 883) investigation of blast furnace construction costs shows, high American wages caused high American construction costs, so P_K was also relatively high in America, but not quite as high as the relative wage.

6. The states were Illinois, Maryland, New Jersey, New York, Ohio, Pennsylvania, and West Virginia in 1899, and Illinois, New York, Ohio, and Pennsylvania in both 1909 and 1919. The data are from the U.S. Bureau of the Census, *Twelfth Census of the United States: Manufactures*, pt. 4, *Special Reports on Selected Industries* (Washington, D.C.), pp. 29, 54–55, 82–83, 88–89; *Thirteenth Census of the United States*, vol. 10, *Manufactures, 1909: Reports for Principal Industries* (Washington, D.C.), pp. 226, 260, *Fourteenth Census of the United States*, vol. 10, *Manufactures, 1919: Reports for Selected Industries* (Washington, D.C.), pp. 323, 347.

References

Allen, R. C. 1979. "International Competition in Iron and Steel, 1850–1913." *Journal of Economic History* 39:911–937.

Berck, P. 1978. "Hard Driving and Efficiency: Iron Production in 1890." *Journal of Economic History* 38:879–900.

Davis, L. E., R. A. Easterlin, W. N. Parker, et al. 1972. *American Economic History*. New York: Harper & Row.

Diewert, W. E. 1976. "Exact and Superlative Index Numbers." *Journal of Econometrics* 4:115–145.

Farrell, M. J. 1957. "The Measurement of Productive Efficiency." *Journal of the Royal Statistical Society*. Ser. A. vol. 120:253–281.

Floud, R., and D. N. McCloskey. 1981. *The Economic History of Britain since 1700*. Cambridge: Cambridge University Press.

Fogel, R. 1966. "The New Economic History: Its Findings and Methods." *Economic History Review*. 2nd ser., 19:642–656.

Landes, D. S. 1969. *The Unbound Prometheus*. Cambridge: Cambridge University Press.

Lau, L. J., and P. A. Yotopoulos. 1971. "A Test for Relative Efficiency and Application to Indian Agriculture." *American Economic Review* 61:94–109.

Marr, W. L., and D. G. Paterson. 1980. *Canada: An Economic History*. Toronto: Macmillan.

McCloskey, D. N. 1968. "Productivity Change in British Pig Iron, 1870–1939." *Quarterly Journal of Economics* 82:281–296.

———— 1973. *Economic Maturity and Entrepreneurial Decline: British Iron and Steel, 1870–1913*. Cambridge, Mass.: Harvard University Press.

Pollak, R. A. 1971. "The Theory of the Cost of Living Index." Research Discussion Paper 11. Washington, D.C.: Bureau of Labor Statistics, Washington, D.C. Reprinted in *Price Level Measurement*, ed. W. E. Diewert and C. Montmarquette, pp. 87–161. Ottawa: Statistics Canada, 1983.

Samuelson, P. A. 1947. *Foundations of Economic Analysis*. Cambridge, Mass.: Harvard University Press.

Solow, R. M. 1957. "Technical Change and the Aggregate Production Function." *Review of Economics and Statistics* 39:312–320.

Webb, S. B. 1980. "Tariffs, Cartels, Technology, and Growth in the German Steel Industry, 1879–1914." *Journal of Economic History* 40:309–329.

Yotopoulos, P. A., and L. J. Lau. 1973. "A Test for Relative Economic Efficiency: Some Further Results." *American Economic Review* 63:214–223.

8

. . .

The Huguenots and the
English Financial Revolution

François Crouzet

As the age of total war, mass murder, and major advances in the techniques of oppression and extermination, the twentieth century has seen the exodus of unprecedented numbers of refugees.[1] Millions have fled the horrors of war and the march of dreaded armies—Belgians and Frenchmen in 1914 and 1940, Spaniards in 1939, "displaced persons" at the end of World War II, Afghans in the 1980s. The refugee phenomenon is not, however, restricted to periods of hostilities and to countries involved in foreign or civil war; the most striking development (which, moreover, results in transfers of population which are permanent and not temporary) has been the multiplying of "political" refugees. This expression covers all individuals who leave their country because they are (or fear to be) victims of "political" persecutions, that is, of harassment and discrimination owing to their religious or political beliefs, and/or to their racial or social origins. The paroxysm of persecution—often in its extreme form of killing—in the twentieth century is, of course, connected with the spread of tyranny, under multifarious guises, from the absolute evil of Hitlerism and Stalinism to the buffooneries of Mitterand and Mussolini.

Still refugees and refuges are not specific to the twentieth century; the great transoceanic migrations of the nineteenth century had basically economic motivations, but the yearning to escape oppressive, indeed, persecuting regimes was instrumental in the emigration of many Germans and, of course, of many Jewish and Polish subjects of the Russian Empire. Moreover, from 1789 to 1905, each of the revolutions and counterrevolutions of the "long" nineteenth century drove people into voluntary or forced exile; true enough, in most cases only small numbers of rulers, activists, and fighters were involved. Still, the *émigration* during the French Revolution was something of a mass movement, but its participants, who were "bad" victims, are not entitled in some eyes to rank as refugees.

There is no refugee if there is no place of refuge. The sine qua non is therefore a "world" which is at least dualistic. There would be no refugee if the

221

planet became politically unified and homogeneous. In cultures such as the Roman Empire or ancient China, which identified with civilization, there was no asylum for dissenters, except the few who would brave the rigors of life in the barbarian periphery. Under the pluralism of cities and states, however, which prevailed in the Mediterranean world before the Pax Romana was imposed, exiles and defectors, that is, "political" refugees, were fairly numerous. Likewise for *fuorisciti* in medieval Italy, with its bitter struggles between Guelphs and Ghibellines.

On the other hand, medieval Christendom could not have any "religious" refuge: there was no place where Albigenses would have found asylum, and only geography preserved the Waldensians in remote Alpine valleys. Admittedly Judaism survived, despite massacres and expulsions, but only because the latter took place in succession and not simultaneously: Jews were never driven out of all Christian countries at the same time, and they had the possibility of fleeing to Muslim countries—as most Spanish Jews did when they were expelled in 1492. Indeed, Islam as the alternative to Christendom and persecution or warfare brought about many migratory movements in the border areas between those two hostile worlds. Nonetheless, they were separate, heterogeneous, impervious worlds; from one to the other (and, indeed, much more from Christendom to Islam than vice versa), men fled as deserters, renegades, and traitors, not as refugees. The exceptions of the Jewish and Moorish fugitives from Spain or of the Greeks who left Constantinople after its fall to the Turks confirm the view that a *refuge* has to be in a separate part of the same civilization, not in a completely different culture. *Se faire Turc* was a desperate solution, one which only hardened rebels and desperadoes could embrace.

In Europe, therefore, refugees were created by the breakup of Christian unity; they were the offspring of modernity, of the Reformation and Counterreformation, of the division of Europe into two camps where the principle *cuius regio, huius religio* was strictly enforced. Luther at Wartburg was the first modern refugee. Possibly the rise of individualism and the improvement in transports were also instrumental: in the Middle Ages, heretics or other dissidents were burned or expelled; later on, they fled. Admittedly, from the sixteenth to the twentieth centuries there was a transition from religious to political, social, and racial persecutions. But this change corresponded to the increasing secularization of Western societies, and the continuity of the process is obvious. There were some lulls, however, such as the decades that preceded the French Revolution, or those before World War I (when the Third French Republic was the only Western regime which persecuted its people—the Catholic majority—for religious reasons, although not harshly enough to trigger an exodus).

Although earlier tragedies pale beside the horrors of the twentieth century—especially the Holocaust—one persecution, followed by the large-scale migration of victims, has left a deep and lasting imprint in collective memory and is often considered a harbinger of things to come. This was the persecution of French Protestants by Louis XIV, marked by the revocation of the Edict of Nantes and the exodus of about 200,000 Huguenots to refuges in several European countries, as well as North America and southern Africa. As P. Joutard has written (quoted in Prestwich 1985, p. 345), this "diaspora inaugurated the long series of migrations for 'ideological' reasons that have multiplied in the twentieth century." (He seems to have overlooked the earlier exoduses of Jews from Spain and Protestants from the Low Countries.)

Of course, there are obvious and significant differences between the persecution of the Huguenots and more recent dramas. The former was self-imposed: a French Protestant could escape all harassment, and even receive various benefits, by converting to Catholicism (and actually most of them did—at least ostensibly). As Jules Michelet put it (quoted in Scouloudi 1987, p. 228), "Let the Protestant but say one word, and he would keep his belongings and his homeland, would be spared terrible dangers." The position was quite different for victims of twentieth-century persecutions, who had no chance to shed their tunic of Nessus. For instance, the fate of individual Jews in Nazi Germany and Europe was determined strictly by parentage. Despite abject letters from Curt and Edgar von Bleichröder, who stressed their good war records and their nationalist, nay, Nazi sympathies, Eichmann turned down the pleas for special treatment by the descendants of Bismarck's banker, who were to him like any other Jews. Likewise, in socialist countries a class enemy, an individual with a bourgeois background, bears an indelible blemish. Stern Protestants have condemned their weaker brethren who recanted, but there was no way for a Jew in Nazi Europe to recant, or a kulak during collectivization, or a descendant of the oppressor class in Maoist China.

True enough, the king's galleys were forerunners of extermination camps—just like the English hulks for French prisoners during the Napoleonic Wars—but on a quite different scale. From 1680 to 1748, 1,551 men were sent to the galleys for reasons of religion; 44 percent of them died *à la peine*. The number of victims of totalitarian regimes in the twentieth century has been estimated at 40 million. Moreover, intolerance was the rule in the seventeenth century and the quasi-obligatory companion of monarchy, whether absolute (France) or limited (England); its prevalence in England and the anti-Catholic repression which was carried out there and in Ireland are too easily neglected. Emmanuel Le Roy Ladurie has courageously exposed the double standard and one-sided moralizing of Whig historiography, including some cynical instances in recent writing. In his view, the behavior of Protestant England toward its Catholics pretty evenly matches that of Catholic France to its Protestants, and the martyrology of British Catholics that of French Huguenots. Thus, between 1678 and 1681, 18 Catholic priests were executed in England and several others died in jail. Likewise, the diaspora of Irish and Jacobite fugitives is often ignored, while its commercial and military advantages to France somewhat balanced the human losses caused by the revocation.

Thus a surprisingly "modern" aspect of the revocation affair does emerge: the intense and remarkably successful propaganda campaign that was conducted at the time and made the Huguenots the first of those "good" victims with whom we are so familiar and for whom every *bien-pensant* must shed a tear. True enough, the revocation was forgotten in the late eighteenth century and in the first half of the nineteenth, but it was rediscovered in 1860 by Jules Michelet, who made it the major crime of the French monarchy, which paid for it with its life. It was Michelet who inscribed the date of 1685 in the memory of the French people, and his actualization of the revocation was immensely successful. It stimulated French Protestants, under the Third Republic, to take stern revenge on their Catholic fellow countrymen for the persecution their forebears had suffered under Louis XIV. Strangely enough, the English public rediscovered the Huguenots at about the same time, mainly thanks to Samuel Smiles's best-selling book of 1867; only the year before, Agnew had revealed to the gentry their Huguenot antecedents!

The persecution of Huguenots and the revocation were not only a crime; they were also a blunder, as France was impoverished by a brain drain which brought wealth to her rivals and enemies. According to the Reverend Isaac Taylor, vicar of Spitalfields in the mid-nineteenth century (Agnew 1886, II, 258):

> The more skilful and intelligent of the artisans were those who had thought for themselves on religious questions, and had embraced the principles of the Reformation. The more cultured members of the nobles and the more thoughtful members of the professional class had been the natural leaders of the Huguenot democracy. Hence it was that almost all of the manual skill, as well as of the brain, the intellect, the wealth and the thrift of France found itself proscribed. The unknown terrors of exile and the difficulties of flight once more morally winnowed the chaff from the wheat . . . Hence, by a process of *natural* selection, the very cream of the manhood of France was lost to her for ever. Her chief industries were destroyed, or rather, transplanted to flourish more vigorously in rival lands.

Correspondingly, the contributions that Huguenot immigrants to the British Isles made to their economic, artistic, and cultural development, and also to England's military victories, have been overestimated, sometimes extravagantly. As early as Queen Anne's reign, this problem was discussed in the polemics between Tories and Whigs; subsequently, the francophobia and the Protestant providentialism of Whig history led many historians to exaggerate the Huguenots' role.[2] Admittedly, similar claims—and counterclaims—have been made about the role of other religious minorities, such as Jews, Quakers, Dissenters, and so on. So this chapter, which deals with Huguenots in England, tries to bring a contribution to the debate on the part played by minorities, especially religious ones, in economic development. When and why do such minorities matter for economic change and progress?

Obviously, answers depend on the nature, the structure, and the values of both the minority and the global society in which the minority operates, that is, the host society when the minority is composed of immigrants and refugees coming from a foreign country. Not much reflection is needed, therefore, to forewarn against an overestimation of the Huguenots' role in England.

Actually, in the late seventeenth century, the English and French economies were not fundamentally different, and England was by no means a backward country in relation to France, from which the English would have had a great deal to learn. "The divergence of England" had in fact already started, and she was ahead of France in several sectors—for instance in agriculture (where technical progress had made the country safe from famine), in her precocious recourse to rural putting-out, in clockmaking and watchmaking, and in colonial trade. In some branches, however, such as the silk, linen, and paper industries, various *métiers d'art,* even public finance (before the 1690s), France had the advantage. One can therefore expect French refugees to have exploited their comparative advantage in branches where they possessed special skills that were relatively scarce in England. And this is what actually happened, but such niches were neither wide nor numerous nor all profitable. Despite the inflow of Huguenot weavers, manufacturers, and designers, the silk industry of Spitalfields was never competitive with that of Lyons, and it survived only as a result of the shelter of prohibition. Eventually, many descendants of refugees were to be stranded in the backwater of a declining manufacture.

Besides, as England was a Protestant country, Huguenots did not bring any new values. Admittedly, they were Calvinists in a country where a large majority of the population was Anglican, and Weberians may consider that they were thus a better nursery for entrepreneurs. Native English Dissenters, however, were close to them from a theological point of view and were also much more numerous. Besides, several French refugee churches soon conformed to Anglicanism.

But for their language, Huguenots were not very different from Englishmen; they resembled the host nation in several critical ways, unlike many immigrant groups in other periods and countries. Their role in the undoubted progress achieved by the English economy in the late seventeenth and early eighteenth centuries (which put England clearly ahead of France) can only have been marginal—a useful contribution but nothing more. It was probably more important in a backward country, such as Brandenburg-Prussia; referring to modern *Gastarbeiter*, R. von Thadden (1987, p. 6) has written that the Huguenots were "first-class immigrants . . . not Turks in Berlin, rather Berliners in Turkey." In England, Huguenots were neither. And of course, things can be much harder for minorities that are very different from their host societies, that have values and attitudes running against the grain. Such groups can be a leaven, as for instance the Chinese in Southeast Asia. In the same way, the refugees from China who settled in Hong Kong—that is, in a Westernized Chinese environment similar to their own—created the industry of the colony, and many of them made fortunes.

At this point, a comparison with refugees from Nazi Germany can be useful, despite their differences from the Huguenots. Some outstanding businessmen have sprung from the ranks of German refugees who settled in Britain and in the United States (for example, Simon Warburg and Robert Maxwell), but the economies of both the country of origin and the host countries were too similar for the macroeconomic contribution of those men to be significant. Conversely, as the social sciences were much more developed in Germany than in America, the arrival there of a handful of German academics gave to those disciplines a remarkable boost. A story of comparative advantage again, but also a reminder that some Jewish intellectuals who left Germany in the 1930s were given chairs in great American universities, while those who did not leave ended in Buchenwald or Auschwitz. Much earlier, in the eighteenth century, a descendant of Huguenot refugees, Charles James d'Albiac, used to say he was eternally grateful to the French ("those damned frogs") for the persecutions that had sent his family to England; and the historian of another well-known family has written of its founder in England, David Bosanquet, that if he had forecast the success of his progeny, "he would have been grateful for the fate that had sent him out of France and established him in this new land of opportunity" (Charrington 1970, p. 11; Lee 1966, p. 124).

This chapter will try to test some of these hypotheses in a case study of the role Huguenots played in the "financial revolution" that England achieved during the late seventeenth and early eighteenth centuries. A major question will be whether the influx of refugees had a snowball effect and started a cumulative process, or whether it was a one-time-only boon, with merely limited impact.

In 1935, W. M. Acres, the historian of the Bank of England "from within," pointed out that the original Court of the Bank, which was elected on July 10–11, 1694, included 7 men "of Huguenot extraction" among its 26 members (24 directors, the governor, and his deputy). Altogether, the 147 directors who were elected during the first 50 years of the bank's existence, from 1694 to 1743, included 24 "Huguenots" (that is, 16 percent of the total); 5 of them became governors (see Table 8.1). Moreover, as a significant share of the

Table 8.1   Directors of the Bank of England with Walloon or Huguenot origins, by year of election.

Year	Director and dates of birth and death
1694	James Houblon, 1629–1700
	John Houblon, 1632–1712 (gov. 1694–1697)
	Abraham Houblon, 1640–1722 (dep. gov. 1701–1703, 1703–1705)
	John Lordell, c. 1630–1726
	James Denew, 1627–1705
	Samuel Lethieullier, 1643–1710
	Theodore Janssen, c. 1654–1748
1697[a]	Charles Chambrelan, 1639–1705
	Samuel Bulteel, 1638–1709
1698	Peter Delmé, 1667–1728 (dep. gov. 1713–1715, 1715–1717)
1700	William Des Bouverie, 1656–1717 (dep. gov. 1707–1709)
1708[a]	John Emilie, 1654–1711
1711[a]	Denis Dutry, 1663–1728
1712	Christopher Lethieullier, 1675–1736
1713	Richard Houblon, 1672–1724
1716	Jean F. Fauquier, ?–1726
1720	Richard Du Cane, 1681–1744
1722	Delillers Carbonnel, 1669–1747 (dep. gov. 1738–1740, 1741–1742)
1723	John Olmius, 1678–1731 (dep. gov. 1731)
1728	James Gaultier, ?–1748
1734	Benjamin Lethieullier, 1688–1760 (dep. gov. 1749–1750)
	Benjamin Longuet, 1685–1761 (dep. gov. 1745–1747, 1747–1749)
1738[a]	John Lequesne, ?–1741
1739[a]	Claude Fonnereau, 1677–1740

Source: Acres (1931, II, 614ff; 1935; 1940).
[a] Served for less than five years.

Bank's stock—and more generally of the early national debt—was subscribed by Huguenots, it has been suggested that Protestant refugees played a major role in the "financial revolution."

True enough, the word *Huguenot,* strictly speaking, applies to Protestants who were French subjects and to their descendants. Actually, the ancestors of many so-called Huguenot Bank directors had emigrated to England from the Spanish Netherlands in the late sixteenth century, and not from the kingdom of France in the seventeenth; they had fled the repression by Alva following the Iconoclastic rioting of 1566, and not the *dragonnades* or the revocation of the Edict of Nantes. Many of these early refugees, however, came from areas that were annexed to France under Louis XIV and have been parts of France since, especially from a narrow zone that stretches along the modern Franco-Belgian frontier, from Armentières to Valenciennes. This point was observed by Samuel Smiles and confirmed by later research, but it has proved too complicated for some English writers, ignorant of or indifferent to continental history, who have called those people Frenchmen. This they never were. So the old appellation of *Walloons* will be used here for such people, while *Huguenot* will be reserved for those who hailed from France.

Prominent in the first Court of the Bank of England were the three Houblon brothers: Sir John, who was elected as the first governor; his elder brother, Sir James; and his younger, Abraham (see Table 8.1). Later on, Abraham's eldest son, Sir Richard, was director from 1713 to 1719. Symbolically, the Bank settled in 1734 on the site of Sir John's house, in Threadneedle Street, and the full uniform of its porters is based on the livery his servants wore.

The three brothers were fourth-generation immigrants; their great-grandfather, Jean Houbelon, son of a merchant of Lille, had fled to England in 1567 and settled as a merchant in London. Their grandfather and their father, James, had followed the same calling and become wealthy. The brothers had reached the top of the merchant hierarchy. They were trading mostly with Portugal, Spain, the Mediterranean, and the Levant; they exported cloth, fish, and colonial produce and imported wine, bullion, and specie on a very large scale. They had been lending to the government before 1694. John and Abraham were among the largest subscribers to the Bank (to the tune of £10,000 each, or about $4.5 million in today's terms); but several of their relatives also subscribed, and by 1702, 15 Houblons were Bank stockholders, with total holdings of £54,760.

Close to the Houblon brothers among the original directors was John Lordell, whose brother and partner, James, had married in 1645 Sara Houblon, their older sister. The Lordells (Lourdel was the likely original name) are said to have been either of Walloon or of French extraction, but were not recent immigrants.

Samuel Lethieullier, director from 1694 to his death, also belonged to a great Walloon family, though settled in England more recently than the Houblons. According to tradition, an ancestor, Jean, had been burned at the stake in Valenciennes, the Geneva of the French-speaking Netherlands, where an outburst of Iconoclasm in 1566 was followed by harsh repression. Actually, Jean Le Thieullier, a rich silk merchant, was beheaded on March 29, 1568. His son, also named Jean, fled to Frankfurt and then settled as a merchant in Cologne; after his death, his widow and son Jean (or John) went to England in 1605. John became a rich London merchant and was naturalized, but during the Civil War he retired to Holland for some years. Thus Samuel was born in Amsterdam and had to be naturalized in 1660; still, he can be considered a second-generation immigrant (and a third-generation refugee). He had four brothers who were also London merchants, engaged, like the Houblons and the Lordells, in trade with southern Europe. Eight Lethieulliers were subscribers of Bank stock in 1694 (although not on the same scale as the Houblons) for £8,200; in subsequent years, however, they increased their holdings. Two nephews of Samuel (sons of his elder brother, Sir Christopher), Christopher and Benjamin, were Bank directors in succession from 1712 to 1760; so, except for short intervals, the court included a Lethieullier for over 60 years.

We do not know much about James Denew, who was a Bank director from 1694 to 1702. According to Acres (1935) he may have been descended from one Philippe de Noued of Caen, who had come to Canterbury in the late sixteenth century. But many De News (or De Neus) who lived in Canterbury in the seventeenth century were Walloons; and the director, through his mother, his wife, and his brother's wife, had close connections with the well-known Walloon families Maurois, de Lilliers, and Du Quesne.

Several men who were elected as directors during the early years after 1694 also had a Walloon background. Samuel Bulteel (director 1697–1708) is a shadowy figure, but he is likely to have descended from one refugee who fled Tournai in 1566 or 1567. On the other hand, Sir William Des Bouverie, baronet, belonged to the most famous of the Walloon clans (he was a fourth-generation immigrant). Laurent Des Bouveries (1542?–1610) was the son of a gentleman of Sainghin-en-Mélantois, southeast of Lille (and close to the battlefield of Bouvines). He disputed with his father over religion and fled to Frankfurt, where he worked as a clerk for a silk manufacturer. From there he moved to England (c. 1567) and settled in Canterbury as a master silk weaver. One of his sons, Edward, became a merchant in London; his grandson, Sir Edward Des Bouveries (1621–1694), was a rich Turkey merchant. He was the father of Sir William, who traded with southern Europe on a very large scale. The Bouveries did not subscribe in 1694, but by 1702 their holdings of Bank stock reached £27,000.

Peter and James Du Cane had invested £6,000 in Bank stock in 1694, but it was Peter's son, Richard, a fifth-generation immigrant, who eventually became a director. The family's original name had been Du Quesne, and their ancestor in England had fled from "Flanders" around 1567; in the third generation the name had been anglicized to Du Cane. The family is said to have been very prosperous at the end of the seventeenth century.

To this Walloon contingent may be added John Olmius and Sir Denis Dutry, who both had roots in modern Belgium—in Arlon for the former, whose father, Herman Olmius, had belonged to the French church on Threadneedle Street. As for Dutry, who became one of the richest financiers of the early eighteenth century, he had been born in Amsterdam, but his family came from Brabant. There is also Sir Peter Delmé, director from 1698 to his death, whose roots (he was a fourth-generation immigrant) also were on the "French borders"

(Gwynn 1985). Adrien de Le Mé had been born in No
mény, in the duchy of Lorraine, then independent. He settled in Norwich, where he died in 1603. His son Philippe Delmé (1588–1653) was minister of the French-Walloon church in Canterbury; he had a son, Peter, who was a dyer and merchant in London and the father of the Peter Delmé who became a Bank director. In the 1690s, Peter the younger was trading on a modest scale, exporting draperies to southern Europe and importing Spanish wool. Later on, however, his business extended greatly, especially in the Levant, and he accumulated one of the largest fortunes in the City (over £400,000). Sir Peter (as he became in 1714) had not bought bank stock in 1694, but his holdings were £20,000 in 1702 and £118,358 in 1723–24 (plus £169,803 in East India and South Sea stock).

Compared with the group from the Spanish Netherlands, the strictly French contribution appears modest. Nonetheless, one (but only one) of the Bank's original directors was a first-generation—indeed a recent—immigrant from France.

Theodore Janssen had been born in Angoulême, but, of course, to a family from the Netherlands (from Gueldre, according to some sources). Angoulême was in the seventeenth century a leading center of the paper industry; it exported to Holland a large share of its output, and a number of Flemish merchants had settled there to buy and ship paper; they also leased some paper mills. According to a local historian, the name Janssen occurs frequently in *minutes notariales* of the third quarter of the seventeenth century, including one Abraham Janssen (this was the name of Theodore's father).

Theodore came to England in 1680 or shortly afterward, with a large sum of money that his father had given him; he was naturalized in 1685 and started as an importer of paper from France, soon on a large scale (in 1695–96 his imports amounted to £22,000, or 93 percent of England's paper imports). Apparently he had fled the persecutions against Protestants and secured part of his family's fortune. His departure may also have had economic reasons, however, as exports of paper from Angoulême had been hit by the Franco-Dutch war of 1672–1678 and were in a decline. Also, in 1687 Janssen was prosecuted by the Company of White Paper Makers in England for having instigated the absconding to France of three Huguenots who were skilled paper makers working for the company; this implied contacts with Barillon, the French envoy in London, who was trying to persuade craftsmen who had fled the *dragonnades* to return to France. This is rather surprising if Janssen was a refugee for reasons of conscience. He was fined £500, reduced to £100 on the plea that he was a "young trader ignorant of the laws" (Coleman 1958, pp. 70–71).

This peccadillo did no serious harm to Janssen, who diversified into finance and started to invest in government securities. His subscription of Bank of England stock in 1694—£10,000—was one of the largest, which explains his election as one of the original directors (he retained his seat up to 1719, but for short statutory intervals). Henceforth, as Alice Carter (1975) wrote, he had his fingers in almost every available financial pie. He subscribed £15,000 to the East India loan of 1698. From 1695 or 1696, he was one of the principal contractors for remittances to the English army on the Continent, and he resumed this prominent role during the War of Spanish Succession. In 1710 he joined the new combination of financiers set up by Harley to take the place—in matters of advances to government and of remittances—of the oligopoly exclusively connected with the fallen Whigs. He had been knighted as early as 1698, and in 1715 he was made a baronet; in 1717 he was elected M.P. for Yarmouth as a Whig. Then things went wrong; he had been a director of the South Sea Company since 1711; when the scandal broke, he was expelled from the House of Commons and his estate—estimated at £243,000—was confiscated. Still, the House decided he might keep £50,000 (which became actually £100,000); he was thus able to live in ease to a ripe old age. Sir Theodore Janssen was one of the great businessmen of his time, but one wonders whether he should be called a French Huguenot.

Seven directors of the Bank during its first 50 years were of genuine French stock, but three of them were not first-generation refugees. Charles Chambrelan (director 1697–1705) was the son of a London merchant-tailor; Acres (1935, p. 242) thinks it is "probable" that he was a descendant of one Peter Chamberlan (*sic*), merchant of Rouen, who had fled to England after the St. Bartholomew massacre, "although," he adds, "there are gaps in the pedigree of the family which I have not yet been able to fill." Delillers Carbonnel was the son of Guillaume Carbonnel, a merchant and elder of the French church, who had been born in Caen (though the name definitely belongs to the South of France); but his mother was a Walloon, daughter of Jean de Lillers and of Anne Maurois, who had married Guillaume in 1654 in London, where the director was born. As for Benjamin Longuet, director from 1734 until his death, with stints as deputy governor and governor, he was likely a grandson of John Longuet, who was born in Bayeux, was naturalized in 1664, and was trading with Spain in the 1690s; Benjamin was a second- or third-generation immigrant.

We are thus left with only four Bank directors who were themselves refugees. John Francis Fauquier (director 1716–1726) was born in Clairac (Agenais), a Protestant stronghold that sent 90 persons to England at the time of the revocation. He came to England with his father and in the early eighteenth century became deputy to the Master of the Mint. James Gaultier (director 1728–1748) came to England from Angoulême and was naturalized in 1700, the same year as Sir John Lequesne, whose family had lived in Rouen in the late seventeenth century. As for Claude Fonnereau, he came to London from La Rochelle, either in 1685 or in 1689; he was naturalized in 1698. He made a fortune (£200,000 according to the press) as a "Hamburg merchant" who imported linen from Germany. In 1735 he bought estates in Essex, and in 1739 he was elected director of the Bank; but he died the following year, just after having reached the top.[3]

Except for Fauquier, the French refugees—and also Longuet, born in England—entered the Court at a later date, over 30 years after the Bank's foundation and near the end of their lives. Claude Fonnereau, however, unlike the others, was the founder of one of the great Huguenot dynasties in England.

Altogether, among the 24 "Huguenots" who were elected directors of the Bank of England during its first 50 years, 10 actually belonged to Walloon families that had long been established in England and 3 more can be linked with them; the origins of 2 others are not clear, possibly French, possibly Walloon, but neither they nor 3 directors with undoubted French roots were first-generation immigrants. Five directors only, including the Dutchman Janssen, had been driven from France by Louis XIV's persecutions. The role of French refugees in the leadership of the Bank of England during its early years was much smaller than some writers have hastily assumed.

This remark, however, does not allow any generalization about the role Huguenots played in England's "divergence" during the late seventeenth and early eighteenth centuries; there were some prominent merchants, from both the first and the second Protestant migrations, who were not involved with the Bank of England (except as stockholders): for instance, Thomas Papillon,[4] Paul Docminicque (a Walloon), Sir John Lambert,[5] and Etienne Seignoret.

Moreover, one must take into account the very small number of Bank directors who had a foreign, but neither Walloon nor Huguenot, background. Indeed, there was only one of them in the original court, Sir James Bateman (c. 1660–1718), who was English-born but with a naturalized father, Joos Bateman, a Flemish immigrant who had become a rich London merchant; he was one of London's merchant-princes and much involved in public finance. Like Sir John Houblon, he accumulated directorships, offices, and honors.[6] Later on, one can find only three or four "foreign" directors; the most prominent was Sir Justus Beck, baronet (d. 1723), who had been born in Amsterdam; he was known as a formidable financier, but was bankrupted in 1720 when the South Sea Bubble collapsed.[7]

On the other hand, it is striking that a few powerful dynasties of Walloon extraction played in the founding of the Bank and in its early management a role that historians have hardly noticed. It is also remarkable—though possibly of antiquarian significance only—that the ancestors of those members of the City elite had been born in or near Lille, Valenciennes, or Tournai—that is, cities without a country—and had emigrated to England at the same time, *au temps des troubles*. Anyhow, it is striking proof of mobility and opportunities within English society that, in three or four generations, descendants of refugees from abroad, who are not likely to have brought much capital, succeeded in rising to the very top of the London bourgeoisie. Generally, families' fortunes were accumulated gradually, but during the wars that raged after 1689, mobility increased and men such as Janssen, Delmé, and Dutry made a lot of money very fast. The overwhelming majority of the refugees were, of course, far less successful.

The founders of those families in England, however, had come from one of the most industrialized and urbanized parts of the Continent, from cities—Lille, Valenciennes, Tournai—that were large for that time, with active trade and manufactures, as well as close relations with Antwerp, then the economic metropolis of northern Europe. We would need to know more about the history of refugee families to ascertain the influence of this background and whether their founders had some special skills that gave them comparative advantages and were instrumental to their business success. The only clear case is that of Laurent des Bouveries, who had been trained in the silk manufacture. It is likely that some other families followed the same path, from silk weaving in Canterbury to the import of silk and the Levant trade in London. On the other hand, when the Bank of England was established, the Houblons, Bouveries, Delmés, and others had been in England for a century or more; they cannot have brought from the Continent any familiarity with or expertise in banking, *rentes,* and other *valeurs mobilières.* Moreover, Acres (1935) was probably right when he wrote that there is no evidence that the Huguenot members of the court of directors acted as a body in opposition to the native English. It is tempting to see a Walloon clique or connection at the origin of the Bank of England and in control during its early days, but it would be rash to do so, even though those families made up a closely knit community and the Houblons and Janssens belonged to the "City group," which had made plans for creating a Bank.

Indeed, one must wonder whether Sir John Clapham was not right in deprecating the role of the so-called Huguenot element among the early Bank directors and in writing about its stockholders (1944, I, 278): "Foreign names there are in plenty . . . but most of those foreign names are of men either by law or in effect English." This raises the difficult problem of the degree of assimilation the Walloon families we are interested in had reached by the 1690s, over a century after their ancestors—or most of them—had landed in England.

James Houblon I, father of the three "founding brothers," wrote, in the 1670s, some "Pious Memoirs," intended for his children. "Be especially charitable to the French Church. I know not of any charity better bestowed or more faithfully managed . . . There your Ancient Father was baptized, there in a

happy day was he married, and in that Congregation were ye all christen'd."
These lines reveal a feeling of double identity, a remembrance of continental
origins. And in 1679 the diarist Evelyn, who was a friend of Sir James Houblon
II, called him "a French merchant." Yet it was the first James who anglicized
his name by dropping the *e* in Houbelon; his fifth son, Jacob, became an
Anglican clergyman; and the family historian (herself a Houblon) was able to
write of a later relative, Jacob Houblon III (1710–1770), a full-blooded country
gentleman, that he had "imbibed the national jealousy of, and dislike for,
France and the French" (Houblon 1907, I, 217; II, 30).

More valid conclusions can be drawn by using an objective criterion of
assimilation—marriage. In the late sixteenth and early seventeenth centuries,
endogamy prevailed in the refugee communities; in particular, several of the
families we are interested in—Houblon, Lethieullier, Denew, Du Quesne (Du
Cane), Des Bouveries, Delmé—became connected by marriage, not so much by
direct matches as through marriages with some other leading Walloon families,
especially de la Forterie and Maurois. The position, however, was quite different in the generation of the early Bank of England directors. Of 13 marriages
contracted by 10 Walloon directors, only 3 were with women who were undoubtedly "foreign" (2 more may have come from foreign families), while 8
were with brides from unquestionably English families. This is a clear sign of
advanced assimilation. Of the 3 Houblon brothers (their mother had been a Du
Quesne), only Sir John had a wife of refugee extraction, Marie Jorion.

As for the directors who had roots in France, all their known marriages were
with Englishwomen, even for those who were first-generation immigrants (not
surprisingly, Janssen married the daughter of a knight and M.P., with a substantial dowry). The only exception is Claude Fonnereau, who twice married
"foreigners." This marriage pattern supports the view that French Huguenots
who came to England in the late seventeenth century assimilated much more
quickly than the Walloons who had arrived a century earlier.

An additional proof of assimilation is to be found in the public offices that
were held by several directors of foreign extraction and in the honors they
received. This is also a sign of a relatively favorable reception by the host
society, especially for refugees who had become wealthy, although it did not
prevent the common people from considering them, with some hostility, as
foreigners. In 1721, during the South Sea scandal, the London mob was crying:
"Break Jansen [*sic*] and Lambert on the wheel—as in their countries they
would have been served" (Dickson 1967, p. 160).

Sir John Houblon was undoubtedly a profiteer of the Glorious Revolution. In
June 1689 he was elected sheriff of London, and in September alderman; in
October he was knighted. In 1690 he was returned as M.P. for Bodmin. In 1693
he was appointed a Lord Commissioner of the Admiralty (the first merchant to

hold this office) and a member of the Board of Trade. In 1695 he was elected Lord Mayor of London, and during his year of office he of course retained his positions at the Bank, at the Admiralty, and in the Commons. He had to leave the Admiralty in 1699, when the Tories came to power, but in 1705, at the age of 73, he was appointed Lord Commissioner of Accounts. Such a plurality of offices and honors, however, was exceptional among the Bank's directors. Sir John's brother James had to be content with being elected alderman and knighted in 1691, and with a short spell as M.P. Theodore Janssen was knighted, made a baronet, and was an M.P. As for Peter Delmé, he served as alderman, sheriff, and Lord Mayor (1723) of London, and was knighted in 1714.

Altogether, the group of 24 Walloon and Huguenot directors includes 6 aldermen of the City, 3 sheriffs of London, 2 lord mayors, and 4 M.P.s; 6 were knighted and 3 were made baronets (Janssen, William Des Bouverie, Dutry). But 11 members of the group held no public office and received no honors. This points to a cleavage—which already appeared from career patterns—between those directors who were "merchant princes" and belonged to the elite of the City, and those who were businessmen of the second or third rank and did not take part in public life.

This pattern, however, was not specific to the Walloon-Huguenot group. The 19 original directors who were "British" included 7 men who were both aldermen and sheriffs of London; 5 of them became lord mayors. There were also 7 M.P.s (5 of whom belonged to the preceding group), 8 knights, and 3 baronets. Altogether, 11 held offices and/or received honors (concentrated among 7 *notables*), while 8 were rank and file.

The foundation of the Bank of England is often described as a coup by a clique of Whig projectors in collusion with Junto ministers; it has been suggested earlier that it might also be seen as the work of a Walloon, or Protestant refugee, clique. The two views are by no means incompatible, as the financiers of foreign extraction at the Bank had held long-standing Whig sympathies and had been associated with the Whig party since its emergence.

Indeed, the origins of this association go back a long way—to the acrimonious attacks by Archbishop Laud on "foreign" churches, with a view to suppressing their privileges and obliging them to conform. These attacks were bitterly resented by the refugee communities, and a large majority of the descendants of the Walloon and French exiles appear to have supported Parliament during the Civil War. At the Threadneedle Street Church in London, a new minister, Louis Hérault, who arrived from France in 1643 and was an enthusiastic royalist, was soon obliged to leave under pressure from the congregation. He was replaced by Jean de la Marche, from Guernsey, whose sermons inveighed against all things royalist and who was among the very first (as early as November 1645) to call for the execution of the king. It is highly significant that the most ardent supporters of de la Marche and of another extremist, Elie Delmé (one of his successors, son of the Canterbury minister, uncle of the Bank's director), included Jacques (James) Houblon (the father of the directors) and members of the Delillers and Duquesne families—though most great City merchants at the time were hostile to radicalism.

The next remarkable episode involved the revival in the 1670s of anti-Catholic feeling and anti-French hysteria in reaction against the policy of Charles II.[8] Rapprochement with an absolutist, popish, expansionist France was seen as a threat to the Protestant religion, the liberties of Englishmen, and the commercial interests of the country. One aspect of this agitation was a campaign against trading with France, which eventually, in 1678, resulted in the prohibition of most French goods. A decisive stage in this campaign was the presentation to a committee of the House of Lords, on November 19, 1674, of a document called "A Scheme of the Trade as it is at present carried on between England and France," generally referred to as the "Scheme of Trade." Its central theme was that England had an unfavorable balance of trade with France to the tune of £1 million per year. This text was extremely influential, both in the short and in the long term. It helped the passing of the act of 1678, and it also encrusted in English opinion for over a century the belief that prohibition of French imports was necessary to prevent the "daily wasting of the Stock of this Nation" (Priestley 1956, p. 207).[9]

The "Scheme" had been signed by 14 merchants, all "men of wealth and established position in the City"; and 5 of them at least were of Walloon or Huguenot extraction: James and John Houblon, Thomas Papillon, John Dubois, and Benjamin Delaune. Moreover, the English signatories included Benjamin and Michael Godfrey; their brother, Sir Edmund Berry Godfrey, was the Whig magistrate who was mysteriously killed in 1678, at the time of the popish plot, and Michael's son—also named Michael—was the first deputy governor of the Bank of England. As for the "leader" and spokesman of the 14, Sir Patience Ward, he had a nephew and heir, Sir John Ward, who was one of the original directors of the Bank and later its governor. There was thus some connection— indeed a striking connection—between the "Scheme" and the Bank between 1674 and 1694.

The motivations of the authors of the "Scheme" were partly ideological: they were staunch Protestants and were strongly opposed to popery. Ward, from a Puritan family, was a rabid anti-Catholic; while Lord Mayor of London, he had an inscription placed on the Monument that attributed the Great Fire to the papists. The Houblon brothers had been told by their father: "Forsake all your goods, yea your very lives, rather than comply with popery" (Houblon 1907, I, 347). Papillon had just been returned as M.P. for Dover by the "fanatic party" and proposed to Parliament a discriminatory tax on Jews.

Now, there was an increasing politicization of commercial questions in the 1670s. On the one hand, it was feared that France, owing to a trade surplus with England, which was paid in specie, would be enabled to build up its army and navy; on the other, retaliatory action against French trade would jeopardize Anglo-French relations and embarrass Charles II. Yet 1674 was not 1685, and, as it has been pointed out, before 1680 some Englishmen at least—especially Dissenters—could still see France in the image of Henry IV and the Edict of Nantes, and therefore as a model for English policy. Moreover, a decisive religious motivation does not fit well with the pro-Spanish stand of the anti-French party (about which more in a moment). Indeed, the Walloons had no personal reason to be hostile to France, which had supported, intermittently, the Protestant rebels in the Low Countries against Spain. There was some irony in their helping, through the Bank of England, to finance the ''War of the Grand Alliance,'' in which Protestant Britain was united to Catholic Spain, the land of the Inquisition and the persecutor of their ancestors (it may be further proof, admittedly, that Walloon families had been anglicized).

Actually there were also business reasons for the campaign against French trade. This was certainly true of Ward, an exporter of cloth to France whose sales had greatly fallen, in part because of the French tariffs of 1664 and 1667. Ward wanted English ministers to exert pressure on France to order to obtain better terms. Similarly, the Houblons and other merchants who were trading with southern Europe, and imported wine from Spain and Portugal, would gain from a prohibition on French wines, imports of which had risen in the 1660s. It was also widely believed that trade with Spain (which was deemed especially advantageous) and trade with France were incompatible: the former would suffer from retaliation by the Spanish government if an Anglo-French commercial treaty were concluded, and even more if the French alliance dragged England into a war with Spain. This had indeed happened under the Commonwealth, and in 1659 the Houblons had joined a host of London merchants in strongly protesting against the war with Spain, which hurt their interests. Some of the 14 were also involved in the import and/or manufacture of silk; they stood to benefit from a prohibition on French silk textiles.

On the other hand, it cannot be maintained—as some historians have done— that English merchants were hurt or even worried by French competition and commercial expansion (particularly in the Levant), of which there was no evidence. Indeed, English trade with southern Europe had been growing and prosperous since 1660 (and would remain so in the 1630s). Moreover, the ''Scheme of Trade'' is replete with serious errors; in particular, the idea that England had an adverse balance of £1 million is ''completely invalid,'' according to Margaret Priestley (1951), who has rightly questioned the intellectual honesty of its authors; nonetheless, this piece of falsification had wide-ranging consequences.

In any event, during the 1670s the Houblons and some other City leaders with a refugee background were active in a campaign that was both anti-French and anticourt. It was almost a matter of course that, during the exclusion crisis that followed, from 1678 to 1681, when political "parties" emerged, this closely knit group, followed by most of the refugees and descendants of refugees, was prominent in support of the Whigs, who were exploiting anti-Catholic feelings and fears aroused by the "popish plot." Then came the beginnings of the *dragonnades* and of a major inflow of refugees, which gave an additional anti-French coloration to those feelings. That same year, 1681, John Houblon, Michael Godfrey, John Dubois, and Thomas Papillon, all of them members of the Grand Jury of Middlesex, which had been packed by Whig sheriffs and had dismissed the prosecution case of high treason against Lord Shaftesbury, were reputedly worth collectively £1 million sterling. In the disputed elections of 1682, Dubois and Papillon stood as Whig candidates for the positions of sheriff in London and Middlesex; after the king's victory, Papillon and Ward fled to Holland.

When the Glorious Revolution came, the refugees, both Walloon and French, supported heartily the anti-Catholic, anti-French faction that triumphed. It has been stressed earlier how the Revolution brought John Houblon offices, influence, and honors: thus in March 1690 Sir John and Sir James Houblon, James Denew, and Thomas Papillon (in addition to two Englishmen who were later directors of the Bank) were members of a committee of 25 Whig leaders who prepared a draft act for a radical and democratic reform of the corporation's constitution. The Whig credentials of the leading directors of the Bank with a foreign background cannot be doubted, and they were obviously part of the "new establishment." This study, then, can only confirm the usual view that the Bank of England—like most institutions of the financial revolution—was "stamped with Whiggism from its inception" (Plumb 1967, p. 138). It was one of the interest groups associated with the Whig party, and it became one of its strongholds, a bulwark of the revolutionary settlement and of the Protestant succession.

Indeed, in the 1690s the refugees supported William III and the Whigs in their vigorous pursuit of the war against Louis XIV's France, which had become an object of odium to all Protestants. Some of them were even ready to engage in privateering, and they were willing to lend to an anti-Catholic, anti-French regime that they felt they could trust. The Bank of England had actually been established to give financial support to William III and his Whig ministers; it did not fail them, and men like the Houblons were staunch advocates of the support that the moneyed interest generally and the Bank in particular gave to the king. To the latter, a chief use of the Bank of England was to facilitate the remittance of money to British forces abroad. From May 1693 up to the end of the war, some directors of the Bank resided by rotation in Antwerp in order to superintend this business. Sir James Houblon and Michael Godfrey went to Flanders, and in a freak accident, the deputy governor had his head taken off by a cannonball while he was observing the siege of Namur in July 1695. The Bank resorted to the help of a number of strong firms with well-established connections both in England and on the Continent, and many of these had "foreign" names—Walloon, Dutch, Huguenot, Jewish—or foreign associates. Theodore Janssen and another recent immigrant and holder of Bank stock, Etienne Seignoret, played a leading role in such remittances to the Low Countries. Seignoret, however, was impeached before the House of Commons in 1698 for having smuggled French silks into England on a large scale, and was fined £10,000.[10] This suggests that the profit motive prevailed over hatred of Louis XIV and of France, at least in some cases.

Meanwhile, moneyed people who had started lending to the new regime—and especially refugees or descendants of refugees—were bound hand and foot to it and felt that their own future depended on its stability. The Revolution had created a vested interest, of which the great "foreign" merchant families were undoubtedly part. It is nonetheless striking that a small group of Walloon merchants, plus a few Huguenots, had a significant impact on England's policy and helped, for reasons both of ideology and of interest, to steer her on a collision course with France that led to the second Hundred Years' War.

Now let us turn from the role played by individuals and families to the contribution of capital.[11]

The study of subscribers and proprietors of Bank of England stock confirms the point made earlier: the significance of the role played in the Bank's early history (and in the City at large) by a few rich merchant families whose ancestors had belonged to the first migration of Protestant refugees in England. Most of these were of Walloon extraction, but some had French origins. They made up a tiny but wealthy group; 27 individuals with this kind of background took part in the 1694 subscription; 22 of them belonged to 5 families: Houblon (5 subscribers), Lethieullier (8), Lordell (3), Du Cane (2), and Chambrelan (4). Those 22 persons subscribed £60,200, or 5.01 percent of the Bank's original capital (and the 27 paid up £64,400, or 5.37 percent of the total). The kinship pattern of Walloon investment in the Bank and its close connection with the directorate are obvious: shareholding by members of this community was almost restricted to directors and their families.

Moreover, the number and value of Walloon holdings rose during the early years of the Bank. The Houblons increased their stake: by 1702, 15 of them were proprietors, with holdings of £54,760. In the Lethieullier family, the elder brother, Sir John, had not subscribed in 1694; but by 1702 he had £5,500 of Bank stock, and he left £30,400 of it at his death. Peter Delmé was not among the early subscribers, and his relative, John Delmé, had taken only £500 of stock in 1694; but in 1697 he subscribed for £4,020 and Peter Delmé for £4,014. The Bouveries had also abstained in 1694, but by 1702, 4 of them had become proprietors, with holdings of £27,047.

So the number of Walloon stockholders rose from 27 in 1694 to 41 in December 1697 and 43 in March 1702; as for the number of their holdings of £2,000 or more, it increased from 13 to 15 and then to 23. Those 23 large holders of 1702 owned £165,182 of stock, or 7.5 percent of the Bank's capital; 6 of them had £10,000 or more (Samuel Lethieullier had £24,420, Peter Delmé £20,000).

The pattern of investment in the Bank by refugees of the second migration—that is, of the late seventeenth century—was somewhat different: the number of subscribers and proprietors from their ranks was higher, large holdings were relatively fewer, family proprietorships were quite rare, and the total contribution was larger.

According to P. G. M. Dickson, 123 Huguenots of *recent domicile* (who had settled in England after 1650) subscribed £104,000 to the Bank in 1694, or 8.7 percent of the first call for £1,200,000. When a second subscription took place in April to June 1697, 60 more Huguenots joined, and by December 1697, about 170 of them were proprietors of Bank stock. Alice Carter reckons that by that date Huguenots of the *second migration* (who had arrived after 1680) held £190,000 of Bank stock, or 8.6 percent of a capital that had grown to £2,200,000. She adds that investment by earlier immigrants, such as the Houblons, brings the total of Huguenot and Walloon holdings to £30,000 (15 percent of total capital).[12]

This may have been the peak of Huguenot involvement in the Bank: by March 1702 the number of holdings by recent refugees had fallen to 126, according to our reckoning. Possibly some refugees had taken advantage of the rise in stock prices after the peace of 1697, while others had sold out when a new war threatened. On the other hand, the Walloons who were closely involved in the Bank's affairs, either personally or through relatives, had retained or even increased their holdings.

Dickson (1967) has calculated that in March 1709, before the Bank's capital was doubled, Huguenots of recent domicile (post-1650) held £139,000, or 6.1 percent, of its stock and subscribed £150,500, or 6.8 percent, of the new call for money. This brought their holdings to £289,500, or 6.4 percent of the total capital.

The estimate, then, made in 1709 by a contemporary, that Huguenot refugees had contributed £500,000 to the Bank's capital and had over £2 million "in the government" was a gross overstatement. It is also likely that Alice Carter (1975, p. 90) went too far when she wrote that the total contribution of Huguenots of recent migration in terms of cash invested or stock held in "the various public loans, what we loosely call the Funds" was roughly of the order of 10 percent and "thus of some importance."

As usual, one can wonder how big is big and how small is small, but such a contribution from a tiny minority of the population is undoubtedly remarkable. Still, Dickson points out that Jews contributed more than Huguenots to the Bank call for capital in 1709. Nonetheless, the figures of Huguenot stockholders must be compared with the estimates that 40,000 to 50,000 French Protestants (and therefore 10,000 heads of families at least) found asylum in Britain from the late 1670s to the reign of Queen Anne, and that about 20,000 of them were living in London in the 1690s and 1700s. The percentage of Huguenots who invested in Bank stock and more generally in the funds then appears minute.

Note that some Huguenots who had found asylum in countries other than England also invested in English funds. Fourteen persons who resided in the United Provinces, but had French names, were subscribers to Bank of England stock in 1694.[13] Then in 1709–1711, 45 residents of Switzerland and Geneva became owners of Bank shares.[14] Still, it was after the South Sea Bubble that permanent foreign investment in English government securities reached a really substantial size; a number of the foreign investors had Huguenot names, and some of them were members of Huguenot families with branches in England. In 1723–24, when there were some 52 Dutch holders of £10,000 or more in the three major stocks (Bank of England, East India Company, and South Sea), 6 were Huguenots, with a total of £83,000.

By March 1724, according to Dickson (1967, p. 282), about 250 owners of Bank of England stock were English Huguenots, or 6 percent of the total number, just as in 1709. Among the biggest holders of stock, Jews now outnumbered Huguenots. Still, Sir Peter Delmé and Sir Denis Dutry held £288,161 and £190,669, respectively, of the three major stocks (£118,358 and £34,738 in Bank stock)—almost half a million between them. Dickson considers that by then "the Huguenot community in London had become fairly well absorbed into English society, and its ownership of securities is therefore no longer of particular significance" (Dickson 1967, p. 282).

On the other hand, Carter (1975) has researched the ownership of stock in the 1760s by the "Huguenot community"—that is, by members of families with roots in France who still worshipped in French churches and were benefactors or on the governing body of the French hospital. As the amount of the public debt was by then very large, she has used a sampling method, finding that English "Huguenots" accounted for around 11 percent of the whole proprietorship of Bank of England stock in 1761–1768; 14 percent of the proprietors of East India stock (17 percent if Dutch-domiciled Huguenots are included); and 22 percent of the proprietors of the 3 percent loan of 1726, in 1754–1756.

The percentage of Huguenot proprietorship was smaller for the large speculative loans floated during the Seven Years' War. Carter (1975, pp. 92, 106) found 14 percent Huguenot names among the proprietors of the 3.5 percent loan of 1756. As for the loan of 1760, 14 of the 106 large holders (with £10,000 of stock or more) were Huguenots and held about 3 to 4 percent of the total. "As the debt grew larger, so did the proportion of it that was taken up by the English themselves . . . It seems that (by the mid-eighteenth century) the proportion of fund holders who were Huguenot is higher than one-tenth, a good deal nearer one-fifth in what we would now call gilt-edged. But the capital thus represented is no longer foreign capital—it is the invested proceeds of much trading as well as financial activity" (Carter 1975, pp. 92, 106). Once more, the estimated percentages are optimistic, but the other remark is most sensible, and it raises a problem that I will consider shortly.

The "Book of the Subscriptions" of 1694 supplies some information about the profession and/or the social status of subscribers. Esquires and gentlemen (plus one knight, the traveler Sir John Chardin, and one marquis), were prominent among French Huguenot subscribers: 36 of the 94 individuals for whom information is given (38 percent). There were also 21 women—mostly widows, but also some spinsters. Eighteen other subscribers were army officers, officials, clergymen, doctors, and apothecaries. This leaves 29 men in business (31 percent of subscribers), who were mostly merchants (22), with a few craftsmen and shopkeepers.

Seventeen subscribers of 1694 appear to belong to the French nobility, but only one of them to a well-known family: the Lady Hester Hervart, Marquise de Governet, who was the daughter of the late controller general of finances, Barthélémy Hervart; she subscribed only £500 in 1694, but by December 1697 her holding of Bank stock had risen to £7,000, and it was still £6,000 in 1702. Four of those noblemen, though obscure, were large subscribers—two for £3,000, one for £4,000, and Jacques (or James) de la Bretonnière for £10,000. This made him one of the largest subscribers; unfortunately there is no information on this wealthy but enigmatic character, except that he died in 1695, having meanwhile increased his holding to £21,800.

As for the distribution of subscriptions according to their amount (see Table 8.2), a majority (62.5 percent) of those by "Huguenots" in 1694 were "substantial" (£500 or more). This is a higher percentage than among the entirety of subscriptions (and it would be still higher if the Walloons, whose holdings were all "substantial," with one exception, were included). Moreover, 15 individuals subscribed £2,000 or more, for a sum of £51,750, or nearly one-half of total subscriptions by persons of French origin. The pattern is roughly the same for the holdings of Bank stock in 1697 and 1702, the subscriptions of 1697 and 1709, with a significant minority—between 12 and 24 percent—of Hugue-

Table 8.2 Distribution of subscriptions and holdings of Bank of England stock.

Size of holdings (£)	1694 subscription	Holdings as of December 25, 1697	Holdings as of March 25, 1702	Holdings of additional stock as of September 24, 1709
Huguenot proprietors				
Under 500	42	79	66	21
500–999	42	33	26	32
1,000–1,999	13	28	20	16
2,000–4,999	13	21	9	13
5,000–9,999	—	7	5	7
10,000 and more	2	2	—	2
Total	112	170	126	91
Walloon proprietors				
Under 500	1	7	4	1
500–999	8	3	9	3
1,000–1,999	5	16	7	4
2,000–4,999	10	10	13	2
5,000–9,999	1	1	4	3
10,000 and more	2	4	6	2
Total	27	41	43	15

Source: Bank of England records.

not proprietors who subscribed or owned stock for £2,000 or more. The pattern of investment is therefore biased toward "substantial" or even "large" holders. Altogether, I have counted 54 individuals of French extraction who, on at least one of those five occasions, made a subscription or owned stock for £2,000 or more. This is a high figure, but only 20 of those persons appear on at least two of those occasions; this suggests a rather rapid turnover among stockholders, under the impact of death and disinvestment; many subscribers of 1694 do not appear on the list of stockholders of 1702; many of those who subscribed additional capital in 1709 had not been proprietors in 1702.

Nonetheless, 17 individuals made a subscription or had a holding of £5,000 or more on at least one of those occasions. These were really "big" proprietors, and they are matched by 12 Walloons, who were in the same £5,000 bracket but made up a much higher proportion of the Walloon group of investors. Symbolically, the 12 subscribers of £10,000 in 1694 included 2 Walloons, Sir John and Abraham Houblon, and 2 Huguenots, Theodore Janssen and James de la Bretonnière.

The Huguenot subscribers of £2,000 or more in 1694 included 8 merchants, and this suggests the emergence in London, in the late seventeenth century, of a group of well-to-do businessmen who had recently immigrated from France; this group, however, was not large. From the tables of "alien merchants" in foreign trade in London during the 1690s, which D. W. Jones (1970) has compiled, one can draw up a list of 73 individuals who are likely to have been French Huguenots of relatively recent arrival (there were also 29 members of Walloon families, long established in England). And most of the trade was concentrated in a few hands; no more than 10 of those Huguenot merchants seem to have had a large turnover (over £10,000). Even if Jones's lists are incomplete, the number of Huguenot merchants was very small in relation to the thousands of adult males who found asylum in England during the 1680s; it was also small in relation to the total number of merchants who were active in London during the reign of William III, which G. S. De Krey (1985, p. 128) has estimated at 1,339.

According to Jones, 33 merchants who were Walloons or Huguenots subscribed to the Bank in 1694, for £56,250; 17 of them—with subscriptions of £21,850—belonged to the second migration. Yet there were some wealthy immigrant merchants who were not Bank proprietors, but who subscribed to the New East India Company of 1698, or to some other financial venture of the 1690s; there were also merchants who did not invest in securities, possibly because all their money was needed in their firms. Taking things altogether, one can catch sight of a small group (possibly a score) of prosperous merchants of recent but not always post-*dragonnades* migration, who were active in the 1690s and 1700s. They included, among others, the silk smuggler and church elder Etienne Seignoret and his partner René Baudouin, the brothers Pierre and Hilaire Reneu, who, like Peter Albert, had come from Bordeaux; James Du Fay from Boulogne; Daniel Hays from Calais; Francis Beuzelin, whose roots were in Rouen; John Delachambre, who had been born in Saint-Quentin; and Georges-Tobie Guiguer from Lyons.[15] Above them towered Theodore Janssen and Sir John Lambert, thanks to their wealth and to their omnipresence. Indeed, they were the only businessmen of the first order who sprang from the ranks of recent refugees; but the careers of both came to a sorry end.

A last point has to be considered. According to Jones's calculations, 58.4 percent of mercantile investment in the Bank of England in 1694 was subscribed by merchants who traded with southern Europe (40 percent by men trading with Iberia) and the western and central Mediterranean, 18.4 percent by Turkey merchants); on the other hand, their share in the imports and exports of London in 1689 was to be only 31.8 percent (East India trade excluded). As for the alien merchants who are listed by Jones (1972) as subscribers to the Bank, 9 out of 33 were importers of wine, 6 were trading to the Mediterranean, and 10 with the

Levant. I have already mentioned that most of the early Bank directors who were Walloons or Huguenots had been involved in those trades.

Jones has explained this ascendancy of "southern" merchants by the fact that, unlike the case of other traders, their capital resources were not fully used in trade during the Nine Years' War, and they thus had liquidities available for investment in stock. Indeed, during the early years of the war, trade with the Mediterranean had been suspended; then, in 1693, the Smyrna convoy was largely destroyed off Lagos by Tourville, and the Levant merchants suffered huge losses. As for wine merchants, there was a sharp drop in their imports because of heavy taxation—higher customs duties plus the land tax, which reduced the disposable income of the landed classes. They "experienced acute resource redundancy" (D. W. Jones 1972, p. 333), but they got out of that predicament by investing first in privateering, which turned easily into inter-loper trade in the waters of the East India Company, and then, in 1694, in the Bank. Thus, the disproportionate role in war finance of southern European merchants, and especially of wine importers, resulted from the differential effects of the war on the various groups of traders and from the redistribution of income within the mercantile community, which in its turn brought about a reallocation of resources.

Actually, the fall in total wine imports during the war is undoubted, but it resulted from the complete interruption of arrivals from France; as a consequence, imports from Iberia greatly increased—from 5,230 tons in 1689 to 18,083 in 1694. Since wine merchants were highly specialized, different firms handled imports from France and from Iberia, and one can suggest that Iberian merchants invested in stock because their trade had boomed and not because it was depressed! As for Levant merchants, they were the wealthiest merchant group in London per capita and had played the role of the elite in the City since early in the century; this may well have had a good deal to do with their large contribution—despite (and not because of) the Lagos disaster. On the other hand, opportunities for the employment of capital in foreign trade had been reduced by the war, so idle funds fell back on domestic projects and became the prey of numerous projectors—the founders of the Bank of England not excluded.

Yet the promoters of the Scheme—men such as the Houblon brothers—were undoubtedly influenced by political factors: the will to support the king and his Whig ministers, the war against France. Since they were leaders among traders to southern Europe, their initiative may well have had a contagious effect on the rank and file, especially those who were of foreign extraction, inasmuch as most of them were staunchly pro-Whig and may have seen the Bank as a Whig enterprise favorable to the "revolutionary settlement." It is also worth observing that most Huguenot merchants in London originated in the Atlantic or

Channel ports or close by; few indeed came from other parts of France, Languedoc included. Such people were familiar with the wine trade—either as exporters if they came from southwestern France, or as importers for those who had
been living north of the Loire. They were also likely to have done some trading
with Spain, with which Brittany and Normandy had active relations. So it is to
be expected that they would exploit their comparative advantage by importing
wine and trading with the Peninsula. It is more surprising to see several of them
engaged in the Levant trade, which in France was a preserve of Marseilles, from
which none of them came; but they may have been influenced by the example
of the Turkey merchants of Walloon extraction, whose ancestors had been
engaged in the manufacture of silks and whose families had moved naturally
into the importing of the raw material and the Levant trade generally.

Investment in stock by Huguenot refugees in the 1690s runs counter to the
view of them as believers who had given up their worldly goods for the sake of
their faith. Actually, while most of the fugitives were all but destitute and in
need of relief, a number of well-to-do individuals and families had managed to
bring over to England a substantial part of their wealth. Herbert Lüthy (1959–
61) has observed that French Protestant historians have glossed over this
problem—possibly because export of capital is considered by French *bien-
pensant* progressives as the most heinous of offenses. Yet both French diplo-
mats and Huguenot propagandists have noted that France was suffering at that
time a hemorrhage of capital. Their "calculations" of the amount of money
imported into England by French refugees in the 1680s yield some amazing
figures—up to £4 or £5 million sterling, roughly twice the yearly savings of
Englishmen, according to Gregory King's estimate for 1688, or the value of the
country's exports. Some historians have been ready to consider these as only
slight exaggerations and to find some justification for them, using adjectives
such as *enormous, considerable,* or *substantial* to describe this capital movement. On the other hand, Daniel Dessert (1984, pp. 182–183) reckons that the
French kingdom lost 850,000 *marcs* of silver between 1683 and 1697, which
ought to amount to under £1 million, and part of this outflow was a consequence
of the war and did not go entirely to England. He thinks that exports of capital
by Huguenots were distinctly marginal. Lüthy, however, rightly observes that
Huguenots succeeded in evading all restrictions against the export of capital:
even poor emigrants took away from specie in their pockets, and rich people,
especially those in business, could resort to ordinary commercial and banking
operations. But he is also right to state that no precise figure, even no order of
magnitude, can be proposed.

Alice Carter (1975, pp. 80, 86) has made great play of "the known migration
of the really rich," but her list boils down to few persons indeed: some relatives
of the late controller general of finances, Barthélémy Hervart, Nicolas Ram-

bouillet de la Sablière and Etienne Monginot de la Salle, both members of the few dynasties of Protestant financiers; François le Coq, *conseiller* at the Parlement of Paris; Antoine Aufrère, *procureur au Châtelet* and sometime elder at Charenton, who had carefully prepared his departure and is said to have exported 225,000 livres tournois—almost £10,000—from France. These people bought English stock and government securities, but they were rentiers and rather elderly. Only one of the individuals mentioned by Carter was an active businessman: Jean Girardot de Tillieux, from a family of timber merchants in Paris, who became in the 1690s a dealer in Bank and other stock on a large scale.

Another group that had resources was the merchants, who were in a good position to transfer capital to England; the first call on their money, however, came from their firms, and, as noted earlier, their number must not be overestimated. The "really rich" were a minute minority among refugees.

Altogether, taking into account the £16,200 subscribed by Huguenots of recent domicile to the Tontine of 1693 (the first English long-term loan to be floated), the £104,000 invested in the Bank in 1694, and various other sums, a wild guess would be that the amount of "new money" that went into "the funds" during the 1690s is not likely to have much exceeded £200,000. This was a substantial but not decisive contribution to war finance; if the Huguenots had not supplied this money, it would have come from some other source, as there was an abundance of liquid capital looking for passive investments. Moreover, long-term borrowing supplied only a small share of total expenditures during the Nine Years' War. True enough, many writers stress the almost unbearable strain to which the English financial system was submitted during this war for survival; it has been said that in 1694 and 1696, England was saved from disaster only by a hair's breadth, thanks first to these new issues, then the intervention of the Bank. But this is overdramatization—though, needless to say, the importance in the long run of the financial innovations of the 1690s must not be underrated. During later years, investment by Huguenots came from profits made in England, from the savings of professional men, officers, and so forth, and from plowing back rentier income.

One strange notion is the idea that many Huguenot refugees had a French financial background and had acquired considerable experience and expertise in government borrowing in the service of the French monarchy; so they brought to England a technical skill and a financial acumen that assisted the country's development "and may well have been a part at least of the leaven at the beginning of the National Debt." There are many contortions by Carter (1975, pp. 79, 84–86) to impute a French connection to a number of Huguenots, with such speculative arguments as: "through his wife he may have been connected with the banking firm of . . ."

Dessert has demonstrated, however, that an overwhelming majority of French financiers were Catholic and only a few Protestant; and the Protestants' role had diminished well before the revocation, as several of the great financial families apostatized. A few members of Huguenot families involved in finance did indeed emigrate to England, but they were passive investors and rentiers. As for technical expertise, one has to recall that the Paris Bourse was not established until 1724, and that before this France had nothing that looked remotely like a market for securities and stock. The *agents de change* of the seventeenth and early eighteenth centuries literally deserved their name; they were engaged in foreign exchange transactions, not stockbroking. (It was actually from Holland that new fiscal and financial techniques were imported into England, by William III and his entourage, which admittedly included some Huguenots.)

On the other hand, Carter and Gwynn have a point: long-term borrowing by government had existed in France since the sixteenth century, much earlier than in England, so Huguenots of means were, as Frenchmen, familiar with *rentes* and used to investing money in fixed-income, long-term government securities. Moreover, those who succeeded in transfering capital to England had it in a liquid form. Most of them settled in towns, especially in London, and it is not surprising that they invested their money in *valeurs mobilières,* rather than in land or houses. Possibly also, as Gwynn (1985, p. 145) suggests, their experience of migration had taught them the usefulness of being as liquid as possible and they used English funds for that purpose, the more so as many thought at first to return to France.

Still, it is remarkable that refugees were ready to invest in a new venture (which the Bank of England was) funds that they had managed to bring through difficulties and dangers and that may have been their only assets. On the other hand, this investment was secure (unless James II was restored); its return was satisfactory; stock could be readily realized on the emerging stock market; and there was a prospect of capital appreciation. Some refugees, moreover, may have seen such investment as a help to their host country and a contribution to the struggle against Louis XIV. Finally, the Huguenots seem to have been readier than the English to invest in securities: we have examples of modest craftsmen putting their savings into Bank stock. This was their comparative advantage, the reason why a small group of 100 to 200 individuals subscribed a share of the new national debt that was quite disproportionate to their actual number.

It is a fact, moreover, that as early as the 1690s, a number of Huguenot refugees in London had become professional dealers in government securities; obviously some large subscribers or holders of stock were playing the market, but there were also operators on a smaller scale who made a living from buying and selling stock, including transactions for the account of third parties. The latter included investors who were resident abroad, especially "Dutch Huguenots." Wealthy merchants such as Lambert, Janssen, Delmé, or Dutry were not above this role, but there were also individuals or firms who acted for relatives abroad. It is worth noting, too, that it was a Huguenot, John Castaing, who started in 1698 (possibly earlier) to publish the first list of market prices in government loans, the *Course of the Exchange;* the idea could not have come from France, however, but rather from Amsterdam. Nonetheless, it shows that the Huguenots had taken to stock like fish to water.

The foundation of the Bank of England has been described earlier as a coup by a clique of Whig projectors; it was also partly the work of "foreign" elements, mixing enterprise, which came mainly from Walloons, long settled in England, and capital, a significant share of which was supplied by recent Huguenot refugees. Gwynn (1985) has suggested that new ideas—especially in matters of banking and public finance—were transmitted from the Huguenot newcomers to the already anglicized members of the foreign churches, and through them to the English merchant community at large. One wonders, however, what kind of new ideas men from Angoulême, Bayonne, Boulogne, even Rouen or Bordeaux (to take the birthplaces of some Bank stockholders) could bring to merchant princes whose families had worked in London for several generations. Nor is there foundation for thinking that the older Walloon group became more willing to hazard its resources in new ventures as a result of its contact with Huguenot refugees and their experience with liquid capital assets! The sensible view is Dickson's (1967, p. 302): "Religious minorities—Huguenots, Jews—were less significant as investors than contemporaries thought, but they included some very important capitalists."

It was not to last. The prominent role played by a small number of those Walloon and Huguenot capitalists in the City and in finance during the late seventeenth and early eighteenth centuries was short-lived because their families were gentrified within one or two generations. They went native: settled in the country, bought estates, married English, became Anglicans, went to English churches. This process—recurrent in English society for successful newcomers—completed their assimilation and anglicization. Here are a few examples.

James Houblon I had 10 sons, and 67 of his grandchildren were alive at his death in 1682; many of his grandsons, however—of whom at least 7 were merchants—did not marry, and only one of them had a son who survived his father, so the family nearly became extinct in the male line! Thus, Jacob Houblon III (1710–1770) inherited inter alia the fortune of Sir Richard, the Bank director and "last of the Houblon merchant-princes" (Houblon 1907, I, 341), who had ordered his personal property to be laid out in the purchase of land because he did not think his heirs could hold their own in the new rough-and-tumble of the business world. Jacob was a rich country gentleman, with no business connections; he was a justice of the peace, high sheriff, lord lieutenant, M.P., colonel of the militia, and a Tory to boot, unlike his Whig ancestors. The christening of his son in 1736 was celebrated with magnificence; the 400 guests included 20 knights and baronets, 150 gentlemen. The later Houblons—or Archer-Houblon from 1800—passed quietly into the (sometimes *fainéant*) gilded gentry: a recent bearer of the name (by marriage), Doreen Archer-Houblon, was a horse trainer, expert in the sidesaddle, who stood in for the queen at rehearsals of the Birthday Parade.

The Lethieulliers, Christopher (d. 1736) and Benjamin (d. 1760), both Bank directors, and their cousin John (1659–1737), son of Sir John, combined activity in business and landownership. But the next generation gave up business. Smart Lethieullier (1701–1760), John's son, was an antiquarian and connoisseur; his brother, Charles (1712–1759), was for a while a fellow of All Souls College—a definite proof of Anglican gentility. Their second cousin, Benjamin, Jr. (1729–1797), is said to have kept some City connections, but he was a gentleman—and an M.P. for 30 years.

The gentrification of the Bouveries started early and was striking. Sir Edward (1621–1694) bought an estate in Hertfordshire and was knighted; his son, Sir William, the Bank director, was made a baronet; one of his brothers was knighted and another was an M.P. Sir Edward (1690–1736), second baronet, a Turkey merchant like his forebears, bought Longford Castle in Wiltshire. He was succeeded by his brother, Sir Jacob (1694–1761), the third baronet. As a younger brother, Jacob started as a Turkey merchant, but he had been educated at Christchurch and the Middle Temple and he inherited money and estates from his father, from an uncle, and finally from his brother. In 1747 he was created baron of Longford and Viscount Folkestone—the first time, it was said, that a merchant was raised to the peerage. His elder son, William (1725–1776), was promoted in 1765 to Baron Pleydell Bouverie of Coleshill, Berkshire, and first earl of Radnor. In 1770 he became governor of the French hospital, a position that has also been held almost continuously by his descendants. Strangely enough, the Radnors, who had no connection at first with France, have by now become the leading Huguenot family, whereas other dynasties of Walloon origin do not seem to have shown much interest in the Huguenot tradition. An Irish peerage was awarded in 1762 to John Olmius, the son of the Bank director (who had bought land in Essex and long pushed for a title), who was made Baron Waltham shortly before his death; but his son died in 1787 without issue and the title became extinct.

Sir Peter Delmé had bought some land, but most of his fortune was personality. His elder son, however, was a landowner and an M.P. His daughter married Sir Henry Liddell, baronet, M.P., a rich northern coal owner, who was madè Lord Ravensworth in 1747; their eldest daughter married the third duke of Grafton. Sir Peter's grandson married the daughter of the earl of Carlisle, Lady Elizabeth Howard, known as the beauty of Queen Charlotte's court. The couple belonged to the smart set and lived on a grand scale, with 100 menservants; but in 1781 racing losses obliged Peter Delmé III to sell horses, dogs, and one of his estates.

As for the Du Canes, Richard had acquired through his marriage in 1710 substantial property near Colchester, where he was returned as M.P. His son Peter was, like him, a director of the Bank, but also high sheriff of Essex in 1745. After him, integration into the gentry appears complete. The same for the Fauquiers: John Francis Fauquier had two sons (both Fellows of the Royal Society); Francis was director of the South Sea Company, but ended his career as lieutenant governor of Virginia (1758–1768); William was a director of London Assurance. In the next generation, one finds an accountant general of the Post Office, one secretary to the controllers of army accounts, and one landowner who became high sheriff of Warwickshire.

There are exceptions. Sir Theodore Janssen failed to found a landed family. Three of his sons succeeded him as baronet, as the first two were unmarried. The third son, Stephen Theodore (d. 1777), was a leading stationer in London and active in City politics (alderman, sheriff, lord mayor, M.P.), but he became a bankrupt in 1756; moreover, he had only a daughter, and the baronetcy expired. At the end of his life he was a director of the French hospital, a sign of Huguenot consciousness.

In sum, full gentrification was achieved in the sixth generation in England for the Houblons (and probably in the seventh for the Du Canes), in the fifth for the Bouveries and Delmés, and in the fourth for the Lethieulliers and Fauquiers, who were more recent immigrants. Henceforth family pedigrees show only country squires, clergymen, army officers, civil servants, and other socially acceptable occupations.

Despite the withdrawal from business by several leading families, the Huguenot presence in the City was still quite strong in the mid-eighteenth century. It has been pointed out many times that the 542 merchants who presented to George II in February 1744 a "loyal address" of support against "a popish pretender" included 100 (99 in this writer's reckoning) names that seem undoubtedly French, most of them belonging to men of Huguenot extraction.[16] Many were plain merchants; some were largely or even mostly involved in stock dealings; but we shall concentrate here on a few top people who were involved in public finance and served as Bank of England directors.[17] Their background was different from those of the Huguenots who had been prominent during the earlier period.

The financiers were active in two different fields; first as underwriters of and subscribers to government loans, during the two great wars in which England was engaged; and second as contractors, who supplied British troops abroad (Gibraltar, Minorca, the West Indies, North America) with food, clothing, and so on, and who made remittances to those garrisons as well as to Britain's allies. Several of them combined the two roles and were also members of Parliament. This is no surprise: only large capitalists could undertake government contracts or underwrite loans; also, M.P.s, especially if they supported the government, were in a better position than outsiders to obtain contracts. So rich men aiming at social advancement sought to enter the Commons.

In both fields financiers of Huguenot extraction had a significant share. They made up 29 percent of the "contributors" (not proprietors) to the loan of half a million pounds floated in 1745 (this percentage is exceptionally high). As for the loan of £3 million that was raised in 1757, the schedule of subscribers includes 13 obvious Huguenot names, for a total of £132,000. The big loan of 1760 was underwritten by 22 firms; 4 of them were "Huguenot" and took just under £1 million of the £7 million that required to be underwritten; moreover £1.2 million went to the Dutch-English-Huguenot firm of Van Neck (of which more later). As for contracting, 6 of the 36 principal contractors who were M.P.s between 1754 and 1790 were of undoubted Huguenot extraction.

We shall now look more closely at eight members of this financial elite: Thomas Fonnereau (1699–1779) and Zacharie (1705–1778), his younger brother; George-René Aufrère (1715–1801); George Amyand (1720–1766); John Durand (c. 1719–1788); Daniel Josias Olivier (1722–1782); Anthony Chamier (1725–1780); and William Devaynes (1730–1809).

Except for Devaynes, they all belonged to a generation active at midcentury, especially during the Seven Years' War. We have no information on the antecedents of Durand and Devaynes, though their identity as Huguenots is proved by their directorships of the French hospital. As for the Fonnereaus, they were second-generation immigrants, being the sons of Claude Fonnereau, the refugee from La Rochelle who became director of the Bank of England toward the end of his life. The four others were third-generation immigrants from the time of the revocation, with roots in Saintonge (Amyand), the Rhône valley (Chamier), Paris (Aufrère) and Nay, near Pau (Olivier).

Interestingly enough, they did not come from a business background, although the fact that four of them were younger sons must have been instrumental in steering them toward a business career. Anthony Chamier alone was the fourth son of a London merchant; but his grandfather, Daniel (1661–1698), had been a minister; he had studied in Die and Geneva and had been ordained in Neuchâtel (1686), but he was refused an appointment there and migrated in 1691 to London, where he became minister of the Savoy Church. His ancestors had been for four generations ministers in various French cities, particularly in

Montélimar; his grandfather, one of the leaders of Reformed theology, had been killed during the siege of Montauban in 1621; a cousin is said to have been broken on the wheel in 1693. D. J. Olivier was son, grandson, and nephew of ministers. As for G. R. Aufrère, his grandfather had been *procureur* in Paris, but his father was a minister in London, and a wealthy one. G. Amyand was the son of the principal surgeon to George II (he was educated at Westminster); his elder brother, Claudius (1718–1774), was a barrister, officeholder, M.P., and undersecretary of state (1750–1756); he married the widow of an earl. So these financiers had a middle-class and "professional" or even "intellectual" background. They also seem to have moved easily in good English society.

G. Amyand started as a successful "Hamburg" merchant (and then became a banker); G. R. Aufrère was a linen draper; Devaynes was partner in a London bank; Chamier was a stockbroker; Olivier was a partner in the large house of Van Neck, where he handled the investment business for foreign clients. As for Durand, he had a more unusual career: he was a captain in the merchant service of the East India Company and a merchant in Calcutta. After returning from India with a fortune, he became a ship's husband, who leased vessels to the company and to government (for instance during the American war). One can add that Amyand and Zacharie Fonnereau were for a time directors of the East India Company, while Devaynes held the post almost continuously from 1770 to 1805 and was three times chairman. He and Aufrère were also directors of insurance companies.

John Durand was solely a government contractor for victualing troops and supplying naval stores in the West Indies and North America. By contrast, Chamier and Aufrère did not engage in contracting and were "pure" financiers, subscribing to and underwriting government loans and dealing in securities. Chamier was one of the largest subscribers to the loans floated during the Seven Years' War and was consulted by the duke of Newcastle. The others, meanwhile, were involved both in lending to government and in contracting. Amyand had contracts for supplies and remittances to Germany during the Seven Years' War; Devaynes was partner in a contract for victualing 12,000 to 14,000 soldiers in America from 1776 to 1782; he also held at times considerable sums in government stock (while the Fonnereaus are said to have subscribed to loans mainly on behalf of third parties).

Except Olivier, all these men were members of Parliament—though in the case of Chamier only for a short time, at the end of his life, long after he had retired from business. The Fonnereaus sat for two boroughs in Suffolk that their father had acquired, while Aufrère was returned for Stamford thanks to the influence of his wife's family (he had married the niece of the countess of Exeter). Durand seems to have bought his first seat after returning from India and sat successively for three different boroughs.

Despite their contribution to the war effort of Britain and their close connection with some leading politicians, these men did not receive any honors, except one baronetcy, which was awarded to George Amyand in 1764, possibly because contracting had a bad name. Sir Lewis Namier has written that the connection between government contracts and membership in the Commons entailed a good deal of jobbery but no wholesale direct corruption. Even so, this charge of jobbery does not accord with the Huguenot reputation for sterling integrity.

For example, in 1756 Sir Joshua Van Neck asked that contracts for supplying Gibraltar be granted to his son-in-law, Thomas Walpole, the Fonnereaus, and John Bristow. He concluded his letter to the duke of Newcastle with the warning: "Your Grace will no doubt consider the inconvenience that may arise from disobliging, in this critical juncture, four gentlemen Members of independent fortunes, and with them their relations and friends" (Namier and Brooke 1964, II, 118). Some years later, in 1762, the Fonnereaus were preparing to desert Newcastle for Lord Bute. The duke, worldly wise, wrote that Zacharie Fonnereau had "owned very plainly that it was his interest, that he had a family; his brother and he had spent thirty thousand pounds in elections; that he had got little from my brother [Henry Pelham] and me, and that he must look out to his interest. I suppose his price is some valuable remittances to Minorca etc.; When a man knows himself that he is bought, one has nothing to say to him" (Namier 1957, pp. 49–51). Actually the contract for Minorca went to George Amyand and another M.P., Nicholas Linwood, but the Fonnereaus retained theirs for Gibraltar, as well as the share which Thomas Walpole had before he was "proscribed," with the friends of Newcastle, at the end of 1762.

A last point is the close business and family relationships that prevailed in London in the mid-eighteenth century between the Huguenot and Dutch communities, the latter being much the smaller, but wealthy and increasingly involved in the financing of England's wars.

The leading Dutch house in the City was that of Van Neck; Gerard (d. 1750) and Joshua Van Neck I (d. 1777) were the sons of a paymaster in the army of the United Provinces. This house played a very large role in the floating of loans during the War of the Austrian Succession and the Seven Years' War, owing to extensive connections in Holland that enabled it to draw on investors there. On the other hand, from about 1730 to 1767, especially in wartime, the house was prominent as agent for the French Farmers-General in the purchasing of American tobacco in Britain and as financial agents for the French government and for unofficial intermediaries to British ministers.

Both brothers had Huguenot wives. Gerard married in 1734 the rich widow of Sir Denis Dutry (d. 1728), the daughter of Hilaire Reneu, a refugee from Bordeaux at the revocation, who had become a leading merchant in London. As for Joshua, in 1731 he married Marie Daubuz. Her grandfather, born in Agen, had been a minister; her father, Stephen Daubuz, was a rich London merchant and stockbroker. Their daughter Elizabeth married in 1753 the Honorable Thomas Walpole, second son of Horatio (Lord) Walpole of Wolterton, younger brother of the prime minister; another Van Neck daughter married Richard Walpole, but he became a partner in another bank. Thomas, along with Daniel Olivier, became partner in the Van Neck firm at the death of Gerard in 1750. This Walpole connection was undoubtedly useful.

Joshua Van Neck I was created a baronet in 1751, but, being foreign-born, he was debarred from Parliament; his son-in-law, however, and his two sons, Sir Gerard (1743–1791) and Sir Joshua Van Neck II (1745–1816), second and third baronets, sat in the Commons. Sir Joshua the elder bought a large estate at Heveningham in Suffolk, where James Wyatt built a Palladian hall for him; and a large part of the Van Neck fortune (Sir Joshua is said to have been one of the richest merchants in Europe at his death) was to be invested in 17,000 acres of Suffolk land. In 1796 Sir Joshua the younger was created a peer of Ireland with the title of Baron Huntingfield, which brought to its climax the process of upward mobility of this Dutch-Huguenot family.

Charles Wilson (1976) observes, however, that this belated change of name was symbolic of the slow assimilation of the powerful representatives of the Huguenot international that the Van Necks had been. The elder Gerard and Joshua had a circle of close friends and business associates who were mainly Dutch or Huguenot. As for Marie Daubuz Van Neck, Wilson (1976, pp. 16, 20–21) writes that she "could hardly be more French or less English"; her letters, written in an amazing mixture of French, Dutch, and English, reveal "how closely the descendants of the refugees still clung together, even as they faded slowly and inevitably into their English background." And yet, when François de la Rochefoucauld visited Heveningham Hall in 1785, Sir Gerard Van Neck and his sister welcomed him, but no allusion was made to their Dutch and Huguenot background.

The Amyand family was quickly gentrified; Sir George Amyand II (1748–1819), second baronet, continued for a time his father's banking business, but he married in 1771 the only daughter and heir of Velters Cornewall of Moccas Court, Herefordshire (a family that pretended to a royal, though illegitimate, descent), and he assumed the surname and arms of Cornewall, which his family has borne since then. His two sisters became countesses. The nephew of Sir George Amyand I, Thomas Amyand (1754–1805), was a director of the Bank from 1798 to 1805.

None of the other financiers who have been discussed created a business dynasty. Anthony Chamier had no children; his name and fortune went to a nephew, who was a servant of the East India Company. G. R. Aufrère had only one daughter, who married Charles A. Pelham (later earl of Yarborough) and inherited his fine collection of paintings. Thomas Fonnereau had no male heir; the Christchurch estate went to his brother, the Reverend Claudius, who was the first in a succession of four clergymen-landowners. Zacharie Fonnereau had a younger son, Martyn, who was a merchant and a director of the Bank of England but who did not marry. Daniel Olivier's only son was a clergyman (as were some of his descendants).

During its second half-century of existence, the Bank of England again selected some "Huguenot" directors, though in smaller numbers than in its early days. Acres (1935) lists seven such men, but two or three more might be added, especially Matthew Clarmont, who belonged to a Bordeaux family, and who reached the chair of governor in 1766. The seven include two men from families who had supplied directors in earlier years: Peter Du Cane (1713–1803), director from 1755 to 1783, and Martyn Fonnereau (1741–1817), director from 1771 to 1783. The others were new men; except Philip de la Haize (1718–1769), merchant, who was the son of a refugee from Dieppe in the 1680s, their names are those of great "Huguenot dynasties."

With Peter Isaac Thellusson (1769–1808, director 1787–1806) we have the most obvious—and possibly the only—representative of the "Protestant international" among the Bank's directors. His ancestors had been in silk passementerie at Saint Symphorien-le-Châtel in the Lyonnais, and had emigrated to Geneva during the French wars of religion. The family prospered for a time, but suffered from the decline of the silk industry in Geneva. Isaac Thellusson (1690–1755) was the son of a small merchant. At 14, he went to Holland and England to learn trade; in 1707 he settled in Paris and entered the great banking house of Tourton and Guiguer (Louis Guiguer was his mother's brother). He did very well, was promoted to chief clerk, and as early as 1715, at the age of 25, became managing partner of the firm, renamed Thellusson et Compagnie. He opposed Law's "System" and became possibly the leading "Protestant" banker in Paris, being involved, for instance, during the 1730s in remittances to the French army in Italy and in supplying grain to France in time of shortage. He resumed relations with his native city, which in 1730 appointed him minister to the Court of Versailles, and retired there in 1744. A self-made man, he was worth over 2 million French livres at his death, and was the leader of the most oligarchic faction in Geneva.

Two of his four sons became bankers, one in Paris, one in London, but there is no continuity between his firm and theirs. Still, George-Tobie (1728–1776) and his partner Jacques Necker—the future minister of Louis XVI—built up a house which, around 1770, was one of the largest private banks in Paris and possibly on the Continent. As for the younger brother Pierre, or Peter (1737–1797), he was sent to England to complete his education. He was naturalized, and in 1761 he married Anne Woodford, sister of Sir Ralph Woodford, M.P. and diplomat (made a baronet in 1791). Setting up as a merchant banker in London with help from his brother in Paris and from Pierre Naville, a London merchant from Geneva who had married his sister, he quickly accumulated a very large fortune. He started in the West Indian trade but also was something of a speculator; and in the 1790s he handled French émigré funds. He purchased the manor of Broadsworth in Yorkshire. His eldest son, Peter Isaac (1761–1808), was elected a director of the Bank at the very early age of 26. He became a Tory M.P. in 1796 and in 1806 was elevated to the peerage of Ireland as Baron Rendlesham. He died two years later.

The last three "Huguenot" Bank directors had a different background. They were descended from refugees who had come from Languedoc at the time of the revocation and belonged to families that had gradually risen in English society.

David Bosanquet I (1661–1732) and his brother Jean (1674–1750) were the sons of a clerk of the royal court at Lunel who apostatized in 1685. But David, who was then in Lyons in the silk trade, fled to Geneva and eventually arrived in London in 1686. There he set up as a mercer and Turkey merchant, an importer of silk, among other things, with Jean, who came over some time later, as partner. They prospered and are said to have been worth £100,000 when they died. Meanwhile, only David married. His sons who grew to adulthood were successful merchants (except one who was a physician), but not of the first rank. The second, Samuel Bosanquet I (1700–1765), married an heiress, bought an estate in Essex, but retained City interests in the Levant trade and in insurance (he was governor of Royal Exchange Assurance). His eldest son, also Samuel (1744–1806), had a strong position in county society, but he devoted his energy to the Bank of England: he was elected a director in 1771 and retained this post until his death, except from 1789 to 1793, when he was deputy governor and then governor. His cousin, Jacob Bosanquet II (c. 1755–1828), was for 46 years director of the East India Company, and three times its chairman between 1798 and 1811. So, during the French wars, both the Bank and the Company had heads who were third-generation Huguenot immigrants, but also ardent "loyalists." A member of the fourth generation, Samuel Bosanquet III (1767–1843), founded his own bank in 1796. Unlike other families that became completely gentrified, the later Bosanquets were to combine landownership and activities in various walks of life, including cricket and philanthropy.

Jean-Pierre (or Peter) Gaussen (1723–1781), who had been elected director in 1771 and was governor in 1777–1779, belonged to a family that intermarried with the Bosanquets. Jean de Gaussen (1639–1729) was born in Lunel, married Marguerite—a sister of David Bosanquet I—and fled at the revocation to Geneva, where he spent the rest of his life. Two of his sons went to England and became well-off merchants in London; but they had no issue. They chose as heir their nephew, Jean-Pierre (son of their brother Paul, who had settled in Geneva), who arrived in London in 1739. In 1755 he married Anna, his second cousin, daughter of Samuel Bosanquet I (so Samuel Bosanquet II, the Bank's governor after him, was also his brother-in-law). The success of this first-generation immigrant is remarkable, but the ground had been prepared by his uncles and by the Bosanquets.

The last Huguenot director—in 1792–1794—was Peter Cazalet (1756–1811). He was a merchant and banker, the grandson or great-grandson of a refugee from Sommières, quite close to Lunel. The fact that Languedoc was the last Protestant stronghold in France to give directors to the Bank might suggest a slower assimilation and acceptance for Méridionaux than for refugees from northern or western France, but it would be rash to generalize from such a small number of cases.

The initial title of this chapter was "The Huguenot International and England," but a more careful look has disclosed that this was a nonsubject! Of course, Protestant refugees, both of the first (sixteenth-century) and of the second (seventeenth-century) migrations, played a minor but significant role in England's economic development. But their contribution to the diversification of England's industrial base, which has been deliberately neglected here, should not be overestimated, the more so as they settled in the South, away from the centers of the Industrial Revolution. Moreover, England was only marginally involved in what is called the Huguenot international, that is, the intricate network of merchant and banking firms that united the various refuges of the Protestant diaspora (which were scattered in the ports and commercial cities of the Continent), with a kind of extraterritorial capital at Geneva). Those firms were thus in a sense predestined to carry on international banking, the essence of which was international correspondence with trusted and trustworthy correspondents. The international's existence depended on the preservation of close relationships—in matters of trade and finance, of course, but also of religion and culture—with the country from which the refugees had fled, on a constant exchange of persons between France and the refuges, and on a nonintegration (or at least an incomplete integration) into the host societies. As Lüthy has stressed, Calvinist France in exile preserved manifold links with the homeland.

Now, the position of English Huguenots in the eighteenth century was quite special (not to speak of the Walloons, whose relations with their land of origin had long been severed). War hindered or even stopped communication with France for long periods. Even in peacetime, Anglo-French trade was severely restricted by both countries' protectionist policies; the bonds between the various refuges and France were therefore weak. Moreover, Huguenots and their descendants who lived in England, where a bitter hatred against their country of origin prevailed (a hatred that many of them shared because of the persecutions they or their families had suffered), were ashamed of their origins, anxious to fit in, to assimilate, to emphasize their loyalty to king and country. We have seen that many of them were most successful in these endeavors, but insofar as they became anglicized, nationalized, insularized, they lost touch not only with France but with the rest of the diaspora as well. To return to the financiers of the mid- and late eighteenth century, who have been discussed in the last part of this chapter, most of them were born in England, and there is no suggestion that they felt different from their fellow Englishmen, even though some of them had close connections with other Huguenot families, kept in touch with one of the French churches, or sat on the board of the French hospital. They were well integrated into English society, indeed, almost or fully assimilated. Because the Huguenots had no organization and no privilege (unlike, say, in Brandenburg-Prussia), they succumbed easily to the temptations of belonging. The rapid decay of their peculiar religious institutions and of the Calvinistic drive that had impelled them to flight separated them in this regard from other, more self-conscious and particularistic minorities such as the Dissenters, Quakers, and Jews.

The very openness and mobility of English society worked against survival as a minority, while making it possible for them to achieve higher positions than they had known in France.[18] (The same social gain occurred in Brandenburg-Prussia, where, as noted earlier, they had even more to contribute to economic modernization.) Few or none of them went back to France after the persecutions had abated, as did the Swiss founders of the *haute banque protestante;* when they did go to visit, they were sometimes appalled by the backwardness of the towns their ancestors had come from. Besides, business was good in England. Englishmen had money to spare, and His Majesty's government was ready to borrow it and, unlike the king of France, was a good debtor. There was no need to jostle to lend to a bankrupt monarchy, as the citizens of Geneva did.

So England had many Huguenot merchants and financiers, but few of them were cosmopolitan, few of them belonged to the international, few of them appear in Lüthy's magnum opus. Exceptions are interesting: they appear, of course, at the time of the diaspora, like the London firm of Tourton and Guiguer, which was part of a family network stretching from Lyons and Geneva to Paris, Amsterdam, and beyond. But the activities, at the beginning of the War of Spanish Succession, of such "international" firms, which were managing remittances not only for England and Holland but also for France, incurred the suspicions of the English government, which thought they were sustaining French credit and prolonging the war; consequently a complete embargo on relations with France was imposed in 1703. Admittedly, the "Système" and the Bubble caused a flurry in international finance, but it was cut short by their collapse. As for the *banque languedocienne* that one historian has detected in

London (Chaussinand-Nogaret 1970, pp. 182–189), its very existence is unproven.

Later on, the house of Van Neck and the firm of Bourdieu and Chollet can be mentioned, but they were involved, the former in the tobacco trade, the latter in the grain trade, in activities which the authorities in London and Versailles tolerated and even encouraged. On the other hand, the prominent position of the Van Necks in public finance depended on their Dutch connections, through which they drew capital toward the English funds. In effect, England had in the United Provinces an open access to the Huguenot international and through them to Geneva. Although basically self-sufficient in finance, England could draw on foreign—Dutch, German, Swiss, even French—capital. But the city on the Léman was only marginal to England, while it was vital for French finance. That was the paradox: the Huguenot international, the product of French persecution, had become geared to promoting and servicing French—rather than British—trade and to lending to an ever impecunious French government. This help, however, encouraged the latter's profligacy and backfired into bankruptcy and revolution.

Notes

1. I am grateful to Patrice Higonnet, David Landes, Henry Rosovsky, and other participants in the Bellagio Conference for helpful comments and suggestions on this chapter. As for my debt to Minna Prestwich, who commented in detail on the original draft, it cannot be stressed too much. Cécile Tardieu, *ingenieur* of the Conseil National de la Recherche Scientifique and attached to the University of Paris IV, has done a great deal of useful research. Geneviève Oger's elegant and perfect typing also deserves notice and gratitude.

Additional notes and bibliographical references, which for reasons of space cannot be included in this volume, are available on request from the author.

2. My thanks to Bernard Cottret for his suggestion on this point.

3. I am grateful to the Borough of Ipswich, Department of Recreation and Amenities, for information on the Fonnereau family tree and other details, following an exhibition on the Fonnereaus that was held in 1985.

4. Thomas Papillon (1623–1702) was a grandson of a gentleman of the bedchamber to Henri IV, son of David Papillon (1579–1659), who emigrated to England, where he worked as an architect, military engineer, and property developer. He was closely associated with the East India Company, to which he supplied victuals, especially beer; he became one of its directors and eventually its deputy governor (1680–1682), but later lost his influence; he was also a contractor for victualing the Royal Navy. He was an M.P. and one of the leaders of the City's opposition to Charles II; from 1690 to 1702 he was commissioner for victualing the navy. He held £1,000 of Bank stock in December 1697 and in 1702; his son, Philippe, a Turkey merchant, subscribed £2,125 in April 1697, and had £1,570 of stock in 1702.

5. Sir John Lambert (1666–1723) had been born in Ile de Ré (his family is said to have been of English origin); he was sent to England to be educated as a Protestant and settled in London around 1680, where he became a great merchant and shipowner; he was very active in the Spanish and wine trades, and claimed later to have exported over £500,000 of English goods in eight years. Later on, he diversified into finance, became an exchange contractor, a stock dealer, and a company promoter

(especially for London Assurance, 1720). Jacob Price (1973) considers that in the 1700s he was also the London agent of the French financier Antoine Crozat and probably of Samuel Bernard, and the paymaster for the French tobacco monopoly, paying for the purchases nominally made by others, such as Tourton and Guiguer. In 1710 he was one of the Whig financiers who supported Harley, for which he was given a baronetcy (1711) and became a director of the South Sea Company. In 1719 he was in Paris and likely involved in speculations during Law's "system" (in 1720 he was expelled from France for maneuvers against the French currency). Shortly afterward, he was engulfed in the South Sea scandal and fled to France. His son and grandsons were bankers in Paris under the name Chevalier Lambert et Cie. He had married the daughter of Benjamin Beuzelin, a merchant refugee from Rouen. His family is still extant. Lambert subscribed only £500 of Bank stock in 1694; by December 1697 he owned £2,875; his holding had fallen to £125 in 1702, but he subscribed £4,500 in 1709.

6. He was on the court of the Bank almost continuously from 1694 to 1711, and governor in 1705–1707 (he owned £10,300 of stock in 1709, before the capital increase). He resigned in 1711 to become subgovernor of the South Sea Company; he was also director of the East India Company. He was sheriff, alderman, and lord mayor of London, and M.P. He was knighted in 1698; his eldest son was created Viscount Bateman (Irish peerage) in 1725.

7. Beck was Bank director from 1710 to 1717; he owned £8,450 of stock before the capital increase of 1709; he also was a promoter of Royal Exchange Assurance. He married a daughter of Charles Cambrelan. The other "foreigners" are William H. Cornelison (d. 1725), of Dutch parentage; Clement Boehm (1660–1734), born in Strasbourg; and possibly John Devink (d. 1722).

8. I am most grateful to Menna Prestwich for drawing my attention to this affair, which had been overlooked in the first draft of this chapter.

9. The idea and figure were not new; they had appeared as early as 1659. In 1663 Samuel Fortrey (from the Walloon family De La Forterie) had published a pamphlet alleging a deficit of £16 million for England. The pamphlet, used by several other writers, was reedited in 1673 and may have been a source for the "Scheme." In 1715 Sir Gilbert Heathcote, a staunch Whig and former governor of the Bank, attacked the commercial treaty with France, using arguments drawn from the "Scheme."

10. Seignoret had been born in Bayonne, but he had lived in Lyons; he had become a denizen in 1686. Despite his smuggling (in which a number of other refugees were involved), he became a respected leader of the Huguenot community in London. He subscribed £2,950 of Bank stock in 1694, £3,710 in 1697, and £6,800 to the capital increase of 1709 (when he also had £14,187 of East India stock). Moreover, his firm—Seignoret and Baudouin (René Baudouin came from Tours and was naturalized in 1678)—subscribed £4,438 in 1697; and one William Seignoret subscribed £2,530 in 1697.

11. The discussion that follows relies on the work of other historians—A. Carter (1975, 1980) and P. G. M. Dickson (1967)—but it has been completed by research in the *Bank of England Records*. From those records the following have been used: the "Book of the Subscriptions," 1694; "Bank Stock list of Subscribers to Capital Issues," 1694 and 1697; "List of the Proprietors in the Stock and Fund of the Bank of England drawn of the Ledgers as they stood dec. 25th 1697" (in 2nd dividend book); a similar list of March 25, 1702; "List of the Proprietors in the Additional Stock of the Bank," September 24, 1709; "Bank Stock Register, Persons deceased," Reg. of Wills, nos. 1, 2, 3, 1694–1721. I am most grateful to the Bank of England for permission to use these documents, to Henry Gillett, archivist, and to Cécile Tardieu, who carried out the research.

There have been the usual difficulties with names which can be either English or French and with anglicized names. Figures must not be taken at their face value, but they give reliable orders of magnitude.

12. Carter (1975, p. 83). My own calculation gives £210,275 (9.6 percent of total capital) for 170 Huguenot holdings and £91,647 (4.2 percent) for Walloon holdings; this gives a total of £301,922, and a percentage of 13.7 percent, slightly less than Carter's. Most of the 1697 subscription was paid in government tallies.

13. Dickson (1967, p. 306). Carter (1975, pp. 83, 89) points out rightly that in 1697, Marc Huguetan, with £10,020 of stock, though not one of the original subscribers, was the second largest

Huguenot holder of Bank shares. From a family of Protestant booksellers of Lyons, he had settled in Amsterdam after 1685 as a publisher and banker. He became a denizen of England in 1696 and is likely to have resided there in 1697. He died in 1702 (with only £1,238 of Bank stock). He was the eldest brother of the notorious Jean-Henri (1665–1749), who was heavily involved in the remittance business conducted by Samuel Bernard for the account of France before defecting to England in 1705. In the late eighteenth century, Pierre Huguetan II, son of another brother, Pierre Huguetan I, a rich Amsterdam publisher, was a very large holder of English stock; he lived in Holland and in London and is said to have left a fortune of £314,000 at his death in 1791.

14. Dickson (1967, p. 310). In 1710 also, the canton of Bern made a loan of £150,000 to the British government; it was converted into South Sea stock in 1711. This holding was gradually increased and completed with Bank of England stock, and on March 1, 1750, reached £357,311. Some citizens of Geneva speculated in South Sea stock during the Bubble (Dickson 1967, pp. 154, 280, 292, 329). Earlier on, three large holders of 1697 and 1709 belonged to famous Geneva families, but were resident in England and denizened or naturalized: Robert Caillé, Jean-Antoine Lullin, and J. M. Couvreu. In the 1720s, most Swiss owners of English funds belonged to well-known patrician families.

15. Daniel Hays (1659–1732) came from Calais as a boy in 1670 and became a substantial merchant. He subscribed £1,000 in 1694, and by 1702 his holdings had risen to £7,200. In 1709 he subscribed £3,500—and also had £20,000 in East India stock. He was a director of the Royal African Company and of the South Sea Company. In 1729–30 he was a tobacco buyer on behalf of the French East India Company (Price 1973, pp. 536–537). Francis Beuzelin was probably the son of Benjamin Beuzelin, merchant in Rouen, friend and correspondent of C. Marescoe and J. David. He had only £1,000 of Bank stock in 1702, but held £6,008 of East India stock in 1709. He was later a director of the Royal African Company.

16. Some had come to England by way of a third country: thus the brothers Anthony and John Louis André, from Nîmes via Genoa, where the family were merchant bankers. Their sister Isabelle married Louis Necker, brother of Louis XVI's minister. Anthony's son was the famous Major John André, hanged as a spy by the Americans in 1780 for his dealings with Benedict Arnold. Beset by wartime interruptions in trade, the Genoa bank liquidated and took advantage of the new consular regime in France to set up in Paris in 1800. The bank it founded is still active today under the name De Neuflize, Schlumberger, Mallet et Cie.

17. Except for G. Amyand, W. Devaynes, and later P. I. Thellusson, this group does not include any Huguenot bankers. Yet there was some overlapping between the families of Bank of England directors and those of the two joint-stock insurance companies set up in 1720, of which "Huguenots" held a significant share. London Assurance, which had been promoted by Sir John Lambert, had 15 percent of its first stock issue owned by Huguenots; 21 of its directors during the eighteenth century appear to have been Huguenots, among them Henry Gaultier, David Bosanquet II, William Fauquier, and Peter Cazalet. As for the Royal Exchange Assurance, at least 20 of 120 eighteenth-century directors were of Huguenot origin: the Bosanquet family, after having had one director of London Assurance (1729–1741), deserted it for the other company, and three of its members were involved in it.

18. Gwynn (1985, p. 174) quotes the views of C. D. Darlington: in England, where refugees bred out, "they yielded over a period of six generations outstanding new individuals in every field of activity and culture"; on the other hand, in France, "the Protestants continued inbred as a useful but not very remarkable section of society."

References

Acres, W. M. 1931. *The Bank of England from Within, 1690–1900.* 2 vols. London.

——— 1935. "Huguenot Directors of the Bank of England." *Proceedings of the Huguenot Society of London* 15, no. 2:238–248.

————— 1940. "Directors of the Bank of England." *Notes and Queries* 179 no. 3–40 (July–September).

Agnew, D. C. A. 1886. *Protestant Exiles from France*. 3rd ed. 2 vols. London.

Ashley, W. J. 1900. "The Tory Origin of Free Trade Policy." In *Surveys: Historic and Economic*. London.

Baker, N. 1967. "John Durand, Stock-Splitter: An Eighteenth-Century Huguenot's Activities in the East India Company." *Proceedings of the Huguenot Society of London* 21, no. 4:280–289.

Barraud, E. M. 1968. *Barraud: The Story of a Family*. London.

Barrie, V. 1973. "The Prohibition of Trade with France: An Issue in English Politics, 1669–1697." Master's thesis. University of Paris IV.

————— 1977. "La prohibition du commerce avec la France dans la politique anglaise à la fin du XVIIe siècle." *Revue du Nord* 59, no. 234 (July–September): 343–364.

Beier, A. L., and R. Finley, eds. 1968. *London, 1500–1700: The Making of the Metropolis*. London.

Beuzart, P. 1930. *La répression à Valenciennes après les troubles religieux de 1566*. Paris.

Black, J. 1986. *Natural and Necessary Enemies: Anglo-French Relations in the Eighteenth Century*. London.

Bosher, J. F. 1987. *The Canada Merchants, 1713–1763*. Oxford.

Brenner, R. 1973. "The Civil War Politics of London's Merchant Community." *Past and Present* 58:53–107.

Briggs, E. R. 1985. *Une évasion de protestants nîmois: la fortune de la famille.*

Bromley, J. S., ed. 1970. *The New Cambridge Modern History*. Vol. 6. Cambridge.

Burn, J. S. 1846. *The History of the French, Walloon, Dutch, and Other Foreign Protestant Refugees Settled in England*. London.

Caldicott, C. E. J., H. Gough, and J. P. Pittion, eds. 1987. *The Huguenots and Ireland: Anatomy of an Emigration*. Dun Laoghaire.

Carswell, J. 1961. *The South Sea Bubble*. London.

Carter, A. C. 1975. *Getting, Spending, and Investing in Early Modern Times: Essays on Dutch, English, and Huguenot Economic History*. Assen.

————— 1980. "The English Public Debt in the Eighteenth Century." In *La dette publique aux XVIIIe et XIXe siècles*, ed. H. Van der Wee. 9th International Colloquium, Spa, September 12–16, 1978, Brussels.

Chapman, S. D. 1977. "The International Houses: The Continental Contribution to British Commerce, 1800–1860." *Journal of European Economic History* 6, no. 1 (Spring): 5–48.

Charrington, E. 1970. *The Family d'Albiac, 1271–1970*. London.

Chaussinand-Nogaret, G. 1970. *Les financiers de Languedoc au XVIIIe siècle*. Paris.

Chown, C. H. I. 1926. "The Lethieullier Family of Aldersbrook House." *Essex Review* 35, no. 140 (October):203–220.

————— 1927. "The Lethieullier Family of Aldersbrook House." *Essex Review* 36, no. 141 (January): 1–21.

Clapham, J. H. 1944. *The Bank of England: A History*. 2 vols. Cambridge.

Clark, P., and P. Slack. 1976. *English Towns in Transition, 1500–1700*. Oxford.

Clay, C. 1978. *Public Finance and Private Wealth: The Career of Sir Stephen Fox, 1627–1716*. Oxford.

Coleman, D. C. 1958. *The British Paper Industry, 1495–1860: A Study in Industrial Growth*. Oxford.

Cottret, B. 1985. *Terre d'exil: l'Angleterre et ses réfugiés français et wallons, de la Réforme à la Révocation de l'Edit de Nantes, 1550–1700*. Paris.

Cunningham, W. [1897] 1969. *Alien Immigrants to England*. London.

Dalton C. 1901–1904. "The Huguenot Huguetans." *Proceedings of the Huguenot Society of London* 7:343–355.

Davies, K. J. [1952] 1962. "Joint-Stock Investment in the Later Seventeenth Century." In *Essays in Economic History*, ed. E. M. Carus-Wilson. Vol. 2. London.

Davis, R. 1967. *Aleppo and Devonshire Square: English Traders in the Levant in the Eighteenth Century*. London.

De Krey, G. S. 1985. *A Fractured Society: The Politics of London in the First Age of Party, 1688–1715.* Oxford.

Dessert, Daniel. 1984. *Argent, pouvoir et société au Grand Siècle.* Paris.

Dickson, P. G. M. 1967. *The Financial Revolution in England: A Study in the Development of Public Credit, 1688–1756.* London.

Douen, E. O. 1894. *La révocation de l'Edit de Nantes à Paris.* 2 vols. Paris.

Drew, B. 1949. *The London Assurance: A Second Chronicle.* London.

Duthoit, J. F. 1933. "The Family of Du Toict, Du Toit, or Duthoit." *Proceedings of the Huguenot Society of London* 14, no. 4:589–594.

Enjalbert, H. 1938. "La circulation, le commerce et les villes dans la vallée de la Charente." *Etudes locales: bulletin de la Charente* no. 2184.

Farnell, J. E. 1961. "The Navigation Act of 1651, the First Dutch War, and the London Merchant Community." *Economic History Review* 16, no. 3 (April):439–454.

Goguel, B. 1969. "François le Coq: Counselor with the Paris Parlement from 1594 to 1626 and his Protestant Entourage." Master's thesis. Sorbonne.

Grassby, R. 1970a. "English Merchant Capitalism in the Late Seventeenth Century: The Composition of Business Fortunes." *Past and Present* 46 (February):87–107.

———— 1970b. "The Personal Wealth of the Business Community in Seventeenth-Century England." *Economic History Review* 23, no. 2 (August):220–234.

Graves, M. A. R., and R. H. Silcock. 1984. *Revolution, Reaction, and the Triumph of Conservatism.* Auckland.

Gravil, R. 1968. "Trading to Spain and Portugal, 1670–1700." *Business History* 10, no. 2 (July): 69–88.

Gwynn, R. D., ed. 1979. *A Calendar of the Letter Books of the French Church of London from the Civil War to the Restoration, 1643–1659.* London.

———— 1985. *Huguenot Heritage: The History and Contribution of the Huguenots in Britain.* London.

Haag, E., and E. Haag. 1857. *La France protestante.* Paris.

Henning, B. D. 1983. *The House of Commons, 1660–1690.* 3 vols. London.

Hoppit, J. 1986. "Financial Crises in Eighteenth-Century England." *Economic History Review* 39, no. 1 (February):39–58.

Houblon, A. 1907. *The Houblon Family: Its Story and Times.* 2 vols. London.

Jones, D. W. 1970. "London Overseas-Merchant Groups at the End of the Seventeenth Century and the Moves against the East India Company." Ph.D. dissertation, Oxford University.

———— 1972. "London Merchants and the Crisis of the 1690s." In *Crisis and Order in English Towns, 1500–1700,* ed. P. Clark and P. Slack. London.

Jones, J. R. 1961. *The First Whigs: The Politics of the Exclusion Crisis, 1678–1683.* London.

———— 1978. *Country and Court England, 1658–1714.* London.

King, Gregory [1696] 1804. *Natural and Political Observations and Conclusions upon the State and Condition of England 1696.* London.

Landed Gentry. (*Burke's Genealogical and Heraldic History of the Landed Gentry.*) 1937 Centenary (95th ed.). London.

La Rochefoucauld, F. de. 1945. *La vie en Angleterre au XVIIIe siècle.* Paris.

Lart, C. E. 1924. *Huguenot Pedigrees.* Vol. 1. London.

Lee, G. L. 1966. *The Story of the Bosanquets.* London.

Lescure, M., ed. 1863. *Journal et mémoires de Mathieu Marais, avocat au Parlement de Paris, sur la Régence et le règne de Louis XV (1715–1737).* Vol. 1. Paris.

Lüthy, Herbert. 1959–61. *La banque protestante en France.* 2 vols. Paris.

Macleod, C. 1986. "The 1690s Patents Boom: Invention or Stock-Jobbing?" *Economic History Review* 39, no. 4 (November):549–571.

Manchée, W. H. 1934. "Some Huguenot Smugglers: The Impeachment of London Silk Merchants, 1698." *Proceedings of the Huguenot Society of London* 15, no. 3:406–427.

McLachlan, J. O. 1940. *Trade and Peace with Old Spain, 1667–1750.* Cambridge.

Melton, F. T. 1986. *Sir Robert Clayton and the Origins of English Deposit Banking, 1658–1685.* Cambridge.

Minet, S. 1947. "Huguenot Directors of the London Assurance." *Proceedings of the Huguenot Society of London* 17, no. 1:90–91.

Namier, L. 1957. *The Structure of Politics at the Accession of George III.* 2nd ed. London.

Namier, L., and J. Brooke, eds. 1964. *The History of Parliament: The House of Commons, 1754–1790.* 3 vols. London.

Neal, L. 1985. "The Integration and Efficiency of the London and Amsterdam Stock Markets in the Eighteenth Century." University of Illinois, Urbana-Champaign, Bureau of Economic and Business Research. Faculty Working Paper no. 1177.

Nicolaï, A. 1935. *Histoire des moulins à papier du Sud-Ouest de la France, 1300–1800.* 2 vols. Paris.

O'Brien, P. K. 1988. "The Political Economy of British Taxation, 1660–1815." *Economic History Review* 41, no. 1 (February):1–32.

Peters, J. 1985. *A Family from Flanders.* London.

Pettegree, A. 1986. *Foreign Protestant Communities in Sixteenth-Century London.* Oxford.

Philips, C. J. 1940. *The East India Company, 1784–1834.* Manchester.

Plumb, J.H. 1967. *The Growth of Political Stability in England, 1675–1725.* London.

Poole, R. L. 1880. *A History of the Huguenots and of the Dispersion at the Recall of the Edict of Nantes.* London.

Poussou, J.-P. 1983. *Bordeaux et le Sud-Ouest au XVIIIe siècle: croissance économique et attraction urbaine.* Paris.

Prestwich, M., ed. 1985. *International Calvinism, 1542–1715.* Oxford.

Price, J. M. 1973. *France and the Chesapeake: A History of the French Tobacco Monopoly, 1674–1791, and of Its Relationship to the British and American Tobacco Trades.* 2 vols. Ann Arbor.

Priestley, M. 1951. "Anglo-French Trade and the 'Unfavourable Balance' Controversy, 1660–1685." *Economic History Review* 4, no. 1:37–52.

——— 1956. "London Merchants and Opposition Politics in Charles II's Reign." *Bulletin of the Institute of Historical Research* 29:205–219.

Quiet Conquest. 1985. (*The Quiet Conquest: The Huguenots, 1685 to 1985.*) Exhibition catalogue compiled by Tessa Murdoch. Museum of London, in association with the Huguenot Society of London.

Rogers, N. 1979. "Money, Land, and Lineage: The Big Bourgeoisie of Hanoverian London." *Social History* 4, no. 3 (October):437–454.

Romilly, S. 1840. *Memoirs of the Life of Sir Samuel Romilly, Written by Himself.* 3 vols. London.

Roseveare, H. G. 1987a. "Jacob David: A Huguenot London Merchant of the Late Seventeenth Century and His Circle." In Scouloudi (1987).

Roseveare, H. G., ed. 1987b. *Markets and Merchants of the Late Seventeenth Century: The Marescoe-David Letters, 1668–1680.* Oxford.

Rubini, D. 1970. "Politics and the Battle for the Banks, 1688–1697." *English Historical Review* 85, no. 337 (October):693–714.

Scouloudi, I. 1947. "Thomas Papillon, Merchant and Whig, 1623–1702." *Proceedings of the Huguenot Society of London* 18, no. 1:49–72.

——— 1969. "L'aide apportée aux refugiés protestants français par l'Eglise de Threadneedle Street: l'Eglise de Londres, 1681–1684." *Bulletin de la Société d'Histoire du Protestantisme français* 115:429–444.

Scouloudi, I., ed. 1987. *Huguenots in Britain and Their French Background, 1550–1800.* Contributions to the Historical Conference of the Huguenot Society of London, September 24–25, 1985. London.

Sedgwick, R., ed. 1970. *The History of Parliament: The House of Commons, 1715–1754.* 2 vols. London.

Shaw, W. A., ed. [1911] 1969. *Letters of Denization and Acts of Naturalization for Aliens in England and Ireland, 1603–1700.* Nendeln.

Sherman, A. A. 1976. "Pressure from Leadenhall: The East India Company Lobby, 1660–1678." *Business History Review* 50, no. 3 (Autumn):329–355.

Smiles, S. [1867] 1889. *The Huguenots: Their Settlements, Churches, and Industries, in England and Ireland.* 6th ed. London.

Stern, F. 1977. *Gold and Iron: Bismarck, Bleichröder, and the Building of the German Empire.* New York.

Stewart, C. P. 1909. "The Régis Family." *Proceedings of the Huguenot Society of London* 9, no. 1:55–107.

——— 1910. "History of the Aufrères." *Proceedings of the Huguenot Society of London* 9, no. 2:145–160.

Supple, B. 1970. *The Royal Exchange Assurance: A History of British Insurance, 1720–1970.* Cambridge.

Sutherland, L. L. 1952. *The East India Company in Eighteenth-Century Politics.* Oxford.

——— 1956. "The City of London in Eighteenth-Century Politics." In *Essays Presented to Sir Lewis Namier,* ed. R. Pares and A. J. P. Taylor. London.

——— 1984. *Politics and Finance in the Eighteenth Century.* London.

Thadden, R. von. 1987. "Eiwanderer in einer ständischen Gesellschaft: Integrationsprobleme den Huguenotten in Preussen und Berlin." In *Berlin und seine Wirtschaft,* ed. Industrie- und Handelskammer zu Berlin. Berlin.

Van Biema, E. 1918. *Les Huguetans de Mercier et de Vrijhoeven: Historie d'une famille de financiers huguenots de la fin du XVIIe jusqu'à la moitié du XVIIIe siècle.* Le Haye.

Viallaneix, P. 1979. "Michelet, Quinet et la légende protestante." In *Actes du Colloque les Protestants dans les débuts de la Troisième République (1871–1885),* ed. A. Encrevé and M. Richard. Paris.

——— 1987. "Michelet et la légende huguenote." In Caldicott, Gough, and Pittion (1987).

Wagner, H. 1912. "The Directors of the French Hospital of La Providence." *Proceedings of the Huguenot Society of London* 10, no. 1:137–155.

Weiss, C. 1853. *Histoire des réfugiés protestants de France, de la révocation de l'Edit de Nantes jusqu'à nos jours.* 2 vols. Paris.

Wilson, C. 1941. *Anglo-Dutch Commerce and Finance in the Eighteenth Century.* Cambridge.

——— 1976. "The Anglo-Dutch Establishment in Eighteenth-Century England." In *The Anglo-Dutch Contribution to the Civilization of Early Modern Society: An Anglo-Netherlands Symposium,* ed. C. Wilson et al. Oxford.

——— 1980. "Dutch Investment in Britain in the Seventeenth-Nineteenth Centuries." In *La dette publique aux XVIIIe et XIXe siècles,* ed. H. Van Der Wee. 9th International Colloquium, Spa, September 12–16, 1978. Brussels.

Wollaston, G. W. 1927. "The Family of Fauquier." *Proceedings of the Huguenot Society of London* 13, no. 4:340–355.

Zysberg, A. 1987. *Les galériens: Vies et destins de 60,000 forcats sur les galères de France, 1680–1748.* Paris.

9
• • •

What Happened to the Theory
of Economic Development?

William Lazonick

Historical Analysis and Economics

Writing in the mid-twentieth century, toward the end of a long academic career, Joseph Schumpeter advised that "if, starting my work in economics afresh, I were told that I could study only one of [the fundamental fields of economic analysis: economic history, statistics, or theory] but could have my choice, it would be economic history that I should choose."

And this on three grounds.
First, the subject matter of economics is essentially a unique process in historic time. Nobody can hope to understand the economic phenomena of any, including the present epoch, who has not an adequate command of historical *facts* and an adequate amount of historical *sense* or of what may be described as *historical experience*.
Second, the historical report cannot be purely economic but must inevitably reflect also "institutional" facts that are not purely economic: therefore it affords the best method for understanding how economic and noneconomic facts *are* related to one another and how the various social sciences *should* be related to one another.
Third, it is, I believe, the fact that most of the fundamental errors currently committed in economic analysis are due to the lack of historical experience more often than to any other shortcoming of the economist's equipment. (Schumpeter 1954, pp. 12–13; emphasis in original)

Schumpeter had started his career some four decades earlier by writing *The Theory of Economic Development* (Schumpeter [1911] 1961), an abstract theoretical investigation that sought to deduce a theory for comprehending the vast expansion of productive capabilities that had occurred in national economies such as those of Britain, Germany, and the United States. By the end of his career, Schumpeter had learned the lesson that a relevant theory of how economies develop must include the history of economic change.

Over the decades that have passed since Schumpeter emphasized the critical role of economic history in the study of economics, the mainstream of the economics profession in the United States has done anything but adopt "historical experience" as a tool—let alone a fundamental tool—of economic analysis. In the decades following World War II, the American economics profession stressed, and indeed became obsessed with, constrained optimization as the fundamental analytical tool. At the same time, with their theoretical vision limited by the marginal significance of their analytical equipment, mainstream economists idealized the market-coordinated economy as the optimal (if not always attainable) form of economic organization.

In the 1950s and 1960s a field of inquiry called economic development was deemed to be relevant for studying the poorer nations of the world. But in sanctioning this endeavor (which by the 1970s had in any case been banished to the periphery of economics), the profession implicitly assumed that the economic successes of the already developed "market economies" were well understood. For purposes of "modern" economic analysis at least, there was no need to construct a theory of economic development. With the search for the nature and causes of the wealth of nations swept under a deductive, mathematical, and statistical rug, mainstream economists lost the ability to think historically.

In their neglect of history, these mainstream economists not only lost touch with evolving economic reality but also ignored (and then forgot) the theoretical insights into the development process of some of their most illustrious predecessors, including Schumpeter himself. And if they could not even savor the insights of the conservative Schumpeter, it is not surprising that they could not stomach the works of the radical Karl Marx, a thinker whom Schumpeter recognized as the pioneer in the integration of theory and history in economic analysis. In Schumpeter's view, there was "one thing of fundamental importance to the methodology of economics that [Marx] actually achieved."

> Economists always have either themselves done work in economic history or else used the historical work of others. But the facts of economic history were assigned to a separate compartment. They entered theory, if at all, merely in the role of illustrations, or possibly as verifications of results. They mixed with it only mechanically. Now Marx's mixture is a chemical one; that is to say, he introduced them into the very argument that produces the results. He was the first economist of top rank to see and to teach systematically how economic theory may be turned into historical analysis and how the historical narrative may be turned into *histoire raisonnée*.   (Schumpeter 1950, p. 44)

Similarly, for Maurice Dobb, the preeminent British Marxist economist, the role of historical analysis was "not a matter simply of verifying particular assumptions but of examining the relationships within a complex set of assumptions and between this set as a whole and changing actuality."

It is a matter of discovering from a study of its growth how a total situation is really constructed: which elements in that situation are more susceptible to change, and which are most influential in producing change in others. It is a matter of putting questions to economic development in order to discover what are the correct questions to ask of the past and of the present and what are the crucial relationships on which to focus attention. (Dobb 1963, pp. vii–viii)

During the 1970s an opportunity existed for economists to take seriously the integration of historical analysis and economic theorizing. Within economics departments, the radical economics movement created an opportunity for economists to study and debate the dynamics of advanced capitalist development, as Marx and Schumpeter had done. At the same time, from outside the economics profession, or at best on its periphery, historians of industrial evolution were uncovering and making accessible the reality of the development process in the advanced capitalist economies; they were providing the foundations of "historical experience" that Schumpeter had deemed so important.

Indeed, back in the 1950s, even as the mainstream of the economics profession was ignoring Schumpeter's call for historically based economic analysis, his ideas were exerting a profound influence on a generation of historians who viewed entrepreneurial decision making and action as central to the process of economic development. Two who stand out are David S. Landes and Alfred D. Chandler, Jr. *The Unbound Prometheus*, published in 1969, and *The Visible Hand*, published in 1977, are landmarks of historical synthesis on the development process in advanced capitalist economies.

Both Landes and Chandler are alumni of the Research Center in Entrepreneurial History, located at Harvard University for a decade beginning in 1948. Schumpeter was a senior member of the center from 1948 until his death in early 1950, but it was not his creation; that honor belonged to Arthur H. Cole. Although inspired by Schumpeter's emphasis on the economic role of the entrepreneur, much of the center's work focused on the sociology and psychology of the entrepreneur—his social background, personality, and social status—rather than on the impact of entrepreneurial activity on economic outcomes (Aitken 1965; Sass 1986). Nevertheless, the center left an intellectual legacy that should have helped today's economists avoid (to use Schumpeter's words) "most of the fundamental errors currently committed in economic analysis" (Schumpeter 1954, p. 13). The Research Center closed down in 1958, but over the longer run the academic institution at which Schumpeter had spent the last sixteen years of his career was to be the main beneficiary. By the beginning of the 1970s both of its primary bearers of "historical experience"—Landes and Chandler—had returned to Harvard.

As distinguished Harvard professors, Landes and Chandler had perspectives on the dynamics of advanced capitalist development that should have, to paraphrase Schumpeter, overcome the most serious shortcoming of the modern economist's analytic equipment. Among economists, moreover, there was at Harvard in the early 1970s a receptive audience: a significant group of radical economists, bent on recapturing and renovating the historical tradition of Marx, in part by taking note of the work of Schumpeter. The intellectual goal of the radical economists was to comprehend the dynamics of capitalist development.

If ever there was an academic setting in the United States at which the confluence of theoretical traditions and historical analysis could at least have made the theory of economic development a matter of debate among economists of different points of view, it was at Harvard in the 1970s. The debate did not take place. An opportunity to make an intellectual impact on the economics profession was lost.

Historians of Capitalist Development

Marxian and Schumpeterian Legacies

The role of economic theory is to provide a simplified framework with which we can analyze complex economic phenomena. Even though a particular analysis, such as those put forth by Marx in the nineteenth century or Schumpeter in the twentieth, may arrive at untenable conclusions, the underlying conceptual framework may serve as a solid foundation on which to build a more adequate theoretical structure. As in the case of Marx and Schumpeter, when an economic theorist asks relevant questions and creates a coherent conceptual framework designed to answer these questions, it is possible to learn as much from the shortcomings of his or her work as from its strengths (see Lazonick 1990, 1991).

Looking at the British Industrial Revolution, Marx saw the conflict between capitalists and workers over the amount of effort expended in the production process as the key determinant of economic development. Capitalist investment in mechanization generated development, in Marx's view, not just because the new technologies were effort-saving and skill-displacing but also because they permitted a shift in social control over the production process from workers to capitalists. Although Marx asked the relevant questions and focused on key causal relationships, he overestimated the extent to which the introduction of mechanized technology enabled British capitalists to render the shop-floor worker "the mere appendage of a machine" (Marx 1977, p. 799; Lazonick 1990, chaps. 1–3).

With his focus on machinery as the solution to the problem of labor effort,

Marx failed to analyze how the persistence of worker control in the organization of the nineteenth-century British enterprise secured the cooperation of labor in the utilization of human and physical resources. These errors in the application of the theoretical framework, however, do not vitiate the insights that can be drawn from it. By focusing on the utilization of resources within the production process, Marx's conceptual framework captured a critical dimension of economic development in a way that no other economic theorist has since done.

For his part, Schumpeter had little conception of the utilization of resources in the production process. Indeed, he rejected precisely that part of Marx's work—the theory of surplus value—that provides a framework for analyzing the ways in which the organization of work affects productivity (see Lazonick 1991, chap. 4). But, undoubtedly influenced by the momentous technological and organizational changes that were occurring in the late nineteenth and early twentieth centuries, especially in Germany and the United States, Schumpeter filled a huge gap in the Marxian analysis of the capitalist enterprise by emphasizing the role of innovation—the development of new productive resources as distinct from the utilization of existing ones—as the prime determinant of the process of economic development.

In line with prevailing individualist ideology, however, Schumpeter initially saw innovation as an entrepreneurial accomplishment, and hence made no attempt to analyze the relation between the internal organization of the enterprise and technological change. Indeed, he weakened his own conception of innovation by treating changes in both technology and organization as aspects of the same general phenomenon. He provided no framework for analyzing the social determinants of successful innovation. Specifically, unlike Marx with his historical methodology, Schumpeter did not focus on the dynamic interaction of the forces and relations of production—of technology and organization—in generating superior economic outcomes.

Nevertheless, over the years, as Schumpeter sought to elaborate his theory of economic development through empirical investigation, he increasingly recognized the collective, and indeed often cooperative, nature of the innovation process. As a result, he came to recognize the evolutionary and dynamic character of economic development, and hence the vital need for historical research to test existing hypotheses and, more important, to generate new ones. As he stated in his 1949 address at the Research Center in Entrepreneurial History (after discussing the various existing definitions of "the entrepreneur"):

> Whether we define the entrepreneur as an "innovator" or in any other way, there remains the task to see how the chosen definition works out in practice as applied to historical materials. In fact it might be argued that the historical investigation holds logical priority and that our definitions of entrepreneur, entrepreneurial function, enterprise, and so on can only grow out of it *a posteriori*. Personally, I believe that there is

an incessant give and take between historical and theoretical analysis and that, though for the investigation of individual questions it may be necessary to sail for a time on one tack only, yet on principle the two should never lose sight of each other. In consequence we might formulate our task as an attempt to write a comprehensive history of entre-preneurship.   (Schumpeter 1949a, pp. 55–56)

If by the "history of entrepreneurship" Schumpeter meant the role of business enterprise in modern economic development, then the most comprehensive histories to date have been written by two alumni of the Research Center. Even if the direct impact of Schumpeter on Chandler or Landes was slight, *The Visible Hand* and *The Unbound Prometheus* take us a long way toward imbuing economic analysis with the "historical experience" of which Schumpeter spoke. Let me assess the main contributions of Chandler and Landes to the theory of economic development.

Chandler

Of the two historians, Chandler's contribution to the theory of economic de-velopment is more clear-cut because of his focus on the evolution of one type of economic institution, the large-scale industrial enterprise (see McCraw 1988). Already by the early 1960s, Chandler had drawn upon his detailed research into business history to enunciate the "strategy and structure" frame-work that forms the core contribution of his work. This Chandlerian framework, as introduced in *Strategy and Structure* (1962) and subsequently developed in *The Visible Hand* (1977) as well as in *Scale and Scope* (1990), provides an analysis of the relation between entrepreneurial strategy and organizational structure in the development of productive resources. Moreover, by emphasiz-ing economies of speed in the success of the industrial enterprise, Chandler offers considerable insight into the institutional arrangements that permit greater utilization of productive resources.

For Chandler, the analysis of modern capitalist development requires a theory of the emergence of the oligopolistic firm, on the grounds that since the late nineteenth century such firms have formed the basis of economic growth in the advanced capitalist economies (for evidence, placed in Chandlerian perspec-tive, see Tedlow 1986; Chandler 1990). The analysis starts with an entrepreneur who chooses a business strategy by investing in particular processes to produce a particular product. The type of entrepreneurial strategies that interest Chandler are those that offer opportunities for substantial economies of scale.

These are industries that require relatively large-scale investments in plant and equipment—what we generally regard as capital-intensive industries. But the determining factor is not, as is typically assumed, "indivisible technology." With its multiplant operations and the vertical integration of technologically separable processes, the modern enterprise far exceeds the size of investments dictated by indivisibility. Indeed, even the size of a single plant is, within limits, a strategic variable that depends on the entrepreneur's expectations of capturing market share, or, in the case of "second movers," a lower-bound parameter set by the successful strategies of the "first movers."

These are industries, moreover, in which not only is the necessary investment in plant and equipment—minimum efficient scale—large, but the processes and products are technologically "complex." High-quality goods produced at low cost cannot immediately be put on the market but must be developed *after* the initial investments in plant and equipment have been made. Technological complexity, therefore, creates the opportunity for the firm to engage in Schumpeterian innovation by combining and developing resources in new ways to achieve superior processes and products. To take advantage of this opportunity, the firm must invest in a number of vertically related processes, the planned development of which is necessary for technological breakthroughs. In addition, it must employ technical and managerial personnel who are able and willing to combine and coordinate their specialized talents to bring the innovation to fruition.

Even if the innovation is ultimately successful, all this investment in plant, equipment, and personnel may take years to generate reasonable returns. It is the lag between investment in innovation and the realization of revenues, rather than technology per se, that subjects these firms to the problem of fixed costs. Unless the firm is willing to incur these fixed costs, however, it cannot hope to generate the process and product innovations that will set it apart from its existing and potential competitors.

Investment in innovation, therefore, creates both an economic problem and an economic possibility for the firm. The economic problem is that, given the high levels of fixed costs incurred, the innovating firm will be at a competitive disadvantage relative to its less venturesome competitors if it does not succeed in capturing a large market share. But the economic possibility is that success in developing superior processes and products will provide it with a basis for increasing *its* share of the market—for achieving high levels of utilization of its productive resources—in ways that its competitors cannot.

Superior products enable the firm to charge a price premium—until competitors imitate the innovation—or forgo some or all of the price premium to extend its market share. Superior processes enable the firm to speed up the flow of work through its production facilities without sacrificing quality, thus cutting unit production costs by spreading out its fixed costs. It is this cost-cutting phenomenon that Chandler calls economies of speed. In a dynamic interaction of supply and demand, as the firm captures a larger market share it spreads out its substantial fixed costs, making possible an even greater share of the market.

Such a dynamic is not automatic, however, even for the innovative firm. To maintain product quality and coordinate the flow of work at high levels of throughput requires further investments in, and development of, managerial organization. The function of such organization is to spread out fixed costs by achieving high levels of throughput while controlling variable costs, so that, as in the standard textbook depiction of the Marshallian firm, increasing costs do not occur as throughput expands.

Provided that the firm has developed the organizational capability to coordinate still higher levels of throughput, the most potent way to control variable costs is to transform them into fixed costs. Rather than rely on the market for the purchase of inputs and the sale of outputs, the firm vertically integrates these activities into its operations. As throughput expands, pressures build for the firm to integrate backward into material supplies in order to ensure a steady and planned flow of inputs of requisite quality. Similarly, pressures build for forward integration into distribution in order to ensure the aggressive marketing of the firm's output required to transform mass production into mass sales.

But controlling variable costs increases the problem of fixed costs, so that the success of such vertical integration strategies depends on the organizational capability that the firm has developed. By achieving economies of speed, the dynamic interaction of organizational capability and ever-increasing investments in technology transforms what would otherwise be the problem of high fixed costs into the source of long-term competitive advantage.

In *The Visible Hand* Chandler focuses primarily on the planned coordination of the flow of work through the processes of production and distribution of the modern industrial enterprise, without, as he puts it in his introductory chapter, trying "to describe the work done by the labor force in these units or the organization and aspirations of the workers" (Chandler 1977, p. 6). Yet, to achieve *economies* of speed, the firm must elicit the labor effort of employees at various levels of the corporate hierarchy while retaining some of the productivity gains to be passed on to buyers in order to increase market share.

Chandler's framework can be elaborated to analyze the social relations that permit the firm to secure the cooperation of labor in the high-throughput investment strategy (see Lazonick 1990, chap. 7). To cope with technological complexity, the firm has to invest in the skills of key employees. But, having incurred these fixed developmental costs, it must then ensure that it retains these workers if it hopes to utilize the human resources in which it has invested. Even if it is successful in retaining these human resources, however, the firm must also motivate its employees to put forth the labor effort necessary to develop high-quality processes and products and achieve high levels of throughput. If the firm, as distinct from its employees, is to reap economies of speed from its investment strategy, it must gain control over a portion of the resultant productivity gains. The surplus value that accrues to the firm will depend not only on the amount of labor effort of requisite quality that employees contribute but also on the share of productivity gains that employees require to secure their cooperation.

In this training, retaining, and motivating of employees whose combined skills enable the firm to conquer technological complexity, the extraction of surplus value cannot be "Marxian exploitation," in which capitalists win and workers lose. Rather, surplus value must result from an institutionalized process of sharing out the benefits of enhanced productivity. The most potent benefits that the firm can offer its employees are not simply high wages and salaries but long-term job security and social mobility within the firm. In effect, as in the case of key physical resources, the generation of productivity through the development and utilization of human resources requires that the firm integrate key personnel into the long-term planning of the enterprise.

The historical experience of successful capitalist development over time and across national economies reveals, moreover, that the definition of the "key" employee has moved farther down the corporate hierarchy to include not only administrative personnel but also production workers (see Lazonick 1991, chap. 2). Increasingly the need for the firm to make long-term commitments to its employees has transformed variable costs into fixed costs, requiring in turn that the firm secure the long-term commitment of its employees if economies of speed are to be generated.

The integration of employees into the long-range planning of the enterprise creates pressures for the further growth of the already successful firm if it is to make good its promises of job security and social mobility in return for labor effort. The saturation of existing product markets or competitive product innovation may limit the growth of the firm on the basis of existing product lines. For sustained growth, the firm must build on those organizational and technological capabilities acquired in capturing existing product markets to move into new product lines. To do so, it must make further investments in physical and human resources, including facilities for systematic research and development. Such investments increase the problem of fixed costs. But they can also generate the product innovations that create opportunities for the firm to achieve economies of *scope* by spreading some of its fixed costs over a number of related product lines. Within each product line, however, economies of scale remain critical for success as high fixed costs must be transformed into low unit costs by extending market share.

Chandler's historical analysis, therefore, fills a large gap in the theory of innovation, and in so doing creates a link with the theory of production. Entrepreneurship, whether individual or collective, is not enough to generate economic development. Innovative entrepreneurial strategies must be followed by the building of organizational structures to plan and coordinate innovation and the flow of work. The success of organizational capability in generating economies of scale and scope depends on the development and utilization of not only physical resources but also, even more fundamentally, human resources. The individual efforts of those involved in the firm's specialized division of labor must be planned and coordinated—in effect, collectivized—to create a powerful productive organization.

Landes

If, as Chandler's account implies, the dynamic interaction of organization and technology determines the course of industrial development, why have some national economies been more successful than others in setting the process in motion? What accounts for the passing of industrial leadership from one nation to another? By placing the historical analysis of technological change in cross-national comparative perspective, David Landes has made pioneering attempts to answer these questions.

Like Schumpeter, Landes begins the analysis of economic development with entrepreneurial activity. In the industrialization of western Europe, he argues, technological change was the outcome of private enterprise engaged in "the rational manipulation of the material and human environment" (Landes 1969, p. 15; page references are from Landes 1969, unless otherwise indicated). But the emergence of entrepreneurial activity where and when it did cannot be understood in abstraction from the social context that created opportunities for private investment and accumulation. For even within western Europe, the timing, rate, and direction of technological change varied across national economies. The comparative economic history of western Europe, therefore, challenges us to identify those aspects of the social environment that support or impede entrepreneurial activity. As Landes (p. 39) says, "If history is the laboratory of the social sciences, the economic evolution of Europe should provide the data for some rewarding experiments."

Let us, therefore, look at the arguments that Landes makes concerning the interaction of entrepreneurship and social context in determining the nature and timing of technological change. For present purposes, the analysis begins with the rise of the factory system in Britain in the late eighteenth century and ends with the long-run relative decline of the British economy from the late nineteenth century. What social forces account for the technological changes that characterized the British Industrial Revolution, and why did the advent of the factory system propel the British economy into a position of industrial leadership? What problems did Germany—ultimately the most successful of the continental economies—face in trying to emulate Britain, and how did it confront

these problems? How and when, in historical retrospect, did Germany ultimately achieve success? And finally, why was Britain, the industrial leader as
late as the 1870s, so unsuccessful in responding to the German challenge?

Landes does not explicitly use the conceptual framework that I have sketched
out in discussing the work of Marx, Schumpeter, and Chandler. In his dichot-
omous definition of "the rational manipulation of the environment," however,
his distinction between "mastery over man and nature" on the one hand and
"the adaptation of means to ends" on the other (p. 21) is akin to Schumpeter's
(1947) important distinction between creative and adaptive response. And in his
analysis of the two ways in which industrialists can respond to their environment, Landes has much to say about the social determinants of innovation and
throughput within the firm.

The technological basis of the British Industrial Revolution was a series of
innovations that substituted machines—"rapid, regular, precise, and tireless"—
for human skill and effort (p. 41). The inventions themselves were the result of
craft-based, as distinct from science-based, activities in which practical "tinkerers" found, by trial and error, workable solutions to mechanical problems.
Because the new technologies were craft-based, they were easily imitated and
diffused, at least once the original patents ran out (see pp. 62ff.).

But, as Landes argues, even when the relevant inventions are ready at hand,
"technological change is never automatic" (p. 42). The main reason is that, in
replacing human skill and effort with machines, technological change creates
only the *potential* for saving on resources and lowering unit costs. Insofar as
investments in a new technology transform what were variable costs into fixed
costs, the entrepreneur must then utilize the new technology in ways that permit
it to outcompete the old. If not, he will become, as Landes puts it, "a prisoner
of his investment" (p. 43).

The task of outcompeting labor-intensive methods is all the more difficult
because of the tendency for those with vested interests in the old technologies
to accede in "compressing the cost of the human factors of production" (p. 42).
A successful adaptive response requires some combination of lower profits to
those capitalists who, because of financial or managerial limitations, continue to
produce on the basis of the old technologies, and lower wages to those workers
who stand to have their skills devalued by the success of the new technology.

A prime example of adaptive response is the putting-out system of textile
manufacture that both preceded the rise of the machine-driven factory system in
Britain and expanded alongside it (pp. 42ff.). An impetus to the early investments in the factory system came from the problem of throughput in the putting-
out system. Particularly during periods of boom, when profitable opportunities
were greatest but labor was in short supply, putters-out found that they lacked
control over the flow of work. With the production process carried out in their

homes, workers had the power to tie up the capital, primarily raw material, supplied by the putters-out, as well as to appropriate some of that capital as their own. Putters-out sought to use the force of law to speed up the flow of work and reduce embezzlement of materials. But, especially in good times, the control of work remained with the workers.

The factory system overcame these internal contradictions of the old mode of production. Despite the higher fixed costs, the factory triumphed because the capitalist gained control over the disposition of materials and the pace of work. In Landes' words:

> The machine imposed a new kind of discipline. No longer could the spinner turn her wheel and the weaver throw his shuttle at home, free of supervision. Now the work had to be done in a factory, at a pace set by tireless, inanimate equipment, as part of a large team that had to begin, pause, and stop in unison—all under the close eye of overseers, enforcing assiduity by moral, pecuniary, occasionally even physical means of compulsion. The factory was a new kind of prison; the clock a new kind of jailer. (p. 43; see also Landes 1983, p. 229, where the depersonified clock becomes a lock)

These words could be right out of Marx, all the more so because Landes recognizes the resistance of British workers to the loss of independence of action inherent in factory work. Indeed, the expansion of the putting-out system in weaving alongside the factory system in spinning during the first four decades of the nineteenth century manifested the willingness of many workers to accept lower wages to work at home rather than submit to factory discipline.

The factory system ultimately won out. By achieving higher levels of throughput and generating economies of speed, it was able to offset both its higher fixed costs and the adaptive response of the putting-out system. To some extent these economies of speed could be achieved by the utilization of relatively docile and cheap segments of the labor force, primarily children and women, even without any radical changes in technology. Over the longer run of the Industrial Revolution, however, the introduction of effort-saving and skill-displacing technology enabled firms to achieve economies of speed even while paying relatively high wages to some of their workers, mainly men, who, to judge from their union organization and strike activity, were anything but docile (Hobsbawm 1984, chaps. 11–14; Lazonick 1979).

Like Marx, however, Landes does not take the analysis of the triumph of the factory system far enough, paying little attention to the contribution of the "aristocracy of labor" to its success. Instead he places all the emphasis on the entrepreneurial motivation to invest—"What distinguished the British economy," he argues, "was an exceptional sensitivity and responsiveness to pecuniary opportunity" (p. 66)—combined with the disciplinary impact of the machine. But, as Landes himself recognizes as he carries the story of industrialization forward in time, the mechanized technology of the Industrial Revolution had a long way to go before skilled labor became dispensable. Hence the notion that, in contrast to the marriage of science and technology later in the nineteenth century, the technology of the Industrial Revolution was craft-based. Landes picks up the story of "the aristocracy of the labour force" only in the late nineteenth century, when these craftsmen had become, in his words, "an obstacle to innovation." Nevertheless, he eloquently describes the productive roles that they played in an era of less complex technology:

> Masters of their techniques, able to maintain their tools as well as use them, they looked upon their equipment as their own even when it belonged to the firm. On the job they were effectively autonomous. Most of them paid their own assistants, and many played the role of subcontractors within the plant, negotiating the price of each job with management, engaging the men required, and organizing their work to their own taste and convenience. The best of them "made" the firms they worked for. (p. 306)

In comparative historical perspective, alongside entrepreneurship and mechanized technology, then, a critical factor in the success of the British Industrial Revolution was the emergence of an abundant supply of skilled operatives who performed many of the day-to-day organizational functions that in later times and other places were taken to be the prerogatives of management. These labor aristocrats were important not only for the utilization of machine technology on the shop floor during the Industrial Revolution but also, through on-the-job apprenticeship systems, for reproducing and expanding the human resource capabilities on the basis of which Britain became, in the third quarter of the nineteenth century, the "workshop of the world."

Continental emulators had no trouble gaining access to the machine technologies of the Industrial Revolution. What they lacked was the skilled labor and shop-floor organization of the British factory system. Unable simply to imitate, Germany in the first half of the nineteenth century made the creative response of making the industrial investments and building the supportive institutions that would ultimately permit its economy to challenge and then surpass the world's first industrial nation.

The investments with the most long-run significance for the shift in national leadership were those that developed human resources. As Landes argues, "The lack of requisite technical skills posed an obstacle to innovation that only time could overcome" (p. 139). In the short run, British immigrants came to the Continent as capitalists or highly paid employees and "trained a generation of skilled workers, many of whom became entrepreneurs in their own right" (p. 150). Landes continues: "The growing technological independence of the Continent resulted largely from man-to-man transmission of skills on the job. Of less immediate importance [in the mid-nineteenth century] was the formal train-

ing of mechanics and engineers in technical schools." As posited by Gerschenkron's (1962) model of economic backwardness, the state, motivated by "a
passionate desire to organize and hasten the process of catching up" (p. 151 and
note), played the major role in planning and financing these investments in
human resources, the return to which was too long-term and uncertain for
private firms or individuals to undertake. From the 1850s on, these investments
in formal education laid the foundations for a new science-based technology:
"What had once been compensation for a handicap turned into a significant
differential asset" (p. 151).

But, for the reasons outlined in my discussion of Chandler's contribution, the
advent of science-based technology greatly increased the problem of fixed costs.
Landes refers to "a gradual institutionalization of technological advance," in
which "the more progressive industrial enterprises were no longer content to
accept innovations and exploit them, but sought them by deliberate, planned
experiment" (p. 325). Because the technological opportunity became more
complex, innovation required greater integration of production activities, firm-
specific investments in training of technical specialists, and the building of a
managerial organization, as well as longer lags between the commitment of
resources and the reaping of uncertain returns. As the problem of fixed costs
increased, so too did the problem of financing the necessary investments.

Even in the British factory system, which itself posed the problem of fixed
costs in comparison to putting-out, private individuals and close partnerships
had been able to mobilize the resources to invest in the craft-based technologies.
In Germany, however, early on, powerful investment banks played a leading
role in industrial development. Citing the authority of Schumpeter and Gerschenkron, Landes argues that, in contrast to the insignificant role of investment
banks in the finance of British industry, "Germany is the best illustration of the
generous yield of systematic investment in a backward economy of high potential" (p. 208). The German banks not only supplied the initial finance to
German industry but also assumed strategic decision-making roles, while permitting the firms that they controlled to organize cartels within their industries
to ensure that individual enterprises would have access to sufficient market share
to transform high fixed costs into low unit costs (p. 350).

Within the German enterprises themselves, the flow of work—what Chandler
calls throughout and Landes calls "the logistics of production" (p. 301)—
became all-important in the achievement of economies of scale. "The basic principle of industrial organization," asserts Landes, "is smooth and direct work
flow from start to finish of the manufacturing process; detours, returns, and halts
are to be avoided as much as possible" (p. 303). Elsewhere in *The Unbound
Prometheus,* he gets at the dynamics of the relation between fixed costs and
throughput: "Efficiency promotes efficiency: indeed, it makes it necessary"

(p. 267). The very size of plants in the German steel industry required the rational organization of work, which in turn required further mechanization to handle the flow of work, which in turn required the standardization of materials and products (pp. 264–268). In the metal-using industries, investment in special-purpose machinery to make interchangeable parts was critical for accelerating the flow of work, a theme on which Landes expands in *Revolution in Time* in discussing the rise of the American watch industry (Landes 1983, chap. 19).

The success of "high-throughput" technologies, however, depended on the restructuring of production relations within the firm. As Landes, referring to the triumph of German industry, goes on to argue: "Reorganization of work entailed reorganization of labour: the relationships of men to one another and to their employers were implicit in the [rationalized] mode of production; technology and social pattern reinforced each other" (Landes 1969, p. 317; see also p. 321).

Summing up, Landes argues, "The reasons for German success in the competition with Britain were not material, but rather social and institutional" (p. 334). What then accounts for the failure of Britain, already an industrial power, to make the necessary social and institutional response? There was the intransigence of the skilled workers, the very same men who, as I have argued, contributed to Britain's rise to industrial supremacy. But in the context of the new international competition based on planned coordination of high-throughput processes, "the skill and virtuosity" of these craftsmen became, to quote Landes, "incompatible with the fundamental principle of industrial technology—the substitution of inanimate accuracy and tirelessness for human touch and effort" (p. 307). The "fundamental *principle* of industrial technology" had, of course, been the same during the British Industrial Revolution. The social organization of German (as well as American) industry, however, had brought the principle closer to practical perfection.

But if, in the late nineteenth century, craft control posed an obstacle to innovation in Britain, why were British industrialists unable to overcome the prevailing institutional constraints? Social power played a role: the craft workers were well organized, their employers were not. At the national level, when Parliament and the judiciary sought to weaken the union movement—most notably by the Taff Vale decision that signaled financial ruin for any union engaged in a prolonged strike—the creative response of the workers was to build a political party that would represent their interests. At the industry level, even when, as in the engineering lockout of 1897–98, the collective power of employers was sufficient to defeat the unions, employers nevertheless remained dependent on craft control to run their individual workplaces because they had no organizational alternative to put in its place. During the tight labor market conditions of the 1910s, the power of the engineering unions reemerged stron-

ger than ever (Zeitlin 1983). As employers who had long relied on their independently organized workers for the supply of technical skills and managerial
coordination, British industrial capitalists simply lacked the organizational capability required to coordinate the use of the new high-throughput technologies,
even when, as was the case in British engineering, firms were pressed by
international competition to invest in them.

But why then didn't British industrialists develop this organizational capability? Here the typical British capitalist found himself in much the same position
as the craft worker who jealously protected his particular job. The capitalist himself had developed specialized managerial skills appropriate to running his particular type of business, and would have had no role to play in a modern corporate
structure. He did not have the ability to make a success of the corporate investment strategy—and he knew it. As a result, he was unable to introduce new technological processes that went beyond the vertically specialized purview of his
existing enterprise. If, as Landes argues, the British industrialist often faced the
problem of "technical interrelatedness" (p. 335), it was because, unlike his more
technologically and organizationally advanced competitors abroad, he would not
undertake the vertically integrated investment strategy that was a prerequisite for
overcoming the problem (for a case study, see Lazonick 1983). He succumbed
to the problem of interrelatedness rather than confront the problem of fixed costs.

If the restricted managerial ability of the British industrialist led him to avoid
the problem of fixed costs, his prior investments in plant and equipment presented him with the alternative of an adaptive response. Rather than invest in
managerial organization and new technologies, he could seek to survive in
international competition by cutting costs on the basis of the existing capabilities, organizational and technological, at his disposal. He could use inferior
materials, seek wage concessions from his workers, accept lower profits, and
deplete his existing capital stock (see, for example, Lazonick and Mass 1984).
In the long run, of course, he would and did lose out. But depending on how
immobile were his workers and how durable his plant and equipment, the long
run could be a matter of decades—by which time he might well be dead. For
him, the strategy of living off his industrial capital was rational. But for British
society as a whole, it meant that the opportunity to invest in superior productive
resources, both human and physical, had passed it by.

Yet, had the adaptive response been confined to old British industries—
textiles, iron and steel, shipbuilding, mechanical engineering—it might have
represented a rational social policy that permitted the expansion of new dynamic
industries while avoiding catastrophic unemployment in the old industrial centers. But the backwardness of the old industries retarded the development of the
social institutions that would support technological change in the new (Elbaum
and Lazonick 1986; Lazonick 1986, 1991, chap. 2). Because late-nineteenth-

century industrialists did not demand science-based technical specialists, the educational system was slow to orient its activities toward supplying them. In the new mechanical industries, such as automobile manufacture, shop-floor control on the craft model became dominant in the first half of the twentieth century even in the absence of unions because industrialists relied on shop-floor workers to coordinate the flow of work while they failed to integrate professional engineers into the managerial structure.

Moreover, because late-nineteenth-century industrialists did not look to financial interests to reorganize their industries, the British banking system, as powerful and concentrated as it was, did not orient its activities toward the mobilization of long-term investment capital. What the British banking system, based in London and handling the world's portfolio investments, did produce was a new wealthy elite that merged with the landed aristocracy and had no interest in technology. Rather than restructure the system of education to effect the marriage of science and technology, the new elite sought to use the system to ratify and reproduce their class privilege. In striving to join the new aristocracy, even those British industrialists who had attained wealth on the basis of technological innovation attempted to partake of this elite culture rather than rid it of its antitechnological bias. One result of such attitudes was to embed the British class structure even in the largest British firms in ways that made it difficult for top management to gain the commitment and coordinate the activities of technical specialists, preventing the organizational cohesion that was becoming increasingly necessary for technological change and international competitive advantage (Lazonick 1986, 1991, chap. 2).

I believe that this summary of the impact of institutional structure on British decline is consistent with the arguments that Landes makes under the heading "Some Reasons Why" (pp. 326ff.; see also pp. 468ff.). In the end, however, it is not social institutions that Landes emphasizes. Rather, he argues that "the decisive consideration was one of attitudes and values" (p. 543). "Even when the British entrepreneur was rational," says Landes, "his calculations were distorted by the shortness of his time horizon, and his estimates were on the conservative side" (p. 354).

But if the profit calculations and time horizons of the British industrialist were adequate to the task in the early nineteenth century, why had they become inadequate by the late nineteenth century? The key to the answer is, in my view, the dramatic transformation of the social determinants of technological change. In the earlier period, the industrial capitalist did not have to engage in an innovative investment strategy or build a cohesive managerial structure. With abundant supplies of skilled labor at hand and craft-based technology readily accessible, the fixed costs of setting up shop were small. He could rely on the market to supply him with inputs and take his outputs. The industrial capitalist could remain an individualist and yet be in the forefront of technological change.

In the later period, however, the British industrialist found himself confronted in international competition by the growing power of collective organization in the development and utilization of productive resources. To set in motion the dynamic interaction between organization and technology now required qualities of human resources and commitments of financial resources readily available to his foreign competitors but not to him. Within his own social environment, moreover, were vested interests, including those inherent in his own limited capabilities combined with his desire to control his own enterprise, that stood in the way of the necessary collective response. Compared to that of his international competitors, his time horizon was short because he was but an adaptive *individual*, not a creative *organization*. His estimates of returns were conservative because his organized competitors had the power to shape their economic environment in ways that he, as an individual proprietor, could not. It should be added that in his comparative analysis of the watch industry in *Revolution in Time,* Landes seems to concur in this analysis, for, in contrast to the individualism rampant in British watchmaking, Landes (1983, p. 303) calls for "a model of *collective* effort and performance" to explain the passing of leadership to the Swiss.

Given the organized power of the new competition, the combination of short planning horizons and conservative profit projections was a recipe not for the quick economic death of British industry but rather for prolonging its economic life. Because British industrialists and workers had already accumulated plant, equipment, and industrial skills, they could for a time live off their physical and human capital. Meanwhile, however, by investing in new technologies and by creating organizations to transform high fixed costs into low unit costs, German, U.S., and then Japanese enterprises would leave their British competitors farther and farther behind.

A Case of Intellectual Failure

In the concluding paragraph of his 1949 address to the Research Center in Entrepreneurial History, Schumpeter called for the integration of theory and history:

> New hypotheses and the marshalling of factual data, old and new, must proceed together . . . In the handling of old and new facts, the historian will gain from keeping in touch with theorists. Neither group should ever be distant from one another—but here the promise from collaboration is particularly great for both parties. As I have said before [see Schumpeter 1947], the study of economic change is an area of research where "economic historians and economic theorists can make an interesting and socially valuable journey together, if they will." (Schumpeter 1949a, pp. 63–64)

Unfortunately, they wouldn't. Even some fifty years before Schumpeter wrote, mainstream economic theorists in the United States such as J. B. Clark and Irving Fisher had embarked on an intellectual journey that would take them ever farther from the study of economic development. They came to view the economic problem as one of the optimal allocation of scarce resources rather than one of generating productivity to overcome conditions of scarcity. In 1932 a British economist, Lionel Robbins, succinctly summed up the emerging neoclassical consensus: "Whatever Economics is concerned with, it is *not* the causes of material welfare as such." Rather, he went on to argue that "Economics is the science which studies human behaviour as a relationship between ends and scarce means which have alternative uses" and that "the technical arts of production are simply to be grouped among the *given* factors influencing the relative scarcity of different economic goods" (Robbins 1932, pp. 9, 16, 33).

Even those prominent American neoclassical economists who have been less dogmatic than Robbins for all intents and purposes have never disputed his definition of "Economics." For example, in *Foundations of Economic Analysis*, first published in 1945, Paul Samuelson (1983, pp. 318–319) was by no means being critical of economists when he wrote: "Often the economist takes as data certain traditionally noneconomic variables such as technology, tastes, social and institutional conditions, etc.; although to the students of other disciplines these are processes to be explained and analyzed, and are not merely history." In the last sentence of his book, Samuelson (p. 355) voiced the hope that sometime in the future economic analysis would confront "the majestic problems of economic development." But his own practice of economics contributed substantially to an intellectual environment in which successive generations of well-trained economists would be unwilling, and increasingly unable, to undertake the task.

To take a line from Landes' discussion of British entrepreneurial failure, we require "some reasons why." Like the study of economic development, so too the study of intellectual development is complex. Nevertheless, I would like to venture a hypothesis of intellectual failure based on the combined interaction of three characteristic features of mainstream economics: individualist ideology, ahistorical methodology, and adaptive professional response.

Ideologically, mainstream economics represents the academic defense of individualism. Neoclassical economists *idealize* an economy in which factors of production have the maximum amount of mobility. It is the existence of "perfect" markets in labor and capital that offer this mobility, permitting the owners of the factors of production to decide where they want to sell their productive resources. In the absence of barriers to entry and exit, the invisible hand of resource allocation reigns supreme. The maximum freedom of the individual to choose, so the story goes, results in the optimal allocation of economic resources. Personal freedom and economic prosperity go hand in hand.

Although very few economists would contend that, in the real world, the perfectly competitive model actually prevails, the vast majority hold it up as an economic (if not political) ideal to be attained. Hence "imperfect" markets are bad; "perfect" markets are good. This view has not gone unchallenged in the history of economic thought, however. Marx argued that by depicting the capitalist economy as an exchange economy, economists were neglecting to analyze the role of social relations of production in generating economic development. Schumpeter argued that a degree of market power, and hence market "imperfection," had become an increasingly necessary basis for economic development, and contended that "perfect competition is not only impossible but inferior, and has no title to being set up as a model of ideal efficiency" (Schumpeter 1950, p. 106).

The historical work of Chandler and Landes supports Schumpeter's contention. Since the British Industrial Revolution, successful capitalist development has become increasingly dependent on the long-term *commitment* of financial, physical, and human resources to particular private and public sector organizations. Market allocation of resources, and the freedom of individual choice that it entails, continues to play an important role in permitting productive enterprises to gain access to readily available inputs. But the analysis of economic activity cannot stop with the process of market exchange without missing the essence of the development process—namely, the growing importance of strategy and structure in overcoming the problem of fixed costs by developing and utilizing productive resources. Fixed costs—the result of investments that must be developed and utilized before they generate returns—manifest nothing other than the immobility of resources that have been allocated to a particular productive organization.

Once allocated, the organization cannot and will not develop and utilize its plant, equipment, and personnel if the owners of these resources are constantly threatening to withdraw them. Rather, the organization will contribute to the development process only if the individuals who participate in it forgo the short-term individualist economic solutions that the market offers for the sake of furthering the long-term collective goals (for elaborations, see Lazonick 1991). Hence the historical fact, so amply demonstrated by Chandler's work, that the visible hand of corporate organization has increasingly replaced the invisible hand of market allocation in the coordination of economic activity and the generation of productivity. Moreover, as Landes' analysis of the Anglo-German rivalry shows, and as more recent Japanese experience confirms, in the process of successful economic development the collectivization of economic activity goes beyond the individual enterprise itself to include groups of enterprises, the educational system, the financial system, and the state.

In their ideological defense of individualism, neoclassical economists have failed to confront the theoretical implications of this evolving historical reality.

With the rise of big business at the turn of the century, as well as big government and big labor from the late 1930s, American economists could either have
reassessed the adequacy of the individualistic vision for understanding evolving
reality or have sought to insulate themselves from that reality by the ever more
intricate elaboration of their prior vision (on the role of "vision" in economics,
see Schumpeter 1949b).

Since the 1890s, at times reacting to the Marxian vision of an impending
transition to socialism (see, for example, Clark 1899), American economic
theorists have chosen the free market vision to the neglect of institutional
reality. These economists did not create the ideology of individualism. Rather,
by equating unfettered independence of action with economic well-being, they
reinforced a deep-seated attachment to the agrarian-democratic vision among
the American population at large. That neoclassical economists have served the
ideological function of making individualist ideology both coherent and legitimate explains the persistence and influence of their approach. But, as the
organizational response to the problem of fixed costs has become ever more
important in determining the success or failure of the economy, the neoclassical
market-coordinated view of the world has increasingly lost touch with social
reality.

The methodological reason for the intellectual failure derives from the manner in which the ideology of individualism has been defended. Once neoclassical economists had embarked on their flight from reality, they required some
other justification for the relevance of their analytical approach. They found that
justification in the quest for a universal, self-contained "science" of economics
that would be independent of prevailing social institutions. The feat could be
accomplished by making the individual the unit of economic analysis in all
times and places, by excluding from the analysis the social context in which
individuals make their choices, and by ignoring or minimizing the failure of
their economic vision to address the theory of economic development.

So, for example, Frank Knight (1952, p. 179) saw no need for a theory of the
business enterprise, arguing that "business organizations are but groups of
ignorant and frail beings, like the individuals with whom they deal." George
Stigler followed Knight in arguing that "the portion of the productive process
carried out in a particular unit is an accidental consideration" (Stigler 1941, p.
76; see also Stigler 1968, p. 62; Stigler 1971; Knight 1952, p. 172). He also
chastised Alfred Marshall for permitting his historical work on business organization "to diminish his contribution to theoretical economics," primarily
because Marshall's emphasis on internal economies made it difficult to explain
"the very existence of competition" (Stigler 1941, pp. 62, 76). Paul Samuelson, as we have seen, thought that the analysis of social phenomena might be
important in other disciplines, but for the sake of scientific generality in eco-

nomics, he cautioned his colleagues not to use a phrase such as "factors of production," which, by attaching productive inputs to particular classes of actors, imbued these inputs with social content (Samuelson 1983, p. 84). We should speak more generally of inputs that differ in terms of their productive contributions, but we should not create any impression that the ways in which these inputs are owned or controlled might affect their productive capabilities and performance.

By the same token, in his American Economic Association presidential address, Samuelson (1962, p. 18) defended the flight from reality by proclaiming to his colleagues that "the economic scholar works for the only coin worth having—our own applause" (which he undoubtedly then received). The explicit message of the address was that the current (early 1960s) practice of the science of economics was the selective cumulation of the "best" that the history of economic thought had to offer. If one accepts this "cumulative selectivity" view of the development of economic analysis, there is little to be gained from the study of the history of economic thought. Hence we can explain the absence for years on end of course offerings in the history of thought in leading economics graduate programs over the past few decades. And we can also explain why many of today's leading economists have little knowledge of the intellectual history of their own discipline.

Ironically, Schumpeter himself contributed to this sad state of affairs. In an article entitled "Science and Ideology," written shortly before his death, Schumpeter argued that all economists bring to their work a preanalytic vision that is based on their ideological preconceptions. It is only on the basis of that vision that economic analysis, or "science," goes forward. For all his recognition of the methodological limitations of neoclassical economics, however, Schumpeter failed to see the ideological underpinnings of the theory of the market economy as captured in his original notion of the "circular flow." Indeed, despite his advocacy of "historical experience," in *History of Economic Analysis* he essentially accepts the "cumulative selectivity" view of the progress of economic "science" (Schumpeter 1954, chap. 1). Perhaps himself overawed by the rise of mathematical technique, he portrayed the neoclassical analysis of the economy as "science," devoid of any ideological content. By succumbing to the scientific pretensions of his colleagues, Schumpeter managed to preserve his respected, if (as it turned out) neglected, status as an economist. But he undermined the methodological critique inherent in his own contribution to the theory of economic development.

Nevertheless, Schumpeter would surely have been astounded to find that, during the 1970s, even the Harvard economics department, from which he had departed just a generation before, had ceased to teach the history of economics as a matter of course to its graduate students. And looking at the content of graduate economics teaching as it now exists, he would surely have agreed that what is passed off as the "best" theory that economists have to offer ignores some of the most relevant contributions in the history of economics. The insights of Marx and Schumpeter himself are cases in point, but so too are those of the "neoclassical" Marshall, who, in contrast to modern neoclassical economists, defined economics as "that part of individual and social action which is most closely connected with the attainment and with the use of the material requisites of well-being" (Marshall 1961, p. 1). To my mind, the most insightful contributions in Marshall's *Principles* have to do *not* with the equilibrium of supply and demand in the determination of market outcomes but rather with the dynamic interaction of internal and external economies—the relations between the growth of firms and the growth of markets—in the process of economic development (see especially Marshall 1961, bk. 4; and, for an elaboration of this argument, Lazonick 1991, chap. 5; for an application to industry, see Mass and Lazonick 1990).

Once economics is defined as an ahistorical science that concerns the allocation of given resources to alternative uses, the equation of science with mathematical technique follows. To succeed, today's leading economic theories do not have to study the *economy* (let alone the history of the economy or the history of economics) to justify the relevance of their fundamental assumptions; they just have to study *economics* to work out more completely the mathematical logic of the exercises performed by (quite literally) yesterday's leading theorists. Not only are such economists not obliged to justify the relevance of their fundamental assumptions; they are typically unaware of what those assumptions are.

As for applied economists, their task is neither to ensure that their quantitative measures do indeed capture the qualitative essence of the underlying reality nor to explore the empirical validity of the causal relations implicit in the models that they estimate. Most empirical work in economics today is undertaken not in order to generate new testable hypotheses, as Schumpeter argued it could and should do, but rather to estimate those models of economic activity that today's leading theorists deem to be of interest. Even then, much more attention centers on the sophistication of the statistical techniques employed than on the implications of the findings for the relevance of the underlying theoretical point of view.

Used properly, mathematical modeling and statistical techniques are important analytical tools. But, like Schumpeter, I believe that these tools of economic analysis serve useful purposes only when they are subordinated to historical analysis so that the scholar can justify the relevance of the models and measures as well as recognize their empirical limitations.

Until two decades or so ago, there was still hope that influential economists might insist on historical analysis as a critical element in the practice of economics. At Harvard (to take a graduate economics program in which I both studied and taught) most of the tenured faculty circa 1970 were veritable institutionalists compared to their counterparts today. Even many of the mathematical neoclassical economists had a keen interest in, and respect for, institutional analyses. But the evolving sociology of the economics profession ensured that the old guard would have little impact on preserving a respected place for the historical analysis of economic change.

The neoclassical vision of the market-coordinated economy coupled with science as mathematical technique dominated the major professional journals and the core requirements of graduate programs. Not surprisingly, adherence to the ideology and methodology of neoclassical economics became the basic credential for securing prestigious academic appointments. At the same time, many of the old guard, who collectively could have had some voice in these matters, exited to spend their time in administrative positions, research institutes, or professional schools. Under the circumstances, graduate students in economics felt considerable pressure—although much less than exists today—to go with the methodological flow or face a future on the periphery of the profession.

Economic historians did not help matters much. The explicit goal of the new economic history that flourished in economics departments in the late 1960s and early 1970s was to use received theory and statistical techniques to transform historical analysis into an applied field of economics (see, for example, Temin 1973, p. 8). In the process, even economic historians ceased to be interested in the theory of economic development. By defining economic history as merely an applied field, economic historians undermined the intellectual justification for requiring all economics graduate students to study economic history (see Field 1987). For if economic history is just another applied, rather than "fundamental," field of economic analysis, why require all economics graduate students to become fluent in it?

Indeed, in the Harvard economics department, the mainstream economists took precisely this position in their attempts to whittle down or eliminate the traditional two-semester economic history requirement. In the 1970s Harvard was perhaps the only major U.S. economics department where a two-semester requirement remained in force. But, after Alexander Gerschenkron retired from the scene, the faculty failed to develop a curriculum or endorse courses that could justify economic history as a fundamental field of economic analysis. Instead, students were simply permitted to take any two courses at Harvard or MIT that had an institutional, historical, or critical bent—that is, anything that did not fit into the mainstream curriculum.

Harvard doctoral candidates did, as a result, become exposed to the study of economic history as well as some unorthodox points of view. But the uncharacteristic freedom of choice accorded students in fulfilling the requirement gave them the distinct, and correct, impression that the faculty viewed it as at best a "liberal arts distribution" (as one graduate student put it), and not as fundamental to the training of a would-be economist. In going along with this free-market solution to the administration of the economic history requirement, economic historians at Harvard had lost an opportunity to exercise some methodological leadership in economics education. Rather than confront the prevailing methodology of economics with an innovative educational response, they adapted to the prevailing professional constraints.

What happened to the theory of economic development was, therefore, not a failure of intellectual *achievement* but rather a failure of intellectual *influence*. As the cases of Chandler and Landes illustrate, intellectual achievements can result from the imaginative and prodigious efforts of individuals who dare to make the grand scheme of things the subject of serious scholarship. But intellectual influence does not necessarily follow. Like innovation in the industrial world, successful innovation in the intellectual world requires long-term commitments of resources, both human and material, and collective organization to overcome vested interests in existing methodologies and ideologies. In intellectual pursuits as in industrial undertakings, the longer the delay in mobilizing and coordinating the resources for innovation, the more entrenched the vested interests become, and the more difficult is the process of change.

Unfortunately, even those who might concur on the need for intellectual innovation in economics often find themselves more divided by ideology than unified by a commitment to understanding the development process. A telling example of the ideological divide is David Landes' critique of "What Do Bosses Do?," an article by his Harvard colleague Stephen Marglin, written around 1970 and first published in 1974. Marglin's arguments exerted considerable influence among radical economists, abroad as well as in the United States, in their efforts to revive and revitalize the theory of capitalist development. Landes' critique, however, displays little understanding of the social context in which the article was written or the nature of the influence that it exercised. In viewing Marglin's piece as an ideological tract, Landes fails to recognize the role it played in helping to open up a window of opportunity for the American economics profession to engage in intellectual innovation.

Landes finds merit in "What Do Bosses Do?" because Marglin "sought to study history and enlist it in his argument" (Landes 1986, p. 621; page references are to Landes 1986, unless otherwise indicated). Indeed, Landes is pleased to find that on the issue of the transition from putting-out to the factory, Marglin "adopts the model of explanation put forward in *The Unbound Prometheus*" (p. 602). Landes does criticize Marglin's failure to recognize the historical role of the capitalist as entrepreneur. But what appears to bother Landes most is that the essay sought to influence the wrong type of people for the wrong kinds of reasons.

Toward the beginning of his critique of Marglin, Landes identifies "What Do Bosses Do?" as a seminal contribution to a "revisionist view" of the economics of work organization, put forth by "the Left, a somewhat vague, heterogeneous cover term that I use to compensate for my ignorance of the sectarian alignments" (p. 589). In the abstract to his critique, Landes states that Marglin's thesis not only "misreads history" but also "is essentially ideological" (p. 585). At the end of the critique, Landes concludes:

> In the last analysis, then, I see Marglin's essays [Marglin 1974, 1984] as exercises in optative economics, useful for the historical questions they raise, but directed primarily to true believers as a vision of what might have been and ought to be. His aim, implicit if not explicit, objective if not subjective, is to delegitimize the capitalist today—*hence the present tense of his title*—and thereby to encourage and justify some unspecified act of expropriation. That is the nature of revolutionary propaganda: to accentuate the negative.   (p. 623; emphasis in original)

Locating Marglin's contribution in a broad political context of the struggle for social change in which, whatever its intent, its influence was minimal, Landes misses out on Marglin's actual achievement, the social context in which it was made, and the intellectual influence that "What Do Bosses Do?" has had. Landes asks: "Where is Marglin coming from?" and answers: "He has to be situated, I think, in a larger stream of criticism of the structures and conditions of work going back to the Industrial Revolution itself" (p. 621). Maybe after the fact. But when Marglin wrote "What Do Bosses Do?" he was coming from a fast-track career as a mathematical economist, in which his training, socialization, and accomplishments (including tenure in the Harvard economics department) should have left him as tightly bound to the mainstream of the profession as was (if I may) Prometheus to the rock. Instead, he wrote "What Do Bosses Do?," the contents of which challenged economists to deal with the social determinants of productivity growth and technological change. Economic outcomes, he argued, are not independent of the exercise of social power as economists are wont to believe.

To make his points, Marglin appealed to the historical record and to cross-cultural comparisons (Landes fails to mention that Marglin's charge of exploitation was aimed not just at the private capitalist but also at the socialist state). Marglin's arguments may be flawed, but, as Landes himself recognizes, at least the relation between history and theory is explicit in them, so that one can go back to the arguments and engage in coherent and fruitful debate. Although I suppose that at the time Marglin had not read Schumpeter's address to the

Research Center in Entrepreneurial History cited earlier, in "What Do Bosses Do?" he did precisely what Schumpeter (1949a, p. 63) urged economists to do: examine the available historical literature to generate new hypotheses.

The issues raised in "What Do Bosses Do?" concerning the interaction of the relations and forces of production provided the most important stimulus to my own decision to do a detailed case study of the role of social organization in the development of cotton textile technology (Lazonick 1979, 1981b). That study evolved into an analysis of the decline of the British cotton textile industry (Lazonick 1983; Lazonick and Mass 1984), as well as critiques of some related work by new economic historians (Lazonick 1981a, 1984, 1987; Mass and Lazonick 1990). Among other things, my analyses revealed some of the conceptual and empirical weaknesses of the new economic historians' attack on Landes himself—so much so that at a conference on British economic decline organized by Bernard Elbaum and me, Donald McCloskey actually accused me of slavishly following the Landes line. So much for "sectarian alignments"! If I am one of the "true believers" to whom Landes refers, so be it. I could name many other scholars upon whom Marglin has, directly or through his writings, had a similar creative influence, but I think it only proper that I leave to them the choice of admitting to so subversive an association.

By his willingness and ability to unbind himself from the rock of mainstream ideology and methodology, moreover, Marglin provided not only intellectual influence but also leadership—a trait that Schumpeter would have well appreciated. True, the fact that Marglin was already a tenured Harvard professor provided him with an opportunity to exercise such leadership that was not available to most others. But the fact is also that among some twenty-five or so other tenured economists who were in the same position, he was unique in risking his professional reputation to mount a much-needed challenge to the status quo.

Nor should it detract from Marglin's role to point out that, by openly espousing radical economics, many other economists who had not been blessed with tenure risked not only their professional reputations but also their future employment prospects. As in all areas of social life, change in academia is a collective phenomenon. In the late 1960s and the early 1970s, for Marglin as for me and many others, the individual choice to make the break from the mainstream approach—to try to change the intellectual constraints rather than merely adapt to them—would not have been possible if not for the political stimulus provided by the social unrest of the time and the growth of a collective movement of radical economists within academia.

Radical economics was certainly of the left. But, contrary to Landes' preconceptions, it was a vibrant intellectual force precisely because, in contrast to the limited scope of the debate between the neoclassical Keynesians and the neoclassical monetarists that held center stage, it was not beset by sectarian dogma. As for "What Do Bosses Do?," what is important about Marglin's particular contribution to radical economics is not that it is ideologically motivated—which it certainly is—but rather that, in contrast to the mainstream economists with their "scientific" and "objective" pretensions, Marglin is quite open about his ideological orientation. Whether or not Marglin's thesis indeed "misreads history," as Landes argues, the fact is that, unlike the vast majority of modern economists, Marglin *read* history and took it seriously. And whether or not Marglin's thesis is "essentially ideological," as Landes contends, the fact is that in being open about his social concerns and political preferences, Marglin did not seek to fortify himself against criticism by proclaiming the scientific objectivity of his approach. Rather, he opened the door to serious debate with those who, like Landes, might choose to disagree.

That ideology enters into even the most careful analytical endeavors is not news to David Landes. For, as he warns his readers at the conclusion of his own analysis of the Anglo-German rivalry:

> When all is said and done, neither empirical evidence nor theoretical reasoning is likely to settle the dispute [over the relative importance of human and nonhuman determinants of economic development]. For one thing, so complex is the matter of history and so unamenable to the replicated analysis of the laboratory, that the precise imputation of weights to each of the many determinants of economic development—even in a limited situation, *a fortiori* in general—is impossible and likely to remain so. For another this very complexity and imprecision precludes demonstration that any given explanation of events, however plausible, is the only possible explanation. And since scholars are human, with many, if not all, of the predilections and biases of other humans, they tend to choose and will no doubt go on choosing those interpretations that they find not only plausible but congenial . . . The identification of the scholar with the problem he studies has often been as important a determinant of his approach as the objective data. (Landes 1969, pp. 357–358)

By the same token, I would argue, it is not ideology acting on its own that creates a barrier to intellectual progress in economics. Rather, given the complexity and evolving nature of the subject matter, the barriers to progress are the institutional suppression of debate among those with different points of view as well as the professional constraints placed on cooperative efforts among those with different methodological skills. If one accepts that "scientific" analysis as currently practiced by mainstream economists is beyond ideology and uses the only relevant methodology, what need could there be for paradigmatic debate or methodological collaboration?

The end result of the rule of "ideology-free science" has been the failure to integrate historical analysis and the theory of economic development into the discipline that calls itself economics. What happened to the theory of economic development, it seems to me, is that those who might have used their influence to transform intellectual opportunity into academic reality have found the ideological orientation of mainstream economists too congenial and their scientific pretensions too overpowering.

The failure to make the study of the nature and causes of the wealth of nations central to the study of economics cannot, therefore, be attributed to limited intellectual capabilities. Given the contributions of the likes of Marx, Schumpeter, and Marshall to the theory of economic development, the intellectual achievements of historians such as Chandler and Landes, as well as many others, have made it intellectually possible to make the historical analysis of the development process fundamental to economic analysis. The opportunity for intellectual innovation in economics exists. Effective leadership and organization could still make it happen.

References

Aitken, Hugh G. J., ed. 1965. *Explorations in Enterprise.* Harvard University Press.

Chandler, Alfred D., Jr. 1962. *Strategy and Structure: Chapters in the History of the American Industrial Enterprise.* MIT Press.

—— 1977. *The Visible Hand: The Managerial Revolution in American Business.* Harvard University Press.

—— 1990. *Scale and Scope: The Dynamics of Industrial Capitalism.* Harvard University Press.

Clark, J. B. 1899. *The Distribution of Wealth.* Macmillan.

Dobb, Maurice. 1963. *Studies in the Development of Capitalism.* International.

Elbaum, Bernard, and William Lazonick, eds. 1986. *The Decline of the British Economy.* Clarendon.

Field, Alexander J., ed. 1987. *The Future of Economic History.* Kluwer-Nijhoff.

Gerschenkron, Alexander. 1962. *Economic Backwardness in Historical Perspective.* Harvard University Press.

Hobsbawm, Eric J. 1984. *Workers: Worlds of Labor.* Pantheon.

Knight, Frank. 1952. "Some Fallacies in the Interpretation of Social Cost." In G. Stigler and K. Boulding, eds., *Readings in Price Theory.* Irwin.

Landes, David S. 1969. *The Unbound Prometheus: Technological Change and Industrial Development in Western Europe from 1750 to the Present.* Cambridge University Press.

—— 1983. *Revolution in Time: Clocks and the Making of the Modern World.* Harvard University Press.

—— 1986. "What Do Bosses Really Do?" *Journal of Economic History* 46 (September).

Lazonick, William. 1979. "Industrial Relations and Technical Change: The Case of the Self-Acting Mule." *Cambridge Journal of Economics* 3 (September).

—— 1981a. "Factor Costs and the Diffusion of Ring Spinning in Britain Prior to World War I." *Quarterly Journal of Economics* 96 (February).

—— 1981b. "Production Relations, Labor Productivity, and Choice of Technique: British and U.S. Cotton Spinning." *Journal of Economic History* 41 (September).

—— 1983. "Industrial Organization and Technological Change: The Decline of the British Cotton Industry." *Business History Review* 57 (Summer).

—— 1984. "Rings and Mules in Britain: Comment." *Quarterly Journal of Economics* 99 (May).

—— 1986. "Strategy, Structure, and Management Development in the United States and Britain."

In Kesaji Kobayashi, ed., *The Development of Managerial Enterprises*. University of Tokyo Press.

―――― 1987. "Stubborn Mules: Some Comments." *Economic History Review*, 2nd ser., 40 (February).

―――― 1990. *Competitive Advantage on the Shop Floor*. Harvard University Press.

―――― 1991. *Business Organization and the Myth of the Market Economy*. Cambridge University Press.

Lazonick, William, and William Mass. 1984. "The Performance of the British Cotton Industry, 1870–1913." *Research in Economic History* 9 (Spring).

Marglin, Stephen. 1974. "What Do Bosses Do? The Origins and Functions of Hierarchy in Capitalist Production." *Review of Radical Political Economics* 6 (Summer).

―――― 1984. "Knowledge and Power." In Frank H. Stephen, ed., *Firms, Organization, and Labour: Approaches to the Economics of Work Organization*. Macmillan.

Marshall, Alfred. 1961. *Principles of Economics*. 9th (variorum) ed. Vol. 1. Macmillan.

Marx, Karl. 1977. *Capital*. Vol. 1. Vintage.

Mass, William, and William Lazonick. 1990. "The British Cotton Industry and International Competitive Advantage." *Business History* 32 (October).

McCraw, Thomas K. 1988. "Introduction: The Intellectual Odyssey of Alfred D. Chandler, Jr." In McCraw, ed., *The Essential Alfred Chandler*. Harvard University Press.

Robbins, Lionel. 1932. *The Nature and Significance of Economic Science*. Macmillan.

Samuelson, Paul. 1962. "Economists and the History of Ideas." *American Economic Review* 52 (May).

―――― 1983. *Foundations of Economic Analysis*. Enlarged ed. Harvard University Press.

Sass, Steven A. 1986. *Entrepreneurial Historians and History: Leadership and Rationality in American Economic Historiography, 1940–1960*. Garland.

Schumpeter, Joseph. [1911] 1961. *The Theory of Economic Development*. Oxford University Press.

―――― 1947. "The Creative Response in Economic History." *Journal of Economic History* 7 (November).

―――― 1949a. "Economic Theory and Entrepreneurial History." In Hugh G. J. Aitken, ed., *Explorations in Enterprise*. Harvard University Press.

―――― 1949b. "Science and Ideology." *American Economic Review* 39 (March).

―――― 1950. *Capitalism, Socialism, and Democracy*. 3rd ed. Harper.

―――― 1954. *History of Economic Analysis*. Oxford University Press.

Stigler, George. 1941. *Production and Distribution Theories*. Macmillan.

―――― 1968. *The Organization of Industry*. Irwin.

―――― 1971. Introduction. In Frank Knight, *Risk, Uncertainty, and Profit*. Reprint ed. University of Chicago Press.

Tedlow, Richard. 1986. "The Process of Concentration in the American Economy." Paper presented at the Ninth International Economic History Congress, Bern, August.

Temin, Peter, ed. 1973. *New Economic History*. Penguin.

Zeitlin, Jonathan. 1983. "The Labour Strategies of British Engineering Employers, 1890–1922." In Howard Gospel and Craig Littler, eds., *Managerial Strategies and Industrial Relations*. Heinemann.

10

· · ·

Public Sector Entrepreneurship

Jonathan Hughes

How shall change be instituted to meet new circumstances in large-scale units which, because they are committed to comparatively static standards of efficiency, limit the capacity of those relatively few men capable of innovation and leadership?

—Walt Rostow, *United States in the World Arena*

Entrepreneurship in the public sector is a subject buried in cynicism, but I shall make a straight run at it. My argument is that for various reasons, including necessity, the public service (bureaucratic) sector should be as innovative and responsive to change as are (one hopes) the competitive firms in the private sector. The argument is mainly subjective, although there should be some way in which innovative advances in the nonmarket sector can be measured objectively. Moreover, improvement in governmental performance does not necessarily imply increased efficiency in a conventional sense—increased output per unit of input.

The issue is most often a matter of sensitivity to changing public needs: finding and supplying (in whatever quantities) the appropriate public service. The country is hardly improved by increasingly efficient outputs of the wrong bureaucratic services. The need to shift bureaucratic output in accord with changes in the country's demand for it implies an entrepreneurial role. It is equally true that entrepreneurial needs arise from within bureaucracies for their own benefit. We now have experience with extensive money-making initiatives by local government bodies, usually in collusion with private interests, to utilize civic powers (including eminent domain) in the interests of revenue-substituting earnings. The New York City Public Development Corporation (formed in 1966) may be the outstanding example, although the techniques have now spread coast to coast *(New York Times,* April 4, 1987). I want to confine my remarks here mainly to appointed bureaucracies.

In my gloomy book *The Governmental Habit* (1977), I could see no clear path to improvement in the performance of government's role in the economy. It seemed to me that what was natural and congenial to us was also inevitably inefficient. Apart from the possibility of social gains' coming from "public goods," government actions mainly reduced output and changed allocation in the economy away from the efficient norms of the market economy. In important dynamic cases, attempts by regulators to tighten up controls necessarily increased the inefficiency.[1] The system could not correct itself.

Then came two presidents who, so they said, were determined to "get the government off the people's back," and, mysteriously, Big Government is now even bigger in every dimension. Moreover, the federal government's expansion has now generated persistent deficits and debt increases of unimagined size, with potential consequences that are not really understood by economists, although dire outcomes of various sorts are routinely forecast.[2] As for the "deregulation" of the Reagan era, that is grossly overrated, like the "frugality" of his budgets.

But there may be options. What can be done to encourage improvement in government from within? If the system will not improve itself left alone, why not agitate it? William Niskanen (1971) suggested competitive bidding between bureaus for the proposed tasks on the government's agenda. Competition, of course, means entrepreneurship. We already have a considerable history of public sector entrepreneurship, without much structural encouragement. Many object to public sector entrepreneurship because of its origins, not the usefulness of the decisions themselves. Public servants are supposed to serve, not invent.

A model of the perfect bureaucrat might be taken from a scene in an Egyptian tomb painting: the loyal scribe seated at Pharaoh's feet, ever willing to do precisely his master's bidding. In modern conditions one might imagine democratically elected legislators projecting their constituents' wishes unambiguously to a pliant and competent corps of public servants who miraculously transform their instructions into reality. If you turn these models on their heads, the scribe instructs Pharaoh, the public servants rule the elected officials, and a mute public is doomed to accept whatever is the outcome. The real world of modern American bureaucracy is neither the pure vision nor its inverse. In a giant and complex governmental establishment, however, the scribe typically knows more than Pharaoh, and power goes with knowledge.

The belief among the bureaucrats that their responsibility expands with their expertise is what has given rise to the best examples of bureaucratic entrepreneurship we have experienced.[3] There are good reasons why such entrepreneurship is a desirable state of affairs, and why every effort should be made to encourage it—obnoxious as that may seem to those who want the scribe's powers strictly confined to Pharaoh's commands.

Modern Public Sector Growth

The modern escalation of government's share of GNP (measured as both net purchases and transfers) makes public sector entrepreneurship a most pressing and vexatious issue.[4] As a spender of money, the federal government is one of the world's prodigies. The estimated $1 trillion it spent in fiscal 1987–88 is more than was spent in any other economy in the world except Japan and the USSR. If we add state and local government expenditures (including all transfer payments), just under $2 trillion was allocated by American governments, the largest spending machine in the world save only the American economy's private sector in aggregate. The amount probably exceeds in present market value all output produced in the continent of Africa. These expenditures were allocations of goods and services, which partly determine future economic growth as well as current distribution.

One of the reasons public entrepreneurship is relatively new as a concern of social scientists is the comparatively short time since the public sector in the industrial countries grew to such magnitudes—that is, since 1945. The main exception is the USSR, whose public sector responsibilities have been huge since 1919. There, any questions about public sector entrepreneurial authority were presumably a muted matter. President Gorbachev must now find an escape hatch from the morass a mindless bureaucracy created over the decades.

Let us consider several dimensions of public sector growth. In 1929 the sum of all American government expenditures was roughly 12 percent of GNP, and the federal government's share alone was only about 3 percent. By 1940, at the end of the peacetime New Deal years, total government expenditures stood at 20 percent of GNP and the federal share had tripled to 9 percent, still less than the combined state and local government share, but only marginally so. In wartime, of course, the federal share was enormous. But in the ensuing postwar period there were certain ratchet effects from earlier peacetime experience. By 1960 total government expenditures were some 30 percent of GNP and by 1986 about 45 percent. By 1960 the federal share had exceeded the sum of state and local government expenditures, and so it has remained. From 1929 to 1986, government measured by expenditures as a proportion of GNP grew four times as fast as did GNP itself—the economy. The federal share grew about seven times as fast *(Historical Statistics* 1960; *Statistical Abstract* 1987).

One major reason for the federal sector's rapid growth is the burden of transfer payments in the American welfare state. Counting only direct purchases of goods and services, the federal sector was actually smaller in 1986 than in 1960 (by about 20 percent) compared to state and local government purchases on GNP account. In 1986 direct federal purchases on GNP account equaled a mere 9 percent of the total. But aggregate federal outlays, including transfers, by 1986 came to 24 percent of GNP, and the 15 percent margin was mainly federal transfer payments, which were roughly double those made by state and local governments. The federal government is unique among American government bodies in that it transfers far more buying power than it utilizes for its own purposes.

The American public sector owns and operates very few productive enterprises. It has been American tradition that productive resources should be mainly privately owned and operated. The federal government, to operate an extensive welfare state, must tax the private sector, and by transferring the funds to transfer recipients, *indirectly* buys from the private sector. The greatest part of the increased federal outlay has become mandatory: entitlement transfers. Governmental growth has also been measured by the ubiquitous expansion of government regulation of the private sector, and also by deregulation—another act of government. A good deal of attention has been paid to individual entrepreneurial contributions in those areas historically. Perhaps, overall, the ideas of regulators, men such as Chief Justice Morrison Waite, Senator John Sherman, or Justice Oliver Wendell Holmes, Jr., have received more attention in the literature than the deregulators, men such as Justice Stephen Field or Alfred Kahn. What is important for our purposes in this literature is the measurable consequences of individual belief and action.[5] Finally, growth of government has meant a proliferation of bureaucracy.

The federal government's organization table alone defies all understanding. What *can* be understood is numbers: the numbers of government employees compared to those in the private (productive) sector. The federal government is, by this measure, the smaller branch. In 1984 there were 2,942,000 full-time civilian employees in the federal government, 3,898,000 employed by state governments, and 9,595,000 employed at local government levels. These outcomes are not surprising considering that education, streets, sanitation, and safety are predominantly state and local government responsibilities. As we have asked for more services of these kinds, we have provided more by expansion of state and local government employment.

Per capita numbers of federal employees have grown immensely. Between 1841 and 1871 there were from 11 to 12 federal employees per 10,000 population. Then the federal government began to grow. By 1921 there were 52 federal employees per 10,000: federal civilian employment in those 50 years grew (at a mean annual rate of 8.6 percent) more than four times as fast as did the general population. In the next 20 years the number doubled again, 161 per 10,000 (growing at a mean annual rate of 10.3 percent), and by 1970 stood at 185 per 10,000 (having slowed in 1940–1970 to a mean annual growth rate of 3.9 percent). Then in the computer age, the numbers of federal employees actually fell (from 2,806,000 in 1970 to 2,498,000 in 1980). The number of federal employees declined sharply to 110 per 10,000. By 1984, however, after the first Reagan administration, the number of federal civilian employees had risen 13.6 percent to stand at 125 per 10,000. Overall (apart from the first Reagan administration), as federal expenditures rose, federal employment fell, and that, in the weird world of public finance, should be counted as an increase in efficiency—

in productivity. Such had *not* happened in state and local government operations: both the total number of employees and the number per 10,000 rose, from 419 in 1970 to 488 in 1980, and to 598 in 1984—a 43 percent increase in a mere four years *(Historical Statistics* 1960, tables A22, Y206, Y210, Y213; *Statistical Abstract* 1987, table 481).

If we bear in mind Parkinson's (1957) first law ("The fact is that the number of the officials and the quantity of the work are not related to each other at all"), it would appear that a more complex society and a vastly more wealthy one, as it grew, acquired government services and bureaucracy at rates far faster than the growth of either output or population. By this measure we must consider growth of government a "superior good." The richer we were, the more government we purchased. Determining and managing the expenditures requires some thought and originality, however; and the huge government economy requires entrepreneurship. Even if one considers all government to be a deadweight loss, it still must be true that some expenditures are less wasteful and destructive than others, that some decisions are less damaging to the commonwealth than others. To some extent the more desirable decisions can be made by the "democracy"—by elected officials. Realistically, however, most of the decision making must be done by appointed officials. Needs change, and there must be new programs to meet them. One can assume, after the Reagan years, that no force within the American political system can or will actually reduce government's fiscal size absolutely, perhaps not even proportionately.

The U.S. government is not a planning system, but existing bureaus can plan their own futures, and do. In fact, because there is no overall plan, five-year or other, new programs are constantly evolving in the bureaus and being advocated.

Bureaucracy is normally a way of reducing the perfect routine the recorded evidences of real-world activity. The origins of bureaucracy are record keeping (the scribe seated at the monarch's feet), and the activity of bureaucracy in its perfected form is perfect routine—nothing out of place, nothing unusual. Record keeping means system. As Max Weber wrote, if left to their own devices, bureaucratic procedures and organization produce outcomes that are utterly conservative and stultifying. Change can come by external force, successfully applied.[6] But it comes also from new ventures, innovations launched from within the bureaucracy itself. The modern activist American agencies, conceiving programs and pushing them on Capitol Hill, are examples of such new ventures. Before the New Deal such activity was not common, apart from such well-established activist bureaus as the Corps of Engineers.

One might imagine the bureaucratic ideal as a world of silent clerks, and that the public would object to new government initiatives coming from the servants—from those who are not elected—but in fact one rarely hears of objections to bureaucratic initiative. IRS form W4, introduced early in 1987, is an outstanding exception.

Oddly enough, probably more constraint on bureaucratic entrepreneurship comes from inside the bureaucracy than from outside. Partly the routine of bureaucracy militates against innovation from within. But more important is the battle for budget shares, how to divide the (temporarily) fixed pool of resources from which all the bureaucrats must draw. The history of bureaucratic entre-preneurship shows that bureaucratic innovation faces the organizational equiv-alents of competition in the marketplace for the innovating private entrepreneur.

Should It Be Encouraged?

There is a fundamental objection to originality, to public sector entrepreneur-ship from the theoretical side, and that is simply that no one in public service can know what the public interest is. Any independent action by a public servant in the public interest is only his or her own vision, and is almost bound to be at least partly wrong and possibly destructive, too. The classic statement in this regard was by Adam Smith himself. In *The Wealth of Nations* Smith set out the doctrine of the free market, made to serve the common good insensibly by the famous invisible hand: public interest was the sum of private interest, privately determined. He stated flatly his opinion of government influence, regulation, or any other supersession of the private contract: "I have never known much good done by those who affected to trade for the public good. It is an affectation . . . not very common among merchants, and very few words need be employed in dissuading them from it . . . That statesman who should attempt to direct people in what manner they ought to employ their capitals . . . [assumes] an authority which could safely be trusted to no council or senate whatever, and which would nowhere be so dangerous as in the hands of a man who had folly and presumption enough to fancy himself fit to exercise it" (Smith 1937, p. 423).

But as I have shown, our private sector—either by taxes or inflation—has already surrendered a huge flow of resources to the public sector. So far as anyone knows, this loss of control is now irreversible. While public sector allocative activity may be broadly directed by democratic processes (and there-fore, we must assume, be in the general interest no matter what), there really is no way under modern conditions, in an economy the size of the United States', for the public allocation to be closely supervised (or even comprehended) in any detail by our elected representatives. Nor can the benefits of policy be fed back into the fiscal mechanism effectively other than by advocacy and/or change (innovation) from within the government sector itself. Pharaoh really cannot tell the scribe what to do in operations on so vast a scale, and so must consider turning the scribe loose, at least to a large extent, because it will make the public sector more productive than it would be if he waited for orders from above, orders which really cannot come in any detail.

From the narrowest view (Kirzner 1973) to the broadest (Schumpeter 1939, vol. 1, chap. 3), it is held that entrepreneurship makes the economic system more efficient than it otherwise would be. The Kirzner view of entrepreneurship is essentially an arbitrage function. The Schumpeterian entrepreneur operates on an altogether more heroic scale, changing the structure of the economy, perhaps even the nature of the social system and the course of history, by introducing into the stream of economic life new ideas, products, services, innovations whose success the entrepreneur alone foresaw. The results, historically, were new firms, new industries, changes in structure, in employment, in location—perhaps a fairly general reordering of the flow of resources in much of total economic life. Innovating entrepreneurs who operated on a vast scale—Andrew Carnegie, Henry Ford, Ray Kroc—achieved such results.

In both conceptions of the entrepreneurial role output expands, and, of course, in the Schumpeterian conception changes in the economy's development path have occurred: the future has been changed. *Necessary* economic improvement is based on the axiom commonly held by economists that what is warranted by the market is per se superior. This is so in theory even if, say, damaging externalities (such as pollution) result. This rule-of-thumb judgment has been attacked for its superficiality by Edward Mishan (1969), who argues that "more is better" is really just a peculiar value judgment of economists that ignores other and perhaps more important measures of social efficiency or desirability; for example, less output with less pollution. The trade-off of cleaner air for a smaller physical output may be the socially preferable option.

Indeed, through extensive use of regulation, society has long acknowledged that purely economic efficiency is most likely not attainable. The regulation is meant to alter or to abolish the decision of the marketplace (on the general nature and limits of modern American regulation, see Hughes 1976b, especially pp. 47–49). Otherwise, regulation would be superfluous. Complete freedom for the entrepreneur is not and never was seen as a desirable social objective in itself.

In fact, entrepreneurial history has always embraced the social-control mechanism imposed by the society around the innovator through its institutions of social constraint: governments at various levels, religion, the common law, the custom of the manor, or whatever. The U.S. Supreme Court's rapping the knuckles of Pierpont Morgan, Edward Harriman, and James J. Hill in the Northern Securities case (1903) illustrates this kind of conflict at the commanding heights. Your average list of weekend drug busts or raids on local horse parlors by the police illustrates the other extreme. The creative or output-inducing role of the entrepreneur has mainly been, and is, a restrained force. In the long run we can see this as positive, because the social-control restraints actually assured the legality of the entrepreneurial role. That made it more effective in the long run: what was both legal and socially acceptable was not necessarily threatened by social and political changes yet to come.

The Public Sector Entrepreneurial Role in the Abstract

We know something about the typical motivations of individuals who become public sector entrepreneurs. But what about corporate ambition? One must know a bureau's objective function—what it collectively strives to achieve, what its maximum expectations might be under its legislative charter, its warrant. There are always limits. Every bureaucracy operates within its constitution. The legal and cultural benchmarks are the boundaries of action; they both direct and deflect it, something like a bobsled run, and those boundaries can be very different. Adolf Eichmann and Colonel Bendetsen organized systems to transport illegally interned civilians in World War II, and Heinrich Himmler and Dillon Myer organized the camps to put them in. One system turned into mass murder, and the other into the War Relocation Authority.[7] The difference was not what they were doing initially but where they were heading, and that was generally determined outside the bureaus involved, even though innovation within the bureaus necessarily had consequences not foreseen in the original warrants. The conception of "indefinite leave" in the WRA camps, whereby the inmates were "relocated" east of the Rockies yet remained in the control of the WRA as to behavior, location, and kind of employment, a sort of parole, was the brainchild of Dillon Myer himself. It was unprecedented in American history as a control of civilian citizens charged with no crimes. It was an innovation, worthy in the eyes of contemporaries in 1952, astonishing now in its ubiquitous illegality (Drinnon 1987, pp. 50–54).

A bureau has a general mission; its continued existence depends, except in the most mindless government structures, on fulfillment of that mission. As conditions change over time, the mission and its procedures must change too, or else the bureau will become dysfunctional (not an unknown occurrence). All this takes place within the established general legal and cultural limitations. Each bureau proceeds on its own way, and innovation allows the bureau to stay abreast of new demands. Changes in the bureau's overall mission, including (occasionally) its abolition, come from the outside. It is rare indeed for a bureau's mission to change because of internal innovation. One does not expect the Department of Commerce to take the Agriculture Department's functions, unless a change is introduced from higher authority.[8] Ordinarily, then, more efficient fulfillment of a bureau's tasks is what we can hope for from internal innovation: entrepreneurship.

The possibilities of public sector entrepreneurship come from both the elective and the appointive parts of the government.

Here I have followed Weber's taxonomy in part. Weber's bureaucrat is *always* appointed, never elected (Miller 1963, p. 68). But I employ a taxonomy in which the appointive personnel are divided into two groups, those appointed by elected authority and those brought aboard on the basis of merit, by tests. The "big swinger" bureaucrats—department secretaries, administrators, commissioners, and the like—are often appointed by elected government officials specifically to shake things up and to launch new initiatives. Although such appointees fall into Weber's appointive category, they clearly have a different attitude toward new ventures than do the "standard" bureaucrats, bound by rules, codes, seniority, and a careerism based on careful conformity to the punctilio of their own bureaus.

Despite all safeguards against outbursts of originality among the bureaucrats, however, pressure for innovation inevitably builds up, and public sector entrepreneurship of some sort must exist, either at the nearly trivial or at the Schumpeterian levels of action, because instructions of modern governments can never be complete. As Lewis (1980) put it: "Legislators, whether they like it or not, tend, like the rest of us, to defer to the possessors of . . . expertise . . . Despite displays of individual virtuosity among elected representatives, the balance of responsibility for initiating policy has long since shifted to professionalized bureaucrats" (p. 6).

There is no way to direct from the top every decision in every part of the bureaucracy by rules alone. So judgment is required, and that judgment is an innovation—something new introduced into the stream of bureaucratic life.

For the bureaucracy, programs, budgets, and procedures are the commodities, the market, and the delivery technologies in the vending of bureaucratic goods. The programs are created to gain budget shares, just as private entrepreneurs create new goods to gain market shares. Opposing bureaus contend for programs and budget shares just as do rival business firms in the private sector. Whereas the consumer (and his income and tastes) determines the size and shares of the private market, elected officials (Congress, for example) determine aggregate markets for bureaucratic goods by taxing and spending, and market shares of separate bureaus through the normal budget processes, including hearings.

Originally this analysis was developed by William Niskanen (1971, p. 3, chaps. 5–8).[9] The bureaus are seen as expenditure-maximizing firms in mutual rivalry for budget shares. The budget itself is the total market for bureaucratic goods and services, and the elected representatives of the people are their surrogates, the consumers—those who actually make the decisions whether to buy. They decide how the bureaus will share the budget. Hence, the bureaucratic entrepreneurs must sell their new ideas to the Congress or to the administration. The general public, whose agents are in Congress and the administration, have almost no direct impact on either side of this market.

There is another way in which the public can have an input, however—through their votes—so sometimes the public entrepreneurs must address the public directly, play to the galleries. A common ploy is to appeal to the electorate over the heads of both the higher-up hierarchical strata and the elected government. The theme of such appeals, as Lewis (1980) phrases it, is selflessness: "A public entrepreneur must never appear to be anything but a seeker of the public good, surrounded and thwarted by lesser men who are interested in their political careers or in 'making it' in the traditional bureaucracy by going along" (p. 85). This refers to the remarkable adroitness of Hyman Rickover in that regard. The appeal to the galleries, if successful, motivates the elected government and removes some of the stench of arbitrary power that must come from public sector innovations activated without the blessings of the democratic process.

Even in a liberal democracy there can never be total absence of arbitrary power exercised by public servants. On a daily basis the need for decision is immediate and the directing power and authority are remote. In modern Big Government many layers of officialdom typically separate decision makers from elected officials who have the powers of oversight, but powers that become increasingly weak as the processes to be supervised multiply in complexity and sheer size. The worst kind of administrative organization separates power from responsibility, and large-scale bureaucratic organizations tend to be models of such imperfection.

With the huge budgets of modern governments the imperfection poses a great dilemma: those who understand the day-to-day workings of the government apparatus do not determine the budgets. Those who determine the budgets cannot know how the expenditures and/or regulations actually affect society. But that is a "micro" problem. There is a larger problem: the determination of policy priorities for the entire government.

In part the national elections are used to advocate policy and to nudge along the bureaucracy, the "permanent government" whose control so vexed President Kennedy when he tried to motivate it (Schlesinger 1965, pp. 679–686). Such a cumbersome instrument cannot determine more than rough outlines at the top. Nor can the representative elected politician, whose main focus, necessarily, is reelection. The detailed expertise of government lies in the part that is not elected, in the bureaus, boards, commissions, administrations, offices— the network of parts and the people in them. And here lies the problem: motivation. There are no profits to be maximized as a measure of efficient effort, and the responsibility and power are both diluted again and again down through the strata of the bureaucracy. Normal career rewards tend to be for strict adherence to the behavioral patterns over time, promotion mainly for longevity of faithful service. In this dimension the motivation of any extraordinary performance is something of a mystery, and major innovation even more so. All of which highlights Rostow's question.

Two Careers

Now I want to introduce two public sector entrepreneurs who will provide some relevant facts to work with. Mary Switzer's career gives us the development of the modern welfare state. The public career of Marriner Eccles gives us the origins of modern public policy in the areas of countercyclical fiscal actions (taxing and spending), and present-day central banking. Mary Switzer's career was made from the humble materials of a graded federal civil servant who worked her way through the ranks. Eccles represents the "big swinger" bureaucrat, the man brought in by elected authority at the top, explicitly to create major innovation. Consider their careers in brief outline (the biographical facts and quotations, except as otherwise noted, are from Hughes 1986; I am indebted to Berkowitz and to Arrington for permission to use their unpublished materials).

Mary Elizabeth Switzer (1900–1971) was largely an *éminence grise* during the formative years of the modern American welfare state. What is known of her achievement is extraordinary. What is not known could well be even more so, since she long strived to maintain a low profile, and our recognition of her achievement today exists partly in spite of her. She served in the federal civil service for 48 years, entering in 1922 when Harding was in the White House. By her own estimate she was an "operator," and for many years devoted her talents to influencing top officials with expertise they did not have. When she was appointed administrator of HEW's new Social and Rehabilitation Services in 1967, she held the highest appointment any woman had ever achieved in the regular civil service. She had been made director of the Office of Vocational Rehabilitation in 1950, and she became the major force in the rehabilitation movement in this country. Her work in rehabilitation of the disabled won her the Lasker Award for international achievement in medicine in 1960. Her citation on that occasion called her "the prime architect of workable rehabilitation service for the nation's physically handicapped." Her work in rehabilitation was taken up by both the Eisenhower and Kennedy administrations, and then in various Great Society programs, as the core of social policy. She arrived at the apex of her career in government service just in time to be greeted by the flaming cities of 1968, and then the Nixon administration. She reached the mandatory retirement age of 70 in 1970 and was replaced by a Nixon political appointee. Her final and short-lived effort to make the American welfare system into a force for social progress failed, as have similar efforts in every administration since her death.

Switzer served first in the treasury (as an economist) in 1922, and remained there in various capacities until 1939. She enjoyed the routine life of a single woman in the Washington social and cultural scene without much drama. She had the dismal job, among others, of clipping newspapers for the discernment of Mellon and Hoover from 1929 to 1932. With the coming of the New Deal her life changed, especially when Josephine Roche was brought in from Colorado by FDR as assistant secretary of the treasury. Roche was a strong feminist and an activist. She took over the Public Health Service (then part of the treasury), and Switzer joined Roche in time to make a national survey of disability, which they hoped (in vain) would influence the social security legislation.[10]

In 1939 Switzer transferred in a departmental reorganization to the Federal Security Administration. That was to be her bureaucratic home (apart from a stint with Paul McNutt in the War Manpower Commission) until she took over Vocational Rehabilitation in 1950.

A most intriguing part of her lifetime achievement came simply from her ability to draft legislation for others; for example, the National Institutes of Health in 1948 and the National Science Foundation in 1950 (when she sand-bagged Truman's attempt to have the agency run by political appointees in the manner of the ICC). Her clandestine skills may be illustrated by the National Institute for Mental Health (1949). Switzer had served on the Board of Visitors of St. Elizabeth's Hospital. In that capacity she met the Menninger brothers and then became a trustee of the Menninger Foundation. When Congressman J. Percy Priest of Tennessee asked the surgeon general for information about mental health, Priest fell into Switzer's grasp and, as Edward Berkowitz wrote in his study (1976) of Switzer, was "presented" with a complete bill Switzer had already written "with the help of the National Committee for Mental Hygiene and the Menninger brothers" (Hughes 1986, pp. 477–478). The National Institute for Mental Health resulted (as well as graffiti urging riders of New York subways to "Fight Mental Health"). The bill went through Congress almost silently.

Switzer collaborated with Roche to create national health insurance and national disability insurance programs, both of which campaigns were unsuc-cessful against powerful opposing forces. Switzer was a virtuoso bureaucratic empire builder and accumulated enemies as well as admirers. She demonstrated two powerful "objective functions." She was an inveterate do-gooder, and pursued a lifelong determination to improve the lives of the poor. A second constant in her motivation was fairly odd for a career bureaucrat: she fought against centralization of power, especially by the Social Security Administration.[11] So far as one can discern, her concern here was owing to her experience in World War II, when germ warfare capability was developed within her old bureau, the Public Health Service. She wrote of her wartime experience: "I resist every increase in the centralization of power over the human soul. In the winning of the war, I don't want to lose the ability to break up central power even at the expense of local inefficiency and scandal" (Hughes 1986, p. 477).

These motivations shaped her techniques of rehabilitation: she worked for maximum local and state agency cooperation with her federal bureau. Her devotion to decentralized authority was reflected dramatically in the Hill-Burton Hospital Construction Act of 1946, in which emphasis was placed on local needs. The Federal Hospital Council, which approved designs and awarded federal subsidies, came from legislation Switzer wrote giving the council real power (Truman wanted it to be only a front), staffing it with medical and hospital professionals. Moreover, Switzer selected the council members herself. The new federally financed hospitals reflected local needs and desires, not just federal criteria. Switzer also used the federal subsidy to remove physical barriers to the handicapped. In connection with the National Commission on Architectural Barriers to Rehabilitation of the Handicapped, she upbraided a convention of architects, "It's your fault [that] there are barriers in hospitals, schools, libraries and court houses" (Hughes 1986, p. 498). The commission's report went to LBJ in 1968, and its consequences may be seen today in every parking lot or building that was subsidized by federal funds.

For an up-from-the-ranks federal civil servant, Switzer's career was a singular achievement, and if one agrees with her motivations and beliefs, caused some of the federal billions to be spent more wisely and more humanely than would otherwise have been the case.

Marriner Stoddard Eccles (1890–1977) is my example of an innovative top-level bureaucratic appointee. To approve of Eccles one must think that countercyclical fiscal policy *could* be a good thing, and that the Federal Reserve System has improved the economy's performance over time. Already a millionaire, and the innovator of the multibank holding company when he joined the New Deal in 1934 as assistant secretary of the treasury, Eccles went to Washington determined to change the American conception of the government's fiscal responsibilities. Eccles had worked out the element of macroeconomics on his own out in Utah sometime between the 1929 crash and his testimony before the lame-duck Senate Finance Committee hearings in February 1933 (Hughes 1986, pp. 518–522).[12] In those hearings Eccles laid out in detail a plan of what the New Deal would in fact come to be.

But not in all ways. Although Eccles wanted compensatory federal finance, the cyclically balanced budget, his ceaseless advocacy of it bore little fruit. Apart from his (marginal) place in the history of economic thought, his missionary efforts with compensatory budget making must be counted as a well-intentioned failure. He wrote of it in 1951, five years before Cary Brown's (1956) famous article in the *American Economic Review* appeared with the same conclusions. Eccles wrote: "We were never able to take up the large amount of slack that existed throughout the economy. We did not take it up because we did not spend enough . . . We were told that the doctrine of compensatory economy was a failure—despite the fact that it had never been tried, except to a mild degree" (Hughes 1986, p. 505).

The entire subject came to be labeled Keynesian economics, after economists had learned their macroeconomics from Keynes (1936). Eccles never read *The General Theory of Employment, Interest, and Money,* and presumably Keynes read little of Eccles' writings on theory. It is unlikely that any federal administration ever took the doctrine of compensatory federal finance seriously (Nixon notwithstanding), apart from the short episode of "fine tuning" under Walther Heller's fescue along the New Frontier.

Eccles was also responsible for the revolution in home mortgage finance in the New Deal's Federal Housing Act (and the subsequent establishment of FNMA, the secondary mortgage market). The basic idea in the FHA was a long payoff period, with small down payments and regular amortization. Before the FHA the opposite conditions generally prevailed, and the secondary market was virtually nonexistent. The FHA ideas remain central in the national mortgage market today, although the FHA itself fell victim to benign neglect in the Reagan years (it was targeted for early oblivion by the neoconservatives when they came to power in 1980).

Most lasting of all was the "Eccles bank bill," the Bank Act of 1935. In that legislation Eccles showed his banker's hand (by all accounts a truly masterful one) and reorganized the Federal Reserve System, shifting its power from New York to the board of governors in Washington, and redefining the monetary base of the American banking system. All of these Eccles banking reforms remain more than half a century later, although the final legislation was less of a thoroughgoing revolution than Eccles wanted (he wanted a single form of federally chartered commercial banking). From 1936 to 1951 Eccles was the guiding light of the Federal Reserve, chairman of the board of governors from 1936 to 1948. He also struggled with Henry Morgenthau during most of the New Deal years for the privilege of FDR's ear on economic policy. Eccles played a leading role in World War II finance, of course, and also in the establishment of the Bretton Woods Institutions, the International Monetary Fund, and the World Bank.

Also lasting until now has been the Fed's policy-making independence. That (formal) independence was reasserted dramatically by Eccles in 1951 when he engaged Harry Truman and treasury secretary John Snyder in a splashy battle over financing the Korean War. Eccles won and the "accord" of 1951 liberated the Federal Reserve system from its "Babylonian captivity"—the obligation existing since 1942 to "pet" (support) the prices of government bonds. That victory was also the occasion for Eccles to exit from the federal government. Although Eccles and Truman did not part company amicably, in later years (1982) a grateful bureaucracy would rename the Federal Reserve Building in Washington, D.C., after Marriner Eccles.

The Lewis Stages

Let us now compare these two careers with the results of Eugene Lewis' (1980) study of the careers of J. Edgar Hoover, Hyman Rickover, and Robert Moses.

After writing a strong caveat on the dangers of generalization from a small sample, Lewis derived a loose "life-cycle" model, in three stages comprising eight subdivisions, from the careers of his three public entrepreneurs. Stage one: (1) recruitment and imperfect socialization to organizational life; (2) mentorship and internalization of appropriate organizational goals. Stage two: (1) the entrepreneurial leap; (2) creation of an apolitical shield; (3) the struggle for autonomy. Stage three: (1) the reduction of uncertainty in task environments; (2) spanning boundaries for purposes of domain expansion; (3) institutionalization and the problems of ultrastability.

Not surprisingly, Lewis found that quite early in their careers his entrepreneurs became internal rebels, chafing to change and reform their bureaus (stage one). Since the bureaucratic existence (to avoid being aborted) involves learning the bureau's elaborate structure and behavior code, the acquisition of a mentor is a necessary substitute for the "early business experience" one finds in histories of private entrepreneurs. In stage two the public sector innovator emerges from the faceless mass. The "entrepreneurial leap" cuts the public sector innovator irrevocably loose from the quiet comfort of the established bureau. His or her entrepreneurial creation must now be buffered from internal competitors, and this is achieved by the creation of an apolitical shield, by playing to the galleries outside the bureaucracy, gaining support from the public and interested parties in the elected government. The entrepreneur, at this stage, must demonstrate that his or her motives are pure, that only the broad public interest motivates his or her innovative actions. Succeeding in this, the entrepreneur must build a base of fiscal and political support separated from the rest of the bureaucracy.

Stage three brings out the demonstrated power and permanence of the entrepreneurial achievement as it moves, along with its entrepreneur, toward old age
and potential stasis. The successful public entrepreneur's new domain is rigor-
ously cleansed of conflicting tasks. He or she then, in a final expansion period,
attempts to protect the empire by expanding into cognate territories. Rickover's
men were placed directly in defense plants. Hoover began to train the nation's
municipal police forces at the FBI academy.

The end state in the Lewis scheme is, alas, another mature bureau, conservative, unbending. Hoover died in the saddle. Rickover was upended by the
DOD "whiz kids" and systems analysis (which denied the need for an all-
nuclear navy). Robert Moses had his ultimate (and oft-used) strategic move, the
threat of resignation, accepted effortlessly by another government entrepreneur
of boundless ambition and prospects, Nelson Rockefeller.

Lewis' life-cycle model is an interesting beginning, worth trying on our own
two bureaucratic entrepreneurs. Switzer fits it best, but not too closely. She
showed no signs of internal rebellion in her stage one. She was a regular at the
salon of Justice Brandeis in Washington, and as a result had a necessarily
restricted vision of government. Her vision was changed abruptly when the
sensational Josephine Roche came to Washington after an unsuccessful run for
governor of Colorado on the Democratic ticket. Switzer did have an early
mentor, Tracy Copp, a professional in the government's small vocational rehabilitation program (under an act of 1920 to benefit veterans of World War I).
Copp seems to have made rehabilitation possibilities a live subject for Switzer.
Later, in World War II, it was Howard Rusk and others in wartime rehabilitation medicine who fired Switzer's imagination.

I cannot identify Switzer's definitive entrepreneurial leap. She built her career
in small increments, but by the mid- and late 1940s, in the Hill-Burton Act and
the legislation for the National Institutes of Health, her powers were apparent
and were used adroitly. When she took over the Office of Vocational Rehabilitation (OVR) in 1950, her entrepreneurial skills were on the loose. She became
an impressive master of steps (2) and (3) of stage two—the creation of medical
and then vocational and social rehabilitation as regions of public policy beyond
politics. In her empire building, her co-opting of local authorities, the use of her
friendships with Rusk, Nelson Rockefeller, Senators Claude Pepper and Lister
Hill, and others, her OVR became a real sacred cow in the Washington bureaucracy. Like J. Edgar Hoover, Mary Switzer got what she wanted from
Congress.

In her stage three Switzer was actively rationalizing the operations of her
rehabilitation bureaucracy when opportunity—actually disaster—came knock-
ing and she opened the door. From 1968 her career was usurped by larger
events, and she failed in the great task of making HEW's welfare operation

a success through rehabilitation. HEW secretary John Gardner had said of Switzer that "she will make history for all of us" (Hughes 1986, p. 497). Martha Derthick (1975) wrote of Switzer's final elevation, "Leaders of [HEW] thought that if anyone could help the welfare poor get to work and show Congress that HEW was trying, Mary Switzer could" (p. 15). They were wrong. History took over in 1968, and Mary Switzer's career was sent to its famous dustbin.

Eccles, as a senior person brought in to create innovation, of course missed all of stage one. In stage two his entrepreneurial leaps were multiple and almost immediate upon his arrival in the nation's capital. He did try to build a buffering apolitical shield for his reorganized Federal Reserve System. In the banking community he already had a powerful built-in clientele outside the government. They owned the system's stock, and it was only half paid up. When Eccles had to struggle for his agency's autonomy, the drama was high indeed, since he had to achieve its independence by facing down the president of the United States. That struggle ended the public career of Marriner Eccles, so there was no real stage three for him in government.

As a mature bureaucracy in its own stage three the Fed, in successive administrations, has proved to be viable indeed, however. Its periodic changes of management (the appointments of new board chairmen) by the president himself, along with new board members, with the advice and consent of the Senate, have kept the Fed's leadership relatively fresh. The district banks, actually parts of the private sector, keep an apolitical shield intact. The Fed, as a result, has proved to be virtually invulnerable to its enemies. But it is not strictly a government bureaucracy (except at the board): it is a remarkable mixture of public and private interests.

Individual Motivation

Why would an individual "step out of line" and become, potentially, an entrepreneur in the public sector? The determinist social scientist might prefer a well-ordered universe in which bureaucratic motivation could be attributed to something systematic: ideological development, economic change, political transmogrifications—something. Arbitrary power should not be a loose cannon on the deck unconnected to identifiable "interests" of some sort. Ideally, public servants should act strictly in the public interest. But what is the public interest? Unless it is asserted by superior authority (and believed), no one can really know.

Studies of individual public sector entrepreneurs in this country reveal innovations in the public sector motivated mainly by private character and private beliefs. This is hardly surprising in a nation without political parties devoted to serious ideology. Nor, probably, would we want it any other way. The whiff of ideology in the Reagan administration was widely regarded as a scandal. We would prefer, it seems, that the public timberlands be cut clean for traditional reasons of greed and corruption than that a Jim Watt warrants it because he believes that the timber should be sold off at auction to let ''market forces'' (the best of all possible worlds to Watt) determine the future extent of forests on the public lands.

Eugene Lewis' three public sector entrepreneurs were actually politically idiosyncratic.

J. Edgar Hoover was an information systems builder mainly, a man devoted to organizational details with only a few informationless political beliefs to guide him. A determinist he was not, and he shied away from organized crime and the drug traffic, when they came, because they might upset the apple cart he already had built.

Hyman Rickover was a man who had a vision of himself and of nuclear reactors in naval vessels, and he fought for that vision against the entrenched hierarchy of his own bureau, the U.S. Navy. Rickover succeeded only by ''playing to the gallery'' in the grand manner. Only Congress, in fact, got him his final promotions and kept him safe from the retirement ax.

Robert Moses was a strange megalomaniac, much akin to the Hollywood moguls of the 1930s, a seeker after public honors and headlines. He was a man of amazing vanity, and he sought praise and publicity. He used the power of eminent domain to destroy more private property than possibly any other single person in American history. Any would-be Marxist revolutionary could well use Robert Moses as a paradigm. Yet he was a conservative politically, and worked equally well with all parties in power.

Hoover the bureaucrat made an empire from the scraps of the 1917 Lever Food Act. Rickover pursued his vision in a navy that was being dismantled after World War II. And Moses, within his public service companies, built vast road transport systems largely designed to exclude buses and trucks. All three were men of highly uncongenial personality, and all three were largely indifferent to serious political commitment. They functioned equally well no matter who was in power. They were driven by internal forces of ego and personality, not by known public needs.

Switzer and Eccles were also apolitical and opportunistic. Switzer operated equally well with Republicans or Democrats in power, and Eccles, the famous New Dealer, was actually a lifelong registered Republican. In fact in the 1952 primary election in Utah he campaigned for the GOP seat in the U.S. Senate (it seemed that the Republicans could not forgive the New Deal stain, even on one of their own).

What Can We Know?

It is unsatisfactory to generalize from so little evidence, because we cannot do it with confidence. We need to know more about public sector entrepreneurs, to produce more case studies. Inevitably, however, the question arises: At what point can we generalize from such evidence? How useful are individual case studies? The answer, alas, is that it depends on the art, originality, or luck of the person utilizing them.

If we now read the summaries of Arthur Cole and others of the old Harvard Center's studies of entrepreneurship, would we know more than we would have by reading only Schumpeter's original treatments of the entrepreneurial role in capitalist economic development? If you say yes, be advised that modern studies of entrepreneurship tend very nearly to ignore the Harvard Center and its findings.[13]

Theory is supposed to be *about something,* and a general theory of public entrepreneurship should be informed about what those phenomena tend to be *im Wirklichkeit.* Niskanen's brilliant and original analysis of the economics of bureaus came from working in them and studying them, not from airy theorizing around ideal states of being. The case study is fact, and there must be facts for knowledge to be generated. The newly measured (thanks to the IRAS satellite) universe in the infrared spectrum, perhaps 50 times the mass of the universe visible in the rest of the spectrum, is a body of fact that will give rise to new theories about structure, history, and change in astrophysics. In the case of public sector entrepreneurs, we need many case studies to form a body of information—a "data base." Like the astronomical phenomena in the infrared spectrum, unseen before 1986, public sector entrepreneurship exists. We simply have not studied it extensively. Our problem was not lack of instruments for the study, but lack of interest.

Options

Our bureaucratic structure has its own history, like the regulatory system, rooted in our own national development. It suits us in a peculiar way. It is democratic in that it is a meritocracy, and access to jobs in it is, in theory, open to anyone. There are various barriers in the form of credentials. But below the appointive positions it is reckoned to be a great improvement over the old spoils system. It is not, however, like a European or Japanese bureaucracy, based on educational elitism. In a society as complex as ours, with so many institutions issuing credentials, the idea of an elite set of American bureaucrats is absurd. The Japanese bureaucracy, perhaps admired currently because of that economy's recent successes, would be unthinkable here (see Vogel 1979, especially chap. 4; also Freedeman 1974). Their method of preserving motivation, dynamism, and fresh ideas is based not only on educational elitism, but on a self-effacing behavior that would be hard to imagine in this society. What we most probably must work with is some variation on what we already have.

Our bureaucracy is congenial, and runs on principles which we do not find foreign, and not surprisingly, therefore, we have a history of public sector entrepreneurship. It could be suppressed, left alone, or encouraged. It is clear that nothing need or should be done to *encourage* innovation among top-level appointees. There will be no lack of people like Marriner Eccles who desire a public service career, either for the change of pace or explicitly to make a contribution for other motives, running through the entire spectrum from altruism to straight greed. The regular turnover of elected political leaders with powers of appointment keeps the door open to such potential innovators, who usually represent well-defined interests or political viewpoints on public policy issues. Their appointments represent the best of all possible worlds in a liberal democracy: choices made by the electorate, however obnoxious. A Jim Watt at the Interior Department may have shocked some, but his viewpoint was the legitimate reflection of a major (or at least vocal) segment of Reagan's supporters.

The issues are different lower down, where entry is by examination and tenure is assured by a combination of longevity and good behavior. The great mass of our bureaucratic expertise is at these lower levels. Is it a potential menace best left strictly harnessed, or even buried in routine, or should ways be found to liberate it?

I have already given my arguments why innovative ideas in the bureaucracy should not be suppressed. In any case, it is unrealistic to suppose that new departures will not be needed in the future. And it is equally unrealistic to suppose that elected representatives, except in the rarest circumstances, can have either the time or the expertise to grasp the details of administration, especially in a world of constant change. The public sector is so vast and so intimately involved in the private sector's own productive efforts that lack of effective responses to new realities is more than an irritant; it can be economically debilitating or even disastrous. The ICC's century-long career of rate setting is often given as the outstanding example of the debilitating consequences of unchanging routine in the face of changing realities (see Hemenway 1973). For an example of bureaucratic disaster consider the Teton Dam, a needless piece of boondoggling by the Corps of Engineers and local construction companies, whose bursting wiped away more than a century of pioneering achievements in the upper Snake River Valley (Rose-Ackerman 1978).

Left alone, the bureaus are always in danger of partial stultification in their own rules and procedures. Their tendency to reject innovation as "trouble making" (and to punish the whistle-blowing miscreants) is too well known to require comment. There is of course the cynical view that minimal government is always the best, and since we cannot reduce the size of what we have, it is best left alone so it will nullify itself by its own inexorable tendencies to stasis. Thus a policy of hands-off is the next best thing to outright abolition. It seems to me, however, that the stakes are too large to leave to chance the solutions of problems of changing needs. The cost of a huge, inert bureaucracy is too high a price to pay just to keep it out of trouble.

A third option is actively to encourage development of public service entrepreneurs from the ranks of the regular civil service. It is not obvious how this could best be done. As I pointed out earlier, Niskanen proposed competition between bureaus for tasks as a way to motivate innovation. What is needed is career protection for those with new ideas. In the free market openings for new initiatives are always there, with rewards and punishments for success or failure dealt out impersonally, measured in dollars and cents. But in the bureaucracy no such impersonal machinery rations out innovation, because there is no profit measure—a problem Niskanen's competitive procedures can partly solve: losers in the competition lose their budget shares. But I think there is a danger that his ingenious scheme to create profit incentives for top officials might well create a bureaucratic Model T, with a frozen "product" design engendering higher profits year after year through cost cutting. One would want the product itself to change as needs change (see Niskanen 1971, pp. 201–209). Also, losers in the marketplace who are removed from control of resources can hope to fight another day. Entry is simple and unrestricted. What happens to public servants who take a chance and fail, whose ideas are rejected and whose bureaus lose funding? Are their careers to end there? The career penalty for failure by a civil servant may be so high as to deflect all but the most daring from pursuing individual initiatives. If lifetime exile from the business world were the price for failure of entrepreneurial initiatives, there would be very few entrepreneurs in the private sector.

One can immediately see a bureaucratic solution to a bureaucratic problem: create an interagency commission on innovation, which would receive suggestions and protect (when necessary) the identities of the internal rebels who made the suggestions. Rewards too could be recommended by such an agency. This plan would have the virtue of being identifiable; responsibility and some power could be placed in focus and could be monitored by elected officials. Such an agency might fall prey to traditional bureaucratic ailments, however, including excess size. A system of ombudsmen, or inspectors general, could be provided, but that implies even more bureaucratic growth.[14]

Private sector experience may provide an escape from the bureaucratic growth problem. Peters and Waterman (1982) studied various solutions to such problems pursued by our most successfully competitive large private firms. Such firms also must overcome productivity-strangling bureaucratic tendencies and must seek out ways to motivate innovation. Recall that Henry Ford tried to do it by firing people, Mao by harassing his officials from office (and some from this life altogether). Our best private firms do not pursue such drastic tactics, but have developed ways to encourage small, off-track, "skunk works" experimentation. These operations are highly informal but regularly supported "idea factories." Some measure of failure is expected as reasonable, but the ideas are tried out. Employees can transfer in and out to work on their own ideas. These are miniresearch centers, without all the expense and formality. Even in cases where large and formal R&D labs are normal parts of the firms, arrangements tend to be made for formal work and free exchanges of new ideas in the early stages of development. Again, potential profit is the permanent measure of value that is lacking in similar small-scale bureaucratic establishments.

Such mini-institutes could easily be made a regular part of any major agency. Niskanen's competitive bureaus would necessarily be smaller than our typical monopoly-service bureaus, and any associated innovation groups would be sized accordingly. It is not that our bureaucracy never experiments. The problem is the lack of a regular structure accessible to the mass of civil servants whose business would be to "manufacture" ideas on the one hand; and on the other, development of well-tested nonmarket criteria to propagate innovations into government as they are warranted by new conditions. Evaluation of new ideas in the bureaus must still be lodged in the hierarchy, but at least regular platforms for innovative ideas would exist for the rank and file beyond the suggestion box, and would not be ritually considered to be disruptive troublemaking.

Such departures may be the best answer to Rostow's question, at least in the career bureaucracy, if there are to be regular channels for new ideas "from below," advanced without the threat of career-ending punishments for those who can see improvements in allocation of publicly controlled resources, or even policy changes, and want to develop their ideas through.[15]

No force can stop the Marriner Eccles kind of governmental entrepreneuring. The Mary Switzers of the civil service are another matter. In particular, the stage of the "entrepreneurial leap" should find some regular provision in the bureaus.

I must confess a premature feeling of futility and defeat at even the mention of this chapter's subject. But the stakes are enormous.

If innovation is the lifeblood of the private economy, why should it be less important in a public sector the size of ours? If the business world should engage, as it does, in attempts to produce hothouses for private sector entrepreneurship with informal "skunk works" and business incubators[16] by the score, which involve governments and universities as well, why should the public sector be without any systematic efforts to promote innovation and entrepreneurship among the millions of public sector employees? Why should the expenditure of more than 40 percent of the GNP be done by blind routine without a known internal system to change its qualities as the economy it serves changes?

Notes

1. The possibilities were given a formal structure in Reiter and Hughes (1981, esp. pp. 1405–6).

2. The major exception, of course, is Eisner (1986).

3. Niskanen (1971) notes the difficulty with the assumption of responsibility along with acquired expertise. "The development of expertise usually generates a sense of dedication, and it is understandable that many bureaucrats identify this dedication with the public interest" (p. 39). In the course of this chapter I will try to shed further light on motivation and identification of the public interest. There is no logical way to say that a bureau established and funded by elected authority is not, per se, in the public interest, even though the bureau's actions are obviously antisocial. In a democracy majority rules, and a bureaucrat may well consider his or her own antisocial expertise to be somehow a contribution to the general welfare because the bureau's activities are warranted by Congress. I can think of no way out of this dilemma.

4. For years economists have pursued, for the most part fruitlessly, the ultimate causes of modern public sector growth. The study by Robert Higgs (1987) attributes growth of government to the ratchet effects of modern crises such as the Great Depression of the 1930s and the world wars of the twentieth century. There is much to be said for this argument, and it is widely supported (see my own discussion in Hughes 1977, pp. 143–145). The courts and Congress, however, have created several fundamental sources of public sector growth, especially in the area of regulation, that cannot be explained by the crisis thesis; for example, the Sherman Antitrust Act, or the outburst of Great Society legislation in the 1960s. I have attempted (Hughes 1976a) to show deep-seated and remote origins of modern public sector growth that are more "constitutional" than episodic.

5. It can be argued, of course, that individuals matter no more on the bench or in the great offices of government than they do in the marketplace. To a Marxist, inexorable historical forces determine the mode of production and the superstructure, and—vulgarly—one would assume, also the opinions in it. A believer in the omnipotent power of market forces in history must come to essentially the same conclusions: individuals, and therefore entrepreneurial action, just do not matter. What happened was bound to happen, no matter what. If your mind is clear of those problems, however, there is the matter of verifiable historical events: the historical facts of critical individual actions in the regulatory system. Those actions came from people, not "forces," historical or market.

6. Changes of administration usually begin with efforts to impose real or imagined mandates for change in the bureaucracy; for example, the endless reorganizations of bureaus dealing with health, welfare, and education as administrations change, or the creation of the Joint Chiefs of Staff, which came from pressure to reduce interservice rivalries.

7. Myer (1971) tells this history from the viewpoint of a dedicated bureaucrat doing his (distasteful) duty. Richard Drinnon (1987) sees Myer's role in a very different light, one refracted through modern experience with racism and the civil rights movement.

8. This would happen, of course, under Niskanen's (1971) scheme for interdepartmental competition for budget shares via competitive bidding for tasks. One might also logically fear that such competition would degenerate into a form of intragovernmental oligopoly.

9. Niskanen sees bureau output as generally oversupplied by a monopoly supplier whose objective function is maximization of its budget share. This is the average case from the model, and of course there must be exceptions in reality. Ruttan (1980) shows that the public sector agricultural research system is actually a high-return (efficient supplier) operation, very efficient in its delivery of product because of its close association with several budgetary sources, at the state as well as at the federal level. The users of the "product" tend to have a direct input into its creation. Agricultural research is not, however, especially efficient in its acquisition of funds. Suppliers can ride free because of the diversity of funding.

10. For the survey, the first ever of disability in the United States, WPA workers interviewed 2.5 million people in 83 cities, and an additional 140,000 in rural areas. Switzer was stunned to discover that some 18 percent of the population between 15 and 64 were in some sense permanently disabled.

11. She may instinctively have known what Niskanen (1971) found decades later: the only logical reason why there should be consolidation of bureaucratic services along lines of specialization would be the existence of potential economies of scale. Niskanen says such economies have rarely been demonstrated, and in any case "the monopoly supply of these activities would prevent any potential economies from being realized by the taxpayers" (p. 196).

12. I translate the English of Marriner Eccles into the jargon of modern macroeconomics so that economists can comprehend what Eccles knew. He was "on the money" *before* Keynes, although, as I point out, others, even less well known to modern scholars, also anticipated the Keynes of 1936.

13. It is very difficult to find mention of the Harvard Center's accomplishment, beyond perhaps a bibliographical reference here and there, in modern works on entrepreneurship, especially among the theorists whom Cole so hoped to influence. Israel M. Kirzner, whose work probably (at least in the United States) is the best accepted among economists, ignores the Harvard people altogether. That is not surprising, considering his conception of entrepreneurship.

14. My Northwestern University colleague, the urbanologist Jonathan McKnight, compares pure bureaucratic growth to a living Christmas tree. The ornaments are the public services. The number of ornaments tends to remain relatively fixed over time while the tree gets bigger and bigger. If services should be cut, for budgetary reasons, the tree remains: a common experience with city services in the 1980s.

15. Schlesinger (1965) quoted President Kennedy's first State of the Union address—"Let public service be a proud and lively career"—and noted that Kennedy took particular pleasure in restoring to official favor certain whistle-blowers from the past who had been punished for their audacity by being ousted from public service.

16. Business incubators are a relatively new technique. My own university, Northwestern, has created one in its technology park, utilizing both private and public funding. It is considered at this writing to be unexpectedly successful. Nationwide, there were 33 incubators in 1983 and 206 by April 1987, with at least 1,000 expected by 1990. These institutions are meant to be innovation hatcheries. In the past, when innovation was predictably abundant in the American economy, such efforts would have been supererogatory. But in modern conditions, with high start-up information costs and complex taxation and regulatory systems to learn, we have, it seems, decided to try giving private innovation a boost by creating a new kind of institution specifically designed for the job. The weight of the argument is simply that what is good for the goose is good for the gander (*New York Times*, May 24, 1987; *Chicago Tribune*, May 26, 1987).

References

Arrington, Leonard J. Unpublished. "Bankers Extraordinary: A History of the First Security Corporation, 1928–1973." First Security Corporation. Manuscript quoted with permission.

Berkowitz, Edward. 1976. "Rehabilitation: The Federal Government's Response to Disability, 1935–1954." Ph.D. dissertation, Northwestern University.

Brown, E. Cary. 1956. "Fiscal Policy in the 'Thirties: A Reappraisal." *American Economic Review* 46, no. 5 (December): 857–879.

Derthick, Martha. 1975. *Uncontrollable Spending for Social Services Grants*. Washington, D.C.: Brookings Institution.

Drinnon, Richard. 1987. *Keeper of Concentration Camps: Dillon S. Myer and American Racism*. Berkeley: University of California Press.

Eisner, Robert. 1986. *How Real Is the Federal Deficit?* New York: Free Press.

Freedeman, Charles Eldon. 1974. *A History of the Conseil d'Etat since 1872*. Ann Arbor: University Microfilms.

Hemenway, David. 1973. "Railroading Antitrust at the ICC." In *The Monopoly Makers: Ralph Nader's Study Group Report on Regulation and Competition*. New York: Grossman.

Higgs, Robert. 1987. *Crisis and Leviathan*. New York: Oxford University Press.

Historical Statistics of the United States. 1960. Ser. F67, Y350, Y601, Y670. Washington, D.C.: Government Printing Office.

Hughes, Jonathan. 1976a. *Social Control in the Colonial Economy*. Charlottesville: University Press of Virginia.

——— 1976b. "Transference and Development of Institutional Constraints on Economic Activity." In *Research in Economic History*, ed. Paul Uselding. Vol. 1. Greenwich: JAI Press.

——— 1977. *The Governmental Habit*. New York: Basic Books.

——— 1986. *The Vital Few: The Entrepreneur and American Economic Progress*. New York: Oxford University Press, Galaxy Editions.

Keynes, J. M. 1936. *The General Theory of Employment, Interest, and Money*. London: Macmillan.

Kirzner, Israel M. 1973. *Competition and Entrepreneurship*. Chicago: University of Chicago Press.

Lewis, Eugene. 1980. *Public Entrepreneurship: Toward a Theory of Bureaucratic Power: The Organization Lives of Hyman Rickover, J. Edgar Hoover, and Robert Moses*. Bloomington: Indiana University Press.

Miller, S. M. 1963. *Max Weber: Selections from His Work*. New York: Thomas Crowell.

Mishan, E. J. 1969. *Technology and Growth: The Price We Pay*. New York: Praeger.

Myer, Dillon S. 1971. *Uprooted Americans: The Japanese Americans and the War Relocation Authority in World War II*. Tucson: University of Arizona Press.

Niskanen, William A., Jr. 1971. *Bureaucracy and Representative Government*. Chicago: Aldine.

Parkinson, C. Northcote. 1957. *Parkinson's Law and Other Studies in Administration*. Boston: Houghton Mifflin.

Peters, Thomas J., and Robert H. Waterman, Jr. 1982. *In Search of Excellence: Lessons from America's Best-Run Companies*. New York: Warner Communications.

Reiter, Stanley, and Jonathan Hughes. 1981. "A Preface on Modelling the Regulated United States Economy." Symposium: The Implications of Social Choice Theory for Legal Decision Making. *Hofstra Law Review* 9, no. 5 (Summer).

Rose-Ackerman, Susan. 1978. *Corruption: A Study in Political Economy*. New York: Academic Press.

Ruttan, V. W. 1980. *Bureaucratic Productivity: The Case of Agricultural Research*. St. Paul: University of Minnesota Economic Development Center.

Schlesinger, Arthur M., Jr. 1965. *A Thousand Days: John F. Kennedy in the White House*. Boston: Houghton Mifflin.

Schumpeter, Joseph. 1939. *Business Cycles: A Theoretical, Historical, and Statistical Analysis of the Capitalist Process*. New York: McGraw-Hill.

Smith, Adam. 1937. *The Wealth of Nations*. New York: Random House, Modern Library Editions.

Statistical Abstract of the United States, 1986. 1987. Tables 441, 491. Washington, D.C.: Government Printing Office.

Vogel, Ezra F. 1979. *Japan as Number One: Lessons for America*. Cambridge, Mass.: Harvard University Press.

11
· · ·

Employment Strategies
and Production Structures in the Swiss
Watchmaking Industry

François Jequier

There has so far been no overall study of the social history of the Swiss watchmaking industry.[1]

I shall try in this chapter to follow the development of the techniques and labor practices of those people who spent their lives in this most unusual industry, with emphasis on the main changes that modified the structures and activities of an occupational category that moved from the farm to the craftsman's cottage, from the smithy to the workshop, from the bench to the factory, and, now, from manufacturing to the multinational holding company.

Hand and Tool

It seems that, in so-called early watchmaking (from the sixteenth to the beginning of the eighteenth century), the craftsman, second only to God in his own workshop, originally made timepieces all by himself with the help of his various tools, each intended for a different operation.[2] He began by designing his caliber himself and finished with a product that embodied his own ideas, workmanship, and abilities. It was the period marked, as Gil Baillod puts it, by "the secret pride of the hand": "The know-how of the hand is allied with that of the mind, but the hand has an intelligence of its own. From long practice, guiding the tool becomes the hand's second nature, to the point of its becoming deformed so as to be more adapted to the tool. The hand knows before the eye, before the ear, that the file is scraping smoothly, that the bevel is not even. The scratch of the burin, the blow with the chasing tool, produces a sensation in the hollow of the hand that tells how precise, how true its movement is" (Baillod 1979, p. 117).

Behind the tool, manipulating the tool, there is always the hand, guided by the ingenuity of the maker. The first period saw a succession of innovations by the best watchmakers—English, French, and Swiss. The marine chronometer, essential for measuring longitude, gave rise to an epic power struggle between Pierre le Roy and Ferdinand Berthoud[3] (Le Bot 1983), and David Landes (1983, pp. 167–170) gives a fine account of their battle over patents. The spirit of enterprise consisted in taking the risk of embarking on the costly development of measuring devices followed by meticulous experiments aboard vessels during interminable voyages on the seven seas. The best craftsmen received substantial prizes from the English Board of Longitude or were awarded pensions as clockmakers to the king of France. Labor relations were confined to the respect shown by the apprentice and the worker for the master, and workshops were privileged places reserved for the carefully picked best workers.

In both Paris and Geneva, the training of future watchmakers was subject to strict regulation intended to prevent any conflict that might disrupt the regularity of work. In a manuscript of February 17, 1792, Ferdinand Berthoud gives a detailed description of the workshop in which he conducted his studies and made his chronometers, emphasizing the primordial importance of his tools: "This collection is the largest of its kind in existence; it is the more valuable in that, the most important of these tools having been created by the inventor of marine clocks himself, there are no others like them, and that, by using these tools and instruments, a skillful artisan could alone, without the help of any other worker, make all the necessary parts of a marine clock ready for placing aboard ship" (Cardinal 1984, p. 231).

In Geneva, watchmaking rapidly rose to the forefront of the city's industries, and the monopoly of the "Fabrique" (the "manufactory") was concentrated in the hands of the "bourgeois," who consigned the tasks they disdained to the other inhabitants and residents of the city. This "closed shop" of the watchmakers was henceforward to be the target of constant attack by the politically disenfranchised until the disturbances of the end of the eighteenth century gave the advantage to the deprived classes, who, through concession after concession, finally secured the abolition of such corporations in 1798.[4]

In the uplands of Neuchâtel, which were spared the shackles of master craftsmen's guilds and other kinds of corporations, wholly manual watchmaking, with the help of simple but often very ingenious tools, developed rapidly, which favored the blossoming of talented youngsters who were trained on the job before leaving to perfect their skills in the best workshops. The watchmaker-peasant combined the work of the farm and the home workshop, following the rhythm of the seasons. From the beginning, however, the Jura watchmakers, from the outskirts of Geneva to the gates of Basel, were dependent on the merchants, who controlled distribution. Technical mastery of manufacture is one thing, but selling the products is quite another, and this strange dichotomy has remained an inherent weakness of Swiss watchmaking for more than a century, right up to the present day.

The Division of Labor and the First Machines

Antony Babel (1938, p. 34) considers that one of the most striking features of the history of the Geneva Fabrique is the speed with which there appeared a division of labor, attributed by him to the pressure of demand, which led to a specialization of tasks. As early as 1660 some craftsmen were concentrating on the production of springs, leaving the easier chores to the women. The most important separation to occur was that between the making of the *ébauches* (rough movements) and the finishing of the watches. This dividing up of production, which came to be called *fabrication en parties brisées* (separate-parts manufacture), facilitated the invention of more and more specialized tools, which in turn led to the first machine tools, despite the opposition of corporations seeking to maintain a certain equality between master craftsmen and to control competition. Workers proved even more vigilant than their masters against this threat of the introduction of ''mechanical instruments'' that could punch out gear wheels, cut springs, or turn parts; and although the abolition of the corporation system in 1798 removed all legal obstacles to mechanization (without, however, giving it any encouragement), Swiss watchmaking was still far from its first ''industrial revolution.''

In the Jura the division of labor occurred painlessly within the family unit, which was a true work community. The variety of products that came out of the workshops adjoining the Jura smithies clearly reveals this gradual passage from one product to the next, from one technique to the next, all involving first the working of iron and then of steel, tempered and more and more finely filed. For example, the Le Coultre family began by making plows, then other farming tools, axes, and knives, before going on to gear wheels, works for music boxes, and razors: ''The work was done in a team at the smithy, and one would have to be quite discerning to be able to say who first had a particular idea. One thing is certain and that is that the good father Jacques-David (1781–1850) worked mainly as a smith and that his brothers and sisters all took to watchmaking'' (Jequier 1983, p. 125).

The pioneers' spirit of enterprise came up against the weight of tradition; the elders were reluctant to innovate, refused to make new investments. Tensions arose within families, amounting in some cases to secessions. Antoine Le Coultre (1803–1881) first left his partnership with his father, then his partnership with his brother, setting up on his own and founding the enterprise Le Coultre & Compagnie, which was destined to have a brilliant future. Inventor of many machines (Lebet 1983, pp. 12ff.; Jequier 1983, pp. 158ff.), he constantly expanded his production capacity, so that by 1850 he was employing more than one hundred workers. He shared the life of his workers; he knew them all personally, and some even lived in his house, as is apparent from his housekeeping inventories. When business was bad, Antoine Le Coultre did not sack anyone, for fear of losing his best assistants. The division of labor and the introduction of the first machines, operated by the worker's hand or foot, constituted no threat to the work communities of the Jura. In Geneva, by contrast, the Association of Watchcase Workers, founded in 1842, opposed a division of labor that "upset watchcase manufacture" (Grospierre 1933, p. 537). This rejection of new production methods led to the establishment of separate factories using machine methods, and the two systems coexisted and competed for a century. Here we may note another characteristic of Swiss watchmaking: the appearance of new manufacturing processes did not eliminate old practices, and usually the two systems operated side by side, which explains the extraordinary heterogeneity of this sector, first as a craft and then as an industry.

These two opposing attitudes toward the division of labor, the one adopted in the Jura area of the canton of Vaud and the other in Geneva, make it clear that social issues arose first in the towns before spreading timidly to the arc of the Jura in the second half of the nineteenth century. The social history of the Swiss watchmaking industry is in fact in many respects a good illustration of the dominance in economic relations exercised by the towns over the countryside and the Jura and neighboring French mountain areas for two centuries. This is shown by the successive waves of emigration. "The town draws the most literate" of the apprentices, as was the case in Lyons and Caen.[5]

From the Machine Tool to Manufacturing

Between the hand tool found in all the specialized home workshops and the automatic machinery installed in the big factories at the end of the nineteenth century stands another category of instrument, the machine tool: "an assemblage of elements designed to move a tool by means of a transmission activated by a motor instead of its being manipulated by the hand of a worker" (*Encyclopaedia Universalis* 1968, X, 234).

As Robert Pinot, disciple of Frederic Le Play, stated in his detailed eyewitness analysis of the situation of workers in the Saint-Imier Valley (in the Bernese Jura):

Machine tools have brought about a veritable revolution in the watchmaking industry: not only have they had their normal effect, that of reducing the production cost and

selling price of each article; not only have they led to an enormous expansion of
consumption; they have also had a powerful impact on the social situation of the worker
. . . When machine-tooling largely replaced working by hand, the type of worker
changed: from being a specialist, an artist, you might say, he became a mere laborer;
access to the entrepreneur level was suddenly closed to him and he was pushed into the
working class. (Pinot 1979, pp. 208, 219)

These changes, though very slow, for they covered a good part of the nineteenth
century, gave rise to the "social question," the first effects of which were the
separation of home from workshop and the building of the first factories—a
development hardly welcome to the watchmaking workers living in the countryside, working at home, and not very inclined to submit to the discipline of
teamwork. This period was marked by resistance to all forms of innovation both
by workers and by employers, and new production techniques were adopted
only under the threat of foreign competition, which was armed with efficient
machines installed in new factories. The first warning came from the French
Jura when Frederic Japy, former apprentice of Jean-Jacques Jeanneret-Gris of
Le Locle, greatly improved machines bought from his former master. By 1795
he was able to produce mechanically some 40,000 articles a year at prices
defying all competition (Lamard 1984). After twenty years of French dominance, the watchmakers of Neuchâtel reacted by building the first factory at
Fontainemelon equipped with the necessary machinery. But this first step toward industrialization remained confined to the sector producing "blanks" (that
is, rough movements, or *ébauches*), until the appearance of the first complete
watchmaking factories, best exemplified by Longines in 1867 (Chollet 1981).

The second shock came from the United States. The Centennial Exhibition of
1876 in Philadelphia suddenly revealed American supremacy based on the
interchangeability of machine-made parts and on the complete integration of the
production system in large plants employing hundreds of workers.[6] The Americans' efficiency resided principally in the rational use of their technical equipment combined with the commercial aggressiveness of the manufacturers whose
vast advertising campaigns served to inundate foreign markets with their products.

The Swiss were not slow to react. In spite of some inevitable resistance the
spirit of enterprise asserted itself, and several *établisseurs* (watch assemblers)
built new factories equipped with the most up-to-date machinery.[7] This structural transformation was particularly rapid toward the end of the nineteenth
century. In 1870 watchmaking employed nearly 35,000 persons, three-quarters
of whom still worked at home. The proportions were completely reversed
toward the end of the century. An official survey of 1905 shows 12,566 working
at home as against 38,728 working in big workshops or factories (Jequier 1972,
pp. 60ff.). The watchmakers converted, enlarged, and multipled their factories

with an eye to machine manufacture and centralized production. The results were not long in coming, and, to revert to the American example, the triumph of the Swiss watchmaking industry was complete at the time of the Chicago World's Fair in 1893. The virtual monopoly was recovered after a close shave. A new generation of employers had taken over.

The emergence and development of plants and factories did not eliminate the old method of production (*établissage*), which underwent similar expansion in the twentieth century despite successive crises, which it overcame by showing flexibility in taking speedy advantage of the smallest openings offered by passing fashions. This coexistence of two modes of production only accentuated the diversity of the watchmaking industry.

Employment Strategies of the New Employers

This reorganization of the industry was to influence labor relations by magnifying inequalities. Plants and factories required large investments, and this compelled many families to resign themselves, albeit reluctantly, to abandoning their status as owners. Joint stock companies gradually replaced the old family associations. These developments did not go unnoticed by trade union leaders. Georges Heymann, secretary of a union section, described the wide-ranging changes that had come about in the factories: "Twenty or thirty years ago there was only one owner, someone the workers knew, almost a companion of theirs, whereas today [1914] these same factories are in the hands of powerful joint stock companies" (*Procès-verbaux* 1914).

The increasing fixed costs led employers to try to hold down wages, while the concentration of their workers in the large establishments they had just built at great expense facilitated the activities of trade unions, whose previously scattered forces, weakened by regional rivalries, began to regroup and consolidate themselves.

At Le Coultre & Compagnie, for example, the number of workers grew rapidly, from 406 in 1889 to 482 in 1890. This distinct expansion of the work force itself created problems of order and discipline, which were exacerbated by the fact that at the slightest slowdown in business, the employers laid off workers in order to cut their variable costs. The gulf between employers and workers widened relentlessly, and the absence of information made any form of dialogue impossible. The fear of the employers was matched by the resentment of the workers. The balance of power favored the employers, who made skillful use of home workers, the "reserve army" so well described by Karl Marx. A new social hierarchy came into being in the sphere of employment. The machine could do without skilled workers, and women, who were considered more docile, were willing to work for lower wages. This helps to explain why they were excluded from the first trade union sections. To manage all these hundreds of workers, foremen were needed, as well as shop superintendents (all plants and factories were divided into workshops), and increasingly strict employment regulations were instituted. In 1897 the Le Coultre brothers decided to revise their factory rules: the 21 rules originally posted in 1880 were replaced by a 20-page printed booklet containing 50 articles of internal administrative regulations and another 10 special rules. The end of the 1890s saw a distinct hardening of employers' attitudes, and it was in this period of growing tension that the first trade unions appeared in the Joux Valley, well after other regions (Jequier 1977). Confronted with this new interlocutor, the employers in turn began to join together in order to coordinate their actions and more especially to exchange information about troublemakers. The organization of workers thus called forth an early form of employers' association, one limited, it is true, by old habits of fierce individualism. Employment strategies varied considerably, depending on the personalities involved and on established regional differences in thinking. For obvious reasons, larger towns such as La Chaux-de-Fonds and Bienne formed the spearhead of the workers' movement, and they sent representatives to try to promote trade union activity in the Jura valleys, which were more tightly controlled by local employers.

Jacques-David Le Coultre and the Social Question

There are few case studies in the social history of employer-worker relations in the Swiss watchmaking industry that compare material from both employer and trade union sources. With some exceptions, the history of Swiss trade unionism confines itself to a formalist, institutional approach and neglects the struggles of remoter regions. The 1907 activities of revolutionary trade unionism and the abortive attempts at a general strike in 1918 have been the subject of more specialized studies centered on a few regions, but their authors have dealt only with the viewpoint of the workers and the trade unions.[8]

The gap is regrettable because there is much to be learned, for example, from the first attempts at employee organization of a prominent employer, whose spirit of enterprise, paternalism, and will to power have left a deep mark on a valley of the Vaud Jura. In September 1906 Jacques-David Le Coultre (1875–1948) inherited a tense labor situation when he took over the management of the family firm, Le Coultre & Compagnie. The systematic rejection by his father and his uncles of all workers' claims had done much to encourage the malcontents to band together, and they had formed a secret trade union.[9] J.-D. Le Coultre's social policy covered half a century, until his death in 1948, and the available material, both from employer and from worker and trade union sources, is sufficiently rich to clarify many issues.

Unlike his elders, the young Le Coultre concluded that he could not ignore his labor force by simply seeking the ringleaders, so he approached his workers to hear their grievances. He developed a dialogue at various levels: one-to-one contacts directly with the workers; formal contact with the trade union, which he recognized in order to combat it more effectively; occasional meetings with the other employers of the Joux Valley so that they might present a united front on trade union demands.

Le Coultre's labor policy can be summed up in a few words: give generously before you are forced to give in. To this end he sought to keep abreast of what was being said among the workers, and he even infiltrated the local trade union to get accurate information. He was thus able to offer his workers more than the local trade union section was likely to demand, and he made certain that this was known, showing a sense of public relations that was ahead of its time. He introduced many benefits: a mutual aid and health insurance society; an assistance fund for elderly workers; a company unemployment fund; a retirement fund; staff quarters offering low-priced meals and recreation rooms; agreements with the local hospital for preferential rates.

Every sum contributed for these purposes was publicized as the employer polished his public image. But these amounts averaged only 4 percent of profits during the years between the two world wars. In 1938, for example, the 15,000 francs thus contributed were a mere pittance compared with the 72,000 francs paid in dividends and the 168,000 francs in extra dividends out of a turnover of 3.2 million francs. Here was a labor policy that was remarkably advanced for the period and did not cost very much.

In fact, we might say that his policy did not cost anything at all, and that Jacques-David Le Coultre managed his workers with as much care as his machinery or his finances; for his active paternalism paid off handsomely. For half a century, Le Coultre & Compagnie remained untouched by the main labor movements; no strike ever disrupted the company, and the loyalty of its workers became legendary. The arrogance of the employers of the preceding generation was superseded by a dialogue of an entirely new kind. The new employer showed real talent as a leader of men, and his labor policy enabled him to avoid the costly confrontations that disturbed other watchmaking regions where employers were less open to compromise.

This particular case constitutes an exception to the generally tense social climate that reigned in the Swiss watchmaking industry during the first third of the twentieth century. What the entire industry had in common was the takeover of the main factories in each watchmaking region. Like Le Coultre in the Joux Valley, the Roberts at Fontainemelon, Longines at Saint-Imier, the Jequiers at

Fleurier, Zenith at Le Locle, the Schilds at Granges, not to mention the innumerable heads of small and medium-sized firms in the towns and villages of the
Jura crescent and the neighboring plateaus around Berne and Solothurn—all of
them had very personal views of the "social question." Faced with the shortage
of housing, they sought various ways of helping the staff they wanted to keep.
For instance, at the beginning of the century, the Tavannes Watch Company
financed a workers' cottages building project that allowed employees to indi-
vidualize their homes by choosing one of the twenty designs offered by the
architect René Chapallaz, whose influence on Le Corbusier seems undeniable
(Emery 1984, p. 220).

Repeated Disturbances of Labor Peace

Strikes and other social disturbances mark the social history of the watchmaking
industry, whose labor traditions—first associative, then cooperative, and finally
trade unionist—go back to the middle of the nineteenth century. Regional
rivalries long prevented the unification of workers' forces, and trade union
movements remained fragmented until the merger in 1915 of the watchmaking
unions with the metalworking unions. The new organization underwent rapid
development, finally becoming the largest trade union federation in Switzerland. The 21,300 membership of 1915 quadrupled by 1919, a year that was one
of the most disturbed in the country's labor history (*Siècle d'union* 1980, p.
220). World War I, which produced a sharp accentuation of social inequalities
in Switzerland, inaugurated a long period of tensions and disputes which was
exacerbated by the depressions of the 1920s and 1930s.

Most of the labor clashes started from minor causes. The equal intransigence
of the two sides, both of them refusing to make the slightest concession, activated mechanisms of escalation that soon led to confrontations. The numerous
strikes were met by lockouts that often lasted for weeks. Starting in the summer
of 1920, the economic depression was marked by the closing of many workshops. In 1921 the number of workers in all factories was reduced by half;
20,400 workers were completely unemployed and 7,400 partly so, the Swiss
watchmaking industry's sales having dropped from 13.7 million units in 1920
to 7.9 million in 1921. Manufacturing disintegrated, and one particular phenomenon is worthy of note: whereas, before the war, production tended to be
concentrated in large factories, the depression encouraged the reappearance of
the small finishers so typical of the industrial organization of the nineteenth
century. Scorning efficient machine tools, having none of the overheads and
fixed costs of the large enterprises, these finishers took advantage of the much
lower cost of home labor and sold inferior merchandise cheaply, using poor-

quality movements and materials. The Swiss watch had already lost much of its prestige during the war, and the launching of these inferior products in all markets further damaged its reputation. The depression dismantled the watchmaking industry further by intensifying its heterogeneity. This extreme fragmentation is apparent from the 1929 survey of enterprises (see Table 11.1), and the prosperous years of the "golden twenties" (1924–1929) had no effect on this splintering of production units (enterprises employing more than 500 persons were mainly manufacturers of rough movements and of finished clocks and watches).

The Swiss watchmaking industry was weakened not only by the small size and geographical dispersion of these thousands of small and medium-sized enterprises but also by a solid tradition of rivalries, both sectoral and regional. Furthermore, it must be remembered that these figures cover the specialized production of all the 130 parts necessary for the making of a finished mechanical watch.

The first collective efforts to reorganize the industry were private in origin. In 1924 the employers' associations of the various regions joined together to form a Fédération Horlogère (Federation of Swiss Watch Manufacturers). The manufacturers of *ébauches* united under the umbrella of a holding company in January 1927, followed in December by the producers of separate parts, who founded the Union des Branches Annexes de l'Horlogerie, or UBAH (Union of Branches Associated with the Watch Industry). In December 1928 agreements were concluded among the various employers' associations determining their relations. A decisive role in the restoration of the watchmaking industry was played by the Chambre Suisse de l'Horlogerie (Swiss Watch Chamber), founded

Table 11.1 Number of persons employed in Swiss watchmaking industry by size of enterprise, 1929.

Number of employees per enterprise	Number of enterprises in category (% total)		Number of persons employed (% total)	
1	421	(15.7%)	421	(0.7%)
2–9	1,268	(47.3%)	6,331	(10.7%)
10–49	764	(28.4%)	16,868	(28.7%)
50–99	134	(5.0%)	9,209	(15.7%)
100–199	56	(2.1%)	7,827	(13.3%)
200–499	30	(1.1%)	8,626	(14.6%)
500 and more	10	(0.4%)	9,517	(16.2%)
Total	2,683	(100.0%)	58,799	(100.0%)

Source: Suisse Recensement Fédéral des Entreprises, Année 1929, II, 2–5.

in 1876, as an organ of liaison between the various watchmaking associations and the public authorities, both cantonal and federal.[10] Optimism revived.

It was short-lived, however. The watchmaking industry, which exported 98 percent of its production, was hit by the depression as early as the end of 1929; the subsequent unprecedented collapse of watch exports mirrored the economic catastrophe of the 1930s. Exports fell from a total of 307 million francs (20.8 million units) in 1929 to 86 million francs (8.2 million units) in 1932. Unemployment beat all previous records. In 1933, out of every 100 unemployed, 19 were from the watchmaking industry. The number of persons employed in the industry fell by 15,000. The expatriation of watchmaking business worried the authorities: shifting of labor abroad, exporting of tools and machines, shipment of bare movements instead of complete watches, resurgence of *chablonnage*[11] in spite of the recently instituted system covered by agreements. The general slump rendered the agreements signed in December 1928 inoperative. The watchmaking regions were the hardest hit by the depression, especially as employers resorted to every possible means of reducing their wage costs: cuts in pay, reduction of paid holidays granted in 1929, mass dismissals, introduction of new work methods deemed more rational. Unbridled competition and free enterprise were stigmatized by all social partners.

It was in these exceptional circumstances that the employers on the one hand and the trade unions on the other (Loertscher-Rouge 1977, p. 160) sought the intervention of a state hitherto reluctant to become involved in the private sector (Ledermann 1941). There appeared to be general agreement that all manufacturers should be even more closely united. It was thus that April 14, 1931, saw the founding at Neuchâtel of ASUAG, the Allgemeine Schweizerische Uhrenindustrie AG (General Corporation of Swiss Horological Industries), a huge holding company incorporating the trusts set up a few years earlier. Its capital came jointly from the Swiss Confederation (six-sixteenths), the banks (five-sixteenths), and the watchmaking organizations (five-sixteenths). Two seats on the board of directors were reserved for trade union representatives, in order to associate the workers with these restructuring efforts. A series of government measures followed, the best known being the Protection of the Watch Industry Order of March 12, 1934, whose purposes were to prevent excessive expansion of the productive apparatus, to maintain production at as constant and regular a level as possible, and to eliminate the effects of reckless competition leading to a price collapse similar to that of the 1930s. Specifically, this statute prohibited henceforth the opening, enlargement, transformation, or removal of watchmaking enterprises, thus protecting the existing enterprises, which would enjoy an assured income once business picked up; and the exporting of watchmaking products other than complete watches (an export license was required), so as to prevent the expatriation of the industry. Lastly, to stabilize selling prices, the order set mandatory price ranges (*prix de barrage*) for the whole of the Swiss watch industry.

Thus, five difficult and troubled years were enough to make the Swiss watchmaking industry abandon its credo of free competition and free enterprise and fit itself to the cartel yoke of price and quota arrangements so contrary to the logic of industrial economics and so conducive to rigidity. We may well ask ourselves today whether other solutions would have been equally effective, for it must be recognized that these repeated interventions by the state, however complicated, enabled a "rectified" Swiss watch industry to recover as early as 1936, before embarking on an unprecedented period of prosperity, which was also due in part to another statute—that proclaiming Swiss neutrality during World War II.[12]

In the realm of employment strategies, the results obtained after bitter negotiations were of capital importance because of the influence they have had on all subsequent collective agreements governing the world of labor in Switzerland right up to the present day.

Françoise Loertscher-Rouge, the author of a detailed study on the policy of the FOMH (Federation of Metal and Watchmaking Workers), repeatedly stresses the willingness of the trade unions to cooperate with the employers (Loertscher-Rouge 1977, pp. 159, 184). As early as 1927, the Union Syndicale Suisse, the trade union umbrella organization, had deleted from its statutes all references to the class struggle, and in the ten years that followed there were numerous moves toward rapprochement both with the employers' associations and with the authorities, despite the persistence in the trade union press of statements as clamorous in their demands as ever. Konrad Ilg (1877–1954), central secretary of the FOMH from 1915 to 1954 and a former revolutionary militant, simmered down considerably, going so far as to "consider the strike weapon unfit for securing a favorable outcome of trade union action. He dissuaded members from using it" (Loertscher-Rouge 1977, p. 165). But since this moderate tone failed to persuade employers opposed to any settlement to negotiate, strikes proved necessary in 1936 and 1937, at the very time when the watchmaking industry was recovering. Once again the state acted as arbiter, in May 1937, when strike movements were under way from Bienne to La Chaux-de-Fonds.

> The employers requested Federal Councillor Hermann Obrecht to intervene, asking him to make use of the enactments adopted following the devaluation [the 34 percent devaluation of the Swiss franc on September 26, 1936, helped to boost watch exports, which rose 58.6 percent from 1936 to 1937], which conferred on the federal authorities sovereign power to arbitrate labor and wage disputes. Although he did not do so, he did convene at Berne a meeting between the representatives of the employers and those of the FOMH, and put before them a draft general agreement dealing mainly with wages

and holidays. In addition, the parties undertook not to resort to strikes or lockouts in case of conflicts but to submit their disputes to an arbitration tribunal to be appointed by them by common accord. This agreement of "labor peace" similar to the one adopted in the metallurgical industry two months later was finalized on May 25. As it entered into force at once, work resumed on May 28 in the factories making metal watch faces. The signature of the agreement was quickly followed in most of the trades it covered by arrangements between the parties whenever that was possible and by arbitration tribunal awards in all other cases. It was in this way that the disputes on wages and holidays were settled. In general, workers obtained six days' fully paid holiday and wage increases of about 10%.[13]

The collective agreement of May 15, 1937, in the watchmaking industry inaugurated an era of social peace; its five articles constituted a stage of fundamental importance in the development of employer-worker relations. This agreement, together with the so-called Labor Peace Agreement of July 19, 1937 (an agreement not much longer than the first, for it contained only nine articles), binding upon the social partners of the Swiss machinery and metalworking industry, signified official recognition of trade unions in the industrial sector that was numerically the largest in Switzerland. From then on, trade unions were regarded as legitimate partners in collective bargaining. At the same time, the two agreements asserted a mutual desire for cooperation and understanding, and they expressly stipulated the absolute obligation to maintain peace, thus putting an end to the era of conflict that had marked the previous half-century.[14]

Both employers' and workers' organizations, exhausted by the Great Depression and eager to take advantage of the economic revival, realized the benefits they could obtain from these agreements, which were widely imitated. Strikes and other labor disputes declined sharply.

I think it can be said without exaggeration that much of Switzerland's prosperity over the past fifty years and more derives directly from this Labor Peace, which has become so completely a part of the country's customs as to modify the thinking of the two sides. A survey carried out in 1981 showed that three Swiss out of four were in favor of the Labor Peace Agreement (*Gazette de Lausanne*, April 29, 1981, p. 11).

The Weight of Tradition versus the Electronic Challenge

The 1934 statute governing the watch industry was tacitly renewed with only minor improvements in 1953 and 1962 and set the structure of the industry until 1971. This officially sanctioned cartelization, which François Schaller (1970, p. 1) described as "the purest economic Malthusianism," stifled initiative and innovation. A widespread attitude of self-satisfaction blinded employers to the consequences of the rapid economic development of the postwar years. The virtual monopoly held by the Swiss watch industry between 1945 and 1960 and the huge profits it generated had a soporific effect on the spirit of enterprise. The fragmentation of production atomized technical progress and confined it to minor improvements. The watchmakers failed to grasp at first the importance of the technical revolution provoked by the introduction of electronics into watch manufacture (Gabus 1983; Milliet 1985). This innovation, which was speedily exploited by foreign competitors, upset habits and tradition and, more important, brought out the weaknesses of the splintered production and small scale of enterprises incapable of undertaking the huge investments necessary for the new modes of production. The average size of enterprises in the watch industry had changed only slowly, from 23.3 employees per establishment in 1929 to 21.7 in 1955, 48 in 1968, and 53 in 1985. The predominance of small enterprises, despite many mergers, most of them doomed to failure, remained one of the endemic weaknesses of the Swiss watch industry. Although highly integrated at the level of the manufacture of movements, it nevertheless remained fragmented and interdependent, split up among hundreds of manufacturers of complete watches, innumerable assemblers, and a host of small subcontractors.

It was in this disorderly state that the Swiss watch industry, after a fine period of expansion between 1961 and 1974, found itself facing the oil shock, the monetary crisis, and the electronic challenge. A fall in exports of 22 percent from 1974 to 1975 led to a drastic cutback in the labor force: between 1975 and 1979 the industry lost 25,000 workers, a third of the total number. Underemployment and partial unemployment revived the social question. But by the late 1980s, the rules of the game had completely changed. The traditional watch industry, with its decentralized structure, its skilled workers, its artisan workshops, its plants and equipment based principally on the production of mechanical watches, saw its share of exports slump from 99 percent in 1974 to 20 percent in 1985 (*Swiss Watchmaking* 1986, p. 29). Conversely, in ten years the share of electronic watches rose from 1 percent to 80 percent, a figure which gives an idea of the magnitude of the technical revolution which was at first suffered, then admitted, and finally accepted by the pioneers of "new watchmaking." Automation has meant a 70 percent reduction in labor costs, which is why the upturn of business in 1985 had very little effect on the number of workers employed, which fell from 76,000 in 1973 to 32,200 in 1985. Furthermore, the skills called for have also greatly changed.

The electronic challenge is now clashing with existing labor legislation. At the end of November 1986 on SMH (Swiss Corporation for Microelectronic and Watchmaking Industries), which took over the assets of the two former giants, ASUAG and SSIH (Société Suisse de l'Industrie Horlogère) reached a new agreement with the watchmaking union. The agreed reorganization of working hours was unheard of for Switzerland, since it provided for continuous operation, twenty-four hours a day, seven days a week. These provisions were, however, contrary to the legislation in force regarding working hours for women. Opposing views were more and more frequently published in the press; the matter is still under adjudication.

A century after its first "industrial revolution," necessitated by the threat of foreign competition, especially American, Swiss watchmaking finds itself facing a second revolution, an electronic one this time, in circumstances offering interesting comparisons. Its belated reaction seriously jeopardized the industry's future, but now that the crisis (yet another one) has passed, fruitful prospects are opening up for the "new watchmaking," of which the SWATCH is one of the outstanding successes. Firmly taken in hand by such managers as Nicolas Hayek, Pierre Arnold, and Stefan Schmidheiny—recognized for their unquestionable achievements in other industries—Swiss watchmaking is finally entering the industrial era. Freed from its backward employers with their limited outlook, the industry has absorbed the quartz shock, and the SMH, its undisputed leader, is large enough to fight the competition from Asia, which is beginning to show the first signs of running out of steam after a period of rapid expansion. This very recent structural mutation will entail new employment strategies, which, it is to be hoped, will extend the achievements of a half-century of labor peace.

Notes

1. As recently as 1983, David Landes expressed surprise that so little attention had been given by scholars to the economic and social aspects of an industry which had existed for centuries (in preface to Jequier 1983, p. 9). He contrasted this with the wealth and variety of works devoted to the technical and artistic aspects of watchmaking—the most important of them mentioned in his masterly survey *Revolution in Time* (1983), which stands as a landmark in world horological history.

In this chapter the terms *watchmaking, watches,* and so on refer also to clocks.

2. This section of the chapter is from Jequier (1987).

3. The story of Ferdinand Berthoud offers a good example of a successful career (Cardinal 1984).

4. On this turbulent period of the social history of watchmaking in Geneva, see Babel (1938).

5. Piuz (1977, p. 206), which cites the work of Maurice Garden concerning Lyons and of Jean-Claude Perrot concerning Caen. See also Jequier (1973).

6. On the development of American watchmaking, see Landes (1983, chap. 19).

7. On Swiss reactions to American competition, see Barrelet (1987).

8. On the history of the workers' movement in Switzerland, see Vuilleumier (1973, 1983). A collective work worth consulting is *Grève générale* (1977). On the social climate of the 1912–1918 period, see Meinrad Inglin's fine novel (1985).

9. A detailed account of these episodes is given in Jequier (1977, 1983).

10. The references to the reorganization of the Swiss watchmaking industry between the two world wars are from Jequier (1972, pp. 152–156).

11. *Chablon:* unassembled set of all or part of the elements of a watch movement except the face, the hands, and the case. *Chablonnage:* sale of *chablons*. The term is applied mainly to the export of *ébauches* and movement components for assembly abroad.

12. On the special situation of the Swiss watchmaking industry during World War II, see the relevant chapters of Jequier (1972, 1983).

13. Loertscher-Rouge (1977, p. 189). For an account of the labor negotiations in the metalworking industry, see Billeter (1985, particularly chap. 7). The text of the May 15, 1937, collective agreement on the watchmaking industry is given on pp. 197–199 of Loertscher-Rouge (1977). Article 1 is worth quoting because of its historical importance: "In view of the country's general economic situation, the Contracting Parties undertake to apply, for the rest of the current year, a system of absolute social peace; in other words, the employers promise not to have recourse to lockouts in any form whatsoever, and the workers promise not to have recourse to strikes in any form whatsoever.

"The parties shall refrain from any concerted action liable to disturb good relations between employers and workers."

14. Aubert (1981) examines this question from a comparative law viewpoint; on the consequences of these collective agreements, see *Paix du travail* (1977).

References

Aubert, G. 1981. *L'obligation de paix du travail: étude de droit suisse et comparé.* Geneva: Georg.

Babel, A. 1938. *La Fabrique genevoise.* Neuchâtel: V. Attinger.

Baillod, G. 1979. *La mesure du temps.* Lausanne: Mondo.

Barrelet, J.-M. 1987. "Les résistances à l'innovation dans l'industrie horlogère des montagnes neuchâteloises à la fin du XIXe siècle." In *Revue suisse d'histoire* 37(4):394–411.

Billeter, G. 1985. *Le pouvoir patronal: les patrons des grandes entreprises suisses des métaux et des machines (1919–1939).* Geneva: Droz.

Cardinal, C. 1984. *Ferdinand Berthoud, 1727–1807: horloger mécanicien du roi et de la marine.* La Chaux-de-Fonds: Musée international d'horlogerie.

Chollet, J.-P. 1981. "Histoire de la Fabrique Longines." *Chronometrophilia* 11 (Winter):10–39.

Emery, M. 1984. "De la ferme à la metropole horlogère." In *Il était une fois l'industrie.* Geneva: Association pour le patrimoine industriel de la Suisse.

Gabus, A. 1983. "Introduction de l'electronique dans la montre." In *La diffusion des nouvelles technologies en Suisse.* Saint-Saphorin: Georgi.

Grève générale de 1918 en Suisse. 1977. Geneva: Gronauer.

Grospierre, A. 1933. "Histoire du syndicalisme ouvrier dans l'industrie horlogère." In *L'Union syndicale suisse, 1880–1930,* ed. F. Heeb. Bern: Union syndicale suisse.

Inglin, M. [1955] 1985. *La Suisse dans un miroir.* Lausanne: Editions de l'Aire.

Jequier, F. 1972. *Une entreprise horlogère du Val-de-Travers: Fleurier Watch Co. S. A.: de l'atelier familial du XIXe siècle aux concentrations du XXe siècle.* Neuchâtel: La Baconnière.

——— 1973. "Les relations économiques entre Genève et la Valée de Joux." *Bulletin de la Société d'histoire et d'archéologie de Genève* 15(2):99–123.

——— 1977. "Fédérations ouvrières et réactions patronales dans une région périphérique au début du XXe siècle: naissance du syndicalisme horloger à la Vallée de Joux." *Revue européenne des sciences sociales et Cahiers Vilfredo Pareto* 15, no. 42:201–265.

——— 1983. *De la forge à la manufacture horlogère (XVIIIe–XXe siècles): cinq générations d'entrepreneurs de la Vallée de Joux au coeur d'une mutation industrielle.* Lausanne: Bibliothèque historique vaudoise.

——— 1987. Preface to *La main et l'outil: collection de machines et d'outils: catalogue de l'exposition temporaire du 27 mars au 27 septembre 1987.* La Chaux-de-Fonds, Musée international d'horlogerie.

Lamard, P. 1984. "Histoire d'un capital familial au XIXe siècle: le capital Japy de 1777 à 1910." Dissertation, University of Franche-Comté.

Landes, D. S. 1983. *Revolution in Time: Clocks and the Making of the Modern World.* Cambridge, Mass.: Harvard University Press.

Lebet, J. 1983. "Notes sur les débuts de la fabrication moderne des pignons d'horlogerie par Antoine Le Coultre." *Chronométrophilia* 15.

Le Bot, J. 1983. *Quand l'art de naviguer devenait science: les chronomètres de marine français au XIIIe siècle.* Grenoble: Terre et Mer.

Ledermann, B. 1941. *Du rôle de l'état dans la réorganisation de l'industrie horlogère suisse.* La Chaux-de-Fonds: Fédération horlogère.

Loertscher-Rouge, F. 1977. "La politique de la FOMH dans l'horlogerie lors de la crise des années trente (1930–1937)." *Revue européenne des sciences sociales et Cahiers Vilfredo Pareto* 15, no. 42:143–199.

Milliet, F. 1985. "La nouvelle horlogerie." *Revue économique et sociale* (Lausanne) (June 2): 89–101.

Paix du travail. 1977. *La Paix du Travail: un enjeu.* Lausanne: Rencontres suisses.

Pinot, R. 1979. *Paysans et horlogers jurassiens.* Geneva: Grounauer. Originally published 1888 and 1889 in the periodical *La science sociale.*

Piuz, A.-M. 1977. "Les relations économiques entre les villes et les campagnes dans les sociétés préindustrielles." *Revue européenne des sciences sociales et Cahiers Vilfredo Pareto* 15, no. 41: 195–231.

Procès-verbaux de la Fédération syndicale horlogère du Sentier. 1914. Vallée de Joux, March 19, 1914.

Schaller, F. 1970. "Les réflexions d'un profane sur l'horlogerie suisse en 1970." *Communications-Ebauches SA,* no. 26 (February).

Siècle d'union syndicale suisse, 1880–1980. 1980. Fribourg: Office du Livre.

Swiss Watchmaking Industry. 1986. Zurich: Union Bank of Switzerland.

Vuilleumier, M. 1973. "Quelques jalons pour une historiographie du mouvement ouvrier en Suisse." *Revue européenne des sciences sociales et Cahiers Vilfredo Pareto* 11, no. 29:5–35.

———— 1983. "Le mouvement ouvrier en Suisse pendant et après la Première Guerre Mondiale." *Le mouvement social,* no. 84 (July–September): 97–126.

12
. . .

Entrepreneurs and Managers

Peter Temin

Any economy is composed of individuals. But while all men are created equal in the sight of God and the U.S. Constitution, not all individuals are equally important to the economy. Entrepreneurs and managers are particularly important for economic progress, and this chapter is concerned with them.

I shall approach several questions. First, is it possible to distinguish between the functions of entrepreneurs and managers in a useful way? One application, for example, is to shed light on the controversy between Stephen Marglin and David Landes about what "bosses"—a loosely defined term—do. Second, can this analytic device help to explain the origin of factory production at the start of the nineteenth century? And third, do the changing functions of managers and entrepreneurs provide any clues to the future health of industrial economies?

Marglin wrote an essay over a decade ago, asking "What Do Bosses Do?" He denied that bosses, the heroes of most economic histories, were anything more than foot soldiers in the class war. Factories, in his view, were organized to steal from workers, not to enhance efficiency. Landes replied in a paper that celebrated the role of bosses and insisted on the efficiency gains of factories.[1] The debate is murky, partly because the function of bosses was not defined by either Marglin or Landes. Clarification of their role provides a good entry into the issues.

There are two kinds of bosses. The first kind, the *Übermenschen,* can be called entrepreneurs. They are the men (typically) who introduce new methods of production, new products, new orientations for their firms. The second kind of bosses are "managers," who actually administer the activity of workers. Managers often work for entrepreneurs, but they may well head their own businesses.

Entrepreneurs are the agents of change, managers of stability. More precisely, as Frank Knight said, entrepreneurs deal with "uncertainty" (that is, unmeasurable risk), while managers handle "risk" (that is, measurable risk) (Knight 1964, chap. 10). Entrepreneurs are needed to introduce new machines

339

and engines; managers are needed to operate them. Entrepreneurs strike out into the unknown; managers implement the known. They perform different economic functions and frequently have contrasting personalities, even though some businessmen—particularly in the early stages of industrialization—have had to undertake both jobs.

Economic theory traditionally had no use for entrepreneurs, just as it had little use for new technologies. Managers, by contrast, fit easily within the economist's traditional model. Landes, by virtue of his training and lifelong work, talked mostly of entrepreneurs. Marglin, also a product of his personal history, spoke largely of managers. The difference has clouded the discussion. Despite a minidebate over terminology, this distinction—crucial to an understanding of the relationship between "bosses" and technological change—has not been made.

Once this distinction *is* made, a fruitful line of argument opens up. Larger economic organizations allow a finer division of labor, as Adam Smith explained. Departing from Smith's discussion, I shall argue that among the divisions of labor, those involving managers are particularly important. But while managers are critical to questions of efficiency, entrepreneurs are critical to those of control. Recent economic theory suggests that it is difficult to hire true entrepreneurs; they consequently were found at the top and in control of economic organizations during the Industrial Revolution. But while transaction costs can explain the locus of control in early factories, Marglin's quest for alternatives points up the shortcomings of this argument when it is applied to contemporary companies.

Consider the manufacture of pins, albeit with the regret (articulated by Clapham) that Adam Smith did not go farther afield to examine a more significant industry. There were, as Smith noted, several functions required to make a pin, and each one was performed by a different person at the end of the eighteenth century. Briefly, wire needed to be drawn, straightened, cut, and pointed. Finer wire for the head needed to be drawn, curled, cut, and attached to the pin. The better grade of pins then had to be placed onto folded sheets of paper. In the 1820s, at least in the British firm described by Ashton (1925), the heading and packaging of pins were done by outworkers.

Ashton's pin factory is comparable to Laslett's early-seventeenth-century London bakery: the archetypal productive household. It contained thirteen or fourteen people, with a clear social organization. At the top stood the baker and his wife. Then there were four paid employees (journeymen), two apprentices, two maidservants, and three or four children (of the baker and his wife). This was a household as opposed to a factory: the baker's food bill (£2 9s. a week) was five times as large as his wage bill (11s. 8d. out of total weekly expenses of £6 10s.). But the wage bill reveals even so the division of labor. The baker and his immediate family received none: they bore the risks of the bakery as economic activity. The journeymen received half a crown a week; the maid-servants tenpence; the apprentices, of course, only training (Laslett 1983, p. 1).

This household was not static. Children and apprentices grew and moved on. Journeymen left for other bakeries or even started their own; the maidservants might go with them or otherwise marry out of the household. But this movement—even the possibility that every member of the household could have been a potential baker or baker's wife—does not deny the existence of hierarchy and the division of labor at any point in time. There is no firm relationship between the size of hierarchies and the extent of economic opportunity.

The division of labor surely promoted efficiency. Less-skilled jobs and those requiring the least physical strength were done by the youngest members of the household. The baker taught his juniors the tricks of the trade. But there is no way to know if the division of labor maximized efficiency or whether the wages paid (both in money and in kind) equaled marginal products. The presence of guilds and the traditional subjection of women in seventeenth-century London, in fact, suggest the contrary. Even small economic hierarchies contained a mixture of efficiency and distributional aspects.

The question, then, is why the size of hierarchies increased in the late eighteenth century. Why were households superseded by factories? To suggest an answer to this question, I should like to turn away from the workers in the manufacture of pins to the boss, one Mr. Stubs at the plant under scrutiny.

Ashton reports the expenses of making 212 pounds of pins in March 1821. The materials cost £13 14s. The cost of manufacture, presumably the labor cost, was £4 1s. 11d., making the total cost £17 15s. 11d. Only one-fifth of this total cost was the labor discussed by Marglin and Landes. The pins sold for £16 17s. 3d.—less than they cost to produce. By-products—leftover heads and scrap metal—brought the revenue up to £17 15s., still about one shilling shy of the cost (Ashton 1925, pp. 287–288).

These costs undoubtedly are current costs. No manufacturer of the time had accounts that dealt with his fixed costs (Pollard 1964, chap. 6). Ashton tells us Stubs had rented space and purchased machinery costing over £300. Once the fixed costs of interest and depreciation are added to the variable costs, they reveal costs to be even further above revenues. Far from exploiting his workers, Stubs seems to have been subsidizing them. Why was he operating at a loss?

Several factors could have been at work. The price of pins had been falling between 1814 and 1821, after the Napoleonic Wars. The price of pins followed the price of raw materials very closely, and manufacturers who held raw material inventories could be caught in a price slide. The trade was reviving from its doldrums in 1821, however, and pin manufacturers were refusing orders in

1822. They were, in fact, trying to organize a pin cartel. It is hard to know whether Stubs's firm had troubles in March 1821 from this cause. The firm also had more long-run problems; it ceased production at the end of the 1820s. Ashton (1925) concludes that Stubs left the business out of moral scruples, "owing to the disgust he felt at the treatment of the infant pin-headers" (p. 292). It would have been convenient to take such a moral stance if the firm also had been losing money and eating up its capital.

What was Stubs doing while his relatively unskilled workers were making pins? Many things. He decided to make pins (and then, later, to stop making pins). He saw, or at least thought he saw, an opportunity to make a profit. He found space to rent, negotiated a price, and made a commitment for a year in advance. He purchased a substantial quantity of machinery, a task that involved the knowledge of which machinery to buy, where to buy it, and how to finance it. He then installed his machinery in his rented space, positioning it in some order, adjusting it to the space, and making sure it worked. He also, we must presume, kept the machinery in working order for the fifteen years or so it was used.

He hired his workers. This was no mean feat. Adult workers were drawn from a wide area. Child workers had to be organized and supervised. The mode of payment—piece rates—had to be determined. The piece rates then had to be decided or negotiated. Stubs had to know or learn how many of each type of worker were needed to keep the process in balance. He undoubtedly did not calculate the output of a wire drawer and a pointer to find the lowest common multiple of their outputs. He had a rough idea from observing the process elsewhere, and he adjusted the proportions by trial and error. In the process, he accumulated inventories, kept track of the throughput, and adjusted his work force. He also supervised the workers, perhaps his most visible activity.

Stubs purchased the raw materials—that is, he knew what was needed, where to get it, and what was a reasonable price. He decided when to buy and how large he wanted his raw material inventories to be. We must presume that he had the contacts and prior credit rating to get financing. Stubs then sold the output. He found markets, selling in both England and America in the difficult postwar years. He decided when to sell and when to hold back for a higher price. He arranged for delivery of his pins and for financing of the sale.

Finally, Stubs kept the books that were the source for Ashton's study. To the best of his ability, Stubs tried to discover if he was making money. As we learned in the 1970s, this is no simple task in a time of rapid price change. Stubs had to contend also with the new distinction between fixed and variable costs. Capital accounting was in its infancy, and Stubs undoubtedly did not understand it. If he was consuming his capital, he would have found out about it only as his machinery wore out and he realized he did not have adequate reserves to replace it.

The man who performed this collection of activities can be termed a manager. It clearly required skill to perform these activities well even for a small firm like Stubs's. More skill is needed to run larger operations. But even a small factory makes the point. Management is a different skill from the skill of drawing, pointing, or heading pins. It needs to be paid according to supply and demand for this skill.

Marglin asks why every worker did not perform these tasks himself or herself. The answer seems clear. The skills required were far different from the skills of drawing, pointing, or heading pins. There was, as Adam Smith asserted, a gain from the division of labor. The discussion has become confused by limiting this concept to the distinction between, say, pointing and heading pins. It needs to be applied as well to the management functions that are implicit in any productive activity.

Doing so makes sense of Marglin's emphatic answer to his questions of why hand-loom weavers did not organize themselves: "To glean rewards from organizing," he asserted, "one had to become a capitalist putter-outer!" (Marglin 1976, p. 21). There were, in other words, gains to becoming a manager, but only if one specialized in this activity. The division of labor in a larger organization—a putting-out network—increased efficiency. But a specialized putter-outer was needed to run the operation. It may or may not have been possible for any given weaver to become a putter-outer. It was not possible for any weaver to be both a putter-outer and a weaver; each activity took too much time. Despite the exclamation point, Marglin's statement is no more than a corollary of Smith's argument on the division of labor.

One thing bosses do, therefore, is manage. It is efficient to have a separate manager for the same reason it is efficient to have separate pinmakers, weavers, and farriers. But how many managers are needed? What determines the size of economic organizations? While Smith said that the division of labor is limited by the extent of the market, it is more useful to think of this problem in terms of the supply and demand for managers.

Consider first the supply of managers. Each manager directs an organization whose size is determined by the extent of his management skills. These depend on his personal attributes: some people can handle larger groups and more complex processes than others. We may presume that the distribution of these qualities in the population is quite stable, although it is affected by the culture of a society and the level of education.[2] The supply of managers changes over time in response to changes in these underlying factors, but changes in the supply are slow. There is little evidence that English education or culture was undergoing a revolution in the eighteenth century. The supply of managers was roughly constant.

The demand for managers is a function of the available technology. New productive techniques required scale for efficient operation—to capture economies of both machinery operation and personnel administration. Stubs ran a factory on the basis of £330 worth of machinery. Hand-loom weaving, baking, and other artisanal activities required less space and equipment for an efficient operation; the proliferation of machinery in the late eighteenth and early nineteenth centuries increased the number of activities that required more. The use of "machines and engines" increased the demand for managers and the size of hierarchies they managed.

The ability to exploit machinery and inanimate power—water and steam—grew over the course of the nineteenth century, and with it the size of factories. This story has been told well by Landes; it needs no repetition here. It is well to remember, however, that technology alone cannot explain the size of factories. Comparisons of twentieth-century factories in different industrialized countries, for example, have shown differences in the use of manpower and the role of bosses inexplicable on the basis of technology (Landes 1969; Crozier 1964).

The growth of factories and large economic organizations did not foreclose economic opportunity. At any moment of time, the existence of hierarchy supposes that there will be people at the bottom. But the existence of a job ladder says nothing about the ease of climbing it. The growth of industry and factories created opportunities for people to rise through the hierarchy. These opportunities were not open to all nor easily accessible to those at the bottom. But the standard of competition is not random assignment of jobs; it is the status quo ante. Economic mobility surely was increased, not decreased, by the advent of industry and factories.

Another function performed by bosses has not yet appeared in this account: they take risks. This is most notable when they are introducing new products or procedures, being Schumpeterian innovators. These bosses can be called entrepreneurs, to distinguish them from managers. Entrepreneurs see new opportunities, invent new machines, discover new markets. They are change agents, performing a different function from that of the manager, who works within a known technology, organization, and market.

Oliver Evans can stand for the early industrial entrepreneur, as Stubs did for the early manager. One of the most brilliant engineers in the new United States, Evans invented the high-pressure steam engine in the early years of the nineteenth century, about a decade earlier than Trevithick in Britain. The engine was widely used; the United States went over to the high-pressure engine substantially earlier than Britain (Temin 1966; Halsey 1981). Evans himself, however, was not an outstanding businessman. He spent a major part of his commercial life extending and defending his steam engine patent. He also invented an automatic flour mill in the 1790s, based on a gravity feed of grain in the milling process that seems to anticipate Henry Ford's assembly line over a century later. Despite the technical virtuosity of Evans' mill, however, it was not a commercial success; the handful of mills built by Evans or under his patent never prospered. The idea of a gravity-feed flour mill, however, did catch on, becoming increasingly common over time. Finally, Evans operated the Mars Works in Philadelphia, a collection of activities clustered around an iron foundry: a blacksmith shop, two air furnaces (to make wrought iron), production facilities for millstones and steam engines. The Mars Works employed thirty-five people in 1811 and burned down in 1819 just before Evans died. It had no assets other than Evans himself. He was an entrepreneur of some distinction, not a successful manager (Bathe and Bathe 1935).

Evans and Stubs were very different. But while they provide clear examples of early industrial entrepreneurs and managers, it must be acknowledged that each performed—as I just noted for Evans—a somewhat mixed job. Risk is present even when conditions are relatively stable, for no commercial activity is without risk of some sort. Stubs was hardly a Schumpeterian innovator; he was engaged in an activity Adam Smith had described a generation earlier. But he was the owner of his pin factory as well as its manager. He therefore took a financial risk with the fixed and circulating capital involved. To this extent he was acting as entrepreneur as well as manager, showing that the functions typically were combined in the early stages of industrialization. The market had not yet grown big enough to make a complete division of labor worthwhile.

The functions of entrepreneur and manager were combined in the career of Josiah Wedgewood. He is particularly interesting because his entrepreneurial activities did not involve new machinery. Instead, Wedgewood introduced new forms of pottery, new methods of manufacture based on a strict division of labor, and new management techniques to operate his factories. But this outstanding eighteenth-century "boss" provides the exception that proves the rule. Stubs and Evans are interesting because they are typical, Wedgewood because he was unique (McKendrick 1960, 1961).

Because he was an exception and because his factories preceded the age of machinery, it is instructive to inquire into the motives behind his hierarchical production. They were, quite clearly, to enhance efficiency. He exerted a powerful control over his workers, extending his reach to their morals as well as their work. He was building an industrial labor force in an age before industrial labor was common, and he had to incorporate the functions now done elsewhere—in schools, armies, other factories—into his factories. This involved coercion and subjection, but there is no doubt that he achieved efficiencies unobtainable by the old guild methods.

Could anyone have done this? Did Wedgewood succeed by restricting access to the *knowledge* of what he was doing? Superficially, the answer is yes.

Wedgewood was obsessed with secrecy, to the point of opening his workers' letters. But the secrets appear to have been Wedgewood's patterns and designs, the skills of making specific shapes or painting particular motifs. The technique of operating a large centralized factory was not a secret; it simply was not duplicatable. Wedgewood was an outlier in the joint distribution of entrepreneurial and managerial skills. He brought something to the pottery business not attainable by any number of master potters. That was the key to his great success, demonstrating that even without new machinery, the successful division of labor was efficiency-enhancing, not simply worker-exploiting.

It was not for another century, until the quarter-century before World War I, that markets and firms had grown enough to make a division of labor between managers and entrepreneurs the rule rather than the exception. The market was expanded by the growth of railroads, telegraph, and telephone; the scale of management by the invention of new machinery. In fact, the scope of management became so large that it required many managers to run an efficient firm. Success in the market entailed a separation of the entrepreneurial function from the many-layered managerial one. Planning needed to be separated from operations (Chandler 1962, 1977).

The distinction between these two functions often is blurred in the literature as well as in practice. The Marglin-Landes debate groups them both under the activities performed by bosses; the business literature does little better. The distinction can be clarified by reference to my description of modes of behavior. I distinguished between "command," "customary," and "instrumental" behavior. The customary mode is used for repeated actions in slowly changing environments; the command mode, for episodic actions amid rapid change. Instrumental behavior, the maximizing actions of most economic theory, occupies an intermediate position in certain conditions. Both entrepreneurs and managers act instrumentally sometimes, but they cannot do so all the time. The manager deals with repeated actions; he works in a stable condition. The entrepreneur, by contrast, deals with change and uncertainty. My analysis implies that managers engage in customary activity; entrepreneurs, in command behavior (Temin 1980).

The different types of behavior are distinguished by the context in which they are exhibited. Customary behavior takes place in loose social structures, command behavior in hierarchies. Business firms are hierarchical, a fact which suggests that both managerial and entrepreneurial activity are forms of command. But the extensive literature on business strategy shows that a business firm in its day-to-day activities resembles a society in many ways.

Barnard, the father of this literature, introduced the point in the 1930s: "An organization can secure the efforts necessary to its existence, then, either by the objective inducement it provides or by changing states of mind. It seems to me improbable that any organization can exist as a practical matter which does not employ both methods in combination.'' Commands are not enough; cooperative activity must come from a sense of shared purpose (Barnard 1938, pp. 141, 233). Selznick extended the argument, distinguishing between two types of decisions: routine and critical. Routine decisions are those involved in the daily functioning of an organization. In the absence of stress necessitating critical decisions, the organization ''runs itself.'' It is a social structure in which people participate according to their state of mind. But even social structures need leaders: ''And the proper tooling of everyday activity is a legitimate and necessary preoccupation of management'' (Barnard 1938, pp. 141, 233; Selznick 1984, pp. 29–35).

Managing a ''bottom-up'' organization is something of an art. The manager needs to project a sense of purpose that helps to guide the actions of people lower down. He or she has to resolve conflicts by political processes internal to the organization. Argyris and Schon (1978) describe techniques for conflict resolution in business firms that resemble family therapy as much as political management. It is a skill that can be taught and learned. But it is not easy to learn, and managers are paid accordingly.

Marglin (1984, p. 146) asserts, ''The ability to organize production . . . is quintessentially a 'public' or 'collective' good.'' This is nonsense. The theory of management is public. It is written in the books I have cited and many, many more. But it is one thing to know the theory and another to be able to practice it. Reading a book on skiing or tennis does not enable one to be an expert skier or tennis player. Reading an economics text, alas, does not an economist make. The theory of management may be a public good, but the ability to manage is a skill like many others. It takes time to exercise, contributes to production, and is compensated in normal circumstances according to its marginal product. Wedgewood, as I have noted, was unique.

Management, in the sense that I have defined the term here, is a necessary part of production. Marglin seems to have been driven to extreme pronouncements to defend the contrary position. But in fact there can be little disagreement, once the merits of any division of labor are recognized. Management is simply another division of labor. The scale of modern management is the result of large markets and large-scale technology. Management in the Industrial Revolution was exercised over much smaller organizations as a result of the size of markets and the scale of technology at that time.

This account of the origin of factories raises another question. Given the need for hierarchy (division of labor), who should control it? While Marglin (1976, p. 17) is correct when he states that firms play no role in the theory of the competitive economy (''It is merely a convenient abstraction for the household in its role as producer''), he ignores the work that has been directed to the organization of industry. This work, which has blossomed since Marglin wrote his original essay, deals with the question of control under the rubric of the principal-agent problem. The manager in this literature is the agent; the question is, who is the principal?

Ownership is a tricky concept. It has had many meanings at different times in history; it needs to be handled with care in any historical discussion. Grossman and Hart define it in the context of the principal-agent literature as the ability to make all decisions not explicitly directed by contract. It is the residual decision-making authority (Grossman and Hart 1987). The government of the United States, according to this definition, owns the states.

A contract specifies the obligations of parties to an agreement or ongoing institutional arrangement. It has to be complete enough to cover most possible outcomes of the activities in question and simple enough to be worth writing, negotiating, and signing. Contracts will be written, therefore, where conditions allow simple, complete agreements to be formulated (Williamson 1985). Employment contracts will be written where the employees' functions fit these characteristics. People will be hired, in other words, if their actions can be monitored.[3]

Managers and entrepreneurs, as I am using the terms, operate in different conditions and perform different jobs. The manager works in stable conditions. His or her actions vary within a relatively narrow range. They are bound both by the constancy of the external environment and by the implicit rules of the firm's internal social structure. This is not to deny that there are problems to be solved. It is rather to identify them as what Selznick calls "routine" decisions. The manager constantly makes decisions needed for the operation of the firm (a few of Stubs's decisions were listed earlier). He does not, typically, make decisions that involve a complete restructuring or reorganizing of the firm.[4]

Managers consequently can be hired. Contracts can be written specifying the nature of their work and the rewards for effort. Chandler (1977) chronicled the growth of what he calls managerial capitalism in the last century. He has argued that firms could exist with very few managers for most of the nineteenth century, perhaps, as in the case of Stubs, with no separation between manager and owner. But the growing scale of markets, of efficient production, and of firms vertically organized to take advantage of a variety of opportunities generated a need for a many-layered managerial hierarchy. The presence of so many managers in turn forced the firm to reorganize to make good use of them, giving rise to the modern multidivisional corporate form.

Chandler ironically blurred the distinction between managers and entrepreneurs even as he made the case for the importance of the former. He was describing the introduction of new corporate forms. He therefore gave prominence to the men who introduced them even as he celebrated the efficiency of these forms. Writing a history rather than an analytic treatise, he focused on change even as he championed a particular form of stability. The men who initiated change therefore were his heroes, although not his managers. They were the men who hired the managers who composed the managerial hierarchy. But since a separate term was not introduced for them, readers could think that they were the managers.

I am reserving the Schumpeterian term *entrepreneur* for these men. They introduced new technologies, new organizational forms, or new marketing concepts. They started new firms—often even new industries—or made dramatic changes in existing firms. They engaged in what I have called command behavior as they reacted to new conditions and created essentially new organizations. They took large risks, sailing in uncharted waters, and made large profits if successful.

The key point here is in the distinction between managerial and entrepreneurial behavior. Superficially similar, one is a response to stable conditions, the other to new opportunities. Simon's distinction between satisficing and maximizing behavior is not rich enough for this application. Managers satisfice. But entrepreneurs do not maximize; they do not have the information to make a calculation that maximizes profits. Instead, they work on intuition, insight, and guts. We remember those who are either truly insightful or lucky. It blurs the analysis to lump together the maximizing behavior undertaken when conditions render satisficing (customary) behavior dysfunctional, but still allow explicit searching and calculating behavior to be effective, and behavior undertaken to break new ground, challenge the accepted wisdom, open up new markets. A distinction between what I have called instrumental (maximizing) behavior and command behavior is needed (Simon 1976, p. xxix; Temin 1980).

It is precisely because command behavior is not instrumental and cannot be anticipated that entrepreneurs cannot be hired. There is no way to write a contract for them to act. The essence of their activities is to do the unexpected; restrictions would conflict with their mission. The entrepreneur retains the residual decision-making authority. He is, in short, the owner—the principal. Klein, Crawford, and Alchian (1978), in an exploration of the choice between contracts and ownership, note that the owner in this sense is also the major capitalist: it would be too costly for the entrepreneur to rent a plant from someone else, because the lessor would need to insure himself against the risk that the entrepreneur would not do whatever he should do with the plant.

Landes, in contrast to Chandler, explicitly celebrated the entrepreneur. His focus was technology, not organization. He therefore made no bones about the importance of pioneers. He in fact did not spend time on the operation of the discoveries once made; his interest was always in the newest innovations (Landes 1969). His statements in the debate with Marglin, however, need to be reformulated slightly to keep the distinction clear. Landes states, for example, that "the ability to combine the factors of production in such a way as to make goods cheaper is one of the central aspects of entrepreneurship" (Landes 1986, p. 594). In the present context, read: management. Landes refers elsewhere in his discussion to what I have been calling entrepreneurship when he asserts: "The biggest and surest source of gain was the application of invention to one's own enterprise—a Schumpeterian headstart" (Landes 1986, p. 614).

Managers, in short, were the workers' bosses, but entrepreneurs were the managers' bosses. Hierarchy is a fact of life, or at least of economic production. Control of productive hierarchies in the first instance went to entrepreneurs who then became bosses. Anyone who had the requisite skills could be a manager. While understandably different, finding a managerial job was the same kind of process as finding a weaving or spinning job. But only those people prepared to "do something different" became entrepreneurs. This critical step in industrialization was omitted from Marglin's analysis.

The identification of entrepreneurship with ownership poses the last set of questions to be considered here. How have the functions of entrepreneurs and managers changed over time? And does this evolution have implications for the future?

At the start of industrialization, from the late eighteenth century through the time of Ashton's Stubs, there was seldom sufficient division of labor to require separate entrepreneurs and managers. The same men performed both functions. The functions began to separate from each other as industrialization progressed, and markets, firms, and the division of labor grew. The integration of both functions in the same person had become dysfunctional by the late nineteenth century in many industries. Entrepreneurs hired managers to run their multidivisional companies. As theory suggests, the entrepreneurs were the owners; the managers, the employees.

The distinction is clear in a famous story about Andrew Carnegie, one of America's preeminent entrepreneurs of the late nineteenth century. As he recounted in his autobiography, Carnegie was anxious to please the extraordinary and creative manager of his Edgar Thomson Works, Captain Bill Jones. Carnegie offered to give Jones a part ownership in the business, with the interest for the loan paid out of profits so that there was no cost to Jones. Jones refused. He was, he said, a working man; a manager in the terminology used here. As Carnegie tells the story, Jones said, "I don't want to have my thoughts running on business. I have enough trouble looking after these works. Just give me a hell of a salary if you think I'm worth it."

"All right, Captain," replied Carnegie, "the salary of the President of the United States is yours." Jones was pleased by both the money and the symbolism, and the Edgar Thomson Works ran spectacularly well. Beyond Jones's pleasure, we can see the division of labor that the large firms of the late nineteenth century required. Carnegie was the top staff officer; Jones, a head line officer. Carnegie was the entrepreneur and owner; Jones, the manager and employee (Carnegie 1920, p. 203; Wall 1970, p. 359).

The separation between managers and entrepreneurs, which became clear only in the late nineteenth century, began to blur again in the early twentieth. In our system of inheritable property, being the son of an entrepreneur was almost as good as being one yourself. Entrepreneurs became bosses through their own abilities; their descendants were appointed bosses by the property system. Inherited property then became more liquid as stock markets grew. The ownership of any individual firm was dispersed, and the children and grandchildren of entrepreneurs were owners in the legal sense without having much control over management. They were the residual claimants of income with severely limited decision-making authority.

As Berle and Mears (1932) publicized half a century ago, the question of how to reward or punish managers has become more difficult as organizations have become more complex and ownership more diffuse. More recent economic analysis has examined the role of corporate takeovers in the control of top executives (Grossman and Hart 1980; Shleifer and Vishny 1986). But if the threat of corporate takeover is the only disciplinary influence on managers, as is sometimes assumed, then the manager has ceased to be an employee in any real sense. Top managers, freed of many traditional constraints, have begun to seem and act very much like owners—that is, entrepreneurs. The two functions have become integrated at this level and blurred again, returning in a curious way to the synthesis of two centuries earlier.

This can be seen clearly in one of the most important executive decisions of our time. AT&T found itself under siege at the end of 1981. The government had rested its antitrust suit against the telephone monopoly in the summer, and AT&T had filed a motion for summary acquittal. Judge Harold Greene replied in a long brief echoing the government's case. Far from rejecting the prosecution's case out of hand, he seemed inclined to accept it. As AT&T's defense presentation approached its conclusion at the end of the year, AT&T's lawyers doubted that they had changed his mind. While no one knew—or knows even now—what Judge Greene would have done had he decided the case, the suspicion was that he would have found AT&T guilty and ordered it to sell Western Electric, its manufacturing arm.

AT&T's end run around the court through Congress was coming to an unhappy conclusion at the same time. The Senate had finally passed a telecommunications bill that could have been an alternative to an antitrust judgment. But the bill was only tolerable to AT&T, the House seemed poised to consider a far more restrictive bill, and the administration was unwilling to enforce the bargain it had struck—or at least that AT&T thought it had struck—to abandon the antitrust case upon congressional passage of a telecommunications bill.

Charles Brown, the chief executive officer of AT&T, firmly believed that the vertical integration of manufacturing and telephone service was essential to the health of the company. He was unwilling to take the chance that Judge Greene did not agree. He thought the House bill also would be too restrictive for a healthy firm, and he knew that key members of Congress did not agree. He was faced with a choice among unpleasant alternatives.

Brown therefore moved to settle the antitrust case, taking the decision out of the hands of Judge Greene and Congress. He agreed to divest the Bell operating companies in return for permission to keep Western Electric and Bell Laboratories part of AT&T and relatively free of restrictions. (In fact, the expectation was that the residual AT&T company would be freed of regulation, a process that is happening gradually today.) This dramatic decision dismantled the largest corporation in the world and changed the future path of telecommunications in the United States and possibly the world (Temin 1987).

Brown obviously was acting as an entrepreneur. He had a chief operating officer who ran the company; Brown's function was to decide its future. No less than Carnegie a century earlier, he had the power to make decisions that determined the shape of his company, its market strategy, and its stance toward competition. Yet—unlike Carnegie—he was not an important owner of AT&T. Ownership was widely diffused among the public. Entrepreneurship had become the function of AT&T's managers, not its owners.

This is not the place to debate the wisdom of Brown's decision. The issue here is how the economy chooses who makes these large decisions. Before the twentieth century, it was the owner-entrepreneurs. They were trained to do so by the experience they acquired creating their companies. Now manager-entrepreneurs such as Brown have this authority. They typically train by rising through the managerial ranks of a large hierarchy and being socialized into the corporate culture of the firm, as described above. Schumpeter realized over forty years ago that this is hardly the best selection process or training for entrepreneurs (Schumpeter 1942).

It is possible to envisage a change in property rights. Ownership of industrial concerns could be given to the workers. But while this would change the distribution of wealth, it would not do much for the selection of entrepreneurial leaders. The new worker-owners would be in the same position as the prior share owners. Ownership would be too diffuse to exert much control; the managers would continue to be entrepreneurs also. A change of ownership does not do away with hierarchies, and it is impossible in an economy as large as ours to concentrate the ownership of most large companies enough for the owners to act as Schumpeterian entrepreneurs.

An exception again proves the rule. Venture capitalists search for entrepreneurs to finance. Aren't they hiring entrepreneurs? No. They do not pay the entrepreneur a salary; they enter into partnership-type arrangements. Ownership, in the sense of residual claimant, is fully shared. That gives the entrepreneur ample incentive to act as a proper residual decision maker as well. He will not have the same interests as a sole owner, but in a small group the entrepreneur identifies with the group. This shared ownership—which has been used in various forms throughout the process of industrialization—is effective only if the group sharing the profits is small. As the group becomes larger, the interests of the entrepreneur diverge ever farther from the interests of his partners (Olson 1965). This exception therefore cannot ever become the norm; there are too many owners of a typical firm.

The division of labor promotes efficiency at any moment of time. Paradoxically, it may limit the improvement of efficiency over time. The men and women at the top of extensive business hierarchies are called upon to perform two dissimilar functions. The role of bosses as managers is clear: they are the bosses who deal with workers, and they work under their own bosses. The position of bosses as entrepreneurs in today's world is less clear-cut. Active in the late eighteenth and nineteenth centuries, the owner-entrepreneurs celebrated by economic historians have given way to manager-entrepreneurs. Even though the combination of functions is reminiscent of a preindustrial world, the conditions in which they operate are not. The managerial structures adopted a century ago may well fail to provide the best selection process and forum for action of today's entrepreneurs.[5]

Notes

1. Marglin (1976, 1984); Landes (1986).

2. John Stuart Mill listed legal rules as well. He thought that the institution of limited liabilities would give rise to worker cooperatives where laborers would hire capital and managers (Mill 1985, p. 132).

3. The usual question in industrial organization is whether a contract is written; in industrial relations, how the contract looks. This discussion asks the former question of the employment contract.

4. Argyris and Schon call these decisions "single-loop learning." The distinction is ubiquitous in the managerial literature, albeit without a unified terminology (Argyris and Schon 1978, p. 3; Selznick 1984, p. 31).

5. Piore and Sabel (1984) argue that a much-reduced hierarchy is today becoming more efficient than vertically integrated, many-layered corporations.

References

Argyris, C., and D. A. Schon. 1978. *Organizational Learning: A Theory of Action Perspective.* Reading, Mass.: Addison-Wesley.

Ashton, T. S. 1925. "The Records of a Pin Manufactory, 1814–21." *Economica* 4 (November): 281–292.

Barnard, C. I. 1938. *The Functions of the Executive.* Cambridge, Mass.: Harvard University Press.

Bathe, G., and D. Bathe. 1935. *Oliver Evans: A Chronicle of Early American Engineering.* Philadelphia: Historical Society of Pennsylvania.

Berle, A. A., and G. C. Mears. 1932. *The Modern Corporation and Private Property.* New York: Macmillan.

Carnegie, A. 1920. *The Autobiography of Andrew Carnegie.* Boston: Houghton Mifflin.

Chandler, A. D., Jr. 1962. *Strategy and Structure: Chapters in the History of the Industrial Enterprise.* Cambridge, Mass.: MIT Press.

———— 1977. *The Visible Hand: The Managerial Revolution in American Business.* Cambridge, Mass.: Harvard University Press.

Crozier, M. 1964. *The Bureaucratic Phenomenon.* Berkeley: University of California Press.

Dutton, H. I., and S. R. H. Jones. 1983. "Invention and Innovation in the British Pin Industry, 1790–1850." *Business History Review* 57 (Summer):175–193.

Grossman, S. J., and O. D. Hart. 1980. "Takeover Bids, the Free-Rider Problem, and the Theory of the Corporation." *Bell Journal of Economics* 11 (Spring):42–64.

———— 1987. "The Costs and Benefits of Ownership: A Theory of Vertical and Lateral Integration." *Journal of Political Economy* 94 (Feburary):691–719.

Halsey, H. I. 1981. "The Choice between High-Pressure and Low-Pressure Steam Power in America in the Early Nineteenth Century." *Journal of Economic History* 41 (December):723–744.

Jones, S. R. H. 1973. "Price Associations and Competition in the British Pin Industry, 1814–40." *Economic History Review* 2nd ser., 26 (May):237–253.

Klein, B., R. G. Crawford, and A. A. Alchian. 1978. "Vertical Integration, Appropriate Rents, and the Competitive Contracting Process." *Journal of Law and Economics* 21 (October):297–326.

Knight, F. H. [1921] 1964. *Risk, Uncertainty, and Profit.* New York: Kelley.

Landes, D. S. 1969. *The Unbound Prometheus: Technological Change and Industrial Development in Western Europe from 1750 to the Present.* Cambridge: Cambridge University Press.

———— 1986. "What Do Bosses Really Do?" *Journal of Economic History* 46 (September):595–624.

Laslett, P. 1983. *The World We Have Lost, Further Considered.* London: Methuen.

Marglin, S. 1976. "What Do Bosses Do?" In *The Division of Labour: The Labour Process and Class Struggle in Modern Capitalism,* ed. A. Gorz. Atlantic Highlands, N.J.: Humanities Press.

———— 1984. "Knowledge and Power." In *Firms, Organization, and Labour: Approaches to the Economics of Work Organization,* ed. F. H. Stephen. New York: St. Martin's.

McKendrick, N. 1960. "Josiah Wedgewood: An Eighteenth-Century Entrepreneur in Salesmanship and Marketing." *Economic History Review* n.s. 12 (December):408–433.

———— 1961. "Josiah Wedgewood and Factory Discipline." *Historical Journal* 4 (March):30–55.

Mill, J. S. 1985. *Principles of Political Economy.* Harmondsworth: Penguin Classics.

Olson, M. 1965. *The Logic of Collective Action.* Cambridge, Mass.: Harvard University Press.

Piore, M. J., and C. F. Sabel. 1984. *The Second Industrial Divide: Possibilities for Prosperity.* New York: Basic Books.

Pollard, S. 1965. *The Genesis of Modern Management.* Cambridge, Mass.: Harvard University Press.

Schumpeter, J. A. 1942. *Capitalism, Socialism, and Democracy.* New York: Harper and Row.

Selznick, P. [1957] 1984. *Leadership in Administration: A Sociological Interpretation.* Berkeley: University of California Press.

Shleifer, A., and R. W. Vishny. 1986. "Large Shareholders and Corporate Control." *Journal of Political Economy* 94 (June):461–488.

Simon, H. A. 1976. *Administrative Behavior: A Study of Decision-Making Processes in Administrative Organization*. 3rd ed. New York: Free Press.

Temin, P. 1966. "Steam and Waterpower." *Journal of Economic History* 26 (June):187–205.

——— 1980. "Modes of Behavior." *Journal of Economic Behavior and Organization* 1 (April): 175–195.

——— 1987. *The Fall of the Bell System: A Study in Prices and Politics*. New York: Cambridge University Press.

Wall, J. F. 1970. *Andrew Carnegie*. New York: Oxford University Press.

Williamson, O. E. 1985. *The Economic Institutions of Capitalism*. New York: Free Press.

III
····

Paths of Economic Growth

13

. . .

Did England's Cities Grow Too Fast during the Industrial Revolution?

Jeffrey G. Williamson

In spite of the appearance of three important books on urbanization—by Anthony Wohl (1983), Jan de Vries (1984), and Paul Hohenberg and Lynn Lees (1985), we still know very little about the impact of urbanization on the other components of modernization. Indeed, we cannot even agree on whether city growth was too fast or too slow. David Landes appears to take the view that fast city growth was a Good Thing. After all, England underwent the Industrial Revolution first and was also more urbanized than its competitors (Landes 1969, pp. 51–52). That historical correlation implies for Landes that England's regime of fast city growth must have been optimal, and that slower city growth would have been a mistake. Wohl takes the contrary view, that England was unprepared for and surprised by the rapid city growth that carried the Industrial Revolution, with disastrous results. City governments did not plan for the event, public health authorities were unprepared for the event, and city social overhead technologies were too backward to deal with the event. Entrepreneurial and technological failure in the public sector and rising land scarcity in the private sector both served to breed levels of crowding, density, mortality, morbidity, and disamenities that even Third World analysts would find hard to comprehend. In Michael Flinn's words, "The 1830s and 1840s saw the appearance of a . . . Malthusian . . . retribution by disease" (1965, p. 14). England was simply unable or unwilling to house itself properly during the First Industrial Revolution. In terms of quality of life indicators, either city growth was too fast, or investment in urban social overhead was too low, or both.

City growth debates have been equally intense in the Third World. Here too pessimists have stressed the city's inability to cope with the social overhead and housing requirements of rapid growth, arguing that city growth has been too fast, requiring public intervention. As a United Nations survey in 1978 showed, this view was certainly the dominant one among government authorities in the developing nations: "Among the 116 developing countries that responded to the

United Nations' 'Fourth Population Inquiry among Governments' . . . [on] the desirability of current rates of rural-urban migration . . . 76 [wished] to slow it down and 14 to reverse it" (Preston 1979, p. 195).

Things had not changed when a similar survey was taken in 1983. In short, the pessimists tend to view Third World city growth as another example of failure in private markets, in this case an example in which a collective resource, the urban commons, is overused. Looking at the Manchester slums in the 1830s, interventionists such as James Kay-Shuttleworth (1832), Frederick Engels (1971), and the social reformers would certainly have agreed. In contrast, laissez-faire optimists view city growth as the central force raising average living standards. Indeed, the optimists tend to attribute any overuse of the urban commons to government-induced price distortions and an urban bias, rather than to failure in private markets (Lipton 1976). While the optimists favor an open, laissez-faire approach to city growth, the pessimists search for efficient legislative devices to close down the cities. Like the Victorian Social Reformers, Third World city planners think city growth has been too fast, and many social scientists would appear to agree (Shaw 1978; Simmons 1979; Preston 1979; United Nations 1980, chap. 9).

Some have argued that cities have grown fast simply by default, and that the Third World has "overurbanized" on these grounds too (Hoselitz 1955, 1957). According to this view, the cities are too large and too numerous, and they got that way somehow through perverse migration behavior. Pushed off the land by labor-displacing events in agriculture and by Malthusian pressures on the land, rural emigrants flood the cities in far greater numbers than new modern-sector jobs can be created for them. Attracted by an irrational optimism that they will be selected for those scarce high-wage city jobs, the rural emigrants keep coming. Lacking high-wage jobs in the growing modern sectors, the glut of rural immigrants spills over into low-wage service sectors, unemployment, and pauperism, while their families crowd into inadequate housing and overload the city's social overhead, blighting an otherwise dynamic urban economy.

In the late 1960s, Michael Todaro (1969) developed a framework which could account for the apparent irrationality of rural immigrants' rushing to the city even in the face of unemployment and underemployment. The Todaro framework and its extensions (Corden and Findlay 1975) have enjoyed considerable popularity, even among economic historians (Pollard 1978, 1981). Todaro stressed *expected* earnings as the critical force motivating migration behavior, fortunate migrants being selected for the good jobs (primarily in manufacturing) and unfortunate migrants making do with low-wage service sector jobs. Certainly Mayhew (1967) made much of London's casual labor and street vending. But while Todaro stresses the role of the low-wage urban service sector as a holding area for the reserve army of immigrants who have come to the city in anticipation of getting those high-wage modern sector jobs, Mayhew's London street people seem instead to have been "pushed" into those low-wage jobs (the residuum). Whether one supports Todaro's "irrational migrant" view or Mayhew's "push" view of city immigration, they both imply that cities grew too fast in the First Industrial Revolution and are growing too fast in the contemporary Third World as well. Society would have been better off had the potential migrants waited for those good urban jobs in England's countryside rather than in the cities themselves.

To make matters even more complex, some have appealed to failure in private factor markets to argue that English cities grew too *slowly*. After all, what are we to make of those wage gaps between city and countryside? Wage gaps and rural labor surpluses would seem to imply insufficient migration and labor market failure. They also imply that urban labor was too expensive and thus that city growth was too slow. Alternatively, they imply capital market failure since it would appear that manufacturing capital failed to move to the countryside in sufficient amounts to exploit the surplus labor fully. And certainly low rates of return in agriculture coexisting with capital scarcity in the city implies a market failure. Factor market failure in any of these dimensions implies a limit to or a constraint on city growth.

So, did cities grow too fast or too slow during the Industrial Revolution? The question is probably too difficult to answer even in a book,[1] but this chapter at least suggests how the answer might be sought.

Did Cities Really Grow Fast?
Demographic Surprises and Dependency Burdens

Was City Growth Fast?

How does the English experience compare with that of the contemporary Third World? Among 29 Third World countries, the rate of urban population growth in the 1960s and 1970s was 4.35 percent per annum (Todaro 1984, p. 13). These city growth rates are double the English rates shown in Table 13.1. Of course, *everything* was growing more rapidly in the Third World. Indeed, the overall population growth rate in the Third World (2.33 percent per annum: Todaro 1984, pp. 10–11) was also about double that of England over the century from 1776 to 1871 (1.23 percent per annum: Wrigley and Schofield 1981, p. 529), implying similar rates of urbanization. While English city growth rates were certainly impressive by the standards of that time, they were quite modest when compared with those of the contemporary Third World.

Oddly enough, while English city growth rates were about half of those recorded in the contemporary Third World, city immigration rates were quite

Table 13.1   Urban immigration and rural emigration, England and Wales, 1776–1871.

| | | I. Urban Immigration | | | | | | |
| | Urban population at starting year (thousands) (1) | Urban population increase (thousands) | | | Percent urban population increase | | Annual percent rates of: | | |
Years		Total (2)	Owing to natural increase (3)	Owing to immigration (4)	Owing to natural increase (5)	Owing to immigration (6)	Urban population increase (7)	Natural increase (8)	City immigration (9)
1776–1781	1,746	191	77	114	40.51%	59.49%	2.08%	0.87%	1.26%
1781–1786	1,937	184	20	169	11.01	88.99	1.81	0.21	1.62
1786–1791	2,121	247	96	151	38.92	61.08	2.20	0.89	1.37
1791–1796	2,368	272	126	146	46.31	53.69	2.17	1.04	1.20
1796–1801	2,640	289	139	150	48.13	51.87	2.08	1.03	1.10
1801–1806	2,929	333	39	294	11.82	88.18	2.15	0.27	1.91
1806–1811	3,262	356	258	98	72.47	27.53	2.07	1.52	0.59
1811–1816	3,618	462	205	257	44.45	55.55	2.40	1.10	1.37
1816–1821	4,080	517	296	221	57.18	42.82	2.39	1.40	1.06
1821–1826	4,597	640	375	265	58.65	41.35	2.61	1.57	1.12
1826–1831	5,237	648	363	285	56.05	43.95	2.33	1.34	1.06
1831–1836	5,885	646	332	314	51.34	48.66	2.08	1.10	1.04
1836–1841	6,531	700	423	277	60.50	39.50	2.04	1.26	0.83
1841–1846	7,231	927	466	461	50.32	49.68	2.41	1.25	1.23
1846–1851	8,158	880	476	404	54.11	45.89	2.05	1.13	0.97
1851–1856	9,038	981	624	357	63.61	36.39	2.06	1.34	0.77
1856–1861	10,019	1,097	791	306	72.08	27.92	2.08	1.52	0.60
1861–1866	11,116	1,387	781	606	56.33	43.67	2.35	1.36	1.06
1866–1871	12,503	1,516	779	737	51.37	48.63	2.29	1.21	1.15

II. Rural Emigration

Years	Rural population at starting year (thousands) (10)	Rural population increase (thousands)			Percent rural population increase		Annual percent rates of:		
		Total (11)	Owing to natural increase (12)	Owing to immigration (13)	Owing to natural increase (14)	Owing to immigration (15)	Rural population increase (16)	Natural increase (17)	Rural immigration (18)
1776–1781	4,995	111	322	−211	All →	None →	0.44%	1.25%	−0.86%
1781–1786	5,106	62	187	−125			0.24	0.72	−0.50
1786–1791	5,168	204	347	−143			0.77	1.30	−0.56
1791–1796	5,372	187	394	−207			0.68	1.42	−0.79
1796–1801	5,559	177	403	−226			0.63	1.40	−0.83
1801–1806	5,736	269	216	53			0.92	0.74	0.18
1806–1811	6,005	263	574	−311			0.86	1.83	−1.07
1811–1816	6,268	304	485	−181			0.95	1.49	−0.59
1816–1821	6,572	323	604	−281			0.96	1.76	−0.87
1821–1826	6,895	279	676	−397			0.79	1.87	−1.19
1826–1831	7,174	225	624	−399			0.62	1.67	−1.14
1831–1836	7,399	176	540	−364			0.47	1.41	−1.01
1836–1841	7,575	165	607	−442			0.43	1.54	−1.20
1841–1846	7,740	36	619	−583			0.09	1.54	−1.57
1846–1851	7,776	−77	569	−646			−0.20	1.41	−1.73
1851–1856	7,699	46	617	−571			0.12	1.54	−1.54
1856–1861	7,745	76	670	−594			0.20	1.66	−1.60
1861–1866	7,821	−158	622	−780			−0.41	1.53	−2.10
1866–1871	7,663	−181	565	−746			−0.48	1.42	−2.05

Sources and notes: The urban and rural populations are derived by applying the share urban to English population totals, the latter taken from Wrigley and Schofield (1981, table A.3.3, pp. 534–535). The urban share is based on Law (1967, 1972). The CBR and CDR underlying the natural increase estimates in columns 3 and 12 are consistent with the economywide CBR and CDR in Wrigley and Schofield (1981). Immigration (+) or emigration (−) is derived as a residual. The remaining columns are self-explanatory. Numbers of rural emigrants (column 4) need not be equal to numbers of urban immigrants (column 13) in the presence of external migration, such as that of the Irish. From Williamson (1990, table 2.5).

similar, ranging between 1.10 and 1.91 in England from 1776 to 1806 (see Table 13.1) and averaging 1.79 in the Third World (Kelley and Williamson 1984). Given that England's rate of city growth was only half that of the Third World, the city immigration rates were really quite spectacular.

It appears that England's cities relied more heavily on immigration than has the Third World. While immigration accounted for 45.8 percent of city population growth in England between 1811 and 1846, it accounted for only 39.3 percent in the Third World in the 1960s and 1970s. The relative importance of immigration to English city growth was even greater in the early years of the First Industrial Revolution: between 1776 and 1811 immigration accounted for a whopping 59.7 percent of city growth. The high immigration rates were necessary because crude death rates were much higher in the cities. These urban-rural crude death rate differentials (Williamson 1990, chap. 2) declined somewhat after 1841, but they were still pronounced in 1866. They continued to decline during the remainder of the nineteenth century, but the switch to a mortality environment in which cities had the lower death rates did not take place until around World War I. The impact of public health and sanitation reform in making the city a relatively benign mortality environment—even in the Third World—is a twentieth-century phenomenon. In nineteenth-century England the cities were killers, a very important fact to remember in understanding the operation of urban labor markets during the First Industrial Revolution.

In the contemporary Third World, crude rates of natural increase are about the same in urban and rural areas (22.5 versus 22.4 per thousand: Rogers 1984, p. 288), whereas in England they were considerably higher in the countryside even as late as 1841 (15.0 versus 11.9 per thousand: Williamson 1990, table 2.1), and the differential was probably far higher in the late eighteenth century. The higher rate of natural increase in the countryside clearly placed great stress on rural-urban labor markets as booming labor demands in the cities were distant from booming labor supplies in the countryside. The Third World has never had to cope with England's poor match between excess city labor demands and excess rural labor supplies. Perhaps this is one key reason why city immigration rates were so high in England even though the rate of industrialization and city growth was so modest by Third World standards.

Were the Cities Faced with Demographic Surprises?

In contrast with the alarmist comments of contemporaries in the 1830s and Wohl's assertion that municipal planners were unprepared for rapid city growth in the early nineteenth century, England's urbanization experience during the First Industrial Revolution was fairly gradual (see Table 13.1, column 7). While there is some evidence of a quickening in city growth rates between 1811 and 1846, which coincides with an acceleration of industrialization after the

French Wars, the surge in city growth is really quite modest. It is the relative stability in city growth rates which is most notable. Only in one half-decade (1781–1786) did the rate of city growth fall below 2 percent per annum, and it never rose above 2.6 percent per annum. The average rate of city growth over the 35 years of most rapid growth (1811–1846) was 2.35 percent per annum, not very much greater than the 2.1 percent per annum rate achieved before and the 2.2 percent rate achieved after. In the face of such evidence, one can hardly argue that municipal planners in the 1830s and 1840s were taken unawares by an unexpected acceleration of city growth since very similar growth rates had been experienced over the previous six decades.

If the housing and the municipal public sectors failed in the early nineteenth century, the explanation did not lie with demographic "surprises." Instead, the failure had its source, at least in part, in the limits on social overhead accumulation imposed by capital market austerity during the French Wars (Ashton 1959, chap. 4; Williamson 1984). The crowding-out effect of the massive increase in the war debt appears to have had its biggest impact on housing and social overhead investment. According to Charles Feinstein's revisions (1978, table XIII, p. 452), the net dwelling stock in constant prices lagged behind population growth up to 1810 (0.85 versus 0.95 percent per annum). The net stock of capital delivering public and social services lagged even further behind population growth up to 1810 (0.62 versus 0.95 percent per annum), and did not begin to catch up until the 1830s. This wartime postponement of housing and social overhead investment eventually became an environmentally nasty peacetime legacy that helped precipitate the Reform Debates of the 1830s.

Did the Cities Suffer Dependency Burdens?

Note, however, that English cities became less dependent on immigrants in satisfying their employment requirements as the Industrial Revolution ensued (see Table 13.1). The explanation here is quite simple: migration was highly selective of young adults. Almost 63 percent of the city immigrants in the 1850s were aged 15 to 29 (Williamson 1990, chap. 2), whereas only a little more than a quarter of the national population fell into that age group. This young adult selectivity bias among the migrants served to twist the age distribution in the cities, heaping the city population in the young adult ages and shrinking the number of very young and very old dependents. This had important implications. The glut of young adults implied high birth rates and low death rates, thus serving to augment the ability of the city to satisfy its employment requirements as time wore on, crowding out future immigrants.

The young adult bias favored the city in other ways too. It created a population which fostered the rate of accumulation of human and physical capital.

In the first place, the inflow of young adults implied a human capital transfer from countryside to city. Indeed, elsewhere I have estimated that the human capital—in the form of rearing costs—embodied in the city's immigrants were from 15 to 18 percent of city investment in 1850 (Williamson 1990, chap. 3). This human capital transfer must have served to take the pressure off conventional capital markets in financing accumulation requirements in England's cities during the Industrial Revolution.

In the second place, by lowering the dependency rate, cities had far lower relief burdens. A very extensive literature explores the sources and impact of the old poor laws in England, and all of it stresses that Speenhamland was an agricultural relief scheme. Nowhere in this literature, however, has anyone explored the extent to which the heavy rural incidence of poor relief might have been due simply to demography—young adults selecting cities and shunning the countryside, leaving behind dependents who were more vulnerable to pauperism. It certainly was true that the incidence of pauperism was higher in the country. This can be seen from data even as late as 1851 (Boyer and Williamson 1989). If we array counties by the share of urban population, then we get the following:

Urban attributes of counties	Number of counties	PAUPC	OLDPC	KIDSPC
urban = 0	16	.0591	.0846	.3630
urban = 1–19%	12	.0553	.0826	.3604
urban = 20–35%	7	.0527	.0786	.3598
urban = 36–65%	7	.0397	.0684	.3523
London	1	.0258	.0611	.3191

PAUPC are numbers relieved per capita, OLDPC is the share of the population aged 60 and older, and KIDSPC is the share of children up to age 14. Note that the pauper rate falls with urbanization, as does the dependency rate. The correlation suggests that the dependency burden should help explain high pauper rates in the countryside and low pauper rates in the cities. When a simple OLS regression is estimated on this data, strong dependency rate effects do indeed emerge:

X variables	Estimated coefficient	t-statistic	
Constant	− 0.192	1.444	
OLDPC	+ 0.755	2.021	
RVPROP	− 0.001	0.566	$R = .494$
IRISH	+ 0.100	0.656	$N = 43$
URBAN	+ 0.027	1.413	Mean PAUPC = .053
AGRIC	+ 0.088	2.770	F-statistic = 7.824
KIDSPC	+ 0.437	1.459	

IRISH is the percent of the population who are Irish, AGRIC is the employment share in agriculture, URBAN is the share in urban areas, and RVPROP is the ratable value of property. The "Speenhamland effect" is confirmed by the significant positive coefficient on AGRIC. The positive (though insignificant) coefficient on URBAN suggests that cities could afford more relief. More important, however, is the fact that the demographic variables perform well, especially the share of elderly. Furthermore, when the regression is used to determine how much of the difference in the predicted PAUPC between rural counties and London is explained by demographic variables, the answer is all of it! The moral of the story is that English cities were favored by the young adult bias. Low dependency rates implied low pauper rates.

As a result of these favorable demographic features, the cities should have had higher savings and accumulation rates. This follows directly from the life-cycle and dependency hypotheses. These hypotheses argue that high dependency rates increase consumption requirements at the expense of savings, and they have been centerpieces in the economic-demographic literature for two decades. Are the rural-urban differences in dependency rates large enough in early nineteenth-century England to have mattered? To answer this question directly would require rural and urban household savings data for early nineteenth-century England—data which are nonexistent. But some indirect evidence can shed light on the question. Nathaniel Leff (1969) found that the dependency rate accounted for a large share of the difference in savings rates for a cross-section of 74 countries in the 1960s, and the variance in the dependency rate for his data was not much greater than the rural-urban differentials for England in 1821 (Williamson 1990, chap. 2). Leff's results suggested that the elasticity of the savings rate with respect to the dependency rate was about -1.5. If we use Leff's elasticity, and assume the savings rate to have been around 10 percent in rural England, then it follows that the urban savings rate would have been 13 percent, a fairly large difference and one owing solely to dependency rate differentials. This dependency rate effect may have been manifested by a direct influence on household savings behavior or, perhaps more likely, indirectly through the impact of dependency rates on poor relief, the tax burden, and thus on disposable income of potential savers. In any case, the inference seems to be that the young adult bias must have had a significant impact on savings and accumulation rate differentials favoring England's cities during the Industrial Revolution.

If England's cities "failed," dependency burdens cannot be viewed as the culprit. On the contrary, they should have made accumulation and growth easier for the cities.

Were City Migrants Todaro-Irrational?

If city immigrants left full employment in the countryside to become underemployed or unemployed in the city, then such migration behavior must be viewed as socially unproductive and city growth too fast. Development economists thought they observed exactly that kind of behavior in the Third World in the 1960s, and many economic historians think they see the same in the nineteenth-century English experience (Pollard 1978, 1981; Matthews et al. 1982, pp. 82–83). Yet, how are we to account for the apparent irrationality of rural immigrants' rushing to the city in the face of unemployment and underemployment? Michael Todaro offered an answer in 1969.

The hypothesis is simple and elegant. While similar statements can be found sprinkled through the literature, the most effective illustration can be found in Max Corden and Ronald Findlay (1975), reproduced in Figure 13.1. Only two sectors are analyzed explicitly in Figure 13.1, but they are sufficient to illustrate the point. Under the extreme assumption of wage equalization through migration, and in the absence of wage rigidities, equilibrium is achieved at E (the point of intersection of the two labor demand curves, AA' and MM'). Here wages are equalized at $w_A^* = w^{M*}$, the urbanization level is $O_M L_M^*/L$ (the share of the total labor force, L, employed in urban jobs, $O_M L_M^*$), where M denotes urban manufacturing and A denotes agriculture. Since wages were never equalized in nineteenth-century England, and since they are not equalized in the contemporary Third World either, the Todaro model incorporates the widely held belief that the wage rate in manufacturing is pegged at artificially high levels by unions, by minimum wage legislation, or by private sector

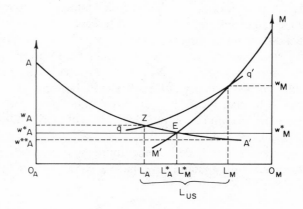

Figure 13.1   The Todaro model according to Corden and Findlay.

emulation of inflated public sector wage rates, say at w_M. If, for the moment, we ignore the realities of unemployment and underemployment, then all those who fail to secure the favored jobs in manufacturing would accept low-wage jobs in agriculture at w_A^{**}. Although this exposition of the model has yet to accommodate Todaro's emphasis on urban unemployment, this incomplete version at least allows for a wage gap between the two sectors, a gap of which so much has been made in both British economic history and the Third World.

Under the assumptions made thus far, Figure 13.1 makes it clear that the level of employment in the urban sector would be choked off by the high wage in manufacturing (by $L_M^* - L_M$), but city immigration need not be forestalled. Indeed, Todaro shows that (excessive and socially nonoptimal) city immigration is likely to be *fostered*, but to get his result we now need to open the analysis to the realities of unemployment and underemployment. Todaro offers an expectations hypothesis which, in its simplest form, states that the favored jobs are allocated by lottery, that the potential migrant calculates the expected value of that lottery ticket, and compares it with the certain employment in the rural sector. Migration then takes place until the urban expected wage is equated to the rural wage. The qq' curve in Figure 13.1 describes the locus of wage-unemployment combinations about which the migrant is indifferent. The equilibrium agricultural wage is now given by W_A, and those underemployed or unemployed in the city[2] (for example, Mayhew's casual laborers and street vendors plus those without any work at all) is thus given by L_{US}.

The new equilibrium at Z in Figure 13.1 seems to offer an attractive explanation for the stylized facts of Third World labor markets. It yields a wage gap, $w_M - w_A$, and urban low-wage underemployment or open unemployment, L_{US}. Furthermore, the total labor force in agriculture is now lower in the presence of "wage expectations" ($O_A L_A < \dot{O}_A L_A^*$), and thus cities are too big and too numerous. Moreover, when the dynamic implications of the model are explored, it turns out that an increase in the rate of manufacturing job creation need not cause any diminution in city unemployment or underemployment. That result is guaranteed if the urban-rural wage gap rises "sufficiently fast" (Todaro 1969, p. 147). As we shall see, a rise in the wage gap can be documented in many parts of the Third World, and it was a striking attribute of British industrialization after the French Wars.

The Todaro model makes some firm assertions about how urban labor markets operate and how immigrants are absorbed into those markets. First, it asserts that immigrants earn lower incomes (and have higher unemployment rates) than nonimmigrants, the latter having first claim to the favored jobs. Second, it asserts that the average immigrant earns less in the cities when he first arrives than he would have earned in the rural area he left (since he has a good chance of ending up unemployed or underemployed). Third, it implies that those immigrants who stay in the city (and do not return discouraged to rural areas) exhibit far steeper age-earnings curves than the nonmigrants. After all, they are likely to be underemployed in low-wage jobs before getting absorbed in the high-wage modern sectors. Now then, do these assertions hold for England during the First Industrial Revolution?

The 1851 *Census of Great Britain* asked a number of questions which are very useful for exploring the employment and wage experience of the migrants who had been pouring into Britain's cities since the end of the French Wars. Besides recording current residence, the census enumerators also asked where the respondent was born; thus, individuals can be identified by migrant status. I have classified people according to five migrant categories (Williamson 1990, chap. 5): nonmigrants (born in the city of residence), migrants from rural areas in Britain, migrants from other urban areas in Britain, migrants from Ireland, and migrants from other foreign countries.[3] In addition to age, sex, and family relationships, the enumerators also asked employment questions. The responses can be classified into five categories: not working (retired, sick, unemployed, pauper, resident of workhouse); working; landed proprietor; family member assisting; and those missing data. For those working, an enormous amount of occupational detail is supplied. I have reconstructed estimates of potential earnings based solely on occupation, sex, and employment status for an urban sample of 20,893 individuals.[4] Obviously, such data must be treated with care, but they appear to be sufficient for our purposes.

The Todaro model implies that earnings of young, new immigrants were likely to have been less than they could have received at home. While the 1851 census enumerators did not identify when an immigrant had arrived at the current location, the data they collected certainly seem to reject the view that young, rural emigrants earned less in the city than they might have earned in the parishes whence they had come. Fully employed farm laborers in England earned about £29 in 1851 (Lindert and Williamson 1983, table 2, p. 4, assuming an implausibly high employment rate of 52 weeks per year), while rural migrants in their twenties earned almost £70 in the cities, even after we adjust for the incidence of unemployment (see Table 13.2: aged 20–29, rural migrants). Even teenage rural immigrants earned far more in the cities than their fathers did in English agriculture (see Table 13.2: aged 15–19, rural male migrants). While young Irish males earned somewhat less (see Table 13.2: aged 20–29, Irish males) than migrants from rural Britain, they certainly earned far more than they could have in Ireland (about £13 in 1836: Mokyr 1983, table 2.6, p. 26). While these comparisons fail to adjust for higher living costs and the greater disamenities of the cities, as I shall show, such factors erode but hardly eliminate the earnings differentials.

Nor do the data in Table 13.2 support the view that male immigrants earned

Table 13.2   1851 earnings estimates for urban adults (£s).

Age	Nonmigrants	Migrants from:				
		Rural	Urban	Irish	Other foreign	Total
Males						
15–19	53.49	55.46	47.19	43.04	23.04	50.15
20–29	68.22	69.89	74.52	53.90	62.09	68.58
30–39	73.06	70.46	69.43	58.76	72.47	69.07
40–49	80.74	68.43	75.79	51.76	100.51	70.88
50–59	62.91	77.91	69.24	73.59	69.84	75.26
60 and over	81.15	50.04	94.95	29.23	203.15	63.81
Average	68.22	67.09	70.19	53.17	82.23	67.22
Females						
15–19	29.46	25.62	28.00	34.59	20.67	27.02
20–29	29.62	24.20	27.90	27.63	22.85	25.39
30–39	25.91	16.69	18.88	15.38	19.11	17.19
40–49	19.77	13.83	19.55	12.22	16.60	15.06
50–59	18.51	15.90	14.97	14.20	14.85	15.56
60 and over	20.41	16.35	30.58	13.43	7.67	18.44
Average	25.86	19.24	23.64	21.10	19.06	20.40

Source: Williamson (1990, table 5.4).

significantly less than nonimmigrants. The average earnings of male nonmigrants were about £68, while migrants earned about £67.

These comparisons already include the impact of unemployment, but since the Todaro model stresses city unemployment experience, we ought to isolate that variable. Table 13.3 reports the percent of adults not working. There is some evidence which confirms the Todaro job search model since the unemployment rate[5] for nonmigrant males, 5.2 percent, was a bit below that of migrant males, 6.6 percent. There is, however, no evidence to support the view that *young* (presumably recent) male immigrants to the cities had significantly higher unemployment rates than nonmigrants of the same age: the unemployment rates for males in their twenties was exactly the same for migrants and nonmigrants, 2.5 percent. Furthermore, Irish males in their twenties had *lower* unemployment rates than nonmigrants. Female migrants, however, did have much higher "unemployment rates" (and lower earnings) than nonmigrants, a result attributable, I assume, to their higher fertility rates.

The evidence in Tables 13.2 and 13.3 seems to support the view that Britain's cities absorbed the flood of migrants rather well. With the exception of the Irish, young males migrating into Britain's cities did not exhibit lower earnings than young male nonmigrants. Nor did they exhibit higher unemployment rates.

Table 13.3   1851 estimates of urban adults not working (%).

		Migrants from:				
Age	Nonmigrants	Rural	Urban	Irish	Other foreign	Total
Males						
15–19	11.0	15.1	22.0	6.5	60.9	17.7
20–29	2.5	2.7	1.6	1.2	7.1	2.5
30–39	1.5	1.6	1.5	6.9	5.7	2.5
40–49	3.2	3.8	3.0	2.7	5.5	3.6
50–59	2.3	4.8	5.6	1.9	10.7	5.0
60 and over	16.1	19.4	21.9	51.2	22.2	23.0
Average	5.2	5.9	6.3	7.6	12.1	6.6
Females						
15–19	32.0	33.9	40.8	20.3	54.5	34.7
20–29	38.3	46.9	46.1	34.5	55.1	45.8
30–39	44.1	67.2	64.6	68.3	68.6	66.8
40–49	55.6	69.2	63.9	74.7	64.5	68.4
50–59	54.5	62.1	66.9	62.5	69.2	63.2
60 and over	55.7	61.9	64.2	75.0	77.8	63.8
Average	43.3	56.7	55.7	52.2	62.9	56.3

Source: Williamson (1990, table 5.5).

Although it is not shown here, they also exhibited the same age-earnings experience. The evidence, therefore, seems to be inconsistent with the view that migrants entered the city in response to expected future high earnings, suffering unemployment or underemployment while they waited for the better jobs. Rather, they appear to have been motivated by *current* job prospects, and those prospects appear to have been confirmed. This is not to say that migrants were rarely unemployed or that they could not be found in the low-wage occupations in large numbers. Rather, they simply had the same experience as nonmigrants.

It appears that English cities did not grow too fast as a result of Todaro-irrational migration. ''Overurbanization'' driven by a flood of overoptimistic migrants was never an attribute of mid-nineteenth-century Britain.

Did Factor Market Failure Limit City Growth?

Did urban-rural wage gaps and inelastic city labor supplies serve to drive up the cost of labor in the cities? Did distortions in factor markets serve to starve industrial firms for finance, suppressing accumulation in the cities and thus lowering the rate of urban job creation? If so, then city growth was too *slow* during the First Industrial Revolution.

Elsewhere (Williamson 1985, p. 49) I have shown that an index of the gap between the average nominal earnings of unskilled nonfarm and farm laborers rose sharply across the first half of the nineteenth century. With the end of the French Wars, the pace of industrialization accelerated, and agriculture resumed its long-run relative demise. Thus, the derived demand for labor shifted dramatically toward urban sectors during an episode when, as we have seen, the natural rates of increase in the labor force favored the countryside. If labor market disequilibrium was ever to appear in England, the time was certainly ripe for it after 1820. Trends in the wage gap index would appear to reflect those disequilibrating forces since it rose by almost 50 percent from 1819 to 1851, when it reached a peak. Thus, if we are looking for evidence of labor market failure that constrained city growth, the 1830s, 1840s, and 1850s are clearly the place to start.

How big was the wage gap during these three decades when the index reached its peak? E. H. Hunt (1973, p. 5) and Nick Crafts (1982, p. 64) both contend that the wage gap between city and countryside is best captured by comparing agricultural wages with those of unskilled laborers in the building trades. Table 13.4 estimates these nominal wage gaps for the 1830s. In the South of England, the wage gap was very large indeed: annual unskilled wages in the London building trades exceeded those of farm laborers in the southern counties by an enormous factor, 106.2 percent. For the North of England, the age gap was much smaller; annual unskilled wages in the five towns of Coventry, Huddersfield, Newcastle, Macclesfield, and Manchester exceeded those of farm laborers in the northern counties by 36.3 percent. The wage gap for England as a whole was 73.2 percent. Compared with nineteen Third World economies in the 1960s and 1970s, and with seven nineteenth-century developing economies, the English wage gaps are very large (Williamson 1990, table 8.3).

As we have already seen in Table 13.1, rural emigration appears to have responded to the labor market disequilibrium produced by the unbalanced growth associated with the industrialization spurt after 1820. In contrast with the conventional wisdom that rural England was full of "a vast, inert mass of redundant" (Redford 1926, p. 84) and "immobile" (p. 94) labor, rural labor responded vigorously to these wage gaps. Indeed, emigration from the English countryside rose dramatically after the French Wars and reached rates in the 1840s (1.6 to 1.7 percent per annum: Table 13.1, column 18) which exceed that of the contemporary Third World by quite a bit (1 to 1.2 percent per annum: Kelley and Williamson 1984, table 3-13, p. 93).

Granted the rural emigration rates were vigorous, but were they vigorous enough? Did they eliminate the wage gaps in *real* terms? After adjusting for the

Table 13.4 Nominal wage gaps in the 1830s.

Region	Annual wages (£)	Description and source
London 1831	48.07	Laborers in the building trades (for bricklayers, plasterers and masons), 21.75 s./week. Assumes 44.2 weeks worked per year. Mayhew estimated that 30 percent of London's workers in the building trades were unemployed during slack seasons. If the slack season is taken as 6 months, then weeks worked per year is 26 + (0.7)26 = 44.2.
Northern towns 1838–1840	36.38	Laborers in the building trades, average summer weekly wages, weighted average of Coventry, Huddersfield, Newcastle, Macclesfield, and Manchester. Also assumes 44.2 weeks worked per year.
Rural south 1833	23.31	Agricultural laborers, average weekly wage (excluding poor relief payments) across 21 shires, where we assume 44.2 weeks worked per year in grain-growing counties of the southeast, and 48 weeks worked per year in southwest. The counties are Middlesex, Surrey, Kent, Sussex, Hants., Berks., Oxford, Herts., Bucks., Northampton, Hunts., Beds., Cambs., Essex, Suffolk, Norfolk, Wilts., Dorset, Devon, Cornwall, and Somerset. The weekly wages range from 8.50 to 13.08 s.
Rural north 1837	26.70	Agricultural laborers, average weekly wage (excluding poor relief payments) across 18 shires, where we assume 48 weeks worked per year. The counties are Glou., Heref., Salop., Staffs., Worc., Warwick, Leic., Lincs., Notts., Derby, Cheshire, the three Yorks, Durham, Northumb., Cumb., and Westmore.
Southern wage gap:	106.2%	
Northern wage gap:	36.3%	
Average (weighted) wage gap:	73.2%	

Source: Williamson (1990, table 7.2, p. 183).

Note: The average wage gap is computed from a weighted average of the north and south wages, where the weights are 1841 county populations for London and 41 northern towns.

The wage gap is computed as the difference between urban and rural relative to the rural wage.

fact that cities were expensive, that cities were environmentally unattractive and required some compensation for the "bads" prevailing there, and that poor relief was used to augment workers' incomes in the countryside during the slack season, Table 13.5 shows that much of the wage gap disappears. This was especially true in the South of England, where city living costs were so high (London rents in particular) and where rural relief was most prevalent. Thus, while the nominal wage gap between London and the rural South was an enormous 106.2 percent, the real gap was 54.7 percent. In the North of England the gap tends to evaporate entirely when it is measured properly. Here the nominal wage gap was 36.3 percent, while the real gap was only 8.7 percent. The wage gap and labor market failure appear to have been mostly southern problems. For England as a whole, the nominal gap was 73.2 percent, while the real gap was far less, 33.2 percent.

Much of the wage gap between city and countryside was illusory, but it fails to disappear entirely when measured properly. Spatial labor market disequilibrium *was* an attribute of the First Industrial Revolution.

The cost of labor was too high in the cities, and the rate of city growth was too slow. How much faster would city growth have been had labor markets been efficient enough to eliminate the wage gaps? It is not possible to answer that question, but we can come close if we are willing to equate rural with agriculture and urban with nonagriculture. Figure 13.2 shows the unemployment distribution between agriculture and nonagriculture in the presence of wage gaps. Given wages in the two sectors, and given the two derived labor demand functions, then employment is at l. If the wage gaps had been eliminated, migrants would have left agriculture for nonagriculture, and employment would have been optimally distributed at l^*. By comparing l and l^*, we can infer, at least roughly, the extent to which city growth was constrained by labor market failure.

Table 13.5 Decomposing the nominal wage gap.

| | Wage gap (%) | | |
Item	South	North	England
(1) Nominal wages	106.2	36.3	73.2
(2) Adjusted by cost of living	79.0	21.9	52.1
(3) Also adjusted by rural poor relief of able-bodied	67.1	21.9	46.1
(4) Also adjusted by disamenities premium for city life	54.7	8.7	33.2

Source: Row 1 is taken from Table 13.4; row 2 is derived by applying cost of living deflators to the nominal wages in Table 13.4. Row 3 is based on Boyer (1986, table 1, p. 421) where poor relief payments to rural laborers are added onto real wages. Row 4 is derived by inflating these rural real wages by disamenity premium estimates in Williamson (1990, table 7.6).

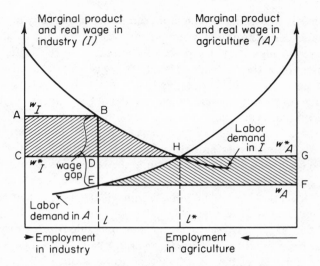

Figure 13.2 General equilibrium analysis of wage gaps in two sectors.

Nor were the constraints on city growth limited to labor market failure. Figure 13.2 also tells us who gains and who loses from the labor market failure. With the disappearance of wage gaps, and with the emigration of labor from agriculture, wages would have risen in agriculture and fallen in industry. Given no change in capital, land, or technology in either of the two sectors, it follows that profits in industry would have risen by ABHC—an increase in their producers' surplus, and rents (or, more likely, farmers' profits) in agriculture would have fallen by EHGF—a decrease in their producers' surplus. As a result, industrial or urban capital accumulation was also choked off by labor market failure. That is, imperfect capital markets ensured that the rate of accumulation in industry was lower, given lower profits. This, after all, is the central premise of the classical labor surplus model.[6]

There were other forces at work which tended to make English cities too small and too few in the 1830s. Imperfect capital markets starved industry for funds, driving a wedge between rates of return in industry and agriculture. Since the industrial capital stock was, therefore, too small, industrial jobs were fewer than they would have been had capital markets been perfect. And they *were* imperfect. To judge from scraps of evidence taken from the mid-nineteenth century, the rates of return in industry were almost two and a half times those of agriculture, an enormous discrepancy (although one that ignores risk differentials and capital gains, it is true).[7]

Elsewhere I have tried to estimate the impact of this private factor market failure by appealing to a simple computable general equilibrium model

(Williamson 1990, chap. 8). Table 13.6 reports the results: it assesses the impact of an elimination of labor market failure (the 1831 real wage gap of 33.2 percent is allowed to disappear), and of an elimination of the capital market failure (the ratio of industrial to agricultural rates of return is reduced to 1 from the 2.4 figure prevailing in the late 1840s).

First, the results suggest that nonagricultural employment in general, and

Table 13.6 The impact of factor market failure.

Impact	Eliminating wage gap and labor market failure	Eliminating rate of return gap and capital market failure	Eliminating both gaps and labor plus capital market failure[a]
Agriculture			
Percent rise in agricultural output (constant prices)	−20.4%	−56.1%	−69.6%
Emigrants from agriculture as % of agricultural labor force	−39.0	−51.4	−57.9
Nonagriculture			
% rise in nonagricultural output (constant prices)	+13.4	+35.8	+39.8
% rise in nonagricultural employment (unskilled labor only)	+15.5	+20.4	+23.0
% rise in nonagricultural profits (nominal)	+11.2	+64.6	+78.1
Manufacturing			
% rise in manufacturing output (constant price)	+24.1	+63.6	+73.4
% rise in manufacturing employment (unskilled labor only)	+25.3	+40.6	+47.2
% rise in manufacturing profits (nominal)	+23.6	+114.7	+141.8

[a] This column is not the sum of the entries in the first two columns, but reports the impact of the joint change.

manufacturing employment in particular, must have been seriously choked off by factor market failure up to the 1840s. While Britain's industrialization performance was certainly impressive after the French Wars, it would have been far more impressive in the absence of these domestic factor market distortions. Indeed, nonagricultural employment would have been 23 percent higher. If that increase is stretched over the three decades between 1811 and 1841, it implies that nonagricultural employment growth would have been about 2.6 percent per annum, not the 1.9 percent per annum actually achieved (Deane and Cole 1962, p. 143). If the impact on city employment had been roughly comparable, then it implies that the rate of city growth would have been 3 percent per annum, not the 2.3 percent per annum actually achieved (see Table 13.1)—a big difference indeed. Manufacturing employment would have been 47.2 percent higher. And if that increase is stretched over the period 1811 to 1841, it implies that manufacturing employment growth would have been about 2.9 percent per annum, not the 1.6 percent per annum actually achieved (Deane and Cole 1962, p. 143).

Second, these distortions had important distributional implications. Profits in nonagriculture would have been much higher (by 78.1 percent), and they would have been increased even more in manufacturing (by 141.8 percent, or more than double the actual profits which accrued to capitalists there). If the reinvestment rate out of nonagricultural profits was relatively high, as most of us believe, then the elimination of factor market distortions would have resulted in a significant rise in savings and accumulation, and most of that accumulation would have centered on the cities, augmenting the rate of job creation and thus city growth. The elimination of the capital market distortions would also have made accessible to all potential savers the high rates of return in city-based activities, and if savings had been responsive to the rate of return, then city-based accumulation would have gotten an even bigger boost.

Those large wage gaps in the South of England still pose a puzzle. One can, of course, offer plausible explanations for the inability of rural emigration to eliminate the labor market disequilibrium between London and the southern countryside. The rate of emigration of the rural work force *was* impressive, but, as we have seen, it was restricted largely to young adults, for whatever the reason, those in their thirties and above rarely emigrated. Even though those in their teens and twenties were very responsive to employment opportunities in London, that age cohort was, after all, a small share of the total rural labor force. Thus, the ability of rural emigration to accommodate the labor market disequilibrium was limited.

But surely there were no such constraints on the migration of manufacturing capital to the countryside in the South. Why didn't Ipswich, Great Yarmouth, and Southhampton become the Prestons, Bradfords, Oldhams, and Huddersfields of the South? Certainly factories migrated to rural labor surplus areas up north. And certainly they did so in New England early in America's antebellum development, as they did in Japan early in the Meiji industrialization effort. Why didn't the factories migrate to rural labor surplus areas in the South of England? Is this another example of market failure's making city growth too slow?

City Housing, Density, Disamenities, and Death

Did Crowding and Mortality Imply That Cities Grew Too Fast?

Analysts and policy makers are sharply divided on the city growth problem. Pessimists stress the Third World's inability to cope with the social overhead and housing requirements of rapid urban growth, citing environmental decay and inadequate housing as evidence of market failure, planning errors, and impending crisis. The pessimists' message is hardly new, since it can be found as early as the 1830s in the parliamentary papers, health surveys, and reformist pamphlets. Then as now, crowding, slums, substandard housing, and nonexistent social services take center stage in the debate.

High density and crowding in England's cities in the early nineteenth century were clearly a response to scarcity and high prices. Rents were also relatively high in the cities, in part because of land scarcity, a scarcity made all the more pronounced by the absence of efficient intraurban transportation, which forced workers to crowd in close to areas of employment. In addition, rents were driven higher by the fact that high nominal wages in the city building trades tended to inflate construction costs. The prices of building materials served to produce the same effect. Baltic and American timber soared in price, as did bricks, partly as a result of war duties and partly owing to the fact that all resource-intensive commodities increased in relative cost. Furthermore, as we have seen, the long period of war from the 1760s to Waterloo tended to crowd out conventional capital accumulation, especially in dwelling construction. With rising urban immigration, excess demand for the urban dwelling stock also rose, and the dwelling stock became of increasingly older vintage. As urbanization quickened after the 1810s and 1820s, urban land got even scarcer, and labor-intensive and resource-intensive products such as dwellings rose in relative cost. Since urban housing was in relatively inelastic supply, and since demand was shifting to the right at an accelerating rate, a rise in its relative scarcity across the Industrial Revolution was guaranteed.

The moral of this tale is that scarce housing bred crowding, and that crowding bred high morbidity and mortality. From that moral, the pessimists leap to the conclusion that England's cities grew too fast. Before we explore that leap, what is the evidence to support the moral?

Dwelling Scarcity and High Rents in the Cities

Table 13.7 shows how strong the upward drift in city rents was. Three city rent series are presented in the table: for some Black Country towns, for Leeds, and for Trentham in Staffordshire. On average, city rents increased at an annual rate of about 2.5 percent between the 1790s and the 1840s. Real rents—that is, those deflated by a cost-of-living index—increased at about the same rate as nominal rents, for a whopping 30 percent each decade. This rent explosion must have encouraged workers to economize on dwelling expenditures by moving to lower-quality housing in more unpleasant districts as well as through greater crowding within all districts, thus creating greater disamenities and mortality risk. To the extent that they did so, it implies that the rise in rents is understated since the quality of the dwelling units must have declined. Certainly many distinguished economic historians think this was the case (Mantoux 1928, pp. 441–442; Ashton 1954, pp. 50–51; Hammond and Hammond 1947, pp. 50–51).

Table 13.7 also confirms Michael Flinn's (1965, p. 6) hunch that the "pressure

Table 13.7   Trends in city rents, 1790–1900 (% per annum growth).

Variable	Early nineteenth century		
	1790–1839/42	1793–1838	1800–40
Black Country town rents			1.7
Leeds rents			
Demand-side estimate	2.0		
Supply-side estimate	3.6		
Average	2.8		
Trentham (Staffs.) rents		2.9	
Cost of living	0.3	0.3	−0.9
Rents relative to cost of living	2.5	2.6	2.6

	Late nineteenth century			
	1850–1900	1850–97	1840–97	1845–98
Black Country town rents	0.8			
Trentham (Staffs.) rents		0.7	0.7	
England and Wales, urban				1.1
Cost of living	−0.2	−0.4	−1.0	−0.6
Rents relative to cost of living	1.0	1.1	1.7	1.7

Source: Williamson (1990, table 9.1).

on housing was possibly at its most acute just at the moment when Chadwick and his colleagues focused their attention on it.'' While real rents increased at about 2.6 percent per annum up to 1840, their growth fell to almost a third of that rate after 1850, to 1 or 1.1 percent per annum. As England emerged from a period of maximum rates of city growth, it appears either that the demand for housing slowed down, or that housing supply made some progress in catching up with past excess demand (as Feinstein's 1978 figures suggest), or both.

By the 1830s, urban rents exceeded rural rents by at least two and a half times. The data underlying that assertion are really quite good. In the early 1830s, the Manchester Statistical Society initiated a set of remarkable housing surveys. The first of these involved 4,102 families in a working-class district of Manchester. To make comparative judgments possible, the society then surveyed rural districts outside Dudley, followed by similar surveys of Rutland and Northumberland. By the 1840s, statistical societies in London, Bristol, Leeds, and elsewhere were imitating the work of the Manchester group. The results of these surveys have been analyzed elsewhere (Williamson 1990, pp. 240–243). While they confirm that working-class rents in London and Manchester were two and a half times those prevailing in the rural North and South, such differentials clearly are an understatement. They ignore the fact that rural dwellings included small gardens, pigsties, and other perquisites; they also ignore the fact that urban families had to share privies with scores of others, that water supplies were distant and of poor quality, and that pollution and other disamenities were part of the urban bargain as well. My guess would be that quality-adjusted rents in the city were three or four times those in the countryside.

The Crowding-Density-Mortality Nexus

High dwelling rents encouraged density and crowding, increasingly so up to the 1840s. What role did such forces play in accounting for the high mortality in England's cities?

Table 13.8 explores the determinants of infant mortality (INFM) in 109 urban parishes surveyed in the 1834 *Poor Law Report* and 72 cities and towns included in a 1905 survey taken by the Board of Trade. Since we are dealing with relatively homogeneous occupations in these data—urban common labor—we can ignore Ratcliffe's (1850) work of more than a century ago which emphasized occupations as one key determinant of mortality and morbidity. In addition, weather variables may have affected infant mortality rates, although such variables were hardly city-specific; thus, the inclusion of temperature (TEMP) in Table 13.8. I have also added city size (POP) and density (DEN) since these variables surely serve as proxies for the difficulty which faced municipal authorities in maintaining the social overhead expenditures necessary to offset the population pressure on the urban environment. In addition, I include a ''dark

Table 13.8   Comparison of infant mortality rates (INFM) in 1834 Poor Law commissioners' urban parishes and 1905 Board of Trade towns.

Variable in log-linear regression	1834 Poor Law parishes		1905 Board of Trade towns	
	$\hat{\beta}$	*t*-statistic	$\hat{\beta}$	*t*-statistic
CONSTANT	6.8509	1.2313[c]	14.432	3.830[a]
DEN	0.0280	1.7024[a]	0.068	2.413[a]
POP	0.0726	3.6174[a]	0.043	2.218[a]
SATMIL	0.0382	1.1744[c]	0.043	1.212
TEMP	−0.5007	0.3520	−2.670	2.759[a]
CROWD	—	—	0.061	2.430[a]
North	0.1902	1.3887[b]	0.086	0.580
York	0.2728	2.1258[a]	0.161	1.132
Lancs.-Cheshire	0.2191	2.0424[a]	0.325	2.430[a]
Midlands	0.3129	2.8812[a]	0.259	1.888[a]
East	0.2850	2.1555[a]	0.352	2.375[a]
South	0.1438	1.4455[b]	0.269	1.915[a]
Wales	0.0923	0.6793	0.294	2.000[a]
R^2	0.449		0.508	
N	109		72	
Mean INFM	200.997		144.569	

Source: Williamson (1990, table 9.4).
[a]   5% significance level.
[b] 10% significance level.
[c] 20% significance level.

satanic mill'' index (SATMIL)—measuring the share employed in manufacturing, mining, and other nonservice or nonagricultural occupations—to capture
the alleged effects of factory work environment and industrial pollution on the
mortality environment. Finally, even before Edwin Chadwick's 1842 *Sanitary
Report,* it was felt that crowded housing conditions were the central contributors
to high urban mortality rates, especially among infants. Thus, the inclusion of
CROWD in the 1905 regression in Table 13.8. Indeed, crowded housing and
poor health were the hypothesized correlates which motivated the 1908 Board
of Trade inquiry in the first place. Unfortunately, neither the *Poor Law Report,*
nor the Registrar General's *Annual Reports,* nor Chadwick's *Sanitary Report*
supplies the necessary data to compute a ''crowded living conditions'' variable
for 1834. We shall have to infer the effect of crowding in the 1830s by reference
to the 1905 results.

Table 13.8 reports the attempt to explain the variance of infant mortality
across urban locations in the 1830s as well as in 1905. The results are very
similar, but with some notable differences. City density (DEN) and size (POP)

both play a consistent and significant role, confirming the conventional wisdom that urbanization bred high mortality in the nineteenth century. More to the point, these results suggest that municipal social overhead expenditures simply could not or did not keep up with the requirements that population density and size generated, thus implying a deterioration in mortality environment. In contrast, the "dark satanic mill" index (SATMIL) only barely plays a significant role early in the century, and it plays no role at all in 1905. It was not industrialization that generated the disamenities associated with high infant mortality rates but rather urbanization. It also appears that the South of England and Wales were regions of very high quality of life in 1834, even after controlling for regional urban and industrial attributes. By 1905, Wales and the South of England has lost that advantage. The really nasty regions stay nasty over the seven decades—Lancashire, Cheshire, Yorkshire, the Midlands, and the eastern counties. Thus, while there are some changes in the relative ranking of regional disamenity levels between 1834 and 1905, these are less notable than the remarkable consistency in the determinants of INFM over these seven decades. Finally, crowding—thought to be an index of low housing quality and unhealthy conditions by the Board of Trade and others since Kay-Shuttleworth's (1832) work on Manchester[8]—does indeed have a significant impact on infant mortality rates in the 1905 regression.

In summary, almost all of the predicted infant mortality variance across cities and towns within regions can be explained by two forces: crowding within dwellings, and density and size of the urban environments within which those dwellings were located.

Overurbanization Once More:
Imperfect Information, Endogenous Mortality, and Externalities

Rapid city population growth generated high and rising density within cities and high and rising crowding within dwelling units. Both served to create unpleasant disamenities and high mortality risk. Can this evidence of ugly-city growth be used to argue that England "overurbanized"?

The answer hinges in part on the value which city dwellers placed on a more benign mortality environment, which they had to forgo under the ugly-city policy regime of fast city growth with low social overhead, or what might be called industrialization on the cheap. If city dwellers had perfect information on mortality environments, if those mortality environments were exogenous, and if there were no externalities associated with disease (for example, if disease were not communicable), then an assessment of the optimality of the ugly-city regime would turn out to be quite simple. If those assumptions do not hold, then the assessment is very difficult indeed.

Since workers placed a value on the good life, employers in the ugly towns were forced to pay high wages to attract and hold their labor force. Higher wages were, of course, necessary to cover higher rents in the crowded cities, but they were also required to compensate workers for the foregone good life. The higher city wages must have had two effects: they must have choked off employment and city growth, and they must have encouraged firms to migrate to the countryside, where labor was cheaper and wages were not inflated by the city-ugliness bribe and scarce housing. As we have seen, city employers paid higher wages, some part of which was a bribe to attract and hold workers in the ugly cities, but some part appears to have reflected disequilibrium in the rural-urban labor market. We have considered a general equilibrium model to estimate the impact on city growth had rural emigration increased sufficiently to eliminate the disequilibrium. This calculation may, however, seriously understate the marginal social cost of city growth and seriously overstate the amount of added rural emigration necessary to eliminate the wage gap. It assumes that the city mortality environment was exogenous. It was not. We have seen that greater crowding and density bred higher mortality. If rural emigrants had been more responsive to real wage gaps, city growth would have been faster, crowding and density would have been greater, and city mortality rates would have been higher. While the supply price of city labor would surely have fallen with the entrance of additional immigrants from the countryside, it would have fallen far less if added crowding had raised city rents and mortality far higher. In short, when city mortality and rents are allowed to rise with density, the number of immigrants necessary to eliminate the real wage gap between city and countryside is smaller. The same argument holds if externalities prevailed: to the extent that diseases were communicable, then the social costs of an added migrant exceeded his private costs, and the former may have increased even more than the latter. In addition, the calculation has assumed that city dwellers had perfect knowledge of the mortality environment. If instead immigrants from environmentally more benign rural areas understated city mortality risk, then their revealed wage-disamenities trade-off understates the social cost of city growth. On all three counts, it follows that our earlier calculation has overstated the extent to which city growth was too slow during the First Industrial Revolution. It does not follow, however, that city growth was too fast.

Public Sector Failure, Underinvestment, and Ugly-City Growth Strategies

Have we been asking the wrong question? Perhaps the right question is whether it was underinvestment in city social overhead that accounts for ugly-city growth during the First Industrial Revolution.

Underinvestment in City Social Overhead

There is a large historical literature on poor public sanitation and overcrowded housing that seems to imply that there was underinvestment in social overhead. Most of that literature is guided by the political rhetoric of the Social Reformers themselves. Indeed, Thomas Southwood Smith, Edwin Chadwick, and John Simon all argued that sanitation investment made good economic sense: they were able to offer calculations showing that lost production, hospital costs, and burial costs from the "fever" (typhus and typhoid) exceeded the cost of the sanitary investment which would have eliminated it; they were also able to show that the cost of sanitary investment was less than the gains owing to a decline in sickness-induced pauperism (Wohl 1983, pp. 146–147). How they made those calculations is another matter entirely.

Greater social overhead investment in the 1830s certainly would have cleaned up England's cities and lowered the mortality environment sooner, but was the social rate of return to investment in municipal overhead higher than returns elsewhere? The "overurbanization" debate clearly hinges on the answer. In spite of the assertions of the Social Reformers, we simply do not know very much about the benefits which additional municipal social overhead investment in the 1830s would have generated. After all, social overhead technology was very primitive early in the nineteenth century, and it is unclear that added investment would have had a significant impact on the mortality environment. It is crucial that we find out, since only then will we be able to assess the importance of public sector failure during the three decades or so following the French Wars. Only then will we be able to assess the importance of the series of acts which gave authority to municipal governments to clean up their cities. If such legislation was truly binding, then there was underinvestment in social overhead during the First Industrial Revolution. We simply do not know the answers to these important questions.

While we cannot yet agree on the impact of social overhead on the mortality environment,[9] let alone agree on the economic value to be attached to mortality improvements, some evidence suggests that Britain underinvested in its cities. It is those unusually low capital-output ratios that offer the circumstantial evidence, but some motivation is needed before I present it.

By the standards of the contemporary Third World and the late nineteenth century, Britain recorded very modest investment shares in national income. That fact has generated a long and active debate centered on the question: Was the investment share low because investment requirements were modest, or was the investment share low because of a savings constraint? The first view argues that investment demand was the critical force driving accumulation during Britain's Industrial Revolution, while the second argues that Britain's growth was savings-constrained. Until very recently, the first view has dominated the literature.

This dominant view sees early-nineteenth-century Britain as so labor-intensive that investment requirements to equip new workers could easily be fulfilled by modest amounts of domestic savings, so easily in fact that domestic savings had to look for outlets overseas. Thus, David Landes (1969, pp. 78–79) brushes problems of accumulation aside with one magisterial sweep, leaving him free to deal with technology and entrepreneurship in the remaining 550 pages of *The Unbound Prometheus:*

> However justified this concern with saving and capital may be in this age of costly equipment and facilities [in] abysmally poor would-be industrial economies, it is less relevant to the British experience . . . the capital requirements of these early innovations were small . . . these critical innovations were [also] concentrated at first in a small sector of the economy, and their appetite for capital was correspondingly limited . . . Under these circumstances, it is not surprising to learn that the aggregate volume of investment was a relatively small proportion of national income in those early decades of the Industrial Revolution, and that it was only later, when a more elaborate technology required large outlays . . . that the proportion rose to the level that economists [look] upon as a characteristic of industrialization.

According to Landes, the explanation for the modest investment requirements during the Industrial Revolution lies with simple labor-intensive technologies, capital-saving innovations, and capital stretching.

Where does this benign view of "modest investment requirements" come from? François Crouzet (1972) tells us in the superb introduction to his *Capital Formation in the Industrial Revolution.* The tradition starts in the 1930s with two very influential papers by Michael Postan (1935) and Herbert Heaton (1937), the latter the source of the statement that the initial capital requirements during the Industrial Revolution were "modest." In the 50 years and more since Postan and Heaton wrote their papers, there have been some amazingly consistent limitations to the debate, from which we must try to escape. First, rarely do we hear any mention of housing, infrastructure, and social overhead. This is surely a puzzling attribute of the accumulation debate since there is another strand of historical literature which stresses crowding in the cities, a deteriorating urban environment, and lack of public investment in social overhead. It is also puzzling since we have come to learn just how large such investments loom in typical industrial revolutions, the Third World included. Indeed, many development economists and historians have argued that such investments are essential complements to the plant and equipment set in place in modern industry. Without them, rates of return in the modern private sector may sag, and industrialization can be choked off. Second, the debate has tended to focus on the modern industrial sector to the exclusion of more traditional sectors, which, as it turns out, continue to dominate the economy well into the late stages of the Industrial Revolution. Third, and most important, the literature has confused what actually was with what should have been. It may be a big mistake to conclude that Britain's labor-intensive growth strategy was a Good Thing. Do Heaton's "modest" investment requirements reflect an attempt to achieve an industrial revolution on the cheap? If so, what did the strategy cost?

We begin by looking at capital-output ratios. Here we have an advantage over Landes since Charles Feinstein's (1978) careful estimates were published almost a decade after *Prometheus.* If investment requirements during the First Industrial Revolution were really modest, this should be reflected in relatively low capital-output ratios.

Table 13.9 collects the evidence for Britain from 1800 to 1860 and for a number of industrial revolutions since. While Feinstein supplies estimates of both average capital-output ratios (ACOR) and incremental capital-output ratios (ICOR), the estimates for the late nineteenth and twentieth centuries are limited to ICORs only. Furthermore, all of the figures in Table 13.9 are for fixed capital.

Section A of the table offers provisional support for the "modest" investment requirements view. Britain's ACOR underwent a spectacular drop from 5.21 in 1800 to 3.55 in 1860, the biggest fall taking place in the first three decades of the nineteenth century. At the margin, therefore, Britain's investment requirements during the Industrial Revolution were far below eighteenth-century averages. Indeed, the economywide ICOR up to 1830 was only 2.65, far below Simon Kuznets' ten-country average for the 1950s (section B), and even below that for contemporary low-income countries and Meiji Japan (the latter viewed by most analysts to have been the classic example of capital-saving development). The margin that mattered during the First Industrial Revolution lay, of course, outside agriculture. As it turns out, agriculture had a far higher ACOR in 1800 than did industry, commerce, and transport combined: 5.93 versus 3.26. Crouzet (1972, p. 29) is quite right, therefore, in stressing that "a large proportion of the new developments were taking place in industries with a relatively low ratio of capital to income." Furthermore, Britain's relatively modest investment requirements at the margin persist into the late nineteenth century. Compared with those of five continental European countries, Britain's ICOR stays low (4.1 versus 6.3: panel C).

In this sense, Landes is correct: Britain's investment requirements on the margin *were* modest during the Industrial Revolution. I believe, however, that the inferences he draws from that observation are incorrect.

First, the case for Britain's unique "modesty" of investment requirements has been overdrawn. Britain's ICOR during the first half of the nineteenth century was 3.1 (section A, total, 1800–1860), not far below the 3.4 figure for low-income countries in the 1950s (section B), especially given the fragile

Table 13.9 Average (ACOR) and incremental (ICOR) capital-output ratios in Britain, 1800–1860, compared with other industrial revolutions.

A. Britain: ACOR	1800	1830	1860
Total	5.21	3.81	3.55
Agriculture	5.93	4.69	3.68
Industry, commerce, and transport	3.26	2.57	3.30
Total *less* agriculture	4.87	3.54	3.52
Total *less* agriculture, housing, and public works	2.15	1.90	2.47
Britain: ICOR	1800–1830	1830–1860	1800–1860
Total	2.65	3.32	3.10
Industry, commerce, and transport	2.19	3.87	3.31
Total *less* agriculture, housing, and public works	1.73	2.94	2.54

B. Twentieth Century: ICOR	1950s	1885/89–1914/18
Total: Ten countries	4.1	
Total: Low-income countries	3.4	
Total: Japan		2.9

C. Late Nineteenth Century: ICOR	Period	ICOR
Germany	1851/55–1911/13	7.4
Italy	1861–1911/13	9.6
Denmark	1870–1914	3.9
Norway	1865–1910/19	6.3
Sweden	1861–1911/20	4.1
Unweighted average		6.3
UK	1851/61–1905/14	4.1

Source: Williamson (1990, table 10.1, p. 271).

character of both estimates. Although Britain's ICOR was relatively low, to argue that savings and capital accumulation were "less relevant" (Landes 1969, p. 78) than in many poor developing countries today is, to say the least, extreme.

Second, one of the key reasons why investment requirements during the First Industrial Revolution were so modest is that Britain failed to commit resources to those urban investment activities which, in Landes' (1969, p. 78) words, make industrialization such a "costly" venture today, and which, in W. Arthur Lewis' (1977) words, make contemporary Third World cities so capital-intensive. Investment in housing and public works simply failed to keep pace with the rest of Britain's economy in the first half of the nineteenth century. One can see this very clearly in section A of Table 13.9. While the total ACOR drops precipitously for 1800–1860, the ACOR for the total economy *less* agriculture, housing, and public works actually *rises* over the same period! While the ACOR outside of agriculture does fall, implying low ICORs and "modest" investment requirements at the margin, the reason for it is that capital-intensive housing and public works were ignored.

To repeat: Landes was correct in stressing the "modest" investment requirements at the margin during the First Industrial Revolution. He was misled, however, by failing to note that those low investment requirements reflect a growth strategy which starved housing, public works, and other urban social overhead investment.

Another way of illustrating this point is to examine the behavior of capital stock growth in what I shall call social overhead—residential housing plus public works and public buildings. Based on Feinstein's data, Table 13.10 documents per annum growth rates in capital stocks per capita (1851–1860 prices). The table's message is clear. Investment requirements during the late eighteenth century were kept modest simply by allowing the stock of social overhead per capita to *fall,* contributing, presumably, to a deterioration in the quality of life, an item which usually fails to be included in "output." This growth strategy continued for the first three decades of the nineteenth century, although not with quite the same intensity. Per capita stocks in public works continued to decline, but dwelling stocks per capita began to rise. The latter did not rise enough, however, to regain the levels of 1760. By 1830, therefore, Britain had accumulated an enormous deficit in social overhead stocks by pursuing 70 years of industrialization on the cheap. It cost her dearly, as the Social Reformers were about to point out. Between 1830 and 1860, there is some evidence of "catching up" in public works—in part a response to the goading of the Social Reformers, but the gap in growth rates between dwelling stocks and all other fixed capital per capita increased.

All of this suggests that while actual investment requirements may have been modest during the First Industrial Revolution, they would *not* have been so

Table 13.10 Capital stock growth per capita by use, 1760–1860 (% per annum).

Use	1760–1800	1800–1830	1830–1860	1800–1860
Social overhead capital	−0.13	0.10	0.39	0.24
Dwellings	−0.13	0.12	0.27	0.19
Public works and buildings	−0.10	−0.09	1.43	0.67
All other fixed capital	0.44	0.27	1.43	0.71
Total fixed capital	0.21	0.21	1.09	0.54

Source: Feinstein (1978, table 8, p. 42) (gross stock of reproducible fixed capital, 1851–1860 prices) divided by population (pp. 84–85).

modest had investment in social overhead kept pace. In fact, had social overhead investment kept up with all other investment after 1800—let alone made good on past deficits through catching up—the ICOR over the first half of the nineteenth century would have been in excess of 4, not the "modest" 3.1 actually achieved.

Low rates of accumulation during the First Industrial Revolution reflect a modest commitment to city social overhead rather than some unique labor-intensive growth strategy.

Circumstantial Evidence: The Problem of Proof

City social overhead was low during the First Industrial Revolution. It lowered investment requirements, perhaps freeing up resources for consumption of foodstuffs and other essential commodities. But it had its price since the cities became ugly, crowded, and polluted, breeding high mortality and morbidity. The price of this ugly-city strategy was high enough so that true welfare gains fell short of measured GNP gains during the First Industrial Revolution (Williamson 1984) while life expectancy improvements lagged behind (Fogel 1986). This correlation invites the inference that more and earlier investment in city social overhead would have lowered mortality and morbidity while raising the quality of life. But what would it have cost? Would it have been a Good Thing? Was *low* investment in city social overhead necessarily evidence of *underinvestment* in city social overhead?

We would get closer to an answer if we knew what accounted for Britain's low investment commitment to city social overhead. The answer is not obvious. Presumably, Landes could argue that the low commitment was consistent with low returns on such investments. He could argue that the demand for city housing was constrained by poverty, and that city social overhead was much too primitive in the early nineteenth century to make a bigger investment commitment profitable. Perhaps. But these investment-demand-side explanations would have to deal with equally plausible saving-constraint and institutional-public-sector-failure explanations. In fact, there is no shortage of explanations for the low commitment to city social overhead investment during the First Industrial Revolution. It could be explained by crowding out and savings constraints. It could be explained by some capital market failure which made it difficult for municipal authorities to secure long-term financing at fair rates. And, of course, it could be explained by a wide gap between private and social rates of return on investment in city social overhead. If it is the last, however, how do we account for the public authorities' unresponsiveness to what were likely to have been high social rates of return? Ignorance? A political mismatch between those who stood to gain from the social overhead investments and those who would have carried the tax burden?

We have come a long way in searching for an answer to the question, Did cities grow too fast during the First Industrial Revolution?

If municipal planners failed, it was not because of demographic surprises after the French Wars or because of dependency burdens. The rate of city growth was not much higher in the 1830s and 1840s—when it is said that England was having her greatest difficulties in coping with city growth—than it had been in the previous six decades. No demographic surprises here. Furthermore, England's cities had unusually low dependency burdens. Poor relief and pauperism were therefore far less burdensome in the city than in the countryside, and thus surplus was freed up for city accumulation. Neither can England's cities be characterized as having been flooded with irrational migrants: they were responding to current job prospects, and the cities absorbed them quite quickly. No evidence of "overurbanization" so far. In fact, when we look to private factor markets, it appears that city growth was too *slow*, not too fast. Capital market distortions starved the city for investment, and labor market imperfections drove wages far above those in the countryside.

If, then, a case is to be made for city failure during the First Industrial Revolution, it must lie with underinvestment in city social overhead. And the villain of that piece will surely be the criminal inactivity of the public sector.

Notes

1. I try to answer this question in Williamson (1990).

2. The qq' curve is a rectangular hyperbola with unitary elasticity. The elasticity of the labor demand curve MM' is assumed to be less than unity in Figure 13.1, an assumption supported by empirical evidence which has been accumulated for the Third World.

3. Unfortunately, the enumerators did *not* ask how long the immigrants had been resident at the current location, so it is not possible to relate earnings experience to length of time in the city's labor market.

4. The long trek from enumerators' manuscripts to earnings estimates for 20,893 individuals in sampled urban areas is described at length in Williamson (1990, chap. 5). I relied on Michael Anderson's tape (Anderson, Collins, and Stott 1980) and Carolyn Crane's work (1985, chap. 4). Here I report only a small portion of the results, and ignore the regression analysis.

5. The terms *unemployment* and *not working* are used interchangeably, although the latter is clearly more accurate. To repeat, adult males not working include unemployed, sick, retired, paupers, and so on.

6. For its modern guise, see W. Arthur Lewis (1954).

7. F. M. L. Thompson (1963, p. 251) estimates the rate of return on industrial capital in 1846 to have been 8 to 9 percent. Paul David (1975, pp. 264–265) uses Thompson's data on estate improvements between 1847 and 1879 to get a rate of return on agricultural capital of 3.6 percent. Thompson himself

feels that between 1846 and 1853 there were "no measurable returns" in agriculture (Thompson 1963, p. 249). David also estimates the rate of return to agricultural mechanization to have been 2 to 4.5 percent between 1846 and 1853. If we take the rate of return to industrial capital at about 8.5 percent (Thompson's 8 to 9 percent in 1846), and the rate of return to agricultural capital at about 3.25 percent (David's 2 to 4.5 percent in 1851), then the ratio was about 2.4, the figure reported in the text and used in subsequent calculations.

8. Frederick Engels (1845) leans very heavily on Kay-Shuttleworth—indeed, plagiarizes him—in describing "social murder" in the great towns of early-nineteenth-century England.

9. Thomas McKeown's *Modern Rise of Population* revolutionized medical and demographic history in 1976. He argued that living standards were the key determinants of mortality trends in the nineteenth century. Municipal improvements and public health took a very poor second, reaching importance only in the late nineteenth century. Simon Szreter (1986) has countered that sanitation and public health investment explain most of the mortality trends in the first two-thirds of the nineteenth century. Each of these scholars leans on very slim evidence, and neither is able to decompose his interpretation into that owing to the marginal impact of a unit of sanitation investment and that owing to the magnitude of the investment. The decomposition is central to the questions posed in the text.

References

Anderson, M., B. Collins, and J. C. Stott. 1980. *Preparation and Analysis of a Machine-Readable National Sample from the Enumerators' Books of the 1851 Census of Great Britain.* Edinburgh: University of Edinburgh.

Ashton, T. S. 1954. "The Treatment of Capitalism by Historians." In *Capitalism and the Historian,* ed. F. A. Hayek. London: Routledge and Kegan Paul.

————— 1959. *Economic Fluctuations in England, 1700–1800.* Oxford: Clarendon Press.

Barnsby, G. J. 1971. "The Standard of Living in the Black Country during the Nineteenth Century." *Economic History Review* 24:220–239.

Bowley, A. L. 1900a. *Wages in the U.K. in the Nineteenth Century.* Cambridge: Cambridge University Press.

————— 1900b. "The Statistics of Wages in the United Kingdom during the Last Hundred Years: Part VI: Wages in the Building Trades—English Towns." *Journal of the Royal Statistical Society* 63: 297–314.

Boyer, G. R. 1986. "The Poor Law, Migration, and Economic Growth." *Journal of Economic History* 46 (June):419–430.

Boyer, G. R., and J. G. Williamson. 1989. "A Quantitative Assessment of the Fertility Transition in England, 1851–1911." *Research in Economic History* 12:93–117.

Corden, W., and R. Findlay. 1975. "Urban Unemployment, Intersectoral Capital Mobility, and Development Policy." *Economica* 42 (February):59–78.

Crafts, N. F. R. 1982. "Regional Price Variations in England in 1843: An Aspect of the Standard of Living Debate." *Explorations in Economic History* 19 (January):51–70.

Crane, C. 1985. "The Role of Children in the Industrial Revolution." Ph.D. dissertation, Northwestern University.

Crouzet, F. 1972. Introduction to *Capital Formation in the Industrial Revolution,* ed. F. Crouzet. London: Methuen.

David, P. A. 1975. *Technical Choice, Innovation, and Economic Growth.* New York: Cambridge University Press.

Deane, P., and W. A. Cole. 1962. *British Economic Growth, 1688–1959.* Cambridge: Cambridge University Press.

de Vries, J. 1984. *European Urbanization, 1500–1800.* Cambridge, Mass.: Harvard University Press.

Engels, F. [1845] 1971. *The Condition of the Working Class in England.* Translated with an introduction by E. Hobsbawm. St. Albans, England: Panther.

Feinstein, C. H. 1978. "Capital Formation in Great Britain." In *The Cambridge Economic History of Europe.* Vol. 8. *The Industrial Economies: Capital, Labour, and Enterprise.* Pt. 1, ed. P. Mathias and M. M. Postan. Cambridge: Cambridge University Press.

Flinn, M. W. [1842] 1965. Introduction to Edwin Chadwick, *Report on the Sanitary Condition of the Labouring Population of Great Britain,* ed. M. W. Flinn. Edinburgh: Edinburgh University Press.

Fogel, R. W. 1986. "Nutrition and the Decline in Mortality since 1700: Some Preliminary Findings." In *Long-Term Factors in American Economic Growth,* ed. S. L. Engerman and R. E. Gallman. National Bureau of Economic Research Studies in Income and Wealth. Vol. 51. Chicago: University of Chicago Press.

Hammond, J. L., and B. Hammond. 1947. *The Bleak Age.* New York: Pelican.

Heaton, H. 1937. "Financing the Industrial Revolution." *Bulletin of the Business Historical Society* 11, no. 1 (February):1–10.

Hohenberg, P. M., and L. H. Lees. 1985. *The Making of Urban Europe, 1000–1950.* Cambridge, Mass.: Harvard University Press.

Hoselitz, B. F. 1955. "Generative and Parasitic Cities." *Economic Development and Cultural Change* 3 (April):278–294.

———— 1957. "Urbanization and Economic Growth in Asia." *Economic Development and Cultural Change* 5 (October):42–54.

Hunt, E. H. 1973. *Regional Wage Variations in Britain, 1850–1914.* Oxford: Clarendon Press.

Jones, G. S. 1971. *Outcast London.* Oxford: Oxford University Press.

Kay-Shuttleworth, J. P. 1832. *The Moral and Physical Condition of the Working Class Employed in the Cotton Manufactures in Manchester.* London: Ridgeway.

Kelley, A. C., and J. G. Williamson. 1984. *What Drives Third World City Growth?* Princeton: Princeton University Press.

Kuznets, S. 1960. "Quantitative Aspects of the Economic Growth of Nations: Pt. 5: Capital Formation Proportions: International Comparisons for Recent Years." *Economic Development and Cultural Change* 3, no. 4, pt. 2 (July):1–96.

———— 1961. "Quantitative Aspects of the Economic Growth of Nations: Pt. 6: Long-Term Trends in Capital Formation Proportions." *Economic Development and Cultural Change* 9, no. 4, pt. 2 (July): 1–124.

Landes, D. S. 1969. *The Unbound Prometheus: Technological Change and Industrial Development in Western Europe from 1750 to the Present.* Cambridge: Cambridge University Press.

Law, C. M. 1967. "The Growth of Urban Population in England and Wales, 1801–1911." *Institute of British Geographers Transactions* 41 (June):125–143.

———— 1972. "Some Notes on the Urban Population of England and Wales in the Eighteenth Century." *Local Historian* 10 (February):13–26.

Leff, N. 1969. "Dependency Rates and Savings Rates," *American Economic Review* 69 (December): 886–895.

Lewis, W. A. 1954. "Economic Development with Unlimited Supplies of Labour." *Manchester School of Economic and Social Studies* 22 (May):139–191.

———— 1977. "The Evolution of the International Economic Order." Discussion Paper no. 74, Woodrow Wilson School, Princeton University.

Lindert, P. H., and J. G. Williamson. 1983. "English Workers' Living Standards during the Industrial Revolution: A New Look." *Economic History Review* 36 (February):1–25.

Lipton, M. 1976. *Why Poor People Stay Poor: Urban Bias in World Development.* Cambridge: Cambridge University Press.

Mantoux, P. 1928. *The Industrial Revolution in the Eighteenth Century.* London: Cape.

Matthews, R. C. O., C. H. Feinstein, and J. C. Odling-Smee. 1982. *British Economic Growth, 1856–1973.* Stanford: Stanford University Press.

Mayhew, H. [1861] 1967. *London Labour and the London Poor*. New York: Augustus M. Kelley.

McKeown, T. 1976. *The Modern Rise of Population*. London: Edward Arnold.

Mokyr, J. 1983. *Why Ireland Starved*. London: Allen and Unwin.

Pollard, S. 1978. "Labour in Great Britain." In *The Cambridge Economic History of Europe*. Vol. 7. *The Industrial Economies: Capital, Labour, and Enterprise*. Pt. 1, ed. P. Mathias and M. M. Postan. Cambridge: Cambridge University Press.

——— 1981. "Sheffield and Sweet Auburn: Amenities and Living Standards in the British Industrial Revolution." *Journal of Economic History* 41 (December):902–904.

Postan, M. 1935. "Recent Trends in the Accumulation of Capital." *Economic History Review* 6, no. 1 (October):1–12.

Preston, S. H. 1979. "Urban Growth in Developing Nations: A Demographic Reappraisal." *Population and Development Review* 5 (June):195–215.

Ratcliffe, H. 1850. *Observations on the Rate of Mortality and Sickness*. Manchester: George Falkner.

Redford, A. 1926. *Labour Migration in England, 1800–1850*. Manchester: Manchester University Press.

Rimmer, W. G. 1960. "Working Men's Cottages in Leeds, 1770–1840." *Publications of the Thoresby Society* 46, pt. 2 (1960):165–199.

Rogers, A. 1984. *Migration, Urbanization, and Spatial Population Dynamics*. Boulder, Colo.: Westview Press.

Shaw, R. P. 1978. "On Modifying Metropolitan Migration." *Economic Development and Cultural Change* 26 (July):677–692.

Simmons, A. B. 1979. "Slowing Metropolitan City Growth in Asia: Policies, Programs, and Results." *Population and Development Review* 5 (March):87–104.

Szreter, S. 1986. "The Importance of Social Intervention in Britain's Mortality Decline c. 1850–1914: A Re-Interpretation." Discussion Paper no. 121, Centre for Economic Policy Research, London, July.

Thompson, F. M. L. 1963. *English Landed Society in the Nineteenth Century*. London: Routledge and Kegan.

Todaro, M. 1969. "A Model of Labor, Migration, and Urban Unemployment in Less Developed Countries." *American Economic Review* 59 (March):138–148.

——— 1984. "Urbanization in Developing Nations: Trends, Prospects, and Policies." In *Urban Development in the Third World*, ed. P. K. Ghosh. Westport, Conn.: Greenwood.

United Nations. 1980. *Patterns of Urban and Rural Population Growth*. New York: United Nations, Department of International and Social Affairs.

Williamson, J. G. 1982. "Was the Industrial Revolution Worth It? Disamenities and Death in Nineteenth-Century British Towns." *Explorations in Economic History* 19 (July):221–245.

——— 1984. "British Mortality and the Value of Life: 1781–1931." *Population Studies* 38 (March):157–172.

——— 1985. *Did British Capitalism Breed Inequality?* Boston: Allen and Unwin.

——— 1990. *Coping with City Growth during the British Industrial Revolution*. Cambridge: Cambridge University Press.

Wohl, A. S. 1983. *Endangered Lives: Public Health in Victorian Britain*. Cambridge, Mass.: Harvard University Press.

Wrigley, E. A., and R. S. Schofield. 1981. *The Population History of England, 1541–1871: A Reconstruction*. Cambridge: Cambridge University Press.

14

• • •

Technology and the Economic Theorist:
Past, Present, and Future

W. W. Rostow

The 1870 Fork in the Road

On the one hand, economic theorists are inclined to regard formulation of marginal analysis around about 1870 as a decisive, creative benchmark in the life of the profession.[1] On the other hand, since that splendid intellectual revolution, mainstream economics has never been able to deal in a satisfactory way with what virtually all economists and economic historians agree is the central distinguishing characteristic of modern economies since the British Industrial Revolution of the late eighteenth century; that is, the regular generation of inventions and, for the first time in recorded history, their absorption into the economy as profitable innovations in an unbroken, if not continuous, flow. Blessedly, economic historians, unencumbered with elegant but illusory dreams of stable equilibrium, have gone on not merely chronicling but also analyzing and debating the origins and consequences of this flow for the performance of economies and the societies of which they are a part.

To some extent the problem lies in the fact that modern economic theory moves from the firm to the economy, from micro- to macroeconomics, blithely skipping the sectors on the Walrasian assumption that the net value product for all productive activity is equated at the margin. But invention and innovation happen primarily in particular sectors rather than in either discrete firms or the economy as a whole. That is why works in economic history are full of homely references to coal mining and cotton textiles, railroads and steel, automobiles and even clocks.

Down to the 1930s macroeconomics consisted almost exclusively of one version or another of the quantity theory of money. It was structured in such a way as effectively to conceal technological change by burying it in Q (or T); that is, the quantity of total output of goods and services. In quantity theory analyses the production variable was treated as exogenous and, as a matter of trend, its rate of change often taken to be constant. The Austrians—from Bohm-

Bawerk to Hayek—dramatized technological change via the somewhat awkward concept of capital deepening.

As macroeconomics evolved in the wake of the Keynesian revolution, it yielded, by way of Harrod-Domar and then neoclassical growth models, formulations that in effect were an aggregate production function. Technological change was subsumed in a marginal capital-output ratio or productivity variable. And when theorists and statisticians sought to account for the determinants of the rate of increase in output, they did so by throwing technological change into a residual left after measuring the supposed contributions of labor and capital inputs. But a modern economy is not driven forward by some sort of productivity factor operating incrementally and evenly across the board—be it called capital deepening, the marginal capital-output ratio, the residual, or what. It is driven forward by the complex direct and indirect structural impact of a limited number of rapidly expanding leading sectors within which new technologies are being efficiently absorbed and diffused. And it is this process of technological absorption that substantially generates, directly and indirectly, the economy's flow of investment via the plowback of profits for plant and equipment, which helps generate enlarged public revenues for infrastructure and enlarged private incomes for residential housing. It is a process fundamental to any serious analysis of growth.

The incapacity of mainstream economic theory to cope with technological change in a useful way is a peculiarly unfortunate deficiency in the present era. Starting in about the mid-1970s the fourth major clustering of innovations in the past two centuries moved into the economy from the R&D process: microelectronics, genetic engineering, the laser, and a range of new materials. These are already restructuring the economies of the older industrial and more advanced developing countries. Their further elaboration and diffusion promise to remain central to the dynamics of the world economy over the next half-century.

Against this background, the present essay sketches briefly how technology was dealt with by a selected sequence of major economists pre-1870, from 1870 to 1939, and in the decades after World War II. It then isolates a series of problems that require solution if economic theory is to come to grips successfully with the problem of technology in the future.

Economists pre-1870

Hume and Adam Smith

Once upon a time economists were pretty sensible.

First, David Hume. I believe the only explicit reference in Hume's economic essays to a particular technology is the following: "Can we expect, that a government will be well modelled by a people, who know not how to make a spinning-wheel, or to employ a loom to advantage?'' (Rotwein 1955, p. 24). But he has a good deal more to say about the ''mechanic arts'' in broader but still discriminating terms. For example, he evokes as a central phenomenon the stimulus provided to invention not only by ''necessity'' but also by the demonstration effect of imported ''luxuries'' (Rotwein 1955, pp. 13, 17–18); he suggests the likelihood of higher rates of increase in productivity in manufacturing than in agriculture, with important consequences for relative price trends (Hume 1802, III, 402–403; IV, 327); and, perhaps of greater relevance to our own day, he analyzes in considerable detail the consequences for and the appropriate response to the narrowing of the technological gap between more and less affluent countries, including the need of the former, in the face of intensified international competition, to make prompt and efficient structural adjustment among the sectors.[2] Hume's great dictum, to which we shall return, is that, on balance, an early comer can gain from the technological and economic rise of a latecomer so long as the early comer remains ''industrious and civilized'' (Rotwein 1955, pp. 78–79).

On this point, as with many others, Adam Smith carried forward along distinctive lines, which nevertheless reflected the work of his older friend:

> The more opulent therefore the society, labour will always be so much dearer and work so much cheaper, and if some opulent countries have lost several of their manufactures and some branches of their commerce by having been undersold in foreign markets by the traders and artisans of poorer countries, who were contented with less profit and smaller wages, this will rarely be found to have been merely the effect of the opulence of one country and the poverty of the other. Some other cause, we may be assured, must have concurred. The rich country must have been guilty of some error in its police [policy].[3]

But Smith, in his treatment of technology, introduced a distinction not to reappear until Schumpeter's *Theory of Economic Development* more than a century and a quarter later. As we are all correctly brought up to understand, the general thrust of his doctrine suggested invention and innovation as an incremental improvement in ways of doing things, evoked by profit possibilities that almost automatically accompanied the widening of the market and the division of labor. He did recognize, however, that over long periods of time, one could identify a few major technological innovations whose high productivity constituted an identifiable discontinuity helping to explain a long period of decline in price. For example, surveying the woolen industry over three centuries, since the time of Edward IV, he identifies ''three very capital improvements'' (Smith 1937, pp. 245–246): the exchange of rock and spindle for the spinning wheel; the use of machines for winding and arranging the yarn before putting it into the loom; and the emergence of the fulling mill, which supplanted treading in water to thicken the cloth. In both his *Lectures* and *The Wealth of Nations*, Smith drew a distinction between inventions contrived by those who actually operated the machines—a kind of incremental learning by doing—and those created by "philosophers," which involved "new powers not formerly applied."[4] He cited the waterwheel, fire machines (steam engines), and wind and water mills as examples of major discontinuous inventions. In *The Wealth of Nations* Smith also allows for creative inventions by specialized "makers of Machines" (Smith 1937, p. 10). In this passage Smith's terse evocation of the creative process is just and memorable: "combining together the powers of the most distant and dissimilar objects."

While recognizing the possibility of major, discontinuous inventive break-throughs and even the likelihood, for a time, of increasing returns in manufactures, Smith envisaged nations' reaching their full complement of riches; that is, a limit to growth. Diminishing returns won out in the end.

Malthus and Ricardo

Although Malthus and Ricardo are generally accounted the creators of the view that economics is the dismal science, their work after the great post-1812 decline in food prices, while focused on Britain's economic malaise from, say, 1815 to 1820, clearly reflected the enlarged role of machinery which had emerged during the generation of warfare with the French, and was quite sanguine about the economy's long-run prospects. Their immediate concern was unemployment, which they interpreted in different ways.

The progress of technology bears in particular on the important final section of Malthus' *Principles*. Written in 1820, it is entitled "Application of Some of the Preceding Principles to the Distresses of the Labouring Classes since 1815, with General Observations." He notes that, unlike the situation during the American and earlier wars, there was now "a more rapid and unsuccessful progress in the use of machinery than was ever before known"; and the "vast increase of productive power" thus generated permitted the burdens of war to be carried while the nation's capital and real income per capita increased. He then argued that the postwar decline in public expenditures and incomes in agriculture reduced the capacity of the rural population to purchase both British manufactures and imports from abroad: "The failure of home demand filled the warehouses of the manufacturers with unsold goods, which urged them to export more largely at all risks" (Malthus 1951, p. 416).

Malthus not only introduced the rise of the machine age into his underconsumptionist explanation for post-1815 distress but also addressed directly the question of whether the introduction of machinery led to chronic unemployment in the long run. Here he inverts Adam Smith by arguing that, with a "most usual'' elasticity of demand, the widening of the market and increased employment can be a function of cost and price reduction brought about by the invention and efficient introduction of machinery (Malthus 1951, pp. 352, 360):

> When a machine is invented, which, by saving labour, will bring goods into the market at a much cheaper rate than before, the most usual effect is such an extension of the demand for the commodity, by its being brought within the power of a much greater number of purchasers, that the value of the whole mass of goods made by the new machinery greatly exceeds their former value; and notwithstanding the saving of labour, more hands, instead of fewer, are required in manufacture.
>
> This effect has been very strikingly exemplified in the cotton machinery of this country . . . But it is known that facilities of production have the strongest tendency to open markets, both at home and abroad. In the actual state of things therefore, there are great advantages to be looked forward to, and little reason to apprehend any permanent evil from the increase of machinery.

Ricardo also took for granted that he lived in a world where machinery and other methods of production were subject to improvement. He regarded total output as a function of ''the application'' of land, labor, machinery, and capital. The separation of the last two thus dramatized the distinction between fixed and working capital. It was on this distinction that Ricardo constructed his analysis of the possibility of technological unemployment on which Marx was to build his concept of the reserve army of the unemployed.

Ricardo treated improvements in agricultural machinery and scientific knowledge as instruments, like cheap grain imports, for fending off diminishing returns in agriculture (Sraffa and Dobb 1955, I, 94, 120, 132); but his fundamental proposition was more stark:

> The natural price of all commodities, excepting raw produce and labour, has a tendency to fall, in the progress of wealth and population; for though, on one hand, they are enhanced in real value, from the rise in the natural price of the raw material of which they are made, this is more than counterbalanced by the improvements in machinery, by the better division and distribution of labour, and by the increasing skill, both in science and art, of the producers. . .
>
> From manufactured commodities always falling, and raw produce always rising, with the progress of society, such a disproportion in their relative value is at length created, that in rich countries a labourer, by the sacrifice of a very small quantity only of his food, is able to provide liberally for all his other wants.   (Sraffa and Dobb 1955, I, 93–94, 97)

Thus, in the wake of the Napoleonic Wars, Ricardo, as well as Malthus, became notably more hopeful about Britain's long-run prospects:

> The richest country in Europe is yet far distant from that degree of improvement [the Stationary State], but if any had arrived at it, by the aid of foreign commerce, even such a country could go on for an indefinite time increasing in wealth and population, for the

only obstacle to this increase would be the scarcity, and the consequent high value, of food and other raw produce. Let these be supplied from abroad in exchange for manufactured goods, and it is difficult to say where the limit is at which you would cease to accumulate wealth and to derive profit from its employment. (Sraffa and Dobb 1955, IV, 179)

Ricardo's famous argument about machinery and technological unemployment has received attention for more than a century and a half whenever technological change converges with unemployment generated by cycles or other forces at work in the economy.[5] In terms of a microeconomic case, Ricardo argued, in effect, that if technological improvement permitted a radical shift in the ratio between fixed capital and labor in manufactures, an increase in unemployment might result. He then went on to adduce wider considerations that might turn the introduction of the new machinery to the advantage of workers as well as capitalists, including reductions in the price of manufactures and enlarged employment opportunities (Sraffa and Dobb 1955, IV, 389–392, 395).

In general, Malthus, much influenced by the indirect as well as direct expansion of employment induced by the new cotton textile machinery, was a long-run optimist about fixed capital; but he allowed for the possibility of a net reduction in the demand for labor if the shift in factor proportions was sudden. Formally, Malthus' analysis of the machinery case is, essentially, macro, Ricardo's micro; although Ricardo's concluding, more hopeful observations on the longer-run impact of machinery embrace structural changes in employment and relate to the economy as a whole. Despite the formal character of their efforts, both were brought to confront the problem by the reality of severe unemployment and a Luddite machine-breaking mood in the working force, notably in the years 1816 and 1819.

J. S. Mill and Marx

While Mill and Marx differed radically on certain fundamental matters, they had, nevertheless, a good deal in common: the first edition of Mill's *Principles* and Marx's *Communist Manifesto* appeared in 1848; both were profoundly affected by the emergence of the railway age in particular, and, in general, by the rapid diversification of new technologies as the midcentury approached; both reflected a heightened consciousness of the new industrial society crystallizing about them; both reacted against the harshness of the emerging industrial system, and Mill seriously contemplated but did not fully embrace socialism as an alternative to capitalism; both envisaged rather romantic, highly affluent, more or less stationary states as the appropriate end product of the process of technological progress and consequent economic growth. But unlike their classical predecessors (and Marshall as well), they envisaged their stationary states as the product of declining relative marginal utility for material goods rather than diminishing returns to natural resources. Taken together, both reflect the end of the first century of modern political economy—focused on growth itself—and the beginning of a second which, assuming growth based on automatically expanding technological virtuosity, concentrated on how best to reconcile its imperatives with enlarged social welfare.

So far as technology is concerned, both Mill and Marx were much influenced by Charles Babbage's bestselling *On the Economy of Machinery and Manufactures,* published in various printings and editions over the period 1832–1841.[6] It was read at a time when the Reform Bill of 1832 dramatized the political rise of a class whose power was rooted in the new technology—a fact to which Babbage refers. Consciousness of a distinctive phase was also heightened by the testimony laid before the 1833 parliamentary select committee on manufacture, commerce, and shipping and by Edward Baines's excellent *History of the Cotton Manufacture* and Andrew Ure's *Philosophy of Manufactures,* both published in 1835.

Babbage's study of machinery and manufactures is remarkable because it combines scientific and engineering expertise with detailed knowledge of production processes, business practice, and basic economic principles. It includes a chapter, "On Over-Manufacturing," which finds in the manufacturing sector, rather than the commercial and financial sectors, the roots of the business cycle. There is, in fact, nothing quite like Babbage's book in the literature of economics. Mill's vigorous advocacy of public support for scientific (and other) research in British universities almost certainly owes a good deal to Babbage. But his most important influence on Mill was more general. Like Marx, Mill was a bookish man. Neither had a direct, hands-on knowledge of factories, machines, or technology. Babbage supplied them with valuable, concrete, even if vicarious knowledge of processes of great significance going forward.

The upshot of Mill's reflections, which, of course, were grounded more widely than just on Babbage's study, was a firmer confidence than even post-1812 Malthus and Ricardo had had that a stationary state would not be imposed by diminishing returns, with which, in best classical style, he nevertheless begins.

Diminishing returns is introduced as "the most important proposition in political economy." Then come the "antagonist principles": "the progress of improvements in production" (Mill 1965, pp. 134, 136). He deals with the accelerated decline in the cost and prices of manufactures owing to "the mechanical inventions of the last seventy or eighty years," which he judges to be "susceptible of being prolonged and extended beyond any limit which it would be safe to specify." But he deals also at greater length than any of his major predecessors with the full range of inventions and innovations capable of exercising "an antagonist influence to the law of diminishing return to agricultural labour." Among these innovations are improved education of the working force, improved systems of taxation and land tenure, and "more solid instruction" of the "rich and idle classes," which would increase their "mental energy," generate "stronger feelings of conscience, public spirit, or philanthropy: and qualify them for roles of constructive social as well as economic innovation" (Mill 1965, pp. 182–184).

Mill was also aware that in the course of the 1830s the emergence of new technologies began to hold out the hope of rendering British farming profitable again after the long period of declining and stagnant agricultural prices which started in 1812: but it was only from about 1837 that the application of the new methods began to yield substantial results and create a new mood.[7] By the time Mill's *Principles* was published in 1848, it was clear that British agriculture would profitably survive despite the repeal of the Corn Laws.

As one might expect, Mill flatly rejected Ricardo's judgment that a shift toward fixed rather than circulating capital is likely to be at the workers' expense (Mill 1965, pp. 750–751): "The conversion of circulating capital into fixed, whether by railways, or manufactories, or ships, or machinery, or canals, or mines, or works of drainage and irrigation, is not likely in any rich country, to diminish the gross produce or the amount of employment for labour . . . All capital sunk in the permanent improvement of land, lessens the cost of food and materials; almost all improvements in machinery cheapen the labourer's clothing or lodging, or the tools with which these are made; improvements in locomotion, such as railways, cheapen to the consumer all things which are brought from a distance."

The British railroad boom of the 1840s, with its massive expansion in fixed capital, and diffuse, strong positive effects on output and productivity, made it clear that Ricardo's proposition held only under extremely restricted assumptions.

So far as I am aware, Marx only once visited a factory. But he was evidently fascinated by machinery; and, like Mill, he drew heavily on Babbage as well as on others writing in this phase of increasing awareness of the ongoing revolution that had unfolded since the 1780s. Engels, actively engaged in manufacture, was evidently a vicarious but important source of information. But Marx went further back into the history of machinery in earlier times. He viewed machinery as a great achievement of capitalism; as a satanic instrument for keeping labor in subjection; and, ultimately, as a major instrument for capitalism's undoing, via the forces set in motion by the rising organic composition of capital.

Marx's ambivalence toward machinery is well reflected in the following passage, in which he begins with an evocation of invention as the business of generating practical applications from science and ends with an analogy from Goethe in which labor is sexually possessed by machinery (Marx 1973, p. 704):

It is, firstly, the analysis and application of mechanical and chemical laws, arising directly out of science, which enables the machine to perform the same labour as that previously performed by the worker. However, the development of machinery along this path occurs only when large industry has already reached a higher stage, and all the sciences have been pressed into the service of capital; and when, secondly, the available machinery itself already provides great capabilities. Invention then becomes a business, and the application of science to direct production itself becomes a prospect which determines and solicits it. But this is not the road along which machinery, by and large, arose, and even less the road on which it progresses in detail. This road is, rather, dissection . . . through the division of labour, which gradually transforms the workers' operations into more and more mechanical ones, so that at a certain point a mechanism can step into their places. Thus, the specific mode of working here appears directly as becoming transferred from the worker to capital in the form of the machine, and his own labour capacity devalued thereby. Hence the workers' struggle against machinery. What was the living worker's activity becomes the activity of the machine. Thus the appropriation of labour by capital confronts the worker in a coarsely sensuous form; capital absorbs labour into itself—"as though its body were by love possessed."[8]

Despite Marx's profound interest in and almost obsession with invention and machinery, and despite his awareness of the link between science and invention, his analysis of the historical transition to modern industrial capitalism is curiously incomplete, and his linkage of technology to capital formation excessively simple. Historically, he moves from the widening of international markets, the "primitive accumulation" brought about by colonization, the slave trade, the expansion of the public debt, and other mercantilist policies, to the diversion of this pool of resources—"dripping from head to foot, from every pore, with blood and dirt"—to machinery and the expansion of fixed capital.[9] There is no role in this story for the scientific revolution, Newton, and the new perception of man's capacity to understand and manipulate nature to his advantage—the Faustian Bargain in Landes' good image. This gap in Marxism was not filled until B. Hessen, a Soviet historian of science, delivered a paper in London in 1931.[10] Hessen argued that Newton "was the typical representative of the rising bourgeoisie," and that "the scheme of physics was mainly determined by the economic and technical tasks which the rising bourgeoisie raised to the forefront." Somewhat similarly, in dealing with the technological change in modern industrial capitalism, Marx subsumes the generation and diffusion of new technology in the whole process of accumulation, driven, as he saw it, by the capitalist's need to maintain the scale of his profits—in the face of intense competition and a falling profit rate—by labor-saving machinery that would sustain the reserve army of the unemployed and ensure a flexible and compliant labor force. Put another way, Marx shared with his classical predecessors and his successors in mainstream economics a tendency to structure his analysis in ways that obscured the complex interplay of science, invention, and innovation despite the critical role it played in his system.

*   *   *

Thus, the work of the pre-1870 classical economists was marked by two characteristics. First, they all assumed that technology and the pace of technological change lay close to the center of economic analysis. This holds even for the pre–take-off economists, Hume and Adam Smith. They introduced technology in a direct, unembarrassed way because the formal structures of their analyses were inherently dynamic. With the exception of Ricardo they all knew a good deal of history, and the great questions on which they focused all concerned movement through time. Under what circumstances would population rise or fall? What were the prospects for technological change and productivity in the economy's major sectors? Would the forces making for increasing returns triumph over those making for diminishing returns; and, if so (in the cases of Mill and Marx), should or would human beings ultimately create an affluent quasi-stationary state? How should more and less technologically advanced countries make the structural adjustments required for them to live together in a civilized way as the latter closed the technological gap separating them from the former (Hume and Smith)?

In short, they had not yet sold their birthright for a mess of equilibrium.

The second characteristic of the classical economists is that they focused on the great issues of their day and, in effect, wrote tracts for the times reflecting those issues: how the expansion of international trade could stimulate technological change to mutual advantage and cease to be a source of bloody conflict; how technological change could expand the market (for example, cotton textiles) as well as vice versa, as Smith thought; how technological change could fend off diminishing returns in agriculture as well as manufactures; how revolutionary technological change could restructure whole societies, not merely their economies (Mill, Marx, and the railroads); whether the workers would gain or lose from the progress of labor-saving technology.

These issues did not wholly disappear from view after 1870, but they ceased to be central.

The 1870–1937 Period

Alfred Marshall

In terms of the 1870 fork in the road, Alfred Marshall is a central figure. Trained as a mathematician, he was, on the one hand, an important participant in the marginalist revolution. Almost a century after the publication of his *Principles*, microeconomics, as conventionally expounded, still bears Marshall's imprint;

and he had a firm grip on general equilibrium analysis as well. On the other hand, rooted as he was in J. S. Mill and the century-old classical tradition that lay behind him, he not only understood but refused to evade the conflict between mathematically formulated equilibrium economics—requiring short-period assumptions—and the economics of the wealth of nations in which the size and quality of the working force, the size of the capital stock, and technology are constantly changing. Although mainly remembered for his elaboration of partial equilibrium analysis, Marshall, from his own perspective, was primarily a growth economist.

At the microeconomic level he perceived and exposed the clash between the static equilibrium analysis—in which the seductive charms of differential calculus could be brought to bear—and the pervasive circumstance of increasing returns in industries; that is, in sectors "which show a tendency to increasing return. Its limitations are so constantly overlooked, especially by those who approach it from an abstract point of view, that there is a danger in throwing it into definite form at all. But, with this caution, the risk may be taken; and a short study of the subject is given in Appendix H" (Marshall 1930, p. 461).

Appendix H then demonstrates that under conditions of increasing returns (decreasing costs)—the normal condition of many firms and sectors in an economy regularly absorbing new technologies—no single stable equilibrium position exists for price and output; when "a casual disturbance" results in a substantial increase in capacity and output (and, thereby, lower costs), a cessation of that disturbance does not result in a return to the initial capacity-output-cost position; and, with respect to demand, a sharp reduction in costs and price may result not merely in increased purchases but also in an irreversible outward shift of the demand curve as consumers become accustomed to the commodity whose price has been greatly reduced (Marshall 1930, pp. 805–812). A reversal in cost and price will, under these circumstances, not return the demand curve to its initial equilibrium position. Thus, not only do both demand and supply curves slope downward but they cease to be independent of each other; and conventional equilibrium microeconomics becomes, in the Watergate phrase, inoperative.

Marshall created various devices for dealing with increasing returns—the trees in the forest, the representative firm, internal and external economics, a historic succession of short-period cost curves moving downward through time in response to improving technology but permitting a definition of equilibrium at a moment of time. With these he could more or less cope with the analysis of firms in existing industries. But he never found a way to deal formally with what he knew to be a major characteristic of technological history; namely, the emergence from time to time of inventions so radical as to create new industries (for example, the railroad and electricity) or profoundly to transform old industries (for example, cotton textiles and steel). Moreover, Marshall was extremely sensitive to the fact that, at any particular period of time in a given country, there were fast-growing, slow-growing, and declining sectors; and that their pace was often related to the historical stages of their underlying technologies.

In the end, he was acutely aware that he had not fully met his own challenge and woven the element of time into "a continuous and harmonious whole." At the close of Appendix H in the *Principles* he reflects on "the imperfection of our analytical methods" and, as often, throws out a clue as to how progress might be made in dealing scientifically with the long run; that is, by dating the time a certain volume of production became "normal." In one sense, the large body of historical and empirical material in Marshall's three major volumes reflects the extraordinarily high goal he set for himself. It was to produce a set of principles which matched reality in its full complexity. Unlike Marx, he visited many factories, met many businessmen, labor leaders, and workers. He understood and often said that the study of "organic growth," which lay at the center of the problem of time in economic theory, was a biological field, not a derivative of or parallel to Newtonian physics.

Marshall, then, firmly brought technological change in the sectors into microeconomic analysis; but he left the gap of "epoch-making" innovations for Schumpeter to fill.

Joseph Schumpeter

In his youthful *Theory of Economic Development* (1911), Schumpeter seized a nettle none of his predecessors was willing to grasp; namely, that the processes of invention and innovation were often neither exogenous nor incremental; or, in his own words, innovation was "spontaneous and discontinuous." Schumpeter does not tell us what led him to make major discontinuous innovations generated by economic incentives the center of his system.[11] Perhaps he did not know. But, objectively, we can identify three suggestive antecedents:

• Adam Smith's distinction between incremental inventions contrived by those who actually operated the machines and those created by "philosophers," which involved "new powers not formerly applied";

• Karl Marx's exposition of a circular flow and then a dynamic economic model at the opening of the second volume of *Capital;* and

• Alfred Marshall's explicit recognition—even dramatization—of the case of increasing returns, the severe theoretical problems it posed, and his effort to resolve them, a recognition Schumpeter respected while regarding Marshall's solution as unsatisfactory.

Schumpeter begins his exposition in *Economic Development* with a particular version of a static-equilibrium Walrasian (or Marxian) system in a state of circular flow. He introduces (or accepts from Walras) a powerful simplifying assumption; namely, that "we shall primarily think of a commercially organized state, one in which private property, division of labor, and free competition prevail" (Schumpeter 1967, p. 5). The acceptance of this assumption blocked off Schumpeter throughout his career from the analysis of the process of growth from underdeveloped beginnings, and thereby limited his range as a growth economist.

Schumpeter's circular flow system is, however, not quite as static as it might at first appear. It does not imply that "year after year 'the same' things happen" (p. 62). It allows for incremental changes in technology which displace the equilibrium point of the system so marginally as to permit new equilibrium positions to be reached from the old "by infinitesimal steps" with which unimaginative managers (as opposed to heroic innovating entrepreneurs) can deal (pp. 61 and 64, n. 1). It also allows for changes in response to powerful exogenous events with economic implications, such as bad harvests, wars, revolutions.

Chapter 2 ("The Fundamental Phenomenon of Economic Development") focuses with great clarity on the one concept that distinguishes development from circular flow—the concept that remained the core of Schumpeter's subsequent work (pp. 64, 66, 132ff.):

Development in our sense is a distinct phenomenon, entirely foreign to what may be observed in the circular flow or in the tendency towards equilibrium. It is spontaneous and discontinuous change in the channels of the flow, disturbance of equilibrium, which forever alters and displaces the equilibrium state previously existing . . .

This concept covers the following five cases: (1) The introduction of a new good—that is one with which consumers are not yet familiar—or of a new quality of a good. (2) The introduction of a new method of production, that is one not yet tested by experience in the branch of manufacture concerned, which need by no means be founded upon a discovery scientifically new, and can also exist in a new way of handling a commodity commercially. (3) The opening of a new market, that is a market into which the particular branch of manufacture of the country in question has not previously entered, whether or not this market has existed before. (4) The conquest of a new source of supply of raw materials or half-manufactured goods, again irrespective of whether this source already exists or whether it has first to be created. (5) The carrying out of the new organization of any industry, like the creation of a monopoly position (for example through trustification) or the breaking up of a monopoly position.

Schumpeter was quite conscious that his assumption that the major economic changes of the capitalist epoch occurred in an irreversible revolutionary way rather than by continuous adaptation was theoretically explosive. He referred, for example, to Marshall's failure to overcome "the difficulties which surround the problem of increasing return.''[12] But he proceeded forward courageously to explore the implications of his proposition that ''spontaneous and discontinuous changes in the channel of the circular flow,'' rooted in technological change, were the heart of capitalist development.

Schumpeter's *Business Cycles* was published in 1939, some 30 years after he had arrived at the basic concepts which form the substance of his *Theory of Economic Development*. The later study is a massive two-volume work of 1,100 pages, almost four times the size of the earlier book. The later study focuses on business cycles, although Schumpeter notes that the subtitle (*A Theoretical Historical and Statistical Analysis of the Capitalist Process*) ''really renders what I have tried to do'' (Schumpeter 1939, I, v). On the whole, there can be few examples of an economist so faithfully trying to turn the ''scaffolding'' of his youth ''into a house.''[13]

Schumpeter's historical passages are designed to buttress his three-cycle theory, which does not concern us here. They reflect much scholarship and a good many debates about both theory and history; but, as he was fully aware, they are peculiarly indecisive (I, v).

The one element in his scheme that comes through persuasively is the three periods of relative concentration of major innovations: cotton textiles, good iron coke, and Watt's steam engine starting in the 1780s; the railroads, starting (awkwardly for Schumpeter's interpretation of the Kondratieff cycle) in the 1830s and 1840s, leading on to steel in the late 1860s; and then, round about the turn of the century, electricity, a batch of new chemicals, and the internal-combustion engine.

In dealing with the interwar years, Schumpeter lays out an important argument bearing on technology and innovation. It starts by reviewing the technical case made, in the late 1930s, for the arrival of secular stagnation. The expansion of the U.S. economy between 1933 and 1937 still left 14 percent unemployed at the peak of what Schumpeter called ''The Disappointing Juglar'' (II, 1011–50). Then came the partially self-inflicted wound of the sharp American recession of 1937–38. In the latter year Alvin Hansen published his *Full Recovery and Stagnation*. For our present purposes, what is significant is that Schumpeter argued that in no objective, technological sense had investment opportunities diminished (II, 1037): ''Nor can it be urged that fundamentally new opportunities of first rate magnitude are not in prospect. Barring the question whether that is so, it is sufficient to reply that in the eighteen-twenties hardly anybody can have foreseen the impending railroad revolution or, in the eighteen-seventies, electrical developments and the motor car.'' After making his case that capitalism was imperiled not by a waning of investment opportunities but by a hostile political, social, and intellectual environment plus self-generated degenerative forces, Schumpeter concludes (II, 1050): ''If our schema is to be trusted, recovery and prosperity should be more, and recession and depression phases less strongly marked during the next three decades than they have been in the last two. But the sociological drift can not be expected to change.'' That was quite a remarkable economic prognosis to make in 1939, even if the period of extraordinary prosperity occurred in a Kondratieff downswing (1951–1973) and the sociological drift toward socialism began to reverse from, roughly, the mid-1970s.

The Young Simon Kuznets

Simon Kuznets' *Secular Movements in Prices and Production* (1930) shares with Schumpeter's *Theory of Economic Development* and *Business Cycles* a few striking similarities and is marked by several equally striking differences.

Like *Economic Development, Secular Movements* is a young person's book incorporating a large vision of the terrain the author intended to explore in his professional career and a definition of his proposed strategy. Both Schumpeter and Kuznets aimed to contribute to the generation of intimately linked dynamic theories of economic growth and business cycles which would combine historical and statistical analysis with theory. Above all, they identified innovation as the critical dimension of growth; they perceived the inherent unevenness of the process of innovation as a key to understanding cycles of differing lengths; they accepted that the pursuit of these insights required not merely aggregate analysis but also detailed analysis of the sectors where innovation actually happened; and they based their analyses on the inescapable path of deceleration followed by a sector caught up in radical innovational change.

In building on these insights, both men broke away from the mainstream preoccupations of their day; although Kuznets had available (and acknowledged the influence of) Schumpeter's *Economic Development;* and, in *Business Cycles,* Schumpeter had available Kuznets' *Secular Movements.*[14] Kuznets begins with a set of observations on the empirical evidence:

If we single out the various nations or the separate branches of industry, the picture becomes less uniform, some nations seem to have led the world at one time, others at another. Some industries were developing most rapidly at the beginning of the century, others at the end . . . Great Britain has relinquished the lead in the economic world because its own growth, so vigorous through the period 1780–1850, has slackened. She has been overtaken by rapidly developing Germany and the United States . . . As we observe the various industries within a given national system, we see that the lead in development shifts from one branch to another. The main reason for this shift seems to be that a rapidly developing industry does not continue its vigorous growth indefinitely, but slackens its pace after a time, and is overtaken by industries whose period of rapid development comes later. Within any country we observe a succession of different branches of activity leading the process of development, and in each mature industry we notice a conspicuous slackening in the rate of increase. But contrasted with our belief in the fairly continuous march of economic progress, it raises a frequently overlooked question. Why is there an abatement in the growth of old industries? Why is not progress uniform in all branches of production, with the inventive and organizing capacity of the nation flowing in an even stream into the various channels of economic activity? What concentrates the forces of growth and development in one or two branches of production at a given time, and what shifts the concentration from one field to another as time passes?

These questions can best be answered by an inspection of the historical records of industrial growth, focused upon the processes that underlie economic development. (Kuznets 1930, pp. 1–5)

At this point Kuznets, having used a series of empirical observations to come to rest on the process of sectoral retardation, introduces some economic theory; but he slides it in with reference to "factors discussed by economic historians" and traces a path that permits him, like Schumpeter, to assert that changes in technique are the decisive factor in growth: "Technical progress comes to be realized in response to some felt needs, which may be brought about by the pressure of population or by changes in demand . . . While all three forces are interdependent, the changes in technique most clearly condition the movements in both population and demand, while the dependence of technical progress upon population and demand is less clear and immediate. In the chain interconnection of the three, this link seems to be most prominent" (pp. 5, 6, 9).

Thus a similar focus on innovation leads Kuznets to much the same hypothesis that had governed Schumpeter's *Economic Development* a generation earlier; but their conceptual framework differs rather sharply.

The second major difference between Schumpeter and the early Kuznets is much narrower. Schumpeter made the creative entrepreneur, and the progressively lesser breeds that swarmed after him, the center of the innovational process; for Kuznets, at the center were his logistic curves (or three-constants Gompertz curves) capturing statistically the process of retardation which suffused the life of sectors in a technologically dynamic economy. Retardation in a sequence of leading sectors was an observed statistical uniformity. He identified four reasons for retardation: the slowing down of technical progress; dependence of the innovational sectors on slower-growing sectors supplying raw material inputs; a relative decline in the funds available for expansion of the innovational sectors; and competition from the same industry in a younger country. Schumpeter's analysis of the waning contribution of an innovational sector to overall growth is not inconsistent with Kuznets'; but it is distinctively different in its emphasis on certain nonstatistical and sociological factors at work.[15]

A third difference between the two approaches to innovation and cycles concerns what might be called the technical or intermediate objective of their work. For Schumpeter, in *Business Cycles* the major objective was to give substance to his innovational interpretation of the long, half-century (Kondratieff) cycle, suggesting also its linkage to sequences of strong and weak decennial (Juglar) cycles. He found that primary trends in production and prices reflected systematically the life cycle of a given technical innovation (or opening up of a new territory or natural resource); that is, a phase of rapid, then decelerating, increase in output and of rapid, then decelerating, decrease in price.

Kuznets did not link his analysis of sectoral retardation to data on the course of national output during the time period with which he dealt. In dealing with secondary movements in production and prices, however, he did speculate at some length on the possible reasons for the concurrence of rapidly expanding output and constrained real wages in the period of rising prices, 1896–1914.

Walther Hoffmann

Hoffmann's *Growth of Industrial Economies,* in effect, made the linkage between sectoral and aggregate growth analysis which Kuznets failed to make.[16] Growth emerges as a process carried forward by a succession of sectors of increasing technological sophistication, with a progressive relative expansion in capital goods. Specifically he finds the following (Hoffmann 1958, pp. 2–3; also chap. 2):

> Whatever the relative amounts of the factors of production, whatever the location factors, whatever the state of technology, the structure of the manufacturing sector of the economy has always followed a uniform pattern. The food, textile, leather and furniture industries—which we define as "consumer goods industries"—always develop first during the process of industrialization. But metal working, vehicle building, engineering and chemical industries—the "capital-goods industries"—soon develop faster than the first group. This can be seen throughout the process of industrialization . . .
>
> For the purposes of our analysis we have divided this gradual process into the following four stages:
>
> Stage I has a ratio of 5(± 1) : 1 [*sic,* for 5(± 1.5) : 1]
> Stage II has a ratio of 2.5(± 1) : 1
> Stage III has a ratio of 1(± 0.5) : 1
> The fourth stage has a still lower ratio.
>
> In Stage I the consumer-goods industries are of overwhelming importance, their net output being on the average five times as large as that of the capital-goods industries. In Stage II the initial lead of the consumer-goods industries has diminished to a point where their net output is only two and one-half times as large as that of the capital-goods industries. In Stage III the net output of the two groups of industries are approximately

equal and in Stage IV the consumer-goods industries have been left far behind by the
rapidly growing capital-goods industries. The main purpose of this book is to show that
these stages of economic development can be identified for all free economies.

By seizing on and pursuing a measurable ratio—the proportion of value
added in a selected group of consumer goods industries relative to a similar
group of capital goods industries—Hoffmann produced an original morphology
of growth in four stages and, along the way, arrayed a wide spectrum of
countries with respect to the timing of their entrance into industrialization. His
work in this area—generally ignored in the literature on development—clearly
belongs among the authentic pioneering efforts.

There is a certain shapeliness in the work of this array of four economists of
the period 1870–1939 who, in different ways, took technology seriously. Marshall, who helped create modern mainstream micro- and macroeconomics, almost alone confronted the challenge posed for formal theory by increasing
returns. He saw clearly how it arose inevitably from the process of technological
innovation; but, despite considerable effort, he could never bring that process
comfortably into the framework of conventional theory. In particular, he found
the problem posed by large revolutionary innovations insoluble. His successors
did not try as hard as Marshall: they simply treated such innovations as exogenous.

Schumpeter seized on that problem and sought to solve it by dynamizing the
Walrasian equilibrium system. His method was to relate the long cyclical waves
in prices, interest rates, and money wages discerned by Kondratieff to the
disequilibrium paths set in motion by clusters of major innovations. He also
tried to relate the decelerating path of these innovations to fluctuations in the
rate of increase in aggregate output via strong and weak Juglar (nine-year)
cycles. As Schumpeter perceived, his effort did not succeed, and, until the end
of his life, his unfulfilled dream was to dynamize the Walrasian model by
rendering technological innovation endogenous.

Kuznets was less haunted than Marshall and Schumpeter by theoretical challenges. He was primarily a skilled statistician and empiricist; but, like his
mentor Wesley Mitchell, he was also a thoroughly literate economic theorist. In
his *Secular Movements* he explored in greater statistical depth than Kondratieff
and Schumpeter the actual paths of output and prices in major sectors driven
along their decelerating paths by major technological innovations.

He also harbored a dream of moving toward a dynamic theory of production
and prices and, indeed, tried to apply his insights to national income accounting
and highly aggregated statistical analyses of growth.

Walther Hoffmann, also primarily a statistician, came at technological change
from quite a different direction. Using historical data on consumer and capital

goods sectors and subsectors, he developed an intriguing stage theory based on the rising relative scale of the latter.

While these four creative figures wrestled directly with the process of technological innovation, the greatly enlarged flow of economists in the seven decades after 1870 focused on other matters: long-term price trends; the refinement of partial equilibrium analysis in factor as well as commodity markets; welfare economics, which led quite directly to efforts to measure national income and its distribution; business cycles and the extraordinary pathology of the world economy during the interwar years. A good deal of this work touched on technological change, and some, at least, of those who did it thought seriously about innovation (for example, D. H. Robertson). But the nature of the most searching policy problems of these decades and the inescapable awkwardness of equilibrium economics in dealing with technological change left the work to be carried forward by a handful of mavericks plus, of course, the economic historians, some of whom foreshadowed the post-1945 approaches to the analysis of technology and growth.

Technological Change and Growth Analysis since 1945

Three Types of Post-1945 Growth Analysis

Growth analysis returned to fashion in three forms in the post–World War II era: Harrod-Domar and neoclassical growth models; statistical analyses of average structural changes associated with different levels of real income per capita, pioneered by Colin Clark, carried forward in the postwar era by Simon Kuznets, Hollis Chenery, and their associates; and development economics, which drew a host of economists to prescription as well as analysis in support of heightened economic modernization efforts in Latin America, Africa, the Middle East, and Asia. There was also, as we shall see, a narrower field of growth accounting, associated notably with the work of Edward F. Denison, which sought to fill the empty boxes of neoclassical growth models.

For our narrow purposes it is sufficient to indicate how each of these three major fields dealt with or failed to deal with the problem of technology. It is almost, but not quite, a catalogue of convenient evasions.

Growth Models

Broadly speaking, growth models have been of two types which aimed to dramatize two quite different problems. The Harrod-Domar model, reflecting the anxieties of the 1930s and an anticipated relapse into depression after the end of the war, aimed to illuminate the inherent instability of a growing capitalist economy. It did so by asserting the unlikelihood (in Harrod's terms) that the warranted rate of growth (^{G}w), which would satisfy private entrepreneurs, would match the natural rate of growth (^{G}n), the maximum long-run rate of advance—required for full employment and determined by the rate of population growth and the flow of innovations. Both the flow of innovations and their productivity (the marginal aggregate capital-output ratio) were given and fixed, as were the proportions of capital and labor in production. The operational focus was on the requirements of public policy to force ^{G}w to approximate ^{G}n.

By the mid-1950s it was apparent that the world economy was not moving along on a knife's edge but enjoying a protracted, robust boom. Neoclassical growth models of two types emerged to explain this cheerful but unexpected circumstance. Type A introduced the assumption of variable proportions between capital and labor to keep growth on an approximation of a full employment path. Type B evoked the shape of the Kahn-Keynes consumption function to achieve a similar outcome: in a boom the rise in income and shift to profits yielded an increase in the savings proportion and a salutary reduction in effective demand; in a slump, the process was reversed and the system was pushed back toward its long-run full employment path by a fall in the savings proportion and rise in effective demand.

With an exception noted herein, the various methods used to cope with the role of invention, innovation, and technology in growth modeling were designed, in a sense, to bypass what might be called the Schumpeter problem; namely his assertion that a significant number of innovations are large, endogenous, discontinuous, and have their initial impact on particular sectors but, in their larger consequences, affect not only the structure of the economy as a whole but virtually all of its major variables; for example, the rate of growth of output, the demand for credit, the price level, real wages, the profit rate. The major growth modelers fastened their attention firmly on forces making for instability or stability in the overall growth path when the determinants of growth were defined in highly aggregated and arbitrary terms.

Here are the major devices for bypassing the problem of technological innovation.

• Assume no technical progress and treat growth as a product of an expanding working force and capital stock.

• Assume technical progress is incremental, exogenous, and a function of the passage of time (disembodied).

• Assume technical progress is embodied in investment and a function of the rate of investment—a kind of return to Smithian incremental technological change in response to the expansion of the market.

• Assume all technical change is endogenous but incremental, induced by factor prices, cumulative experience in production, education and other improvement of human capital, and/or by R&D investment.

This world of incremental technological change, exogenous or endogenous, was rendered even more manageable by the generous use of the assumption of neutral technical progress, which is usually defined as an unchanged ratio of the marginal products of capital and labor so long as the overall capital-labor proportion is constant. But capital-saving and labor-saving forms of technical progress were, in some cases, introduced.

It should be noted that one major growth modeler (Type B), Nicholas Kaldor, did, to his credit, seek to reconcile Schumpeter's insight with growth modeling (Kaldor 1954). His line of argument can be summarized tersely as follows:

• All (then) current growth models consisted in the superimposition of an exogenous unexplained linear trend on an otherwise trendless model. In no sense do the resultant theories provide "the basis for a theory of economic growth." (p. 65)

• A theory of growth must explain variations in rates of growth "in different ages or in different parts of the world." (p. 65)

• Variations in rates of population growth, technical progress, and capital accumulation are not independent of human action but are a function of "basic social forces," especially "human attitudes to risk-taking and money-making." (pp. 66–67)

• Thus it is not the trend rate of growth that determines the strength and duration of booms but "the strength and duration of booms which shapes the trend rate of growth . . . Schumpeter's hero, the 'innovating entrepreneur' . . . is found, after all, to have an honourable place, or even key role, in the drama." (pp. 68–71)

Kaldor drew back from the profound implications of this bold foray into what he regarded as the forbidden fields of sociology and social history; but in the rather arid world of model building his essay is something of an oasis.

Growth modeling fell away rapidly in the 1970s and 1980s. It provided in none of its variants either an explanation for the postwar boom of the 1950s and 1960s or for its demise. The three great forces yielding the unexampled postwar boom were: the large backlog of hitherto unapplied technologies available to Western Europe and an even larger backlog for Japan; an array of new technologies, mainly prewar in origin, but available to all advanced industrial states for rapid innovation (television, synthetic fibers, plastics, new pharmaceuticals, and so on); and protracted improvement in the terms of trade for advanced industrial countries after 1951.[17] The latter sharply reversed at the close of 1972; the stimulus of the old and new innovations waned from the mid-1960s forward in a perfectly natural way.

Without including an explanation for trend movements in relative prices and a much more disaggregated analysis of the generation and diffusion of technologies, growth models of the post–World War II quarter-century were not particularly useful; although they provided considerable high-grade economic talent relatively innocent fun for some time. But there is an element of truth in A. K. Sen's (1970, p. 9) rather bitter summation: "It is as if a poor man collected money for his food and blew it all on alcohol."

The Statisticians of Growth

The statisticians of growth are certainly not vulnerable to Sen's charge of frivolous self-indulgence. Kuznets, picking up from Colin Clark's work, and backed from 1949 on by the Social Science Research Council, carried forward one of the great social science enterprises of the century, embracing eleven countries in addition to the United States. The purpose, as we all know, was to assemble in a uniform, comparable manner and analyze the data on the structural changes accompanying the process of modern economic growth. This is conventionally measured in terms of real national income per capita. The degree of disaggregation varies in Kuznets' studies of structural changes in demand, production, trade, and employment. But a good deal of his analysis is conducted in terms of the three Colin Clark categories: agriculture, industry, and services.

Kuznets did not confine himself, however, to reporting the average behavior of growing economies at different levels of real income per capita. He analyzed the fundamental nature of accelerated modern growth itself. He concluded, like most analysts, that, at its core, it was caused by the application of modern scientific thought technology to industry. Thus, Kuznets regarded the measurable statistical phenomena he cited as evidence of entrance into modern growth as a result of a deeper process. These secondary, measurable phenomena were, notably, an accelerated rate of urbanization (which he used to date entrance into modern growth); a sustained and rapid increase in real product per capita, usually associated with high rates of population growth; a shift of the working force out of agriculture to industry and services; enlarged contacts with the outside world.

For the author of *Secular Movements* some 30 years earlier, Kuznets' analytic emphasis on the application of modern scientific thought and technology to the economy is wholly comprehensible, focused as that book was on the sequence of leading sectors resulting from the diffusion of a succession of new technologies. But two aspects of Kuznets' massive exercise in statistical morphology denied him access to what he himself regarded as the Hamlet of the story of modern economic growth. First, his three basic categories were so broad that they could not be directly linked to the introduction and diffusion of major, particular technologies. Second, having made reasonably precise statistical measurability the overriding criterion for his work, Kuznets found it impossible to deal with technological changes within the framework of his enterprise. In his 1971 *Economic Growth of Nations,* near the end of his most productive period, Kuznets (1971, p. 315), after some 300 pages of statistical and analytic summary of previous findings, suddenly expresses his frustration: "Since the high and accelerated rate of technological change is a major source of the high rates of growth per capita product and productivity in modern times, and is also responsible for striking shifts in production structure, it is frustrating that the available sectoral classifications fail to separate new industries from old, and distinguish those affected by technological innovations."[18]

In the following 28 pages, Kuznets illustrates the need for greater disaggregation, if growth is to be linked to the coming in of new technologies. He discusses leading sectors, old and new, and presents a highly disaggregated table to capture their evolution in the United States over the period 1880–1948. Against that background he then sets up a model to illustrate the impact on aggregate growth rates of new rapid growth sectors and new products. It is a joy to be back with the author of *Secular Movements* and to observe his sensitive appreciation of the innovational process hitherto masked by his overriding preoccupation with large national income aggregates.

But in fact Kuznets was never able to resolve his fundamental dilemma: he defined modern growth in terms of the effective absorption of new technologies; but he measured it in terms of product per capita, a quite different, if related, variable. And his successors in comparative statistical growth analysis, led by Hollis Chenery, productive in many ways, were also not able to break out of this prison of their own construction.

With respect to uniformities, Chenery's 1975 *Patterns of Development, 1950–1970,* written with Moises Syrquin, perhaps best captures his method and achievement; although Chenery moved beyond in several major subsequent publications.

Its cross-sectional method differs from Kuznets' comparison of long historical time series in several respects. Chenery and Syrquin use correlation analysis to establish their average patterns (or "stylized facts"); disaggregate systematically a bit beyond Kuznets' strictly economic categories; and helpfully include several social categories, notably education and the demographic transition.

Chenery went further in three major directions. First, in an article written with Lance Taylor, he disaggregated industries into "early," "middle," and "late."[19] These roughly approximate the sequence of leading sectors which characterize my take-off, drive to technological maturity, and high mass consumption, as well as Walther Hoffmann's industrial stages. Second, Chenery gave a great deal more attention to trade and capital flows (including foreign aid) than Kuznets and defined categories for developing countries according to the relative scale and composition of their foreign trade. Third, Chenery had the advantage of having worked intensively on the problems of particular countries, such as Italy, Japan, Pakistan, and Israel. He was a substantial figure in policy-oriented development analysis from the late 1950s forward. He understood better than some the gap between average behavior (and deviations) derived from correlation analysis and the kind of data required to render responsible policy recommendations. Analytically, he quite consciously sought to combine the virtues of historical and cross-sectional analysis with a sense of the uniqueness of particular cases.

Evidently, I find the Chenery extension of Clark-Kuznets structural analysis of growth more useful than the Harrod-Domar and neoclassical growth models. The two major weaknesses are, in my view, the inadequacy of the treatment of technological change and the failure to relate its findings to the relevant non-economic factors which often are the major source of deviations from average behavior. But this is, after all, an almost universal weakness in formal growth modeling as well as in statistical analyses of the morphology of growth.

Growth Accounting: Edward F. Denison

A method for analyzing changes in the determinants of growth on the basis of painstaking disaggregation was developed by Edward F. Denison of the Brookings Institution. His method is incorporated in six books of his own (the first published in 1978) and similar studies by others. Taken all together, this literature embraces recent experience in Canada, Western Europe, Japan, India, and the Republic of Korea, as well as the United States, especially over the period 1929–1982 (Denison 1985).

Table 14.1 indicates the extent of Denison's disaggregation as well as his estimate of the various sources of American growth over the 53 years for which he has developed comparable data.

For our purposes, the key variable is quantitatively the most important: "advances in knowledge." It covers both technological change and improvements in "managerial and organizational knowledge" (Denison 1985, p. 28). Despite heroic efforts, including linkage to the estimates of the productivity of R&D by Edwin Mansfield and others, Denison has thus far been forced to settle for treating advances in knowledge as a residual.[20] Denison provides reasonably convincing reasons for believing his residual is a fair approximation of improvements in knowledge for the period 1948–1973. With admirable candor, however, he finds that the collapse in the rate of productivity increase after 1973 beyond the explanatory power of his analytic system (pp. 29–30).

In short, growth accounting is a promising method for studying economic progress; but, like mainstream economic theory and the statistical morphology

Table 14.1 U.S. contributions to growth rates, 1929–1982.

	Potential national income				Actual national income			
	Total		Per person employed		Total		Per person employed	
	Whole economy	Nonresidential business	Whole economy	Nonresidential business	Whole economy	Nonresidential business	Whole economy	Nonresidential business
Growth rate	3.2	3.1	1.6	1.7	2.9	2.8	1.5	1.6
Percent of growth rate								
All sources	100	100	100	100	100	100	100	100
Labor input except education	34	25	-13	-23	32	20	-12	-25
Education per worker	13	16	26	30	14	19	27	34
Capital	17	12	15	10	19	14	20	13
Advances in knowledge	26	34	54	64	28	39	55	68
Improved resource allocation	8	11	16	19	8	11	16	18
Economies of scale	8	11	17	20	9	12	18	22
Changes in legal and human environment	-1	-2	-3	-4	-1	-2	-3	-4
Land	0	0	-3	-4	0	0	-3	-3
Irregular factors	0	0	0	0	-3	-5	-7	-8
Other determinants	-5	-7	-10	-13	-5	-8	-10	-13

Source: Denison (1985, p. 30).

of growth, it has not yet developed a grip on the process by which new technologies are generated in particular sectors and diffused.

Development Economics

There is a certain paradox in the field of development economics as it enjoyed its period of glory in the 1950s and 1960s and experienced subsequently a period of retrospective criticism, debate, and even counterrevolution. In essence it was, in its heyday, the study of and prescription for societies which had failed to absorb substantially (or fully) the pool of relevant technologies which had been cumulatively created over the two previous centuries.

On the other hand, with an exception noted herein, the great issues of analytic and policy debate in the field of development economics have not focused directly on technology, its generation and diffusion. The three major, partially related issues in contention were, stated crudely,[21] national planning versus reliance on the market; import substitution versus export-led growth; and priority for agriculture versus priority for industry. All relate to the central question of the pace at which a developing society absorbs efficiently the pool of hitherto unapplied, relevant technology available to it. But that question was mainly debated at one remove.

The question of technology did arise directly, however, around the issue of "appropriate technology," centered on Ernst Schumaker's "small is beautiful" doctrine. The now familiar Schumaker argument was that the capital-labor ratios prevailing in advanced countries generated capital-intensive, labor-saving technologies inappropriate to developing countries with quite different capital-labor ratios: "intermediate technologies" were, therefore, required: more sophisticated than those of the traditional society, more labor-intensive (and more human) than those of the advanced industrial world.

There is a strong prima facie case for Schumaker's view. An economic historian immediately thinks of Japan's great success with two-tier industrial development, starting with the silk industry, combining labor-intensive production in the villages with modern factory production. This system, requiring a literate farm population, efficient organization, and good quality control, has never been duplicated on a large scale elsewhere. And, in general, the extent to which Schumaker's proposition could be efficiently applied has never been satisfactorily established. In one sense, Mao's disastrous Great Leap Forward of 1958 was a romantic, ill-conceived experiment in this direction. As the backyard iron furnaces of the Great Leap Forward demonstrated, the production possibility curves of microeconomic textbooks, with their array of incremental gradations of technology, do not exist in real life. Nature and human ingenuity may not be capable of providing efficient possibilities between a backyard iron furnace and a modern steel mill. On the other hand, it can be, and has been, argued that we do not know. The technology now generally available has been generated in the labor-expensive North. Thus, *some* creative talent in the South might focus usefully on filling in the production possibility curves at the labor-intensive end.[22]

Economists often fail to take account, however, of an important mitigating circumstance. The working force involved in a production process is much larger than the sum of those actually engaged with machines on the floor of the factory or steel mill. Factory production has a large and usually long logistical tail engaging not only administrative personnel but material handling, transport, the production of essential raw material inputs, infrastructure, housing, and other services to the working force, and so forth—in short, the whole Leontief input chain. As anyone who has observed economic and social life in a low-wage developing country knows, these activities are normally and quite sensibly much more labor-intensive than in advanced industrial countries. Thus the whole production process associated with a final product may conform much better to Schumaker's criteria than the final production or assembly stage.

The Direct Study of Technology: Its Generation and Absorption

For differing reasons, then, the growth modelers, statistical morphologists, and development economists for the most part dealt with technology as an exogenous aggregate. As Jacob Schmookler (1972, p. 70) wrote: "While neoclassical economic theory has many important applications, it is poorly related to what really happens in the long run. It suffers from this deficiency mainly because it makes no provision for changes in technological knowledge . . . Technological change has to be introduced into the analysis from the outside. It is assumed, not explained." For example, the best-known theoretical formulation and statistical measurement of the contribution of technology ("knowledge") to growth is "the residual," to which concept a whole series of economists contributed over three decades.[23]

On the other hand, the paradox incorporated in Schmookler's observation was recognized by many postwar scholars who, in one way or another, set about studying directly the generation and diffusion of technology.

This is not the occasion for a bibliographical essay on a quite massive field;[24] but some examples should be noted.

Among economic historians, for example, Paul A. David and Nathan Rosenberg have carried forward in more sophisticated style the pioneering studies of Abbot Payson Usher, who had considerable impact on Schumpeter's formulation of Kondratieff cycles.[25]

In this field it is somewhat difficult to separate economic historians from other analysts of technological generation and diffusion because virtually all thoughtful students are driven back into history to track out the inherently prolonged dynamic processes involved. W. Rupert Maclaurin, architect of the remarkable post-1945 rise of the economics department at MIT, was also a pioneer in the analysis of change in communication technology.[26] Jacob Schmookler made a number of sophisticated contributions to the study of technology, perhaps most strikingly in the complex relations between science and inventions.[27] Edwin Mansfield and Zvi Griliches pioneered the effort to measure the rate of return from research and development.[28]

From a quite different perspective, several major analysts have attempted to isolate the disproportionate impact on overall output, investment, and productivity change of sectors incorporating relatively new, rapidly diffusing technologies; that is, the young Kuznets' leading sectors of *Secular Movements*. Here the National Bureau of Economic Research (NBER) study of Daniel Creamer and his colleagues and W. E. G. Salter's *Productivity and Technical Change* have been invaluable, as well as Solomon Fabricant's earlier NBER analysis of industrial production growth rates.[29]

There have also been those who, in the past few decades, have returned to the study of innovation and its diffusion under the inspiration of Schumpeter's *Business Cycles*. Here the stimulus was, clearly, the end of the great boom of 1951–1972 and the emergence of a protracted period of deceleration and irregular fluctuations which fit no pattern familiar in mainstream economics. Gerhard Mensch and Christopher Freeman and his colleagues at Sussex have been major figures in this branch of the invention-innovation renaissance.[30]

Finally, there has been a great deal of work addressed directly to the generation, diffusion, and impact on output and employment of the clustering of innovations which asserted itself in the mid-1970s. The immensely fertile IC^2 Institute at the University of Texas at Austin is one major source of work of this kind.[31]

Nathan Rosenberg has written fruitfully about almost all these dimensions of the study of technology; but neither he nor his colleagues in this specialist exploration of the field have produced a unified view of the various phenomena they have isolated or linked technology generation and diffusion to the main body of economics.

Problems for the Future

The Fourth Technological Revolution: Character and Significance

The unification of technology analysis and its linkage to micro- and macroanalysis is, as suggested at the beginning of this chapter, urgent as one looks at the present and speculates about the future. We are living in the midst of the fourth great technological revolution of the past two centuries, and the relative fate of both advanced industrial and developing countries will depend over the next half-century and beyond on the pace at which its scientific potentialities are unfolded and, especially, the pace at which the subsequent inventions are efficiently woven into the societies of the world economy, rich and poor alike.

Following the sequence Schumpeter derived from economic historians—which should be taken seriously but not too seriously—there were three distinct concentrations of major innovations between the 1780s and, say, the 1960s. Factor-manufactured textiles, Cort's method for making iron from coke, and Watt's steam engine all came onstage in a substantial way in Britain of the 1780s; then the railroads, making considerable commercial headway in the 1830s but generating substantial booms in Britain, the American Northeast, and Germany in the 1840s and leading on to the revolution in steelmaking in the 1870s; and finally, electricity, a new batch of chemicals, and the internal-combustion engine. These became significant round about the opening of the twentieth century and, in various elaborations, carried economic growth forward through the 1960s in the advanced industrial countries.

The measurement of degree of development in terms of the capacity to absorb and apply efficiently the global pool of relevant technologies is heightened, as I suggested earlier, by the character of the Fourth Technological Revolution. The new technologies have four distinctive characteristics: a close linkage to areas of basic science also undergoing revolutionary change; a capacity to galvanize the old basic industries as well as agriculture, forestry, animal husbandry and the whole range of services; an immediate relevance to developing countries to a degree depending on their stage of growth; and a degree of diversification such that no single country is likely to dominate them as, for example, Britain dominated the early stage of cotton textiles and the United States the early stage of the mass-produced automobile. The diversified character of this cluster of technologies is already yielding large-scale trade and cooperation across international boundaries as comparative advantage asserts itself, as well as evident intense international cooperation.

While the old industrial countries of the North have been spawning this glamorous, much-discussed revolution in technology, the developing regions of the South have been mounting a little-noted human revolution of their own.

Overall, the proportion of the population aged 20 to 24 enrolled in higher education in what the World Bank calls "lower middle income" countries rose from 3 percent to 10 percent between 1960 and 1982; for "upper middle income" countries the figure increased from 4 percent to 14 percent. For Brazil, fated to be a major actor in this drama, the proportion rose from 1 percent in 1965 to 12 percent in 1982. In India, with low per capita income but a vital education system, the figure rose from 3 percent to 9 percent. To understand the meaning of these figures, one should recall that in 1960 the proportion for the United Kingdom was 9 percent, for Japan 10 percent.

There has been, moreover, a radical shift toward science and engineering. In India, for example, the pool of scientists and engineers has increased from about 190,000 in 1960 to 2.4 million in 1984—a critical mass exceeded only in the United States and the Soviet Union. In Mexico the annual average increase of graduates in natural science was about 3 percent, and in engineering 5 percent, in the period 1957 to 1973. From 1973 to 1981 the comparable figures were an astonishing 14 percent and 24 percent, respectively, an almost fivefold acceleration.

Even discounting for problems of educational quality, the potential absorptive capacity for the new technologies in the more advanced developing countries is high. Their central problem—like that of most advanced industrial countries—is how to make effective use of the increasingly abundant scientific and engineering skills they already command. This requires, in turn, an ability to generate and maintain flexible interactive partnerships among scientists, engineers, entrepreneurs, and the working force.

These figures, signaling a surge in technological absorptive capacity, mark the arrival of a stage where national growth rates are, under normal circumstances, at a maximum. Despite current vicissitudes, India, the developing countries of the Pacific Basin (including China), and those containing most of the population of Latin America are likely to absorb the new technologies and move rapidly forward over the next several generations. Much the same would happen, I believe, if the Middle East could find its way from its chronic bloodletting to a twentieth-century version of the Treaty of Westphalia, which ended the Thirty Years' War in 1648.

Thus, the world economy and polity face a familiar adjustment in which latecomers narrow and finally close the gap with front-runners. But this time it is likely to occur on an unprecedented scale. The advanced industrial countries (including the USSR and the East European nations) now constitute about 1.1 billion people, or approximately one-quarter of the world's population. At least 2.6 billion people, about 56 percent, live in countries that will, I estimate, acquire technological virtuosity within the next half-century. Moreover, population growth rates in the decades ahead will be higher in the latter group than in the former. We are talking about a great historical transformation; and technological generation and diffusion is at the heart of the process.

Eight Tasks Ahead

If economic historians and economists are to make a maximum contribution to an understanding of the technological dimension of the process under way, they must unify the eight following dimensions of the task and link them to the main body of economic theory; although it should be immediately noted that linkage will transform and dynamize micro- and macroeconomics. For purposes of clarity, conservation of space, and, perhaps, to stimulate controversy, I shall state them tersely and bluntly, without reference to their roots in the literature already summarized earlier in this essay.

First, and most fundamental, *invention*—that is, the whole R&D process— should be regarded as a subsector of total investment; that is, it represents current allocation of human talent and other resources to achieve an expected future rate of return over cost that, taking risk and appropriability into account, at least matches allocations in other directions. It is possible to argue, as Schumpeter did, that not all inventions are born of Mother Necessity. Some represent creations that generate a hitherto unsuspected market. But we are dealing, in the end, with an investment governed by not unfamiliar laws of expected future profitability.

Second, R&D is a *complex spectrum* in which investment is involved at each stage from basic science to pilot projects. The criteria governing investment in each type of activity in the spectrum will vary; and the relations among them are complex, notably the often oblique relation between basic science and invention. For present purposes it is sufficient to note that a range of conceptually distinguishable but interacting creative investment activities are in play within the R&D spectrum; and that the linkages and interactions have never been as close as they are in the Fourth Technological Revolution.

Third, it is useful if oversimple to regard inventions and innovations as made up of two broad types: *incremental and discontinuous*, in the tradition of Adam Smith and Schumpeter. In fact, however, we are dealing with a spectrum of degrees of discontinuity and, therefore, degrees of creativity and heroism in innovation. Nevertheless, the distinction between profit maximization under conditions of fixed production functions and entrepreneurship under degrees of risk imposed by the need to change production functions should not be wholly lost.

Fourth, scientific and inventive as well as entrepreneurial talent tends to *cluster;* but none of us can yet explain precisely and confidently why this important phenomenon occurs. The literature contains various notions of clustering as well as various explanations for the degree to which the phenomenon exists. A good deal of further work on this problem is required. Three clues appear worth pursuing: the working out and refinement of a given innovational breakthrough is clearly a long-term process, transcending a number of conventional (say, nine-year) business cycles; the logistical path of a sector affected by a major innovational breakthrough results in a withdrawal from that sector of R&D creative talent as the sector's rate of growth decelerates; the clusters of apparently independent technological systems may not be as independent as they look. Thus, for example, the impact of Watt's steam engine on both the cotton textile and iron fabrication industries; the impact of the railroad on the modernization of both the iron and steel and engineering industries as well as on agriculture and raw material production; the internal combustion engine on chemical, electricity, steel, and machinery industries; and the ubiquitous role of the computer in the current technological revolution.

Fifth, we must find a way to deal systematically with the phenomenon of a *technological backlog:* its size and the circumstances which determine whether and at what pace that backlog can be efficiently absorbed. This proposition obviously relates to the analysis of underdevelopment but also to the problems which underlie the current Soviet aspiration for perestroika and those underlying the challenge faced by certain U.S. sectors that have failed to absorb promptly and efficiently the full potentialities of the technologies of the Fourth Technological Revolution.

Sixth, we need to clarify the relation between the pace of technological absorption and the *investment rate.* A high proportion of investment in plant and equipment is financed in advanced industrial societies by the plowback of profits. There is considerable evidence that industrial investment is disproportionately concentrated in sectors rapidly absorbing new technologies or technologies, hitherto out of reach, drawn from the technological backlog. The pace of technological absorption in leading sectors also substantially determines the rate of growth of real GNP, thus public revenues and thus also real private income available for consumption. One can argue, therefore, that the rate of investment is substantially (not wholly) determined by the pace of technological absorption: plant and equipment outlays directly; infrastructure investment via the course of public revenues; residential housing via the course of real private income net of taxes.

Seventh, official *statistical data* on employment should be reorganized to permit measurement of total employment associated with a given sector or innovation. The Standard Industrial Classification (SIC) numbers cannot be easily grouped to measure, for example, total employment associated with steel, or computer output. One needs estimates for each stage in the Leontief input-output chain, including services. The motor vehicle industry in the United States is virtually the only sector for which such estimates have been made.[32] The inability to make such calculations is felt with particular strength at a time of technological revolution such as the present.

Eighth, more research is required on the *impact of innovations* generated by problems and profit possibilities in one sector on productivity and by output in other sectors. As I noted earlier, both history and the contemporary scene are full of examples of such unforeseen, secondary benefits—from the steam engine to the computer. In particular, such linkages help explain why the phenomenon of diminishing returns to basic commodity production—built into classical economics—has been fended off for the better part of two centuries in the advanced industrial world.

These eight problems embrace virtually all of the issues to which historians and other analysts of technology have addressed themselves. I believe that, if pushed further, these areas for research would yield not only a more coherent specialist field but also a way of linking technological generation and diffusion to mainstream economics.

The keys to the linkage are, of course, the treatment of the whole R&D process as a complex endogenous investment subsector or sectors; the distinction between incremental and discontinuous innovations; the tendency of major innovations to cluster; the phenomenon of the technology backlog; and the multidimensional role of the pace of technology absorption in determining the rate of investment.

When made, these linkages would of course rather radically transform existing growth models—indeed, contemporary mainstream economics as a whole. But so much the better.

Notes

1. W. S. Jevons and Carl Menger published their formulations in 1871, Leon Walras in 1874, although Jevons' "coefficient of utility" made its appearance as early as 1862.

2. Rotwein (1955, pp. 80–82). The lively and theoretically fruitful eighteenth-century debate on this subject is well summarized in Hont and Ignatieff (1983).

3. This quotation is to be found in Hont and Ignatieff (1983, p. 300), where original sources are provided. See also Smith (1937, p. 462).

4. Cannan (1896, pp. 167–168); Smith (1937, pp. 9–10). The meaning of "philosophers" in Smith's usage, "whose trade it is not to do anything, but to observe everything," is suggested by his listing of their several areas of specialization (Cannan 1896, p. 168): "mechanical, moral, political, chemical."

5. See, for example, chap. 5 in Rostow (1981).

6. The first edition of Babbage (1832) sold some 3,000 copies in two months—the equivalent of about 40,000 copies in the United States today. Two further printings followed shortly, and an enlarged fourth edition was published in 1841. Babbage is quoted on eight occasions by Mill in his *Principles*, sometimes at length.

7. See, for example, Gayer et al. (1953, I, 295–296). See also Matthews (1954, p. 32).

8. "Als hatt' es Lieb im Leibe," Goethe, *Faust*, pt. I, act 5 (Auerbach's cellar in Leipzig).

9. See especially Marx (1954, vol. 1, chap. 31, "Genesis of the Industrial Capitalist").

10. For precise references and discussion, see Rostow (1975, pp. 148–151, 251). These passages and references include G. N. Clark's reply to Hessen's interpretation of Newton.

11. Loring Allen points out that there are foreshadowings of *The Theory of Economic Development* in Schumpeter's first book (1908). In his most vivid comment (pp. 182–183), Schumpeter argues that statics and dynamics are completely different fields, with different problems, methods, and subject

matter. He notes that his current work is within the terrain of statics; but he concludes: "Dynamics, still in its infancy [*Anfangen*], is a 'Land of the Future.' "

12. Schumpeter (1967, p. 63, n. 1). The reference to Marshall is in the later English edition. It is unclear whether Marshall's bold confrontation of the problem on increasing returns—and failure fully to solve it—influenced Schumpeter's thought in formulating *The Theory of Economic Development*.

13. Schumpeter (1939, I, v). Three other examples come to mind: Adam Smith's *Wealth of Nations* and Karl Marx's *Communist Manifesto* and the first volume of *Capital*.

14. Kuznets (1930, pp. 299–330) includes a brief paraphrase of Schumpeter's development theory in a section entitled "Innovations, Progress, and the Cyclical Fluctuations." He notes that it is among the theories he is using "as a point of departure for our reasoning" (p. 300, n. 1).

15. Schumpeter (1939, pp. 497–500). There is a certain grudging character to Schumpeter's refer-. ences to Kuznets on retardation. He calls it an "old idea" (p. 497, n. 2) and characterizes Kuznets' analysis as a "partial success."

16. The 1931 edition, entitled *Stadien und Type der Industrialisierung*, was published in Kiel by the Institut für Weltwirtschaft of the University of Kiel. The 1958 edition, *The Growth of Industrial Societies*, translated from the German by W. O. Henderson and W. H. Chaloner, was published in Manchester by the Manchester University Press.

17. For an elaboration of this argument, see Rostow (1985).

18. One of Kuznets' final scientific papers (1981) focused substantially on the same theme, that is, the centrality of technological innovation and its structural consequences.

19. Chenery's 1960 "Patterns of Industrial Growth" foreshadowed to a degree the conclusions of the 1968 article (Chenery and Taylor 1968).

20. See especially Denison (1985, pp. 27–32), including notes on Edwin Mansfield and others.

21. For a more extensive list of "development dichotomies" and an interesting effort to reconcile them, see Streeten (1984).

22. See, for example, Urquidi (1986). This issue was also taken up in the report by an international commission chaired by Felipe Herrera (OAS 1980).

23. The work of Edward F. Denison (for example, Denison 1985) and others in growth accounting has a considerable intellectual background, including Schmookler (1952), Fabricant (1954), Cairncross (1955), Abramovitz (1956), Solow (1957). See also a critical response to emphasis on technology rather than total physical inputs as the source of productivity increase (Jorgenson and Griliches 1967).

24. The bibliographic references at the close of each chapter of Stoneman (1983) provide a useful sense of the scale and direction of recent analytic work on the economics of technological change. But Klein's *Prices, Wages, and Business Cycles: A Dynamic Theory* (1984) should be added, despite its title.

25. See, notably, David (1975) and Rosenberg (1976). These works provide a good view of the perspectives of both scholars incorporated in other books and essays. For an effort to bridge the gap between mainstream economics and economic historians, including considerable discussion of problems posed by technology, see Parker (1986).

26. Maclaurin focused primarily on various aspects of radio and television technology. See, for example, Maclaurin (1949).

27. In addition to Schmookler (1972), see Schmookler (1966).

28. See, for example, Mansfield (1968a, 1968b). Griliches' seminal study was an effort to measure the social rate of return for 1910–1955 on R&D resources invested in the development of hybrid corn (1957; see also Griliches 1958).

29. Fabricant (1940); Creamer, Dobrovolsky, and Berenstein (1960); Salter (1966). In his belated return to a disaggregated approach to the linkage of technology to growth, Kuznets uses extensively the study of Creamer et al. (Kuznets, 1971, pp. 314–343).

30. Mensch's hypothesis is incorporated in his *Stalemate in Technology* (1979). Freeman's views are fully elaborated in Freeman, Clark, and Soete (1982). The references in the latter (pp. 203–210) list the principal work at that time on long cycles as well as the older literature; although work on long cycles continued to swarm in the 1980s. My evaluation of the Mensch-Freeman debate is in my review of the

latter's study in the *Journal of Economic Literature* 20 (March 1983):129–131. See also Kleinknecht (1987).

31. A few of IC²'s many monographs in this terrain are Abetti et al. (1987); Abetti, LeMaistre, and Smilor (1987); Konecci et al. (1985, 1986); Konecci and Kuhn (1985); Kozmetsky (1985); and Mahajan and Wind (1986).

32. See Rostow (1978, appendix C, pp. 670–675), where various estimates for the U.S. motor vehicle industry have been assembled.

References

Abetti, P. A., C. W. LeMaistre, and R. W. Smilor, eds. 1987. *Industrial Innovation, Productivity, and Employment.* Austin: IC² Institute, University of Texas.

Abetti, P. A., C. W. LeMaistre, R. W. Smilor, and W. A. Wallace, eds. 1987. *Technological Innovation and Economic Growth.* Austin: IC² Institute, University of Texas.

Abramovitz, M. 1956. "Resources and Output in the United States since 1870." *American Economic Review, Proceedings* 46.

Babbage, C. 1832. *On the Economy of Machinery and Manufactures.* London: Charles Knight.

Cairncross, A. 1962. "The Place of Capital in Economic Progress." Reprinted in Cairncross, *Factors in Economic Development*, pp. 75–88. New York: Praeger.

Cannan, E., ed. 1896. *Lectures by Adam Smith.* Oxford: Clarendon Press.

Chenery, H. 1960. "Patterns of Industrial Growth." *American Economic Review* 50 (September): 624–654.

Chenery, H., and M. Syrquin. 1975. *Patterns of Development, 1950–1970.* London: Oxford University Press.

Chenery, H., and L. Taylor. 1968. "Development Patterns among Countries and over Time." *Review of Economics and Statistics* 50 (November):391–416.

Creamer, D., S. P. Dobrovolsky, and I. Berenstein. 1960. *Capital in Manufacturing and Mining: Its Formation and Financing.* Princeton: Princeton University Press.

David, P. A. 1975. *Technical Choice, Innovation, and Economic Growth.* Cambridge: Cambridge University Press.

Denison, E. F. 1985. *Trends in American Economic Growth, 1929–1982.* Washington, D.C.: The Brookings Institution.

Fabricant, S. 1940. *The Output of Manufacturing Industries, 1899–1937.* New York: National Bureau of Economic Research.

——— 1954. "Economic Progress and Economic Change." In 36th Annual Report. New York: National Bureau of Economic Research.

Freeman, C., J. Clark, and L. Soete. 1982. *Unemployment and Technical Innovation.* Westport, Conn.: Greenwood Press.

Gayer, A. D., et al. 1953. *The Growth and Fluctuations of the British Economy, 1790–1850.* Oxford: Clarendon Press.

Griliches, Z. 1957. "Hybrid Corn: An Exploration in the Economics of Technological Change." *Econometrica* 25, no. 4 (October):501–522.

——— 1958. "Research Costs and Social Returns: Hybrid Corn and Related Innovations." *Journal of Political Economy* 66, no. 5 (October):419–431.

Hoffmann, W. G. [1931] 1958. *The Growth of Industrial Economies.* Trans. W. O. Henderson and W. H. Chaloner. Manchester: Manchester University Press.

Hont, I., and M. Ignatieff, eds. 1983. *Wealth and Virtue: The Shaping of the Scottish Enlightenment.* Cambridge: Cambridge University Press.

Hume, D. 1802. *History of England.* London: Strahan (printer).

Jorgenson, D. W., and Z. Griliches. 1967. "The Explanation of Productivity Change." *Review of Economic Studies* 34, no. 99 (July):249–283.

Kaldor, N. 1954. "The Relation of Economic Growth and Cyclical Fluctuations." *Economic Journal* 64 (March):53–76.

Klein, B. H. 1984. *Prices, Wages, and Business Cycles: A Dynamic Theory.* Elmsford, N.Y.: Pergamon Press.

Kleinknecht, A. 1987. *Innovations Patterns in Crisis and Prosperity: Schumpeter's Long Cycle Reconsidered.* New York: St. Martin's.

Konecci, E. B., and L. Kuhn, eds. 1985. *Technology Venturing: American Innovation and Risk-Taking.* New York: Praeger.

Konecci, E. B., G. Kozmetsky, R. W. Smilor, and M. D. Gill, Jr., eds. 1985. *Technology Venturing: Making and Securing the Future.* Austin: IC² Institute, University of Texas.

—— 1986. *Commercializing Technology Resources for Competitive Advantages.* Austin: IC² Institute, University of Texas.

Kozmetsky, G. 1985. *Transformational Management.* Cambridge, Mass.: Ballinger.

Kuznets, S. 1930. *Secular Movements in Prices and Production.* Boston: Houghton Mifflin.

—— 1971. *Economic Growth of Nations: Total Output and Production Structure.* Cambridge, Mass.: Harvard University Press.

—— 1981. "Driving Forces of Economic Growth: What Can We Learn from History?" In *Towards an Explanation of Economic Growth,* ed. H. Giersch. Tübingen: J. C. G. Mohr.

Maclaurin, W. R. 1949. *Invention and Innovation in the Radio Industry.* New York: Macmillan.

Mahajan, V., and Y. Wind, eds. 1986. *Innovation Diffusion Models of New Product Acceptance.* Cambridge, Mass.: Ballinger.

Malthus, T. R. 1951. *Principles of Political Economy.* 2nd ed. New York: Augustus Kelley.

Mansfield, E. 1968a. *The Economics of Technological Change.* New York: W. W. Norton.

—— 1968b. *Industrial Research and Technological Innovation.* New York: W. W. Norton.

Marshall, A. 1930. *Principles of Economics.* 8th ed. London: Macmillan.

Marx, K. 1954. *Capital.* London: Lawrence and Wishart.

—— 1973. *Grundrisse: Foundations of the Critique of Political Economy.* Rough draft. Trans. with a foreword by M. Nicolaus. London: Allen Lane.

Matthews, R. C. O. 1954. *A Study in Trade Cycle History: Economic Fluctuations in Great Britain, 1833–1842.* Cambridge: Cambridge University Press.

Mensch, G. [1975] 1979. *Stalemate in Technology: Innovations Overcome the Depression.* Trans. New York: Ballinger.

Mill, J. S. [1848] 1965. *Principles of Political Economy.* V. W. Bladen and G. M. Robson, eds. London: Routledge.

Organization of American States (OAS). 1980. "Hemispheric Cooperation and Integral Development." OEA/Ser. T/11, OIC 15–80. Washington, D.C., August 6.

Parker, W. N., ed. 1986. *Economic History and the Modern Economist.* Oxford: Blackwell.

Rosenberg, N. 1976. *Perspectives on Technology.* Cambridge: Cambridge University Press.

Rostow, W. W. [1948] 1981. *British Economy of the Nineteenth Century.* Westport, Conn.: Greenwood Press.

—— 1975. *How It All Began.* New York: McGraw-Hill.

—— 1978. *The World Economy: History and Prospect.* Austin: University of Texas Press.

—— 1983. Review of Freeman, Clark, and Soete (1982). *Journal of Economic Literature* 20 (March):129–131.

—— 1985. "The World Economy since 1945: A Stylized Historical Analysis." *Economic History Review* 37, 2nd ser., no. 2 (May):252–275.

Rotwein, E., ed. 1955. *David Hume: Writings on Economics.* Madison: University of Wisconsin Press.

Salter, W. E. G. 1966. *Productivity and Technical Change.* 2nd ed. with addendum by W. B. Reddaway. Cambridge: Cambridge University Press.

Schmookler, J. 1952. "The Changing Efficiency of the American Economy, 1869–1938." *Review of Economic Statistics* 34, no. 3 (August): 214–231.

——— 1966. *Invention and Economic Growth.* Cambridge, Mass.: Harvard University Press.

——— 1972. *Patents, Invention, and Economic Change: Data and Selected Essays,* ed. Z. Griliches and L. Hurwicz. Cambridge, Mass.: Harvard University Press.

Schumpeter, J. 1908. *Das Wesen und der Hauptinhalt der Theoretischen Nationaloekonomie.* Leipzig: Duncker and Humblot.

——— [1911] 1967. *The Theory of Economic Development.* New York: Oxford University Press.

——— 1939. *Business Cycles.* New York: McGraw-Hill.

Sen, A. K., ed. 1970. *Growth Economics.* Harmondsworth: Penguin.

Smith, A. 1937. *Wealth of Nations,* ed. E. Cannan, with an introduction by M. Lerner. New York: Random House.

Solow, R. M. 1957. "Technical Change and the Aggregate Production Function." *Review of Economics and Statistics* 39, no. 3 (August):312–320.

Sraffa, P., and Dobb, M. H., eds. 1955. *The Works and Correspondence of David Ricardo.* Cambridge: Cambridge University Press.

Stoneman, P. 1983. *The Economic Analysis of Technological Change.* Oxford: Oxford University Press.

Streeten, P. 1984. "Development Dichotomies." In *Pioneers in Development,* ed. G. M. Meier and D. Seers. New York: Oxford University Press for the World Bank.

Urquidi, V. L. 1986. "Scientific and Technological Cooperation for Development: Towards a New Outlook." Lincoln-Juarez Lecture, 1982, Washington, D.C., November 13.

15

...

Creating Competitive Capability: Innovation and Investment in the United States, Great Britain, and Germany from the 1870s to World War I

Alfred D. Chandler, Jr.

In the last decades of the nineteenth century, "a cluster of innovations that have earned the name of the Second Industrial Revolution . . . marked the start of a new upswing, a second cycle of industrial growth which is still in course and whose technological possibilities are still far from exhausted" (Landes 1969, p. 235). In this chapter, I attempt to build on this concept by relating the innovations of the "second wind" to entrepreneurial success and failure by focusing on the link between the two: investment—the investment that was required to exploit fully the potential of the new technologies, not only in terms of market and profit, but also in making available the new and improved products and processes throughout the world. The entrepreneurs who made investments large enough to exploit fully the economic potential of these new processes and products developed competitive capabilities that permitted their enterprises and their nations' industries to dominate markets abroad as well as at home.

My basic argument is that such exploitation required the creation of what could be termed the modern industrial enterprise. That enterprise was, in turn, the result of three sets of investments. Most essential was the investment in production large enough to utilize the economies of scale and scope inherent in the technological innovation. A second set was the investment in marketing and distribution large enough to sell the goods produced by the new processes of production in the volume in which they were made. Finally, the success of the resulting enterprise called for the recruitment of a managerial hierarchy to manage and coordinate the day-to-day processes of production and distribution and to allocate resources for future production and distribution.

The purpose of this essay, then, is to analyze this three-pronged investment, the institution that it created, and the competitive capabilities it developed. The first part defines in general terms the modern industrial enterprise, its attributes, the reasons for its appearance, and the development of its competitive strength. The second part reviews the historical story of four sets of major industries— chemicals, metals, machinery, and food—in three leading industrial nations— the United States, Britain, and Germany—in the four decades before the coming of World War I.

The Modern Industrial Enterprise

This new institution carried out more than a production function. It was a governance structure. It governed and so integrated units carrying out different production functions as well as commercial, research, and financial functions. In such a multiunit enterprise each unit had its own administrative office, its own managers and staff, its own set of books, as well as its own resources in terms of physical facilities and personnel to carry out the specific functions involved in the production and distribution of a specific product in a specific geographical area. Each unit could theoretically act as an independent business enterprise. The activities of these units were coordinated and monitored by middle managers, whose work in turn was coordinated and monitored by full-time top managers who planned and allocated resources for the operating units and the enterprise as a whole (see Figure 15.1).

Such multiunit, multifunctional, multiregional enterprises had three important historical attributes. Not only did such enterprises appear quite suddenly in the last quarter of the nineteenth century, but they also clustered from the start in industries with much the same characteristics. Finally, they were born and continued to grow in much the same manner.

The historical experiences related later in this chapter document the timing of the appearance of this institution. They also describe the similar patterns of beginnings and continued growth. They do not, however, fully indicate the industries in which the new industrial enterprises first appeared and continued to cluster throughout the twentieth century. This clustering is indicated by Tables 15.1–15.4. Table 15.1 gives the location, country by country and industry by industry, of all the industrial corporations in the world that employed more than 20,000 workers in 1973. It indicates that 289 (72 percent) of the 401 companies that made the list were in food, chemicals, oil, primary metals, machinery, electrical machinery, and transportation equipment. (These are two-digit industrial groups as defined by the U.S. Census in its Standard Industrial Classification [SIC] and listed in the tables.) Just under 30 percent were in three-digit categories of other two-digit groups—subcategories that had the same high-volume, capital-intensive technologies of production as those in which the 65

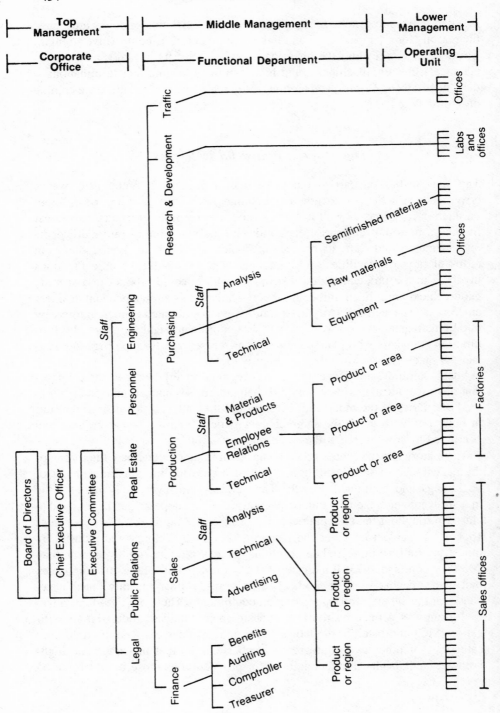

Figure 15.1 The multiunit, multifunctional enterprise (source: Chandler 1990, p. 16).

Table 15.1 Distribution of world's largest industrial enterprises with more than 20,000 employees, by industry and country, 1973.[a]

SIC group[b]	Industry	United States	Outside United States	Great Britain	West Germany	Japan	France	Others	Total
20	Food	22	17	13	0	1	1	2	39
21	Tobacco	3	4	3	1	0	0	0	7
22	Textiles	7	6	3	0	2	1	0	13
23	Apparel	6	0	0	0	0	0	0	6
24	Lumber	4	2	0	0	0	0	2	6
25	Furniture	0	0	0	0	0	0	0	0
26	Paper	7	3	3	0	0	0	0	10
27	Printing and publishing	0	0	0	0	0	0	0	0
28	Chemicals	24	28	4	5	3	6	10	52
29	Petroleum	14	12	2	0	0	2	8	26
30	Rubber	5	5	1	1	1	1	1	10
31	Leather	2	0	0	0	0	0	0	2
32	Stone, clay, and glass	7	8	3	0	0	3	2	15
33	Primary metals	13	35	2	9	5	4	15	48
34	Fabricated metals	8	6	5	1	0	0	0	14
35	Machinery	22	12	2	3	2	0	5	34
36	Electrical machinery	20	25	4	5	7	2	7	45
37	Transportation equipment	22	23	3	3	7	4	6	45
38	Instruments[c]	4	1	0	0	0	0	0	5
39	Miscellaneous	2	0	0	0	0	0	0	2
—	Conglomerate	19	3	2	1	0	0	0	22
	Total	211	190	50	29	28	24	59	401

Sources: Compiled from "The Fortune Directory of the 500 Largest Industrial Corporations," *Fortune*, May 1974, pp. 230–257; "The Fortune Directory of the 300 Largest Industrial Corporations outside the U.S.," *Fortune*, August 1974, pp. 174–181.

[a] The *Fortune* lists include enterprises of noncommunist countries only.

[b] These are the two-digit industrial groups as defined by the U.S. Census in its Standard Industrial Classification (SIC).

[c] Medical equipment and supplies, photographic equipment and supplies, and watches and clocks.

percent clustered, that is, cigarettes in tobacco; tires in rubber; newsprint in paper; plate and flat glass in stone, glass, and clay; cans and razor blades in fabricated metals; and mass-produced cameras in instruments. Only 21 companies (5.2 percent) were in the remaining two-digit categories—apparel, lumber, furniture, leather, publishing and printing, instruments, and miscellaneous—industries characterized by relatively low-volume, labor-intensive processes of production. Table 15.2 shows that large industrial corporations had clustered

Table 15.2 Distribution of the 200 largest industrial enterprises in the United States, by industry, 1917–1973.[a]

SIC group	Industry	1917	1930	1948	1973
20	Food	29	31	27	22
21	Tobacco	6	5	5	3
22	Textiles	6	4	8	3
23	Apparel	3	0	0	0
24	Lumber	3	4	2	4
25	Furniture	0	1	1	0
26	Paper	5	8	6	9
27	Printing and publishing	2	2	2	1
28	Chemicals	20	20	23	28
29	Petroleum	22	26	22	22
30	Rubber	5	5	5	5
31	Leather	4	2	2	0
32	Stone, clay, and glass	5	8	6	7
33	Primary metals	31	23	23	19
34	Fabricated metals	11	10	6	5
35	Machinery	17	19	23	16
36	Electrical machinery	5	5	7	13
37	Transportation equipment	24	23	29	19
38	Instruments	1	2	1	4
39	Miscellaneous	1	2	2	1
—	Conglomerate	0	0	0	19
	Total	200	200	200	200

Sources: Chandler (1990, appendixes A.1–A.3 for 1917, 1930, and 1948); figures for 1973 compiled from Fortune, May 1974, pp. 230–257.

[a] Ranked by assets.

throughout the twentieth century in the United States in much the same industrial groups in which they were concentrated in 1973. Tables 15.3 and 15.4 indicate that the pattern was much the same for Britain and Germany (after World War II, numbers are for West Germany only).

The Economies of Scale and Scope in Production

How then to account for these three common attributes? Let us begin by examining the characteristics of the major production innovations of the Second Industrial Revolution. What differentiated these processes from earlier ones was

Table 15.3   Distribution of the 200 largest industrial enterprises in Great Britain, by industry, 1919–1973.[a]

SIC group	Industry	1919	1930	1948	1973
20	Food	61	63	53	33
21	Tobacco	3	4	6	4
22	Textiles	26	21	17	10
23	Apparel	0	1	2	0
24	Lumber	0	0	0	2
25	Furniture	0	0	0	0
26	Paper	3	5	6	7
27	Printing and publishing	5	10	7	7
28	Chemicals	14	11	17	21
29	Petroleum	3	4	3	8
30	Rubber	3	3	2	6
31	Leather	1	1	1	3
32	Stone, clay, and glass	2	7	8	16
33	Primary metals	40	24	25	14
34	Fabricated metals	1	8	7	7
35	Machinery	7	6	10	26
36	Electrical machinery	6	10	11	14
37	Transportation equipment	23	17	21	16
38	Instruments	0	2	1	3
39	Miscellaneous	2	3	3	1
—	Conglomerate	0	0	0	2
	Total	200	200	200	200

Sources: Chandler (1990, appendixes B.1–B.3 for 1919, 1930, and 1948); figures for 1973 compiled from *The Times 1000, 1974/75* (London, 1974, table 15).

[a] Ranked by market value of quoted capital.

the potential for exploiting unprecedented cost advantages of the economies of scale and scope. In the older labor-intensive industries, increases in production resulted almost wholly from adding more machinery and more workers to operate the additional machines. In the industries in which the modern industrial firm came to concentrate, increasing output resulted from improving and rearranging inputs; from improving machinery, furnaces, stills, and other equipment; from reorienting the process of production within the plant; from placing the several intermediary processes involved in production of a final product within a single works; and from increasing the application of energy (particularly that generated by fossil fuel). The first set of industries remained labor-intensive; the second set became capital-intensive.

Table 15.4 Distribution of the 200 largest industrial enterprises in Germany, by industry, 1913–1973.[a]

SIC group	Industry	1913	1929	1953[b]	1973[b]
20	Food	26	28	22	24
21	Tobacco	1	1	0	6
22	Textiles	15	24	26	4
23	Apparel	1	1	1	0
24	Lumber	1	0	0	0
25	Furniture	0	0	0	0
26	Paper	4	5	3	2
27	Printing and publishing	0	1	0	6
28	Chemicals	30	24	24	30
29	Petroleum	5	7	6	8
30	Rubber	4	2	5	3
31	Leather	2	5	2	1
32	Stone, clay, and glass	7	7	6	15
33	Primary metals	49	33	40	19
34	Fabricated metals	5	3	5	14
35	Machinery	25	19	28	29
36	Electrical machinery	7	11	8	21
37	Transportation equipment	16	24	18	14
38	Instruments	2	3	3	2
39	Miscellaneous	0	2	3	1
—	Conglomerate	0	0	0	1
	Total	200	200	200	200

Sources: Chandler (1990, appendixes C.1–C.3 for 1913, 1929, and 1953); figures for 1973 compiled from *Handbuch der deutschen Aktiengesellschaften, 1974–75.*

[a] Ranked by sales for 1973 and by assets for the other three years.

[b] Data for West Germany alone.

In these new capital-intensive industries, production units achieved much greater economies of scale (or scope)—that is, their cost per unit dropped much more quickly as the volume of materials processed increased—than in the labor-intensive industries. In these capital industries large plants operating at their optimal efficient scale (that is, the scale of operation that brought the lowest unit cost) had a much greater cost advantage over smaller plants than was the case in industries using more labor-intensive technologies.

Such potential cost advantages could not be fully realized, however, unless a constant flow of materials through the plant or factory was maintained to ensure effective capacity utilization. Unit costs rose sharply as volume of flow was reduced. The decisive figure in determining costs and profits was and still is, then, not rated capacity for a specified time period but rather throughput—that is, the amount actually processed in a specific time period. Throughput became, then, the proper economic measure of capacity utilization. In the capital-intensive industries, the throughput needed to maintain minimum efficient scale required careful coordination not only of flow through the processes of production but also of the flow of inputs from the suppliers and the flow of outputs to the retailers and final consumers.

Such coordination did not and indeed could not happen automatically. It demanded the constant attention of a managerial team or hierarchy. The potential economies of scale and scope were and still are, then, characteristics of a technology. The actual economies of scale or of scope, as measured by throughput, are organizational. Such economies depend on knowledge, skill, experience, and teamwork—on the organized human capabilities essential to exploit the potential of technological processes.

The significance of the resulting economies of scale, as indicated by throughput, can be illustrated by the well-known example of one of the very first modern industrial (as opposed to transportation, communication, or distribution) enterprises in the United States, the Standard Oil Company (its successor, Exxon, is still the world's largest oil company). The oldest and still largest German chemical companies provide as striking an example of the economies of scope.

In 1882 the Standard Oil "alliance" formed the Standard Oil Trust. The purpose was not to obtain control over the industry's output. That alliance, a loose federation of 40 companies, each with its own legal and administrative identity but tied to John D. Rockefeller's Standard Oil Company through interchange of stock and other financial devices, already had a virtual monopoly (Chandler and Tedlow 1985, pp. 346–360). The members of the alliance of that time produced 90 percent of America's output of kerosene. Instead, the trust was formed to provide a legal instrument to rationalize the industry so as to exploit more fully economies of scale. The trust provided the essential legal means to create a corporate or central office that could, first, reorganize the processes of production by shutting down some refineries, reshaping others, and building new ones and, second, coordinate the flow of materials, not only through the several refineries, but also from the oil fields to the refineries and from the refineries to the consumers. The resulting rationalization made it possible to concentrate close to a quarter of the world's production of kerosene in three refineries, each with an average daily charging capacity of 6,500 barrels, with two-thirds of their product going to overseas markets. (At this time, refined petroleum products were by far the nation's largest nonagricultural export.) Imagine the diseconomies of scale—that is, the increase in units costs—that would result from placing one-fourth of the world's production of shoes or textiles or lumber into three factories or mills! The administrative coordination of the operation of miles and miles of machines and the huge concentration of labor needed to man these machines would make no economic or social sense.

This reorganization of the trust's refining facilities brought a sharp reduction in average cost of production of a gallon of kerosene. It dropped from 1.5 cents a gallon before reorganization to 0.54 cent in 1884 and 0.45 cent in 1885. Profit margin rose from 0.53 cent in 1884 to 1.003 cents in 1885. (That increase was the source of the largest industrial fortune in modern times.) The costs at the giant refineries were still lower—costs far below those of any competitor. Maintaining this cost advantage, however, required these large refineries to have a continuing daily throughput of from 5,000 to 6,500 barrels, or a three-fold to fourfold increase over the earlier daily flow of 1,500 to 2,000 barrels, with the resulting increases in transactions handled and in the complexity of coordinating the flow of materials through the process of production and distribution.

In the same years that Standard Oil was investing in its large refineries to exploit the economies of scale, the German dye makers were making an even larger investment to permit them to exploit fully the economies of scope. The enlarged plants came to produce literally hundreds of dyes and in addition many pharmaceuticals from the same raw materials and the same set of intermediate chemical compounds. The first three enterprises to make such an investment, initially to exploit the cost advantages of scale and then those of scope—Bayer, Hoechst, and BASF—reduced the price of the new synthetic dye blue alizarin from 270 marks per kilo in 1869 to 23 marks in 1878 and 9 marks in 1886 and to make comparable price reductions in their other dyes.[1] The addition of a new dye or pharmaceutical to their total product line added little cost for the production of that dye and at the same time reduced the unit cost of the other dye products. On the other hand, each addition involved the development of a specialized product—one requiring constant supervision to ensure the necessary quality—and each increased the need for organizational coordination.

These stories of Standard Oil and the three German chemical firms are by no means unique. Indeed, in the last two decades of the nineteenth century comparable investments were made in new production technologies in nearly all the industries where the modern industrial enterprise would continue to cluster for the next century—in the refining, distilling, processing, and packaging of food products; in the production of a wide variety of chemicals, rubber, glass, abrasives, and other materials; in the making of steel, copper, and other nonferrous metals; and in the production of machines made through the fabrication and assembling of interchangeable parts, and also in heavier machinery, including electrical equipment, that provided the furnaces, refineries, and a wide variety of processing equipment used in the many new industries.

The differentials in potential scale and scope economies of different production technologies indicate not only why the large hierarchical firms appeared in some industries and not in others, but also why they appeared suddenly in the last two decades of the nineteenth century. Only with the completion of the modern transportation and communication networks—those of the railroad, telegraph, steamship, and cable—and the organizational innovations essential to operate them as integrated systems, could materials flow into a factory or processing plant and finished goods move out at a rate of speed and volume required to achieve substantial economies of throughput. Transportation that depended on the power of animals, wind, and current was too slow, too irregular, and too uncertain to maintain a level of throughput necessary to achieve the potential economies of the new technologies.

Economies of Scale and Scope in Distribution

If the cost advantages of the economies of scale and scope can account for when and where the modern industrial enterprise made its appearance, they cannot explain the second investment essential to its initial growth, that is, the investment in a national and often international marketing and distributing organization. The explanation requires an understanding of the operations of the new types of enterprise that appeared in distribution. For the new, all-weather, regularly scheduled, and historically unprecedented fast transportation and communication brought as profound a revolution in distribution as they did in production. The new commercial intermediaries that arose in response to the new opportunities included the full-line wholesalers and the new mass retailers—the department stores, the mail-order houses, and the chains or multiple shops. These enterprises made their profit on markup rather than on commissions, as had the traditional merchants; and they did so on the basis of high-volume sales at low price, for the profits depended on the maintenance of high-volume flow. For them, "stockturn" (that is, the volume processed in relation to inventory by a single set of facilities and personnel within a specified period of time) became as significant a criterion for performance as throughput was for the new high-volume producers.

These commercial intermediaries grew large by exploiting the cost advantages of both scale and scope. Because they handled the products of many manufacturers, they could ship and market more cheaply than could a single producer. They further reduced costs by using the same sets of facilities to sell many related products. These commercial intermediaries could, however, lose their cost advantages to the new producers in two situations. One was when a manufacturer's output reached the minimum efficient volume for the distribution of that line. The other was when marketing and distribution of a product required an investment in specialized skills and facilities that could be used only to market and distribute that one product. They had little incentive to make such investments in marketing and distribution not only because they would lose the advantages of scope, but also because the profitability of the investment would depend wholly on the decisions of the handful of manufacturers volume-producing that product. In other words, if they made that investment, they became captives of the producers.

For these reasons the entrepreneurs who made the investment in production large enough to exploit the economies of scale and scope usually had to invest in national and often international marketing and distribution networks. This product-specific investment involved both the provision of marketing services and the building of distribution facilities. Thus the makers of the new American mass-produced machinery—whether sewing, agricultural, or office (typewriters, cash registers, mimeograph machines, and the like)—had to provide demonstration, after-sales service and repair, and consumer credit. For the producers of heavy machinery, close contact with customers was even more necessary, for the machines had to be designed to the users' special needs and often required even more complex after-sales service and even more extensive consumer credit. So also the makers of dyes not only had to show their customers—producers of thread, cloth, leather, and other fabrics and finishes—how to use the new synthetic dyes but also often provided machinery to facilitate the process. And if the producers of the new powerful explosive—dynamite—failed to instruct carefully on its use, they often lost their customers.

Oil refiners, chemical manufacturers, and meat packers and canners and other food processors required more in the way of product-specific distribution facilities than of marketing services. The two pioneers in the oil industry, Rockefeller in the United States and the Nobel brothers in Russia, after building the world's largest refineries, invested heavily during the 1880s in pipelines, railway tank cars, oceangoing tankers, and storage depots in order to ensure steady, scheduled distribution of their products in the volume in which they could be produced.

The profitable utilization of extensive investment in production and in distribution required a third investment—in personnel. The founders of the new enterprises had to recruit full-time salaried managers, not only to administer each set of facilities, but also to coordinate the flow of materials from purchasing to distribution to the retailer or final customer. The founders, therefore, had to build a managerial hierarchy in which lower and middle managers handled production, distribution, purchasing, and other functions, while they, assisted by the top managers, coordinated and monitored their activities and planned and allocated resources for future production and distribution.

First Mover Advantages and the New Oligopolistic Competition

As soon as a handful of firms had made such investments, they dominated their markets. Their industries quickly became and remained oligopolistic and occasionally monopolistic, for the first to make the three-pronged investment acquired powerful competitive advantages. To compete with the first movers, rivals had to build plants of comparable size and make the necessary investments in distribution and, in some industries, in research. They also had to recruit and train a managerial hierarchy. The construction of a plant of the size needed to achieve comparable economies of scale or scope often meant, however, that the total capacity of an industry came to exceed existing demand. If newcomers were to maintain capacity utilization essential to ensure competitive unit costs, they had to take customers from the pioneers.

This was a challenging task. While the newcomer's production managers were learning the unique characteristics of a new or altered technology, and while its sales forces were being recruited and trained, the first movers often had already begun to work out the bugs in the production processes and had taken strides in ensuring prompt delivery, in meeting customers' special needs, and in providing the basic marketing services. In branded packaged products, where advertising was an important competitive weapon, the first movers were already investing some of the high profits resulting from high-volume throughput into massive advertising campaigns.

The first movers had other advantages. In the more technologically complex industries the first to install research laboratories and to train technicians in very product-specific development skills had a comparable advantage, one that was often reinforced and expanded by patents obtained on both product and process. Moreover, in most of the new industries the latecomers had to make a much larger initial capital outlay than did their predecessors, for they could not finance the initial increases in the scale of production or expand their marketing networks from retained earnings as could the first movers. Not only did the latecomers' investment have to be larger, but it was also riskier, precisely because of the first movers' competitive strength. Thus, not only were the pioneers the first to exploit the cost advantages of scale and scope, but their head start in developing capabilities in all functional activities—production, distribution, purchasing, research, finance, and general management—meant that they were often well down the learning curve in each of these functional activities before the newcomers were into full operation.

Although these barriers to entry were intimidating, newcomers did appear, particularly when new sources of supply were opened, when rapid demographic changes altered existing markets, and when technological change created new markets and diminished old ones. In those industries where scale and scope provided cost advantages, the number of players remained small, however. There was little turnover among the leaders between the 1890s and the 1950s.

In these industries the few large integrated firms competed for market share and profits in national and often world markets in what was a new, oligopolistic manner. That is, they no longer competed, as firms had done previously and as firms continued to do in the more fragmented labor-intensive industries, primarily on price. In the new capital-intensive industries the largest (usually the first to make the three-pronged investment in production, distribution, and management) became the price leader, basing prices on the estimates of demand in relation to its plant capacities and those of its competitors.

Although price remained a competitive weapon, these firms competed more forcefully for market share and increased profits with functional and strategic efficiency. That is, they competed by attempting to carry out more capably the several processes of production and distribution, by developing and improving both product and process through systematic research and development, by locating new and more suitable sources of supply, by providing more effective marketing services, by product differentiation (in branded packaged products primarily through advertising), and finally by moving more quickly into new and expanding markets and out of old and declining ones. The test of such competition was changing market share, and in most of the new oligopolistic industries, market share and profits changed constantly.

Such competition for market share and profits tended to sharpen the capabilities of the middle managers responsible for each of the functional activities. It also tested and enlarged the skills of the top managers in coordination, strategic planning, and resource allocation. Their combined capabilities can be considered those of the organization itself. These highly product-specific and process-specific organizational capabilities and skills affected, indeed often determined, the direction and pace of the continuing growth of the industrial enterprise and of the industries and the national economies in which they operated.

The Historical Experience

This description of the beginnings and growth of the modern industrial enterprise is much oversimplified. The details differ from nation to nation, industry to industry, and even firm to firm; but the general sequence holds. The historical experience demonstrates the significance of the critical entrepreneurial act—the making of the three-pronged investment. It shows that those who made it also developed competitive capabilities that permitted them to capture and then to hold, often for decades, international markets. It was the success of American and German entrepreneurs in making these investments and the failure of British entrepreneurs to do so that helped to permit American and German industries quickly to outstrip those of Britain in the quarter-century before World War I.

These investments also had a critical impact on the continuing accumulative innovations within these industries. The first movers created the organization in which so much of the continuing small, cumulative improvements in product and process occurred. As both David Landes and Nathan Rosenberg have so rightly and eloquently stressed, technological innovations are interdependent and interrelated. Innovation in one industry and one sector in an economy has a profound impact on the supply and demand for products of other industries and for technological change within them.[2] Thus the coming of high-volume generation of electricity in the 1880s created needs and opportunities for technological and organizational innovation in a wide variety of industries. Once the three-pronged investment was made to exploit fully sets of often interrelated technological innovations, however, the managers of the resulting enterprises decided the direction of, and the resources devoted to, continuing innovation in that industry.

Because of these interrelationships and interdependencies the innovations of the second wind—of the Second Industrial Revolution—that swept through the United States and Europe in the latter half of the nineteenth century were so widespread and took place in so many more industries than did those of the First Industrial Revolution, the following brief review must be very selective. It considers investments in four industries: the new chemical industries, in which the Germans and, to a lesser extent, the American entrepreneurs made the critical investments; the heavy and light machinery industries, where the Americans made them in the light volume-produced machinery and the Germans in more specialized heavy industrial equipment; the metals industries, where again Germans and Americans acquired competitive capabilities; and finally one set of industries—the production and distribution of branded packaged products— where British entrepreneurs invested enough to become major players in international markets.

Chemicals

The history of the new organic chemical industry provides a striking example of the ways in which the three-pronged investment in production, distribution, and management created competitive capabilities. In 1870 the British dye makers enjoyed nearly every possible economic advantage. An Englishman, William Perkin, was the pioneer, producing the first synthetic dye in 1856. The world's largest market for dyes was the British textile industry, and it remained so until after World War II. Dyes were made of coal, and Britain had an abundance of readily available, high-quality coal. The only advantage the German producers had was the better training available in chemistry in Germany. By 1870, however, leading German chemists were employed by British firms. By any economic criterion the British dye producers should quickly have dominated international markets.

In the 1870s German firms—Bayer, BASF, Hoechst, AGFA, and two others—"scaled up" their production of aniline and alizarin dyes. It was this investment that increased throughput and drove the price of alizarin dye from 270 marks a kilo in 1869 to 23 marks in 1878. Then, in the late 1870s and early 1880s, three—Bayer, BASF, and Hoechst—began to build much larger plants in order to exploit the economies of scope by producing many dyes and also pharmaceuticals from the same set of intermediates, an investment that permitted the reduction in the price of alizarin to 8 marks by 1886.[3] In the 1880s these firms extended their marketing organizations throughout the world. At the same time they offered salaries that quickly brought the German chemists in Britain back to Germany to work in the new research laboratories that would long lead the world in the development of new products and processes based on organic chemistry. By the 1890s, too, these firms had recruited and trained what were the world's largest managerial hierarchies in industrial enterprise. Because of the resulting competitive capabilities of these enterprises, German firms accounted for 140,000 tons (Bayer, BASF, and Hoechst producing 77 percent of this output) of the 160,000 tons of dyes produced in 1913. Three smaller Swiss neighbors produced 10,000, and the British pioneers 4,000 (Haber 1971, pp. 121, 123, 145). Thus, although British entrepreneurs in this industry had every economic advantage, Germans made the investments that created the critical competitive advantages.

Nor were such competitive capabilities developed in just dyes. Many more specialized pharmaceutical firms, including Merck, Schering, and Heyden, made comparable though somewhat smaller investments which permitted them to compete successfully at home and abroad. In Europe and even the United States their leading competitors remained the pharmaceutical lines produced by the German dye makers. In the new electrochemical industry DEGUSSA and Griesheim became and then remained the leaders in Europe. DEGUSSA's American subsidiary, Roessler & Hasslacher, became a major producer in the United States. So, too, Rutgerswerke and Holtzverkohlungs did the same in the less technologically complex tar- and wood-based chemical industries; as did Bayerische Stickstoffwerke in agricultural chemicals shortly after the turn of the century.

Although American chemical manufacturers made little attempt to compete with the Germans even within the United States in dyes and pharmaceuticals, they did make comparable investments in other branches of the industry. National Carbon and Union Carbide competed successfully with DEGUSSA's subsidiary; Barrett in tar- and wood-based chemicals and a little later American Cyanamid in agricultural chemicals more than held their own outside Europe. In 1891 Rowland Hazard formed the Solvay Process Company and made the investments necessary to exploit fully that new capital-intensive process for producing synthetic alkalies in the United States. A little more than a decade later the du Pont cousins consolidated the explosives industry and rationalized it so that it could realize more effectively the economies of scale, particularly in the production and marketing of dynamite.

Only in these last two chemical industries did British entrepreneurs make the investments essential to have their enterprises become players in their global oligopolies. Significantly, it was the merger in 1926 of these two—Brunner, Mond, producers of alkalies by the Solvay process, and Nobel Industries, Ltd., makers of dynamite—that created Imperial Chemical Industries, the one major British producer of industrial chemicals established between the 1880s and the 1950s.

Machinery

If British industrialists failed before the 1920s to create international competitive capabilities in new chemical industries, they were even less successful in machinery. In electrical equipment, which, like chemicals, was becoming science-based, the first movers—General Electric and Westinghouse in the United States and Siemens and AEG in Germany—made their investments in the 1880s and early 1890s in the production of equipment to generate, transfer, and use electric power, created their international marketing organizations, and recruited their managerial hierarchies. Mather & Platt, a leading British textile machinery firm, obtained Edison patents at the same time that Emil Rathenau, the founder of AEG, obtained them. There appears to be no economic reason why Sir William Mather could not have made an investment in production, distribution, and management comparable to that of Rathenau. Nevertheless, neither he nor any other British entrepreneur did so (Byatt 1979, pp. 141, 143, 148). As a result, by 1911–1913 two-thirds of electrical equipment machinery made in British factories was produced by subsidiaries of General Electric, Westinghouse, and Siemens.[4] The largest domestic producer, Dick Kerr, accounted for less than 8 percent of total output, and Mather & Platt had become a minor producer of electrical equipment for factories. As in the case of chemicals, continuing research and improvement of product and process in this critical industry was carried on not in Britain but in the United States and Germany.

In the production of nonelectrical heavy machinery—the machinery that processed, shaped, and finished the new products of the Second Industrial Revolution—German enterprises quickly came to have a unique position. They

built large plants to produce, from much the same raw and semifinished materials with much the same forges, foundries, pressing and stamping machines,
and other processing equipment, an extraordinary range of machinery and equipment for railroads, ships, shipping terminals, mines, and for the metalmaking,
metal fabricating, glass, chemical, food, textile, lumber, leather, and other
industries. These firms included MAN, Humboldt, Borsig, BEMAG, DEMAG,
HANOMAG, Buchau Wolf, and even the steelmaker GHH. No comparable
heavy machinery enterprises appeared in either the United States or Britain. In
both countries industrial companies designed much of the equipment they
needed and had it produced in job shops. By 1900 these German firms were
equipping factories not only in Europe but throughout the world, including the
United States.

If the Germans, through their investments in production and distribution in
the 1880s and 1890s, quickly led the world in the making of heavy machinery,
the Americans acquired an even greater global dominance in the same decades
in light machinery produced by the fabrication and assembling of interchangeable parts. It was in the early 1880s that the innovators in sewing machines and
agricultural equipment made the investments that ensured them close to a global
monopoly for more than half a century. Between 1881 and 1883 Singer Sewing
Machine's investment in production at its Elizabethport, New Jersey, plant
(built in 1876)—an investment that incorporated for the first time fully interchangeable parts production—increased throughput to over 8,000 machines a
week and then to 10,000 (Hounshell 1984, pp. 99–121, 178–182). In 1884 the
company built a plant with a comparable capacity near Glasgow, Scotland. The
two works were soon producing over 75 percent of the world's sewing machines. In 1881 the McCormick Harvester works were making 30,000 machines
a year. By the middle of the decade their throughput had doubled to 60,000. In
these same years Singer filled in its international sales network and McCormick
its national one.

By World War I Singer and International Harvester (the successor to McCormick) completely dominated European markets. The latter had built a large plant
in Germany and then, as had Singer, in Russia. Indeed, by 1913 subsidiaries of
these two American companies were the two largest commercial enterprises in
imperial Russia. By then Singer was producing 79,000 machines annually in its
Moscow factory with a work force of 2,500 wage earners and 300 salaried employees; while its sales force of 27,439 covered the vast territory from the Sea of
Japan to the Baltic (Carstensen 1984, pp. 65, 78, 193–195, 208).

In office machinery—typewriters, cash registers, mimeograph machines, cal-
culators, tabulators, and the like—the Americans had almost as impressive a
dominance. This was also the case in larger volume-produced machinery such
as elevators and printing presses.[5] Occasionally German entrepreneurs built
comparable enterprises to mass-produce machinery. Deutz in stationary gaso-

line engines, Linde in refrigeration machinery, and a little later Bosch in magnetos and other electrical equipment are examples. British entrepreneurs never seriously entered into the production of either light volume-produced machinery or heavier, more specialized equipment, however. Their successful machinery firms remained established ones that provided equipment for the older industries, primarily textiles and mining.

Mining

The experience of the metal industries, especially steel, is better known than that of chemicals or machinery. That experience is summarized in Table 15.5, which gives the output of steel mass-produced by the Bessemer process, invented in 1856, and the Siemens-Martin open-hearth technology, perfected in the late 1860s. Because the output of the Bessemer converter was more brittle than that of the open hearth, it was used primarily for making rails, tubes, and some sheet, whereas the higher-grade open-hearth steel was used for beams and for other structures and for ship plate. In steel the British led the way, building small mills to meet a still relatively small demand. In 1880 Britain remained the largest steel producer, although only barely so. Then, as the world emerged from the severe depression of the late 1870s, German and American entrepreneurs began to make the investments that fully utilized the cost advantages of the new technologies. In 1879 Andrew Carnegie added blast furnaces to his Edgar Thomson rail mill to make it the world's most efficient rail producer.[6] In 1883 he converted the Homestead works, which he had purchased in 1881, from rails to structures, replacing Bessemer converters with open-hearth furnaces. In 1888 the new Duquesne works (which Carnegie acquired in 1891) went into production using the new "direct rolling" processes (Livesay 1975, p. 132). By 1886 the South Chicago Works, the largest rail mills outside of Pittsburgh, came on stream, as did, at about the same time, the large Joliet works (in Illinois) and Jones and Laughlin in Pittsburgh. At precisely the same moment German firms—Rheinische Stahlwerke, Hoerder Verein, Dortmunder Union, Krupp, and GHH—began installing Bessemer and open-hearth facilities to produce "basic" steel by the Thomas Gilchrist process. Here, although less so in the United States, the invention in 1879 of that new process permitted German steelmakers to use low-grade phosphorus ores essential to high-volume production in both processes (see Table 15.5).[7]

In both countries the new mills were able to meet the rising demand in the 1880s for pipes, wire, cables, bridges, and above all rails and structures as the United States and Europe rapidly urbanized and industrialized. As throughput soared (see Table 15.5), prices fell in both the United States and Germany. The price of rails "in works at Pittsburgh" fell from $67.50 in 1880 to $29.25 in 1889.[8] British producers could no longer compete on either continent. Imports

Table 15.5 Production of steel ingots and castings, by process, Great Britain, United States, and Germany, 1875–1914 (in thousand metric tons).

Year	Bessemer process			Open-hearth process			Other processes	Total
	Acid	Basic	Total	Acid	Basic	Total		
Great Britain, 1875–1914								
1875	—	—	630	—	—	89	—	719
1880	—	—	1,061	—	—	255	—	1,316
1885	—	—	1,324	—	—	594	—	1,918
1890	—	—	2,048	—	—	1,590	—	3,638
1895	—	—	1,560	—	—	1,753	—	3,313
1900	1,275	499	1,774	2,910	298	3,208	—	4,981
1905	1,419	587	2,006	3,093	808	3,901	—	5,907
1910	1,157	651	1,808	3,066	1,604	4,670	—	6,478
1914	810	490	1,300	3,741	2,922	6,663	—	7,963
United States, 1875–1914								
1875	304	—	304	—	—	7	42	353
1880	975	—	975	—	—	92	65	1,132
1885	1,378	—	1,378	—	—	121	54	1,553
1890	3,348	—	3,348	—	—	466	67	3,881
1900	6,066	—	6,066	774	2,309	3,038	96	9,245
1905	9,928	—	9,928	1,049	7,093	8,142	101	18,171
1910	8,541	—	8,541	1,100	13,876	14,976	162	23,679
1914	5,645	—	5,645	820	14,765	15,585	107	21,337
Germany, 1880–1914								
1880	679	18	697	—	—	36	—	733
1885	379	548	927	—	—	276	—	1,203
1890	351	1,493	1,844	—	—	388	—	2,232
1895	316	2,520	3,836	—	—	1,189	—	4,025
1900	223	4,142	4,365	148	1,997	2,145	136	6,646
1905	424	6,204	6,628	166	3,087	3,253	186	10,067
1910	171	8,031	8,202	140	4,974	5,114	383	13,699
1914	100	8,144	8,244	275	5,946	6,221	481	14,946

Sources: For the United States, compiled from American Iron and Steel Institute, *Annual Statistical Report, 1914*, pp. 28–29; for Great Britain and Germany, compiled from [British] National Federation of Iron and Steel Manufacturers, *Statistics of the Iron and Steel Industries, 1922*, pp. 14, 57.

of British rails into the United States from 1880 to 1883 were substantial, although not quite as large as they had been in the years before 1874 when the depression struck. After 1883 they all but disappeared. Tariffs cannot account for the British loss of the American market since the only change in tariffs in the decade of the 1880s was a reduction in 1883.[9] In the same years the British lost markets in continental countries and then in Latin America and Asia—markets where the Germans had to pay the same tariff as the British.

During the 1890s output continued to rise in both Germany and the United States. As costs fell, prices dropped. First mover profits soared. By the late 1890s, when Carnegie's costs had fallen to $11.25 a ton, rail prices had dropped from $18.75 in 1897 to $17.63 in 1898. Carnegie's profits rose from $7 million in 1897 to $11 million in 1898. Then in 1899, when boom times raised steel prices to $28.12 a ton, Carnegie's profits reached $21 million. In the next year they were $40 million (Livesay 1975, p. 166). As in the case of Rockefeller, reduced costs and increased profit margins generated another of the world's largest industrial fortunes.

By World War I American and German steelmakers had captured nearly all the world markets except for the British empire and Britain itself (Temin 1966, p. 148). As the British producers lost their overseas markets, they turned to concentrating on meeting domestic demand, particularly the British shipbuilding industry, still the world's largest. In the late 1880s and 1890s they shifted from Bessemer to open hearth to meet this market. During the decade of the 1890s roughly half of the open-hearth steel produced in Britain (over a quarter of the total output) went to shipbuilding (McCloskey 1973, p. 84). By 1914 Britain was importing 15 percent of the world's steel exports, 58 percent from Germany and the rest primarily from Belgium and the United States (Temin 1966, p. 148). By the end of the 1880s German and American first movers had powerful competitive advantages in international markets. Only a courageous and somewhat irrational British steelmaker would have made the investment required to build an integrated works in Britain large enough to compete with those in Pittsburgh and in the Ruhr in order to regain these more distant markets. By not doing so, however, the British lost these markets forever.

If by 1890 British entrepreneurs had missed their chance to compete abroad in steel, they still had every opportunity to do so by exploiting the new technologies of production that transformed the copper industry in the late 1880s and early 1890s. In the 1880s copper smelting was being rapidly altered by an adaptation of the Bessemer converter. It was, however, the development in 1891 of a generator powerful enough to permit large-scale electrolytic refining of copper that transformed the industry. In the next two years, five large refineries were built to exploit the scale economies of the new process. Indeed, these economies were so large that only seventeen more refineries were built in the

United States during the next 90 years, five of these before 1910 (Navin 1978, pp. 63–69).

Shortly after the turn of the century the four firms—Anaconda, American Smelting and Refining, Phelps, Dodge, and Kennecott—had made the investment necessary to dominate the industry. The fifth member of the global oligopoly was the German firm Metallgesellschaft. It immediately invested in two of the new refineries in the United States, then expanded its mining activities in Mexico and built an extensive sales force for the United States and Europe. Its former subsidiary, American Metals (AMEX), remains a leading member of the oligopoly, while Metallgesellschaft is still Europe's largest processor and distributor of nonferrous metals.

The response of British entrepreneurs to the new technology was minimal. Three leading copper processors installed small electrolytic furnaces. Two of these then immediately made arrangements to be the sole suppliers to each of the two leading British copper cable companies. Nor did the largest British-owned and operated enterprise, the Rio Tinto Company, with its mines in Spain, take the opportunity to build a copper-processing complex on the banks of the Mersey or the Bristol Channel comparable to that built by American and German entrepreneurs on the shores of the greater New York harbor. At that time, Rio Tinto's Spanish mines produced close to one-quarter of the world's copper output. The distance from the ores to British processing plants and from the refineries to British and continental markets were much shorter and transportation less expensive than was the case in New York. In 1884 the Rio Tinto company built a smelter near Swansea, Wales. "Between this time and the turn of the century, however," the company's historian has written, "there are few signs that the company was interested in the revolutionary change that was taking place in associated industries throughout the world" (Harvey 1979, p. 15). By 1900 the opportunity for a British firm to become a player in the oligopoly was gone, never again to return.

Branded Packaged Products

If British entrepreneurs failed to make the investment necessary to create competitive capabilities in chemicals, machinery, and metals, they were much more successful in the production and distribution of branded packaged products. Two reasons may help to account for the British success here. One was that the world's first industrial nation also became the world's first consumer society. The golden quadrangle between London, Cardiff, Glasgow, and Edinburgh remained the world's most concentrated consumer market until well after World War II. The other may have been that of all the capital-intensive industries in which the modern industrial enterprise appeared and then continued to cluster, the cost advantages of scale remained the smallest, and product-specific marketing and distribution of services and facilities the least necessary, in the production and distribution of branded packaged products.

Those food, drink, and consumer chemical industries in which the economies of scale existed, including soap, chocolate, cigarettes, biscuits, breakfast cereals, canned milk, and matches, quickly became concentrated. Again, the 1880s were the decade where the first to exploit these advantages by making the three-pronged investment in production, distribution, and management became the first movers in their industries. Thus, in 1888 William H. Lever built Port Sunlight, a model factory patterned after Procter and Gamble's Ivorydale, completed in Cincinnati in 1885.[10] In the second half of the 1880s the Wills brothers in Britain and James B. Duke in the United States invested in the new Bonsack cigarette machine that could produce 125,000 cigarettes a day, as compared to 3,000 made by the fastest handworker. The two quickly dominated world markets. (They divided the globe between them in 1904 with the formation of Imperial Tobacco and British-American Tobacco.) In the 1880s, too, the British chocolate makers—the Cadburys—built their "factory in a garden," and Rowntree and Fry expanded their plants in a comparable fashion. So, too, did the German chocolate maker Gerbrüder Stollwerke, one of the very few successful German mass producers of branded packaged products. In that decade Nestlé in Switzerland and Borden in the United States became the first movers in processing milk. (Nestlé soon moved into chocolate making.) In the 1880s, too, the continental margarine makers—the Dutch Van den Bergh and Jurgens and the Austrian company of Schicht (the three were to make up the European side of the 1929 merger that formed Unilever)—all built their large plants. So in the United States did such first movers as Quaker Oats, Diamond Match, and Heinz. All these firms recruited large forces of "travelers" or salesmen and built branch houses and other distributing facilities needed to sell their products in the volume in which they were produced. All reinforced their first mover positions by pouring profits coming from the cost advantages of scale into massive advertising campaigns. As one historian of advertising has pointed out, the producers of branded packaged products helped provide a financial base for a new literary vehicle for mass culture—weekly and monthly magazines such as the *Ladies Home Journal* and *McClures* and an increasingly popular literary form, the short story (Pope 1983, pp. 8–9, 43–45, 137).

Labor-Intensive Industries

If the multiunit, multifunctional enterprise came to dominate industries where the new technology of production offered potential cost advantages of scale and scope and where sales required product-specific marketing and distribution personnel and facilities, there was far less reason for its growth in industries where this was not the case. In those industries where, given the technology of production, the minimum efficient size of the plant was even smaller than those in branded packaged products, where mass distribution did not call for product-specific skills and facilities, and where coordination of flows was a relatively simple task, manufacturers had much less incentive to make the three-pronged investment in production, distribution, and management. In such industries as publishing and printing, lumber, furniture, textiles, apparel, leather, seasonal and specialized food processing, and specialized instruments and machinery, the large integrated firm had few competitive advantages. Indeed, it often had competitive disadvantages, for size in production facilities not only failed to bring lower costs but also made the firm even less flexible in meeting changes in demand. This was normally the case in apparel (both cloth and leather), furniture, a number of food processing industries, hardware, and specialized metalworking trades. Even where scale and scope and the integration of production and distribution brought cost reductions, as occurred in textiles and lumber, they were rarely sharp enough to permit a small number of firms to dominate the industry. In all these industrial categories many small single-unit firms continued to prosper. In these labor-intensive industries the competition remained more on the basis of price and the ability to move quickly to meet changing demand.

On the other hand, where technology and innovation led to substantial economies of scale and scope, where volume distribution of goods required investments in product-specific facilities and skills, and where managerial hierarchies were needed to coordinate, monitor, and plan if the cost advantages of the new technologies were to be reaped, the first to create modern industrial enterprise by making the three-pronged investment quickly dominated their industries—industries all central to the development and continuation of growth of the modern industrial urban nations. And it was the resulting competitive capabilities of the new enterprises that permitted the United States and Germany to outstrip Britain and to so become quickly the world's industrial leaders at the beginning of this century.

Entrepreneurial Success and Failure

The analysis presented here emphasizes that the critical entrepreneurial act in exploiting so many of the technological innovations of the Second Industrial Revolution was the three-pronged investment in production, distribution, and management. It further emphasizes that the time in which to make those investments was short. Failure to act within a period of a very few years meant the loss of markets, often permanently, abroad and even at home.

In some cases the failure to invest was a rational entrepreneurial response. In steel, British entrepreneurs may have been paying the price of being first comers but not becoming first movers. Their relatively small initial investment in new production technologies, their reliance on commercial intermediaries, and their personal management all reflected a market that was still limited. When American and European markets for rails, structures, tubes, and other steel products took off in the 1880s, the American and German producers had a far greater incentive to make the investments that would fully utilize the cost advantages of the new technologies. They were much closer geographically and also culturally to these markets. Once they had made the investments and acquired the first mover advantages, their British competitors had little choice but to turn their production to meeting the still sizable demands of the domestic British market and particularly its still rapidly growing shipbuilding industry. Rational too was the British failure in machinery. In the mass production of light machinery the American first movers had such a head start on both the new processes of production and the new ways of distribution that they remained virtually unchallenged until the 1960s. So, too, the German producers who initially exploited the economies of scope to build heavy machinery for the many new and enlarged industries continued to maintain their competitive advantages.

On the other hand, in chemicals, electrical equipment, and copper British (and French) entrepreneurs had almost the same opportunities as Americans and Germans. In dyes and pharmaceuticals the British entrepreneurs had even greater opportunities and incentives than German industrials to create the new enterprises. In electrical equipment British inventors were as prolific as Thomas Edison, Elihu Thomson, George Westinghouse, and Werner von Siemens. In copper the owners and operators of the Rio Tinto Company and the three leading processors had an even greater opportunity to dominate the European markets than did the Mertons, who established Metallgesellschaft.

In these industries the availability of capital in Britain was hardly a constraint, for London was the largest and most sophisticated capital market in the world and German and American firms financed their subsidiaries in London. Nor, of course, was the availability of trained labor a problem, since the workers in the factories of these subsidiaries were all British. In these industries the answer lies, as Landes (1969) has stressed, more in cultural factors, and Landes' explanation of these factors remains by far the most convincing. Precisely how education, legal requirements, and individual expectations affected the investment decisions in these three industries during the short period of opportunity requires a more detailed and thorough investigation based on personal and company records than has yet been made.

Whatever the exact reasons, the moment of opportunity was brief. Once the window was closed, it was difficult to reopen. One reason was that so many of the continuing cumulative innovations occurred within the established enterprises. Thus, when British steelmakers attempted to modernize their industry in the interwar years, they had to rely wholly on American techniques and methods. In chemicals—organic, electrical, agricultural—research and development remained concentrated in Germany and the United States, at least until the formation of ICI. In electrical equipment, innovation and particularly commercialization of products and processes continued to be carried on primarily in Berlin, Schenectady, and Pittsburgh. Moreover, in both Germany and the United States the coming and continued growth of the new industrial enterprises created demands for technical scientific and commercial knowledge and skills that expanded the nations' educational infrastructure in ways that rarely occurred in Britain.

For this and other reasons outlined in this chapter, the investments required to utilize fully the economic potentials of the technological innovations of the Second Industrial Revolution became central to the growth and wealth of industrializing economies. Not only were they essential in developing the capabilities that permitted the United States and Germany to outperform Great Britain in many of these new industries, but they also made it possible for Germany to regain so quickly its place in international markets in a brief period after 1924—markets that had been lost through a decade of war, occupation, and inflation. Comparable investments by British entrepreneurs in glass (Pilkington), rayon (Courtaulds), and rubber (Dunlop) made their enterprises and their industries internationally competitive before 1914, as did those in oil (Anglo Persian [British Petroleum]), chemicals (ICI), and containers (Metal Box) during the interwar years. And comparable investments in many of these and other capital-intensive industries provided the nations of Western Europe and Japan with the necessary competitive capabilities to challenge the American hegemony in international markets since the 1960s.

Notes

1. Beer (1959, p. 119); Haber (1958, pp. 128–136); Kaku (1979, p. 78).

2. Nathan Rosenberg (1979) makes this point most effectively, as does Landes (1969) in his chapter "Short Breath and Second Wind."

3. Haber (1958, pp. 128–136). Detailed documentation for individual firms listed here and throughout the rest of this article are given in Chandler (1990).

4. Byatt (1979, pp. 150–152). In addition, imports of electrical equipment from Germany, largely from AEG, rose from £121,000 in 1904 to £348,000 in 1910.

5. Particularly useful on the dominance of American light machinery firms in Germany, the home of Europe's most sophisticated machinery production, is Blaich (1984).

6. Temin (1964, pp. 170–175, 179–183); Chandler (1977, pp. 259–266). Carnegie was the first to use commercially the basic Thomas Gilchrist process in American open hearth (Clark 1928, pp. 269, 655).

7. Particularly useful here is Wangenroth (1986, chaps. 5 and 6, particularly pp. 196–197).

8. Prices and imports are given in Temin (1964, pp. 282, 284).

9. Tausigg (1929, p. 159). In Germany, as Steven B. Webb (1980, pp. 310, 312) notes, "tariffs were redundant in many cases, however, because Germans produced steel cheaply enough to export." He adds, "Even with free trade, Germans would have regularly imported only tin plate and special types of pig and bar iron."

10. Wilson (1968, pp. 33–38); Chandler (1977, p. 296). For other American companies, see Chandler (1977, pp. 289–302). Documentation for the British and German companies are in Chandler (1990).

References

Beer, J. J. 1959. *The Emergence of the German Dye Industry*. Urbana: University of Illinois Press.

Blaich, F. 1984. *Amerikanische Firmen in Deutschland, 1890–1918: U.S.-Direktinvestitionen im deutschen Maschinenbau*. Wiesbaden: Franz Steiner Verlag.

Byatt, I. C. R. 1979. *The British Electrical Industry, 1875–1914: The Economic Returns of a New Technology*. Oxford: Clarendon Press.

Carstensen, F. V. 1984. *American Enterprise in Foreign Markets: Studies of Singer and International Harvester in Imperial Russia*. Chapel Hill: University of North Carolina Press.

Chandler, A. D., Jr. 1977. *The Visible Hand: The Managerial Revolution in American Business*. Cambridge, Mass.: Harvard University Press.

——— 1984. "The Emergence of Managerial Capitalism." *Business History Review* 58 (Winter): 479–484.

——— 1990. *Scale and Scope: The Dynamics of Industrial Enterprise*. Cambridge, Mass.: Harvard University Press.

Chandler, A. D., Jr., and R. S. Tedlow. 1985. *The Coming of Managerial Capitalism: A Casebook on the History of American Economic Institutions*. Homewood, Ill.: Richard D. Irwin.

Clark, V. 1928. *History of Manufacturing in the United States, 1860–1914*. Washington, D.C.: Carnegie Institution.

Haber, L. G. 1958. *The Chemical Industry during the Nineteenth Century*. Oxford: Clarendon Press.

——— 1971. *The Chemical Industry, 1900–1930: International Growth and Technological Change*. Oxford: Clarendon Press.

Harvey, C. E. 1979. "Business History and the Problem of Entrepreneurship: The Case of the Rio Tinto Company, 1878–1939." *Business History* 21, no. 1 (January):3–22.

Hounshell, D. 1984. *From the American System to Mass Production, 1800–1932: The Development of Manufacturing Technology in the United States*. Baltimore: Johns Hopkins University Press.

Kaku, S. 1979. "The Development and Structure of the German Coal-Tar Dyestuff Firms." In *Development and Diffusion of Technology*, ed. A. Okochi and H. Uchido. Tokyo: Tokyo University Press.

Landes, D. S. 1969. *The Unbound Prometheus: Technological Change and Industrial Development in Western Europe from 1750 to the Present*. Cambridge: Cambridge University Press.

Livesay, H. C. 1975. *Andrew Carnegie and the Rise of Big Business*. Boston: Little, Brown.

McCloskey, D. M. 1973. *Economic Maturity and Entrepreneurial Decline: The British Iron and Steel Industry, 1879–1913*. Cambridge, Mass.: Harvard University Press.

Navin, T. R. 1978. *Copper Mining and Management*. Tucson: University of Arizona Press.

Pope, D. 1983. *The Making of Modern Advertising*. New York: Basic Books.

Rosenberg, N. 1979. "Technological Interdependence in the American Economy." *Technology and Culture* 20 (January):25–50.

Tausigg, F. W. 1929. *Some Aspects of the Tariff Question.* Cambride, Mass.: Harvard University Press.

Temin, P. 1964. *Iron and Steel in Nineteenth-Century America: An Economic Inquiry.* Cambridge, Mass.: MIT Press.

———— 1966. "The Relative Decline of the British Steel Industry, 1880–1913." In *Industrialization in Two Systems,* ed. H. Rosovsky. New York: John Wiley & Sons.

Wangenroth, U. 1986. *Unternehmensstrategien und Technischer Fortschritt: Die deutsche und die britische Stahlindustrie, 1865–1895.* Göttingen: Vandenhoeck & Ruprecht.

Webb, S. B. 1980. "Tariffs, Cartels, Technology, and the Growth of the German Steel Industry, 1879–1914." *Journal of Economic History* 40, no. 2 (June):309–330.

Wilson, C. 1968. *The History of Unilever: A Study in Economic Growth and Social Change.* New York: Frederick A. Praeger.

16

•••

Benefits and Costs of Late Development

Anne O. Krueger

To what extent is development in the last half of the twentieth century easier, and to what extent is it harder, than in the nineteenth century?[1] In one sense, the answer is almost trivial: in almost all dimensions, the opportunity set is larger than it was a century ago. Leaving aside for the moment the few ways in which opportunities have shrunk, one might simply conclude that more opportunities are self-evidently better than fewer; development in the twentieth century has necessarily been "easier" than it was a hundred years earlier.

In another sense, however, the question goes much deeper: there is an opportunity set now that provides technical alternatives; there is also a set of tastes subject to which people make their choices; and there are the instruments chosen to implement those choices. While most elements of the opportunity set are much larger, tastes may have changed (possibly because of information as to what levels of living standards are technically achievable), and when instruments chosen are inappropriate, that too must be a function of the times. I shall leave the issue of tastes aside and concentrate on the opportunity set and the choice of instruments, noting only in passing that awareness of the living standards achieved in the West has clearly cut both ways in developing countries: the demonstration effect may lead to more consumption, but it may also motivate persons to attain more than they would have in the absence of knowledge of consumption possibilities.

For many purposes, it is important to define development whether as growth of total output, output per head, or other measures of well-being. For purposes of comparing the nineteenth and twentieth centuries, however, the correlation between growth rates of total and per capita incomes and other measures of well-being is sufficiently high that the issue of definition is secondary. I shall simply assume that development is the process of raising output per person, and focus on whether more or less growth could be attained with a given increment of resources in the twentieth century than in the nineteenth, with only a passing glance at the ease of resource accumulation.

In a nutshell, I shall argue that growth is unequivocally easier: not only could more growth be attained, but a lot more has been attained than a century ago. While technological improvements in the normal sense (especially in transport, communications, and power) have contributed significantly to this quantitative difference, the largest advantage of growing in the twentieth century has been the availability and buoyancy of the international market, which have permitted a degree of reliance on comparative advantage and division of labor not possible in the nineteenth century.

Gaining access to this potential source of growth, however, has required a policy regime that has run counter to many of the ideas of the twentieth century. In that sense, more rapid growth has been attainable as an economic phenomenon, but attaining it has probably been more difficult as a political phenomenon. Many developing countries have fared far less well than the opportunities open to them would have permitted, as some now recognize.

Growth Rates in the Nineteenth and Twentieth Centuries

The simplest proof that development in the twentieth century could be faster than in the nineteenth is empirical: it has been.[2] Estimates are that the most rapidly growing countries in the nineteenth century experienced growth at an average annual rate of 1.5 percent per capita (Kenwood and Lougheed 1983, pp. 33–34). For three straight decades Korea, Singapore, Hong Kong, and Taiwan have achieved the same growth rate *per decade* that those countries previously had per century.

But while rapid growth has certainly been possible, at least for those countries, it has not been universally achieved. Table 16.1 provides some data on investment rates, growth rates, and per capita incomes over a 20-year period for a sample of developing countries. For the points I wish to make, I shall treat the real rate of growth of per capita income over the 1960–1981[3] period as an indicator of the "success" of development.[4]

To focus the argument, I have grouped countries into several categories. The "highly successful" developing countries are defined as those that have achieved a minimum average annual rate of growth of per capita income of 5 percent for two decades or more (thus, living standards are at least two and a half times what they were 20 years earlier and decadal growth has achieved as much as growth in the most rapidly growing countries during the entire nineteenth century). The "successful" developing countries are those that have achieved at least 3.5 percent annual per capita income growth over the same time period (and thus have at least doubled per capita incomes in that interval). "Satisficing" developing countries are those that have attained some growth in

Table 16.1 Indicators of real per capita income, investment rates, and growth, 1960–1981.

Country	Per capita average annual growth rate (percent)	Per capita income (1981 dollars)		Gross domestic investment as share of GNP	
		1960	1981	1960	1981
Unsuccessful					
Niger	−1.6	450	330	13	27
Ghana	−1.1	500	400	24	6
Zaire	−0.1	215	210	12	33
Zambia	0.0	600	600	25	23
Satisficers					
Burma	1.4	140	190	12	24
India	1.4	200	260	17	23
Jamaica	0.8	1,010	1,180	30	16
Peru	1.0	960	1,170	25	19
Argentina	1.9	1,760	2,560	22	26
Successful					
Indonesia	4.1	240	530	8	21
Thailand	4.6	313	770	16	28
Turkey	3.5	730	1,540	16	25
Tunisia	4.8	560	1,420	17	31
Highly successful					
Korea	6.9	450	1,700	11	26
Brazil	5.1	820	2,220	22	20
Yugoslavia	5.0	1,050	2,790	37	32
Hong Kong	6.9	1,340	5,100	18	30
Singapore	7.4	1,260	5,240	11	42

Source: World Bank (1983).

living standards but less than the successful countries, and "unsuccessful" countries are those whose living standards are estimated to have fallen below their 1960 levels by 1980 (and, for most of them, living standards and real incomes have dropped further since).[5] While substantial errors of measurement of growth rates are possible for individual countries, these categories are sufficiently far apart that there is no likelihood that a country that was really successful would be recorded as a failure, and vice versa.

The choice of countries was more or less arbitrary, made with a view to illustrating the importance of economic policies in determining growth rates.[6]

As can be seen, the significant differences between the groups of countries lie not in their investment rates but in other aspects of development.[7] Some "unsuccessful" countries had high initial savings rates, and some experienced significant increases in their investment rates without a commensurate improvement in growth performance. All categories of developing countries except the unsuccessful ones have achieved marked increases in their savings rates and rates of capital accumulation. In India, the savings rate rose well above that regarded by the planners as necessary to achieve a successful growth performance (which, despite that, India did not achieve). Even among the failures, savings rates have risen, although not to the same extent as for more successful developing countries, for reasons to which I shall return.

By contrast with the relatively small variation in savings rates, especially once differences in per capita incomes are taken into account, differences in growth rates (and hence in the efficiency with which accumulated resources are employed) are much greater. In the early 1960s, for example, the Korean savings rate was below the Indian, and yet the Korean growth rate over the next two decades was almost three times higher. This implies a much greater efficiency in the use of incremental resources or a much larger increase in the efficiency with which existing resources were used, or some combination of the two. Regardless of exactly how this came about, it is indisputable that some countries were far more successful in encouraging the efficient use (or reallocation) of resources than were others.

Any satisfactory model of development today must incorporate not only the determinants of the rate of resource accumulation but also the determinants of the efficiency with which existing and incremental resources are used. Thus a development economist today, seeing an aggregate production function with a "technical change" parameter, would be inclined to read into it much more than technical change as normally understood. The production function, as the term is usually defined, describes the maximal combinations of outputs attainable from given inputs. In most economies, a number of factors result in the economy's operation inside the production possibility frontier. Growth can originate either through an outward shift in the frontier (assuming that is accompanied by no increase in the degree to which the actual operation is inside the frontier)[8] or in a reduction in the divergence between the actual operating point and the frontier.

While informed analysts differ to some extent on the emphasis they would place on the various determinants of the efficiency with which incremental resources were employed (and/or existing resources reallocated) in different developing countries at different times, there would be considerable agreement on the basics. For cross-section analysis, these include differences in trade and payments regimes, and therefore in the extent to which countries were open to the international economy and willing to avail themselves of the potential benefit it offers. They also include the degree of government control over private-sector activity and efforts by governments to ''regulate'' prices and markets. Finally, they include macroeconomic policies and the extent to which the economy was subjected to intense pressures of excess demand and inflation.

Given different developing countries' policies, over time the state of the international economy significantly affects all growth rates: a country with an open trade and payments regime, stable macroeconomic policy, and government policies geared to supporting growth normally grows significantly more rapidly in periods of rapid growth of the international economy than in periods of slow growth; but a country with an inner-oriented trade regime, severe macroeconomic imbalance, and pervasive controls over private economic activity also grows less rapidly in periods of slow worldwide growth. Combining time series and cross-section, the country with policies geared to development will probably grow more rapidly during periods of a sluggish international economy than the country with inappropriate policies will during periods of rapid growth.

Any consideration of the contrast between nineteenth-century and twentieth-century growth must therefore address three key issues: the difference in the production function then and now; the difference in the rate of growth of the international economy as it affects opportunities for developing countries; and the determinants of economic policy.

Differences in Environment

If one thinks of an aggregate production function for per capita output, with resource availability per capita, the state of technology, the state of the international economy, and the determinants of economic efficiency (and therefore of economic policies) as its four arguments, one can organize a discussion of contrasts between nineteenth- and twentieth-century developments around these four headings. Because the state of technology is the contrast that comes to most people's minds first, and because it interacts so strongly with each of the other factors, I will consider it first, and then proceed to a discussion of the role of the international economy, both in providing opportunities for trade and in potential factor flows. I will consider it first, and then proceed to a discussion of the role of the international economy, both in providing opportunities for trade and in potential factor flows. I will consider determinants of policy in the next section.

Technological Differences

There is no doubt that technologies of all kinds are available in the twentieth century that were not available in the nineteenth. In the early days of development efforts, it was fashionable to regard the availability of all of the blueprints developed over the past several hundred years as a major source of advantage to developing countries. Some went so far as to regard "technology transfer" as the essence of development.

Experience and research both suggest that the potential benefits are considerably smaller than the "free blueprint" notion would suggest (see Johnson 1975). It is clear that there are some technologies that are strongly saving of both capital and labor, and these represent a source of significant advantage for latecomers. Yet, many other technologies were developed in response to changing needs of increasingly labor-scarce, capital-abundant economies, and some of these have represented irresistible temptations to politicians in developing countries. The steel mill erected in a country without iron ore or coal and automobile assembly factories with far smaller production runs than are economic are perhaps the best-known symbols of this tendency, but there have been far greater wastes of scarce capital.

The lesson of the past three decades or so is that the availability of technology per se is seldom of much use: as Teece (1977), Rosenberg and Birdzell (1986), and many others have stressed, a considerable amount of specialized skill is normally needed to translate blueprints into meaningful production possibilities. When technologies are inappropriate, the net benefits may in fact be negative. Hayami and Ruttan (1985), for example, have carefully demonstrated how the development of agricultural technology in Japan and the United States followed very different patterns: American development was laborsaving, and by and large consisted in the invention of mechanical products that permitted a farmer to cultivate more relatively abundant land. In Japan, by contrast, most technological developments were chemical based and land saving. When poor, labor-abundant countries invest heavily in mechanical, laborsaving machinery, it is problematic whether real incomes rise or fall.[9] The evidence from the Green Revolution is that considerable research into local conditions is essential if increases in productivity are to be achieved and sustained.

In general, when countries have provided incentives that reasonably reflected relative international prices and domestic factor scarcities, the availability of a greater choice set in the twentieth century has permitted more effective use of resources than would otherwise have been possible. Adoption of inappropriate technology has been sufficiently costly, however, and sufficiently intermingled with the policy choices to be discussed later, that it is difficult to conclude that technological availability, per se, constitutes a significant plus for twentieth-century development over earlier efforts. Different types of technology have had diverse consequences, however, and further analysis must distinguish among them. Four types can usefully be identified: communications, power, and transport; agricultural technology; industrial technology; and technology impinging on health and social welfare.

Transport, communications, and power. Although it is difficult to imagine how one would test the hypothesis, the very large declines in costs of transport and communications are surely the greatest benefit from technological advances that developing countries have today relative to the early developers a century ago. North (1958) estimates that the real cost of ocean transport fell to 3 percent of what it had been a century earlier by 1913.[10] Such a dramatic decline certainly must free resources for other uses, but in addition it permits rapid integration of domestic markets with consequent opportunities for utilizing comparative advantage among regions at an earlier stage of development. Insofar as the size of the market is a critical factor in affecting the costs of many activities, the availability of low-cost transport must make development substantially easier within countries. But in addition, the availability of world markets for many commodities, with very low transport costs for accessing them, is a clear benefit, as we shall see.[11]

Modern communications technology must, too, be regarded as a substantial net plus, even in countries where high tech is always purchased regardless of the benefit-cost calculus. In part this is because the link to the rest of the world is potentially so valuable; in part, however, the availability of low-cost communications has undoubtedly saved enough resources to more than offset whatever waste there has been.[12]

The same conclusion probably holds, although perhaps with less quantitative significance, with respect to power. Despite the construction of occasional uneconomic plants (typically either of too large a size or with technical flaws resulting largely from overly ambitious projects), the availability of cheap electrical power must be counted as a large net benefit to countries attempting to develop in the second half of the twentieth century.

Indeed, it can be argued that the "unsuccessful" and "satisficing" developing countries have erred in devoting too few public resources to the efficient development of low-cost power, transport, and communications, and have allocated too many resources to developing capital-intensive industries where the benefits for growth are dubious at their stage of development. The successful countries, and even more the highly successful countries, have availed themselves to the full of the opportunities provided by the infrastructure technologies.

Agricultural technology. As is widely known, a large number of developing countries have attempted to tax their agricultural sectors heavily in order to subsidize industrial growth. In some instances, these taxes and subsidies have been implicit, administered through a combination of an overvalued exchange rate and heavy protection of domestic industrial production. In other instances, marketing boards and other government interventions have effectively suppressed producer and farm gate prices well below their border price equivalents.[13]

In that policy environment, neither the direct incentive of prices nor the indirect support of agricultural extension and research has been available to support increases in farm output. Growth in agricultural productivity has been slow, but the problem has been with the incentives structure (through both relative prices and direct controls).

In circumstances in which governments have not attempted heavy subsidization of urban activities and taxation of agriculture, the advantages of modern technology have been great. The contribution of the Green Revolution to increasing incomes and outputs in agricultural areas is too well known to require much comment.[14] The Green Revolution has in large part focused on improved combinations of chemicals, pesticides, and seeds, which are relatively labor-using in their application, to increase the productivity of land. It is, therefore, "appropriate technology" for labor-abundant, land-scarce countries. As with most technical changes, however, using the right combination of chemicals, water, and other inputs requires both specialized knowledge of individual farming areas and ability on the part of cultivators to understand and regulate the timing and quantities of the various inputs. It thus represents a potential gain for countries with adequate agricultural research and extension institutions and capabilities but is by no means a "free gift."

Industrial technology. The degree to which the availability of more advanced industrial technology improves the opportunity set of developing countries is problematic.[15] Much of the industrial technology available in the twentieth century was developed in response to altered factor proportions and relative prices: insofar as that technology is capital intensive and laborsaving, it is not of significant benefit to countries in the early stages of development. To be sure, there have been a large number of instances in which technical advance has been Hicks neutral or even labor using, and these may have improved opportunities for rapid development. And, to the extent that even laborsaving technical progress may have lowered the cost of imports from developed countries, there may have been a net advantage.

It is clear that improvements in industrial technology could not make development more difficult in the twentieth century than in the nineteenth under appropriate policies. The visibility of high-tech industries, however, and the inevitable temptations of politicians to install them in their countries has resulted in uneconomic factories and industries in a number of countries. As with so many other issues of development, the real question is whether developing countries' policies and incentives are conducive to exploiting opportunities or lead to inappropriate choices. One has to conjecture that in the appropriate environment, the availability of resource-saving new technologies certainly improved the potential increment in real output per unit of resource accumulation, but relative to technical changes in agriculture and infrastructure, these improved opportunities may have been somewhat less important.

Health and social welfare. It can hardly be disputed that advances in medical knowledge, especially in such public-health areas as malarial eradication and inoculation, have contributed to a sharp increase in life expectancy in all developing countries. And, insofar as the object of development is to improve the quality of life, these advances must be judged to provide greater twentieth-century than nineteenth-century opportunities. Indeed, life expectancy in many developing countries today exceeds that in most developed countries at the turn of the century.

This conclusion is reinforced only if it is recognized that human capital is a scarce resource, and that the reduction in the severity of epidemics and other causes of death in the age range from 15 to 50 has increased the return on education and other investments in the quality of labor inputs.

The only conceivable way in which the positive impact of health technology can be questioned is through its effects on the rate of population growth, and, in turn, the effects of more rapid population growth on prospects for raising per capita incomes.[16] Even here, a first point to be noted is that if individuals can choose whether to have higher living standards or larger families and choose the latter, the fact that they choose larger families indicates their improved well-being. There are also questions as to how negative the effects of population growth may be (see Kelley 1988). To the extent that the rate of population growth is an endogenous function of other variables, and people are choosing larger families as family income rises, one must count improved health technology as a contributor to development (and regard income per family, rather than income per capita, as the criterion by which to judge success).

Nonetheless, it can hardly be denied that if there were two otherwise identical societies (in the sense of having the same initial technology, land, and capital per person, and so on), and one ''accidentally'' had a higher rate of population growth than the other, the rate of growth of per capita income would surely be lower in the higher-population-growth country, although the rate of growth of real GNP would presumably be faster. Whether the difference were larger or smaller would presumably depend on a variety of factors, including the existing standard of living and the availability of additional arable land.

For most developing countries, however, rates of growth of real GNP are sufficiently higher than they were in the nineteenth century that there must be presumed to be a large number of offsets to more rapid production growth. This was seen in the data in Table 16.1. The possible exceptions are the countries, mostly in sub-Saharan Africa, with rates of population growth in excess of 3 percent. In those countries for which they are available, survey data indicate that the number of children per household exceeds the desired level. In these circumstances, it must be concluded that some deceleration in the rate of population growth would constitute a sensible object of development policy, and that failure to reduce those growth rates will be a significant obstacle to raising living standards (see World Bank 1985). Even then, it must be recognized that a considerably wider variety of techniques for family planning are now available than existed a century ago. In that sense, even in countries where the rate of population growth is deemed to be higher than is socially desired, the possibility of a rapid reduction in the rate of growth through voluntary means is greater than it was a century ago, a fact evidenced by rapid slowdowns in growth rates in South Korea, Taiwan, Thailand, and Indonesia, among others.

Social welfare is affected not only by public health measures, which clearly improve the quality of life for the already existing population, but also by other investments in man. Most observers would regard literacy, and more generally education, as a major determinant of the quality of life and the opportunity set open to individuals. It is perhaps noteworthy that one does not hear discussions of educational technology mentioned among the differences between the nineteenth and twentieth centuries. In fact, however, it may be that one of the significant contributions to policy formulation that has benefited development prospects in the twentieth century has been the recognition of the potential role of universal primary education. Equally interesting is whether there has been any technical change in elementary education: there is clearly more knowledge to be transmitted at higher educational levels. But it seems doubtful whether the technology for producing primary education has altered much, although the availability of lower real-cost communications may have lowered costs significantly.

The International Economy

The international economy impinges on developing countries in a number of ways; it provides a market for commodities with significant resource rents; it can also permit developing countries to make use of comparative advantage in labor-intensive manufactures (which interacts with the state of technology in ways noted later in this chapter); and it can provide additional resources through aid and capital flows or permit their removal through outmigration of labor. This last item is germane to the rate of resource accumulation (see the discussion of resource accumulation which follows).

Market for primary commodities. Little needs to be said about resource rents. Their importance for development is usually greatly exaggerated, and the supply response of both agriculture and minerals is generally much larger than policy makers anticipate. Nonetheless, it is surely true that (except for political repercussions) it should be easier to develop with more favorable terms of trade for primary commodity exports than with less favorable terms of trade, and fluctuations in the terms of trade may inhibit development.[17] The key issue, therefore, is the level and rate of change in the terms of trade in the latter half of the twentieth century contrasted with the nineteenth.

With regard to the terms of trade, there are genuine questions as to what commodities should be regarded as "developing country commodities" and which should be treated as "developed country" commodities (see Michaely 1984). In 1984 manufactured exports of developing countries stood at $150.8 billion, whereas their primary commodity exports were $319.3 billion.[18]

If one takes the terms of trade between primary commodities and manufactures as the relevant indicator, it is difficult to ascertain any significant difference between terms of trade changes in the nineteenth and twentieth centuries. Uncertainties as to quality changes (in both manufactures and primary commodities), data problems, and the statistical margin of error resulting from efforts to distinguish between trends and cyclical fluctuations obscure the issue. The 1950–1980 period seems to have been one of greater-than-average buoyancy of primary commodity prices, even if one excludes oil. As a consequence, even if the terms of trade between primary commodities and manufactures did deteriorate mildly over the century preceding 1950, there is reason to believe that they improved somewhat secularly thereafter, at least to 1980. Indeed, the evidence suggests that the terms of trade were improving for latecomers after World War II, and were probably not significantly different, once quality improvements are taken into account, in 1980 than they were in 1880.[19]

The evidence is clearer when it comes to cyclical fluctuations. The quarter-century ending in 1973 was a period of unprecedented expansion and minimum cyclical fluctuations by contrast with both the nineteenth century and the interwar period. While some observers have suggested that the 1980s represented a reversion to earlier patterns of slow growth and cyclical fluctuations, the evidence for the 1950–1980 period strongly indicates that the international economy was more stable than it had been in earlier periods. The fluctuations in the terms of trade were certainly no more pronounced than in earlier periods. Overall, then, it is likely that the first 35 years after World War II offered terms of trade at least as conducive to resource accumulation and growth for primary commodity producers as did the nineteenth century.

Opportunities for trade in manufactures. One characteristic that has differentiated the highly successful developing countries from others has been their adherence to an outer-oriented trade regime.[20] There appear to be at least two distinct sources of gain (or avoidance of loss) from an outer-oriented trade strategy. One is the resulting competitive pressure on domestic firms, which seems to increase efficiency in many firms in virtually all industries.[21] The other is the opportunity provided to use abundant unskilled labor in the production of labor-intensive goods for domestic consumption and export, rather than to use scarce capital (both human and physical) in producing a wider variety of goods domestically. Available evidence strongly suggests that the same rate of re-source accumulation will lead to more rapid growth in outer-oriented regimes than in ones oriented toward import substitution (IS), regardless of the state of the world economy. There is ample evidence, however, that the growth attainable from outer-oriented policies is significantly higher when the international economy is growing rapidly.[22] In large measure this is because of the second contribution of outer-oriented regimes to development: it is possible to expand exports of labor-intensive manufactures and to increase market shares more rapidly, and with less effect on the terms of trade, when the international economy is growing rapidly.

On this score, development was surely easier in the first three decades after 1950 than it was at any time in the nineteenth century. Not only was the market much larger (and therefore able to absorb a larger increase in imports more easily than would otherwise have been possible), but transport costs were lower. This made more goods tradable with a smaller fraction of the f.o.b. value-added absorbed in shipping.

Moreover, from 1955 to 1980 the volume of world trade grew at an average annual rate of 5.8 percent. This contrasts with Kuznets' estimates that world trade per capita grew at an average annual rate of 2.9 percent from 1800 to 1913. If one takes the world rate of population growth to have been 0.6 percent annually,[23] that yields an estimated annual rate of growth of the volume of world trade of 3.5 percent. A difference in excess of 2 percent annually is huge, especially for new entrants attempting to penetrate markets. Developing countries (of which the highly successful accounted for an increasingly large share) were able to realize an average annual rate of growth of manufactured exports of 13 percent in that environment from 1950 to 1980.

Not only was the growth of world trade much more rapid in the 1950–1980 period than in the nineteenth century, but it also took place in an environment where the ''support facilities''—communications, wholesalers, finance, and insurance which would have been expensive for poor countries to provide and would have put them at a disadvantage competitively—were readily available from other trading nations. Moreover, the differences in costs of production of manufactured goods between rich nations and poor in the twentieth century probably have exceeded most such differences in the nineteenth, simply because real-wage differences among trading nations were nowhere nearly as large then as they are now. This would suggest that the opportunities for growing through trade are far greater today than they were a century ago both because the gains from trade per unit of trade are greater (that is, the ''pretrade'' prices differ by more now than they would have a century ago), and because entry into new lines of activity, and expansion in those lines, is facilitated by the more rapid growth of trade.[24]

Resource Accumulation

Resource accumulation occurs either through the postponement of present consumption (domestic saving) or receipt of capital inflows. Four possible reasons have been given as to why saving may be more difficult in the latter half of the twentieth century than it was in the nineteenth. First, it is conceivable that per capita incomes are lower in the countries embarking on development in the twentieth century than they were in the last century. The force of this argument would vary significantly across countries. Second, there may be heavier political pressures for current government consumption than there were a century ago (see the next section), but that pertains to economic policies. Third, there may be a "demonstration effect" inducing individuals to allocate a larger share of income to current consumption. Finally, the worldwide real interest rate may be lower now than it was in the nineteenth century. While it is difficult to evaluate the quantitative importance of these arguments, the fact is that savings rates in almost all developed countries exceed those of the industrialized countries at the time they were developing.

There is, however, the question of international flows of factors of production. With regard to capital flows, it would appear that differences in magnitudes for recipient countries between the twentieth century and the nineteenth are not very large: capital flows into the United States seldom exceeded 1 percent of GNP in any decade; in some smaller developing countries such as Argentina they were significantly larger, but those flows went to the richer among the latecomers and were important mostly in the smaller lands that were newly settled or opened up.[25]

The chief difference between capital flows in the nineteenth and twentieth centuries has originated not in their magnitude but in their source: nineteenth-century flows were amost entirely private, while capital flows to developing countries in the 1950s and 1960s were largely public. In the 1960s a few highly successful developing countries began accessing private capital markets, and for them private capital flows were an important source of additional resources.[26] Since official flows were more often concessional than were private, it might even be argued that the economic value of the resources transferred by official capital flows in the twentieth century was greater than that of the predominantly private in the nineteenth. This would be especially true for the 1950–1980 period if one added the reduction in real value of outstanding debt associated with worldwide inflation. Given subsequent events, however, it would be difficult and unwise to try to press that point too far.

In addition to capital flows, much has been made of the "brain drain" as a negative factor in twentieth-century growth, contrasted with the supposedly positive impetus provided in the nineteenth century by the ease with which those left out of the growth process could migrate. The nineteenth-century outmigration from Europe appears to have been part of the rural-to-urban movement, and as such presumably speeded up the economic transformation from an agrarian to an industrial society. Analysts seem to be unanimous in the view that nineteenth-century migration benefited the growth of both the countries of origin and destination (see Kenwood and Lougheed 1983, chap. 3). By contrast, the migration of unskilled workers has generally been a far less significant phenomenon in the latter half of the twentieth century, although Turkish workers' migration to Europe may be on the same scale. Even for Indian and Pakistani migrant workers in the Middle East, the magnitude of the movement relative to the size of the economies of the migrants' countries of origin is small compared to the nineteenth-century flows. To the extent that outmigration speeded up development in the nineteenth century, therefore, it has not provided a similar spur in the twentieth.

Moreover, largely because of the immigration laws of the industrial countries, much of the outmigration that has taken place from developing countries has consisted of skilled and highly educated persons and has on that account been alleged to have been detrimental to development in the countries of origin.[27] The issue is a complex one. Even in countries with well-functioning labor markets, the absolute gap in real incomes to professionals between developed and developing countries is much larger than it was a century ago. The issue is confounded, however, by the overproduction of highly educated personnel in developing countries (see Krueger 1972), and by government policies that suppress earnings differentials between highly skilled persons and others in the labor force to extremely low levels.

Overall, there are differences in the opportunities for inflows and outflows of factors of production between the nineteenth and the twentieth centuries, but their net impact on development prospects is unclear. If one were to consider flows of factors of production alone, one might conclude that the nineteenth century was marginally more conducive to development than the twentieth. If these flows are considered in the context of the international economy, however, it must be judged that the opportunities offered by trade did much more than offset any potential disadvantages associated with flows of factors of production. Korea, for example, shifted from 70 percent rural to 70 percent urban in the course of three decades; such a shift could not have occurred without the benefit of the international economy, and it represented a far more rapid demographic transition than any experienced in the nineteenth century. Indeed, for the very rapidly growing developing countries, the major benefit of the twentieth-century environment was the buoyant, open international economy, and its greater buoyancy surely provided greater opportunity for economic development than did outmigration in the nineteenth century.

Determinants of Government Policies

Despite possible negative outcomes with respect to capital flows and population growth, the evidence is overwhelming that the economic environment in the second half of the twentieth century has been more conducive to rapid increases in real per capita incomes than it was in the nineteenth, for the same rate of resource accumulation. As we saw in Table 16.1, some countries have used that environment to grow at previously unheard-of rates. The second striking feature of Table 16.1, however, is the great disparity between countries. Some have been highly successful; some have satisficed; some have even retrogressed. Although a number of factors have contributed, and a full exploration of the determinants of growth rates on a cross-section basis is well beyond the scope of this essay, there is little doubt that economic policies have varied widely between the highly successful countries and the failures. Given that economic policies are determined within the environment of the time, some attention to policies, and the reasons why the twentieth century may have made adoption of appropriate policies more difficult than the nineteenth, seems warranted.

Nineteenth-century development "just happened." To be sure, governments helped build railroads, developed agricultural extension services, and otherwise contributed to growth. But they undertook these activities on a one-by-one basis in response to the political and, hopefully, economic merits of each case. There was no presumption that governments were responsible for growth rates and therefore had to "do something."[28] In the twentieth century, by contrast, development has been a conscious goal of policy, and is deemed to be the responsibility of the policy makers. That difference in view, and therefore in policy, may in itself be the result of catch-up: the body politic in developing countries in the twentieth century is cognizant of the tremendous gaps in living standards between developing and developed countries; there is thus an imperative for catch-up, or at least for providing reasons why it is not happening.

It is at this stage that the economist's analytical tool kit lets him down: on the one hand, it is straightforward to conclude that, for example, when the real return to cocoa farmers in Ghana fell to 2 percent of its former level in two decades (see Strykker 1987), the resultant shrinkage in output was attributable to policy; on the other hand, it is difficult to say *why* policies so inimical to development were adopted. Yet avoiding the issue completely would be like looking for a lost item under a lamppost in full knowledge that it had been misplaced in a distant dark corner.

The underlying beliefs on which development policies were based in the first decades after 1945 were a deep-seated distrust of markets and a strong commitment to government as the lead agent in economic activity.[29] It should either itself undertake production and distribution, or it should regulate private economic activity. These views were held by policy makers in almost all developing countries, as well as by a majority of "development economists"; many stated that development economics was "different" because developing countries' economies were "different" in the sense that markets did not work and developing countries' economies were not responsive to changes in incentives.[30] At its most sophisticated, development economics was reflected in documents such as the Indian Five-Year Plans, which set forth which activities would be reserved for the government sector, which ones might be joint, and which might (subject to licensing) be undertaken privately, and in planning models developed to help government officials decide what to produce (see Chakravarty 1987). At a more mundane level, these beliefs were manifest in requirements for licensing of imports, exports, and investment; in government-owned manufacturing establishments and state marketing boards with monopoly over distribution of numerous commodities; and in price controls and pervasive regulations over the movement of goods and the activities of individuals and firms.[31]

Not only did governments institute detailed and pervasive regulation of those activities they did not directly undertake themselves, but they also failed to carry out adequate investment in and maintenance of essential infrastructure and to provide the other essential services that form the basis on which development can take place. Although low-cost transport, communications, and power may be the greatest potential technological legacy of the industrial countries to the prospects for development of the latecomers, these activities were sadly neglected[32] as governments concentrated on establishing new high-cost (and often technologically advanced, capital-intensive) industries, and suppressing prices of traditional commodities to subsidize, implicity or explicitly, these new high-cost activities. Thus, the potential benefits from the low real cost of imports via reliance on trade and comparative advantage were lost, and the availability of high-tech, capital-intensive activities became a detriment rather than a positive factor in development. The pervasiveness of controls and regulations varied in both intensity and duration from country to country. At its most extreme, economic activity has been virtually strangled in some countries of sub-Saharan Africa. In many other countries, the potential benefits of late development were offset to a greater or lesser degree by the policy environment in which development was occurring.

The critical question that must be addressed here, however, is not how detrimental policies were, but rather what were their determinants. For those determinants, I suspect, are a key difference between development in the twentieth and nineteenth centuries. Uncomfortable as it may be to move from the realm of economic determinants to the determinants of ideas, it is ideas that have been crucially important, at least in legitimizing, if not in motivating, development policies. The topic is therefore worth a few paragraphs of speculation. And, if one takes "knowledge" as reflected in technological advance to be a positive contribution of the twentieth century, one must surely also weigh the contribution of the "knowledge" base on which policy was formulated.

Three key determinants of policy come immediately to mind: the colonial legacy, the ideology inherent in the view of government as a benevolent Platonic guardian, and the distrust of market mechanisms inherent in the ideas originating in the Great Depression.

It is entirely understandable that a newly independent nation might well reject the international economy after years of colonial rule. Such a rejection clearly played a key part emotionally in the initially universal adoption of quantitative restrictions, exchange controls, and import licensing.[33] A belief that the international economy would keep developing countries the "hewers of wood and drawers of water" for the developed world was probably in large measure an emotional response to colonialism and its legacy. But it found intellectual validation in the infant industry argument, and in the pessimistic conclusions of Nurkse (1959) and others about the prospects for the international economy. The "export pessimism," articulated by Nurkse and others, was used to support arguments for protection, exchange control, and isolation from the international economy. Whether these arguments were the real reasons or the rationalizations is difficult to judge, but the evidence is overwhelming that damage done by highly restrictive trade regimes was enormous.[34]

Whether export pessimism and a belief in the infant industry argument (which seemed natural when observers thought the major difference between developed and developing countries lay in the larger size of industry in the former) were convincing or not, the colonial legacy surely provided strong emotional grounds on which to base economic policies essentially dissimilar to those that had prevailed during nineteenth-century development.

The second contributor was clearly the notion of the state as a Platonic guardian. Much economic thinking of the nineteenth century, including Bentham and his followers and the Webbs, was based on the explicit or implicit premise that governments were the benevolent guardians of society. Whether stated or not, this assumption led economists to accept the notion that if there were a market failure, the government *should* intervene to avoid it. That government intervention itself could have costs attached to it, or that bureaucrats, pressure groups, and others would attempt to use the power of the state for their own ends, was largely overlooked. That government failure might loom as large as or larger than market failure, and that therefore the costs of intervention should be weighed against the potential benefits, was seldom articulated in theories that derived formulas for optimal taxation, optimal tariffs, or other interventions. Indeed, in the late 1960s and early 1970s, when economists were beginning to address the irrationality of some government interventions, the

argument (which was itself an important contribution) that not every intervention will necessarily achieve a desired goal, and that some might even be
counterproductive, was a major step forward.[35]

The third determinant of ideas underlying policy formulation was undoubtedly the distrust of markets that originated in the experiences of the Great
Depression. Not only did that experience provide direct proof to policy makers
of the unreliability of the international economy, but it also led to the Keynesian
revolution, with its emphasis on the unreliability of the private economy. To be
sure, the implications of the Keynesian revolution were focused largely on the
role of government in macroeconomic stabilization, but the implications were
nonetheless largely that an activist government would, as a Platonic guardian,
improve social welfare through its expenditures (which could, if aggregate
demand was inadequate, actually be costless). Despite the fact that the urgency
of development originates from the scarcity of resources and poverty of the
citizenry in developing countries, the intellectual milieu created by the legacy of
the Great Depression deflected attention from that scarcity and seemed to imply
that the central economic issues lay elsewhere.

Given the interaction between a natural distrust of the industrial countries
associated with the colonial legacy, economists' emphasis on market failures
and neglect of the costs of intervention, and the distrust of markets associated
with the legacy of the Great Depression and Keynesian economics, it is small
wonder that politicians in developing countries adopted some of the policies
they did. To the extent that this was the intellectual environment of the 1950s,
it must be concluded that development was, at least in that regard, more difficult
in the twentieth century than it was in the nineteenth.

What, then, should be concluded? Was development easier in the nineteenth
century than in the 1950–1980 period, or was it harder? The answer, it would
seem, is that aside from political pressures and the policy issues discussed in the
section on government policies, it has been far easier. Indeed, except for sub-
Saharan Africa, developing countries' growth rates have exceeded those of the
now-industrialized countries in the last century by a considerable margin. Moreover, they exceeded those of developed countries, so that there has on average
been some catch-up.

The role of ideas in policy formulation is the difficult question. A highly
plausible case can be made that the West could not have developed had the role
of government now widely accepted as standard been the norm in the nineteenth
century. Insofar as ideas concerning the role and obligations of the state are
readily transmitted internationally, those same ideas that limit further growth of
the now rich countries certainly render political pressures for nondevelopmental
government activities all the greater.

One must conclude, then, that the 1950–1980 period provided a very hospitable international environment for those countries whose economic policies could be formulated outside the influence of deep-seated distrust of markets. Indeed, the international economy was so hospitable that even countries whose economic policies were demonstrably inefficient were nonetheless able to grow, unless those policies were too extreme: they just grew less rapidly than countries fully available themselves of the international economy and the opportunities it presented. There can be no question but that growth could proceed at rates unheard of in the nineteenth century, as the evidence from the successful developing countries, and even the satisficers, indicates.

The question may be asked, in conclusion, whether the environment of the quarter-century after 1980 will be as favorable. It is clear that the international economy of the early 1980s was far less conducive to growth than in the three preceding decades (although a number of countries nonetheless registered very good, and even highly successful, growth records). The terms of trade for primary commodities have sharply deteriorated; the rate of growth of world trade has slowed down markedly; official capital flows have not increased, while private flows have diminished; and threats of protection and a collapse of the multilateral trading system are very real.

The answer must be that, even on very optimistic assumptions, it is difficult to imagine that the growth of the international economy will be as rapid over the present quarter-century as it was over the quarter-century beginning in 1950. In that sense, the opportunities offered by the international economy will no longer be as favorable as those of the recent past. Ironically, however, in a less permissive international environment, it is possible that policy formulation in developing countries will improve, in the sense of eschewing, or at least reducing the impact of, policies highly inimical to growth. The international environment of 1950–1980 did not penalize policy mistakes quickly or severely. In that sense it was permissive, with little feedback to policy makers or voters that the forgone growth costs were significant. In the present environment, feedback is more rapid, and the penalties for policy mistakes are significantly greater. It may well be that the post-1985 period will turn out to be one of more rapid growth in the developing countries than the 1950–1980 period, if the benefits from more appropriate domestic economic policies outweigh the costs of a less buoyant international economy. Much has been learned about development over the past several decades, and especially in the 1980s. If that knowledge pays off in more rapid growth, the benefits of being a latecomer will be even greater as the mistakes of the past become avoidable.

Notes

1. I am indebted to Robert Bates, James M. Henderson, Allen Kelley, T. N. Srinivasan, and to participants in the Korea Development Institute seminar (Seoul) and at the Bellagio conference of August 30–September 4, 1987, for helpful comments on earlier drafts of this chapter.

2. There is a school of thought among some political scientists that development in the twentieth century has been more difficult because the power of the developed countries could be and has been used to prevent catch-up. The fact that catch-up has taken place should be sufficient to belie the notion.

3. The choice of years was based largely on the consideration that the 1980s were turbulent ones for many developing countries, and it seemed preferable to choose a period in which growth rates were not dominated by recent events. The categorization of countries would change little (although almost all average growth rates would fall) were the years 1982–1985 included in the calculations.

4. While cross-country comparisons of growth rates must be interpreted with care, they are nonetheless correlated fairly well with advances in life expectancy and other measures of health and in social indicators such as literacy and educational attainment. While there are many grounds on which it might be possible to believe that, for example, a 4 percent growth rate in one country represents a greater social advance than a 4.5 percent growth rate in another, the difference in experience among developing countries is much greater than that. Few observers have questioned the validity of the growth rates in Table 16.1 as a general indicator of economic performance in the countries listed.

5. For purposes of comparison, all countries in the OECD (Organization for Economic Cooperation and Development) except Switzerland (1.9 percent) and New Zealand experienced growth rates of per capita income in excess of 2 percent over the same period. Data are from World Bank (1985).

6. For more systematic analyses of the differences among countries, see the World Bank's *World Development Report* for various years, but especially 1983 and 1985.

7. W. Arthur Lewis' (1954) famous dictum that the central problem of development is for an economy to "somehow convert itself" from saving 4 to 5 percent of GNP to saving 12 to 15 percent (Agarwala and Singh 1963, p. 416) was conventional wisdom in the late 1950s and 1960s. But partly because policy makers focused on raising savings rates, and partly because experience has demonstrated that savings rates can rise sharply without a commensurate increase in growth rates, that optimistic view of the development process no longer seems tenable.

8. It is well established in the theory of international trade that resource accumulation can actually decrease welfare in the presence of some departures from economic efficiency. See Bhagwati and Srinivasan (1978) for a discussion of negative shadow prices.

9. See Hirsch and Hirsch (1963) for an evaluation of the Turkish mechanization program in the 1950s, under which tractors were imported, forest land was cleared and converted to wheat production, and cattle grazing and forestry declined. They estimate that real agricultural output in Turkey fell as a consequence.

10. See also Kenwood and Lougheed (1983) for a more general discussion of the decline in transport costs.

11. To be sure, six-lane highways have been built to interiors, and almost all developing countries have their own subsidized and usually costly airlines and expensive airports. This is not to deny that some countries have a comparative advantage in the provision of international jet travel; the clear preference of many travelers for some of the Southeast Asian airlines, and their profitability, attests to this.

Some have argued that the transport patterns imposed by colonial rulers, with major routes leading to the coast or to the capital, were not highly conducive to commercial development. That argument, however, suggests that the benefits would have been even greater had commercial, rather than political, considerations guided the choice of routes. It does not imply a negative benefit.

12. I assume that the political imperative for communications would have resulted in large resource expenditures even had low-cost communications techniques been unavailable. A partial counterargument, to which I shall return, is that the ease of communication makes developing countries' economic

policies even more politicized than they would otherwise be, and that there may be costs to that. On the other side of the coin, however, it can similarly be argued that the availability of low-cost communications permits educational outreach well beyond what would otherwise be attainable, given scarce resources.

13. See Krueger, Schiff, and Valdés (1988) for documentation of this phenomenon. See also World Bank (1986) for a survey of agricultural taxation rates in the nineteenth century.

14. For a survey of the accomplishments of the Green Revolution, see Hayami and Ruttan (1985, chap. 11).

15. To the extent that technological changes in capital-intensive industries have increased the comparative advantage of the now industrialized countries in those industries, the opportunities for specialization in more labor-using manufactured products by the now developing countries are greater than they would otherwise be. In this section, however, I consider the ways in which direct adoption of technological advances may affect development prospects.

16. I ignore here the sometimes heard contention that the early developers had the advantage of cheap and abundant raw materials. That assertion is patently inconsistent with the allegation that the terms of trade have turned against primary commodities. And, as we have seen, the evidence suggests little secular change in the terms of trade between primary and other commodities.

17. It may be significant, however, that oil-exporting developing countries as a group fared worse than oil-importing developing countries in the 1970s. The availability of resource rents may simply intensify political maneuvering to gain control over them.

18. Estimates here and elsewhere pertaining to world trade in recent periods are from General Agreement on Tariffs and Trade (GATT 1985, table A39).

19. Indeed, it is highly likely that the reduction in costs of transport was so large that the terms of trade of both exporters and importers improved. For a review of the evidence regarding long-term trends in the terms of trade, see Spraos (1980).

20. By outer-oriented I mean a trade regime that permits internal price relationships between import-competing and exportable goods to reflect fairly closely the border prices of those same bundles of goods. That, in turn, implies the absence of significant quantitative restrictions or high tariffs and the maintenance of a realistic exchange rate. For a fuller exposition, and an analysis of why these policies have been so crucial to growth, see Krueger (1983, 1984).

21. Corbo and de Melo (1985) analyzed the effects of the opening up of the Chilean trade and payments regime after 1973. To their surprise, they found very large productivity gains, ranging up to 800 percent, among existing firms who had rationalized after pressure from imports was felt. See Krueger (1984) for a discussion of why these efforts seem so strong.

22. Perhaps as important, the political consensus necessary to adopt outer-oriented policies may be easier to achieve in periods of buoyancy in the international economy than it is during periods of slow growth or stagnation. There is also the consideration that if very many developing countries were to try to achieve rapid growth through export promotion in the face of slow or stagnant world demand, they would almost surely collectively meet with limited success, as capturing markets away from existing suppliers is inherently more difficult than increasing share in an expanding market.

23. Kenwood and Lougheed (1983) estimate world population to have been 906 million in 1800 and 1.608 billion in 1900, which yields an estimated growth rate of 0.575 percent annually. Even for Britain, the fastest-growing country, in the peak period of the rate of growth of trade, 1840–1870, Kuznets (1967, p. 4) estimates the decennial growth rate to have been 64.4 percent, which is 5.1 percent annually.

24. As I have already noted, the marked drop in transport costs implies that more of the cost difference accrues to exporting and importing nations and less is absorbed in transport costs.

25. See World Bank (1986). Capital outflows from some industrial countries constituted a larger portion of GNP in the nineteenth century than have those flows in the twentieth.

26. See Frank, Kim, and Westphal (1975, chap. 7) for an analysis of the role of private capital flows in Korea.

27. See Bhagwati (1985, pt. 4) for an analysis of the issues associated with the "brain drain" as a phenomenon of twentieth-century development.

28. Indeed, the shift from mercantilism to more laissez-faire policies marked the acceleration of the industrialization process.

29. The distrust originated, of course, with the historical legacy, which included colonialism, slavery, and the worldwide impact of the Great Depression. Moreover, many developing countries inherited complex apparatuses of government intervention when they became independent. Marketing boards, state trading companies, price controls, and parastatals were all part of the colonial legacy.

30. See Hirschman (1982) for a discussion of this viewpoint and, for contrasting views, Lal (1983) and Little (1982).

31. The government of India established "food zones," across which it was illegal to transport major food grains; permits were also needed to transport a number of key commodities across state lines; and expansion, or even operating above licensed capacity, was illegal without the appropriate licenses. Regulations of this sort are still common in a number of countries today; for example, in Brazil, government permission is required before a firm may legally move a computer from one floor of its building to another.

32. In correspondence, T. N. Srinivasan noted that in some instances, notably India, the problem was not one of neglecting investment in power, but rather that huge sums were spent inefficiently.

33. Even here, however, caution must be exercised. The restrictiveness of most developing countries' trade regimes increased sharply in the aftermath of the commodity price boom associated with the Korean War, and there is substantial evidence that controls over international transactions were much intensified in response to "foreign exchange shortage." Even then, questions must be asked as to why controls, rather than devaluation and incentives, were the initial response.

34. See Little, Scitovsky, and Scott (1970); Bhagwati (1978); and Krueger (1978) for some of the evidence.

35. See Krueger (1986) for a further discussion of the evolution of thought in development economics. On the determinants of government policies in sub-Saharan Africa, see Bates (1984). It should also be recognized that there was a widespread belief that the Soviet Union had rapidly achieved development.

References

Agarwala, A. N., and S. P. Singh, eds. 1963. *The Economics of Underdevelopment*. New York: Oxford University Press.

Bates, R. H. 1984. *Markets and States in Tropical Africa*. Berkeley: University of California Press.

Bhagwati, J. N. 1978. *Foreign Trade Regimes and Economic Development: Anatomy and Consequences of Exchange Control*. New York: National Bureau of Economic Research.

———— 1985. *Dependence and Interdependence: Essays in Development Economics*, ed. G. Grossman. Oxford: Basil Blackwell.

Bhagwati, J. N., and T. N. Srinivasan. 1978. "Shadow Prices for Project Selection in the Presence of Distortions: Effective Rates of Protection and Domestic Resource Costs." *Journal of Political Economy* (February):97–116.

Chakravarty, S. 1987. *Development Planning: The Indian Experience*. Oxford: Oxford University Press.

Corbo, V., and J. de Melo. 1985. "Scrambling for Survival: How Firms Adjusted to the Recent Reforms in Chile, Uruguay, and Argentina." *World Bank Staff Working Paper*, no. 764.

Frank, C. R., Jr., K. S. Kim, and L. E. Westphal. 1975. *Foreign Trade Regimes and Economic Development: South Korea*. New York: National Bureau of Economic Research.

General Agreement on Tariffs and Trade (GATT). 1985. *International Trade 1984–85*. Geneva.

Hayami, Y., and V. W. Ruttan. 1985. *Agricultural Development: An International Perspective*. Baltimore: Johns Hopkins University Press.

Hirsch, E., and A. Hirsch. 1963. "Changes in Agricultural Output per Capita of Rural Population in Turkey, 1927–1960." *Economic Development and Cultural Change* 11, no. 4 (July):372–394.

Hirschman, A. 1982. "The Rise and Decline of Development Economics." In *The Theory and Experience of Development*, ed. M. Gersovitz. London: Allen and Unwin.

Johnson, H. G. 1975. *Technology and Economic Interdependence*. London: St. Martin's.

Kelley, A. C. 1988. "Demographic Change and Economic Development in the Third World." *Journal of Economic Literature*. 26, no. 4 (December):1685–1728.

Kenwood, A. C., and A. L. Lougheed. 1983. *The Growth of the International Economy, 1820–1980*. London: Allen and Unwin.

Krueger, A. O. 1972. "Rates of Return to Turkish Higher Education." *Journal of Human Resources*. 7, no. 4 (Fall):482–499.

――――― 1978. *Foreign Trade Regimes and Economic Development: Liberalization Attempts and Consequences*. Lexington, Mass.: Ballinger.

――――― 1983. *Trade and Employment in Developing Countries*. Vol. 3. *Synthesis and Conclusions*. Chicago: University of Chicago Press.

――――― 1984. "Comparative Advantage and Development Policy Twenty Years Later." In *Economic Structure and Performance*, ed. M. Syrquin, L. Taylor, and L. E. Westphal. Orlando, Fla.: Academic Press.

――――― 1986. "Changing Perspectives on Development Economics and World Bank Research." *Development Policy Review* 4, no. 3 (September):195–210.

Krueger, A. O., M. Schiff, and A. Valdés. 1988. "Agricultural Incentives in Developing Countries: Measuring the Effect of Sectoral and Economywide Policies." *World Bank Economic Review* 2, no. 3 (September):255–271.

Kuznets, S. 1967. "Quantitative Aspects of the Economic Growth of Nations: Part 10: Level and Structure of Foreign Trade: Long-Term Trends." *Economic Development and Cultural Change* 15, no. 2, pt. 11 (January):1–140.

Lal, D. 1983. *The Poverty of "Development Economics."* London: Institute of Economic Affairs.

Lewis, W. A. 1954. "Economic Development with Unlimited Supplies of Labour." *Manchester School of Economic and Social Studies*. 22 (May):139–195. Reprinted in Agarwala and Singh (1963, pp. 400–449).

Little, I. M. D. 1982. *Economic Development: Theory, Policy, and International Relations*. New York: Basic Books.

Little, I. M. D., T. Scitovsky, and M. Scott. 1970. *Industry and Trade in Some Developing Countries*. London: Oxford University Press.

Michaely, M. 1984. *Trade, Income Levels, and Dependence*. Amsterdam: North-Holland.

North, D. C. 1958. "Ocean Freight Rates and Economic Development, 1750–1913." *Journal of Economic History* 18, no. 4:537–555.

Nurkse, R. 1959. *Patterns of Trade and Development*. Stockholm: Almquist and Wiksell.

Rosenberg, N., and L. E. Birdzell, Jr. 1986. *How the West Grew Rich*. New York: Basic Books.

Spraos, J. 1980. "The Statistical Debate on the Net Barter Terms of Trade between Primary Commodities and Manufactures." *Economic Journal* 90:197–228.

Strykker, D. 1987. "The Political Economy of Agricultural Price Policy: Ghana." World Bank Comparative Study Working Paper.

Teece, D. J. 1977. "Technology Transfer by Multinational Firms: The Resource Cost of Transferring Technological Know-How." *Economic Journal* 87, no. 346 (June):242–261.

World Bank. 1983, 1985, 1986. *World Development Reports*. New York: Oxford University Press.

17

...

Prometheus Unbound and Developing Countries

Irma Adelman

What has been the development experience of less developed countries over the last several decades? Had we approached their development in the 1950s from the perspective of the economic history of the diffusion of the British Industrial Revolution to the European continent and to overseas territories, what would have been a reasonable set of expectations for contemporary developing countries? Have there been any real surprises?

Contrasts with the Nineteenth Century

A comparison between nineteenth-century growth and the first quarter-century of economic development starts with a brief discussion of the major differences in initial conditions and political and technological environment between the two time periods.

First, the political and ideological climates in which developing countries operate today are very different from those in the nineteenth century. The end of colonialism and the revolution in rising expectations have put the governments of developing countries under considerable pressure to deliver rapid improvements in standards of living, at least to the urban middle class and workers, whose rising expectations, when not met, destabilize governments. The growth of formal education and exposure to Western cultures through communications media not available in the nineteenth century have led to ideologies, shared by a significant percentage of developing countries' politically active citizens, that emphasize widespread economic opportunities and equality. These ideologies contrast with the very unequal distributions of wealth and access to opportunities that characterize the great majority of developing nations. National governments are under pressure to deliver more widespread sharing of the benefits of growth than their policies, institutions, distributions of wealth, and development strategies can provide. At the same time, political forces for the maintenance of the status quo and for benefiting entrenched elites remain as strong as they were in many countries during the nineteenth century. Attempts to respond to these pressures by some governments lead to vacillating policies, now favoring the demands of those elites, now those of the middle class and workers. Other governments try to deliver all goods to all people through populist policies that lead to inflation and balance-of-payments difficulties. The army is always in the wings, and steps in when the economic crisis gets out of hand. When it, too, cannot respond to the pressures on policy or correct the overhang of past mistakes, there is a sharp loss of legitimacy and widespread political protest, and a democratic regime takes over temporarily, alas, only to continue the cycle. The result is significantly more fragile government structures, which are generally unequal to the task of sustained economic development. Whether the task entails liberalization, structural adjustment, or land reform, most governments of less developed countries (LDCs) are generally unable to implement the requisite changes and keep on track under the pressures of the macroconstraints and the interest-group demands that they face. Governments in the nineteenth century were more stable, were expected to deliver much less, and had administrative capacities that were more equal to the tasks they were expected to perform.

Population growth is a far greater burden in today's Third World than it was in the nineteenth century. Rates of population increase in western Europe in the early nineteenth century were about half of what they are in today's underdeveloped world. In addition, governments are now expected to provide primary education facilities, with a greater burden on the public treasury. Population growth in many developing countries has been too rapid relative to possibilities for absorbing the increase in nonagricultural employment. The supply of cultivable but uncultivated land—the internal frontier—has been largely exhausted. Large-scale emigration comparable to that in the nineteenth century is not possible today.

The distribution of world income has remained constant between 1950 and 1980, implying that the more rapid growth of LDCs has enabled them just to maintain the absolute income gaps over the period. The income levels of developing countries at the end of World War II were much lower, however, than those of European countries in the nineteenth century, a situation that poses a much more difficult task for mobilizing savings. Administrative capacities of even the European latecomers to development were much higher than those of most developing countries in the 1950s. Finally, technology gaps between today's developing and developed countries far exceed those in the nineteenth century. And gaps in the capital-intensity of available technologies are much wider than in the nineteenth century, posing problems of inappropriate technology transfer, and leading to lower growth and worse distribution of income than would have existed otherwise.

These contrasts in initial conditions between underdeveloped countries in the nineteenth century and developing countries today all add up to one result: development is much more difficult to achieve in today's developing countries than it had been in the nineteenth century, despite the disappearance of colonialism as an obstacle to domestic-oriented development. And yet, developing countries had done much better in growth terms and no worse in the distributional consequences of growth.

Typical Growth Patterns and Their Variants

Both in the nineteenth century and in the period after World War II, countries followed a variety of growth paths. The variety of growth patterns has been smaller, however, in contemporary developing countries than that which characterized the nineteenth century, in large part because of the exhaustion of some opportunities.

Growth Paths between 1850 and 1914

The generalizations that follow are derived from the historical analysis of Morris and Adelman (1988), comparing statistically the growth patterns of 23 countries between 1850 and 1914. The Morris-Adelman statistical analysis focuses on both conventional economic factors and on institutional, social, and political forces, and comprises a wide range of development levels. It includes most of the currently developed countries as well as about half a dozen countries that are still underdeveloped today.

Historically, one can distinguish five paths of growth typical of groups of countries in the nineteenth century: two industrial paths, two agricultural paths, and one balanced growth path. One industrial path, followed by the firstcomers to the Industrial Revolution (Great Britain, Belgium, France, and the United States), resulted in the effective spread of industrialization, substantial manufacturing exports, and widespread improvements in agricultural technology. Along this path, prior agricultural development, the evolution of the market system, and political institutions that limited the political power of landed elites were strongly linked with widespread industrialization.

Along the second industrial path, followed by the latecomers to the Industrial Revolution with large populations (Germany, Japan, Italy, Spain, and Russia), governments promoted import-substitute industrialization in an effort to catch up with the firstcomers. They implemented laws that facilitated market exchange and factor mobility, introduced measures for political unification, and used tariffs as a major weapon for industrialization. Along this path success with industralization varied greatly; agriculture lagged behind industrial expansions; and dualistic, inequitable growth was the outcome. Only Germany achieved more widespread growth before 1914, and this only after the implementation of institutional and policy reforms sponsored by governments in which landed elites were no longer as powerful as they had been.

The primary export expansion path was undertaken by countries with quite different types of initial conditions: land-abundant countries, such as Australia, New Zealand, Brazil, and Canada; and densely populated countries with very low productivity in food production, such as Burma, China, Egypt, and India. The results of primary export expansion differed sharply between the two types of nations.

In the densely populated agricultural countries, low levels of agricultural productivity severely constrained the supply of food, raw materials, and income for purchasing manufactured goods. Expatriates dominated trade, and there was little modern industrial growth. Export expansion proceeded rapidly, but its pace was not systematically related to agricultural progress, industrial expansion, or increases in average income or wages. Primary export expansion in land-scarce countries thus resulted in enclave development with little positive impact on the rest of the economy.

In the land-abundant countries, resources attracted foreign settlers, capital, and entrepreneurship, thus greatly accelerating export expansion and economic growth and making up for deficiencies in local factor and commodity markets. Governments dominated by expatriate exporters and indigenous large landowners pushed laws freeing land transactions, promoting large landholdings, and subsidizing immigration. Industrialization came late and occurred behind tariff walls. In this group of countries, the early phase of primary export expansion resulted in limited but very dualistic growth. The ultimate outcome depended on whether small farmers, domestic manufacturers, and labor wrested power from the landed elites. Where they did, land policies were altered in favor of small farmers; moderate tariff protection was granted to infant industries; and wage-goods–based growth resulted in more widespread development. Where the political power of landed elites continued strong, as in Argentina and Brazil, most food was supplied by tenant farmers with low productivity, and luxury goods were significant in both imports and production.

The final path in the nineteenth century was one of open-economy balanced growth, adopted by a few small European nations (Belgium, Denmark, the Netherlands, and Sweden). They followed a path of export expansion that involved both heavy trade dependence and widespread domestic economic growth. Substantial agricultural progress preceded their industrialization. In the last quarter of the nineteenth century, extensive agriculture was widely replaced by intensive farming based on livestock, dairy products, or other specialized high-value crops. The small size of their domestic markets put pressure on them to develop internationally competitive processes of production, and deficiencies in their natural resources led them to specialize in exports of human-resource–intensive products. Agrarian institutional reforms that preceded industrialization contributed to the diversification of exports, to per capita income growth, and to the widespread diffusion of benefits from growth.

The five paths resulted in very different growth rates, economic structures, agriculture-industry interactions, agricultural and industrial development, and diffusion of growth and of its benefits. Of the five paths, only two culminated in sustained widespread domestic growth before 1914: the industrialization strategy of the firstcomers to the Industrial Revolution and the small, open-economy, European balanced-growth strategy. Important common characteristics of these two strategies were: functioning factor markets; land-tenure systems that gave incentives and property rights to small cultivators; effective parliamentary institutions; above-average levels of human-resource development; open development strategies; and substantial improvements in agricultural productivity preceding industrialization.

The expectations about economic development generated by nineteenth-century experience were therefore rather pessimistic. Developing countries could not be firstcomers to the Industrial Revolution. And of the remaining four paths among which countries could choose, only the open-economy, balanced-growth path chosen by the small European countries had led to widespread growth and development. This strategy entailed institutional and agricultural initial conditions that were lacking in virtually all developing countries in the 1950s. It also applied only to small countries. What of the development prospects of the large countries? At best, nineteenth-century experience indicated paths of growth without development in the Kuznets sense. In both the large latecomers to the Industrial Revolution and in the land-abundant immigration-absorbing countries, growth had on the average been narrowly based, dualistic, and inequitable throughout most of the period. Fewer than a handful of these countries had achieved somewhat more widespread growth by the end of the nineteenth century, but only if and when (as in Australia) indigenous modernizing groups became influential in setting economic policy and in selecting domestic institutions.

Development thus looked difficult and risky, and offered a few role models for large countries. It was no accident that the dominant development models in the 1950s stressed dualistic growth; that arguments for balanced growth entailing a big push were advanced by the development forerunners; and that institutional and political development seemed a necessary but difficult task whose importance was emphasized by historians writing on economic development.

Contemporary Growth Patterns in Developing Countries

The growth process of currently developing countries between 1955 and 1973 was more favorable than empirically based historical expectations in some respects and replicated historical experience in others. The speed of economic growth, the rate of growth of exports, and the rates of transformation of the structures of production, exports, and consumption were four to five times more rapid in the average developing country than in the average country in the nineteenth century. There was also an acceleration of social change relative to the period before World War I, and some important modernizing institutions were introduced with little difficulty, though perhaps adopted only superficially. But the prevalence of dualistic, inequitable growth patterns replicated itself in most developing countries. The superstars were relatively small countries. And the "large-country" development problem remains to be solved, although there are glimmers of hope on the horizon in the performance of China, India, and Indonesia.

As in the nineteenth century, contemporary development experience has also been marked by noticeable differences in development patterns among groups of countries. The patterns of structural change documented by Chenery and various coauthors (1975, 1986) portray the transition process of an average developing country, and three significant variations from the average pattern. The variants on the average pattern have been defined by differences in initial conditions, particularly country size and natural resources, and by differences in development strategies with respect to the relations between industrialization and international trade.

Average contemporary development pattern. The structural research program started by Colin Clark and Kuznets and studied econometrically in great detail by Chenery and his coauthors has described the transformations that have taken place in less developed countries during the transition process from very underdeveloped to semi-industrial nations. The average transition pattern has resembled that of the latecomers to the nineteenth-century Industrial Revolution. The government-promoted transition has entailed the accumulation of physical and human capital and shifts in the composition of demand, production, employment, and international trade. Uniformly, the core transitional process has been one of industrialization, with an increasing share of total value added, investment, and employment in the manufacturing sector. The first 20 years of the process have involved import-substitute industrialization, sheltered behind tariff walls, and discrimination in investment and price policy against food agriculture. As in the nineteenth century, the average process has resulted in moderately dualistic growth, with worsening distribution of income.

In the Chenery story, the earliest phase in the transition process of an average developing country has involved a substantial rise in exports, mostly of primary commodities, accompanied by a gradual but steady shift in export structure toward manufacturing exports. The expansion and transformation in exports have been accompanied by a substantial increase in investment, first in human and then in physical capital, and by a sharp drop in the share of primary production in total output.

The next phase of the transition of the average country has entailed shifts in the composition of consumption from food to nonfood, which have generated increases in demand for manufactured consumer goods. Technology has been imported from labor-scarce countries. The share of manufacturing in total domestic output has risen, but the shift of labor from primary production has lagged substantially behind the transformation in the structure of production. The relative productivity of labor in agriculture in this middle phase therefore declines to about half that in manufacturing. Partly as a result of the dualistic character of growth, the distribution of income worsens as well.

The final phase in the transition of the average country to a semi-industrial state has been characterized by manufacturing exports about equal in value to primary exports; industrial output about three times primary output; industrial employment about the same as primary employment; relative productivities between sectors that are almost the same; and a distribution of income that is starting to recover.

Alternative development patterns. The systematic differences from the average pattern in the period after World War II have been between large and small countries, and between land-abundant and human-resource–abundant countries. Large countries have more diversified resource bases and potentially more important domestic markets. They have therefore relied less on international trade for resources and markets and have had lower levels of primary exports and manufacturing imports. They have pushed import-substitute industrialization more heavily; they have developed heavy industry earlier; and they have been less efficient in their use of both capital and labor. As in the nineteenth century, the growth rates of the large countries have been lower and their income distributions worse than those of the average countries.

Small developing countries have had to pursue more open development strategies willy-nilly. The natural-resource–poor small countries have concentrated on education, labor-intensive and, later, skill-intensive exports, and early industrialization; they have had less-than-average primary and heavy industry. After an initial phase of import substitution in consumer manufactures, they shifted to export-led growth early rather than continuing to industrialize through import substitution in heavy manufactures. They have tended to use heavy foreign borrowing in the initial phase of their development to build up labor-intensive industries and exports very rapidly, and with low capital-output ratios. This strategy then enabled them to continue rapid growth when foreign capital inflows were reduced. Their farming systems have tended to rely on owner-operated farms using intensive farming methods to overcome their small farm sizes. They have been very sensitive to changes in the international environment and have tended to adapt quickly and successfully to changes in the world economy. Their strategy has resembled that of the small, open European economies, with very similar favorable outcomes for the diffusion of growth, for income distribution, for the growth and diversification of exports, and for increases in per capita incomes. It is in this group of countries that the superstars among the newly industrializing countries can be found.

By contrast, the natural-resource–rich small countries have concentrated on primary exports, have delayed their industrialization, and, except for the oil exporters, have experienced difficulties in growing beyond middle-income levels. Low levels of agricultural productivity in food production have constrained food supplies and foreign exchange for industrial imports. They have tended to undergo long periods of inefficient import substitution and to experience foreign exchange crises and slow growth. When commodity prices were high, they suffered from the "Dutch disease" phenomenon (that is, the effects of windfall wealth), and when commodity prices were low, they suffered from foreign exchange crises. In both periods industrialization suffered. Expatriates have tended to play an important role in export agriculture, in commerce, and in politics. Agriculture has been very dualistic, with food agriculture using subsistence technology and commercial export farms and plantations using modern techniques.

The contemporary experience of the small resource-rich countries has historically resembled that of the densely settled agricultural countries, even though their initial conditions have been quite different. The similarities in development patterns are probably due to the political dominance of primary exporters and the classes with which they are allied in both groups of countries. They have set price, fiscal, investment, tariff, immigration, land, and trade policies that discriminate against food agriculture and indigenous entrepreneurship. The results, both then and now, have been low productivity in food agriculture and severe foreign exchange shortages constraining economic growth.

There have been no contemporary analogues among developing countries to the firstcomers to the Industrial Revolution. Except perhaps for Hong Kong, no developing countries have fit the purely neoclassical story, in which economic development is the result of the invisible hand operating through market mechanisms that arise spontaneously in a free-trade regime in which ·governments merely promulgate laws aimed at making markets more complete and more perfect, reducing transaction costs and enforcing property rights. The other small, balanced-growth developing countries have resembled "Japan, Inc." rather than Belgium or Great Britain. Governments have taken the lead in investment; development strategies have been planned, and the plans have been vigorously enforced, both through macroeconomic measures and through micromanagement of individual firms; myriads of specific price and nonprice incentives have been employed to ensure compliance of firms with the plans; and governments have used a steel fist rather than an invisible hand to enforce "liberalization" policies.

Similarly, the pattern of the land-abundant countries, in which the prime mover was immigrant settlement accompanied by massive capital inflows, has no analogue in the period after World War II. The legacies of this pattern are, however, still evident in the land-abundant Latin American countries, in which landed elites have continued to exercise a great deal of influence on domestic institutions, on trade and exchange rate policy, and on public investment, to the detriment of food agriculture, agricultural terms of trade, income distribution, industrialization, and economic growth. Argentina exemplifies this point: there appears to be a stalemate there between the landed elite and populist prourban forces, which has led to vacillating and conflicting policies, sometimes favoring landed elites and sometimes urban workers.

There has been one extra path in the period since World War II—that of the centrally planned socialist countries. In some respects, their path has been similar to that of the large countries. But they industrialized earlier than even the large countries, shifted more and earlier into heavy industry, and had relatively closed economies maintained by quantity controls on imports rather than tariffs. Here the similarity with large countries ends, however. The centrally planned economies achieved higher rates of growth of GNP than the average developing country. But their higher growth came at the cost of lower rates of growth of consumption: their investment rates and capital-output ratios were much higher than in the average developing country pattern, and their rates of growth in total factor productivity lower. Despite their import-substitute industrialization, they achieved better distributions of income through wage policies and by subsidizing the basic-needs bundle (except for housing) both in their pricing and supply policies. While similar to the path of the large countries, their path was in some respects more successful.

Contrasts with the Nineteenth Century

A nineteenth-century analyst of contemporary developing countries would find few surprises in their growth patterns and in the varied outcomes of their growth strategies. Then as now, development changed the structure of production and exports from mostly primary to mostly manufacturing. Then as now, different groups of countries followed different growth paths. And the outcomes of the different paths followed by countries with similar initial conditions have been qualitatively quite similar, although growth and structural change has been greatly accelerated in the postwar era.

Our nineteenth-century analyst might, perhaps, be somewhat surprised at how few countries have followed the small, open-economy, high–agricultural-productivity, balanced-growth pattern that had been so very successful during his time. He might be saddened by the repetition of the policy mistakes of the large countries in the nineteenth century, with the same detrimental effects on the spread of growth and on social justice and by the lack of different modern alternatives to their development dilemmas. And he might also yearn for the autonomous neoclassical growth path of the firstcomers to the Industrial Revolution, though not for the distributional consequences of market-led growth in the early phase. Having been exposed to the variety of nineteenth-century experiences, however, he would realize how very special the experiences of the firstcomers to the Industrial Revolution had been and how inapplicable the institutional, technological, political, and international conditions that had been critical for the success of the firstcomers were to today's underdeveloped countries.

While the imaginary nineteenth-century analyst would find contemporary development patterns familiar, he would be astounded by the speed of economic and social change in developing countries since World War II. He would ask himself whether the effects of the acceleration in speed of growth and structural change had been good or bad. The answer would not be obvious. He would have to weigh many countervailing effects of accelerated growth against one another. Arguing for slower growth would be the worse income distributions than would have resulted from more rapid growth; the higher rates of urbanization; the greater population and more rapid degradation of renewable resources and environment; the population explosion resulting from the difficulty of fertility rates' adjusting to the rapid drop in mortality rates; and the pronounced social and political strains on the fragile polities of the (mostly) newly independent or rapidly transforming less developed countries, with their ensuing threats to human rights and individual liberties. Arguing for accelerated growth would be the higher average income levels resulting from the more rapid growth of developing countries; the more rapid reductions in absolute poverty in those developing countries that had reached fairly advanced levels of development in food agriculture and were pursuing labor-intensive growth strategies; the lower levels of infant mortality; the catching up to developed countries by the average developing country as its rate of growth of income and manufacturing exports exceeded that of virtually all developed countries; the greater infrastructure and environmental sanitation levels; and the increased economic and social modernization.

It is hard to say whether our Rip Van Winkle would find the more rapid modern growth preferable to the slower speed of change of the nineteenth century. On the one hand, nineteenth-century growth, though slower, had, after all, not been free of most of the currently intensified negative effects of accelerated growth. On the other hand, although nineteenth-century growth had been slower, it had led to the growth of many countries and the development of some. In the end, he would be glad that he did not have to resolve the issue, since whatever he decided would be irrelevant to the current growth of developing countries. This is a thought that I find comforting as well.

Prime Movers of Growth

Both in the nineteenth century and in current LDCs, governments and exports have played a significant causal role in determining growth patterns and patterns of institutional and economic development.

Nineteenth Century: Governments

The prime movers of economic growth in the nineteenth century were governments, international trade, and international factor movements. Of these, governments, which played a pervasive role in initiating growth, were the most important (Adelman, Lohmoller, and Morris 1988).

Even among the firstcomers to the Industrial Revolution, whose governments were least instrumental in growth initiation, the state played a significant part in determining the institutional structure of the economy, investing in education and transport, and setting tariff policies. Governments of moderately backward European nations worked to initiate growth more directly: they substituted government demand and foreign inputs for capital, skills, and domestic demand that were inadequate because of deficient institutions and significant underdevelopment. In land-abundant immigrant-settled countries, foreign-dominated governments initially substituted foreign trade, imports of capital, credit, and immigration for scarce domestic resources; limited the development of market institutions; and generated insufficient incentive structures for domestically oriented economic growth. Eventually, however, these substitutions became inadequate to support further economic expansion. Growth became blocked unless governments responding to political pressures from domestic nonlanded, nonprimary-export–oriented elites promulgated laws promoting the spread of domestic commodity and factor markets, land reform widely redistributing the ownership of land, and complementary inputs for owner-cultivators. Finally, part of the reason for the stagnation of the densely settled, low-productivity countries was the inability of their economically dependent governments to engage in investment programs, institution building, and policies designed to foster the growth of the domestic economy. Politics, especially the structure of political power, thus determined the institutions and policies on which the structure of growth depended.

The nature of government influence varied among countries in the nineteenth century. A primary determinant of the impact of governments on development was the structure of political power. In European-settled countries in which marked reductions in the political influence of large estate owners occurred, there was significant development of food agriculture, domestic manufacturing, internal transport, and education. Where the landed elites lost their dominant political position, governments changed land laws in ways that helped market farming, promoted literacy, protected the early phases of wage-goods manufacturing, and built feeder roads and rural schools. By contrast, where landlords continued to dominate politically, the benefits from growth did not reach most peasants. There was little public education and local government and few feeder roads, and most peasants were producing food with primitive techniques on large estates or subsistence-size plots. The structure of political power was, in turn, influenced by the extent to which countries were economically and politically dependent on foreign metropolitan powers. The more dependent the countries, the more powerful the local landed elites and the more control over tariff and investment policies exercised by them and by colonizing powers. Heavy dependence on foreigners was likely to restrict domestic economic growth: the alliance of domestic resource-owning elites with strong foreign interests concentrating on production for exports tended to strengthen biases against food agriculture, wage-goods production for the home market, rural education, and rural farm-to-market transportation.

Everywhere, the ability of governments to continue to substitute for missing domestic institutions and factors declined as growth proceeded regardless of initial conditions, power structure, and development strategies. Eventually, sustained widespread growth became blocked in the absence of policies and institutions enabling farmers profitably to market their produce at home and small manufacturers profitably to provide wage goods for domestic consumption. The adoption of the appropriate land, trade, education, and transport policies and institutions in turn required the weakening of the political power of landed elites and/or metropolitan powers, and the classes with which they were allied. International trade continued to be important to economic growth, but as a complement to, rather than a substitute for, domestic development.

Nineteenth Century: Exports and International Factor Flows

We have already seen the dynamic role of exports for the economic growth of countries in the nineteenth century and the varied effects that export growth had on domestic growth linkages and on the diffusion of the benefits from growth to workers in the urban sector and to the agricultural poor. The more economically dependent the countries were and the less politically influential their domestic nonlanded elites, the lower the domestic growth linkages and the more concentrated the distribution of benefits. We have also seen the negative effects that import-substitute industrialization had on growth rates and income distribution in the large latecomers to the Industrial Revolution.

On the average, export-led growth raised rates of growth of per capita GNP during the nineteenth century, though there were significant variations in the importance of export-led growth in different countries and during different subperiods. The rates of expansion in both foreign trade and economic growth were much slower, however, than in the period following World War II, and the mechanisms used to induce export growth and the effects of export growth varied substantially across countries. In France, for example, high tariffs slowed resource transfer to industry. By contrast, in Great Britain the failure to protect agriculture accelerated the movement of resources out of agriculture. Free trade in the colonies destroyed handicraft industry, while the low tariffs in the Netherlands, Denmark, and Switzerland induced a rapid shift from grains to specialized high-value agricultural exports. The outcome of primary export expansion also varied across countries. Where tenure conditions were conducive to the generation of an agricultural surplus that was widely distributed, and where government policies reflected the interests of domestic manufacturers and farmers producing food for the domestic market in setting trade policies, staple exports generated positive linkages throughout the economy and resulted in successful development. Otherwise, export growth, while associated with GNP growth, resulted in narrowly based, dualistic growth with few positive spread effects.

Not only was international trade important to nineteenth-century growth, but international migration and capital movements also provided key sources of growth. International migration led other phases of structural change in the second half of the nineteenth century (Adelman and Morris 1984) and, as stressed by Thomas (1973), played an initiating role in the long swings in the economic activity of the Atlantic community during the period. Malthusian pressures coupled with laborsaving innovations in agriculture in the Old World generated a push toward emigration, while wage differentials between the two worlds generated a pull toward the new one. Immigration was associated with capital movements from the Old World and, as links with the metropolitan centers increased, generated a complementary, dependent pattern of economic growth in the newly settled territories. Immigration and foreign capital inflows led to infrastructure investment, linking ports with export-producing centers and lowering transport costs and increasing the competitiveness of exports. Subsequent increases in export and GNP growth were the result. But, at the same time, immigration also exerted a dampening influence on both agricultural and industrial wages, thereby limiting the spread effects from export expansion.

Prime Movers of Growth in Developing Countries

Governments and international trade have been prime movers of growth in developing countries as well. But the role of international factor transfers has been much less important than during the nineteenth century and trade more important.

LDC governments have played a major part in accelerating the process of industrialization—the major aim of economic policy in all developing countries. They have pursued this aim by focusing on two necessary conditions for industrialization: the mobilization of finance—savings and foreign exchange— and the creation of markets for manufacturing output. The primary differences in development patterns among countries have related to these two aspects of development policy. There have been systematic differences among groups of countries in the manner in which finance for development was raised, particularly in the relative role of agriculture, trade, and foreign capital as sources of saving for capital accumulation in manufacturing. Similarly, the search for markets—domestic or foreign—also varied by country, by phase of development, by ideology, and by state of the world economy. Industrialization and trade policy have been intimately linked, since foreign exchange is necessary to purchase intermediate goods and machinery for industrialization and to enable a decoupling of production patterns from consumption patterns.

The major noninstitutional instruments at the commands of governments have been price policy, investment policy, and trade policy. These have interacted wtih macropolicies and constraints to create, in most countries, stop-go policy regimes. Except when macroconstraints on the balance of payments or fiscal side have been very binding, governments have tried to use the instruments at their disposal to accelerate industrial growth.

In price policy, LDC governments have set agricultural prices below world prices and used the difference to finance investment in manufacturing and keep nominal wages in manufacturing low so as to be competitive in export markets despite low productivity. Governments have also intervened in factor markets, primarily by lowering the price of capital, both generally and selectively, and by rationing or selectively subsidizing foreign exchange to foster the growth of particular industries. In investment policy, they have concentrated on the infrastructure necessary for industrialization and on direct investment in intermediate-goods manufacturing.

In trade policy, a combination of overvalued exchange rates and tariffs has been used initially by all LDC governments to foster import-substitute industrialization at the expense of exports, whether agricultural or industrial. The result has been a combination of an agricultural sector starved of resources and discriminated against by low terms of trade; periodic foreign exchange crises, since import-substitute industrialization is foreign-exchange–intensive; and domestic inflation. Next came a bifurcation in trade policies: most countries continued into the secondary stage of import substitution, in intermediates and capital goods; a few newly industrializing countries liberalized their trade policies and started exporting the light manufacturing goods that they had previously produced under an import-substitution regime. There is a vast literature by development economists with a trade orientation on the superiority of the latter strategy for economic growth, adjustment to trade shocks, and the diffusion of benefits from growth. Most developing countries, even the Four Little Tigers (Singapore, Taiwan, Hong Kong, and Korea), have used elements of both strategies in various combinations and sequences.

As in the nineteenth century, the nature of government policies in LDCs has been determined by the political interests reflected in the state and by the capacity of governments to implement their policies. In a few small economies, challenged by survival imperatives and endowed with good human resources, governments with a great deal of autonomy and capacity to act shifted out of import substitution into export-led growth early, adopted institutions and price policies designed to foster productivity growth in both agriculture and industry, and flexibly shifted policies and institutions as growth proceeded or as the world economy changed. Most developing country governments have been less technocratic and less autonomous in their approach to policy. Their policies have been shaped by ideological preconceptions, by pressures from political elites, domestic or foreign, or even motivated by personal gain. These considerations have led to policy distortions away from optimal policy, retarding growth and increasing income disparities. In these countries performance has been poorer, on the average, and policy has been more inflexible, more crisis prone, and with less satisfactory adjustment to crisis.

While trade and trade policy have continued to be critical determinants of economic growth in today's LDCs, immigration and international factor flows have been less significant, on the average, than during the nineteenth century. Except in a few small countries foreign capital flows and foreign direct investment have been much smaller than in the nineteenth century, and international migration has been almost negligible by comparison.

Contrasts with the Nineteenth Century

The primary difference between the nineteenth and twentieth centuries is not in the nature of the prime movers—governments and international trade—but rather in the vastly greater speed of growth in both exports and per capita GNP that the prime movers induced. The volume of world trade grew at a historically unprecedented rate between 1950 and 1973, with very small cyclical interruptions, largely owing to the unprecedentedly rapid growth of income and mass purchasing power in the OECD countries. As a result, the impetus that the rapid growth in world trade imparted to the growth of developing countries was much greater as well. Indeed, on the average the growth rates of LDCs were more rapid than those of the developed countries, though the dispersion in growth rates among developing countries widened.

In the nineteenth century the contribution to economic growth of primary exports and of manufacturing exports was almost the same, but in twentieth-century LDCs primary exporters have benefited much less from the growth in world trade than have manufacturing exporters. In the postwar era, import-replacing innovations (synthetics, artificial sweeteners) and changes in consumer tastes in developed countries have made primary-export strategies less advantageous, on the average, than manufacturing export strategies. Also, primary prices have behaved more cyclically than manufacturing prices. Partially as a result, LDCs have endeavored to increase the share of manufacturing exports, and the proportion of manufactured exports originating in developing countries has risen.

The slowdown in the growth of income in the OECD countries since the first and second oil shocks is probably a change in trend rather than a mere cyclical break. A slowdown in population growth and the aging of the population in the OECD countries suggest a downturn in the Kondratieff cycle. In addition, there has been a loss in comparative advantage of the OECD countries in manufacturing and, partially as a result, a shift in the composition of production into sectors with inherently less potential for total factor productivity growth—services and government. Finally, the economies of the OECD countries have become more cyclical and inflation-prone, and there has been a shift in policy goals toward more concern with avoiding inflation than with increasing employment. The combination is likely to induce slower growth in OECD incomes and hence, to a lesser extent, in world trade over the next decade or so.

As OECD growth slowed down in the 1970s, developing countries borrowed heavily, at variable interest rates, in an effort to keep up their rates of growth in the face of decelerating growth in OECD demand for their exports. The petrodollars were recycled to developing countries through the banking systems of the OECD countries, leaving developing countries with a debt overhang and developed countries with shaky financial systems.

These factors all point to the likelihood that world growth rates will return to a level somewhat above their nineteenth-century trends in the next decade or so. Growth rates in developing countries will then more closely resemble those of the nineteenth century.

Sources of Growth

The differences between today's developing countries and their nineteenth-century counterparts have been more pronounced with respect to sources of growth than to growth patterns and prime movers of growth.

While governments and international trade were the prime movers in the nineteenth century, the primary sources of growth were technological and institutional change (Landes 1969) and the resource accumulation they induced. It is impossible to do a strict Denison-type growth-accounting decomposition for the nineteenth century, since data on capital accumulation is unobtainable for the whole range of nineteenth-century countries. Nonetheless, a regression equation fitted to the Morris-Adelman nineteenth-century data for 23 countries (Adelman, Lohmoller, and Morris 1988) accounts for 50 percent of the inter-country variance in growth rates of per capita GNP between 1850 and 1914 by reference to only four (latent) variables: technological change in industry; the degree of imbalance between technological change in industry and agriculture; the diffusion of commodity and factor markets; and the growth of exports. (The definition of these latent variables and the technique used to compute the regression equation are explained in Adelman, Lohmoller, and Morris 1988. Since the regression results reported here are part of a simultaneous equation system, the coefficients represent only the net direct effects of the included variables.)

Nineteenth Century: Technological Change

The diffusion of Industrial Revolution technology played a key role in raising rates of economic growth in the latter part of the nineteenth century. Landes (1969), Marshall (1920), and Kuznets (1968) emphasize that the dynamic forces for change in the nineteenth century were the revolution in textile and steel technology and the revolution in transport technology embodied in the introduction of the steamship and the railroads. My econometric model fitted to nineteenth-century data (Adelman, Lohmoller, and Morris 1988) indicates that almost a third of the explained variance in growth rates was accounted for by technical change in industry and agriculture.

Where improvements in agricultural technology kept pace with improvements in industrial technology, higher rates of growth of per capita GNP were the result (Adelman, Lohmoller, and Morris 1988). The importance of an agricultural output sufficient to provide a marketable surplus was pervasive. Whether countries were industrializing or exporting primary products or both, growth did not spread widely without abundant land or productive food agriculture. In the early phase of industrialization, a marketable surplus above the subsistence needs of the domestic population was necessary to expand exports. For a time, food imports could substitute for domestic food production. But raising the productivity of food agriculture became essential to continued growth once immigrant populations grew dramatically and demand for foreign exchange to import intermediate goods expanded. The economic history of the nineteenth century thus lends support to the balanced-growth theorists, Nurkse (1953) and Rosenstein-Rodan (1943), who argued for the adoption of balanced-growth strategies in current developing countries. Then as now, failure to improve agricultural technology in line with industrial technology retarded growth by leading to bottlenecks in foreign exchange earnings and by lowering domestic savings and domestic demand for manufactures as export earnings from agricultural staples became insufficient to pay for the imports of food and intermediates required to support growing immigrant populations and industrialization. The importance of high-productivity agriculture for economic growth is a theme of nineteenth-century growth and development.

Nineteenth Century: Institutional Change

In addition to technological improvement in both industry and agriculture, linkages between technological and institutional change were also a significant source of growth in the nineteenth century, a point stressed by Landes (1969). Legal institutions reducing market transaction costs emphasized by North and Thomas (1970), the drastic social changes implicit in the establishment of functioning market systems stressed by Polanyi (1944), and the revival of Roman law providing for fixity of contracts, predictability of economic transactions, and establishment of unconditional property rights underlined by Anderson (1974) all played a major role in nineteenth-century growth. Indeed, our econometric estimates (Adelman, Lohmoller, and Morris 1988) suggest that the institutional changes in economic, social, and legal conditions involved in promoting the effective functioning of commodity and factor markets played an even more important role than technological change in the explanation of nineteenth-century capitalist development: the net direct effect of these forces accounted for half of the explained variance in economic growth rates; and the direct and indirect multiplier of improvements in market institutions and of higher levels of market development was about three times the corresponding multiplier for improvements in industrial and agricultural technology.

While the spread of market systems was a central process for modern economic growth, its effects on the diffusion of growth and its benefits varied. Whether the evolution of market systems resulted in dualistic, export-enclave growth or in more generalized development depended on the extent of foreign economic dependence and on whether landed elites or indigenous manufacturers, wage earners, or small farmers were politically influential in setting land, tariff, financial, immigration, and investment policies. Where modernizing elites gained political power, governments took a more active role. The destruction of communal land arrangements and the concentration of land in export-oriented estates tended to proceed more slowly than in more dependent countries. Domestic markets for local manufactures, rural banking institutions serving food farmers, roads for marketing agricultural wage goods, and rural education tended to develop and spread more rapidly. Internal growth linkages and a wider diffusion of benefits were the result. By contrast, in more dependent countries growth patterns remained narrow, and benefits were concentrated in the hands of a few staple exporters.

Appropriate land institutions were critical to nineteenth-century development. But the nature of appropriate land institutions changed as development proceeded. In the initial phases of development, in which a marketable agricultural surplus was essential for expanding exports, concentrated forms of land ownership and dualistic agricultural structures helped growth by concentrating the limited investable surplus where land was abundant. As industrialization and growth proceeded, a domestic agricultural surplus capable of at least matching population growth with expanded food production became essential. For a time, governments could substitute for a productive agriculture by importing food, but eventually domestic productive agriculture capable of providing food for urban consumption and markets for domestic industrial output became essential for further economic growth. At this point the institutional requisites for further agricultural growth shifted. Unimodal agricultural growth strategies for distributing the agricultural surplus widely among the peasant populations became necessary. Agrarian institutions providing incentives to farmers who were owner-cultivators and well-distributed ownership of land were required to generate the widespread agricultural improvements on which the expansion of food production and home markets rested, provided that a level of agricultural productivity had been achieved that yielded a sizable marketable surplus. Inequality in land ownership slowed growth at this stage.

Appropriate institutions in agriculture interacted with the spread of market institutions to determine the distributional impact of economic growth. For the poorest agricultural-export economies, the more concentrated land ownership, the more negative the impact of commercialization accompanying export expansion. There, commercialization accelerated cash cropping and weakened extended-family safety net arrangements so that during bad harvests or price declines, peasant indebtedness and land losses increased. By contrast, when land ownership was well dispersed, as in the small open economies of Europe that started with favorable land and political institutions and human resources, the strengthening of market systems ultimately spread economic growth and its benefits widely.

Developing Countries: Technical Change as a Source of Growth

The importance of technical change to the growth of semi-industrial less developed countries, the subsample of developing countries in which technical change has contributed most, has been studied by Chenery, Robinson, and Syrquin (1986). Their Denison-type decomposition of sources of growth indicates that 70 percent of the growth of total GNP in semi-industrial countries from 1950 to 1973, the period of rapid growth, came from increases in factor supplies and only 30 percent came from growth in total factor productivity. Furthermore, of the 30 percent of growth attributable to improvement in total factor productivity, about half came from resource reallocations from low- to high-productivity sectors associated with industrialization. In the growth of semi-industrial countries, the contribution to overall output growth of technological change within given industrial sectors (that is, technological change per se) has therefore been limited to at most 15 percent. This is about half what it was during the nineteenth century. Even in the industrial sectors of the miracle-growth less developed countries (the Four Little Tigers), Westphal, Kim, and Dahlman (1985) attribute a small role to technological innovation. They find that most of the growth in total factor productivity in manufacturing of these countries was due to resource reallocations among manufacturing sectors; the rest was due to mastering existing industrial technologies and translating them into efficient production.

Capital accumulation has contributed the lion's share of sources of growth in developing countries. Chenery, Robinson, and Syrquin (1986) estimate that, of the overall growth in factors, the growth in capital has accounted for 60 percent of the contribution of factor growth to GNP growth, while growth in employment has accounted for 40 percent. This bears out the emphasis on problems of capital accumulation by the early development economists of the 1950s, particularly Lewis (1954), the socialist writers Robinson (1956) and Kalecki (1971), and the "Big Push" theorists such as Rosenstein-Rodan (1943).

It is interesting to speculate why technological change has contributed so little to the growth of even the most advanced LDCs. In the industrial sectors of LDCs, the limited contribution of technical change may in part be due to the fact that the modern factories that have been established in less developed countries have generally been "turnkey" operations involving the combined transfer of both capital and technology. The small contribution of technical change in industry to overall growth may thus in part be a statistical illusion; since the new technology has been embodied in capital, a significant part of its contribution may be misattributed to capital accumulation in the Denison-type growth accounting. The relatively small contribution of technical change to the growth of less developed countries has also, in part, been a real phenomenon, however: the new industrial enterprises that were established started out with the most modern technology available. The scope for incremental technological change has therefore been smaller. In addition, the macropolicies in trade and finance associated with import substitution in less developed countries have generally led to "stop-go" policy regimes in which nonembodied technological change of the slow adaptive variety did not have much chance to flourish. It was constrained by the unavailability of critical intermediate inputs, replacement parts, and low levels of aggregate demand owing to bad macropolicies. The Chenery, Robinson, and Syrquin (1986) studies of total factor productivity growth in individual sectors of a few newly industrialized countries indicate clearly that during import substitution phases of their industrialization, total factor productivity growth was negative. It was only if and when countries switched to open trade regimes that total factor productivity growth in these industries became positive.

In LDC agriculture the contribution of technological improvement to productivity change has, on the average, also been small. But the potential is evident. In the fewer than half-dozen countries that have introduced high-yielding varieties of rice and wheat and coupled the introduction with policies, programs, and institutions conducive to productivity change, the contribution of growth in agricultural productivity to overall growth has been large. In these countries, the effect of the diffusion of the high-yield varieties has been to allow transfer of resources out of agriculture, raise rural incomes and rural purchasing power for manufacturing goods, increase GNP growth, and affect, though not necessarily reduce, the rate of growth of grain imports. The measures required for the diffusion of the high-yield varieties were infrastructure investment in irrigation, extension, and roads; the availability of complementary factors (fertilizer and credit); a predominance of owner-operated farms responsive to price incentives; and price policies that do not take away from farmers all the gains from productivity improvement. The conditions for successful productivity change in agriculture to result from the adoption of new high-yield varieties are thus demanding. In addition, development policy, at least before the food crisis of 1973, had a significant urban-industrial bias. Governments have tended to substitute cheap grain imports for domestic increases in agricultural productivity and "tax" the agricultural sector by terms-of-trade policies that keep grain prices below world market prices and use the difference to finance industrial investment and the government budget. The combination of this policy bias in favor of industrialization with the complex requirements of diffusion of technical change in agriculture explains why the conditions for productivity change in food agriculture have not been met in most LDCs and changes in agricultural technology have so far contributed little to the growth of the average developing country. The potential impact of improvements in agricultural technologies on the growth of LDCs is large, but remains to be realized by most of them.

Compared to nineteenth-century growth, then, developing country growth has tended to be more resource-intensive. Technological change, in the form of innovation or adaptation, has as yet to play a major role.

Technological change has contributed less to the economic growth of developing countries for a variety of reasons: it has been more abrupt; it has been capital-embodied and capital- and foreign-exchange intensive; in most countries, macroeconomic policies have been unpropitious to the more continual variety of adaptive technical change, even where human and institutional resources were favorable; there have been complex interactions, especially in agriculture but also in industry, between technological and institutional change; technological change in agriculture has been infrastructure-intensive and has required either fertilizer imports or domestic fertilizer industries; governments have been unwilling to allocate capital and foreign exchange to food agriculture; and price and exchange rate policies have worked against technical change in agriculture.

But there may be more basic reasons why technical change has contributed less to the growth of developing countries than it did during the nineteenth century. The gap in technology between today's developing and developed countries is much larger than it was in the nineteenth century. As a result, the technologies available for transfer to today's developing countries are less suited to their resource endowments, and more difficult to master. The new industrial technologies transferred to developing countries have also not been as revolutionary for their time as the new Industrial Revolution technologies in textiles, steel, and transport were for their time. The recent communication, information, and transport technologies, which have enabled new patterns of global division of labor to take place, have as yet had little impact on the great majority of developing countries. The new high-yield varieties introduced in agriculture in a few regions of a few developing countries, while tripling yields when combined with optimal amounts of water, fertilizer, and labor, have been produced with traditional biotechnologies rather than by new gene-splicing genetic engineering. The potential of these new research techniques for accelerating agricultural innovations appropriate for the agroclimatic and economic conditions of developing countries is large and largely untapped. Thus, the new technological revolutions in both agriculture and industry that are currently technologically feasible have barely been exploited in practice. Not surprisingly, the current technological revolution has not yet impinged significantly on developing countries.

Developing countries: institutional change as a source of growth. By contrast with technological change, institutional change has been just as important to the growth of developing countries as it was to countries in the nineteenth century. Now as then, economic and political institutions were especially critical to the diffusion of benefits from economic growth, and the nature of requisite institutional transformations varied with development levels.

Changes in the economic institutions of developing countries have been more significant and multifaceted in agriculture than in industry. In agriculture there have been changes in tenurial systems, in marketing institutions, and in transaction modes. But just as in the land-abundant, low-income, densely settled countries of the nineteenth century, the effect of these changes has not always been to raise productivity.

The tenurial reforms in agriculture have tended to replace precapitalist relations with commercial agriculture, thus making cultivators more sensitive to changes in economic incentives. At one extreme, communal forms of landownership have been replaced with ownership and cultivation by household firms. At the other extreme, noncommercial, low-productivity latifundia have been replaced by commercial farming in large estates or by farmer cooperatives. Subsistence farming has been reduced by proletarianization of subsistence farmers into landless workers at one extreme, and by shifts into commercial food and export crops at the other. The reforms that have led to owner-cultivation have tended to improve the productivity of land and sometimes total factor productivity as well. The introduction of cooperatives has had mixed productivity results. And the introduction of commercial estates for export crops has tended to raise productivity over latifundia. While these changes in agrarian systems have led to greater sensitivity to market incentives, the evidence suggests that incentives have influenced cropping patterns more strongly than aggregate agricultural output. The resulting increases in total factor productivity have therefore, on the average, been due more to resource reallocation effects than to increases in the productivity of individual crops.

Furthermore, the generally positive effects of tenurial reforms in agriculture have tended to be counteracted by reforms in marketing institutions, with negative productivity effects. Parastatals have been introduced in most LDCs for the marketing of staples and export crops in order to facilitate the transfer of the agricultural surplus to the state, as a partial substitute for other forms of tax that are more difficult to collect. The parastatals have kept agricultural prices below world market prices and used the surplus to finance both industrial development and the government budget. These policies have generally had negative and sometimes disastrous effects on agricultural output and productivity.

Other institutional reforms in agriculture in less developed countries have been productivity-neutral, though they have generally led to a shifting of more of the output and market risk from the landowner to the cultivator and the farm worker. The bundled work-credit or work-factor-input precapitalist relations between cultivator and landowner, and between hired labor and farmer, have tended to become unbundled market relations. As in poor, densely settled nineteenth-century countries, these changes have had major effects on income distribution and on the food security of landless workers and subsistence tenant farmers, but only minor effects on overall agricultural production.

Institutions for agricultural extension and for agricultural credit have been introduced in most less developed countries and have worked in very variable ways, generally favoring export crops over food agriculture and large farmers over small ones.

In the industrial sectors of developing countries, institutional changes have been fewer than in agriculture and of lesser significance for industrial growth. As in nineteenth-century Europe, the family firm continues to play a leading role in the industrial sectors of most developing countries, as do nonbank sources of industrial finance. The contract law developed arduously over the nineteenth century has been introduced wholesale into developing countries. The spheres of applicability of contract law, of limited-liability companies, banking institutions financing long-term investment, and export-import commercial institutions have been extended through industrialization, foreign trade, and the growth of market institutions. Major institutional innovations in industry, introduced in a few newly industrializing countries, have been industrial analogues of "trading houses," multinational firms, government enterprises, and joint foreign-domestic and public-private ventures. But in the main, as in the latecomers to the Industrial Revolution, governments and international trade have tended to substitute for missing domestic factors in industry and to complement domestic institutional gaps for industrial development.

Institutions and development in developing countries. The description presented herein, of how the impact of economic, social, and political institutions on economic growth rates changes during the process of economic development, is drawn from Adelman and Morris (1967). Our statistical analysis of the relations between institutional change and economic growth for 74 developing countries from 1950 to 1964 remains the only systematic investigation of these interactions over a large number of countries representing a significant range in development levels. Our results indicate that the process of economic growth has been closely related to changes in economic, social, and political institutions, and suggest that one can look at the entire process of economic growth as the progressive differentiation of the social, economic, and political spheres from one another and the development of specialized institutions and attitudes within each sphere.

In sub-Saharan Africa, the relationship between the penetration of market institutions and the breakdown of traditional tribal controls has been very close. A small foreign or expatriate market sector has provided incentives that have led to a crumbling of tribal controls over land and to reductions in the dominance of tribal structures and values. The extent of erosion in the economic content of tribal social organization has extended the sphere in which purely economic considerations govern economic activity. This in turn has influenced the degree of responsiveness to economic incentives, the extent of the country's absorptive capacity, and the productivity of investment in both physical and human capital. In the Adelman-Morris study, this process of socioeconomic differentiation explained 72 percent of intercountry differences in rates of economic growth between 1950 and 1964 at this lowest level of development.

The intermediate level of development has been characterized by much greater differentiation of the economic sphere from the social, and by much greater diversity in patterns of economic and social development. At the social level the dominant theme has been one of extreme disequilibrium, considerable social tensions, and very uneven social development. In the political sphere the primary systematic association has been between an increase in political insta-bility and the rate of economic progress; there have been no reliable associations between economic growth and either the form of political system or leadership commitment to development. As a result of the great diversity in paths of social development, the degree of association of economic growth with changes in social and political institutions appears very small statistically across the entire group of intermediate transitional countries. The dominant forces in the growth of transitional countries at this level of development seem to be economic, and they reflect the processes of accumulation and change in economic institution associated with more rapid industrialization.

At the "high" level of development, which includes most of the newly industrializing countries, higher levels of social and political development have been established, and the social and political tensions characteristic of the intermediate stage have been eased. Also, the development of market systems has become pervasive, and moderately effective financial institutions and fairly adequate levels of physical overhead capital have been attained. The Adelman-Morris analysis indicates that the rate of economic progress of countries at this level of development becomes conditioned primarily by improvements in economic institutions, accumulation, and by the political climate of the nation, particularly the extent of commitment of its leadership to economic development. The major obstacles to development become the political conditions that hamper the adoption or execution of rational economic policies. The variables indicating the extent of leadership commitment to development—the scope and commitment to purposive attempts by leaders to alter institutional arrangements and policies that clearly block the attainment of development goals—by themselves explained 60 percent of intercountry differences in the Adelman and Morris analysis of growth rates of countries at this level of development between 1950 and 1964.

Institutional forces have acted in today's developing countries much as they did in the nineteenth century. As in the nineteenth century, institutional change stressed by the classical economists, by "stage theorists" (Rostow 1960), by modernization theorists, and by historians writing about economic development (Kuznets 1968), has clearly been important to the growth of less developed countries. As in the nineteenth century, different institutions mattered most for growth and development at different phases of the evolution of currently developing countries. Institutions required to initiate growth had to be changed to sustain growth. As in the nineteenth century, different institutional changes were important for growth and for economic development in the sense of widespread growth with widely distributed benefits.

Initially, interactions between economic growth, the expansion in market institutions, and social change were the most significant. The dominant economic processes were quite similar to those in the land-abundant, non-European countries historically: the dualistic expansion of a modern, export-oriented sector based on the exploitation of abundant natural resource endowments. As with these countries, the result was narrowly based growth with little development, little diffusion of benefits from growth, and steep deterioration in the distribution of income.

The penetration of market institutions in transitional countries induced rapid social change, with varying lags in different countries. The tensions between economic modernization and lagging social development induced political and social unrest (one cannot help thinking of Iran here), with some negative effects on economic growth. One would have to go back earlier than 1850 to find historical analogues in western European history; but the Communist Revolution in backward Russia can be viewed as a modern counterpart occurring just after World War I. As during the nineteenth century, growth rates in transitional countries have been lower than those at higher levels of development, and slower but more broadly based than at lower levels of development. As in the large land-abundant countries of the nineteenth century, the growth of transitional developing countries has been associated with industrialization based on import substitution, the buildup of infrastructure, especially transport and electrical power networks, and the evolution of economic institutions for mobilizing savings.

As in the nineteenth century, once market institutions, social development, and political institutions enhancing the capacity to govern reached certain threshold levels of development, subsequent growth was no longer tied to the further evolution of these institutions. Instead, what mattered was the degree to which political institutions came to reflect the interests of domestic modernizing non-landed elites in their trade and investment policies and in the economic institutions they adopted in agriculture and industry. As among the nineteenth-century latecomers, the critical institutional forces for developing countries at this level of development were the effectiveness of government initiatives in overall economic planning and coordination and in the reform of economic institutions.

I suspect that the near future will see a much greater impact of both technological and institutional change on developing countries. Neither the new biotechnologies nor the new communication and information technologies have as
yet had a significant impact on the world economy and on less developed
countries. These technological innovations are likely to have major effects on
technical change and comparative advantage, with both positive and negative
consequences for less developed countries. The diffusion of these innovations
will also lead to new institutions for international trade and factor movements as
well as to new institutions for managing globalized manufacturing production.
Thus, were we to compare 20 years from now the sources of growth of less
developed countries with those in the nineteenth century, we would find greater
similarities. It is even quite conceivable that in 20 years we may conclude that
technological and institutional changes have been more significant sources of
growth in currently less developed countries than they were in the nineteenth
century. In short, the contemporary Prometheus is still in shackles and has not
yet been unbound.

Which expectations based on nineteenth-century growth were borne out by the
Third World experience during the first quarter-century of development?

First, growth patterns in the Third World have exhibited a similar variety in
patterns as in the nineteenth century. Where the same pattern has been repeated,
it has had much the same consequences qualitatively. The primary export pattern has been rather less successful than it was in the nineteenth century; export
expansion, the growth of manufacturing exports from developing countries, and
growth rates of per capita GNP have been significantly higher; and some
nineteenth-century patterns have been missing. Flexibility in institutional and
policy responses has been just as critical to sustained developing country growth
as it was in the nineteenth century.

Second, institutional development has been just as important to economic
development as in the nineteenth century. But the diffusion of market-oriented
growth has not had as strong a positive impact in the initial phases of rapid
export expansion, except in agriculture, where it has been a major force for
change. Widening the process of economic growth has required weakening the
power of traditional elites, just as in the nineteenth century, but historical
expectations concerning specific alternative power structures' helping to widen
economic growth do not mesh with recent Third World experience. Expectations concerning the negative impact of heavy foreign dependence are borne out
in broad outline but not in detail, since the specific forms of dependence are
different now.

Third, technical progress has been less influential in the growth of developing
countries than it was in the nineteenth century, in part because the technology

transferred has been less revolutionary than in the nineteenth century, in part because the capital intensity of technology has been high, and in part because macroeconomic constraints have led to stop-go policy regimes.

Fourth, historical expectations about the crucial importance to growth of governments and international trade have been borne out. Export-led growth was quite potent in inducing growth during the regime of high world trade growth up to 1973. But in contrast to the nineteenth century, export-led growth has been a better policy in manufacturing than in primary exports. The consequences of government-led growth have spanned the spectrum, with government failure rivaling market failure as a source of stagnation, misallocation of resources, and maldistribution of the fruits of growth.

On the whole, our nineteenth-century Rip Van Winkle would not be surprised by the contrasts with nineteenth-century development. There is broad agreement on the nature of the general processes and moving forces. Some of the specific differences that have emerged may well be temporary, and all of them can be explained as a result of changing circumstances and differences in initial conditions. Indeed, given the vastly varied initial conditions and circumstances facing today's Third World, he might well be astounded by the extent of similarity.

References

Adelman, I., and C. T. Morris. 1967. *Society, Politics, and Economic Development: A Quantitative Approach.* Baltimore: Johns Hopkins University Press.

——— 1984. "Patterns of Economic Growth, 1850–1914, or Chenery-Syrquin in Historical Perspective." In *Economic Structure and Performance,* ed. M. Syrquin, L. Taylor, and L. Westphal. Orlando, Fla.: Academic Press.

Adelman, I., J.-B. Lohmoller, and C. T. Morris. 1988. "A Latent Variable Regression Model of Nineteenth-Century Economic Development." Giannini Foundation Working Paper no. 439. University of California, Berkeley.

Anderson, P. 1974. *Lineages of the Absolutist State.* London: New Left Books.

Chenery, H., and M. Syrquin. 1975. *Patterns of Development, 1950–1970.* London: Oxford University Press.

Chenery, H., S. Robinson, and M. Syrquin. 1986. *Industrialization and Growth: A Comparative Study.* London: Oxford University Press.

Kalecki, M. 1971. *Selected Essays on the Dynamics of the Capitalist Economy.* Cambridge: Cambridge University Press.

Kuznets, S. S. 1968. *Toward a Theory of Economic Growth with "Reflections on the Economic Growth of Nations."* New York: Norton.

Landes, D. S. 1969. *The Unbound Prometheus: Technological Change and Industrial Development in Western Europe from 1750 to the Present.* Cambridge: Cambridge University Press.

Lewis, A. W. 1954. "Economic Development with Unlimited Supplies of Labour." *Manchester School of Economic and Social Studies* 22:139–191.

Marshall, A. 1920. *Principles of Economics.* London: Macmillan.

Morris, C. T., and I. Adelman. 1988. *Comparative Patterns of Economic Growth*. Baltimore: Johns Hopkins University Press.

North, D. C., and R. B. Thomas. 1970. "An Economic Theory of Growth of the Western World." *Economic History Review* 23, 2nd ser.:1–17.

Nurkse, R. 1953. *Problems of Capital Formation in Underdeveloped Countries*. Oxford: Oxford University Press.

Polanyi, K. 1944. *The Great Transformation: The Political and Economic Origins of Our Time*. Boston: Beacon Paperback.

Robinson, J. 1956. *Accumulation of Capital*. London: Macmillan.

Rosenstein-Rodan, P. N. 1943. "Problems of Industrialization in Eastern and Southeastern Europe." *Economic Journal* 53:205–217.

Rostow, W. W. 1960. *The Stages of Economic Growth: A Non-Communist Manifesto*. Cambridge: Cambridge University Press.

Thomas, B. 1973. *Migration and Economic Growth: A Study of Great Britain and the Atlantic Economy*. Cambridge: Cambridge University Press.

Westphal, L. E., L. Kim, and C. J. Dahlman. 1985. "Reflections on Korea's Acquisition of Technological Capability." In *International Technology Transfer: Concepts, Measures, and Comparisons*, ed. N. Rosenberg and C. Frischtak, pp. 167–221. New York: Praeger.

18

∙ ∙ ∙

Marriage Bars:
Discrimination against Married Women Workers
from the 1920s to the 1950s

Claudia Goldin

The participation of married women in the American labor force has expanded since 1920, slowly at first but with continued acceleration after World War II.[1] Many of the forces that eventually effected change—increased education, a markedly reduced birth rate, and the emergence of the clerical sector—were apparent as early as the 1920s. Yet the process was extremely protracted. Conditions in the 1930s had much to do with the slowness of change in the economic role of women, but the impact of the depression often worked through preexisting social norms and other restrictions.

Many offices and school boards during the first two decades of this century adopted "marriage bars," by which married women were not hired and single women who married were fired. The bar against those who married while in service was the more restrictive of the two because women in the 1920s were just beginning to extend their working time after marriage. The bar against hiring married women was somewhat ancillary; one could hardly fire a woman who married while in service yet hire a married woman. But the older married woman who sought white-collar employment was in an extreme minority in the 1920s, in part because changes in education and fertility primarily affected cohorts born after 1900. Furthermore, older women in the 1920s lacked prior work experience in the clerical sector, which was often a precondition for work in the field.

The majority of young women in the 1920s left the work force at the precise time of marriage, and most who did not left soon thereafter. Firms were therefore reluctant to keep recently married women, who might treat their jobs as temporary positions, and had little motivation to accommodate the rare older married woman who might want employment. The cost to firms of firing women who married was low because the ancillary rule barring all married women entailed little sacrifice. Costs were further minimized by the types of occupa-

511

tions routinely offered women. In the majority of offices women were easily replaced by other female workers. Jobs in the clerical sector were highly segregated by sex—men were routinely barred from some occupations, women from others. Thus firms did not lose much by having policies that required them to dismiss women when they married. With little to lose and everything to gain, a substantial percentage of firms instituted a marriage bar prior to the Great Depression, and many extended the bar as a socially acceptable means of rationing employment during the 1930s.

Discrimination against married women and older workers came rather cheaply to firms in the period before World War II: the reduction in supply was small, and the loss in training was mitigated by the limited kinds of positions women were offered. Firms also perceived that there were gains to policies that guaranteed homogeneity across sex, race, age, and marital status within occupations. But many aspects of this equilibrium were deceptively fragile and were to change radically in the 1950s.

The 1950s mark a sharp break in the way the labor market accommodated married women, older women, and women with household responsibilities. I do not mean to imply that all discrimination disappeared or that child-care centers flourished. But one must not forget that prior to 1950 the marriage bar expanded and part-time work was exceptionally rare. After 1950 the marriage bar vanished almost entirely (except for flight attendants)[2] and part-time work became widespread. The factors that account for these changes amount to nothing short of a revolution in the demographics of labor supply.[3]

Three-quarters of all female workers around 1900, and over one-half in the (nonwar) years prior to 1950, were single. Not surprisingly, they were exceptionally young. Their median age was only around 22 in 1900, but it increased to over 36 by 1950. Employers in the 1920s and 1930s routinely hired only inexperienced high school girls; ''Younger, untrained people direct from [high] school prove more satisfactory'' was the frequent response of personnel officers.[4] They had little reason to look elsewhere. Young single women flooded the labor market in those years; they were docile, educated, and had few home responsibilities. The labor market for women workers was organized to accommodate the young and was structured around the presumption that women would remain at work only until marriage.

Demographic shifts of the 1920s and 1930s made many changes inevitable. The decreased birth rate meant the population had to age in the coming years and the supply of young women and female high school graduates had to decline as a proportion of the population. The squeeze in labor supply was further exacerbated by a related change—the post–World War II increase in marriages and the baby boom.[5] Fewer young women were available for employment after the late 1940s, and those who might have been were marrying earlier and having larger families. For all these reasons the supply of young single female workers simply dried up.

The inversion in labor supply was accompanied by a mounting desire of older married women to seek gainful employment. The young women of the 1910s and 1920s who left high school and took clerical positions eventually became the older married women of the 1930s and 1940s. They were past child-rearing age, besides having few children by historical comparison, and they had skills and work experience. In the absence of the depression they would surely have increased their labor force participation earlier than the 1950s; their notable participation during World War II creates a prima facie case for that counterfactual.

By the 1950s firms could no longer ignore older married women, and certain aspects of the workplace were accommodated to their needs. The marriage bar, which had at its height affected 75 percent of all local school boards and over 50 percent of all office workers, was virtually abandoned. The rhetoric of the workplace changed as well. Where a married woman was once the anomaly and was perceived to be inefficient, she was now seen as the perfect employee. In the mid-1950s one personnel director, whose firm had previously barred married women, praised older women's "maturity and steadiness"; another noted, "They are more reliable than the younger ones" (1957 Hussey Report: Penn Mutual Life Insurance Co., August 22, 1956, Brown Instrument, March 29, 1957). But before the accommodations can be discussed, the prohibitions and their rationale must be addressed.

Prohibitions against the Employment of Married Woman

Discrimination against women can be revealed in a variety of ways. In its most typical and pervasive form, no prescribed barriers exist. Rather, employers, employees, and customers can express their prejudices against women workers by preferring not to associate with them. The existence of this type of discrimination is often inferred from its effects on earnings and occupations. Prescribed barriers against the training and employment of women are more easily observed forms of discrimination. Rules can exist barring the education and training of women, as was the case in the professions of law and medicine and among certain medieval guilds and more modern unions.[6] In other circumstances, rules restrict the employment of women, as in the armed forces, post office, local fire departments, and legal profession. The distinction between the two types of discrimination—the more or less subtle revealing of preferences and the rather obvious prohibitions—is often blurred when written rules do not exist but custom dictates the result.

Bars concerning the hiring and firing of married women arose in teaching and clerical work from the late 1800s to the early 1900s and provide the most numerically significant form of all prohibitions in their impact on the employment of married women. The occupations covered by the prohibitions were to become the most frequently encountered positions for married women during the post-1950s era. In 1920 just 11 percent of all married women in the labor force were teachers and clerical workers, but the figure practically quadrupled over the next half-century, reaching 41 percent by 1970. In contrast, prohibitions against the employment of women as doctors and lawyers, probably the best known of all bans, affected a trivial percentage of women.[7]

Prohibitions against the employment of married women consisted generally of two bans—one against the hiring of married women and a second concerning the retention of existing workers when they married. I will refer to the first ban as the *hire bar* and to the second as the *retain bar*. It was uncommon for a firm to hire married women but fire single women when they married, but the reverse frequently occurred. That is, firms with single women in their employ might choose to retain a woman when she married but not hire one already married. If firms could effectively screen workers for certain traits, or if they invested considerably in training their workers, firing existing workers could be costly. Some firms and many school boards allowed women who married in service to remain with the organization as temporary workers or substitute teachers, who could be dismissed at will and whose salaries were not based on tenure. Firms often imposed both the retain bar and the hire bar. It was rare, however, for a firm to impose the same prohibitions on men.[8]

Extent of the Marriage Bar

The extent of the bans across the entire economy have been difficult to assess. These were, after all, the policies of individual firms and, in the case of school boards, individual localities. Prohibitions against the employment of married women teachers are the easiest to track through comprehensive surveys of local school boards by the National Education Association (NEA) beginning in the late 1920s.

Marriage bars were instituted in public school teaching sometime in the late 1800s and were expanded in the early 1900s. Extensive surveys of local school boards, which began in 1928, indicate that 61 percent of all school boards would not hire a married woman teacher and 52 percent would not retain any who married while under contract (see Table 18.1). Because the data are grouped in the NEA reports by size of locality, Table 18.1 also weights the percentages by population. The unweighted data are generally higher than the

Table 18.1 Marriage bars among school boards, 1928–1951, and firms hiring office workers, 1920s and 1930s (in percent).

	Do not retain single women when married		Do not hire married women	
	Weighted	Not weighted	Weighted	Not weighted
Teachers				
1928	47.3	52.2	61.9	61.0
1930–31	52.2	62.9	72.2	76.6
1942	58.4	70.0	77.7	87.0
1950–51	9.4	10.0	19.5	18.0

Office workers	Do not retain		Do not hire	
Year (no. of observations)	Weighted	Not weighted	Weighted	Not weighted
1920s (178)	25.0	12.0	36.0	29.2
Philadelphia (44)	26.4	14.3	40.4	31.8
1930s				
Philadelphia (106)	26.6	23.6	41.1	50.9
Kansas City (83)	28.4	15.7	41.7	31.3
Los Angeles (139)	9.4	8.6	24.4	15.8

	Do not retain (policy and discretionary)		Do not hire (policy and discretionary)	
	Weighted	Not weighted	Weighted	Not weighted
1920s	34.7	27.3	51.7	52.8
Philadelphia	36.9	35.7	60.7	59.1
1930s				
Philadelphia	34.5	34.9	58.5	60.4
Kansas City	46.0	30.1	57.8	43.4
Los Angeles	25.1	15.7	38.8	26.6

Sources: Teachers: National Education Association (1928, 1932, 1942, 1952), from citations in Oppenheimer (1976). Office workers: 1931, 1940 Office Worker Survey, Firm Records (see data appendix).

Notes: Teachers: Weighted figures use city population weights; the unweighted are simple averages by number of school boards, independent of population. City population weights are from Bureau of the Census, 1975. Office workers: Weighted figures are weighted by the firm's female employment; the unweighted are simple averages across firms in the sample. The 1920s sample includes Chicago, Hartford, New York City, and Philadelphia. Where possible, the responses apply to practices predating the depression, although the interviews were conducted in 1931–32. The 1930s sample includes Los Angeles, Kansas City, and Philadelphia and refers to practices during the Great Depression (interviews were conducted in 1939). "Discretionary" means that firms stated that single women were preferred, married women were placed on special probation, or policy was up to the department head.

weighted data, reflecting the fact that large cities had proportionately fewer bars. Both types of bars increased during the depression, and on the eve of American entry into World War II, fully 87 percent of all school boards had the hire bar and 70 percent the retain bar. But sometime during World War II both bars disappeared. By 1951 only 18 percent of the school boards had the hire bar and 10 percent the retain bar.

The extent of the marriage bar in office work can be inferred from information in two comprehensive surveys conducted by the Women's Bureau (1931 Office Worker Survey, Firm Records; 1940 Office Worker Survey, Firm Records; see data appendix). Original firm-level manuscripts from these surveys reveal much about the nature of the bans and their origin. The earlier one, taken in 1931, yields information about the 1920s and the later one, taken in 1940, covers the changes during the Great Depression.[9]

The 1931 survey sampled mainly large firms in seven cities, of which 178 firms in Chicago, New York, Philadelphia, and Hartford are included here. The 1940 survey was taken in five cities and sampled a wider range of firms; the sample here includes 328 firms in Kansas City, Los Angeles, and Philadelphia. Only Philadelphia is included in both surveys. The firms in the 1931 survey include insurance companies, investment houses, banks, publishing firms, advertising companies, public utilities, and mail order firms. Added to the 1940 survey are manufacturing firms, retail stores, wholesale outlets, small professional offices, and firms in the transportation and communications sector.[10]

Both surveys contain information of a rather confidential nature regarding firm personnel practices—occupations offered only to women and to men separately, discrimination against blacks and Jews, the retention of single women when they married, the barring of married women, the use of salary scales, promotion from within, and minimum and maximum age limits. Information of this type would be virtually impossible to obtain in today's litigious environment. But personnel officers and other firm managers interviewed by the Women's Bureau were exceptionally candid, as their remarks indicate.[11] The surveys also contain more mundane personnel matters: the numbers of female and male employees, number of new employees, hours of work, personnel benefits (retirement plan, group insurance), union activity, the bureaucratic organization of the firm, and various paternalistic practices. Because the two surveys were executed by the same government agency (the Women's Bureau of the Department of Labor) they bear a striking resemblance, although the one for 1940 is more comprehensive.[12]

In the 1920s about 12 percent of all firms in the sample had a formal policy of not retaining single women when they married (see Table 18.1), but 25 percent of all female employees were in firms having such a policy. The policy, therefore, increased with firm size. Some firms did not have a strict marriage bar policy, but had discretionary rules allowing them to retain able workers, to hire married women when single ones were unavailable, or to leave the policy up to department heads. These I have termed the "discretionary" cases. About 35 percent of all female employees were working in firms that would not retain them as a condition of both policy and discretion. Considerably more firms had policies against hiring married women than against the retention of single women who married. About 29 percent of all firms had such policies in the 1920s and the policies affected 36 percent of all female employees across these firms. Over 50 percent of all firms and all female employees were affected by the dismissal of women when they married as a condition of policy and discretion.[13]

The policy of firing and hiring married women varied considerably by the type of firm and by firm size (see Table 18.2). Insurance offices, publishing firms, banks, and public utilities had the most extensive controls in the 1920s; insurance offices, banks, public utilities, and the office portion of manufacturing firms had the most in the 1930s. Large firms, measured by the number of female employees, were more likely to institute such policies than were small firms for both years.[14] Although the marriage bar policy varied considerably by city for the 1930s sample, it did not for the 1920s sample, given the industrial distribution.

The data in Tables 18.1 and 18.2 suggest some increase in the marriage bar policy during the Great Depression. But the extent and even the existence of the increase is difficult to discern because the 1931 survey, which yields the data for the 1920s, included only large firms, and the industrial distribution of firms as well as the cities covered changed over the two surveys. The data in Table 18.2 that array policies by size of firm show some increase over time, particularly for the marriage bar as policy. The Kansas City and Philadelphia percentages for the retain and hire bars in the 1930s are, with one exception, larger than the average for the 1920s, but the Los Angeles data are not (see Table 18.1).[15]

One way of handling the problem of composition is to pool the two samples and include firm size, industry, and city dummy variables, and a year variable to estimate the impact of the depression. Equations estimated in this fashion exhibit a positive, large, and significant effect of the depression, in the case of the hire and the retain bar as policy. But the discretionary-policy version of both the hire and retain bars did not change over time.[16] The depression, it seems, led firms to extend a discretionary marriage bar into the realm of firm policy. Where firms had exercised discretion in the hiring and firing of married women before the depression, they instituted strict policies not to hire and not to retain married women in the 1930s.

Philadelphia was the only city sampled in both years and provides further evidence for the extension of the marriage bar during the depression. Of the 41 firms in the 1920s sample, 23 were also sampled by the Women's Bureau in the

Table 18.2 Marriage bars by sector and size of firm, clerical sector.

Size of firm (no. of female clerical employees)	Policy		Policy and discretionary		Distribution	
	Do not hire	Do not retain	Do not hire	Do not retain	Firms	Female employees
1920s						
11–20	0.0%	0.0%	0.0%	0.0%	1.1%	0.1%
21–50	25.9	10.9	46.7	21.0	27.5	3.3
51–100	40.4	8.4	63.5	28.9	24.2	6.0
101–200	17.4	3.5	41.8	26.0	18.5	9.4
201–400	31.0	22.2	59.5	47.5	11.8	11.3
401–700	39.0	32.2	89.8	45.7	5.1	8.6
701 and more	39.5	30.4	45.6	33.5	11.8	61.3
No. of observations					178	51,597
1930s (Kansas City and Philadelphia)						
11–20	41.0%	17.9%	43.6%	25.6%	24.2%	3.7%
21–50	43.6	18.2	49.1	25.5	34.2	11.2
51–100	46.9	25.0	65.6	56.3	19.9	15.7
101–200	50.0	25.0	75.0	43.8	9.9	13.8
201–400	62.5	50.0	62.5	62.5	5.0	12.0
401 and more	27.3	18.2	54.5	27.3	6.8	43.6
No. of observations					161	25,358

Sector	Policy		Policy and discretionary		No. of firms
	Do not hire	Do not retain	Do not hire	Do not retain	
1920s					
Insurance	61.1%	45.7%	73.2%	59.5%	58
Publishing	37.0	34.7	56.1	36.0	34
Banking	35.4	21.2	41.9	30.2	27
Public utilities	32.9	13.5	93.9	42.9	13
Investment	11.3	1.4	26.6	9.8	27
Advertising	11.1	0.0	28.2	0.0	13
1930s (Kansas City and Philadelphia)[a]					
Insurance	50.0%	42.3%	53.8%	53.8%	26
Publishing	33.3	13.3	46.7	33.3	15
Banking	54.5	9.1	72.7	45.4	11
Public utilities	50.0	33.3	66.7	50.0	6
Investment	16.7	16.7	50.0	16.7	6
Manufacturing	57.6	22.0	67.8	37.3	59
Sales	17.2	10.3	24.1	13.8	29

Sources: Teachers: National Education Association (1928, 1932, 1942, 1952), from citations in Oppenheimer (1976). Office workers: 1931, 1940 Office Worker Survey, Firm Records (see data appendix).

[a] Includes only firms with more than nine female employees, for comparability with 1920s.

1930s survey. Of these 23 firms, 11 experienced no change in policy, 2 reversed their prohibitions, and fully 10, or 43 percent, increased their prohibitions.[17]

The marriage bar, in both the retain and hire versions, therefore predated the depression, but was expanded during the 1930s among local school boards and firms hiring office workers. Marriage bars have been mistakenly portrayed as originating in the unemployment of the 1930s, but the depression only reinforced and extended bans against the employment of married women (see, for example, Scharf 1980). The extensions, however, often took the form of government regulations that greatly strengthened preexisting social norms and conventions.

Federal Order 213, passed in 1932 as part of the Federal Economy Act, mandated that executive branch officials, in the face of layoffs, fire workers whose spouses were employed by the federal government. The regulation almost always entailed the firing of married women, although many husbands could also have been furloughed. By 1940, 26 states had proposed legislation to restrict married women's employment and 9 others had some form of restriction already in place (Shallcross 1940). Similar regulations became effective among various local governments and served to expand the group of affected occupations to include librarians and nurses, although they too were probably covered by prohibitions prior to the depression.[18]

Federal Order 213 and the actions of state and local government lent credibility to predepression policies of businesses and local school boards and enabled the extension of a system already in place. The bar was extended to occupations, such as nurse and librarian, and to sectors, such as manufacturing, where it was not extensively used before the depression. It is inconceivable that marriage bars could have gained such wide acceptance during the depression had it not been for previous policies and the social consensus built around them. But the depression did more than sanction the bans. It helped extend them and reinforced social norms that kept married women, particularly the emerging middle class, out of the labor force.

Explaining the Marriage Bar

Social consensus has so often been built around barring the employment of married women that the original reason for the marriage bar has been obscured. The bans arose in various occupations at a time when single women were just extending the period of time they planned to stay in the labor force after marriage and when a small but growing number of married women were deciding to enter the labor force. The vast majority of married women in the period before 1940 (at least 81 percent for the group aged 40 to 49) left the labor force at the precise time of marriage, and few would again work for pay until they were considerably older.[19] Thus, prior to the advent of the marriage bars there were few older married women in the labor force and even fewer, proportionately, in the occupations that would eventually be covered by the bans. Marriage bars, at the time of their initial adoption, did not appreciably reduce the supply of married women to the covered occupations. The affected group, for the immediate time period, consisted of young single women who were contemplating marriage in the near future.

A frequently encountered interpretation of these prohibitions involves discrimination against educated, middle-class married women, particularly native-born and white women (see, for example, Kessler-Harris 1981). The covered occupations, teaching and clerical work, almost always required a high school education, and thus many have claimed that the bans were intended to limit the employment of educated, middle-class married women. Female operatives in manufacturing, waitresses, and domestic servants, on the other hand, were often foreign-born or black, and their positions were generally unaffected by marriage bans. In this view, the bans served to maintain a threatened status quo, keeping middle-class women in the home to take care of their families, and were a reaffirmation of a legal and social system characterized by patriarchy.

Another explanation of bans is that employers in firms with rigid wage systems tied to their workers' seniority desired a young, inexperienced work force, particularly in times of unemployment. When managers are unable to set wage scales for separate jobs, as might be the case when there is a strong union, certain positions could have earnings that rise more rapidly than productivity. At some point, therefore, earnings for certain individuals will exceed their productivity, and the firm will want to terminate their employment. Routine clerical work in large-scale firms provides a possible instance in which the job was simple, repetitive, and not accompanied by a continued increase in productivity with experience. The marriage bar was a socially acceptable way of terminating the employment of women whose wages would eventually exceed their addition to firm revenue.

The hypothesis is explored in Samuel Cohn's (1985) fine study of occupational sex-typing, with examples drawn from the experiences of two large and unique British firms: the Great Western Railway and the General Post Office.[20] Both organizations had strong unions, tenure-based wage systems for all workers, and large numbers of routine jobs for women only. Both firms offered substantial dowries to women who married after at least six years of company service. According to Cohn, the dowries were meant to encourage young women to marry and thus leave the firm, in the face of their rising real wages but constant productivity. These two organizations, Cohn claims, used tenure-based wages for all positions, but had to reconcile the constraint with their need for low-wage workers to perform routine tasks. They accomplished this by hiring young women who would be terminated in about six to ten years in a socially acceptable manner—by retirement at marriage.[21]

Each of the reasons presented does not fit all the facts for the American case over the first half of the twentieth century. Marriage bars were often put in place in the clerical sector during the 1920s, well before the unemployment of the depression, and they ended abruptly during the 1950s when older married women began to provide a larger proportion of the female labor supply. They were adopted in the absence of strong labor unions, as opposed to the British case, and by firms with highly sex-segregated labor forces, often with gender-based salary scales. There were considerably more firms with bans against the hiring of married women than against the retention of single women who married. Thus it appears that many firms wanted to screen women prior to marriage but did not want to lose skilled and trusted employees. In fact, the sectors with the most restrictive policies often had female employees with the longest tenure.[22]

Marriage bars constituted an odd form of discrimination against women. The covered occupations were almost always female-intensive ones, so it might even be said that women as a group were not discriminated against. It has been asserted that the bars were discriminatory, because by upholding outmoded norms, they impeded social change. But the bars do not appear to have been policies to realign a threatened status quo. Although social consensus was formed around the rules, the dominant underlying rationale was not necessarily a prejudice against middle-class married women's working. Rather, the rationale can be discerned through an investigation of firm-level records for which information exists on whether the firm had the retain bar, the hire bar, or both, as well as other characteristics, such as the number of employees, the existence of various personnel policies, hours of work, and the growth rate of the firm.

Firm-Level Evidence for the 1920s and 1930s

The correlates of the policy of not retaining single women at the time of marriage (retain) are explored in Table 18.3. For both the 1920s and 1930s samples, there is a positive yet weak relationship between the number of employees in the firm and the probability of not retaining women who marry (also see Table 18.2 on the effect of firm size). But in both samples, the magnitude of the impact of firm size declines when factors concerning personnel relations are included. Size, therefore, is merely a proxy here for the internal structure of firms and related employee policies. Firms having a policy of internal promotion, fixed salary scales, or regular salary increments with time on the job (promote) had a higher probability of not retaining single women upon marriage. The probability also increases with policies that set a maximum age for new hires (maximum age) and with the existence of pensions (pensions); yet it decreases with unionization for the 1930s (union), contrary to the inference from the British case. Furthermore, the lower the number of scheduled hours per week (hours), and the smaller the growth rate of the firm for the 1930s (growth), the greater the probability of not retaining single women.

Firms almost always had a maximum age policy if they had a regular internal promotion ladder, and the policy was generally in effect for both men and women. Another variable related to internal promotion was the existence of certain jobs for which only men would be considered (male only). Although some of these jobs were supervisory and others were professional, the vast majority were starting jobs, such as messenger, mail boy, and file clerk, and thus also indicate internal promotion ladders.[23]

The results imply that firms with established personnel practices regarding internal promotion and salary increments did not retain female employees when they married. Their policies, however, were tempered by the tightness of their labor market, so that firms with lower hours (possibly owing to work-sharing

Table 18.3 Explaining marriage bars: logit regressions for retain bar, 1920s and 1930s.

1920s retain	As policy		As policy and discretionary	
	Coefficient	Coefficient	Coefficient	Mean
	(1)	(2)	(3)	
No. of employees $\times 10^{-3}$	1.00	0.671	0.186	581
	(2.12)	(1.33)	(0.41)	
(No. of employees$^2 \times 10^{-7}$)	-1.26	-0.906	-0.58	
	(1.47)	(1.06)	(0.70)	
Promote	1.58	1.49	1.94	0.536
	(2.40)	(2.18)	(4.27)	
Maximum age		0.775	0.991	0.223
		(1.29)	(2.03)	
Pensions		1.32	0.892	0.289
		(2.32)	(1.99)	
Hours	-0.172	-0.228	-0.225	40.2
	(1.61)	(1.95)	(2.51)	
Constant	3.27	4.91	6.29	
	(0.76)	(1.05)	(1.77)	
Log likelihood ratio	-54.1	-46.6	-78.3	
No. of observations	174	166	166	
Mean of dependent variable (unweighted)	0.121	0.120	0.289	

Table 18.3 (continued)

1930s retain	As policy		As policy and discretionary	
	Coefficient	Coefficient	Coefficient	Mean
No. of employees $\times 10^{-3}$	1.90	0.671	0.382	149
	(1.20)	(1.33)	(0.77)	
(No. of employees$^2 \times 10^{-6}$)	−1.41			
	(1.20)			
Promote	0.593	0.155	0.227	0.347
	(1.64)	(0.37)	(0.65)	
Maximum age		1.12	1.03	0.151
		(2.62)	(2.73)	
Pensions		1.11	0.724	0.188
		(2.32)	(1.85)	
Union		−0.845	−1.10	0.074
		(1.01)	(1.54)	
Male only		0.340	0.593	0.450
		(0.90)	(1.93)	
Hours	−0.170	−0.110	−0.093	40.4
	(2.46)	(1.42)	(1.46)	
Growth		−1.93	−2.05	0.162
		(1.20)	(1.61)	
Constant	4.65	2.51	2.67	
	(1.68)	(0.78)	(1.01)	
Log likelihood ratio	−126.7	−99.5	−135.3	
No. of observations	317	271	271	
Mean of dependent variable (unweighted)	0.151	0.151	0.258	

Sources: Teachers: National Education Association (1928, 1932, 1942, 1952), from citations in Oppenheimer (1976). Office workers: 1931, 1940 Office Worker Survey, Firm Records (see data appendix).

Notes: Promote = 1 if policy of firm was to promote from within or if there were graded salary steps or annual increases in salary; maximum age = 1 if the firm had a stated maximum age for new hires; pensions = 1 if the firm had a pension plan; union = 1 if the firm's office workers were unionized; male only = 1 if the firm had at least one job from which women were excluded by policy; hours = normal weekly hours of office workers; growth = (new hires in 1939) / (employment in 1939). Means refer to the regression in the last column. Dummy variables for cities and a variable indicating whether salary grades were used are also included in the 1930s regression. Absolute values of *t*-statistics are in parentheses.

policies) and lower growth rates were more likely to have the marriage bar.[24]

The coefficients on most variables are sufficiently large to have greatly influenced the marriage bar policy. In the 1920s data, for example, a firm with 300 employees and a work week of 40 hours would stand a nearly negligible chance, 3.5 percent, of having the retain bar as policy. But had the firm, in addition, a policy of internal promotion, the probability would rise to 14.9

percent. If hours fell from 40 to 35, say, because of depressed economic conditions, the probability of the retain bar would rise further to 29.3 percent. In the 1930s data the same original firm, however, would have a 15.4 percent probability of the retain bar, increasing to 24.7 percent with a policy of internal promotion, and to 43.4 percent with a decrease in hours to 35 from the original 40. Thus the 1930s firms had a much greater chance of having the marriage bar independent of their personnel practices and hours. Furthermore, the impact of the promote variable is less for the 1930s data than for the 1920s data. The implied change in the probability of the retain bar with the internal promotion policy is 0.168 for the 1920s but 0.076 for the 1930s, computed around the means.[25]

All of this implies that during the depression, firms joined a bandwagon that had sanctioned the firing of women who married and their wholesale banning as employees. Some firms in the depression enacted the bar for reasons similar to those of firms in the 1920s, but many others, particularly in the manufacturing sector, were seeking ways to cope with employment cutbacks. They found precedent and consensus in discrimination against married women.

The presence of the maximum age policy raises further questions about the hiring of women. In some instances the policy was related to the existence of pensions or group insurance that were not experience-rated, and maximum age rules shielded the firm from paying out more to employees than had been accumulated.[26] The policy constrained both men and women searching for jobs in midlife, but provided greater restrictions for women who lacked continuity in the work force. For men, the new personnel practices often meant that tenure with firms was encouraged and frequently ensured. But for women, the new institutional arrangements became added bars to their initial entry at midlife.

The Women's Bureau schedules contain, in addition to the easily quantifiable information, comments of personnel directors and agents of the firms revealing their justifications for marriage bar policies. The reasons elicited for the marriage bars often confound the firms' actual constraints, individual prejudices, and societal norms. Some firms expressed concern that women who married while in their employ might become less efficient because they would leave in the near future. A personnel officer in a Philadelphia insurance firm noted that although his firm had no official policy, he would prefer that women leave on marriage because "they were less efficient after marriage—too much temporary didn't care attitude" (1931 Office Worker Survey, Firm Records, Indemnity Insurance Company of North American, Philadelphia). Other agents, concerned that by firing women who married they would lose valued employees, put them on probation. A Philadelphia bank official stated that "those who marry are told that the company reserves the right to dismiss them at any time so that those whose work deteriorates after marriage can be dispensed with" (1931 Office

Worker Survey, Firm Records, Provident Trust Company, Philadelphia). Some firms actually reversed earlier bars, such as Philadelphia's Provident Mutual, which had a bar in 1924 but found that "too many valuable [employees] were lost" (1931 Office Worker Survey, Firm Records, Provident Mutual Life Insurance, Philadelphia).

Most officers, however, gave no rationale for their policies, and a few offered personal reasons. An agent in the publishing industry noted that "men are too selfish and should have to support their wives," and another thought "personally that married women should plan to be in their homes if possible" (1931 Office Worker Survey, Firm Records, F. A. Davis Company, Presbyterian Board of Christian Education, Philadelphia). Many personnel officers and other agents appeared to take great pride in answering that their firms gave preference to married men in hiring and in salaries, and to married women whose husbands were unemployable. After all, social consensus in the 1930s labor market was built around rationing jobs by need, the notion that men should earn a "family wage," and norms circumscribing the economic role of married women.

One surprising aspect of the comments is that various firms did mention that they gave small dowries or vacations when female employees married, but these were always firms that retained women who married and hired married women. In Hartford, where most insurance companies had both the hire and retain bars, Phoenix Mutual Life, which had no policy, had a "special wedding vacation" (1931 Office Worker Survey, Firm Records). It does not appear, then, that firms encouraged young women to marry, as was the inference from the British data, in the same manner that pensions encourage retirement.

Marriage bars therefore were instituted by large firms, with centralized hiring, promotion from within, and salary schedules that were often fixed. Such evidence points to the role of salaries based on tenure with the firm, internal labor markets, and modern employment practices among large firms in sectors hiring clerical workers. This still leaves open the possibility, raised in the British case, that firms wanted to encourage turnover when productivity rose less rapidly than earnings but when the earnings schedule increased continuously with experience. But that does not appear to have been the case. Salaries did not increase considerably with tenure; increments, moreover, were gender-specific; and many firms that had no bar encouraged marriage. Instead, a related possibility seems more plausible.

Productivity in the workplace may have declined or been perceived to decline with marriage. The decline in productivity may have been caused by the fact that most women who did not leave the labor force at the time of marriage left soon after. Many of these women may have been unwilling in their temporary capacities to accept the routine, discipline, and monotony that office work entailed. A firm might gain by uniformly dismissing women at the time of marriage rather than singling some out later to fire, if the costs of the policy were sufficiently low. Circumstances of the 1920s, and to an even greater degree those of the 1930s, much reduced the costs. Furthermore, various personnel policies rendered rules, rather than discretion, the preferable route regarding the dismissal of workers.

Firms often adopt internal promotion, fixed salary scales, and benefit packages to conserve on supervision costs and encourage efficiency and effort among employees (see, for example, Lazear 1979; Lazear and Rosen 1981). Discretionary firing could result in greater wage demands to compensate employees for the increased probability of being terminated. In various incentive-based models of the labor market (Lazear 1981, 1979; Bulow and Summers 1986) employees base their salary demands on the expected probability of being furloughed. The gains from having rules rather than discretion increase if the reduction in labor supply from curtailing the employment of married women is small.

Therefore, the bar against retaining women at marriage emerged from the various policies of modern personnel departments. These policies made discretionary firing costly, and resulted in salary scales and promotion procedures that severed the relationship between wages and productivity. The ban eliminated the potential for any supervisor to fire a married woman whose actual or perceived productivity declined. The same firms almost always then instituted a ban against the employment of married women per se.

Complementary Evidence from Local School Boards

The experience of school boards with the marriage bar echoes that of firms hiring clerical workers, although the evidence is at a more aggregated level. Sometime in the early twentieth century, school boards instituted contractual obligations with teachers and fixed salary schedules. Although the precise timing is not clear, bars against the hiring and retention of married women appear to be linked to these arrangements.[27] Salary schedules varied widely across the thousands of American school boards by the stipulation of minimum and maximum salaries, salary increments, and thus the number of years of possible increase. By 1923 the vast majority of school boards had adopted a salary schedule, and the average elementary school teacher would have taken six to eight years to achieve maximum salary (see National Education Association 1923). School boards realized that experience alone was but one consideration, and the schedules were further complicated by provisions for increases with training and summer school, and for off-scale increments called supermaximum salaries.

The stated purpose of salary schedules was to elicit appropriate effort from teachers with a minimum of bickering. Because salary schedules did not rise limitlessly, it is unreasonable to presume that marriage bars were used to terminate employment of individuals whose productivity was maintained. Rather, it seems more likely, as in the case of office workers, that school boards wanted to avoid the problem of firing workers whose productivity declined. As in the case of office workers, the policy was pursued more vigorously when the potential labor supply of already married women seemed slender and when general economic conditions called for reductions in personnel.[28] It should also be noted that the legality of the marriage bar was often in doubt, and in 1941 courts in fully 22 states ruled the marriage bar "capricious and unjust."[29]

The firing of married schoolteachers was justified by contemporaries in various ways. There was a reason to fit anyone's prejudice, ranging from the moralistic (that married women with children should be at home taking care of their own) to the Victorian (that pregnant women would be objectionable in the classroom) to the economic (that married women were less efficient and became entrenched).[30] As in the case of office workers, the marriage bar for teachers was successful because most Americans could justify and rationalize it.

Thus the evidence from local school boards and firms hiring office workers suggest that marriage bars appeared when the cost of retaining or firing unproductive workers was high and when the potential sacrifice from limiting labor supply was low. The bars, interestingly, were rarely found among firms hiring factory operatives for whom piece-rate payment was often used (47 percent of all female operatives in the 1890s were on incentive pay) and for whom, therefore, the relationship between earnings and productivity was strictly maintained. The only important exception I have encountered is that of electrical machinery operatives (Schatz 1983) in two large manufacturing firms (General Electric and Westinghouse) both having extensive, modern personnel practices similar to those in office work.[31] The marriage bar was most often found among firms and sectors having internal promotion and regular salary advances, and among local school boards having fixed salary scales. The sectoral distribution creates a prima facie case that the marriage bar emerged when the relationship between pay and productivity was severed. There were few costs, and there was much to gain, from both forms of the marriage bar in the 1920s, and the possible benefit grew during the depression. But increased costs were lurking in the background.

The Decline of the Marriage Bar in the 1950s

The constraints facing firms changed considerably with World War II. No longer did they operate in an environment of unemployment. No longer could they bar the hiring of married women without placing formidable restrictions on their labor supply. Personnel policies quickly reflected these constraints. The new practices and the rhetoric accompanying them are revealed in original schedules of a 1957 study on personnel policies (Hussey 1958; called here the 1957 Hussey Report; see data appendix).

Older female workers in the mid-1950s were suddenly being praised for their maturity, reliability, neat appearance, and less chatty nature. Employers, particularly in the clerical sector, were pleased to "rehire those who . . . previously served in that capacity," as did Penn Mutual Life Insurance, which prior to World War II had a marriage bar. Scott Paper hired married women who could "offer skills gained earlier, before marriage," underscoring the finding that a woman's first occupation affected her chance of future employment (Goldin 1989).[32] But in retail trades, particularly in the suburbs, the older married woman with absolutely no previous training was now the "ideal employee"; the middle-class woman, "naturally courteous" and "well-bred," and who did not have to work was preferred by the major department stores (1957 Hussey Report: Lord and Taylor, October 30, 1956).

Not all personnel officers viewed the hiring of the older married woman with equanimity. There were detriments as well as benefits. In retail trade many older married women, "housewives who have never worked or have not worked for fifteen to twenty years, are found to be inexperienced in arithmetic and have difficulty in learning to operate the cash registers." In banking, "older women may work more slowly," but most added as well that "the type of service they can give a company is of great value" (1957 Hussey Report: Strawbridge and Clothier, November 14, 1956; Central-Penn National Bank, October 19, 1956).

Firms were still leery of hiring young married women, and some adopted a policy of not hiring those with small children or of firing women who became pregnant. The sequel to the marriage bar was the pregnancy bar. All in all, the best female employee was, in the words of a Sears, Roebuck officer, "a married woman with a mortgage on her house and her children partially raised" (1957 Hussey Report: Sears, Roebuck, and Company, November 7, 1956).

By the 1950s married women were welcomed employees in almost all the large, paternalistic companies that just prior to World War II had barred their hiring. The complete turnaround was the consquence of changes in a variety of constraints. The unemployment of the 1930s that compelled firms to ration jobs through means including the firing of married women had vanished and in its place was an extremely tight labor market. The young woman of two decades earlier, who gave a firm several years before marriage, was replaced by one who left school later and married earlier. Firm managers knew the constraints, although they often overstated them: "In the earlier years, the girl of 18 might work until she married at 23 or 24 . . . Now she is more likely to marry within

6 months or a year of starting work and resign within another'' (1957 Hussey Report: Fidelity Mutual, August 17, 1956). But it should also be remembered that the older married woman of the 1950s had been the young woman of the 1920s and 1930s. The point did not escape the attention of firm officers in the Hussey Report, who spoke of women returning to positions they held decades before. Despite their rusty mathematical skills, older married women of the 1950s were considerably better equipped to handle modern clerical and sales work than older married women had been in the 1920s.

Altered constraints were not the only factors that brought a shift in hiring practices. World War II awakened firms to the fact that bans against the hiring of married women were lessening their supply of female employees. The number of working women during World War II increased most among those over 45 years old. From March 1940 to July 1944, the peak of the wartime employment for women, those aged 45 to 64 increased in numbers by 165 percent and those over 64 by 197 percent; in contrast those 25 to 44 years old increased by only 128 percent (U.S. Bureau of the Census 1946).

The bans had little impact on potential labor supply in the early 1920s, when the majority of older married women would not have joined the labor force in any event. But the bans became considerably more binding and thus more restrictive as cohorts of educated young women advanced in age. By the 1940s many in the cohorts who had served as office workers when young were the mothers of grown children, and by the 1950s the vast majority of adult married women had high school diplomas. It had been easy in the 1920s for firms to issue blanket policies against the hiring of married women, but it was far harder in the 1950s for them to bar certain kinds of married women—those with young children, those with demanding husbands, and so on. So the bans were lifted, almost in their entirety, and the participation of married women in the American labor force advanced in the absence of perhaps the most blatant form of employment discrimination in the history of women's work.

The Long-Run Impact of the Marriage Bar

The bans restricted the participation of married women in the American economy in several senses. In the most obvious fashion they barred married women from employment in a variety of occupations during the first half of this century. But the marriage bars that preceded the Great Depression may have been less overtly and intentionally discriminatory than is apparent. As characterized in this paper, the bars were initially the result of an actual or perceived difference in the efficiency of young single and married female employees in firms with modern personnel practices. Such views were not necessarily formulated in an unbiased fashion. Discrimination against married women may have caused employers to have a jaundiced view of their productivity. Less harmless, in addition, were the social norms against their employment that preceded and fostered the bans, and the extension of both the bans and social norms during the Great Depression were a great setback to working women.

The immediate impact of the bans in the 1920s on the labor force participation of married women may have been trivial, but their longer-range effects were likely of great significance. Young women had little encouragement to invest in skills that were valued in the sectors covered by the bars. They might become typists and possibly machine operators, but they had less incentive to become accountants. The bars also prevented firms from recognizing the hidden labor supply of older married women. As the bars expanded in the late 1920s and during the depression, many married women who might otherwise have looked for employment were discouraged from doing so. As the potential pool of educated and experienced married women climbed, firms may have underestimated the costs of the marriage bar policy.

The bars in office work both before and during the depression restricted the employment of married women but did not block their hiring. Smaller firms without modern personnel practices hired married women and did not fire single women when they married. Sectors such as banking, insurance, and public utilities, however, were off limits to married women, as were a large percentage of local school boards around the country. For office workers these prohibitions often meant that married women were restricted from precisely those firms having internal promotion possibilities. While internal promotion was never substantial for women in any sector, the added restrictions lowered married women's rate of return to education. A sample of female clerical workers from the 1940 Women's Bureau survey reveals differences between married and single women's earnings, given years with the current employer, total job experience, education, and time spent between jobs in the home, among other relevant factors. Married and single women earned approximately the same on average, but the return to education varied by marital status. Returns were considerably lower for married women, so that while women with lower-than-average education received higher earnings if they were married, those with higher-than-average education received lower earnings. Returns to a year of education were 4.6 percent for single women but only 1 percent for married women.[33] The data suggest that married women were channeled into firms, sectors, and jobs for which education was of lower value, particularly within the internal promotion scheme.

The extensive movement to ration jobs during the Great Depression by firing married women can be blamed on the marriage bars that preceded 1929. Firms could hardly have built a solid consensus around the firing of married women had it not been for the marriage bars prior to the depression. The bars, through a peculiar quirk of history, were responsible for the numerous setbacks to women's employment during the depression. In these many ways, then, marriage bars served to delay the period of increased female labor force participation in America.

Data Appendix

Many of the data sets used in this paper were collected from original survey schedules, some located in the National Archives, Washington, D.C. They are described briefly to alert the reader to their origin, features, and readily available documentation. (I will be making these data sets accessible through the Inter-University Consortium for Political and Social Research at the University of Michigan.) I have also included here qualitative data. Each set has been given a short code name and is listed chronologically by that name. The date listed approximates that of the actual survey, not that of the published report.

1931 Office Worker Survey, Firm Records: National Archives, Record Group 86, Boxes 280–281 (see U.S. Department of Labor, Women's Bureau 1934). Only the firm-level records of this survey survive. The data came from "general interviews with the management on numbers of men and women employed, policies and practices as to hours of work, overtime, vacations, promotions, and welfare activities, restrictions based on age or marital status, kinds of office machines used, and effect of mechanization on employment in the preceding 5-year period" (p. 2). The firms covered in this survey are larger than those in the similar 1940 survey and include only banks, public utilities, insurance companies, investment houses, publishing companies, and advertising firms. Records for 178 firms in four cities (Chicago, Hartford, New York, and Philadelphia) were used, and information was coded on numbers of female and male office workers, scheduled hours, and personnel relations (whether firm hired married women, fired women if they married, had internal promotion, age restrictions, pensions, and group insurance). The comments of the interviewee were also recorded regarding the reasons for various policies and whether policies regarding marriage were due to the onset of the depression.

1939 Retrospective Survey: National Archives, Record Group 86, Boxes 446–450 (see U.S. Department of Labor, Women's Bureau 1941; see also Goldin 1989). Only 532 of the original schedules were found in the archives, although coded cards for others survive. The cards include information on over 2,800 women (including 742 currently married women) working in Cleveland in 1939; the surviving original schedules contain information on 532 married women who were not currently working but who had worked in the past. The

Women's Bureau coded work time for the currently working sample in five-year intervals and dropped other information that exists for the sample of women not currently working; thus the samples of working and nonworking women contain somewhat different information. All records were collected. Information was included on marital status, age, foreign birth, education, complete retrospective work histories, first occupation, last occupation, date at which work began, and, frequently, dates of marriage and pregnancy. It is my belief that this is the first large-scale retrospective survey of women's work patterns in America.

1940 Office Worker Survey, Firm Records: National Archives, Record Group 86, Boxes 496–500 (see U.S. Department of Labor, Women's Bureau 1942). Both firm- and individual-level records of this survey survive. Information was gathered by the Women's Bureau from payroll records and from interviews with personnel officers and other agents of the firms. Firms of all sizes were surveyed, and include those in the sectors listed for the 1931 survey plus the office portion of the manufacturing, meat packing, petroleum, and transportation and communications industries; also nonprofits, government agencies, retail and wholesale businesses, and small offices (such as lawyers). The surveys were extensive; for example, fully one-fourth of Philadelphia's office workers were included in the survey (no. 188–5, p. 2). Records for 328 firms in Kansas City, Los Angeles, and Philadelphia were collected, and information was coded on the variables listed for the 1931 survey plus new hires in 1939, personnel policies regarding discrimination on the basis of race and sex (whether the firm had policies against the employment of women or men in certain occupations), and the presence of unions. The interviewees often noted whether the firm favored married men in hiring, promotion, and salaries. Only firms with more than 9 female employees and more than 19 total employees were coded in Philadelphia. No government agencies were used in the sample.

1940 Office Worker Survey, Individual Records: National Archives, Record Group 86, Boxes 472–486 (see U.S. Department of Labor, Women's Bureau 1942; also Goldin 1984, 1986). A sample of 724 female office workers and 481 male office workers was collected for Philadelphia. Information was coded for each on age, marital status, education (years and diploma for grade school, high school, college, and various vocational and graduate programs), total work experience, experience with current firm, experience with office work, other experience, current earnings, earnings when worker began at the firm, whether worker had been furloughed, and whether work with the current firm was continuous.

1957 Hussey Report: The files containing these schedules are in box 167 of the (as yet unarchived) papers of Gladys Palmer, generously lent to me by Ann Miller of the Sociology Department of the University of Pennsylvania. They are referred to here as the Hussey Report after Miriam Hussey, who conducted the surveys as Gladys Palmer's assistant (see Hussey 1958). Approximátely 40 complete interviews exist and cover a range of Philadelphia firms and retail stores for the period 1956–57. Many of the same firms are included in the 1931 and 1940 Office Worker Surveys.

Notes

1. Much of the information in this chapter can be found in Goldin (1990, chap. 6).

2. United Airlines in the mid-1980s lost a Title VII class action case *(Romasanta v. United Air Lines, Inc.)* for firing stewardesses when they married.

3. Oppenheimer (1976, chap. 5) contains such a theory about the evolution of married women's labor market work.

4. 1931 Office Worker Survey, Firm Records: Hartford. See data appendix for a description of the survey and others used in this chapter.

5. Easterlin (1978, 1980) causally connects the two swings in fertility through a model of relative income.

6. See Morello (1986) on law; Harris (1978) on the professions in general.

7. In 1980, for example, only 1.4 percent of all labor force participants were physicians and lawyers, broadly defined.

8. Airlines imposed both forms of the marriage bar in the 1950s, which initially affected both male stewards and female stewardesses. Cambridge and Oxford universities at one time mandated that male instructors be unmarried, a continuation of the previous cleric status of professors.

9. The earlier survey was taken in 1931 in the four cities sampled; other cities were surveyed in 1932.

10. Government offices were excluded from the sample because they used civil service procedures.

11. Personnel officers and other agents of the firms freely admitted to having discriminated against blacks in hiring office workers and gave various reasons for their prejudices. Security Title Insurance in Los Angeles hired "only caucasians . . . for positions which entail meeting the public"; Philadelphia Electric Company admitted that "employees refuse to work with colored people in the clerical field" (1940 Office Worker Survey, Firm Records). Such candor is echoed in the remarks on sex discrimination.

12. The Women's Bureau also recorded individual-level data from personnel records in each of the firms surveyed. These records do not exist for the 1931 survey but do for the 1940 one (see Goldin 1984, 1986).

13. These summary data are in general agreement with those from a national survey cited in Cohn (1985, p. 99). In that sample 51 percent of all offices did not hire married women and 30 percent did not retain them in 1936 (when "supervisor's discretion" is treated as no bar). For factory employment the figures are 39 percent and 18 percent, but there is little evidence that factories had as extensive bars for operatives in the 1920s as they did for clerical workers. Rather, it appears that operatives were almost entirely unaffected by the marriage bar until the depression.

14. Because the 1931 survey included only firms that had more than nine female employees, only such firms are included for the 1940 survey information in Table 18.2. Note the very small numbers of firms in the smallest group for the 1931 survey and the substantial fraction of total female employees in firms with more than 700 employees.

15. It is not clear why Los Angeles is an outlier. Perhaps only large cities in eastern and midwestern states had extensive marriage bars; western cities may have had less restrictive policies, in general, against female employment.

16. The coefficients on the dummy variable for the 1930s sample are: 0.904 ($t = 1.67$) for the case of the retain bar as policy and 0.928 ($t = 2.20$) for the case of the fire bar as policy. An insurance

company in Philadelphia with 300 employees, for example, would have had a 23.4 percent probability of the retain bar in the 1920s, but a 43.0 percent probability in the 1930s.

17. One firm actually changed each bar in the opposite direction and is included with the group experiencing no net change. Of the ten that increased the bar, four changed the retain bar only, three changed the hire bar only, and three changed both retain and hire. The increased bar occurred in three ways: five firms moved from a discretionary bar to a bar policy; two moved from no bar to discretionary; and three moved from no bar to a bar policy. Fully 50 percent of the increase reflects a change from discretion to rule, providing further evidence to support the pooled regression results that many firms during the depression merely changed discretionary policies.

18. On the legislation passed and proposed during the depression, see Shallcross (1940) and Kessler-Harris (1981); a detailed history of Federal Order 213 can be found in Scharf (1980, chap. 3).

19. Among married women 40 to 49 years old who had worked in the past but who were not presently in the labor force in 1939, 62 percent had left the labor force at the time of marriage, 5 percent had worked only after marriage, and 33 percent had worked before and after marriage but left before 1939. Of these 33 percent, 86 percent had left at marriage but returned to work sometime after, to leave again before 1939. Of the married women 40 to 49 years old in the labor force in 1939, 31 percent had worked continuously, but information is not available about when the others married. The labor force participation rate among urban married women 40 to 49 years old in the 1940 census was approximately 15 percent. Therefore, of those who were working at or around the time of marriage, between 81 percent and 85 percent would have exited the labor force at that precise time. The lower bound assumes that no women at work in 1939 had left the labor force at marriage; the upper bound excludes from the group exiting at marriage only the 31 percent who had continuous work experience. These data are from Goldin (1989), with additional information from the 1939 Retrospective Survey (see data appendix).

20. See also Cohn (1988), who analyzes one of the surveys used here and finds support for his theory of "synthetic turnover." Although my findings differ somewhat from Cohn's on the details of the marriage bar, our substantive conclusions are similar.

21. The economic reasoning here is similar to that in models of hours restrictions and mandatory retirement (see Lazear 1979, 1981).

22. In New York, for example, 32 percent of all female office workers had spent five or more years with the present firm; but 44 percent of those in insurance companies and 38 percent of those in public utilities had (U.S. Department of Labor, Women's Bureau 1934, p. 27). The evidence for the other cities supports the conclusion here that there is no clear relationship between experience with a firm and the existence of a marriage bar.

23. A similar variable for "female only" jobs, those for which men would not be considered, was not significant and was omitted.

24. Note that the 1920s results may reflect the decline in hours during the initial onset of the Great Depression.

25. The computations use the logit regression coefficients in Table 18.3, column 1 (retain as policy) for both years. To compute the chance of having the retain bar, the coefficients (β) are multiplied by their mean values (X), in this case the 40- or 35-hour week, the 300 employees, and 0 or 1 for the promote variable. The equation for the probability (P) in a logit estimation is: $P = 1/[1 + \exp(-X\beta)]$. The computations for the change in the retain bar with the adoption of the internal promotion policy use the formula $\partial P/\partial \text{promote} = P(1 - P)\beta$, where β is the coefficient on the promote variable. The computed data for the 1930s implicitly apply to either Philadelphia or Kansas City because of the inclusion of city dummy variables.

26. This discussion raises the possibility that retirement and group insurance policies changed between the 1920s and 1950s and became experience-rated. If so, women, particularly older women, would have benefited. The possibility that some personnel practices changed raises a further one that tenure-based wage systems and promotion from within were also altered in the 1950s to accommodate the large supply of female employees.

27. Peters (1934, p. 25), a volume on married women teachers in Virginia, contains the only

published evidence I have encountered on the urban-rural breakdown of the marriage ban over time. According to his figures, the majority of urban school boards in Virginia instituted a ban against hiring married women before 1928, while the majority of rural school boards instituted the ban at the start of the Great Depression. About one-third of all urban school boards having a ban after 1932 had one before 1918, while only one-tenth of the rural school boards had such a ban before 1918. This chronology fits that of the institution of fixed salary scales.

28. Margo and Rotella (1981) consider the case of Houston, in which the marriage bar was established before World War I, then dropped during the war, only to be reinstituted after.

29. See Peterson (1987), who notes that in St. Louis, where the bar was established in 1897, no woman challenged it until 1941.

30. See Lewis (1925, pp. 185–188), who lists 31 frequently heard reasons why married women should not be employed as teachers and 31 equally touted reasons why they should.

31. There are probably other exceptions, particularly in manufacturing. Orra Langhorne (1886; cited in Scott 1970, p. 122), for example, noted that "married women are not admitted" in the cigarette factories of Lynchburg in which white single women and black women worked.

32. 1957 Hussey Report: Penn Mutual Life Insurance, August 22, 1956; Scott Paper, March 28, 1957.

33. The sample (1940 Office Worker Survey, Individual Records), described in the data appendix, consists of 724 women, 168 of whom were married. It is discussed at length in Goldin (1984, 1986). In a regression on the log of full-time yearly earnings, the coefficient on a dummy variable indicating marital status (1 = married) is 0.424, but that on an interaction between the dummy variable and years of education is -0.0362. The coefficient on years of education for the entire sample is 0.0458.

References

Bulow, J., and L. Summers. 1986. "A Theory of Dual Labor Markets with Application to Industrial Policy, Discrimination, and Keynesian Unemployment." *Journal of Labor Economics* 4 (January):376–414.

Cohn, S. 1985. *The Process of Occupational Sex-Typing: The Feminization of Clerical Labor in Great Britain*. Philadelphia: Temple University Press.

——— 1988. "Firm-Level Economics and Synthetic Turnover: Determinants of the Use of Marriage Bars in American Offices during the Great Depression." Unpublished ms.

Easterlin, R. 1978. "What Will 1984 Be Like? Socioeconomic Implications of Recent Twists in Age Structure." *Demography* 15:397–432.

——— 1980. *Birth and Fortune: The Impact of Numbers on Personal Welfare*. New York: Basic Books.

Goldin, C. 1984. "The Historical Evolution of Female Earnings Functions and Occupations." *Explorations in Economic History* 21 (January):1–27.

——— 1986. "Monitoring Costs and Occupational Segregation by Sex: A Historical Analysis." *Journal of Labor Economics* 4 (January):1–27.

——— 1989. "Life Cycle Labor Force Participation of Married Women: Historical Evidence and Implications." *Journal of Labor Economics* 7 (January):20–47.

——— 1990. *Understanding the Gender Gap: An Economic History of American Women*. New York: Oxford University Press.

Harris, B. J. 1978. *Beyond Her Sphere: Women and the Professions in American History*. Westport, Conn.: Greenwood Press.

Hussey, M. 1958. *Personnel Policies during a Period of Shortage of Young Women Workers in Philadelphia*. Philadelphia: Industrial Research Unit, Wharton School of Finance and Commerce, University of Pennsylvania.

Kessler-Harris, A. 1981. *Out to Work: A History of Wage-Earning Women in the United States*. New York: Oxford University Press.

Lazear, E. 1979. "Why Is There Mandatory Retirement?" *Journal of Political Economy* 87 (December):1261–84.

———— 1981. "Agency, Earnings Profiles, Productivity, and Hours Restrictions." *American Economic Review* 71 (September):606–620.

Lazear, E., and S. Rosen. 1981. "Rank-Order Tournaments as Optimum Labor Contracts." *Journal of Political Economy* 89 (October):841–864.

Lewis, E. E. 1925. *Personnel Problems of the Teaching Staff.* New York: Century Company.

Margo, R., and E. Rotella. 1981. "Sex Differences in the Labor Market for Public School Personnel: The Case of Houston, Texas, 1892–1923." Unpublished ms.

Morello, K. B. 1986. *The Invisible Bar: The Woman Lawyer in America.* New York: Random House.

National Education Association. 1923. "Teachers' Salaries and Salary Trends in 1923." *Report of the Salary Committee of the NEA* 1, no. 3 (July). Washington, D.C.

———— 1928. "Practices Affecting Teacher Personnel." *Research Bulletin of the NEA* 6, no. 4 (September). Washington, D.C.

———— 1932. "Administrative Practices Affecting Classroom Teachers: Part I: The Selection and Appointment of Teachers," and "Part II: The Retention, Promotion, and Improvement of Teachers." *Research Bulletin of the NEA* 10, no. 1 (January). Washington, D.C.

———— 1942. "Teacher Personnel Procedures: Selection and Appointment." *Research Bulletin of the NEA* 20, no. 2 (March). Washington, D.C.

———— 1952. "Teacher Personnel Practices, 1950–51: Appointment and Termination of Service." *Research Bulletin of the NEA* 30, no. 1 (February). Washington, D.C.

Oppenheimer, V. K. [1970] 1976. *The Female Labor Force in the United States: Demographic and Economic Factors Governing Its Growth and Changing Composition.* Westport, Conn.: Greenwood Press.

Peters, D. W. 1934. *The Status of the Married Woman Teacher.* New York: Teachers College, Columbia University.

Peterson, S. 1987. "Married Women and the Right to Teach in St. Louis, 1941–1948." *Missouri Historical Review* 81 (January):141–158.

Scharf, L. 1980. *To Work and to Wed: Female Employment, Feminism, and the Great Depression.* Westport, Conn.: Greenwood Press.

Schatz, R. W. 1983. *The Electrical Workers: A History of Labor at General Electric and Westinghouse, 1923–60.* Urbana: University of Illinois Press.

Scott, A. F. 1970. *The Southern Lady: From Pedestal to Politics, 1830–1930.* Chicago: University of Chicago Press.

Shallcross, R. 1940. *Should Married Women Work?* Public Affairs Pamphlets no. 49. New York: National Federation of Business and Professional Women's Clubs.

U.S. Bureau of the Census. 1946. *Labor Force, Employment, and Unemployment in the United States, 1940 to 1946.* Current Population Reports, ser. P-50, no. 2. Washington, D.C.: Government Printing Office.

———— 1975. *Historical Statistics of the United States: Colonial Times to 1970.* Washington, D.C.: Government Printing Office.

U.S. Department of Labor, Women's Bureau. 1934. "The Employment of Women in Offices," by Ethel Erickson. Bulletin no. 120. Washington, D.C.: Government Printing Office.

———— 1941. "Women Workers in Their Family Environment." Bulletin no. 183. Washington, D.C.: Government Printing Office.

———— 1942. "Office Work in [Houston, Los Angeles, Kansas City, Richmond, Philadelphia]." Bulletins no. 188-1,2,3,4,5. Washington, D.C.: Government Printing Office.

Contributors

• • •

Index

Contributors

• • •

Irma Adelman, Thomas Forsyth Hunt Chair, Economics and Agriculture and Resource Economics, University of California at Berkeley, is coauthor of "Is Structural Adjustment with a Human Face Possible? The Case of Mexico," *Journal of Development Studies* (1990) and *Patterns of Economic Development, 1850–1914* (1989).

Robert C. Allen, Professor of Economics, University of British Columbia, Vancouver, is author of "The Growth of Labour Productivity in Early Modern English Agriculture," *Explorations in Economic History* (1988) and "The Price of Freehold Land and the Interest Rate in the Seventeenth and Eighteenth Centuries," *Economic History Review* (1988).

Paul Bairoch, Professor, Director of the Department of Economic History, University of Geneva, is author of *Cities and Economic Development: From the Dawn of History to the Present* (1988) and *The Economic Development of the Third World* (1977).

Rudolf Braun, Professor of Modern History and the History of Switzerland, University of Zurich, is author of *Industrialisation and Everyday Life* (1990), and *Französische Übersetzung: Le déclin de l'Ancien Régime en Suisse* (1988).

Alfred D. Chandler, Jr., Straus Professor of Business History, Emeritus, Harvard Graduate School of Business Administration, is author of *Scale and Scope: The Dynamics of Industrial Capitalism* (1990) and coauthor of *The Coming of Managerial Capitalism* (1985).

François Crouzet, Professor of Modern History, University of Paris-Sorbonne, is author of *Britain Ascendant: Comparative Studies in Franco-British Economic History* (1990) and *The First Industrialists: The Problem of Origins* (1985).

Paul A. David, William Robertson Coe Professor of American Economic History and Professor of Economics, Stanford University, is coauthor of "Priority, Secrecy, Patents and the Socio-Economics of Science and Technology," *Sci-*

539

ence in Context (1991) and "The Economics of Compatibility Standards: An Introduction to Recent Research," *Economics of Innovation and New Technology* (1990).

Wolfram Fischer, Professor of Economic and Social History, Free University of Berlin, is editor of *Handbuch der europäischen Wirtschafts und Sozialgeschichte, vol. 5 (1850–1914)* (1985) and *vol. 6 (1914–1980)* (1987), and author of *Armut in der Geschichte* (1982).

Robert W. Fogel, Charles R. Walgreen Professor of American Institutions, University of Chicago, Graduate School of Business, is author of "Second Thoughts on the European Escape from Hunger: Famines, Price Elasticities, Entitlements, Chronic Malnutrition, and Mortality Rates," in S. R. Osmani, ed., *Nutrition and Poverty* (1991) and *Without Consent or Contract: The Rise and Fall of American Slavery* (1989).

Claudia Goldin, Professor of Economics, Harvard University, and Program Director and Research Associate, National Bureau of Economic Research, is coeditor of *Strategic Factors in Nineteenth-Century American Economic Development* (1991) and author of *Understanding the Gender Gap: An Economic History of American Women* (1990).

Jonathan Hughes, Professor of Economics, Northwestern University, is author of *The Governmental Habit Redux: Economic Controls from Colonial Times to the Present* (1991) and *The Vital Few: The Entrepreneur and American Economic Progress* (1986).

François Jequier, Professor of Contemporary History, University of Lausanne, is author of "Fondements éthiques et réalisations pratiques de patrons paternalistes en Suisse romande (XIXe–XXe siècles)," in Erik Aerts, Claude Beaud, and Jean Stengers, eds., *Liberalism and Paternalism in the Nineteenth Century* (1990) and *Charles Veillon (1900–1971): Essai sur l'émergence d'une éthique patronale* (1985).

Anne O. Krueger, Arts and Sciences Professor of Economics, Duke University, is author of *Perspectives on Trade and Development* (1990) and *The Political Economy of International Trade* (1990).

William Lazonick, Professor of Economics, Barnard College, Columbia University, is author of *Business Organization and the Myth of the Market Economy* (1991) and *Competitive Advantage on the Shop Floor* (1990).

Joel Mokyr, Professor of Economics and History, Northwestern University, is author of *The Lever of Riches: Technological Creativity and Economic Progress* (1990) and "Is There Still Life in the Pessimist Case? Consumption during the Industrial Revolution," *Journal of Economic History* (1988).

W. W. Rostow, Professor Emeritus of Economics and History, University of Texas at Austin, is author of *Theorists of Economic Growth from David Hume to the Present, with a Perspective on the Next Century* (1990) and *The World Economy: History and Prospect* (1978).

Peter Temin, Professor and Head, Department of Economics, Massachusetts Institute of Technology, is author of *Lessons from the Great Depression* (1989) and *The Fall of the Bell System: A Study in Prices and Politics* (1987).

Jeffrey G. Williamson, Laird Bell Professor of Economics and Master of Mather House, Harvard University, is author of *Inequality, Poverty, and History: The Kuznets Memorial Lectures* (1991) and *Coping with City Growth during the British Industrial Revolution* (1990).

Index

• • •